W9-ADM-614

THE GREAT GAME

Other books by the author

Foreign Devils on the Silk Road
Trespassers on the Roof of the World
Setting the East Ablaze

THE
GREAT GAME

The Struggle for Empire in Central Asia

PETER HOPKIRK

'Now I shall go far and far
into the North, playing the
Great Game...'

Rudyard Kipling, *Kim*, 1901

Kodansha International
New York • Tokyo • London

Kodansha America, Inc.,
114 Fifth Avenue,
New York, New York 10011, U.S.A.

Kodansha International Ltd.,
17-14 Otowa 1-chome,
Bunkyo-ku, Tokyo 112, Japan

Published in 1992 by Kodansha America, Inc.

First published in Great Britain in 1990 as
The Great Game: On Secret Service in High Asia
by John Murray (Publishers) Ltd.

Copyright © 1990, 1992 by Peter Hopkirk.
All rights reserved.

Printed in the United States of America

92 93 94 95 7 6 5 4 3 2

Library of Congress Cataloging-in-Publication Data
Hopkirk, Peter.
     The great game : the struggle for empire in central Asia / Peter
Hopkirk.
     p. cm.
     Includes bibliographical references (p. 527-542) and index.
     ISBN 4-7700-1703-0
     1. Asia, Central—Politics and Government. 2. Asia, Central—
Relations—Soviet Union. 3. Soviet Union—Relations—Asia,
Central. 4. Asia, Central—Relations—Great Britain. 5. Great
Britain—Relations—Asia, Central. I. Title.
DS329.4.H67 1992
320.958—dc20   92-16925
                                                               CIP

Printed and bound by
Arcata Graphics
Fairfield, Pennsylvania

For Kath

Contents

Maps   xi
Illustrations   xiii
Foreword   xv
Acknowledgements   xix
Prologue   1

THE BEGINNINGS   9
1. The Yellow Peril   11
2. Napoleonic Nightmare   24
3. Rehearsal for the Great Game   38
4. The Russian Bogy   57
5. All Roads Lead to India   69
6. The First of the Russian Players   77
7. A Strange Tale of Two Dogs   89
8. Death on the Oxus   99
9. The Barometer Falls   109

THE MIDDLE YEARS   121
10. 'The Great Game'   123
11. Enter 'Bokhara' Burnes   135
12. The Greatest Fortress in the World   153
13. The Mysterious Vitkevich   165
14. Hero of Herat   175
15. The Kingmakers   188
16. The Race for Khiva   202
17. The Freeing of the Slaves   213
18. Night of the Long Knives   230
19. Catastrophe   243

CONTENTS

20. Massacre in the Passes   257
21. The Last Hours of Conolly and Stoddart   270
22. Half-time   281

THE CLIMACTIC YEARS   293
23. The Great Russian Advance Begins   295
24. Lion of Tashkent   306
25. Spies Along the Silk Road   321
26. The Feel of Cold Steel Across His Throat   339
27. 'A Physician from the North'   355
28. Captain Burnaby's Ride to Khiva   365
29. Bloodbath at the Bala Hissar   384
30. The Last Stand of the Turcomans   402
31. To the Brink of War   418
32. The Railway Race to the East   430
33. Where Three Empires Meet   447
34. Flashpoint in the High Pamirs   465
35. The Race for Chitral   483
36. The Beginning of the End   502
37. End-game   513

Bibliography   527
Index   543

Maps

The Battlefield of the New Great Game   xvi

The Caucasus   xxi

Central Asia   xxii

The Far East   xxiv

Afghanistan and the N.W. Frontier   194

The Pamir Region   341

Illustrations

(*between pages 104 and 105*)
1. Henry Pottinger
2. Arthur Conolly (India Office Library)
3. General Yermolov
4. General Paskievich
5. Imam Shamyl
6. Russian troops preparing to lay siege to an *aul*
7. The Indus at Attock (India Office Library)
8. Sir Alexander Burnes
9. Lieutenant Eldred Pottinger
10. Ranjit Singh
11. Shah Shujah (National Army Museum)
12. Dost Mohammed
13. British troops entering the Bolan Pass in 1839 on their way to Kabul (National Army Museum)
14. Sir William Macnaghten
15. Mohan Lal
16. The fall of Ghazni, 1839 (National Army Museum)
17. The last stand at Gandamak (India Office Library)

(*between pages 264 and 265*)
18. Captain Conolly and Colonel Stoddart
19. Emir Nasrullah of Bokhara
20. The Ark, or citadel, at Bokhara
21. Turcoman slavers in action
22. General Konstantin Kaufman
23. General Mikhail Skobelev
24. Lieutenant Alikhanov
25. Sir Henry Rawlinson
26. George Hayward (Royal Geographical Society)
27. Scanning the passes
28. Map-making in High Asia

ILLUSTRATIONS

(*between pages 424 and 425*)
29. Sir Louis Cavagnari
30. The Bala Hissar fortress, Kabul (India Office Library)
31. General Sir Frederick Roberts, VC
32. Newsbill announcing Roberts's Triumph (National Army Museum)
33. Abdur Rahman
34. A contemporary cartoon from *Punch* (National Army Museum)
35. An anonymous political officer with friendly Afghan tribesmen (India Office Library)
36. Cossacks manning a machine-gun post in the Pamirs
37. The celebrated meeting of Captains Younghusband and Gromchevsky
38. Francis Younghusband
39. Gurkha troops showing the flag in Tibet (India Office Library)

Foreword

Since this book was written, momentous events have taken place in Great Game country, adding considerably to the significance of my narrative. Suddenly, after many years of almost total obscurity, Central Asia and the Caucasus find themselves once more back in the headlines, a position they frequently occupied during the nineteenth century. The map-makers too have been hard-pressed to keep up with the rapidly developing picture. With the collapse of Communism, more than half a dozen entirely new countries have sprung up among the ruins of Moscow's 'Evil Empire' in Asia, which stretched from the Caucasus in the west to China's frontiers in the east. Local wars have been fought, Russian names expunged from the map, and foreign embassies opened in brand-new capital cities.

Meanwhile, a new struggle is under way as rival outside powers compete to fill the political and economic void left by Moscow's abrupt departure. Already political analysts and headline writers are calling this manoeuvring for long-term advantage 'the new Great Game'. For, while the stakes are far higher and the players mostly new, they see it today as a continuation of the age-old struggle. It is this which gives the following narrative an even greater significance. For it tells, in full and graphic detail for the first time, how a succession of ambitious Tsars and ruthless generals crushed the Muslim peoples of Central Asia and occupied their lands. Fearing that the Russians would not stop until India too was theirs, the British sent young officers northwards through the passes to spy on them. At times the Great Game spilled over into Afghanistan, Persia, China and Tibet - as it could again today if it is allowed to escalate.

Most powerful of the players in today's Great Game is the last of the superpowers, the United States of America. Washington sees the region, so long in limbo, as an extension of the Middle East, fraught with the same perils and problems. Fearing the nightmarish consequences for the rest of the world if hot-headed

THE NEW GREAT GAME
BATTLEFIELD

Astrakhan

RUSSIA

KA

CASPIAN SEA

GEORGIA

Batum

Tbilisi (Tiflis)

ARMENIA

AZERBAIJAN

Erzurum

Yerivan

NAGORNO-
KARABAGH

Baku

Krasnovodsk

KARA

TURKEY

NAKHI-
CHEVAN

TURKM

DES

Van

Lenkoran

Ashk

Tabriz

Kazvin

IRAQ

R. Tigris

R. Euphrates

Teheran

Qum

Baghdad

Isfahan

IRAN

Ken

Basra

Shiraz

KUWAIT

PERSIAN
GULF

Bushire

xvi

mullahs armed with nuclear weapons were to gain control there, it seeks to nurture stability in this volatile region. Other rival powers energetically pursuing a stake in Central Asia's future include Iran, Turkey, Saudi Arabia, Pakistan and Libya. All are busy opening embassies and consulates, not to mention mosques and Koranic schools, in the region's new capitals. Japan and Korea, with a long-term eye on its raw materials and markets, are also actively seeking footholds in Central Asia.

Then there is Moscow itself, one of the original players in the Great Game of this book. Still haunted by the trauma of the Mongol conquest, it is determined that no Asian neighbour should ever again pose such a threat, especially considering the growing danger of weapons of mass destruction becoming freely available to all. Like its new ally, the United States, Moscow is grimly anxious to ensure that power does not get into the hands of irresponsible leaders in its former Asiatic domains. It also fears for the safety of its many nationals living there.

Yet another intensely worried player is neighbouring China, whose own Central Asian Muslims look yearningly across the frontier to where - in Kazakhstan, Tajikistan, Kyrgyzstan, Uzbekistan, Turkmenistan and Azerbaijan - their co-religionists bask, at least for the moment, in their newfound freedom. For Peking, with restive Tibetans already on its hands, the collapse of Communism in Soviet Central Asia is an alarming and threatening development which could imperil its own presence in the region.

It is impossible to guess, at the time of writing, how things will work out in the Muslim republics, and which of the rival players in today's Great Game will triumph. For the collapse of Soviet rule has tossed Central Asia back into the melting pot of history. Almost anything could happen there, and it would take a brave, or foolish, man to forecast what. But one thing seems certain. Central Asia, for good or for ill, is back once more in the thick of the news, and looks like staying there for a long time to come.

Peter Hopkirk

Acknowledgements

Forty years ago, when a subaltern of 19, I read Fitzroy Maclean's classic work of Central Asian travel, *Eastern Approaches*. This heady tale of high adventure and politics, set in the Caucasus and Turkestan during the darkest years of Stalinist rule, had a powerful effect on me, and no doubt on many others. From that moment onwards I devoured everything I could lay hands on dealing with Central Asia, and as soon as it was opened to foreigners I began to travel there. Thus, if only indirectly, Sir Fitzroy is partly responsible – some might say to blame – for the four books, including this latest one, which I have myself written on Central Asia. I therefore owe him a considerable debt of gratitude for first setting my footsteps in the direction of Tbilisi and Tashkent, Kashgar and Khotan. No finer book than *Eastern Approaches* has yet been written about Central Asia, and even today I cannot pick it up without a frisson of excitement.

But in piecing together this narrative, my overriding debt must be to those remarkable individuals who took part in the Great Game and who left accounts of their adventures and misadventures among the deserts and mountains. These provide most of the drama of this tale, and without them it could never have been told in this form. There exist biographies of a number of individual players, and these too have proved valuable. For the political and diplomatic background to the struggle I have made full use of the latest scholarship by specialist historians of the period, to whom I am greatly indebted. I must also thank the staff of the India Office Library and Records for making available to me numerous records and other material from that vast repository of British imperial history.

The individual to whom I perhaps owe most is my wife Kath, whose thoroughness in all things has contributed so much to the writing and researching of this, and my earlier books, at all stages, and on whom I tried out the narrative as it unfolded. In addition to preparing drafts for the five maps, she also compiled the index. Finally, I was most fortunate in having Gail Pirkis as my editor. Her eagle-eyed professionalism, calm good humour and unfailing tact proved to be an immense support during the long months of seeing this book through to publication. It is worth adding that Gail, when with Oxford University Press in Hong Kong, was responsible for rescuing from virtual oblivion a number of important works on Central Asia, at least two of them by Great Game heroes, and having them reprinted in attractive new editions.

Note on Spellings

Many of the names of peoples and places occurring in this narrative have been spelt or romanised in a variety of ways over the years. Thus Tartar/Tatar; Erzerum/Erzurum; Turcoman/Turkmen; Kashgar/Kashi; Tiflis/Tbilisi. For the sake of consistency and simplicity I have mostly settled for the spelling which would have been familiar to those who took part in these events.

THE CAUCASUS

300 Miles

Kilometres 0   100   200   300   400   500

R U S S I A

River Volga

Astrakhan

River Kuban

Oudjuk Kale

Armavir

C I R C A S S I A

Cherkessk

CASPIAN

Teberda

River Terek

DAGHESTAN

SEA

BLACK

SEA

G E O R G I A

Petrovsk

Batum

Trebizond

Tiflis

Derbent

Artvin

River Kura

KHANATE

Kars

OF

Lake
Sevan

Erzerum

Erivan

AZERBAIJAN

ERIVAN

Mount
Ararat

Baku

KARABAGH

Lake Van

River Aras

Araxes
Valley

Nakitchevan

Lenkoran

T U R K E Y

Tabriz

Lake
Urmia

Area of the main map

Maragheh

P E R S I A

Tiflis

Baku

Tabriz

To Teheran

xxi

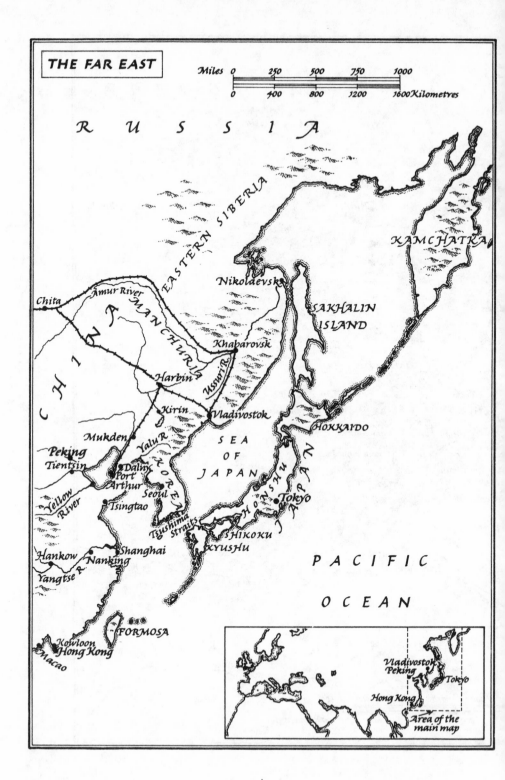

THE FAR EAST

Miles 0 250 500 750 1000

0 400 800 1200 1600 Kilometres

RUSSIA

EASTERN SIBERIA

KAMCHATKA

Nikolaevsk

SAKHALIN ISLAND

Chita

Amur River

MANCHURIA

CHINA

Khabarovsk

Harbin

Ussuri R.

Kirin

Vladivostok

HOKKAIDO

Mukden

Yalu R.

KOREA

SEA OF JAPAN

Peking

Tientsin

Dalny

Port Arthur

Seoul

HONSHU

JAPAN

Tokyo

Yellow River

Tsingtao

Tsushima Straits

SHIKOKU

KYUSHU

Hankow

Nanking

Shanghai

PACIFIC

Yangtse R.

OCEAN

Kowloon

Hong Kong

FORMOSA

Macao

Vladivostok

Peking

Tokyo

Hong Kong

Area of the main map

Prologue

On a June morning in 1842, in the Central Asian town of Bokhara, two ragged figures could be seen kneeling in the dust in the great square before the Emir's palace. Their arms were tied tightly behind their backs, and they were in a pitiful condition. Filthy and half-starved, their bodies were covered with sores, their hair, beards and clothes alive with lice. Not far away were two freshly dug graves. Looking on in silence was a small crowd of Bokharans. Normally executions attracted little attention in this remote, and still medieval, caravan town, for under the Emir's vicious and despotic rule they were all too frequent. But this one was different. The two men kneeling in the blazing midday sun at the executioner's feet were British officers.

For months they had been kept by the Emir in a dark, stinking pit beneath the mud-built citadel, with rats and other vermin as their sole companions. The two men – Colonel Charles Stoddart and Captain Arthur Conolly – were about to face death together, 4,000 miles from home, at a spot where today foreign tourists step down from their Russian buses, unaware of what once happened there. Stoddart and Conolly were paying the price of engaging in a highly dangerous game – the Great Game, as it became known to those who risked their necks playing it. Ironically, it was Conolly himself who had first coined the phrase, although it was Kipling who was to immortalise it many years later in his novel *Kim*.

The first of the two men to die on that June morning,

while his friend looked on, was Stoddart. He had been sent to
Bokhara by the East India Company to try to forge an alliance
with the Emir against the Russians, whose advance into Central
Asia was giving rise to fears about their future intentions.
But things had gone badly wrong. When Conolly, who had
volunteered to try to obtain his brother officer's freedom,
reached Bokhara, he too had ended up in the Emir's grim
dungeon. Moments after Stoddart's beheading, Conolly was
also dispatched, and today the two men's remains lie, together
with the Emir's many other victims, in a grisly and long-
forgotten graveyard somewhere beneath the square.

Stoddart and Conolly were merely two of the many officers
and explorers, both British and Russian, who over the best
part of a century took part in the Great Game, and whose
adventures and misadventures while so engaged form the narrative of this book. The vast chessboard on which this shadowy
struggle for political ascendancy took place stretched from the
snow-capped Caucasus in the west, across the great deserts
and mountain ranges of Central Asia, to Chinese Turkestan
and Tibet in the east. The ultimate prize, or so it was feared
in London and Calcutta, and fervently hoped by ambitious
Russian officers serving in Asia, was British India.

It all began in the early years of the nineteenth century,
when Russian troops started to fight their way southwards
through the Caucasus, then inhabited by fierce Muslim and
Christian tribesmen, towards northern Persia. At first, like
Russia's great march eastwards across Siberia two centuries
earlier, this did not seem to pose any serious threat to British
interests. Catherine the Great, it was true, had toyed with the
idea of marching on India, while in 1801 her son Paul had got
as far as dispatching an invasion force in that direction, only
for it to be hastily recalled on his death shortly afterwards. But
somehow no one took the Russians too seriously in those days,
and their nearest frontier posts were too far distant to pose any
real threat to the East India Company's possessions.

Then, in 1807, intelligence reached London which was to
cause considerable alarm to both the British government and
the Company's directors. Napoleon Bonaparte, emboldened
by his run of brilliant victories in Europe, had put it to Paul's

successor, Tsar Alexander I, that they should together invade
India and wrest it from British domination. Eventually, he told
Alexander, they might with their combined armies conquer
the entire world and divide it between them. It was no secret
in London and Calcutta that Napoleon had long had his eye
on India. He was also thirsting to avenge the humiliating
defeats inflicted by the British on his countrymen during their
earlier struggle for its possession.

His breathtaking plan was to march 50,000 French troops
across Persia and Afghanistan, and there join forces with Alexander's Cossacks for the final thrust across the Indus into
India. But this was not Europe, with its ready supplies, roads,
bridges and temperate climate, and Napoleon had little idea of
the terrible hardships and obstacles which would have to be
overcome by an army taking this route. His ignorance of the
intervening terrain, with its great waterless deserts and mountain barriers, was matched only by that of the British themselves. Until then, having arrived originally by sea, the latter
had given scant attention to the strategic land routes to India,
being more concerned with keeping the seaways open.

Overnight this complacency vanished. Whereas the Russians
by themselves might not present much of a threat, the combined armies of Napoleon and Alexander were a very different
matter, especially if led by a soldier of the former's undoubted
genius. Orders were hastily issued for the routes by which
an invader might reach India to be thoroughly explored and
mapped, so that it could be decided by the Company's defence
chiefs where best he might be halted and destroyed. At the
same time diplomatic missions were dispatched to the Shah of
Persia and the Emir of Afghanistan, through whose domains
the aggressor would have to pass, in the hope of discouraging
them from entering into any liaisons with the foe.

The threat never materialised, for Napoleon and Alexander
soon fell out. As French troops swept into Russia and entered
a burning Moscow, India was temporarily forgotten. But no
sooner had Napoleon been driven back into Europe with terrible losses than a new threat to India arose. This time it was
the Russians, brimming with self-confidence and ambition,
and this time it was not going to go away. As the battle-

hardened Russian troops began their southwards advance through the Caucasus once again, fears for the safety of India deepened.

Having crushed the Caucasian tribes, though only after a long and bitter resistance in which a handful of Englishmen took part, the Russians then switched their covetous gaze eastwards. There, in a vast arena of desert and mountain to the north of India, lay the ancient Muslim khanates of Khiva, Bokhara and Khokand. As the Russian advance towards them gathered momentum, London and Calcutta became increasingly alarmed. Before very long this great political no-man's-land was to become a vast adventure playground for ambitious young officers and explorers of both sides as they mapped the passes and deserts across which armies would have to march if war came to the region.

By the middle of the nineteenth century Central Asia was rarely out of the headlines, as one by one the ancient caravan towns and khanates of the former Silk Road fell to Russian arms. Every week seemed to bring news that the hard-riding Cossacks, who always spearheaded each advance, were getting closer and closer to India's ill-guarded frontiers. In 1865 the great walled city of Tashkent submitted to the Tsar. Three years later it was the turn of Samarkand and Bokhara, and five years after that, at the second attempt, the Russians took Khiva. The carnage inflicted by the Russian guns on those brave but unwise enough to resist was horrifying. 'But in Asia,' one Russian general explained, 'the harder you hit them, the longer they remain quiet.'

Despite St Petersburg's repeated assurances that it had no hostile intent towards India, and that each advance was its last, it looked to many as though it was all part of a grand design to bring the whole of Central Asia under Tsarist sway. And once that was accomplished, it was feared, the final advance would begin on India – the greatest of all imperial prizes. For it was no secret that several of the Tsar's ablest generals had drawn up plans for such an invasion, and that to a man the Russian army was raring to go.

As the gap between the two front lines gradually narrowed, the Great Game intensified. Despite the dangers, principally from hostile tribes and rulers, there was no shortage of intrepid young officers eager to risk their lives beyond the frontier, filling in the blanks on the map, reporting on Russian movements, and trying to win the allegiance of suspicious khans. Stoddart and Conolly, as will be seen, were by no means the only ones who failed to return from the treacherous north. Most of the players in this shadowy struggle were professionals, Indian Army officers or political agents, sent by their superiors in Calcutta to gather intelligence of every kind. Others, no less capable, were amateurs, often travellers of independent means, who chose to play what one of the Tsar's ministers called 'this tournament of shadows'. Some went in disguise, others in full regimentals.

Certain areas were judged too perilous, or politically sensitive, for Europeans to venture into, even in disguise. And yet these parts had to be explored and mapped, if India was to be defended. An ingenious solution to this was soon found. Indian hillmen of exceptional intelligence and resource, specially trained in clandestine surveying techniques, were dispatched across the frontier disguised as Muslim holy men or Buddhist pilgrims. In this way, often at great risk to their lives, they secretly mapped thousands of square miles of previously unexplored terrain with remarkable accuracy. For their part, the Russians used Mongolian Buddhists to penetrate regions considered too dangerous for Europeans.

The Russian threat to India seemed real enough at the time, whatever historians may say with hindsight today. The evidence, after all, was there for anyone who chose to look at the map. For four centuries the Russian Empire had been steadily expanding at the rate of some 55 square miles a day, or around 20,000 square miles a year. At the beginning of the nineteenth century, more than 2,000 miles separated the British and Russian empires in Asia. By the end of it this had shrunk to a few hundred, and in parts of the Pamir region to less than twenty. No wonder many feared that the Cossacks would only rein in their horses when India too was theirs.

Besides those professionally involved in the Great Game, at home a host of amateur strategists followed it from the sidelines, giving freely of their advice in a torrent of books, articles, impassioned pamphlets and letters to the newspapers. For the most part these commentators and critics were Russophobes of strongly hawkish views. They argued that the only way to halt the Russian advance was by 'forward' policies. This meant getting there first, either by invasion, or by creating compliant 'buffer' states, or satellites, astride the likely invasion routes. Also of the forward school were the ambitious young officers of the Indian Army and political department engaged in this exciting new sport in the deserts and passes of High Asia. It offered adventure and promotion, and perhaps even a place in imperial history. The alternative was the tedium of regimental life on the sweltering plains of India.

But not everyone was convinced that the Russians intended to try to wrest India from Britain's grasp, or that they were militarily capable of doing so. These opponents of forward policies argued that India's best defence lay in its unique geographical setting – bordered by towering mountain systems, mighty rivers, waterless deserts and warlike tribes. A Russian force which reached India after overcoming all these obstacles, they insisted, would be so weakened by then that it would be no match for a waiting British army. It was thus more sensible to force an invader to overextend his lines of communication than for the British to stretch theirs. This policy – the 'backward' or 'masterly inactivity' school, as it was called – had the additional merit of being considerably cheaper than the rival forward school. Each, however, was to have its day.

Wherever possible I have tried to tell the story through the individuals, on either side, who took part in the great imperial struggle, rather than through historical forces or geopolitics. This book does not pretend to be a history of Anglo-Russian relations during this period. These have been thoroughly dealt with by academic historians like Anderson, Gleason, Ingram, Marriott and Yapp, whose works are listed in my bibliography. Nor is there room here to go into the complex and continually evolving relationship between London and Calcutta. This is a subject in its own right which has been explored in detail in numerous histories of the British in India, most recently by Sir Penderel Moon in his monumental, 1,235-page study of the Raj, *The British Conquest and Domination of India*.

Being primarily about people, this story has a large cast. It includes more than a hundred individuals, and embraces at least three generations. It opens with Henry Pottinger and Charles Christie in 1810, and closes with Francis Young-husband nearly a century later. The Russian players, who were every bit as able as their British counterparts, are here too, beginning with the intrepid Muraviev and the shadowy Vit-kevich, and ending with the formidable Gromchevsky and the devious Badmayev. While taking a very different view of these events, modern Soviet scholars have begun to show more inter-est (and not a little pride) in the exploits of their players. Having no convenient phrase of their own for it, some even refer to the struggle as the *Bolshaya Igra* ('Great Game'). I have tried, when describing the deeds of both Britons and Russians, to remain as neutral as possible, allowing men's actions to speak for themselves, and leaving judgements to the reader.

If this narrative tells us nothing else, it at least shows that not much has changed in the last hundred years. The storming of embassies by frenzied mobs, the murder of diplomats, and the dispatch of warships to the Persian Gulf – all these were only too familiar to our Victorian forebears. Indeed, the head-lines of today are often indistinguishable from those of a century or more ago. However, little appears to have been learned from the painful lessons of the past. Had the Russians in December 1979 remembered Britain's unhappy experiences in Afghanistan in 1842, in not dissimilar circumstances, then they might not have fallen into the same terrible trap, thereby sparing some 15,000 young Russian lives, not to mention untold numbers of innocent Afghan victims. The Afghans, Moscow found too late, were an unbeatable foe. Not only had they lost none of their formidable fighting ability, especially in terrain of their own choosing, but they were quick to embrace the latest techniques of warfare. Those deadly, long-barrelled *jezails*, which once wrought such slaughter among the British redcoats, had as their modern counterparts the heat-seeking Stinger, which proved so lethal against Russian helicopter-gunships.

Some would maintain that the Great Game never really

ceased, and that it was merely the forerunner of the Cold War of our own times, fuelled by the same fears, suspicions and misunderstandings. Indeed, men like Conolly and Stoddart, Pottinger and Younghusband, would have had little difficulty in recognising the twentieth-century struggle as essentially the same as theirs, albeit played for infinitely higher stakes.

But before we set out across the snow-filled passes and treacherous deserts towards Central Asia, where this narrative took place, we must first go back seven centuries in Russian history. For it was then that a cataclysmic event took place which was to leave an indelible mark on the Russian character. Not only did it give the Russians an abiding fear of encirclement, whether by nomadic hordes or by nuclear missile sites, but it also launched them on their relentless drive eastwards and southwards into Asia, and eventually into collision with the British in India.

THE BEGINNINGS

'Scratch a Russian, and
you will find a Tartar.'

Russian proverb

·1·

The Yellow Peril

You could smell them coming, it was said, even before you heard the thunder of their hooves. But by then it was too late. Within seconds came the first murderous torrent of arrows, blotting out the sun and turning day into night. Then they were upon you – slaughtering, raping, pillaging and burning. Like molten lava, they destroyed everything in their path. Behind them they left a trail of smoking cities and bleached bones, leading all the way back to their homeland in Central Asia. 'Soldiers of Antichrist come to reap the last dreadful harvest,' one thirteenth-century scholar called the Mongol hordes.

The sheer speed of their horse-borne archers, and the brilliance and unfamiliarity of their tactics, caught army after army off balance. Old ruses, long used in tribal warfare, enabled them to rout greatly superior numbers at negligible loss to themselves. Time and again their feigned flight from the battlefield lured seasoned commanders to their doom. Strongholds, considered impregnable, were swiftly overwhelmed by the barbaric practice of herding prisoners – men, women and children – ahead of the storming parties, their corpses then forming a human bridge across ditches and moats. Those who survived were forced to carry the Mongols' long scaling ladders up to the very walls of the fortress, while others were made to erect their siege engines under heavy fire. Often the defenders recognised their own families and friends among these captives and refused to fire on them.

Masters at black propaganda, the Mongols saw to it that hair-raising tales of their barbarity were carried ahead of them as they advanced across Asia, devastating kingdom after kingdom, towards a quaking Europe. Cannibalism was said to be among their many vices, and the breasts of captured virgins were reputedly kept for the senior Mongol commanders. Only instant surrender held out the slightest hope of mercy. After one engagement the beaten enemy leaders were slowly crushed to death beneath planks upon which the victorious Mongols were feasting and celebrating. Often, if no more prisoners were required, entire populations of captured cities were put to the sword to prevent them from ever becoming a threat again. At other times they would be sold into slavery *en masse*.

The dreadful Mongol whirlwind had been unleashed on the world in 1206 by an illiterate military genius named Teumjin, formerly the unknown chief of a minor tribe, whose fame was destined shortly to eclipse even that of Alexander the Great. It was the dream of Genghis Khan, as he was to become known, to conquer the earth, a task which he believed he had been chosen by God to carry out. During the next thirty years, he and his successors almost achieved this. At the height of their power their empire was to stretch from the Pacific coast to the Polish frontier. It embraced the whole of China, Persia, Afghanistan, present-day Central Asia, and parts of northern India and the Caucasus. But more important still, and particularly to our narrative, it included vast tracts of Russia and Siberia.

At this time Russia consisted of a dozen or so principalities, which were frequently at war with one another. Between 1219 and 1240 these fell one by one to the ruthless Mongol war-machine, having failed to unite in resisting this common foe. They were to regret it for a very long time to come. Once the Mongols had conquered a region it was their policy to impose their rule through a system of vassal princes. Provided sufficient tribute was forthcoming, they rarely interfered in the details. They were merciless, however, if it fell short of their demands. The inevitable result was a tyrannical rule by the vassal princes – the shadow of which hangs heavily over Russia to this day – together with lasting impoverishment and backwardness which it is still struggling to overcome.

For well over two centuries the Russians were to stagnate and suffer under the Mongol yoke – or the Golden Horde, as these merchants of death called themselves, after the great tent with golden poles which was the headquarters of their western empire. In addition to the appalling material destruction wrought by the invaders, their predatory rule was to leave the Russian economy in ruins, bring commerce and industry to a halt, and reduce the Russian people to serfdom. The years of Tartar domination, as the Russians term this black chapter in their history, also witnessed the introduction of Asiatic methods of administration and other oriental customs, which were superimposed on the existing Byzantine system. Cut off from the liberalising influence of western Europe, moreover, the people became more and more eastern in outlook and culture. 'Scratch a Russian,' it was said, 'and you will find a Tartar.'

Meanwhile, taking advantage of its reduced circumstances and military weakness, Russia's European neighbours began to help themselves freely to its territory. The German principalities, Lithuania, Poland and Sweden all joined in. The Mongols, so long as the tribute continued to reach them, were unperturbed by this, being far more concerned about their Asiatic domains. For there lay Samarkand and Bokhara, Herat and Baghdad, cities of incomparable wealth and splendour, which greatly outshone the wooden-built Russian ones. Crushed thus between their European foes to the west and the Mongols to the east, the Russians were to develop a paranoid dread of invasion and encirclement which has bedevilled their foreign relations ever since.

Rarely has an experience left such deep and long-lasting scars on a nation's psyche as this did on the Russians. It goes far towards explaining their historic xenophobia (especially towards eastern peoples), their often aggressive foreign policy, and their stoical acceptance of tyranny at home. The invasions of Napoleon and Hitler, though unsuccessful, merely reinforced these fears. Only now do the Russian people show signs of shaking off this unhappy legacy. Those ferocious little horsemen whom Genghis Khan let loose upon the world have much to answer for, more than four centuries after their power was finally broken and they themselves sank back into the obscurity from which they had come.

The man to whom the Russians owe their freedom from Mongol oppression was Ivan III, known also as Ivan the Great, then Grand Prince of Moscow. At the time of the Mongol conquest Moscow was a small and insignificant provincial town, overshadowed by and subservient to its powerful neighbours. But no vassal princes were more assiduous than those of Moscow in paying tribute and homage to their alien rulers. In return for their allegiance they had gradually been entrusted with more power and freedom by the unsuspecting Mongols. Over the years Moscow, by now the principality of Muscovy, thus grew in strength and size, eventually coming to dominate all its neighbours. Preoccupied with their own internal rifts, the Mongols failed to see, until too late, what a threat Muscovy had become.

The showdown came in 1480. In a fit of rage, it is said, Ivan trampled on a portrait of Ahmed Khan, leader of the Golden Horde, and at the same time put several of his envoys to death. One escaped, however, and bore the news of this undreamed-of act of defiance to his master. Determined to teach this rebellious underling a lesson he would never forget, Ahmed turned his army against Muscovy. To his astonishment he found a large and well-equipped force awaiting him on the far bank of the River Ugra, 150 miles from Moscow. For weeks the two armies glowered at one another across the river, neither side seeming inclined to make the first move to cross it. But soon, with the arrival of winter, it began to freeze. A ferocious battle appeared inevitable.

It was then that something extraordinary happened. Without any warning, both sides suddenly turned and fled, as though simultaneously seized by panic. Despite their own inglorious behaviour, the Russians knew that their centuries-long ordeal was all but over. Their oppressors had clearly lost their stomach for the fight. The Mongol war-machine, once so dreaded, was no longer invincible. Their centralised authority in the West had finally collapsed, leaving three widely separated khanates – at Kazan, Astrakhan and in the Crimea – as the last remnants of the once mighty empire of Genghis Khan and his successors. Although the overall Mongol grip had been broken, these three remaining strongholds still constituted a threat, and would eventually have to be destroyed if anyone was to feel safe.

It fell to one of Ivan's successors, Ivan the Terrible, to seize the first two of these and incorporate them in Muscovy's rapidly expanding empire. Thirsting for revenge, his troops stormed the fortress of Kazan on the upper Volga in 1553, slaughtering the defenders just as the Mongols had done when they laid waste Russia's great cities. Two years later the Khanate of Astrakhan, where the Volga flows into the Caspian, met with a similar fate. Only the Crimea, the last remaining Tartar redoubt, still held out, and then merely because it enjoyed the protection of the Ottoman sultans, who regarded it as a valuable bulwark against the Russians. Thus, save for the occasional raid by the Crimean Tartars, the Mongol threat had been eliminated for ever. It would leave the way open for the greatest colonial enterprise in history – Russia's expansion eastwards into Asia.

The first phase of this was to carry Muscovy's explorers, soldiers and traders 4,000 miles across the immensity of Siberia, with its mighty rivers, frozen wastes and impenetrable forests. Comparable in many ways to the early American settlers' conquest of the West, it was to take more than a century and only end when the Russians had reached the Pacific seaboard and established themselves there permanently. But the conquest of Siberia, which is one of the great epics of human history, lies outside the scope of this narrative. This vast inhospitable region was too far away from anywhere for any other power, least of all the British in India, to feel threatened by it. Its colonisation, however, was only the first stage of a process of expansion which would not cease until Russia had become the largest country on earth, and, in British eyes at least, an ever-increasing threat to India.

*　　*　　*

The first of the Tsars to turn his gaze towards India was Peter the Great. Painfully conscious of his country's extreme backwardness, and of its vulnerability to attack – largely the result of the 'lost' Mongol centuries – he determined not only to catch up, economically and socially, with the rest of Europe, but also to make his armed forces a match for those of any other power. But to do this he desperately needed vast sums of money, having emptied the treasury by going to war with Sweden and Turkey simultaneously. By a happy coincidence, at around this time, reports began to reach him from Central Asia that rich deposits of gold were to be found there on the banks of the River Oxus, a remote and hostile region where few Russians or other Europeans had ever set foot. Peter was also aware, from the accounts of Russian travellers, that beyond the deserts and mountains of Central Asia lay India, a land of legendary riches. These, he knew, were already being carried away by sea on a massive scale by his European rivals, and by the British in particular. His fertile brain now conceived a plan for getting his hands on both the gold of Central Asia and his share of India's treasures.

Some years before, Peter had been approached by the Khan of Khiva, a Muslim potentate whose desert kingdom lay astride the River Oxus, seeking his assistance in suppressing the unruly tribes of the region. In exchange for Russian protection, the Khan had offered to become his vassal. Having little or no interest in Central Asia at that time, and more than enough on his hands at home and in Europe, Peter had forgotten all about the offer. It now occurred to him that possession of Khiva, which lay midway between his own frontiers and those of India, would provide him with the staging point he needed in the region. From here his geologists could search for gold, while it would also serve as a half-way house for the Russian caravans which he soon hoped to see returning from India laden with exotic luxuries for both the domestic and European markets. By exploiting the direct overland route, he could seriously damage the existing sea trade which took anything up to a year to travel between India and home. A friendly Khan, moreover, might even provide armed escorts for the caravans, thus saving him the enormous expense of employing Russian troops.

Peter decided to send a heavily armed expedition to Khiva

to take up, somewhat belatedly, the Khan's offer. In return, the ruler would be provided with a permanent Russian guard for his own protection, while his family would be guaranteed hereditary possession of the throne. Should he prove to have changed his mind, or be short-sighted enough to resist the expedition, then the accompanying artillery could knock sense into him by reducing the medieval mud architecture of Khiva to dust. Once in possession of Khiva, preferably on an amicable basis, then the search for the Oxus gold, and for a caravan route to India, would begin. Chosen to lead this important expedition was a Muslim prince from the Caucasus, a convert to Christianity and now a regular officer in the élite Life Guards regiment, Prince Alexander Bekovich. Because of his background Bekovich was judged by Peter to be the ideal man to deal with a fellow oriental. His party consisted of 4,000 men, including infantry, cavalry, artillery and a number of Russian merchants, and was accompanied by 500 horses and camels.

Apart from hostile Turcoman tribesmen who roamed this desolate region, the principal obstacle facing Bekovich was a dangerous stretch of desert, more than 500 miles wide, lying between the eastern shore of the Caspian and Khiva. Not only would the expedition have to negotiate this, but eventually the heavily laden Russian caravans returning from India would also have to cross it. But here a friendly Turcoman chieftain came to their assistance. He told Peter that many years before, instead of flowing into the Aral Sea, the River Oxus used to discharge into the Caspian, and that it had been diverted by the local tribes to its present course by means of dams. If this was true, Peter reasoned, it would not be difficult for his engineers to destroy the dams and restore the river to its original course. Goods travelling between India and Russia, and vice versa, could then be conveyed for much of the way by boat, thus avoiding the hazardous desert crossing. The prospects for this began to look promising when a Russian reconnaissance party reported finding what appeared to be the old Oxus river bed in the desert not far from the Caspian shore.

After celebrating the Russian Easter, Bekovich and his party set sail from Astrakhan, at the northern end of the Caspian, in

April 1717. Conveyed across the great inland sea by a flotilla of nearly a hundred small vessels, they carried with them enough provisions to last a year. But everything took much longer than had been expected, and it was not until mid-June that they entered the desert and headed eastward towards Khiva. Already they were beginning to suffer from the extreme heat and from thirst, and soon they were losing men through heat-stroke and other sickness. At the same time they had to fight off the attacks of marauding tribesmen determined to prevent their advance. But there could be no question of turning back now and risking the fury of the Tsar, and the party struggled stoically on towards distant Khiva. Finally, in the middle of August, after more than two months in the desert, they found themselves within a few days' march of the capital.

Far from certain how they would be received, Bekovich sent couriers ahead bearing lavish gifts for the Khan, together with assurances that their mission was strictly a friendly one. Hopes of successfully accomplishing it looked promising when the Khan himself came out to welcome the Tsar's emissary. After exchanging courtesies, and listening to the mission's band together, Bekovich and the Khan rode on towards the town, the former's somewhat depleted force following at a distance. As they approached the city gates, the Khan explained to Bekovich that it would not be possible to accommodate and feed so many men in Khiva. He proposed instead that the Russians should be split up into several groups so that they could be properly housed and entertained in villages just outside the capital.

Anxious not to offend the Khan, Bekovich agreed and told Major Frankenburg, his second-in-command, to divide the men into five parties and to send them to the quarters assigned to them by their hosts. Frankenburg objected, expressing his misgivings over allowing the force to be dispersed in this way. But he was overruled by Bekovich, who insisted that his order be obeyed. When Frankenburg continued to argue with him, Bekovich warned him that he would have him court-martialled when they got back if he did not do as he was told. The troops were then led away in small groups by their hosts. It was just what the Khivans had been waiting for.

Everywhere they fell upon the unsuspecting Russians. Among the first to die was Bekovich himself. He was seized, stripped of his uniform, and while the Khan looked on, brutally hacked to death. Finally his head was severed, stuffed with straw, and displayed, together with those of Frankenburg and the other senior officers, to the jubilant mob. Meanwhile the Russian troops, separated from their officers, were being systematically slaughtered. Forty or so of the Russians managed to escape the bloodbath, but when it was over the Khan ordered them to be lined up in the main square for execution before the entire town. Their lives were saved, however, by the intervention of one man. He was Khiva's *akhund*, or spiritual leader, who reminded the Khan that his victory had been won through treachery, and warned him that butchering the prisoners would merely worsen the crime in the eyes of God.

It was the act of a very brave man, but the Khan was impressed. The Russians were spared. Some were sold by their captors into slavery, while the remainder were allowed to make their painful way back across the desert towards the Caspian. Those who survived the journey broke the dreadful tidings to their colleagues manning the two small wooden forts which they had built there before setting out for Khiva. From there the news was carried back to Peter the Great at his newly finished capital of St Petersburg. In Khiva, meanwhile, to boast of his triumph over the Russians, the Khan dispatched the head of Bekovich, the Muslim prince who had sold his soul to the infidel Tsar, to his Central Asian neighbour, the Emir of Bokhara, while keeping the rest of him on display in Khiva. But the gruesome trophy was hastily returned, its nervous recipient declaring that he had no wish to be a party to such perfidy. More likely, one suspects, he feared bringing down the wrath of the Russians on his own head.

The Khan of Khiva was luckier than he probably realised, having little concept of the size and military might of his northern neighbour. For no retribution was to follow. Khiva was too far away, and Peter too busy advancing his frontiers elsewhere, notably in the Caucasus, to send a punitive expedition to avenge Bekovich and his men. That would have to wait until his hands were freer. In fact, many years would pass before the Russians once more attempted to absorb Khiva into their domains. But if the Khan's treachery went unpunished, it was certainly not forgotten, merely confirming Russian distrust of orientals. It was to ensure that little quarter would be given when they embarked on their subjection of the Muslim tribes of Central Asia and the Caucasus, and in our own times of the *mujahedin* of Afghanistan (although this was to prove rather less successful).

In the event, Peter was never again to pursue his dream of opening up a golden road to India, along which would flow unimagined wealth. He had already taken on more than one man could hope to achieve in a lifetime, and accomplished much of it. But long after his death in 1725 a strange and persistent story began to circulate through Europe about Peter's last will and testament. From his death bed, it was said, he had secretly commanded his heirs and successors to pursue what he believed to be Russia's historical destiny – the domination of the world. Possession of India and Constantinople were the twin keys to this, and he urged them not to rest until both were firmly in Russian hands. No one has ever seen this document, and most historians believe that it never existed. Yet such was the awe and fear surrounding Peter the Great that at times it came to be widely believed, and versions of its supposed text to be published. It was, after all, just the sort of command that this restless and ambitious genius might have given to posterity. Russia's subsequent drive towards both India and Constantinople seemed, to many, confirmation enough, and until very recently there existed a strong belief in Russia's long-term aim of world domination.

* * *

It was not for another forty years, however, until the reign of Catherine the Great, that Russia once again began to show signs of interest in India, where the British East India Company had been steadily gaining ground, principally at the expense of the French. In fact one of Catherine's predecessors, the pleasure-loving Anne, had returned all Peter's hard-won gains in the Caucasus to the Shah of Persia (hardly in keeping with

Peter's supposed will) on the grounds that they were draining her treasury. But Catherine, like Peter, was an expansionist. It was no secret that she dreamed of expelling the Turks from Constantinople and restoring Byzantine rule there, albeit under her firm control. This would give her fleet access to the Mediterranean, then very much a British lake, from the Black Sea, still very much a Turkish one.

In 1791, towards the end of her reign, Catherine is known to have carefully considered a plan to wrest India from Britain's ever-tightening grip. Not surprisingly, perhaps, this idea was the brain-child of a Frenchman, a somewhat mysterious individual named Monsieur de St Génie. He proposed to Catherine that her troops should march overland via Bokhara and Kabul, announcing as they advanced that they had come to restore Muslim rule under the Moguls to its former glory. This would attract to Catherine's standard, he argued, the armies of the Muslim khanates along the invasion route, and foment mass uprisings against the British within India as word of their coming spread. Although the plan got no further than that (she was dissuaded from it by her chief minister and former lover, the one-eyed Count Potemkin), this was the first of a long succession of such schemes for the invasion of India which Russian rulers were to toy with during the next century or so.

If Catherine failed to add either India or Constantinople to her domains, she nonetheless took a number of steps in that direction. Not only did she win back from the Persians the Caucasian territories which Anne had restored to them, but she also took possession of the Crimea, that last surviving stronghold of the Mongol empire. For three centuries it had enjoyed the protection of the Turks, who saw it as a valuable shield against the increasingly aggressive colossus to the north. But by the end of the eighteenth century, the once warlike Crimean Tartars had ceased to be a force to be reckoned with. Taking advantage of territorial gains she had made at the expense of the Turks on the northern coast of the Black Sea, and of internal strife among the Tartars, Catherine was able to add the Crimean khanate to her empire without a shot being fired. She achieved this, in her own words, simply by 'placing posters in important locations to announce to the Crimeans our receiving them as our subjects'. Blaming their troubles on the Turks, the descendants of Genghis Khan meekly accepted their fate.

The Black Sea now ceased to be a Turkish lake, for not only were the Russians to build a giant new naval arsenal and base at Sebastopol, but also their warships were within two days' sailing of Constantinople. Fortunately for the Turks, however, a freak storm not long afterwards sent the entire Russian Black Sea fleet to the bottom, temporarily removing the threat. But although the great city astride the Bosporus which she had dreamed of liberating from Muslim rule was still firmly in Turkish hands when Catherine died, the road leading to it was now appreciably shorter. For the first time Russia's increasing presence in the Near East and the Caucasus began to give cause for concern among senior officials of the East India Company. Among the earliest to sense this was Henry Dundas, President of the Company's new Board of Control, who warned of the danger of allowing the Russians to supplant the Turks and the Persians in these regions, and the long-term threat this might pose to British interests in India if the cordial relations then existing between London and St Petersburg were ever to deteriorate or collapse altogether.

However, in the light of what happened next, such fears were momentarily forgotten. A new spectre had suddenly arisen, representing a far more immediate threat to Britain's position in India. Still only in his twenties, and burning to avenge French defeats at the hands of the British there, Napoleon Bonaparte had turned his predatory gaze eastwards. Fresh from his triumphs in Europe, he now vowed to humble the arrogant British by cutting them off from India, the source of their power and riches, and eventually driving them from this greatest of all imperial prizes. A strategic foothold in the Near East, he believed, was the first step towards this. 'To conquer India we must first make ourselves masters of Egypt,' he declared.

Napoleon wasted no time in setting about this, borrowing every book on the region which he could discover, and marking heavily those passages which interested him. 'I was full of dreams,' he explained long afterwards. 'I saw myself founding a new religion, marching into Asia riding an elephant, a turban on my head and in my hands the new Koran I would have written to suit my needs.' By the spring of 1798 all was ready, and on May 19 an armada carrying French troops sailed secretly from the ports of Toulon and Marseilles.

·2·

Napoleonic Nightmare

It was from the lips of a native of Bengal that Lord Wellesley, the new Governor-General of India, first heard the sensational and unwelcome news that Napoleon had landed in Egypt with 40,000 troops. The man had just arrived in Calcutta from Jeddah, on the Red Sea, aboard a fast Arab vessel. A full week was to pass before the tidings were officially confirmed by intelligence reaching Bombay via a British warship. One reason for the delay was that the French invasion force had managed to give the British Mediterranean fleet the slip, and it had not been known for some weeks whether it was bound for Egypt, or was heading round the Cape for India.

The fact that Napoleon was on the move with so large a force had caused grave alarm in London, especially to Dundas and his colleagues at the Board of Control. For the East India Company's position in India was still far from secure, even if it was now the paramount European power there, with a virtual monopoly of the country's commerce. Fighting the French and others had almost reduced it to bankruptcy, and the Company was in no position to take on Napoleon. It was with some relief, therefore, that it was learned that he had got no further than Egypt, although this was threat enough. Widespread conjecture now followed as to what Napoleon's next step would be. There were two schools of thought. One argued that he would advance overland through Syria or Turkey, and attack India from Afghanistan or Baluchistan, while the other was

convinced that he would come by sea, setting sail from somewhere on Egypt's Red Sea coast.

Dundas was sure that he would take the land route, and even
urged the government to hire Russian troops to intercept him.
The Company's own military experts believed that the
invasion, if it came, would be sea-borne, although the Red Sea
was closed for much of the year by contrary winds. To guard
against this danger, a British force was hastily dispatched round
the Cape to block the exit to the Red Sea, and another sent
from Bombay. The strategic significance of the Red Sea route
was not lost on Calcutta. Some years earlier, news of the
outbreak of war between Britain and France had reached India
this way in record time, enabling the Company's troops to steal
a march on the unsuspecting French there. Although, as yet,
there was no regular transportation service via the Red Sea and
Egypt, urgent messages and travellers in a hurry occasionally
went that way rather than by the usual route around the Cape,
which could take up to nine months or more, depending on
the winds and weather. But Napoleon's occupation of Egypt
was to put a stop to this short cut for a while.

Unlike senior government and Company officials in London,
Wellesley himself did not lose too much sleep over Napoleon's
presence in Egypt. He was frankly far from convinced that it
was possible to launch a successful invasion from there,
whether by land or by sea. This, however, did not prevent him
from turning the fears of those in London to his own advantage.
A firm believer in forward policies, he was as keen to advance
the Company's frontiers in India as the directors were to keep
them where they were. They simply wanted profits for their
impatient shareholders, not costly territorial gains. As it was,
the Company had found itself drawn reluctantly and expensively into the vacuum created by the disintegration of Mogul
rule in India, and therefore increasingly involved in government and administration. Consequently, instead of being able
to provide their shareholders with the annual dividend they
had been guaranteed, the directors faced ever-mounting debts
and the perpetual threat of bankruptcy. Fighting off an
invasion, they knew, would be totally ruinous, even if successful, as little assistance could be expected from the government

at home which was itself engaged in the life-and-death struggle with France.

The crisis gave Wellesley the opportunity he needed, however. This was the excuse to crush and dispossess those native rulers who showed themselves to be friendly with the French, whose agents were still extremely active in India. But he was not to stop there. As he took full advantage of the free hand London was forced to give him to protect its valuable interests, large new areas of the country came under British control. Because his reports took so long to reach London, and anyway were always deliberately vague, Wellesley was able to continue these expropriations throughout his seven-year tenure as Governor-General. Thus, by the time of his recall in 1805, Company territory, its subsidiary states and regions partially controlled by it had expanded dramatically from the original three coastal presidencies of Calcutta, Madras and Bombay to include the greater part of India as we know it today. Only Sind, the Punjab and Kashmir still retained their independence.

The initial impetus, or pretext, for this spectacular piece of empire-building had been provided by Napoleon's precipitate move. Yet that threat, which had caused such panic in London, proved to be extremely short-lived. Making up for his failure to find and intercept the French armada before it reached Egypt, Admiral Horatio Nelson finally came upon it anchored in Aboukir Bay, east of Alexandria. There, on August 1, 1798, he trapped and destroyed it, only two vessels managing to escape. He thus cut Napoleon off from France, severing his supply lines, and leaving him to get his troops home as best he could. But if this defeat enabled Company chiefs in London to breathe again, the young Napoleon had far from abandoned his dream of driving the British out of India and building a great French empire in the East. Indeed, wholly undisturbed by his failure in Egypt, he was, on his return to France, to move from strength to strength with a succession of brilliant victories in Europe.

Before embarking on these, however, he was to receive a startling proposition from St Petersburg. It came, early in 1801, from Tsar Paul I, Catherine the Great's successor, and offered him the opportunity to avenge himself on the British and further his ambitions in the East. Paul, who shared his dislike of the British, had decided to revive the plan, which Catherine had turned down a decade earlier, for an invasion of India. It too involved a long advance southwards across Central Asia by Russian troops. But he had a better idea. It should be a combined attack by both Russia and France, which would make victory over the Company's armies virtually certain. He put his grandiose plan secretly to Napoleon, whom he admired almost to the point of infatuation, and awaited his reply.

Paul's idea was for a force of 35,000 Cossacks to advance across Turkestan, recruiting the warlike Turcoman tribes there as it went with promises of unimaginable plunder if they helped to drive the British from India. At the same time a French army of similar size would descend the Danube, cross the Black Sea in Russian vessels, and continue by the same means via the Don, Volga and Caspian Sea to Astrabad, on the south-eastern shore of the latter. Here they would rendezvous with the Cossacks before proceeding eastwards through Persia and Afghanistan to the River Indus. From there they would launch their massive onslaught together against the British. Paul had plotted their progress almost to the hour. It would take the French, he calculated, twenty days to reach the Black Sea. Fifty-five days later they would enter Persia with their Russian allies, while a further forty-five would see them on the Indus – just four months from start to finish. To try to win the sympathy and co-operation of the Persians and Afghans through whose territory they would pass, envoys would ride ahead explaining the reason for their coming. 'The sufferings under which the population of India groans', they would be told, 'have inspired France and Russia with compassion', and the two powers had united for the sole purpose of freeing India's millions 'from the tyrannical and barbarous yoke of the English'.

Napoleon was unimpressed by Paul's scheme. 'Supposing the combined army be united at Astrabad,' he asked him, 'how do you propose that it should get to India, across a barren and almost savage country, a march of nearly 1,000 miles?' The region he referred to, Paul wrote back, was neither barren nor

savage. 'It has long been traversed by open and spacious roads,'
he insisted. 'Rivers water it at almost every step. There is no
want of grass for fodder. Rice grows in abundance ...' From
whom he obtained this highly coloured account of the grim
tract of desert and mountain which they would have to negotiate before reaching their objective is not known, though he
may simply have been carried away by his own enthusiasm.
Paul concluded his letter with this exhortation to his hero:
'The French and Russian armies are eager for glory. They are
brave, patient and unwearied. Their courage, their perseverance and the wisdom of their commanders will enable
them to surmount all obstacles.' Napoleon remained unconvinced and declined Paul's invitation to join him in the venture.
However, as will be seen in due course, a not dissimilar scheme
was already beginning to take shape in Napoleon's own mind.
Disappointed, but undeterred, Paul decided to go it alone.

*   *   *

On January 24, 1801, Paul issued orders to the chief of the
Don Cossacks to raise a large force of fighting men at the
frontier town of Orenburg, and prepare to march on India. In
the event, the number mustered was only 22,000, far short of
that originally deemed necessary by Paul's advisers for such
an operation. Accompanied by artillery, they were to proceed
via Khiva and Bokhara to the Indus, a journey which Paul
calculated would take them three months. On reaching Khiva
they were to free Russian subjects held in slavery there, and at
Bokhara to do the same. Their main task, however, was to
drive the British out of India, and bring it, together with its
trade, under St Petersburg's control. 'You are to offer peace to
all who are against the British,' Paul ordered the Cossack
leader, 'and assure them of the friendship of Russia.' He concluded with these words: 'All the wealth of the Indies shall be
your reward. Such an enterprise will cover you with immortal
glory, secure you my goodwill, load you with riches, give an
opening to our commerce, and strike the enemy a mortal blow.'
    It is quite evident that Paul and his advisers knew virtually
nothing about the approach routes to India, or about the
country itself and the British dispositions there. Paul frankly

admitted as much in his written instructions to the expedition's leader. 'My maps', he told him, 'only go as far as Khiva and the River Oxus. Beyond these points it is your affair to gain information about the possessions of the English, and the condition of the native population subject to their rule.' Paul advised him to send ahead scouts to reconnoitre the route and to 'repair the roads', though how he came to believe in the existence of the latter in this vast, desolate and largely uninhabited region he does not say. Finally, at the last minute, he dispatched to the Cossack chief 'a new and detailed map of India' which he had just managed to obtain, together with the promise of infantry support as soon as this could be spared.

From all this it is clear that no serious thought or study had been given to this wild adventure. It is equally clear, as Napoleon had almost certainly realised, that Paul, a lifelong manic-depressive, was rapidly losing his reason. But the dutiful Cossacks, who had spearheaded Russia's conquest of Siberia and were soon to do the same in Central Asia, never thought to question the wisdom of the Tsar, least of all his sanity. Thus, ill-equipped and ill-provisioned for such a momentous undertaking, they rode out of Orenburg in the depths of winter and headed for distant Khiva, nearly 1,000 miles to the south. The going proved cruel, even for the hardened Cossacks. With great difficulty they got their artillery, 44,000 horses (for every man had a spare) and several weeks' supply of food across the frozen Volga and struck into the snowy Kirghiz Steppe. Little is known about their journey, for the British only learned of it long afterwards, but in a month they had ridden nearly 400 miles, reaching a point just north of the Aral Sea.

It was there one morning that one of the look-outs spotted in the distance a tiny figure against the snow. Minutes later a galloping horseman caught up with them. Utterly exhausted, he had ridden night and day to bring them the news. Tsar Paul, he told them breathlessly, was dead – assassinated. On March 23, at midnight, a group of court officials, alarmed at Paul's worsening megalomania (he had shortly before ordered the arrest of the Tsarina and his son and heir Alexander), had entered his bedroom intending to force him to sign abdication papers. Paul had leapt from his bed and tried to escape by scrambling up the chimney, only to be dragged down by his feet. When he refused to sign the document, he was unceremoniously strangled. Alexander, strongly suspected of being privy to the plot, had been proclaimed Tsar the next day. Having no wish to be dragged into an unnecessary war with Britain because of a hair-brained scheme of his father's, he had at once ordered the recall of the Cossacks.

In dispatching a messenger to stop them at all costs, Alexander undoubtedly prevented a terrible catastrophe, for the 22,000 Cossacks were riding to almost certain death. Brave and disciplined though they were, it is unlikely that they could have got even half-way to the Indus before disaster struck. Already they were having difficulty in providing for themselves and their horses, and before long frost-bite and sickness would have begun to take their toll. Those who managed to survive these hazards had still to run the gauntlet of hostile Turcoman tribesmen waiting to fall upon anyone entering their domains, not to mention the armies of Khiva and Bokhara. If by a miracle any of them had come through all that alive, and ridden down through the passes to the first British outposts, then it was there that they would have had to face the most formidable foe of all – the well-trained, artillery-backed European and native regiments of the Company's army. Thanks to Alexander's promptness, however, they now turned back, just in time, thus living to fight another day.

*   *   *

Wholly unaware of any of this, or of any malevolent intentions towards them by St Petersburg, the British in India were nonetheless becoming increasingly conscious of their vulnerability to outside attack. The more they extended their frontiers, the less well guarded these inevitably became. Although the immediate threat from Napoleon had receded, following his Egyptian setback, few doubted that sooner or later he would set his sights again on the East. Indeed, his agents were already rumoured to be active in Persia. Were that to fall under his influence, it would represent a far graver menace to India than his brief presence in Egypt had. Another potential aggressor was neighbouring Afghanistan, a warlike kingdom about which little was then known, except that in the past it had launched a number of devastating raids on India. Wellesley determined to neutralise both these threats with a single move.

In the summer of 1800 there arrived at the royal court in Teheran a British diplomatic mission led by one of Wellesley's ablest young officers, Captain John Malcolm. Commissioned at the age of only 13, and a fluent Persian speaker and brilliant horseman, he had been transferred to the Company's political department after attracting the favourable attention of the Governor-General. Laden with lavish gifts, and accompanied by an impressive retinue of 500 men, including 100 Indian cavalry and infantry, and 300 servants and attendants, he reached the Persian capital after marching up from the Gulf. His instructions were to win the friendship of the Shah at any cost (buying it if necessary) and to get it in writing in the form of a defensive treaty. Its aims were to be twofold. First of all it was to include a guarantee that no Frenchman would be allowed to set foot in the Shah's domains. Second, it was to contain an undertaking that the Shah would declare war on Afghanistan, a long-standing adversary of his, were it to make any hostile move against India. In return, were either the French or the Afghans to attack Persia, then the British would supply the Shah with the necessary 'warlike stores' to drive them out. In the event of a French invasion, moreover, the British would undertake to send him ships and troops as well. Put another way, they would be able to attack a French invasion force attempting to reach India across Persia both on the Shah's territory and in his territorial waters.

The Shah was delighted by the persuasive Malcolm, who was exceptionally adept at oriental flattery, and even more pleased with the sumptuous gifts he bore, each carefully chosen to appeal to Persian cupidity. These included richly chased guns and pistols, jewelled watches and other instruments, powerful telescopes and huge gilded mirrors for the Shah's palace. To help smooth the way there were also generous gifts for his senior officials. By the time Malcolm left Teheran for the coast in January 1801, amid much pomp and panoply and protestations of undying friendship, he had obtained, in writing, all the undertakings he had come for. Two treaties, one political and the other commercial, were signed by Malcolm and the Shah's chief minister on behalf of their respective governments. However, as these were never formally ratified, there was some doubt in London as to just how binding they were. This legalistic nicety, while lost on the Persians, suited the British. For his part, except for the sumptuous presents, the Shah had got little or nothing in return for his own solemn undertakings, as he would shortly discover.

Not long after the British mission's departure from Persia, something occurred on the Shah's northern frontier which gave him good reason – or so he believed – to congratulate himself on having acquired such a powerful ally and protector. He began to feel threatened, not by Napoleon or the Afghans, but by aggressive Russian moves in the Caucasus, that wild and mountainous region where his and the Tsar's empires met. In September 1801, Tsar Alexander annexed the ancient and independent kingdom of Georgia, which Persia regarded as lying within its own sphere of influence, a move which brought Russian troops rather too close to Teheran for the Shah's comfort. But although Persian feelings ran high, actual hostilities did not break out between the two powers until June 1804, when the Russians thrust even further south, laying siege to Erivan, the capital of Armenia, a Christian possession of the Shah's.

The latter sent urgent pleas to the British, reminding them of the treaty they had signed, in which they agreed to help him if he was attacked. But things had changed since then. Britain and Russia were now allies against the growing menace of Napoleon in Europe. In 1802, after overthrowing the five-man Directory, which had ruled France since the Revolution, Napoleon had appointed himself First Consul, and two years later crowned himself Emperor. He was now at the height of his power, and it was clear that he would not be content until the whole of Europe lay at his feet. The British therefore chose to ignore the Shah's call for help against the Russians. As it happened, they were quite within their rights, for Malcolm's treaty made no mention of Russia, only of France and Afghanistan. The Persians were deeply affronted though, seeing this as a betrayal in their hour of need by a people they believed to be their ally. Whatever the rights and wrongs of it, their apparent abandonment of the Shah was very shortly to cost the British dear.

Early in 1804, informed of what had happened by his agents, Napoleon approached the Shah, offering to help him drive back the Russians in return for the use of Persia as a land-bridge for a French invasion of India. At first the Shah demurred, for he had not given up hope of the British, who were nearer at hand, coming to his assistance, and he therefore played for time with Napoleon's envoys. But when it became clear that no help would come from Calcutta or London, he signed a treaty with Napoleon, on May 4, 1807, in which he agreed to sever all political and commercial relations with Britain, declare war on her, and allow French troops the right of passage to India. At the same time he agreed to receive a large military and diplomatic mission, commanded by a general, which among other things would reorganise and train his army along modern European lines. Officially this was to enable him to win back territories which he had lost to the Russians, but there seemed little doubt to those responsible for the defence of India that Napoleon intended to include the reinvigorated Persian troops in his designs against them.

It was a brilliant coup by Napoleon, but worse was to follow. In the summer of 1807, after subduing Austria and Prussia, he defeated the Russians at Friedland, forcing them to sue for peace and to join his so-called Continental System, the block-ade aimed at bringing Britain to her knees. The peace talks took place at Tilsit, amid great secrecy, aboard a giant raft decked with flags moored in the middle of the River Niemen. This curious choice of venue was to ensure that the two emperors were not overheard, especially by the British, who were known to have spies everywhere. Despite this precaution, however, the British secret service, which had an annual vote of £170,000, devoted principally to bribery, appears to have smuggled its own man on board – a disaffected Russian noble-man who sat hidden beneath the barge, his legs dangling in the water, listening to every word.

Whether or not this was true, London was quick to discover

that the two men, having patched up their differences, were now proposing to join forces and divide the world between them. France was to have the West, and Russia the East, including India. But when Alexander demanded Constantinople, the meeting point of East and West, for himself, Napoleon had shaken his head. 'Never!' he said, 'For that would make you Emperor of the world.' Not long afterwards intelligence reached London that just as Alexander's father had put a plan for the invasion of India to Napoleon, so the latter had proposed a similar but greatly improved scheme to his new Russian ally. The first step would be the seizure of Constantinople, which they would share. Then, after marching the length of a defeated Turkey and a friendly Persia, they would together attack India.

Greatly alarmed by this news, and by the arrival of the powerful French mission at Teheran, the British acted swiftly – too swiftly in fact. Without consulting one another, both London and Calcutta dispatched trouble-shooters to Persia to try to prevail upon the Shah to eject the French – 'the advance guard of a French army,' Lord Minto, Wellesley's successor as Governor-General, called them. The first to arrive was John Malcolm, hurriedly promoted to Brigadier-General to give him added weight in his dealings with the Shah. In May 1808, eight years after his previous visit, Malcolm arrived at Bushire in the Persian Gulf. There, to his intense irritation, he was kept waiting by the Persians (under pressure, he was convinced, from the French), who refused to allow him to proceed any further. The real reason for the delay was that the Shah had just learned of Napoleon's secret deal with Alexander, and it was dawning on him that the French, like the British before them, were in no position to help him against the Russians. Napoleon's men, realising that their days in Teheran were numbered, were trying to persuade the wavering Shah that because they were no longer at war with the Russians, but their allies, they were now in an even stronger position to restrain Alexander.

Becoming increasingly annoyed at being kept waiting on the coast while his French rivals remained in the capital, enjoying the Shah's ear, Malcolm sent a sharp note to the Persian ruler warning him of the grave consequences if the mission was not expelled forthwith. After all, had not the Persians, under the treaty that he himself had negotiated with them, solemnly undertaken to have no dealings whatsoever with the French? But the Shah, who had long ago torn up the treaty he had signed with the British, was merely angered by Malcolm's high-handed ultimatum. The latter thus continued to be debarred from visiting the capital and putting the British case in person. As it was, he decided to return at once to India and report in full to the Governor-General on the Shah's intransigence, with the strong recommendation that only a show of force would knock any sense into his head and see the French on their way.

Shortly after his departure, Sir Harford Jones, London's emissary, arrived. By good luck he did so just as the Shah had reconciled himself to the fact that it would take rather more than the good offices of the French to get the Russians to withdraw from his Caucasian territories. The Persians proceeded to take another U-turn. The French general and his staff were handed their passports, and Jones and his accompanying staff fêted. The Shah was desperately looking for friends, and was only too happy to forget the past – especially as Jones had brought with him as a gift from George III one of the largest diamonds he had ever set eyes on. If he was puzzled by the arrival, in such quick succession, of two British missions, one breathing fire and the other bearing gifts, he was tactful enough to say nothing about it.

Although relations between Britain and Persia were now cordial again, those between London and Calcutta were not. Smarting from the easy success of London's man where his own had failed, Lord Minto was determined to reassert his responsibility for British relations with Persia. The somewhat undignified quarrel which ensued marked the beginning of a rivalry which would bedevil relations between British India and the home government for the next century and a half. In order to keep India's interests paramount, the Governor-General wanted his own man, Malcolm, to negotiate the proposed new treaty with the Shah, while London opposed this. A face-saving compromise was eventually reached, under which Sir Harford Jones, a highly experienced diplomat, would stay on and complete the negotiations, while Malcolm, promoted to Major-General for the occasion, would be sent to Teheran to ensure that this time its terms were firmly adhered to.

Under the new agreement the Shah undertook not to allow the forces of any other power to cross his territory for the purpose of attacking India, or himself to engage in dealings inimical to Britain's interests, or those of India. In return, were Persia itself threatened by an aggressor, Britain would send troops to its assistance. Were this to prove impossible, she would send instead sufficient arms and advisers to expel the invader, even if she herself were at peace with the latter. Clearly this meant Russia. The Shah was not going to make the same mistake again. In addition he would receive an annual subsidy of £120,000, and the services of British officers to train and modernise his army in place of the French. Malcolm would be responsible for supervising the latter. However, there was another compelling reason why Lord Minto was so anxious to send Malcolm back to Teheran.

Fears of a Franco-Russian attack on India had brought home to those responsible for its defence how little they knew about the territories through which an invading army would have to march. Something had to be done quickly to remedy this, for all the treaties in the world would not stop a determined aggressor like Napoleon. In Minto's view, there was no one better equipped to organise this than Malcolm, who already knew more about Persia than any other Englishman. In February 1810, he arrived once again at Bushire and made his way, unhindered this time, to the Persian capital. Accompanying him was a small group of hand-picked officers, ostensibly there to train the Shah's army in the arts of European warfare, but also to discover all they could about the military geography of Persia – just as Napoleon's men had been doing before them.

However, that was not all. Further to the east, in the wilds of Baluchistan and Afghanistan, regions through which an invader would have to pass after crossing Persia, other British officers were already at work, secretly spying out the land for

Malcolm. It was a hazardous game, calling for cool nerves and a strong sense of adventure.

·3·

Rehearsal for the
Great Game

Had one been travelling through northern Baluchistan in the spring of 1810, one might have observed a small party of armed men mounted on camels leaving the remote oasis-village of Nushki and making for the Afghan frontier. Ahead of them in the distance, vivid sheets of lightning lit up the blackened sky, while now and again in the surrounding mountains the rumble of thunder could be heard. A heavy storm seemed imminent, and instinctively the riders drew their cloaks about them as they headed into the desert.

One of the men stood out from the others, his skin being noticeably lighter than that of his companions. They believed him to be a Tartar horse-dealer, for that is what he had told them, and never having seen one before they had no reason to doubt him. He had hired them to escort him through the dangerous, bandit-infested country lying between Nushki and the ancient walled city of Herat, 400 miles to the north-west, on the Afghan–Persian frontier. There, the fair-complexioned one explained, he hoped to purchase horses for his rich Hindu master in far-off India. For Herat was one of the great caravan towns of Central Asia, and especially renowned for its horses. It also happened to be of considerable interest to those responsible for the defence of India.

The stranger had arrived in Nushki a few days earlier, accompanied by another man of like complexion whom he had introduced as his younger brother who worked for the same Hindu merchant. They had reached Nushki from Kelat, Balu-

chistan's mud-built capital, after disembarking on the coast
from a small native vessel which had brought them from
Bombay. The journey up from the coast had taken them the
best part of two months, for they had not hurried, asking many
questions on the way, while trying not to appear too inquisitive.
It was at Nushki that the two had separated, the elder heading
for Herat with his escort, while the other struck westwards
towards Kerman, in southern Persia, where he said he too
hoped to buy horses for their employer.

Before going their own ways, the two men had taken leave
of one another in the privacy of the native house they had
rented for their brief stay in Nushki. They were most careful
to ensure that they were neither observed nor overheard.
Indeed, had an inquisitive person happened to peer through a
crack he might well have been puzzled by what he saw and
heard. For it was obvious that this was more than simply the
parting of two brothers. With lowered voices and a careful eye
on the door, the two men discussed, with an un-Asiatic degree
of precision, the details of their respective routes, and last-
minute arrangements should anything go amiss. They discussed other matters too which an eavesdropper would have
had difficulty in following. For had the truth been known (and
it would have meant instant death for both), neither of them
was a horse-dealer, let alone a Tartar. Nor for that matter were
they even brothers. They were young British officers engaged
on a secret reconnaissance for General Malcolm through wild
and lawless regions which had never previously been explored.

Captain Charles Christie and Lieutenant Henry Pottinger,
both of the 5th Bombay Native Infantry, were now about to
embark on the most dangerous and – to those who had sent
them – the most valuable part of their mission. Already, during
their apparently leisurely journey up from the coast they had
managed to gather considerable intelligence concerning the
tribes, their leaders and the numbers of fighting men they
controlled. They had also taken careful note of the defensive
possibilities of the terrain through which they had travelled.
As strangers, even as Tartars professing the Muslim faith, they
were looked upon with intense suspicion. More than once they
had had to lie their way out of trouble by embellishing and

improving their cover story to suit the circumstances. Had the fiercely independent Baluchis discovered what they were up to, it would immediately have been assumed that the British were exploring their lands preparatory to seizing them. But fortunately for Christie and Pottinger no one living in this remote region had ever set eyes on a European. So far nobody had penetrated their disguise – or so it appeared.

Nonetheless, as they parted, each wishing the other good luck, they were aware that this might be their last meeting. Assuming all went well, however, their plan was to meet up again at an agreed rendezvous, in the relative safety of the Shah's domains, after completing their respective reconnaissances. If by a certain date one of them had failed to arrive, then the other should assume that he had either been forced to abandon the journey, or had been killed, in which case the one who did make the rendezvous would proceed to Teheran alone and report to General Malcolm. If either found himself in difficulties, he would try to get a message to the other, or to the British mission in Teheran, so that some kind of help might be organised.

After Christie's departure with his men on March 22, Pottinger remained in Nushki preparing his own small caravan. Malcolm had given him the task of exploring the great deserts which were thought to lie to the west, presenting a major obstacle, it was hoped, to an advancing army. But on March 23 he received alarming news. A message sent by friends whom he and Christie had made in Kelat, the Baluchi capital, warned him that men had arrived there from neighbouring Sind with orders to arrest the two of them. They had told the Khan of Kelat that Christie and Pottinger were no more horse-dealers than they were, and that they had adopted this guise to survey the country for military purposes, a move which threatened both their peoples.

The two Englishmen were to be seized and taken back to Hyderabad, the capital of Sind, where they would be severely dealt with. The armed Sindians, the message warned, were on their way to Nushki, a distance of only fifty miles across the desert. He and his companion, it advised, should leave while there was still time, as the Sindians made no secret of the fact that they were to be bastinadoed. Aware that this was the least of the fates he might expect in Hyderabad, Pottinger made plans to leave immediately. The following morning, with an armed escort of five Baluchis, he hastily set off westwards, profoundly grateful to their friends at Kelat who had endangered their own lives to protect his and Christie's.

*   *   *

Meanwhile, oblivious to all this, Christie had encountered another hazard as he and his small party approached the Afghan frontier. Not long after leaving Nushki he had been warned by a friendly shepherd that thirty armed Afghans were planning to rob him, and were at that moment waiting in ambush in a gully some distance ahead. To add to Christie's discomfort, the storm which had been brewing as he rode out of Nushki now broke with a vengeance, soaking everyone to the skin, as well as their possessions, and forcing them to seek what little shelter they could find in that barren landscape. It was hardly an encouraging start to an unimaginably lonely assignment. But by the following morning the storm had passed, and so too, it transpired, had their foes. Nonetheless the fear of raiders in this lawless realm was a perpetual trial to both Christie and Pottinger, as it would be to all subsequent players in the Great Game.

In the hope that it might offer him some protection against bandits, Christie decided to abandon his horse-dealer's guise and adopt that of a pious hadji, or Muslim pilgrim returning from Mecca. In his account of his journey he does not go into details, but this transformation appears to have been conducted with the help of an Indian merchant to whom he bore a secret letter, and between the signing off of one escort and the acquisition of another. His new cover, however, was not without its own problems and dangers, and he soon found himself embarrassingly out of his depth when a mullah engaged him in a theological discussion. He managed to avoid exposure by explaining that he was a Sunni Muslim and not, like his interlocutor, a Shiite. Christie must have been an exceptionally resourceful individual for at one point he managed to obtain a forged *laissez-passer*, purportedly from the tyrannical local khan and bearing his genuine seal. With the aid of this he ensured himself a warm welcome from the khan of the neighbouring region who even entertained him in his palace.

By now Christie was within four days of his goal, the mysterious city of Herat which only one other living European had dared to visit. It lay on Afghanistan's frontier with eastern Persia, astride the great network of trans-Asian caravan routes. Its bazaars displayed goods from Khokand and Kashgar, Bokhara and Samarkand, Khiva and Merv, while other roads led westwards to the ancient caravan cities of Persia – Meshed, Teheran, Kerman and Isfahan. But to the British in India, fearing invasion from the west, Herat possessed a more ominous significance. It stood on one of the traditional conqueror's routes to India, along which a hostile force could reach either of its two great gateways, the Khyber and Bolan Passes. Worse, in a region of vast deserts and impenetrable mountain ranges, it stood in a rich and fertile valley which – or so it was believed in India – was capable of provisioning and watering an entire army. Christie's task was to discover the truth of this.

On April 18, four months after he and Pottinger had sailed from Bombay, Christie rode through the principal gateway of the great walled city of Herat. He had abandoned his disguise as a holy man and had reverted to that of a horse-dealer, for he carried with him letters of introduction to a Hindu merchant living in the town. He was to remain there for a month, taking careful notes of all that caught his soldier's eye, or ear. 'The city of Heerat', he observed, 'is situated in a valley, surrounded by lofty mountains.' The valley, running from east to west, was thirty miles long and fifteen wide. It was watered by a river which rose in the mountains and ran the length of the valley which was intensively cultivated, with villages and gardens stretching as far as the eye could see. The city itself covered an area of four square miles, and was surrounded by a massive wall and moat. At its northern end, raised up on a hill, was a citadel built of baked brick, with a tower at each corner. Surrounding this was a second moat, spanned by a drawbridge, and beyond this another high wall and a third moat, albeit dry. Spectacular as all this appeared to anyone approaching the city, it failed to impress Christie. 'On the whole,' he wrote, 'it is very contemptible as a fortification.'

But if he was not struck by Herat's capacity to defend itself against attack by an army supplied with modern artillery, like that of Napoleon or Tsar Alexander, Christie was much impressed by its obvious prosperity and fecundity, and capacity therefore to support and supply any invading army into whose hands it might fall. In the surrounding countryside there was excellent grazing, an ample supply of horses and camels, and an abundance of wheat, barley and fresh fruit of all kinds. The population of Herat and its suburbs Christie put at 100,000, including 600 Hindus, mainly wealthy merchants.

On May 18, satisfied that he had nothing more of value to discover, Christie announced that before returning to India with the horses he proposed to buy for his employer he would make a brief pilgrimage to the holy city of Meshed, 200 miles to the north-west, in Persia. He was thus able to leave Herat without having to buy the horses which his cover story demanded. The following day, with considerable relief, he crossed into eastern Persia. After months of lying and subterfuge, he at last felt reasonably safe. Even if it was discovered that he was an East India Company officer in disguise, Britain's now good relations with Persia would ensure that no serious harm befell him. Nine days later he turned off the old pilgrim road to Meshed, striking south-westwards across the desert to Isfahan, which he calculated Lieutenant Pottinger should by now have reached.

*　　*　　*

During the two months since they had parted company at Nushki, much had happened to his brother officer. Without a map to guide him (none then existed), the 20-year-old subaltern had set off on a 900-mile journey across Baluchistan and Persia. He chose a route which for a further century no other European was to attempt, though earlier invaders had passed that way. The journey was to last three months and take him across two hazardous deserts, with only local guides to steer him between wells and the bands of murderous brigands.

Despite sickness and other hardships, he maintained a surreptitious but detailed day-to-day record of all he saw and heard which could be of value to an invading army. He noted down wells and rivers, crops and other vegetation, rainfall and climate. He pinpointed the best defensive positions, described the fortifications of villages along the route, and detailed the idiosyncrasies and alliances of the local khans. He even recorded the ruins and monuments he passed, although not being an antiquarian he had to rely on the dubious stories of the locals as to their age and history. In addition, he secretly charted his route on a sketch map, which later was turned into the first military map of the approaches to India from the west. Just how he managed to do this without detection he did not disclose in his otherwise detailed account of the journey, perhaps wishing to retain his secret for subsequent use.

On March 31, after skirting the south-eastern corner of the mighty Helmund desert, whose existence and approximate location were thus confirmed, Pottinger and his five-man party struck into the first of the two deserts they were now forced to cross. The presence of such vast natural obstacles astride an invader's path, Pottinger knew, would be extremely welcome news to those responsible for the defence of India. He was soon to discover for himself why these deserts enjoyed so ill a reputation among the Baluchis, for within a few miles they ran into a succession of near-vertical dunes of fine red sand, some of them twenty feet high. 'Most of these', he recounts, 'rise perpendicularly on the opposite side to that from which the prevailing wind blows ... and might readily be fancied, at a distance, to resemble a new brick wall.' The windward side, however, sloped gently to the base of the succeeding dune, leaving a pathway between them. 'I kept as much in these paths as the direction I had to travel in would admit of,' he added, 'but had nevertheless exceeding difficulty and fatigue in urging the camels over the waves when it was requisite to do so, and more particularly where we had to clamber up the leeward face of them, in which attempt we were many times defeated.' The next day conditions got worse. Their continuing battle with the sand dunes was, in Pottinger's words, 'trifling compared with the distress suffered, not only by myself and people, but even the camels, from the floating particles of sand.' For a layer of abrasive red dust hovered over the desert, getting into their eyes, noses and mouths, and causing extreme discomfort, not to mention thirst, which was aggravated by the intense heat of the sun.

Before long they reached the dry bed of a river, 500 yards wide, with a recently abandoned village beside it, its inhabitants driven out by the drought. Here they halted, and after much digging managed to obtain two skins of water. The nature of the desert now changed from sand to hard black gravel. Not long afterwards the air began to feel sultry and dust-devils or whirlwinds sprang up, followed shortly by a violent storm. 'The rain fell in the largest drops I ever remember to have seen,' Pottinger recounts. 'The air was so completely darkened that I was absolutely unable to discern anything at the distance of even five yards.' Yet this storm was mild, his guide told him, compared with those which sometimes struck the desert at the height of summer, when it was considered impassable to travellers. The furnace-hot wind which accompanied these storms was known to the Baluchis as the 'flame' or the 'pestilence'. Not only could it kill camels with its violence, but it could flay alive an unprotected human being. According to Pottinger's men, who claimed to have witnessed its effects, 'the muscles of the unhappy sufferer become rigid, the skin shrivels, an agonising sensation, as if the flesh was on fire, pervades the whole frame . . .' The victim's skin, they assured him, cracked 'into deep gashes, producing haemorrhage that quickly ends this misery', although sometimes the sufferer might survive in agony for hours if not days. (That this was clearly a wild exaggeration may be obvious today, but in Pottinger's time little was known about desert travel, and anything must have seemed possible in previously unexplored regions such as this.)

Since the desert was without landmarks of any kind, the guide plotted their course by means of a distant range of mountains. Once, however, when Pottinger decided to leave at midnight to avoid the terrible heat of the day, they quickly found themselves lost, not knowing in which direction to proceed. Concealed on him, Pottinger carried a compass. Unknown to his men, he surreptitiously produced this, and after forcing the glass from it, he managed to feel the needle with his thumb, thus establishing the direction they should be heading in. When at daylight this proved to be accurate, his men were astonished, and for days spoke of it 'as wonderful proof of my wisdom'. Normally Pottinger only used his compass in secrecy to take bearings for his sketch map, but once or twice he was unable to prevent it from being seen. He would explain that it was a *Kiblah nooma*, or Mecca-pointer, which showed him the direction in which the Kiblah, or Muhammad's tomb, lay so that he could prostrate himself towards it when praying.

That day they rode for nineteen hours, travelling forty-eight miles and exhausting both men and camels. Food and water were now running dangerously low, and Pottinger wanted to continue until they reached the mountains where at least there would be water. However his men were too fatigued to go on, so they halted for the night, sharing the remains of the water between them, but eating nothing. The following afternoon they approached the village of Kullugan, in a region known as the Makran, which was notorious for its lawlessness. Pottinger's guide, who turned out to be married to the daughter of the Sirdar, or headman, insisted on entering the village first, explaining that it was customary with strangers in this dangerous region. Shortly afterwards he returned to say that Pottinger would be welcome, but that the Sirdar had ordered that, for his own security, he should adopt the guise of a hadji, otherwise he could not be responsible for his safety, even in his own house.

'You are no longer in the Khan of Kelat's territories,' it was explained to him. He must not expect the same good order and security that he had enjoyed there. 'We are now in the Makran, where every individual is a robber by caste, and where they do not hesitate to plunder brothers and neighbours.' As a horse-dealer employed by a rich merchant in India he would be particularly vulnerable, for it would be assumed that he must be carrying money, even if it was not his own. Pottinger had been warned of Makran's ill reputation by the Sirdar of Nushki, so he immediately assumed 'the religious air and mien' appropriate to his new calling.

On entering the village he halted and dismounted by the mosque where he was formally received by the Sirdar and other elders. Later he was conducted to his lodgings, a miserable hovel with two rooms, where food was brought for him and his men. This they fell upon with gusto and gratitude, not having eaten anything for thirty hours. Buying food for their onward journey proved more difficult. Because of the drought, it was explained, food was in very short supply and its price had risen astronomically as a result. All that could be spared, therefore, were a few dates and a little barley flour from the Sirdar's own supplies.

Pottinger was warned that the next village on his 700-mile ride to Kerman was at war with Kullugan, its inhabitants having raided and plundered them only three weeks previously. Not only would it be suicide for him to attempt to travel there, but he would be ill-advised to proceed any further westwards without additional armed men. Indeed, his guide told him he was not prepared to proceed without such protection, offering instead to escort him back to Nushki. Pottinger reluctantly agreed to hire six more men armed with matchlocks for the next leg of their journey, and a new route, bypassing the hostile neighbour, was worked out.

That night the village elders, including the Sirdar himself, descended on Pottinger's lodgings to discuss with him various topics including, to his alarm, religion. For as a holy man his views were eagerly canvassed and respectfully listened to. Despite an almost total ignorance of Muslim theology, he managed to bluff his way through without inviting suspicion. Not only did he avoid making elementary mistakes, but he also settled a number of points at issue. One of these was over the nature of the sun and moon. One of the villagers maintained that they were the same. But if that was so, queried another, why was it that sometimes both could be seen simultaneously? Ah, replied the first, one was merely the reflection of the other. At this point the view of Pottinger was sought. He was now beginning to get irritated by this uninvited audience, and moreover wished to get to sleep, so he adjudicated in favour of the latter view, thus definitively settling a debate which, he feared, would have continued for some hours, the villagers having little else to do.

The following day the Sirdar suggested that before leaving Pottinger should attend prayers at the mosque. This was, Pottinger later wrote, 'an act of duplicity I had hitherto evaded.' But he was given little choice, for the Sirdar came to his lodgings to collect him. 'I perceived there was no alternative,' Pottinger relates, 'so I simply went through the motions of prostration, keeping my eye fixed on the Sirdar, and muttering to myself.' Amazingly, no one appears to have suspected him. The friendly Sirdar, who had suggested the new disguise, knew full well that he was not a holy man, but had no idea that he was a Christian and a British officer, assuming him to be a devout Muslim. Nor was this to be the last time that Pottinger's disguise as a holy man would cause him intense anxiety. After riding all night they reached the village of Gull, where Pottinger was warmly welcomed by the mullah who invited him to breakfast. 'I found four or five well-dressed and respectable men sitting on carpets spread under a shady tree, with bread and butter-milk in wooden dishes before them,' Pottinger tells us. They rose to their feet to welcome him, and he found himself seated on the mullah's right. After they had eaten, one of the men called upon Pottinger to say a prayer of thanksgiving. 'This', Pottinger recounts, 'was as unexpected as it was unwelcome, and I was greatly perplexed for an instant.' Fortunately, however, before leaving Bombay he had taken the trouble to learn a Muslim prayer or two from a servant, never dreaming that this would later save him from an unpleasant fate. He and Christie had intended to carry out their mission as horse-dealers, not as holy men, or he might have taken pains to learn these prayers more thoroughly. Desperately trying to remember one, Pottinger now stood up, uncomfortably aware that all eyes were fixed on him. 'I assumed a very grave air,' he recalled, 'stroked down my beard with all imaginable significance, and muttered a few sentences.' He was careful to pronounce – 'rather distinctly' – such words as *Allah*, *Rusool* (the Prophet) and *Shookr* (Thanks). These words were the most likely, he felt, to recur in a prayer of this kind. The risky subterfuge worked once again, for the unsuspecting mullah and his companions smiled benignly upon their pious visitor.

Pottinger's next close shave occurred the following day, in another village. He was buying a pair of shoes in the market (for one of his had been carried off by a jackal during the night) when an old man in the crowd which had gathered round him pointed to his feet. Pottinger, he declared, was clearly not a man accustomed to a life of toil or poverty. 'I instantly went to my shoes and put them on,' Pottinger recounts, 'for notwithstanding I had persevered in exposing my feet to the sun, I could never get them to assume the weather-beaten colour of my hands and face.' Wishing to avoid further interrogation, he returned to his camel, followed closely by the man, and left the village rather hastily.

Two days later, Pottinger and his party entered the small, mud-walled village of Mughsee, where they had planned to halt for the night. But on discovering what was happening there, they decided not to linger. Only a few days earlier, they were told, a gang of armed brigands had murdered the Sirdar and his family and taken over the village. One of his sons had managed to escape, and at that very moment the brigands were laying siege to the house in which he was sheltering, and which was pointed out to Pottinger and his party. The unfortunate youth, whose father had refused to let the brigands cultivate land near the village, had been told that he might as well come out and be put to death like the rest of his family, for otherwise they would starve him out. None of the villagers attempted to go to his defence, and Pottinger's small party was powerless to intercede. They had little choice but to continue on their way, leaving him to his fate.

Three days later, Pottinger was to find himself wondering if his own last moment had not come. He had arrived at the village of Puhra bearing with him a letter of introduction from the Sirdar of a previous village. This he presented to the Khan of Puhra, who called upon his *mirza*, or clerk, to read it aloud. To Pottinger's acute embarrassment, it expressed the writer's suspicion that this holy man who was passing through their territories was really an individual of high birth, possibly a prince even, who had forsworn a life of privilege to become a humble holy man. That it had been written with the best of intentions, to ensure that he would be well received, Pottinger had no doubt. But it was to lead directly, and dramatically, to his being exposed not only as a bogus pilgrim – an infidel Christian, moreover – but also as an Englishman. And his exposure came from a totally unexpected quarter.

After the Sirdar's letter had been read out, the crowd of villagers surrounding Pottinger had looked at him with new interest. It was at this moment that a small boy aged 10 or 12 suddenly raised his voice. 'If he hadn't said that he was a holy man, I would swear that he is the brother of Grant, the European, who came to Bampur last year ...' The sharp-eyed youngster had come within an inch of the truth. The previous year Captain W. P. Grant of the Bengal Native Infantry had been sent to explore the coastline of the Makran to see whether a hostile army would be able to advance towards India by this route (he had reported that it would). During his reconnaissance he had journeyed some way inland to the town of Bampur, in eastern Persia, which Pottinger was now approaching. By sheer ill-chance, this boy – perhaps the only one present ever to have set eyes on a European – must have seen him and spotted some resemblance between the two men.

Pottinger, badly shaken, tried to conceal his dismay. 'I endeavoured to let the lad's remark pass unnoticed,' he wrote, 'but the confusion of my looks betrayed me.' Seeing this, the Khan asked him if it was true that he was really a European. To Pottinger's relief, he went on to say that if he was he need not fear, for no harm would come to him. Realising that there was no point in further pretence, Pottinger confessed that he was indeed a European, but in the service of a rich Hindu merchant. Such a confession earlier in his journey would very likely have cost him his life, for it would immediately have been assumed that he was an English spy, but he was now quite close to the Persian frontier and consequently felt safer, although still not totally so. Moreover, his disguise had only been partially penetrated. His profession and the real purpose of his presence had not been detected.

The Khan, fortunately, was amused by the subterfuge,

finding no offence in an infidel posing as a Muslim holy man. But Pottinger's guide, who had clearly been made a fool of, was incensed. At first he refused to accept Pottinger's confession and regaled the Khan and the crowd with accounts of the theological debates he had engaged in with the holy man. The Khan laughed heartily when he described how Pottinger had even taken him to task over points of religion, a religion it now transpired that he did not believe in. The guide's anger and discomfiture were exacerbated by the claim of another of Pottinger's men that he had known all along that he was no holy man, although he had not suspected him of being a European.

A furious argument now broke out, with the guide accusing the other man of being an accessory to Pottinger's elaborate deception. In the end the good humour of the Khan, who pointed out that others including himself had also been deceived, saved the day, and by the time of their departure from the village forty-eight hours later Pottinger found that he had been forgiven by his guide. In the meantime he had become a celebrity, and his lodgings were besieged by what he described as 'a concourse of idle and obstreperous Baluchis who harassed me with preposterous queries and remarks.' That afternoon, however, a genuine holy man – this time a Hindu fakir – arrived, thus relieving Pottinger of 'the task of entertaining the whole village'.

Five days later Pottinger rode into the nondescript village of Basman, the last inhabited place in Baluchistan to the east of the great desert he would have to cross before reaching the safety of the Shah's domains. On April 21, after halting overnight in the village, Pottinger and his men headed towards the desert which they entered in the early hours of the following morning. There was no water or vegetation of any kind, while the heat, Pottinger recounts, 'was greater and more oppressive than I had hitherto experienced since leaving India.' They were also taunted by mirages or – as the Baluchis called them – the *suhrab*, or 'waters of the desert'.

In the fashion of his day, Pottinger constantly underplays the hazards and discomforts of his journey, but in describing the desert crossing he for once allows the reader to share with him the hell of thirst. 'A person may endure,' he writes, 'with patience and hope, the presence of fatigue or hunger, heat or cold, and even a total deprivation of natural rest for a considerable length of time.' But to feel one's throat 'so parched and dry that you respire with difficulty, to dread moving your tongue in your mouth from the apprehensions of suffocation it causes, and not to have the means of allaying those dreadful sensations, are ... the extreme pitch of a traveller's calamities.'

After two days' hard riding, usually at night to escape the heat, they reached the small Persian frontier village of Regan, on the far side of the desert. It was surrounded by a high wall, each of its sides 250 yards long, 5 or 6 feet thick at the base, and excellently maintained. The villagers, Pottinger learned, lived in permanent fear of the Baluchi tribesmen who, he tells us, 'seldom fail to pay them, or some other part of the Persian domains, a hostile visit once or twice a year.' In addition to the guards on the single gate, there were sentinels armed with matchlocks positioned at intervals along the wall who kept watch all night – 'frequently hallooing and shouting to encourage each other and warn any skulkers who may be outside that they are on the alert.'

Pottinger's unexpected arrival from out of the desert caused considerable consternation. 'For none could divine', he wrote, 'how we had entered the country unperceived.' The Khan, who received him warmly, expressed astonishment that the Baluchis had allowed him to pass through their country unmolested. Even so he had to spend the night outside the fort, for it was an absolute rule that no stranger should be allowed to sleep within its walls.

Pottinger now pressed on towards Kerman, the provincial capital, a large and heavily fortified town governed by a Persian prince and celebrated throughout Central Asia for its fine shawls and matchlock guns. It was here that he and Christie had agreed to rendezvous on the completion of their secret missions. Eight days later, after leaving the desert and riding through neatly tended villages and snow-capped mountain scenery, he arrived there, hiring himself a room in a caravanserai near the bazaar. Word of his arrival spread quickly, and soon the usual inquisitive crowd, this time several hundred strong, assembled at the door of his lodgings and began to pester him with questions. For although he no longer needed to conceal his identity, Pottinger was still dressed like a native in a faded blue turban, a coarse Baluchi shirt and a pair of filthy and tattered trousers which had once been white. But that evening, he tells us, having disposed of his inquisitors and purchased the best meal he had enjoyed in weeks, 'I lay down and slept with more composure than I had done any night for the preceding three months.'

On arrival he had sent a message to the Prince, seeking an audience. At the same time he had dispatched a courier to Shiraz where he believed (wrongly, as it turned out) his chief, General Malcolm, to be, advising him that he had come through safely and that his mission had been successfully accomplished. The Prince sent back a message welcoming him, and inviting him to his palace the following day. This presented Pottinger with a slight problem, for clearly he could not see the Prince in the clothes he had arrived in. Fortunately, however, he was able to borrow a change of dress from a Hindu merchant living near the caravanserai, and at ten o'clock the next morning he presented himself at the palace gates.

After crossing several inner courtyards, he was met by the Urz Begee, or Master of Ceremonies, who led him into the royal presence. The Prince, a handsome bearded man wearing a black lambskin cap, was seated at a window some ten feet above them, looking down into a small court with a fountain playing in the centre of it. 'We made a low bow,' Pottinger recounts, 'then we advanced a few yards and made a second, and in like manner a third, all of which the Prince acknowledged by a slight inclination of the head.' Pottinger had expected to be invited to be seated. 'But my dress not being of the first order,' he wrote afterwards, 'I suppose I was not thought respectable enough for that honour, and therefore I was placed opposite the Prince in the courtyard, round the walls of which all the officers of government were standing, with their arms folded across their bodies.' The Prince then called out 'in a very loud voice to know where I had been, and what could have induced me to undertake the journey I had performed, or how I had escaped from the dangers that must have attended it.'

Although he could now safely admit to being a European, indeed an English officer, the real purpose of his journey could not be revealed, even to the Persians. He therefore told the Prince how he and another officer had been sent to Kelat to buy horses for the Indian Army. His companion had returned by another route, while he had travelled overland through Baluchistan and Persia where he hoped to join Malcolm. The Prince seemed to accept his story and after half an hour dismissed him. There was no sign yet of Christie, nor any word from him, so Pottinger decided to stay a little longer in Kerman before attempting to report to Malcolm. This the Prince agreed to, and Pottinger filled in the time usefully by garnering all he could about the character and customs of the Persians, and in particular the city's defences.

When he had been in Kerman for some days, he was able to observe Persian justice in action. Seated at the same window from which he had addressed Pottinger, the Prince passed both judgement and sentence on a number of men accused of murdering one of his servants. The city that day was in a state of great excitement. The gates were closed and all official business halted. The sentences were carried out on the spot, in the courtyard where Pottinger had stood, the Prince looking on with satisfaction at the horrifying spectacle. 'Some,' wrote Pottinger, 'were blinded of both eyes, had their ears, noses and lips cut off, their tongues slit, and one or both hands lopped off. Others were deprived of their manhood, also having their fingers and toes chopped off, and all were turned out into the streets with a warning to the inhabitants not to assist or hold any intercourse with them.' When dispensing justice, Pottinger was told, the Prince wore a special yellow robe called the Ghuzub Poshak, or Dress of Vengeance.

Not long afterwards Pottinger received first-hand experience of the Prince's devious ways when he was paid a furtive visit by a middle-aged court official who asked to speak to him in private. No sooner had Pottinger closed the door than his visitor launched into a long oration extolling the virtues of Christianity, finally declaring that he wished to embrace it. Suspecting that the man was an *agent provocateur* sent by the Prince, Pottinger told him that regrettably he had neither the knowledge nor the authority to instruct him in this or any other religion. His visitor tried a new tack. There were at that very moment, he assured Pottinger, 6,000 men living in Kerman praying that the English would come and liberate them from the Prince's tyrannical rule. When, he asked, might they expect the English army to arrive? Anxious to avoid being drawn into such a dangerous conversation, Pottinger pretended not to understand the question. At that moment another visitor arrived and the man hastily departed.

Pottinger had now been in Kerman for three weeks and there was still no sign or news of his brother officer. Hearing that a caravan was about to leave for Isfahan, he decided to join it. Eleven days later he reached Shiraz and after a further sixteen days entered Isfahan, only to learn that Malcolm was in Maragheh, in north-western Persia. While resting in Isfahan, luxuriating in the comforts of a palace set aside for important visitors, Pottinger was informed one evening that there was a man wishing to speak to him. 'I went down', he wrote later, 'and as it was then quite dark I could not recognise his features.' For several minutes he conversed with the stranger before it suddenly dawned on him that this shabby, travel-stained figure was Christie. Christie had learned on reaching Isfahan that there was another *firingee*, or European, in town, and had asked to be taken to him. Like Pottinger he at first failed to recognise his deeply tanned friend, dressed in Persian costume. But seconds later the two men were embracing, overwhelmed with relief and joy at the other's survival. 'The moment', wrote Pottinger, 'was one of the happiest of my life.'

It was June 30, 1810, more than three months since their parting at Nushki. In all, since first setting foot in Baluchistan, Christie had ridden 2,250 miles through some of the most dangerous country in the world, while Pottinger had exceeded this by a further 162 miles. These were astonishing feats of daring and endurance, not to say of discovery. Had it been twenty years later, when the Royal Geographical Society was founded, both men would certainly have won its coveted gold medal for exploration, which so many of their fellow players in the Great Game were to carry off for journeys equally perilous.

As it turned out, their enterprise and courage did not go unrecognised by their superiors who were delighted by the valuable intelligence they had brought back. Both were now earmarked as young officers of outstanding enterprise and ability. Lieutenant Pottinger, who was not yet 21, was destined for rapid promotion, a long and distinguished role in the coming Great Game, and eventually a knighthood. In addition to the secret reports that he and Christie had prepared on the military and political aspects of their journeys, Pottinger was to write an account of their adventures which thrilled readers at home, and which is today still sought after by collectors of rare and important works of exploration. For their adoption of a pilgrim's robes to penetrate forbidden regions was undertaken nearly half a century before Sir Richard Burton won himself immortal fame by doing likewise.

Christie, sadly, was less fortunate than Pottinger, his days already being numbered. When Pottinger was recalled for duty in India, Christie was invited by General Malcolm to stay behind in Persia to help, under the terms of the new treaty, to train the Shah's troops to withstand Russian or French aggression. Two years later, while leading Persian infantry he had trained against the Cossacks in the southern Caucasus, he was to die in singularly dramatic circumstances. But we are moving ahead of the narrative, for much was to happen before that. Early in 1812, to the immense relief of London and Calcutta, the alarming partnership between Napoleon and Alexander had broken up. In June of that year Napoleon attacked, not India, but Russia, and to the astonishment of the world suffered the most catastrophic reverse in history. The threat to India had been lifted. Or so it seemed to a wildly rejoicing Britain.

·4·

The Russian Bogy

In the Baltic town of Vilnius, through which Napoleon's troops marched to their doom in the summer of 1812, there stands today a simple monument bearing two plaques. Together they tell the whole story. On the side with its back towards Moscow is written: 'Napoleon Bonaparte passed this way in 1812 with 400,000 men.' On the other side are the words: 'Napoleon Bonaparte passed this way in 1812 with 9,000 men.'

The news that the Grande Armée was streaming back through the Russian snows in total disorder was received at first in Britain with utter disbelief. The overwhelming forces which he had hurled against the Russians made a French victory appear certain. Word that Moscow had fallen to Napoleon's troops, and was in flames, seemed merely to confirm this. But then, after weeks of conflicting rumours, the truth began to emerge. It was not the French but the Russians themselves who had set fire to Moscow in order to deny Napoleon the food and other supplies he had hoped to find. The story of what followed is too well known to need retelling here. With winter approaching, and already desperately short of food, the French were forced to withdraw, first to Smolensk, and finally from Russia altogether.

Harassed continuously by Cossack and guerrilla bands, Napoleon's men soon found themselves forced to eat their own horses to survive. The retreat now turned into a rout, and soon the French soldiers were dying in tens of thousands, from frost-bite, sickness and starvation as much as from enemy action. As Marshal Ney's rearguard crossed the frozen Dnieper, the ice gave way, plunging two-thirds of the men to their deaths. In the end, only a shattered and demoralised remnant of Napoleon's once great army, which had been ear-marked for the conquest of the East, including India, succeeded in escaping from Russia. But Alexander, convinced now that he had been ordained by the Almighty to rid the world of Napoleon, was not content simply to drive them back beyond his own frontiers. He pursued the French half-way across Europe to Paris, entering it in triumph on March 30, 1814.

In Britain, as elsewhere, news of Napoleon's downfall was greeted with euphoria. Alexander's earlier duplicity in joining forces with him against Britain was conveniently forgotten, as relief overcame every other consideration. The newspapers vied with one another in heaping praise upon the Russians and extolling their many virtues, imaginary or otherwise. The heroism and sacrifice of the ordinary Russian soldier, especially of the splendid Cossacks, caught the imagination of the British public. Touching stories reached London from Europe of how ferocious Cossacks preferred to sleep on straw palliasses beside their horses rather than on comfortable beds in the best hotels, and how others turned their hand to help housewives on whom they were billeted with the domestic chores. One Cossack private who arrived in London that spring received a rapturous welcome – as did the Cossack chieftain who, fourteen years earlier, had led his men on that short-lived expedition against India on the orders of Tsar Paul. If anyone remembered, they said nothing. Instead, he was festooned with honours – including an honorary degree from Oxford – and was sent home laden with gifts.

This love affair with Russia was not, however, destined to last. For an uneasy feeling had already begun to dawn on some that a new monster had been created in Napoleon's place. Among them was the British Foreign Secretary, Lord Castle-reagh. When Alexander demanded at the Congress of Vienna, called in 1814 to redraw the map of Europe, that the whole of Poland should come under his control, Castlereagh objected strongly, believing Russia to be already powerful enough in

Europe. But the Tsar was insistent, and the two powers came close to war, this only being averted when Alexander agreed to share Poland with Austria and Prussia. However, the lion's share went to Russia. Nonetheless the European frontiers with which Russia finally emerged when Napoleon was safely imprisoned on St Helena were to mark the limits of its westward expansion for a century to come. In Asia, however, where there was no Congress of Vienna to curb St Petersburg's ambitions, it would soon be a very different story.

*   *   *

If one man could be said to be responsible for the creation of the Russian bogy, it was a much-decorated British general named Sir Robert Wilson. A veteran of many campaigns, with a reputation for hot-headedness both on and off the battlefield, he had long taken a close interest in the affairs of Russia. It was he who had been the first to report Alexander's now notorious words as he stepped aboard the barge at Tilsit in 1807. 'I hate the English as much as you do, and am ready to assist you in any undertaking against them,' one of Wilson's contacts overheard him declare. Wilson had begun by greatly admiring the Russians, and even after this had remained on good terms with them. When Napoleon turned on Russia, Wilson had been sent as official British observer with Alexander's armies. Despite his non-combatant status, he had thrown himself as frequently as possible into the battle against the invader. This gallantry had won him the admiration and friendship of the Tsar, who had added a Russian knighthood to those of Austria, Prussia, Saxony and Turkey which he already possessed. The general was to witness the burning of Moscow, and was the first to send back news of Napoleon's defeat to a disbelieving Britain.

It was on his return to London that Wilson drew official wrath upon himself by launching a one-man campaign against the Russians, Britain's allies, and in the eyes of most people the saviours of Europe. He began by demolishing romantic notions about the chivalry of the Russian soldier, especially those darlings of press and public, the Cossacks. The atrocities and cruelties perpetrated by them against their French captives, he alleged, were horrifying by the accepted standards of European armies. Large numbers of defenceless prisoners were buried alive, while others were lined up and clubbed to death by peasants armed with sticks and flails. While awaiting their fate, they were invariably robbed of their clothes and kept standing naked in the snow. The Russian women, he claimed, were especially barbaric towards those Frenchmen unfortunate enough to fall into their hands.

Few at home were in any position to challenge Wilson, a soldier of great distinction and experience, who had witnessed these things at first hand, including acts of cannibalism. Nor did he have much time for the Tsar's generals, then still basking in the glory of their victory. He accused them of professional incompetence in failing to attack the retreating French, thus allowing Napoleon himself, together with an entire army corps, to escape. They had been content, he reported, to allow the Russian winter to destroy the invader. 'Had I commanded 10,000, or I might say 5,000 men,' he noted in his diary at the time, 'Buonaparte would never again have sat upon the throne of France.' He even claimed that the Tsar had confided to him his own lack of confidence in the abilities of Marshal Kutuzov, his commander-in-chief, but explained that it was not possible to sack him because he enjoyed the support of powerful friends.

But Wilson's most violent onslaught was still to come. In 1817, four years after his return from Russia and after successfully standing for Parliament, he published a diatribe against Britain's ally. Entitled *A Sketch of the Military and Political Power of Russia*, and written anonymously (although no one was in any doubt as to its author), it was quickly to prove a bestseller and run to five editions in rapid succession. In it he claimed that the Russians, emboldened by their sudden rise to power, were planning to carry out Peter the Great's supposed death-bed command that they conquer the world. Constantinople would be their first target, followed by the absorption of the remains of the Sultan's huge but dying empire. After that would come India. In support of his sensational claim, Wilson pointed to the massive and continuing build-up of Russia's armed forces, and the remorseless expansion of the Tsar's domains. 'Alexander', he warned, 'already has a much larger army than his defensive line requires or his finances can satisfy, and yet he continues to increase his force.'

During Alexander's sixteen years on the throne of Russia, Wilson calculated, he had added 200,000 square miles to his empire, together with thirteen million new subjects. To underline this, his book included a folding map on which Russia's latest frontiers were marked in red, and its previous ones in green. This demonstrated just how close Alexander's armies now were to the capitals of Western Europe, and also to Constantinople, the key to the crumbling Ottoman Empire and eventually to the most direct route to India. The Ottoman capital was vulnerable to an attack by Russia from three directions. One was down the western littoral of the Black Sea from what is now Romania. Another was across the same sea from the Crimea. A third was from the Caucasus and westwards through Anatolia. Once Alexander was in possession of the Sultan's Near Eastern territories, he would be in a position to strike against India, either through Persia – and papers captured from Napoleon showed that he considered such a route feasible – or by a sea-borne force from the Persian Gulf, a voyage taking under a month.

Ten years previously, Wilson wrote, the Tsar had had an army only 80,000 strong. This had now grown to 640,000, not including second-line troops, militia, Tartar cavalry, and so on. There was 'none more brave', moreover, than the ordinary Russian soldier. He might also be cruel, but no other troops could 'march, starve or suffer physical privation' to the same degree. Wilson blamed Russia's spectacular rise to power on the short-sightedness of its allies, most especially Britain. 'Russia,' he declared, 'profiting by the events which have afflicted Europe, has been handed the sceptre of universal domination.' As a result the Tsar – a man 'inebriated with power', he claimed – was now an even greater potential threat to Britain's interests than Napoleon had ever been. It only remained to be seen how he intended to use his vast army to extend Russia's already vast empire. 'There is evidence amounting to conviction', Wilson concluded, 'that he has always proposed to accomplish the instructions of Peter the Great.'

Wilson's once close acquaintance with the Russian sovereign (who had after all honoured him with a knighthood), as well as with his army on the battlefield, invested his book with an authority which could not be ignored. However much it might enrage those who wished to see Britain and Russia brought closer, the general's alarmist and sensational message guaranteed him widespread attention in the press and among his parliamentary colleagues. Some editorials and reviews welcomed his warning as timely, while others condemned Wilson for slandering a friendly power and spreading what they claimed to be needless alarm. In an extended review of the book, running to no fewer than forty pages, the then pro-Russian *Quarterly Review* declared: 'Let us not, on the mere possibility that she might one day become too dangerous, dissolve our union with an ancient ally from whose greatness we now derive, and are likely to derive, increasing benefits.' Instead, in words which might have been taken from a leading article today on Anglo-Russian relations, it proposed that any rivalry should be restricted to 'which shall govern best'.

Although Wilson had no lack of supporters among the intelligentsia and the liberals, who abhorred Alexander's authoritarian rule, and from newspapers and journals of like view, he was largely shouted down. Nonetheless his book, much of which was based on false assumptions, gave birth to a debate on Russia's every move which would continue for a hundred years or more, in press and Parliament, on platform and in pamphlet. The first seeds of Russophobia had been sown. Fear and suspicion of this new great power, with its vast resources and unlimited manpower, and about which so little was known, had been planted firmly and permanently in British minds. The Russian bogy was there to stay.

*   *   *

Wilson was not alone in fearing that the Russians would use their Caucasian possessions as a springboard for an advance on Constantinople, or even Teheran. The Turks and Persians had long had similar worries, and in the summer of 1811, shortly before Napoleon's invasion of Russia, they had agreed to set aside their ancient rivalries and fight the infidel intruder together. Things had looked promising for them when Alexander began to withdraw his troops from the Caucasus for service at home, and the remaining Russian units began to suffer heavy casualties. In one engagement the Persians forced an entire regiment to surrender, together with its colours – an unheard-of humiliation for the Russians. 'The rejoicings at the Persian court can be imagined,' wrote one commentator. 'The Russians were no longer invincible.' At least that is how it appeared to the Shah, who had visions of further victories which would restore to him all his lost possessions.

Any such hopes, however, were quickly dashed. Locked now in a life-and-death struggle with Napoleon, the desperate Alexander had managed to negotiate a separate peace with the Turkish Sultan, the Shah's supposed ally. In return for an end to all fighting, the Russians agreed to return to the Turks virtually all the territory they had won from them during the previous few years. It was a painful decision for Alexander, but it gave his badly depleted forces in the Caucasus the respite they desperately needed, enabling them to concentrate all their efforts now against the Persians. Still smarting from their earlier disgrace at the hands of the Shah's troops, who had clearly benefited from the presence of General Malcolm's team of British officers, the Russians were burning to avenge themselves. The opportunity was not long in presenting itself.

One moonless night in 1812, a small Russian force led by a young general of only 29 named Kotliarevsky secretly crossed the River Aras, the Araxes of Alexander the Great's time, which nowadays marks the frontier between Iran and Azerbaijan. On the far bank was encamped a much larger but unsuspecting Persian force commanded by the Shah's headstrong son and heir, Abbas Mirza. He had been lulled into complacency by his earlier successes against the weakened Russian forces and by reports, very likely spread by the Russians themselves, that they went in great fear of him. So confident was he that he ignored the warning of his two British advisers to post pickets to watch the river, and even withdrew those they had placed there. His advisers were Captain Christie, Lieutenant Pottinger's former travelling companion, seconded to the Persians as an infantry expert, and Lieutenant Henry Lindsay, a massively built artillery officer, nearly seven foot tall, whom his men likened to their own legendary hero, the great Rustum.

Now that Britain and Russia were allies against Napoleon, members of Malcolm's mission had orders to leave the units to which they were attached in the event of hostilities breaking out, so as to avoid any risk of political embarrassment. But the Russians struck so swiftly that Christie and Lindsay, not wishing to be thought by the Persians to be running away, decided to ignore the order and fight with their men for whom they had formed a strong attachment. They tried desperately therefore to rally their troops, and for a whole day managed to hold off the fierce Russian attacks, even driving them back. But that night Kotliarevsky's troops struck again in the darkness, causing the Persians to fire into their own ranks in the confusion. Abbas Mirza, convinced that all was now lost, ordered his men to retreat. When Christie ignored this order, Abbas himself galloped up, seized the colours, and again called upon his men to abandon the position. In the chaos which ensued, Christie fell, shot through the neck by a Russian bullet.

Such was his men's devotion to him, according to the account of another member of Malcolm's mission, Lieutenant William Monteith, that 'more than half the battalion he had raised and disciplined himself' were killed or wounded trying to get him off the battlefield to safety. Their efforts were in vain, however. The next morning a Russian patrol found the British officer lying mortally wounded. 'He had determined never to be taken alive,' Monteith reported. If he was to face court martial for disobeying orders, he was reported to have said, 'it should be for fighting and not for running away.' A man of immense strength, Christie promptly cut down the unfortunate Russian officer who tried to raise him.

Word was hurriedly sent to Kotliarevsky that there was a severely wounded British officer lying out on the battlefield who was refusing to surrender. Orders came back that, whatever the risk to his captors, he was to be disarmed and secured.

'Christie made a most desperate resistance,' Monteith tells us, 'and is said to have killed six men before he was dispatched, being shot by a Cossack.' His body was later found by the mission's British doctor who buried him where he lay. 'Thus fell as brave an officer and amiable a man as ever existed,' Monteith concludes, though the Russians had seen little of this amiability during their brief encounter with him. Abbas Mirza's complacency, which had allowed his troops to be taken by surprise, cost 10,000 Persian lives, according to one account, while the Russians lost only 124 men and 3 officers. In addition to annihilating the Persian army, Kotliarevsky captured a dozen of Lieutenant Lindsay's fourteen precious guns, each ornately inscribed (or so the Russians claimed): 'From the King of Kings to the Shah of Shahs'. The earlier Russian defeat had been more than amply avenged.

The victorious Kotliarevsky now marched eastwards through the snow towards the Caspian where stood the great Persian stronghold of Lenkoran, only 300 miles from Teheran, and recently rebuilt along modern lines by British engineers. Believing it now to be siege-proof, the Persian defenders ignored Kotliarevsky's call to them to surrender, and drove back his first assault with considerable loss of life. But finally, after five days of bloody fighting, and with Kotliarevsky at the head of his troops, the Russians succeeded in breaking through the defences. Having turned down the Russian offer of an honourable surrender, the Persians were slaughtered to a man. Even so, Kotliarevsky lost nearly two-thirds of his troops, and was himself found semi-conscious and suffering from severe head wounds among the heaps of Russian and Persian dead beneath the breach his sappers had blown in the wall. Later, from his hospital bed, he reported to Alexander: 'The extreme exasperation of the soldiers at the obstinacy of the defence caused them to bayonet every one of the 4,000 Persians, not a single officer or man escaping.'

General Kotliarevsky himself never fought again, so grave were his injuries. Regretfully he had to turn down the Tsar's offer of the command of all Russian troops in the Caucasus, one of the greatest prizes to which a soldier could aspire. But for his victory, costly as it had been, he was to receive the highest award the Tsar could bestow, the coveted Order of St George, roughly the equivalent of the Victoria Cross. It was the second time he had won it, an unprecedented feat at so young an age. Years later, when he knew he was dying, Kotliarevsky summoned his family together and unlocked a small casket, the only key to which he always kept on his person. 'This', he told them with emotion, 'is why I was unable to serve my Tsar and fight for him and my country to the grave.' Opening the casket, he removed from it, one by one, no fewer than forty pieces of bone which Russian army surgeons had extracted from his shattered skull so many years before.

Following their two devastating defeats at Kotliarevsky's hands, the Persians had by now lost all stomach for the fight, and when the British, who were anxious to halt the Russian advance by diplomatic means if possible, offered to mediate a ceasefire, the Shah was only too glad to accept. The Russians, too, were grateful for a breather and the chance to rebuild their strength. And as the victors they were able to dictate the terms, and retain most of the territory they had won from the Persians. Thus, in 1813, under the Treaty of Gulistan, the Shah was obliged to surrender almost all his domains north of the River Aras, including his claims to Georgia and Baku, as well as renouncing all naval rights on the Caspian Sea. The latter effectively turned the Caspian into a Russian lake, bringing the Tsar's armed might another 250 miles closer to India's northern frontiers. The alternative would have been to allow his troops to continue their remorseless advance further and further into Persia. All that the Shah got in return, apart from an end to hostilities, was an undertaking from the Tsar that he would support the claim of Abbas Mirza, his son and heir apparent, to the Persian throne if this were ever disputed.

For his part, however, the Shah had no intention of honouring this treaty which had been forced upon him by his aggressive neighbours, regarding it as no more than a short-term expedient to halt their immediate advance. With Britain's continued help he hoped to rebuild his army, momentarily vanquished, along the latest modern lines, and at the opportune moment to seize back all his lost territories. After all, the Persians had once been a great conquering power, while their initial victories over the Russians in the recent war had shown what they were still capable of doing. But the Shah appeared not to appreciate that Britain and Russia, faced by a common foe in far-off Europe, were now officially allies, and that London, having successfully checked the Russian advance by peaceful means, had no wish to quarrel with St Petersburg over someone else's tribulations. For Russia's military build-up in the Caucasus was not yet widely viewed in Britain as posing a serious threat to India, at least not in government circles, where Sir Robert Wilson and his like were regarded as scaremongers.

With the Napoleonic menace towards India now over, and to the grave disappointment of the Shah, the British military mission to Persia was considerably reduced, while strict orders were issued that never again were British officers to lead Persian troops into battle against the Russians. The Christie affair had been overshadowed by the stirring events in Europe, and no protests had ensued from St Petersburg, but no one in London or Calcutta wished to risk a repetition. The Shah was in no position to argue, for any defensive treaty with Britain, then still the world's leading power, was better than none. Even a request that Persian officers might be sent to India for training was turned down, it being feared – according to a confidential note by the Governor-General – that their 'arrogance, licentiousness and depravity' might undermine the discipline and morals of the Company's native troops. However, if Wilson and his fellow Russophobes had failed to win much support in official circles for their fears of a new colossus arising in Napoleon's place, members of the British mission in Teheran had for some time been gravely concerned about Russia's growing power in the East.

Some of the mission's officers had already felt the hot breath of the monster to the north. Among those who had served as advisers to the Persian forces on the Russian front was a young Indian Army captain named John Macdonald Kinneir. Later he was to drop the Kinneir, and adopt Macdonald as his surname, but for simplicity's sake I have stuck to his original name. Seconded from the Madras Native Infantry to the Company's political department, he had served for some years in

Persia, where one of the first tasks entrusted to him by General Malcolm was the assembly into one volume of all the geographical intelligence gathered by Christie, Pottinger and other officers in the team. Published in 1813 under the title *A Geographical Memoir of the Persian Empire*, it was to remain for many years the principal source of such intelligence. In addition, Kinneir had himself travelled widely in these regions, and was extremely well qualified to air his views on the question of a potential Russian threat to Britain's interests in the East. This he was shortly to do, in a lengthy appendix to a second work, this time devoted to his own travels in the East, which appeared a year or so after Wilson's.

If Christie and Pottinger were the earliest players in the Great Game, albeit in its Napoleonic era, and Wilson its first polemicist, then Kinneir can lay claim to being its first serious analyst. Just how vulnerable, he now asked, was India to attack?

·5·

All Roads
Lead to India

The glittering riches of India have always attracted covetous eyes, and long before the British first arrived there her rulers had learned to live with the perpetual threat of invasion. This went back to the very earliest times when, some 3,000 years before the East India Company drove out its European rivals, successive waves of Aryan invaders had crossed the north-western passes, forcing the aborigines southwards. Numerous invasions, both great and small, followed, among them those of Darius the Persian *circa* 500 BC, and Alexander the Great two centuries later, although neither stayed for long. Between AD 997 and 1026, the great Muslim conqueror Mahmoud of Ghazni (which now forms part of Afghanistan) made no fewer than fifteen raids into northern India, carrying off vast quantities of booty with which to embellish his capital. Mohammed of Gor (today in northern Pakistan), having in his turn conquered Ghazni, led six invasions of India between 1175 and 1206, one of his generals becoming ruler of Delhi. After Tamerlane's troops sacked Delhi in 1398, another Central Asian warrior, Babur the Turk, invaded India from Kabul and in 1526 founded the great Mogul Empire, with Delhi as its capital. But even he was not the last of the Asiatic invaders. In 1739, with an army spearheaded by 16,000 Pathan horsemen, the ambitious Nadir Shah of Persia briefly seized Delhi, then still the Mogul capital, and carried off the world-famous Peacock Throne and Koh-i-noor ('Mountain of Light') diamond to grace his own capital.

Finally, in 1756, the Afghan ruler, Ahmad Shah Durrani, invaded northern India, sacking Delhi and removing as much loot as he could struggle back with over the passes.

Every one of these invaders had reached India overland, and it was not until the Portuguese navigators opened up the sea route from Europe at the end of the fifteenth century that her Mogul rulers began to worry about the possibility of an invader arriving by sea. Because the British themselves had come that way, it was perhaps natural for John Kinneir, in what is today called a 'risk assessment', to look first at the prospects of success of a sea-borne invasion. After all, India's 3,000-mile coastline appeared vulnerable, being ill-watched and virtually unguarded against a surprise attack. Not only the British, but also the Portuguese, Dutch and French had come that way, while as long before as the year AD 711 an Arab army, 6,000 strong, had sailed down the Persian Gulf and conquered Sind. Wilson warned that the Russians might do likewise.

Kinneir, however, who knew the Gulf region well from his own travels (he had even had a brush with Arab pirates there) and had access to the latest intelligence, argued that the obstacles facing a sea-borne aggressor were sufficient to rule out such an operation. 'We have little to dread from this quarter,' he wrote. To begin with, a hostile power would somehow have to gain possession of suitable harbours within reasonable sailing distance of India. Only the Red Sea or Persian Gulf, he believed, would provide the sheltered anchorage necessary for the preparation and launching of an invasion fleet. First the fleet would have to be built, which could hardly fail to attract the attention of the Royal Navy. And where would the materials come from? 'Neither the borders of the Red Sea, nor those of the Persian Gulf, afford timber or naval stores,' wrote Kinneir. 'Nor could materials be brought from a distance by water, or a fleet be collected, without our express permission.' The entrances to both these waterways were so narrow that, if the need arose, they could easily be blocked.

That he and his colleagues had not been wasting their time during their fact-finding travels in Persia was evident from the kind of detail that he was able to produce. While it was true, he reported, that forests of oak abounded in south-western

Persia, the trees (and he had seen them himself) were too small for building ships. Furthermore, they grew at a considerable distance inland, and would have to be transported to the shores of the Gulf at great expense and 'over stupendous rocks and frightful precipices'. Although timber of sorts could be found on the Ethiopian shore of the Red Sea, this, he tells us, was inferior even to that of Persia. It was not surprising therefore, he added, that all Arabian and Persian dhows were either built in India or from timber brought from there.

Ultimately, India's protection from such an invasion lay in the Royal Navy's domination of the seas. 'Were it even possible', Kinneir wrote, 'for an enemy to succeed in constructing a fleet with materials conveyed, at vast trouble and expense, from the interior of Syria, or the shores of the Mediterranean ... there is no harbour which could protect such a fleet from the attack of our cruisers.' And even supposing there was, he added, the invasion fleet would face certain destruction the moment it put to sea.

Kinneir now turned his attention to the several overland routes which an invader might use. Essentially there were two – directly eastwards through the Middle East, or south-eastwards through Central Asia. The former was the route most likely to be taken by an invader from Europe ('a Napoleon', as Kinneir put it), while the latter would be Russia's most obvious choice. An invader marching directly eastwards would be faced by several alternatives. If starting from, say, Constantinople, he could either approach the Indian frontier-lands by first marching the length of Turkey and Persia, or he could all but bypass Turkey by transporting his invasion force across the Black Sea to north-eastern Turkey, or through the Mediterranean to the Syrian coast, entering Persia from there. The latter, Kinneir pointed out, would expose him to the full fury of the British Mediterranean fleet. The former, on the other hand, would put his troopships safely out of its reach.

Ideally, rather than having to fight every inch of the way, an invader would try to come to some sort of an accommodation with those whose territories he had to cross, although the British were unlikely to stand idly by and let this happen. But even if he did manage to achieve this – and here Kinneir spoke from first-hand experience of the terrain – he would be faced by a series of extremely formidable obstacles all the way to India. These would include high mountain ranges; passes so steep or narrow as to be impassable to artillery; waterless deserts; areas so poor that they could hardly support the existing population, let alone a passing army; and hostile tribes and cruel winters which, as history had shown, could annihilate an army almost overnight. Even Alexander the Great, military genius though he was, had nearly come to grief in the icy passes of the Hindu Kush, which had been left unguarded because they were thought to be impenetrable in winter. Thousands of his men had been frozen alive – many literally bonded to the rocks in the sub-zero temperatures – or had died of frost-bite. He is said to have lost more men during the crossing than in all his Central Asian campaigns put together.

The last great natural obstacle facing an invader was the mighty River Indus and its network of tributaries. Fourteen hundred miles long, it had to be crossed before an invader could hope to conquer India. That this was not impossible, numerous early invaders had proved. But none of them had had to face a highly disciplined force, led and trained by European officers schooled in the most advanced defensive tactics of the day. The defenders would be fresh, well fed and regularly supplied, while the invaders would be exhausted from months of marching and hardships, short of food and ammunition, and greatly reduced in numbers. If the invader got that far, then there were two obvious points, Kinneir noted, at which he might try to cross the Indus. Were he to approach India via Kabul and the Khyber Pass, as a number of earlier invaders had, then he would most likely choose Attock. Here, he reported, the Indus was 'of great breadth, black, rapid and interspersed with many islands, all of which may be easily defended.' However, there were a number of fordable spots in the vicinity.

Were the invader to take the more southerly route through Afghanistan, via Kandahar and that other great gateway to India, the Bolan Pass, then he would probably attempt to cross the Indus near Multan, 300 miles down river from Attock. It was at this point that a Mongol army had once swum the Indus, and Kinneir described it as 'perhaps our most vulnerable frontier'. A more southerly route still, across Baluchistan, he appears to have ruled out, for he did not so much as mention it, perhaps because Pottinger and Christie had reported it to be impassable to a force of any size, while the coastal route, although once used by Alexander the Great, was deemed too vulnerable from the sea for an invader to consider it.

All roads ultimately led through Afghanistan, whatever route an invader came by. Even the Russians – and now Kinneir switched specifically to them – must approach India through Afghanistan, whether they set out from their new stronghold in the Caucasus or from their forward base at Orenburg, on the edge of the Kazakh Steppe. If they used the former, he warned, they could avoid having to march the length of Persia by making use of the Caspian, which they now controlled, to transport troops eastwards to its far shore. From there they could march to the Oxus, up which they could be ferried as far as Balkh, in northern Afghanistan. After crossing Afghanistan, they could approach India via the Khyber Pass. This, it will be recalled, was the route which Peter the Great had hoped to use to make contact with India's Mogul rulers – a dream which had ended with the massacre of the Khivan expedition. Kinneir was clearly unaware of the appalling difficulties of this route, for it was not until 1873, long after his death, that a detailed account of the expedition, and the hardships which it had to overcome, was translated from the Russian. In fact, once beyond the confines of the Persian and Turkish empires, Kinneir was as much out of his depth as anyone, having to admit that he had 'failed in every endeavour to gain such information as can be relied upon' about the terrain between the eastern shore of the Caspian and the Oxus.

Kinneir recognised, however, that supplying an invasion force attempting to cross Central Asia would present a colossal problem. 'The great hordes', he wrote, 'which formerly issued from the plains of Tartary to invade the more civilised kingdoms of the south, generally carried with their flocks the means of their sustenance.' Nor were they encumbered with the heavy equipment necessary for modern warfare. They were thus able to perform marches 'which it would be utterly impossible for European soldiers to achieve.'

The final option for the Russians lay in an advance from Orenburg, the fortress they had built in 1737 as a base from which to bring under their control the warlike Kazakhs who roamed the vast steppe region to the south and east. This would involve a 1,000-mile march southwards to Bokhara – 'said to be forty days' journey' away, according to Kinneir, but in fact several times that – followed by another long march across the desert and over the Oxus to Balkh. The route, Kinneir reported (correctly enough), was infested with murderous tribes, all hostile to the Russians. 'Before therefore the Russians can invade us from this quarter,' he wrote, 'the power of the Tartars must be broken.' Until that had been achieved, he believed India to be secure from invasion from the north. Curiously, Kinneir seems not to have seen the crossing of Afghanistan as perhaps the most formidable obstacle of all. For an invader would somehow have to get his weary troops, plus artillery, ammunition and other heavy equipment, not only across the Hindu Kush, but also through the lands of the fanatically xenophobic and warlike Afghans themselves. However, there was at that time an almost total ignorance, even among men as well informed as Kinneir, of the vast mountain systems and peoples surrounding northern India. For the era of the great Himalayan explorers still lay far off.

Unlike Wilson, Kinneir was not fully convinced that Tsar Alexander was planning to seize India: 'I suspect that the Russians are by no means desirous of extending their empire in this quarter; it is already too unwieldy, and may probably, ere long, crumble into pieces from its own accumulated weight.' He considered Constantinople a far more likely target for Alexander's ambitions. On the other hand, if the Tsar did wish to strike a crippling blow against the British in India, at minimal risk or cost to himself, there was another option which Kinneir could foresee. When the ageing Shah of Persia died, it would give the Russians the opportunity to gain control of the throne, 'if not reduce it entirely to their authority'.

Of the Shah's forty sons, there was not one, Kinneir wrote, who did not have his eye on the throne. As governors of provinces or towns, nearly half of them had their own troops and arsenals. Were St Petersburg to support one of these rival claimants (despite an undertaking to back the heir apparent, Abbas Mirza), Kinneir believed that during the inevitable turmoil which would ensue, 'the superior skill and discipline of the Russian troops would ... enable them to place their own creature on the throne.' Once they had the Shah in their pocket, it would not be difficult for them to incite the Persians, renowned for their love of plunder, to march on India. After all, had not Nadir Shah, the present Shah's ancestor, acquired the Peacock Throne and the Koh-i-noor diamond that way? The invasion could even be planned by Russian officers, although none of their troops would be involved, thus allowing the Tsar to wash his hands of it.

Kinneir's careful and detailed study of the invasion routes would be the first of many such assessments, official or otherwise, to see the light of day during the coming years. Despite the gradual filling in of the blanks on the map of the surrounding regions, most of the routes which he considered were to recur again and again, with minor variations, in subsequent studies. However, as the memory of Napoleon faded and fears of the Russian peril grew, the emphasis would gradually move northwards, from Persia to Central Asia, while Afghanistan, the funnel through which an invader must pass, was to loom increasingly large in the minds of those responsible for the defence of British India. But all that lay in the future. Despite the heated debate which Wilson's alarmist treatise had sparked off, most people were still not convinced that Russia, officially Britain's ally, bore her any ill-will or had designs on India.

Momentarily anyway, the Russian advance southwards into Persia had been blocked by British diplomacy, giving cause for considerable satisfaction in London. However, even as Kinneir was writing, General Alexis Yermolov, the Russian Military Governor of the Caucasus, had begun to look covetously eastwards, across the Caspian Sea, to Turkestan. It was there, exactly a century earlier, that the Russians had been so treacherously outwitted and defeated by the Khivans. What now followed was the first tentative step in a process which, during the next fifty years, would deliver the great khanates and caravan cities of Central Asia into the hands of the Tsar.

·6·

The First of the Russian Players

In the summer of 1819, in the Georgian capital of Tiflis – then the Russian military headquarters in the Caucasus – a young officer in uniform might have been observed at prayer in a quiet corner of the new Orthodox cathedral. He had good reason to be there that day, for he had much to ask of his Maker. At the age of 24, Captain Nikolai Muraviev was about to embark on a mission which most men would have considered suicidal. Disguised as a Turcoman tribesman, and following the same hazardous route as the ill-fated 1717 expedition, he was to try, on General Yermolov's orders, to reach Khiva, more than 800 miles to the east.

If he succeeded in crossing the bleak Karakum desert without being murdered or sold into slavery by the hostile and lawless Turcomans, he was to deliver in person to the Khan of Khiva, together with lavish gifts, a message of friendship from Yermolov. After a century without any contact, the Russians hoped thus to open the way for an alliance with the khanate. Yermolov's bait was commerce – the opportunity for the Khan to acquire luxury goods from Europe and the latest in Russian technology. It was a classic Great Game strategy, which the Russians were to use again and again, for Yermolov's long-term aim, when the moment was right, was annexation.

Befriending the Khan, therefore, was only part of Captain Muraviev's task. That was dangerous enough, for the Khivan ruler was widely known to be a tyrant who terrorised not just his own subjects but also the surrounding Turcoman tribes.

But Muraviev had been entrusted with a further role, which was even more perilous. He was to observe carefully, and note down secretly, everything he could discover about Khiva's defences – from the locations and depths of the wells along the route, to the numerical strength and military capacity of the Khan's armed forces. He was also to collect as much economic intelligence as he could about the khanate, so that the truth about its legendary wealth could be properly judged.

The Russians had one further interest in this remote medieval kingdom. Over the years large numbers of Russian citizens – men, women and children – had been sold into lifelong bondage in the flourishing slave-markets of Khiva and Bokhara. Originally they had included survivors from the 1717 expedition, but they were now mostly soldiers and settlers kidnapped or captured by the Kirghiz tribes around Orenburg, or fishermen and their families seized by the Turcomans on the shores of the Caspian. Very little was known about their plight, for escape was virtually impossible. It was Muraviev's final task to try to discover all he could about them.

Yermolov had chosen his man with care. Muraviev, the son of a general, and one of five brothers all of whom were serving officers, had already shown himself to be exceptionally able and resourceful. As an ensign of only 17, he had been five times mentioned in dispatches in the war against Napoleon. But he had other qualifications which fitted him exactly for this mission. In addition to being a trained military surveyor, he had carried out a number of clandestine journeys, including one behind Persian lines when he had travelled with false papers and disguised as a Muslim pilgrim. Thus not only did he have a soldier's eye for the terrain, but he was also fully aware of the dangers to which he was exposing himself.

Even so, Yermolov had reminded him that were he to fail, and the Khivans to imprison, enslave or execute him, he would have to be disowned by the Russian government. There would be no possible way of rescuing him, and the Tsar could not afford to lose face at the hands of a petty Central Asian ruler. Muraviev had one other quality which Yermolov told him to exercise without shame on the Khan, and that was his exceptional charm. To this was added a fluency in the local tongues.

'Your capacity for making yourself liked,' the general told him, 'together with your acquaintance with the Tartar language, can be turned to great advantage. Do not regard the arts of flattery from a European point of view. They are constantly used by Asiatics and you need never fear of being too lavish in this respect.'

As he prayed in the cathedral on the eve of his departure, the prospects of his returning alive to tell the tale must have seemed slender. For in the Khan's last communication, received some years earlier, he had warned that an unpleasant fate lay in store for any Russian envoy who approached Khiva. And yet, if anyone could pull it off, Yermolov was convinced that it was the brilliant young Muraviev.

A month after leaving Tiflis, Muraviev sailed from Baku in a Russian warship, calling in briefly at the coastal fortress of Lenkoran before crossing to the wild and desolate eastern shore of the Caspian. Here he was to remain for several weeks, making contact with the scattered Turcoman settlements while still enjoying the protection of Russian sailors and guns. At first the people were frightened and suspicious, but with the help of gifts to their chieftains he gradually won their confidence. Finally it was agreed that for a payment of forty gold ducats he could accompany a caravan which was shortly due to leave for Khiva across the treacherous Karakum desert. Half that sum would be paid on departure, and the rest on his safe return to the Russian warship. It was decided that it would be wise for him to travel disguised as a Turcoman of the Jafir Bey tribe, one Murad Beg, although the caravan men knew that he was really a Russian carrying gifts and important messages for the Khan of Khiva. The disguise was intended to protect him, not to mention the gifts, from the raiders and slavers who lurked in the desert. Even so, Muraviev carried a pair of loaded pistols and a dagger hidden beneath his robe.

On September 21 the caravan, consisting of seventeen camels, four of them Muraviev's, set off into the Karakum, being joined by other merchants as they proceeded. Eventually their numbers swelled to 40 men and 200 camels. 'The heat was great but not intolerable,' Muraviev was to write. 'The desert presented ... a very picture of death. Not an object betrayed signs of life . . . only here and there a stunted patch of bush struggled for existence in the sand.' Although he was constantly haunted by the fear of slavers, the journey passed largely without incident until they were just five days short of Khiva. They had halted to allow a large caravan of 1,000 camels and 200 men to pass when, to Muraviev's horror, someone pointed at him. They now crowded around him, asking his own caravan men who he was. Realising that his disguise had been penetrated, they replied with great presence of mind that he was a Russian they had captured and that they were taking him to Khiva for sale. The others congratulated them, saying that they had just sold three Russians in Khiva and got a good price for them.

When just thirty miles short of the capital, Muraviev sent ahead two men. One he dispatched to Khiva to advise the Khan of his approach, while the other carried a similar message to the nearest military commander, for he was anxious to prevent any wild or alarming rumours from preceding him – least of all any suggestion that he was the advance guard of a force coming to avenge the treacherous massacre of 1717. As they rode out of the desert into the oasis surrounding the capital, Muraviev noticed how prosperous the villages were. 'The fields, covered with the richest crops,' he wrote, 'presented a very different aspect to the sandy wastes of yesterday.' Even in Europe, he added, he had not seen such well-cultivated land. 'Our course lay through lonely meadows covered with fruit trees in which the birds sang sweetly.' All this he recorded discreetly in his notebook.

Muraviev planned to make his entry into Khiva the next morning, but had ridden only a few miles when he was intercepted by a breathless horseman who ordered him, in the name of the Khan, to proceed no further, but to await the imminent arrival of two senior palace officials. Shortly afterwards they rode into view, accompanied by an armed escort. The elder, Muraviev observed, had 'the face of a monkey . . . and jabbered at a tremendous pace . . . betraying at every word a vile character.' He was know as Att Chapar – meaning 'galloping horse' – for it was his official function to travel throughout the country proclaiming the Khan's orders. His companion, a tall, noble-looking man with a short beard, proved to be a senior officer in the Khivan armed forces. Chapar promised Muraviev that the Khan would receive him the following morning, but explained that in the meantime he would have to wait in a small fort a few miles away.

The walls of the fort were made of stone set in mud, and were about 20 feet high and 150 feet long. The fort itself was built in the form of a square, with a watch-tower at each corner. 'There was only one entrance,' Muraviev observed, 'and that through a large gate secured with a powerful padlock.' The room he was allocated was dark and squalid, although it provided welcome shelter from the intense heat. Food and tea were brought to him, and he was allowed to wander about the fort, although always accompanied by a guard. It did not take him very long to realise, however, that he was a prisoner. Unknown to him, someone had seen him taking surreptitious notes, and word of this had quickly reached the Khan. The arrival of a Russian envoy was disturbing enough, but it was clear that Muraviev was also a spy. If he was allowed to go free he would next appear at the head of an army. His arrival had caused consternation at the palace, and disagreement among the Khan's advisers as to what should be done with him.

The Khan had angrily cursed Muraviev's Turcoman companions for not robbing him and murdering him far out in the desert, thus sparing himself from any involvement or blame. The Qazi, his spiritual adviser, had recommended that the Russian be taken out into the desert and buried alive, but the Khan had pointed out that were word of it ever to get back to the Russians, then retribution in the form of a punitive expedition would speedily follow. It was generally agreed that Muraviev already knew too much, and must somehow be liquidated. But how? Had there been some way of disposing of him without the Russians ever discovering who was to blame, the Khan would not have hesitated for a second. The Khivans, normally so proficient in such matters, were for once baffled.

After seven nerve-wracking weeks, while Muraviev languished in the fort, it was finally agreed that the Khan should see the Russian and try to find out exactly what his game was. Just as Muraviev was despairing of ever getting away alive, and was making elaborate plans for a daring escape across the desert on horseback to the Persian frontier, he received a message to say that the Khan would see him at the palace. The next day, under escort, he was taken into Khiva. 'The city presents a very beautiful appearance,' he later recounted. Outside the walls stood the palaces and well-tended gardens of the rich. Ahead, in the distance, he could see the great mosque rising above the city's forty-foot-high walls, its blue-tiled dome, surmounted by a massive golden ball, shimmering in the sunlight.

His entry caused a sensation among the townsfolk, who turned out in strength to glimpse this strange apparition in a Russian officer's uniform. A large crowd accompanied him through the narrow streets to the elegantly furnished apartments which had been prepared for him, some even forcing their way in after him and having to be violently ejected by his Khivan escort. Now, for the first time, Muraviev became aware that among the crowd, staring at him in disbelief, were Russians – the pitiful victims of the slavers. They took off their hats respectfully to him, he later wrote, 'and begged me in whispers to try to obtain their release.' The memory of those lost souls was to haunt Muraviev for the rest of his life, but there was nothing he could do for them, his own position being precarious enough. Indeed, there seemed every likelihood that he might very soon be joining them. Even now, though his situation had improved, a close watch was kept on his every movement, with spies listening constantly at his door.

Having dispatched General Yermolov's letter and gifts to the royal palace, two days later Muraviev received a summons to appear before the Khan that evening. Putting on his full dress uniform (he had been advised that it would be a breach of etiquette to wear his sword), he set out for the palace preceded by men armed with heavy sticks who brutally cleared a way through the crowds. Even the roofs were lined with spectators, and once again Muraviev could hear 'the imploring voices' of his fellow countrymen among the multitude. Making his way past Khiva's great tiled mosques and *madrasahs*, its covered bazaars and bath-houses, he finally reached the main palace gateway. Entering, he crossed three courtyards, in the first of which were waiting sixty envoys from the surrounding regions who had come to pay their respects to the Khan. Eventually he was led down some steps and found himself in a fourth courtyard. In the middle of this, somewhat incongruously, stood the royal yurt – the circular tent of Central Asia. Seated in the entrance, cross-legged on a beautiful Persian rug, was the Khan himself.

Then, just as Muraviev was hesitating over how he should approach the Khan, he suddenly found himself seized from behind by a man in a dirty sheepskin coat. For a split second he feared he had been tricked. 'The thought flashed through my mind that I was betrayed,' he wrote, 'and that I had been brought here unarmed, not for negotiation, but for execution.' He shook himself free and prepared to fight for his life. But hastily it was explained to him that this was an ancient Khivan custom, and that all envoys were dragged before the Khan as a sign of voluntary submission. Muraviev now advanced across the courtyard towards the yurt, halting at the entrance and saluting the Khan in the local fashion. He then remained standing, waiting to be addressed. 'The Khan', he reported later, 'has a very striking appearance. He must be six feet high ... his beard is short and red, his voice pleasant, and he speaks distinctly, fluently and with dignity.' He was dressed in a turban and a red robe. The latter, Muraviev was gratified to see, was newly made up from material included among the gifts he had brought.

After stroking his beard for several minutes and studying the Russian carefully, the Khan at last spoke. 'Envoy,' he enquired, 'wherefore art thou come, and what dost thou wish of me?' This was the moment Muraviev had been waiting for ever since leaving Tiflis. He answered: 'The Governor of the Russian possessions lying between the Black Sea and the Caspian Sea, under whose rule are Tiflis, Ganja, Grusia, Karabagh, Shusha, Nakha, Shekin, Shirvan, Baku, Kubin, Daghestan, Astrakhan, Lenkoran, Saljan and all the fortresses and provinces taken by force from the Persians, has sent me to express his deep respect, and to deliver you a letter.'

The Khan: 'I have perused this letter.'

Muraviev: 'I am also commanded to make certain verbal

representations to thee, and only await thy order to discharge myself of the message now, or at any time that may be suitable.'

The Khan: 'Speak now.'

Muraviev explained that the Tsar of all the Russias wished to see a prosperous commerce grow up between their two kingdoms for their mutual profit and well-being. At present there was little trade because all caravans had to march for thirty days across a bandit-infested and waterless desert. But there was a shorter route which could be used. This lay between Khiva and the new harbour which the Russians were planning to build on the eastern shore of the Caspian at Krasnovodsk. There, Muraviev told the Khan, his merchants would always find vessels waiting, laden with all the Russian luxuries and goods that he and his subjects most desired. Moreover, the route between Khiva and Krasnovodsk would only take seventeen days, little more than half the present journey. But the Khan shook his head. While it was true that this was a far shorter route, the Turcoman tribes inhabiting that region were subject to Persian rule. 'My caravans would thus run the risk of being plundered,' he added, which effectively ruled it out.

This was the opening the Russian had been hoping for. 'Sire,' he declared, 'if thou wilt but ally thyself to us, thy enemies shall also be our enemies.' Why not therefore allow a Khivan official to visit Tiflis as a guest of the Tsar so that important matters of mutual interest, such as this, could be discussed with General Yermolov, who was eager for the Khan's friendship? The suggestion clearly fell into line with the Khan's own thinking, for he told Muraviev that he would send trusted officials back with him, adding: 'I myself desire that firm and sincere friendship may grow between our two countries.' With that he gave a sign that the audience was at an end. Muraviev, relieved that it had gone so well and that his life no longer appeared to be at stake, bowed and withdrew from the royal presence.

He was now anxious to leave Khiva before the winter closed in, as there was a risk that the warship which had orders to await his return might be trapped in the ice until the following spring. It was while the Khan's officials prepared for their journey to Tiflis with him that the Russian slaves managed to smuggle a brief and poignant message to him about their plight. Hidden in the barrel of a gun which he had sent for repair, it read: 'We venture to inform Your Honour that there are over 3,000 Russian slaves in this country who have to endure unheard-of suffering from hunger, cold and overwork, as well as every kind of insult. Take pity on our plight and lay it before His Majesty the Emperor. In gratitude we poor prisoners pray to God for your welfare.'

Muraviev, who had been making his own discreet enquiries into the situation of the slaves, was much moved by this. 'It made me very conscious of the gratitude which I owed to Providence for delivering me from danger,' he wrote afterwards. But there was little that he could do for his fellow countrymen there and then, beyond discovering all he could about them so that St Petersburg might be informed. 'I resolved that as soon as I returned I would do everything that I could to deliver them,' he added.

One elderly Russian he managed to speak to had been a slave for thirty years. He had been seized by the Kirghiz just a week after his wedding and sold in the Khiva slave-market. For years he had worked for long hours under terrible conditions to try to scrape together enough money to buy his freedom. But his master had cheated him of all his savings and then had sold him to someone else. 'We consider you as our deliverer,' he told Muraviev, 'and pray to God for you. For two years more we will bear our sufferings in expectation of your return. If you do not come back, several of us will try to escape together across the Kirghiz Steppe. If God pleases that we should die, be it so. But we shall not fall alive into the hands of our tormentors.' Young Russian males, Muraviev learned, fetched the highest prices in the Khivan slave-market. Persian males fetched considerably less, and Kurds least of all. 'On the other hand,' he reported, 'a Persian female slave commanded a far higher price than a Russian one.' Slaves caught trying to escape were nailed by their ears to a door, being too valuable to execute.

By now the Khan's men were ready to leave, and more than two months after first arriving there, Muraviev struck out once again into the desert. Among the huge crowds which turned out to see him off he noticed small, sad-faced groups of Russian slaves waving to him. One man, obviously from a good family, ran for a while at his stirrups, beseeching him not to forget 'us poor people'. After a bitterly cold journey across the desert, they finally reached the Caspian on December 13, 1819. Muraviev was greatly relieved to see the Russian corvette which had brought him still anchored off-shore. He hoisted his hat on a pole to attract attention, and a boat was sent to collect him. There was great rejoicing at his safe return, but he learned that the crew had suffered badly during the five months which had passed since they sailed from Baku. Only twenty of the original one hundred and twenty were still fit enough to carry out their duties. Five had died, thirty had scurvy, while the rest were so debilitated that they could hardly drag themselves around the decks.

They put into Baku on Christmas Eve. There Muraviev learned that General Yermolov was at Derbent, further up the coast, and he immediately set off to report his safe return to his superior. The general sent orders for the Khivan envoys to be brought to Tiflis where he would receive them. Meanwhile Muraviev sat down to prepare a full report on his mission, and his own recommendations over what action could be taken to free the Tsar's subjects from bondage. It covered everything from the strength of the Khan's armed forces, the weaknesses of his defences, the size of his arsenals and the best approach routes for an advancing army, to the economy, the system of government, crime, punishment, torture and methods of execution (impalement being a favourite). Muraviev also described the Khan's 'monstrous cruelty' and his penchant for devising new methods of torture and punishment. Those caught drinking alcohol or smoking, which were forbidden after he himself had decided to give them up, had their mouths slit open to the ears. The permanent grin which resulted was intended as a macabre warning to others.

Muraviev argued passionately for the early conquest of Khiva. Not only would this free the Russian slaves from their bonds, but it would also bring to an end the tyranny under which most of the Khan's subjects were forced to live. Furthermore, possession of Khiva would enable Russia to break the British monopoly of India's priceless trade. For with Khiva in its hands 'the whole trade of Asia, including that of India' could be re-routed via there to the Caspian, and thence up the Volga to Russia and the European markets – an altogether shorter and cheaper route than via the Cape. This would seriously undermine, and eventually destroy, British rule in India, while providing badly needed new markets there and in Central Asia for Russian goods.

The conquest of Khiva, moreover, would not be difficult or costly, Muraviev argued. He believed that it could be achieved by a determined commander with as few as 'three thousand brave soldiers'. An invading force would discover very quickly that it had valuable allies awaiting it. For a start there were the warlike Turcoman tribes living in the deserts through which it must pass to reach Khiva. Muraviev could vouch from his own experience of them that they went in as much fear of the Khan as his own subjects did, and would rally eagerly to anyone coming to overthrow him. Inside the capital the invader would enjoy the desperate support of a large fifth column. In addition to the 3,000 Russian slaves, many of whom had once been soldiers, there were 30,000 Persians and Kurds held in bondage by the Khivans. All were men with everything to gain and nothing to lose.

Despite all the perils that the young Muraviev had faced to gather intelligence for his chiefs, his grandiose plan for the annexation of Khiva and the release of the Russian and other slaves was to go unheeded. The moment had passed, for the once-great Yermolov had begun the slow slide from grace which would end with his replacement as Military Governor of the Caucasus. Moreover, Tsar Alexander himself had more urgent problems to contend with at home where his own position was threatened by disaffection. Nonetheless, Muraviev was at least able to keep his promise to the hapless Russians he had left behind in Khiva. Summoned by the Tsar to St Petersburg to be commended on his daring, he briefed the Emperor personally on the plight of his subjects there. Even if Muraviev was unable to do anything to hasten their freedom, his revelations were to provide the Russians with an excellent excuse for their subsequent expansion into Muslim Central

Asia. Thus his journey was destined to mark the beginning of the end of the independent khanates of Central Asia.

One man who foresaw this only too clearly was an official of the East India Company named William Moorcroft, who had spent several years travelling in the extreme north of India on the fringes of Turkestan. From remote camps on the upper Indus, where no European had ever set foot before, he was urging his superiors in Calcutta to pursue a forward policy in Central Asia and thus pre-empt Russian moves there. Not only, he repeatedly warned them, would the Russians seize the whole of Turkestan and Afghanistan, with their vast untapped markets, but very likely British India too. But whereas Muraviev, the first Russian player in the Great Game, was to be rewarded by his country, ending his career as Commander-in-Chief in the Caucasus, Moorcroft would be disowned by his chiefs, and finish up in a lonely, unmarked grave beside the Oxus.

·7·

A Strange Tale
of Two Dogs

North of the Himalayan passes, on the storm-swept Tibetan plateau, stands the sacred mountain of Kailas. Wreathed in mystery, superstition and perpetual snow, the 22,000-foot peak is believed by both Buddhists and Hindus to lie at the very centre of existence. For as long as anyone can remember, devotees of both faiths have risked their lives to reach this remote mountain, one circuit of which is said to wash away the sins of a lifetime. To the faithful the bleak landscape around Kailas abounds in religious associations, including, some say, the footprints of the Buddha himself. There are holy lakes to bathe in, the tombs of saints to visit, sacred caves in which to meditate and pray, and monasteries where the exhausted traveller may rest.

The pilgrims come from as far away as Mongolia and Nepal, India and Ceylon, China and Japan, as well as from Tibet itself. Over the years many have perished in the icy passes, the victims of frost-bite or starvation, avalanches or bandits. However, it has taken more than the fear of death to deter men from making the hazardous journey through the mountains to Kailas. Even today they come, with their prayer-wheels and amulets, some carrying heavy rocks on their arduous circuit of the holy mountain as an act of extreme penance. But nowadays the ragged pilgrims have to share this sacred terrain with jeep-loads of Western tourists who have added it to their list of exotic destinations.

Until quite recently the Kailas region was one of the least

accessible places on earth. Only a handful of Europeans had ever set foot there, the first being two Jesuit priests who passed through it in 1715, describing the mountain as 'horrible, barren, steep and bitterly cold', before hastening on to Lhasa. A further century was to pass before the next European set eyes on it, this time a British veterinary surgeon travelling the far north of India and beyond in search of horses for the East India Company's cavalry, and combining this with a bit of unofficial exploration. His name was William Moorcroft, and he had come to India in 1808 at the Company's invitation to be superintendent of its stud. He soon became convinced that somewhere to the north, in the wilds of Central Asia or Tibet, there was to be found a breed of horse of great speed and stamina which could be used to revitalise the Company's bloodstock. It was in the course of the second of three long journeys he made in search of these horses – this one to the Kailas region of Tibet – that something happened which gave birth to an obsession that haunted him for the rest of his life.

It occurred in the house of a Tibetan official. There, to the Englishman's astonishment, he was greeted by two strange dogs which he knew at once to be of European origin. One was a terrier and the other a pug, both of them breeds unheard of in Central Asia. But where had they come from? Very soon Moorcroft guessed the answer. Clearly recognising him as a European, the two dogs jumped all over him, licking him and barking excitedly. Then, after begging, the creatures put on a passable imitation of military drill. To Moorcroft this meant only one thing. The two dogs had once belonged to soldiers. The villagers told him that they had acquired them from Russian traders, but Moorcroft was persuaded otherwise. Either way, however, it demonstrated that the Russians had already been there. From then until his death in 1825, Moorcroft was to deluge his superiors in Calcutta with impassioned warnings about Russian intentions in Central Asia.

St Petersburg, he was convinced, was out to seize the great untapped markets of Central Asia. The East India Company, he wrote, must decide whether the natives of Turkestan and Tibet 'shall be clothed with the broadcloth of Russia or of England', and whether they should purchase their 'implements

of iron and steel from St Petersburg or from Birmingham.'
More than that, he believed that the Russians were intent on
conquest. First it would be the khanates of Central Asia, and
then India itself. In one letter to his superiors he explained
how a handful of British officers commanding native irregulars
might halt an entire Russian army advancing southwards
through the passes by rolling huge boulders down on it from
the heights above.

But these were early days yet. In both Britain and India the
Russophobes were still very much in a minority, enjoying little
or no support from either the government or the Company.
Indeed, although they shared similar views, it is unlikely that
Sir Robert Wilson, the father of Russophobia, and Moorcroft
had ever heard of one another, let alone corresponded. Meanwhile, the Company's directors remained far from convinced
that St Petersburg, officially still Britain's ally, harboured any
ill intentions towards India. Their own first priority was the
consolidation and protection of the territories they had already
acquired, which was proving costly enough, rather than
winning new ones in the Himalayas and beyond, as Moorcroft
was urging them to do. His warnings were thus dismissed by
his superiors as resulting from excessive zeal rather than from
sound judgement. They were simply filed away in the Company's archives, ignored and unread, and were not destined to
see the light again until after his death.

It had long been the dream of Moorcroft, in his quest for
horses, to visit the great caravan city of Bokhara, the capital of
the richest of the Central Asian khanates. For in the markets
there, he was convinced, he would find the horses he needed
for the Company's stud, which so far had eluded him. These
were the legendary Turcoman steeds, of whose speed, stamina
and manoeuvrability he had heard so much in the bazaars of
northern India. In the spring of 1819 his persistence was
rewarded, and finance and approval were granted for the 2,000-
mile expedition, which was to be his third and last. But, like the
Russian traveller Muraviev on his mission to Khiva, Moorcroft
was given no official status, so that he could be disowned if he
got into difficulties, or if his visit to a city so far beyond India's
frontiers were to lead to protests from St Petersburg.

To purchase horses was only one of Moorcroft's objectives. He also planned to open up the markets of the far north to British goods, and so pre-empt the Russians whom he believed to have similar aims. So it was that on 16 March, 1820, he and his party crossed out of Company-held territory followed by a large and slow-moving caravan laden with the finest British exports, ranging from porcelain to pistols, cutlery to cotton, and deliberately chosen to outshine the greatly inferior Russian goods. Apart from the many pony men and servants, Moorcroft's companions for this long-distance raid across the Oxus were a young Englishman named George Trebeck, and an Anglo-Indian, George Guthrie. Both men would prove not only capable and reliable, but also steadfast friends when things became difficult. Though none of them could have foreseen it, due to long and frequent delays their journey into the unknown was to take them no less than six years to complete, and then it would end in tragedy.

*　　*　　*

The most direct route to Bokhara, Moorcroft knew from his earlier travels in the north, lay through Afghanistan. Unfortunately a bitter civil war was raging there which, despite their small Gurkha escort, would expose the expedition to the gravest danger, especially when word got around that their camels were weighed down with valuables intended for the markets of Turkestan. Moorcroft decided therefore to try to bypass Afghanistan, and approach Bokhara from the east, from Kashgar in Chinese Turkestan. This was most easily reached across the Karakoram passes from Leh, the capital of Ladakh. By approaching Bokhara this way, moreover, Moorcroft also hoped to open up the markets of Chinese Turkestan to British goods. In September 1820, after innumerable delays in the Punjab, and more than a year on the road, Moorcroft and his companions finally arrived in Leh, the first Englishmen ever to set foot there. They at once set about trying to establish contact with the Chinese authorities in Yarkand, on the far side of the Karakorams, seeking leave to enter their domains. But it was not to be that easy, as Moorcroft soon discovered.

For a start, Yarkand lay 300 miles away to the north, across some of the most difficult passes in the world, especially in winter, and it could take months to get a reply from officials there who, at the best of times, were not given to hurrying themselves. However, although it was some time before he realised it, there were other factors conspiring against Moorcroft's efforts to enter Chinese Turkestan, or Sinkiang as it is now called. The powerful local merchants had for generations held a monopoly over the caravan trade between Leh and Yarkand, and had no wish to lose this to the British. Even when Moorcroft offered to appoint the most prominent of them as the East India Company's agent, they continued to sabotage his efforts. Only afterwards was he to discover that they had warned the Chinese that the British were planning to bring an army with them the moment they were allowed through the passes.

Moorcroft had not been long in Leh when he discovered that he had what he most feared, a Russian rival. Ostensibly he was a native trader who operated across the passes between Leh and the caravan cities of Chinese Turkestan. In fact, as Moorcroft soon found out, he was a highly regarded Tsarist agent, of Persian-Jewish origin, who carried out sensitive political and commercial missions for his superiors in St Petersburg. His name was Aga Mehdi, and he had begun his singular career as a small-time pedlar. Soon he was dealing in Kashmiri shawls, celebrated throughout Asia for their great warmth and beauty. Then, with remarkable enterprise, he had made his way across Central Asia, eventually reaching St Petersburg, where his shawls had attracted the attention of Tsar Alexander himself, who had expressed a wish to meet this enterprising merchant.

Alexander had been much impressed by him, and had sent him back to Central Asia with instructions to try to establish commercial contacts with Ladakh and Kashmir. This he had succeeded in doing, and some Russian goods now began to appear in the bazaars there. On his return to St Petersburg the delighted Tsar had presented him with a gold medal and chain, as well as a Russian name, Mehkti Rafailov. A more ambitious mission was next planned for him, this time with political as well as purely commercial objectives. His orders were to proceed considerably further south than ever before, to the independent Sikh kingdom of the Punjab. There he was to try to establish friendly contacts with its ageing but extremely astute ruler, Ranjit Singh, who was known to be on excellent terms with the British. He bore with him a letter of introduction from the Tsar, signed by his Foreign Minister, Count Nesselrode. This, innocent enough on the face of it, declared that Russia wished to trade with Ranjit Singh's merchants, who would be welcome to visit Russia in return.

Moorcroft was not slow in discovering all this, and through his own agents even managed to obtain a copy of the Tsar's letter. It appeared to confirm his worst suspicions about Russian intentions. He also found out that this enterprising rival was expected shortly in Leh, on his way to Lahore, Ranjit Singh's capital. 'I was anxious to see him,' Moorcroft observed in his journal, 'that I might be able better to ascertain his real designs, as well as those of the ambitious power under whose patronage and authority he was employed.' Moorcroft learned too that Rafailov, to use his new name, was carrying not only a considerable sum of money, but also rubies and emeralds, some of great size and value. The latter, Moorcroft suspected, were almost certainly intended as gifts from the Tsar to Ranjit Singh and others, being too valuable for local sale or barter.

The Englishman also heard, from those returning across the passes from the north, of Rafailov's worrying activities in this strongly Muslim corner of the Chinese Empire. In Kashgar, it was reported, he had secretly promised local leaders the Tsar's support in casting off the Manchu yoke. Were they to dispatch to St Petersburg the rightful heir to the throne of Kashgar, Rafailov was said to have told them, then he would be sent back at the head of a Russian-trained army to recover the domains of his ancestors. Whatever the truth of this, Moorcroft observed, the local populace appeared only too happy to believe that the Tsar was their friend. Rafailov, it was clear, was a formidable adversary. His knowledge of the peoples and languages of the region, not to mention his intelligence and enterprise, equipped him superbly for the task with which Moorcroft believed he had been entrusted – 'to extend the influence of Russia to the confines of British India', and to gather political and geographical intelligence from the intervening territories.

All this Moorcroft reported in his dispatches to his superiors, 1,100 miles away in Calcutta, together with his discovery that Rafailov had been escorted across the most treacherous stretch of his journey, the lawless Kazakh Steppe, by a troop of Cossack cavalry. Moorcroft was now more than ever convinced that behind St Petersburg's bid for the markets of India's far north lay what he called 'a monstrous plan of aggrandisement'. Where caravans of Russian goods could go, the Cossacks would surely follow. Rafailov was merely a scout, feeling the way forward and preparing the ground. Believing that the destiny of northern India lay in their hands, and that this wily newcomer, now only a fortnight or so away, had somehow to be foiled, Moorcroft and his companions awaited his arrival with some excitement.

It was never to be, however. Precisely how the Tsar's man died is not clear. But somewhere high up in the Karakoram passes he perished, his remains joining the thousands of skeletons, human and animal, strewn along what one later traveller called 'this via dolorosa'. Moorcroft tells us little except that his rival's death was 'of a sudden and violent disorder'. One can only guess that he died of a sudden heart attack or from mountain sickness, for in places the trail carried the traveller up to nearly 19,000 feet above sea level. Possibly even Moorcroft, an experienced medical man as well as a vet, did not know the cause of Rafailov's death, or perhaps the answer lies buried somewhere among the 10,000 pages of manuscript which represent his reports and correspondence. Any suggestion that Moorcroft himself had anything to do with it can almost certainly be discounted. Not only was he an extremely honourable man, but he was also generous to a fault. According to his biographer, Dr Garry Alder, perhaps the only man to have thoroughly explored the Moorcroft papers, he saw to it that his adversary's small orphaned son was adequately provided for and educated, although that is all we are told. Until the Russian secret archives of the period are made available to Western scholars, the precise truth about Rafailov will not be known for certain. Moorcroft, however, was genuinely convinced that he was a highly trusted agent of Russian imperialism – just as Soviet scholars today brand Moorcroft himself as a British master spy sent to pave the way for the annexation of Central Asia. Had Rafailov lived a few years longer, Moorcroft maintained in a letter to a friend in London, then 'he might have produced scenes in Asia that would have astonished some of the Cabinets of Europe.'

Rafailov's unexpected removal from the scene did little to lessen Moorcroft's near-paranoia about Russian designs on the northern Indian states. Without consulting his superiors in Calcutta first, and with no authority to so act, he now negotiated a commercial treaty with the ruler of Ladakh on behalf of 'British merchants'. It was, he was convinced, a master stroke which would eventually open up the markets of Central Asia to manufacturers at home, then still suffering from the economic ravages of the Napoleonic wars. His enthusiasm, however, was not shared by his chiefs. When news of the unauthorised treaty reached them, they at once disowned it. Not only were they unconvinced of Russia's designs on Central Asia, let alone India, but they were also anxious to avoid doing anything likely to offend Ranjit Singh, ruler of the Punjab, whom they regarded as a most valuable friend and neighbour. The very last thing they wanted was to have him, and his powerful, well-trained army of Sikhs, as a foe. And it was no secret in Calcutta that Ranjit Singh, following his earlier annexation of Kashmir, jealously viewed Ladakh as lying within his own sphere of influence.

It was too late, however, to prevent him from finding out about the treaty. Moorcroft had already written to him warning him that Ladakh was an independent state in whose affairs he must not meddle, and adding that it was the ruler's wish to become a British protectorate. An abject apology for Moorcroft's transgression, together with a total retraction of the treaty, was hastily sent to Ranjit, but not in time, it seems, to save Moorcroft from the Sikh's fury (let alone that of his own chiefs, who had still to deal with him). For not long afterwards there began a series of mysterious attempts on the lives of Moorcroft and his two companions.

The first of these was made by an unidentified gunman who fired at them through the window at night, narrowly missing George Trebeck as he sat writing, the would-be assassin perhaps mistaking him for Moorcroft who spent hours at his portable desk preparing reports and writing up his journal. Subsequently two further attempts were made on Moorcroft's life by nocturnal intruders, one of whom he shot dead. The frustrated assassins now tried a new tack. Before long Moorcroft and his companions experienced unexplained pains, which they attributed to some kind of fever. But if they had fallen foul of Ranjit Singh (not to mention those local merchants whose monopoly they threatened), they still had friends among the Ladakhis, some of whom clearly knew what was going on. One night, as Moorcroft was racking his brains over the cause of their malady, he was visited by two strangers, their faces covered to conceal their identity. By means of gestures they made it unmistakably clear that he and his companions were being poisoned. After some suspect tea had been disposed of, the aches and pains abruptly ceased. And so, oddly, did the assassination attempts.

But if Moorcroft had survived the vengeance of these foes, he was now to face the displeasure of his own employers. So far the directors had been surprisingly tolerant of their Superintendent of Stud and his endless and costly quest for fresh bloodstock. After two fruitless expeditions, they had even allowed him to embark on another, his present journey to Bokhara. There was no doubt that they badly needed the horses, and Moorcroft had, in the course of his travels, sent back a great deal of valuable topographical and political intelligence. Even his increasing Russophobia did not perturb them too much. They merely closed their ears to it. However, interfering with the East India Company's highly sensitive relations with neighbouring rulers was an altogether different matter.

Their first move was to suspend Moorcroft, together with his salary, and a letter to this effect was dispatched to him. This was followed not long afterwards by another letter, ordering his recall. It appears that Moorcroft received word of his suspension, but not of his recall to Calcutta. He was nonetheless mortified. 'I secured for my country', he protested, 'an influence over a state which, lying on the British frontier, offered a central mart for the expansion of her commerce to Turkestan and China, and a strong outwork against an enemy from the north.' The humiliation of being disowned by his own side must have been hard for him to stomach. On top of that he had signally failed to arouse the directors' interest in the great untapped markets of Central Asia, or to convince anyone in Calcutta or London of the menace which he believed Russia posed to British interests in Asia.

Anyone less determined than Moorcroft would have given up in disappointment. After all, he could have returned to London and resumed his career as a successful vet. But he had not forgotten the horses which he had come so far to find. If the approach to Bokhara through Chinese Turkestan was blocked, then they would have to take the more dangerous route across Afghanistan after all. What Moorcroft did not realise was that their many months in Ladakh spent trying to negotiate with the Chinese across the mountains had been pointless almost from the start. For the artful Rafailov, whom Moorcroft held in such esteem, had successfully poisoned the minds of the senior Chinese officials against them before setting out on his own fateful journey through the passes.

Moorcroft and his companions now tried to make up for lost time, leaving Leh before the letter summoning them home could reach them. In the late spring of 1824, after travelling through Kashmir and the Punjab (taking care to steer well north of Ranjit Singh's capital, Lahore), they crossed the Indus and entered the Khyber Pass. Beyond it lay Afghanistan, and beyond that Bokhara.

·8·

Death on the Oxus

To take an ill-armed caravan laden with precious goods, and rumoured to be carrying gold, through the heart of Afghanistan was at the best of times a perilous undertaking. To attempt this when the country was in the grip of anarchy, and teetering on the brink of civil war, called for courage, or perhaps foolhardiness, of the highest order. Yet this is what Moorcroft and his companions now boldly set out to do. The prospects of their coming out alive, of reaching the River Oxus with themselves and their merchandise intact, seemed slender. Some of the wild stories which preceded them, moreover, were hardly calculated to improve their chances.

According to one of these they were really the secret advance guard of a British invasion force, and they had come to spy out the land prior to its annexation. Perhaps the Afghans could read Moorcroft's thoughts, for before very long he was writing to Calcutta proposing just that. If the British did not get their hands on Afghanistan first, he warned, then the Russians almost certainly would. And what better moment than the present, when two rival factions were vying for the Afghan throne? A single British regiment, Moorcroft argued, was all that would be needed to place a suitably compliant candidate on the throne. As usual, his suggestion fell on deaf ears. However, it would not be long before other, far more influential, voices were clamouring for precisely this, and claiming the idea as their own. For Afghanistan was destined to loom large in British imperial history, and Moorcroft merely to be ahead of his time.

Another rumour which greatly embarrassed them was that they were prepared to pay those tribes whose territories they traversed generously for safe passage. They went in constant fear of attack or treachery, but also won friends through Moorcroft's veterinary skills, which were much sought after in a land almost entirely dependent upon domestic animals for its livelihood. The ferocity of the Afghan summer was a severe trial for them all, affecting even their dogs, two of which died from sunstroke. The heat, observed Moorcroft, 'was as if it had been blown from a blacksmith's forge'. As always, while they travelled, he made copious notes about the people and topography, wildlife and livestock, agriculture and antiquities. At the great Buddhist site of Bamian, which they were the first Europeans ever to see, they gazed up in awe at the two colossal figures carved from the cliff face, the taller of which they calculated to be 150 feet high, an underestimate of some 30 feet. They also wrote their names in a cave in charcoal, and a century and a half later Moorcroft's was still there.

Finally, nearly eight months after entering the Khyber Pass, and after overcoming a wearying succession of obstacles, they reached the banks of the Oxus, becoming the first Englishmen ever to set foot there. Considering the dangers and difficulties they had faced, it was an astonishing feat of courage and determination. Even today few Europeans have seen the Oxus, so remote is its course, and those who have done so have mostly viewed it from the air when flying between Tashkent, in Soviet Central Asia, and Kabul. The strategic importance of the mighty river was not lost on Moorcroft, who no doubt could visualise the Cossacks swimming with their horses across it. 'The current', he noted, 'was less rapid than I expected to have found it, not exceeding two miles an hour. The banks were low, and the soil loose, like those of the Ganges, and the water was similarly discoloured by sand.'

At Khwaja Salah, the main crossing point, the river appeared to be no wider than the Thames at Charing Cross, although elsewhere it was far broader. In spring, they were told, when the snow in the Pamirs, where the Oxus has its source, began to melt, the river was in some places a mile or more in width. From Khwaja Salah three flat-bottomed wooden boats operated a ferry service, each capable of carrying twenty camels or horses.

By now it was winter and the snow added to their discomfort, reducing the desert to a quagmire, often knee deep, and greatly reducing the caravan's progress. Five days after crossing the Oxus they reached Kashi, the second largest town in the kingdom of Bokhara, whose 16-year-old governor, Prince Tora Bahadar, was the Emir's second son. To reach his palace, in order to pay their respects, they had to struggle through rivers of mud beneath which lurked cavernous holes, invisible from above, into which a man might momentarily vanish. Their brief audience with the youthful governor, Moorcroft reported, passed off cordially, 'and augured well for our reception at Bokhara'. What he did not know was that behind the teenager's charming manner and 'constant smile' were hidden a ruthless ambition and evil nature. Not only would he murder his elder brother and seize the throne of Bokhara on their father's death, but he would also later cast two British officers into a rat-infested pit before having them beheaded in the square overlooked by his palace.

On February 25, 1825, Moorcroft and his companions were able to make out in the distance the unmistakable line of minarets and domes which they knew were those of Bokhara, the holiest city in Muslim Central Asia. So holy was it said to be that while elsewhere on earth the daylight shone downwards from the skies, from Bokhara it radiated upwards to illuminate the heavens. For Moorcroft and his weary party it must have been a triumphant sight, justifying all that they had been through since leaving Calcutta. 'We found ourselves', he wrote that night in his journal, 'at the gates of that city which had for five years been the object of our wanderings, privations and perils.' Sadly, their elation was to prove short-lived. As they entered the city the following morning they were greeted by excited children crying 'Ooroos ... Ooroos' – 'Russians ... Russians'. Moorcroft knew in that moment that they must already have seen Europeans, and that he had been beaten to his goal by his foes from the north.

It had happened, he soon learned, more than four years earlier. But news travelled so slowly in the vast Asian heartland that neither he, in the far north of India, nor his superiors in Calcutta had learned of it. The Russians, for their part, were happy that it should remain that way, for they regarded Muslim Central Asia as lying firmly within their own sphere of influence. The mission, officially a diplomatic and commercial one, had set out in October 1820 from Orenburg. It had brought with it a fulsome letter from the Tsar to the Emir who, through native go-betweens, had agreed to receive it. To further smooth the way, the Russians also brought lavish gifts, including guns and furs, watches and European porcelain. It was hoped that these would create an appetite among rich Bokharans for more such goods. For the Russian factories – of which there were now some 5,000, employing 200,000 workers – were becoming desperate for new markets.

The home market was too small and impoverished to absorb the rapidly growing volume of goods being produced, while their British rivals, using more sophisticated machinery, were able to undercut them in both Europe and America. However, in Central Asia, on their own doorstep, lay a vast potential market where, so far anyway, they faced no competition. The British must, at all costs, be kept out of Central Asia. The bazaars of the ancient Silk Road were to be filled with Russian goods only. To St Petersburg the Great Game was as much about commercial penetration as about political and military expansion, especially in those early years, although inevitably the flag – the two-headed imperial eagle – followed the caravans of Russian merchandise. It was a remorseless process which, on the British side, only Moorcroft had yet foreseen. And here, in far-off Bokhara, he himself had come face to face with it for the first time, for already the bazaars were filled with Russian goods.

Inevitably, there had been more to the Russian mission of 1820 than a purely commercial reconnaissance, as Moorcroft must have guessed. It had had orders, it would later transpire, to bring back detailed plans of Bokhara's defences, and as much military, political and other intelligence as possible. One of its members, a German-born doctor named Eversmann, had undertaken the almost suicidal task of entering the capital in disguise and mingling with the Emir's subjects to glean all he could there, on the assumption that the mission and its escort would be kept outside the city's walls. Although the Emir had agreed to receive the Russians, they were taking no chances, for they had not forgotten the treachery which had led to the massacre of the Khivan mission. In addition therefore to the cavalry and infantry escort, they took with them two powerful artillery pieces which, if the need arose, would make short work of Bokhara's mud walls, palaces and mosques.

The 1,000-mile march across steppe and desert was to prove a gruelling one for both men and animals, and they lost many of their horses long before reaching the Emir's territory. Although the Kazakhs, through whose domains they first had to pass, gave them little trouble, at one spot they came upon more than a hundred corpses lying in the desert, the remains of a Bokharan caravan which had been attacked by raiders. They served as a grim reminder of the problems that their own merchants' caravans would face if the predatory Kazakhs were not first brought to heel. More than two months after setting out they reached the first Bokharan outpost, and the following day were met by a caravan bearing fresh fruit, bread and fodder for their horses, thoughtfully sent by the Emir himself – but not something that an invading force from the north could look forward to. Four days later they pitched their camp outside the gates of the capital and awaited the Emir's summons.

Here was Dr Eversmann's chance. Under cover of the excitement caused by the arrival of the 'Ooroos', and posing as a merchant, he managed to slip unnoticed into the city and find lodgings in a caravanserai. While the members of the mission and their escort were accommodated in a village outside the walls, this somewhat shadowy figure, about whom little appears to be known, set to work gathering information ranging from military matters to the sexual proclivities of the Bokharans. Of the latter he was to write: 'Were I not constrained by shame, I could relate incredible facts.' Apparently things went on in Bokhara which 'even in Constantinople' were taboo. The people, Eversmann tells us, had no notion of 'refined sentiments', but thought only of sexual gratification, despite the brutal punishments inflicted on those caught indulging in these unnamed 'enormities'. The Emir himself was no exception. In addition to his harem, the doctor reported, he enjoyed the services of 'forty or fifty degraded beings' in this city where 'all the horrors and abominations of Sodom and Gomorrah' were practised.

Eversmann's disguise, the precise details of which are not known, must have been remarkably convincing, for the Emir's secret police, with informers everywhere, appear to have suspected nothing during his three-month stay in Bokhara. But he was acutely aware of the dangerous game he was playing. Asking a question, or even taking a stroll, he wrote, was enough to arouse suspicions, and thereby invite unwelcome attention. All intelligence which he gleaned during the day had to be copied down 'clandestinely at night'. The doctor's luck, however, was eventually to run out. By ill chance he was recognised by a Bokharan who remembered him from Orenburg, and who denounced him to the secret police. He had planned to pass all his notes to a member of the mission and then himself join a caravan bound for Kashgar, in Chinese Turkestan, where it seems he proposed to gather similar intelligence for his masters. But he was warned that the moment he left town, and was clear of any Russian protection, he was to be murdered.

The Emir did not allow his discovery of this piece of Russian duplicity to sully the cordial relations which he had just established with his powerful neighbours. Presumably this was why Eversmann was to be quietly done away with when he and his companions had gone their separate ways. The doctor now hastily changed his plans and decided to return to Orenburg with the mission which, having completed its tasks (including the discreet drawing of a plan of the city walls), was sitting it out until the worst of the Central Asian winter was over.

On March 10, 1821, amid protestations of undying friendship, the Russians departed the Emir's capital, from which he ruled over a kingdom almost the size of the British Isles. Fifteen days later they left the last of his territories. Their one regret, like Muraviev at Khiva, was at having to leave behind them numbers of their fellow countrymen whom they had

1. Henry Pottinger (1789–1856), who as a subaltern explored the approach routes to India disguised as a horse-dealer and a holy man.

2. Arthur Conolly (1807–42), who first coined the phrase 'The Great Game' and who was later beheaded in Bokhara. Seen here in Persian disguise.

3. General Yermolov (1772–1861), conqueror of the Caucasus. His men wept when he was later disgraced.

4. General Paskievich (1782–1856), who replaced Yermolov and continued Russia's ruthless drive southwards.

6. Russian troops preparing to lay siege to an *aul*, or Caucasian
   hilltop village

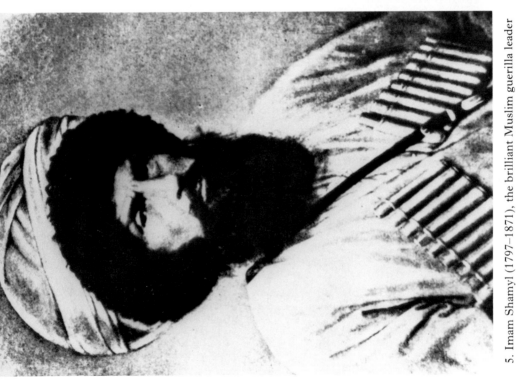

5. Imam Shamyl (1797–1871), the brilliant Muslim guerilla leader
   in the Caucasus, who resisted the Russian conquest for many years

7. The Indus at Attock, where it was feared that a Russian army coming through the Khyber Pass might enter British India.

8. Sir Alexander Burnes (1805–41), in Afghan dress. He was finally
hacked to death by a fanatical Kabul mob.

Opposite:
9. (*above left*) Lieutenant Eldred Pottinger (1811–43), 'Hero of Herat' and nephew
of Henry Pottinger.

10. (*above right*) The charismatic Ranjit Singh (1780–1839), one-eyed ruler of the
Punjab, whose domains were seen by the British as a bulwark against invasion.

11. (*below left*) The British puppet Shah Shujah (1780–1842), who briefly replaced
Dost Mohammed but was assassinated by his own countrymen.

12. (*below right*) Dost Mohammed (1791–1863), Emir of Afghanistan. Dethroned by
the British, who feared his contacts with Russia, he had to be reinstated after the
First Afghan War.

13. British troops entering the Bolan Pass in 1839 on their way to Kabul. The Bolan and Khyber passes, it was feared, could also bring Russian troops into India.

14. Sir William Macnaghten (1793–1841), who forcibly placed Shah Shujah on the throne of Kabul, but soon paid for this with his life.

Mohan Lal (1812–77), Burnes's Kashmiri confidant and spy. uable to his British masters, he warned Burnes in vain of the dangers facing him in Kabul.

16. The British advance into Afghanistan in 1839. Ghazni, the last enemy stronghold before Kabul, falls after the gates are blown open by Lieutenant Henry Durand.

17. The British retreat from Afghanistan in 1842. The last stand of the 44th at the village of Gandamak, where their bones can still be found.

found among the slaves of Bokhara. Some of them had been so long in bondage that they had almost forgotten their mother tongue. 'At the sight of us,' one of the mission reported, 'they were unable to hold back their tears.' But whatever the mission's feelings, there was little they could do for these poor wretches other than publicise their plight, as Muraviev had done, and pray for the day when Russian rule would prevail in Central Asia, and such cruel and barbaric practices would be outlawed for ever.

If St Petersburg had entertained thoughts of taking Bokhara by force, nothing in fact came of them. Indeed another four decades were to pass before it finally came under Tsarist sway. However, to Moorcroft the danger of the Russians returning with a conquering army seemed real enough. During his own stay in Bokhara, where he had been well received by the Emir, he had made two more uncomfortable discoveries. One was that the Russian-made goods in the bazaars, despite their inferiority, were actually preferred to those which he and his companions had faced so many perils and hardships to bring to Bokhara. No less disappointing was the discovery that the horses – those fleet and hardy beasts he had dreamed of for so long – were no longer to be found in any numbers in the Emir's kingdom.

Bitterly disappointed at this final failure, Moorcroft decided to head for home before the passes into northern India were closed by snow for the winter. Taking with him those few horses he had managed to acquire, he and his companions set off back along the route by which they had come. Once across the Oxus, however, Moorcroft decided to make one last attempt to buy horses at a remote desert village to the south-west where he had heard they were to be found. Leaving Trebeck and Guthrie at Balkh, he set off with a handful of men. It was the last that they would ever see of him.

* * *

Mystery will always surround the fate of Moorcroft, as well as that of his companions. Officially he died of fever on or about August 27, 1825. He was nearly 60, by Indian standards an old man, and had been complaining of ill-health for some months. His body, too decomposed to indicate the cause of death, was brought back not long afterwards to Balkh by his men and buried there by his companions. Within a short time Guthrie too was dead, followed not long afterwards by Trebeck, both deaths apparently due to natural causes. Meanwhile the expedition's interpreter, long in Moorcroft's service, had also died. It seemed too much of a coincidence, and soon rumours began to circulate in India that they had been murdered, probably poisoned, by Russian agents. Another version, rather less sensational, was that they had been killed for their possessions. In the view of his biographer, Dr Alder, Moorcroft almost certainly did die from some kind of fever, his will to live perhaps finally broken by the discovery that there were no horses of the type he sought at the village on which he had pinned his last hopes.

But there is one last twist to the story. More than twenty years after his supposed death, two French missionary explorers who reached Lhasa, 1,500 miles away to the east, were told a curious tale before being expelled by the Tibetans. An Englishman named Moorcroft, pretending to be a Kashmiri, had lived there for twelve years, they were assured. It was only after his death, while on his way to Ladakh, that the truth had come to light. For in his home were discovered maps and plans of the forbidden city which this mysterious stranger had apparently been preparing. Neither of the two French priests had ever heard of Moorcroft before, but they reported that a Kashmiri who claimed to have been his servant had corroborated the Tibetans' story. When first published in 1852, in an English-language account of their travels, this extraordinary revelation was to cause a minor sensation in Britain. For it raised the question of whether it really was Moorcroft's decomposing body which his companions had buried at Balkh, or that of someone else.

Moorcroft's biographer, while not totally ruling out the possibility that he could have faked his own death rather than return home to face his critics and official censure, nevertheless believes this to be highly unlikely, 'the great weight of evidence and probability' being against it. Only temporary insanity, Dr

Alder concludes, 'perhaps under the influence of high fever, could account for actions so utterly inconsistent with Moorcroft's character, his record and everything he stood for'. One possible explanation which has been suggested for the Frenchmen's story is that when Moorcroft's caravan broke up after his own and his companions' deaths, one of his Kashmiri servants may have found his way to Lhasa with maps and papers belonging to him. When the servant subsequently died on his way home to Kashmir, these – bearing Moorcroft's name – might well have been found in his house. The unsophisticated Tibetans, ever suspicious of outsiders' intentions, would have assumed the maps to be of their country, and the dead servant to be the Englishman whose name they bore, who evidently had been spying on them all those years.

However, if Moorcroft was written off by his superiors during his lifetime, only death saving him from the humiliation of official censure, then he was to be more than compensated for this afterwards. Today he is honoured by geographers for his immense contribution to the exploration of the region during his endless quest for horses, and regarded by many as the father of Himalayan discovery. No one cares about his failure to find those horses, or to open up Bokhara to British merchandise, even if these meant so much to Moorcroft himself. But it is in the realm of geopolitics that his real vindication, so far as we are concerned, lies. For it was not so long after his death that his repeated but unheeded warnings about Russian ambitions in Central Asia began to come true. These, together with his remarkable travels through Great Game country, were soon to make him the idol of the young British officers who were destined to follow in his footsteps.

Perhaps Moorcroft's final vindication lies in the location of his lonely grave, last seen in 1832 by Alexander Burnes, a fellow countryman and player of the game, who was also on his way northwards to Bokhara. With some difficulty he found it by moonlight, unmarked and half covered by a mud wall, outside the town of Balkh. For his wearied companions, as infidels, had not been allowed to bury him within its limits. Moorcroft thus lies not far from the spot where, more than a century and a half later, Soviet troops and armour poured southwards across the River Oxus into Afghanistan. He could have asked for no finer epitaph.

·9·
The Barometer Falls

The truce in the Caucasus between Russia and Persia, which had halted the Cossacks' advance and turned St Petersburg's covetous gaze towards Central Asia, was not to last long. Both Tsar and Shah had looked upon the Treaty of Gulistan, which the British had negotiated between them in 1813, as no more than a temporary expedient which would allow them to strengthen their forces prior to the next round. It was the Shah's aim to win back his lost territories, ceded under the treaty to the Russian victors, while St Petersburg intended, when the moment was right, to extend and consolidate its southern frontier with Persia. Within a year of Moorcroft's death the two neighbours were at war again, to the dismay of the British who had no wish to see Persia overrun by the Russians.

The immediate cause of hostilities this time was a dispute over the wording of the treaty, which failed to make it clear to whom one particular region, lying between Erivan and Lake Sevan, belonged. Talks were held between General Yermolov, the Russian Governor-General of the Caucasus, and Abbas Mirza, the Persian Crown Prince, to try to resolve this. But these broke down, and in November 1825 Yermolov's troops occupied the disputed territory. The Persians demanded their withdrawal, but Yermolov refused. The Shah was incensed, as were his subjects, and recruits for a holy war against the infidel Russians flocked to Abbas Mirza's standard from all parts of the country.

The Persians were aware that the Russians were not yet

ready for a war. Not only was St Petersburg embroiled on the side of the Greeks in their struggle for independence against the Turks, but at home, especially within the army, it was facing serious disorders following the sudden death of Tsar Alexander in December 1825. Encouraged by his own recent success against the Turks, Abbas Mirza decided to strike the Russians while they were off their guard. Suddenly and without warning a 30,000-strong Persian force crossed the Russian frontier, carrying all before it. An entire Russian regiment was captured, as were a number of key towns once belonging to the Shah, while Persian irregulars carried out raids right up to the very gates of Tiflis, Yermolov's Caucasian headquarters. The triumphant Persians also managed to recover the great fortress of Lenkoran, on the Caspian shore.

For the first time in his long and brilliant career, Yermolov, known as the 'Lion of the Caucasus', had been taken by surprise. Mortified, St Petersburg accused London of inciting the Persians to attack, for it was no secret that there were British officers serving with Abbas Mirza's force as advisers, and some even directing his artillery. The new Tsar, Nicholas I, immediately decided to relieve Yermolov of his command, and replace him with one of Russia's most brilliant young generals, Count Paskievich. But if the ageing 'Lion' had lost the confidence of his superiors, he still retained the respect and affection of his troops, who blamed St Petersburg for the débâcle. When he drove away from Tiflis, in a carriage he had to pay for himself, many of his men wept openly.

With the help of reinforcements, Paskievich now turned the tide against the invaders. Before long Abbas Mirza suffered a succession of defeats, which culminated in the capture of Erivan, today capital of Soviet Armenia. To commemorate his victory, Nicholas appointed Paskievich 'Count of Erivan', a move calculated to enrage the Persians. In return, Paskievich presented Nicholas with a sword said to have been that of Tamerlane himself, which had been taken from a Persian general. The Shah now called urgently on his ally Britain for help under their recently signed defence pact. This caused considerable embarrassment in London. Militarily speaking, Britain was in no position to help, having no troops within reach of the Caucasus. Moreover, she was extremely unwilling to tangle with Russia, still officially her ally.

The original purpose of the pact between London and Teheran had, so far as the British were concerned, been the protection of India from attack by an invader marching across Persia. Despite the warnings of Wilson and others, there seemed to be little immediate risk of this happening. Fortunately for the British, the pact contained an escape clause. Under this they were only obliged to go to the Shah's assistance if he were attacked, and not if he were the aggressor. And legally speaking, despite much provocation and humiliation, he was the aggressor, for it was his troops which had crossed the Russian frontier, whose demarcation he had agreed to under the Treaty of Gulistan. Thus was Britain able to wriggle off the hook, for the second time in twenty-two years. But it was to do considerable harm to her reputation, not merely among the Persians, but throughout the East. For it was immediately assumed that the British were too frightened of the Russians to come to the help of their friends. Rather more worrying, the Russians were beginning to believe this too.

Without the help they had expected from their British allies, the Persians had no choice but to sue once again for peace. Luckily for them, however, the Russians were at that moment at war with the Turks, or the surrender terms agreed in 1828 at Turkmanchi might have been harsher than they were. As it was, Tsar Nicholas added the rich provinces of Erivan and Nakitchevan permanently to his empire. The Persians, for their part, had learned a bitter lesson about great power politics, not to mention the deviousness of the British. For London, aware that the unfortunate Shah was desperate for funds, now persuaded him to waive any remaining liability on the part of Britain to come to his assistance if he was attacked, in exchange for a substantial sum of money. With that, British influence in Persia, hitherto paramount, evaporated, to be replaced by that of Russia. The Persians now found themselves a virtual protectorate of their giant northern neighbour, which had the right to station its consuls wherever it wished in the country, and whose merchants were entitled to special privileges.

In the winter of 1828 the new Russian ambassador to the Shah's court, Alexander Griboyedov, arrived in Teheran where he was received with much formal politeness and official ceremony, despite the hostility felt towards him and his government. A distinguished literary figure with strong liberal leanings, and one-time political secretary to Yermolov, it was Griboyedov who had negotiated the humiliating terms of the Persian surrender. Now it was his task to see that these were fully carried out, including the payment by Persia of a crippling war indemnity. To the more fanatical religious elements, his presence in their midst served as a red rag. It was unfortunate, moreover, that he arrived in Teheran in January 1829 during the holy month of Muharram, when feelings run high and the faithful slash themselves with swords and pour glowing cinders on their heads. Hatred of the infidel Russians was thus at flashpoint. It was Griboyedov himself who provided the spark.

*　　*　　*

Under the terms of the peace treaty it had been agreed that Armenians living in Persia might, if they so wished, return to their homeland now that it had become part of the Russian Empire, and was therefore under Christian rule. Among those who sought to take advantage of this was a eunuch employed in the Shah's own harem, and two young girls from that of his son-in-law. All three fled to the Russian legation where they were given sanctuary by Griboyedov while arrangements were being made for their journey home. When the Shah learned of this, he immediately asked Griboyedov to return all three of them. The Russian refused, arguing that only Count Nesselrode, the Tsar's Foreign Minister, could make exceptions to the terms of the treaty, and that the Shah's request would have to be referred to him. It was a brave decision, for it would have been only too easy to return them for the sake of better relations, but Griboyedov knew very well the fate which would befall the three were he to hand them over.

Word of this insult to their sovereign by the detested infidel spread quickly through the city's population. The bazaars were closed on the orders of the mullahs and the people summoned to the mosques. There they were told to march on the Russian legation and seize the three being given asylum there. In no time a mob several thousand strong had gathered, encircling the building and screaming for Russian blood. The crowd was growing by the minute, and Griboyedov realised that the legation's small Cossack guard could never hold it off. They were all in mortal danger, and reluctantly he decided to offer to return the Armenians. But it was too late. Moments later, urged on by the mullahs, the mob stormed the building.

For more than an hour the Cossacks tried to hold the invaders back but, greatly outnumbered, they themselves were gradually driven back, first from the courtyard, then room by room. Among the crowd's early victims was the eunuch, who was cornered and torn to pieces. What happened to the two girls is not known. The Russians' last stand was made in Griboyedov's study, where he and several Cossacks held out for some time. But the mob had by now got on to the roof where they tore off the tiles, burst through the ceiling and attacked the Russians below. Griboyedov, sword in hand to the last, was finally overwhelmed and brutally slaughtered, his body being tossed from the window into the street. There his head was hacked off by a kebab vendor, who exhibited it, to the delight of the crowd, spectacles and all, on his stall. Even more unspeakable things were done to the rest of his corpse which finally ended up on a refuse heap. It was later identified by a deformity of one of his little fingers, the result of a duel in his youth. All this time there had been no sign of any troops being sent to disperse the mob or rescue Griboyedov and his companions.

The following June the poet Alexander Pushkin, a friend of Griboyedov's, was travelling through the southern Caucasus when he came upon some men leading an ox-wagon. They were heading towards Tiflis. 'Where are you from?' he asked them. 'Teheran,' they replied. 'What have you there?' he enquired, pointing to the wagon. 'Griboyedov,' they told him. Today Griboyedov's body lies in the little monastery of St David on a hillside above Tiflis, or Tbilisi as it has since been renamed. From Teheran meanwhile, fearing terrible retribution from the Russians, the Shah had hastily dispatched his grandson to St Petersburg to express his horror at what had happened, and to offer his profoundest apologies. On being received by Nicholas, the young prince is said to have held out his naked sword, the point towards himself, offering his own life in exchange for Griboyedov's. But he was ordered to return the weapon to its scabbard, and told that it would be enough if those responsible for the murders were severely punished.

In fact, being still at war with the Turks, Nicholas was anxious to avoid doing anything which might provoke the unpredictable and hot-tempered Persians into hasty action, least of all into joining forces with the Turks against him. As it was, some in St Petersburg suspected that agents of the hard-pressed Sultan were behind the attack on the legation, their aim being to revive the war between Russia and Persia, and so take some of the pressure off their own troops. For since the ceasefire, General Paskievich's forces had managed to drive the Turks from their remaining positions in the southern Caucasus and had begun to advance into Turkey proper. Others in St Petersburg, on hearing of Griboyedov's murder, at once suspected the British, still nominally their allies, of being behind it, a suspicion which still lingers among Soviet historians today.

Just as Russia's Caucasian adventures had caused concern in London, Paskievich's westward advance into Turkey now began to give rise to alarm, lest Constantinople and the Turkish straits be Nicholas's ultimate objective. By the summer of 1829 the great garrison town of Erzerum had fallen to Paskievich, leaving the road from the east all but undefended. At the same time, in the Sultan's European territories, Russian troops were fighting their way southwards towards Constantinople through what are today Romania and Bulgaria. Two months after Erzerum's surrender, Edirne, in European Turkey, fell to the advancing Russians. Only a few days later, Russian cavalry units were within forty miles of the capital. With the generals pressing St Petersburg to be allowed to go in for the kill, the end of the ancient Ottoman Empire seemed to be in sight at last. It was very much as Sir Robert Wilson had warned some twelve years earlier.

Now that Constantinople was all but in his grasp, Nicholas

must have been sorely tempted to let the advance go on. But wiser counsels, both in St Petersburg and among the other European powers, urged caution. If the Russians attacked the capital, foreign ambassadors there warned, a wholesale massacre might follow of the Christian minorities – the very people whose interests Nicholas professed to represent. The geopolitical consequences too were worrying. If the Ottoman Empire were to break up, with Russia occupying Constantinople and commanding the straits, a scramble would follow among the major European powers, including Britain, France and Austria, for what was left. Not only might a general European war result, but with British and French bases in the eastern Mediterranean, Russia's southern flank would be permanently threatened. It would be altogether safer to let the Sultan keep his ramshackle empire intact, even if he were to be made to pay for the privilege.

Therefore, to the disappointment of Paskievich and the other Russian commanders, the war was speedily brought to an end. A major confrontation between the powers was thus averted, for the British and French were already preparing to send their fleets to the straits to prevent this crucial waterway from falling into Russian hands. Within a matter of days the outline terms of the Turkish surrender had been settled, and on September 14, 1829, at Edirne, or Adrianople as it was then called, a peace treaty was signed. Under this the Russians were guaranteed free passage for their merchant ships through the straits – the next best thing to having a warm-water port on the Mediterranean – although nothing was said about warships. Russian merchants were also to have the freedom to trade in all parts of the Ottoman Empire. In addition the Sultan was obliged to concede any claims to Georgia and to his former possessions in the southern Caucasus, including two important ports on the Black Sea. The Russians, in return, handed back the garrison towns of Erzerum and Kars, together with most of the territory they had seized in European Turkey.

Although the crisis was over, the British government, led by the Duke of Wellington, had had a fright. Not only had the Russians defeated two major Asiatic powers, Persia and Turkey, in swift succession, thereby greatly strengthening their hand in the Caucasus, but they had come perilously close to occupying Constantinople, the key to the domination of the Near East and the most direct routes to India. The Russian generals, as a result, were bursting with confidence, and the brilliant Paskievich was said to be speaking openly, if vaguely, of the coming war with Britain. The barometer of Anglo-Russian relations now began to plunge. Could it be, people asked, that the story of Peter the Great's dying exhortation to his heirs to conquer the world might be true after all?

*   *   *

One man who had long been convinced that it was true was Colonel George de Lacy Evans, a distinguished soldier who, like Sir Robert Wilson, had turned polemicist and pamphleteer. Already he had published one controversial book, entitled *On the Designs of Russia*, in which he claimed that St Petersburg was planning, before very long, to attack India and other British possessions. That had appeared, however, in 1828, when there was less cause for such suspicions. But immediately after the Russian victory over the Turks, he followed this up with another, this time called *On the Practicability of an Invasion of British India*. Whereas his first book had attracted many hostile reviews, this one, because of its timing, was assured of a more sympathetic audience, especially in the higher realms of government.

Quoting (often highly selectively) the evidence and opinions of both British and Russian travellers, including Pottinger, Kinneir, Muraviev and Moorcroft, Evans set out to prove the feasibility of a Russian thrust against India. St Petersburg's immediate aim, he believed, would be not so much the conquest and occupation of India as an attempt to destabilise British rule there. If there was one thing the directors of the East India Company feared more than bankruptcy, it was trouble with the natives, who so vastly outnumbered the British in their midst. Evans next examined the possible approach routes. Although Persia was now all but in the Tsar's pocket, he thought it unlikely that a Russian army would choose to come that way. Its flanks and lines of communication would be

vulnerable to attack by British forces which could be landed at
the head of the Gulf. More likely, he believed, it would follow
the route envisaged by Kinneir eleven years earlier. Drawing
on several Russian sources, he argued that St Petersburg could
move a 30,000-strong force from the eastern shore of the
Caspian to Khiva, whence it would sail up the Oxus to Balkh.
From there it would march via Kabul to the Khyber Pass.

By appending a mass of persuasive detail, Evans managed
to make it sound all too easy – especially to those, like himself,
who were ignorant of the terrain. Indeed, outside Russia, there
was no one with any first-hand experience of it. Nonetheless
he saw the crossing of the Karakum desert to Khiva as presenting no insuperable problem, pointing out that both British
and French armies had successfully traversed such waterless
tracts in Egypt and Syria. As for transporting the invasion
force up the Oxus, there were, he said, 'numerous large fishing
boats employed by the natives' on the Aral Sea which could
be commandeered for this purpose. Evans also recommended
that the crucial passes of the Hindu Kush, lying between an
invader from the north and the Khyber, be thoroughly
explored, while 'some sort of agent' should be stationed at
Bokhara to give early warning of a Russian advance. Furthermore, he proposed that political agents should be based
permanently in Kabul and Peshawar where, he argued, they
would be of greater value than in Teheran.

Despite its shortcomings, which were less apparent then
than now, his book was to have a profound influence on policy-
makers in London and Calcutta, and was to become the virtual
bible of a generation of Great Game players, until its deficien-
cies began to show up. Even if it contained nothing that was
very new, and which had not already been said by Wilson,
Kinneir or Moorcroft, the recent aggressive moves by Russia
gave it a force and sense of urgency which their warnings had
lacked. These were heightened by a disturbing announcement
from St Petersburg (fortuitously coinciding with the publication of the book in the autumn of 1829) that an Afghan
chief had come to pay his respects to Tsar Nicholas, as also
had an ambassador from Ranjit Singh, ruler of the Punjab,
whom the British considered to be their friend.

One influential figure much impressed by Evans's arguments was Lord Ellenborough, a member of the Duke of Wellington's Cabinet, who had recently become President of the Board of Control for India. Already anxious about Russian intentions in the Near East, Ellenborough found the book both disturbing and convincing, and at once sent copies of it to Sir John Kinneir (as he had now become), the Company's envoy at Teheran, and to Sir John Malcolm, Kinneir's former chief, who was Governor of Bombay. At the same time in his diary he noted: 'I feel confident that we shall have to fight the Russians on the Indus.' Eight weeks later he amended this to: 'What I fear is an occupation of Khiva unknown to us ... so that in three or four months from leaving Khiva the enemy might be at Cabul. I am sure we can defeat the enterprise. We ought to defeat it before the enemy reaches the Indus. If 20,000 Russians should reach the Indus, it will be a sharp fight.' The Russians, Britain's allies against Napoleon, were no longer to be trusted, and this time it was official.

A hawk by nature, Ellenborough strongly favoured presenting St Petersburg with an ultimatum warning that any further incursions into Persia would be regarded as a hostile act. This was rejected by his Cabinet colleagues who argued that short of going to war they had no way of enforcing such an ultimatum. That old India hand the Duke of Wellington was confident that a Russian army approaching India through Afghanistan, whether from Persia or from Khiva, could be destroyed long before it reached the Indus. But what did worry him was the unsettling effect the advance of a 'liberating' force might have on the native population. For this reason it was vital that an invader should be dealt with swiftly, and as far from India's frontiers as possible. However, that would call for detailed maps of the approach routes. Enquiries by Ellenborough soon disclosed that such maps as did exist were wildly inaccurate and largely based on hearsay. No official efforts had been made to fill in the blanks beyond India's frontiers since Christie and Pottinger twenty years earlier.

Ellenborough now set about making up for lost time. From every possible source he gathered military, political, topographical and commercial intelligence on the countries surrounding India. He sought information on everything, from the size of the Russian navy on the Caspian Sea to the volume of their trade with the khanates of Muslim Central Asia. He wanted to know about the routes taken by the Russian caravans, as well as their size and frequency. He sifted through all that was known about Khiva, Bokhara, Khokand and Kashgar, and their capacity to withstand a Russian attack. Had Moorcroft been alive still he would have been able to supply many of the answers. As it was, almost the only intelligence from this region was to be obtained in St Petersburg. There the British ambassador, Lord Heytesbury, had obtained the services of a spy who produced for him copies of top-secret documents. These, he told London, showed that Russia was in no position, militarily or economically, to embark on an adventure against India. However, he was written off by Ellenborough as a Russophile because of his known sympathies, and his dispatches were therefore read with scepticism.

Ellenborough was determined wherever possible to obtain his intelligence at first hand, through his own men. Until then, with their missions to Khiva and Bokhara, the Russians had been making all the running. Individual enterprise, as Moorcroft had discovered, was discouraged. But now, under Ellenborough, all that was to change. A succession of young Indian Army officers, political agents, explorers and surveyors were to criss-cross immense areas of Central Asia, mapping the passes and deserts, tracing rivers to their source, noting strategic features, observing which routes were negotiable by artillery, studying the languages and customs of the tribes, and seeking to win the confidence and friendship of their rulers. They kept their ears open for political intelligence and tribal gossip – which ruler was planning to go to war with which, and who was plotting to overthrow whom. But above all they watched for the slightest sign of Russian encroachment in the vast no-man's-land lying between the two rival empires. By this way or that, what they learned eventually found its way back to their superiors, who in turn passed it on to theirs.

The Great Game had begun in earnest.

THE MIDDLE YEARS

'A scrimmage in a Border Station –
A canter down some dark defile –
Two thousand pounds of education
Drops to a ten-rupee jèzail –
The Crammer's boast, the Squadron's pride,
Shot like a rabbit in a ride!'

Rudyard Kipling

·10·

'The Great Game'

On January 14, 1831, a bearded and dishevelled figure in native dress arrived out of the desert at the remote village of Tibbee, on India's north-west frontier. The village has long since vanished from the map, but at that time it served as a border post between British India and the group of small independent states lying to the west, then collectively known as Sind. It was with relief that the stranger had reached the safety of Company territory, and the reassuring sight of the Indian Army sepoys manning the frontier. He had been travelling for more than a year, often exposed to great danger, and at times doubting whether he would return alive. For beneath his darkened complexion, burned almost black by months in the sun, his features were clearly those of a European.

He was in fact a British officer in disguise – Lieutenant Arthur Conolly of the 6th Bengal Native Light Cavalry – and the first of Lord Ellenborough's young bloods to be sent into the field to reconnoitre the military and political no-man's-land between the Caucasus and the Khyber, through which a Russian army might march. Daring, resourceful and ambitious, Conolly was the archetypal Great Game player, and it was he, fittingly enough, who first coined this memorable phrase in a letter to a friend. He had an astonishing tale to tell, as well as a wealth of advice for those who were to follow him into the wild and lawless regions of Central Asia. It was on all these matters that Lieutenant Conolly, not yet 24, now reported to his superiors. Despite his junior rank and tender years, his views were to carry much weight and to have a considerable influence on his chiefs in those early years of Anglo-Russian rivalry in Asia.

Orphaned at the age of 12, when both his parents died within a few days of each other, Conolly was one of six brothers, three of whom, himself included, were to suffer violent deaths in the service of the East India Company. After schooling at Rugby, he sailed for India where in 1823, aged 16, he joined his regiment as a cornet. Although often described as being shy and sensitive, his subsequent career shows him to have been an officer of exceptional toughness and determination, not to mention courage, while his portrait depicts him as a powerfully built, formidable-looking man. But Conolly possessed one further quality which was to have a bearing on his career. Like many other officers of that time, he had a strongly religious nature. In his case, however, this had been heightened during the long sea voyage out to India by contact with the charismatic Reginald Heber, the celebrated hymn-writer and newly appointed Bishop of Calcutta.

Conolly, in common with most of his generation, believed in the civilising mission of Christianity, and in the duty of its adherents to bring its message of salvation to others less fortunate. British rule, being based on Christian principles, was the ultimate benefit which could be bestowed upon barbaric peoples. Even Russian rule, provided it kept well away from the frontiers of India, was preferable to that of Muslim tyrants, for at least the Russians were Christians of a sort. He was also sympathetic to St Petersburg's desire to free its Christian subjects, and those of other faiths, from slavery in the khanates of Central Asia. It was these convictions, together with a thirst for adventure, which drove him to risk his life among the (to him) heathen tribes of the interior.

Officially returning overland to India at the end of his leave, Conolly had left Moscow for the Caucasus in the autumn of 1829. Britain and Russia were still officially allies, and although relations were becoming increasingly strained, he was warmly received by Russian officers in Tiflis and even provided with a Cossack escort for the most hazardous stages of his journey through the Caucasus to the Persian frontier. 'The Russians', he explained, 'do not yet command free passage through the Caucasus, for they are obliged to be very vigilant against surprise by the Circassian sons of the mist who still cherish the bitterest hatred against them.' But he badly underestimated the Circassians when he predicted that Russian troops would have little difficulty in subjugating 'these ferocious mountaineers' now that their Turkish allies had been driven from the Caucasus. Neither he nor his Russian hosts were able to foresee the violent holy war which was soon to convulse this mountainous corner of the Tsar's dominions.

As Conolly rode southwards he observed all he could of the Russian army, appraising officers and men, and their equipment, training and morale, with a keen professional eye. These, after all, were the troops which, if it ever came to it, would march on India. By the time he crossed into northern Persia he was much impressed by what he had seen. He had been astonished at the stoicism and hardiness of the troops who slept out in the snow in mid-winter without tents and made light of every obstacle and difficulty. As a cavalry officer himself he was stirred by the feat of one regiment of dragoons he visited which had captured an enemy fort by galloping into it before the defenders could close the gates.

So far, while under the protection of the Russians, Conolly had not had to worry about concealing his identity or adopting a disguise. But what he proposed to do next was a very different matter, and unthinkable for a British officer to attempt. It was his intention to try to reach Khiva by crossing the great Karakum desert, and discover, among many other things, what the Russians were up to there. No longer accompanied by his Cossack escort, and about to enter some of the most dangerous country on earth, disguise now became imperative. It was a subject to which Conolly was to devote considerable thought. However well a European spoke the native tongue, he wrote later, it was extremely difficult when travelling among Asiatics to escape detection. 'His mode of delivery, his manner of sitting, walking or riding ... is different from that of the Asiatic.' The more self-conscious he became in trying to imitate the latter, the more likely he was to attract unwelcome attention. Discovery would almost certainly spell death, for an Englishman (or a Russian for that matter) caught travelling in disguise in these regions would automatically be assumed to be a spy preparing the way for an invading army.

An excellent disguise for an Englishman, Conolly suggested, was not as a native at all, but as a doctor, preferably French or Italian. 'These itinerant gentry are sometimes met with,' he reported, 'and they are not viewed with distrust.' For a doctor, even an infidel one, was ever welcome among a people constantly at the mercy of sickness. 'Few', he added, 'will question you.' This alone was reason enough for using such a disguise, for it spared one the ordeal and nuisance of constant interrogation about the motive for travelling in these sensitive parts. Among such people, moreover, one needed only a basic knowledge of medicine to acquire a reputation as a great *hakeem*, or doctor, Conolly pointed out. He himself had treated a number of patients. 'The simplest medicines', he added, 'will cure most of their ailments, and you may tell those who are beyond your skill that it is not their *nusseeb*, or fortune, to be cured.'

However, if one did decide to travel disguised as a native, Conolly advised, then it should be as a poor one. Robbery and extortion, as he was to learn to his cost, were perpetual threats in these lawless regions. Not having the medicines or implements to pass himself off as a European doctor, he decided for his attempt to reach Khiva to adopt the guise of a merchant, purchasing silk scarves, shawls, furs, pepper and other spices for sale in the bazaars there. After hiring a guide, servants and camels, he set off for Khiva, 500 miles across the desert to the north-east, from the town of Astrabad, at the southern end of the Caspian Sea. As he left, after arranging to rendezvous with a large Khiva-bound caravan further along the route, a Persian friend observed: 'I don't like those dogs you're amongst.' But Conolly did not take the warning seriously, assuming perhaps that he was a match for any native treachery.

At first all went well as they hastened to catch up the main caravan, for this would afford them protection during the Karakum crossing. The caravan and pilgrim trails, they knew, were regularly raided by Turcoman slavers. 'It is generally in the grey of the morning that the Toorkmuns wait for the pilgrims,' Conolly reported. This was when the travellers, half asleep after a long night's march, were at prayer. The aged and those who resisted were immediately killed, while the strong and the beautiful were carried off to be sold in the slave-markets of the khanates. Conolly was well aware of the enormous risk he was taking, but the lure of Khiva outweighed this.

He and his party had been riding hard for several days, and believed themselves to be very close to the Khiva-bound caravan, when trouble suddenly struck. Early one morning, as they were about to break camp, four villainous-looking horsemen galloped towards them, causing Conolly to reach for his concealed weapons. But ignoring him, their leader began to address the Englishman's native guide. He spoke, Conolly noted, 'with much earnestness, in a low tone', and every now and again looked towards him in a manner clearly not friendly. Finally he addressed Conolly in Persian, saying that they had been sent to protect him from others who were on their way to murder him. It was fairly evident to Conolly that this was a fabrication, though their intentions were far from clear. But against these four well-armed men he knew he would stand little chance, and it was only too clear that he was their prisoner. The prospect of his joining the main caravan now looked extremely remote.

Conolly soon discovered that the four men had been sent by a neighbouring chief to arrest him after a confused tale had begun to circulate that he was a Russian agent employed by the Shah of Persia to spy out the Turcoman lands prior to their annexation. He was said to be carrying large quantities of gold with which to buy the allegiance of dissident tribal leaders and others. Conolly had told his captors that the story was nonsense, insisting that he was a merchant from India on his way to Khiva to sell his merchandise, and suggested that they search his baggage to satisfy themselves that he was not carrying any gold. After rummaging through his belongings and finding nothing besides a brass astrolabe (which they seemed to think might be made of solid gold), his captors appeared uncertain what to do next, keeping him moving aimlessly from place to place.

At first Conolly thought that they might be awaiting further orders. Only later did he discover the truth. The men could not agree among themselves about what to do with him. The choice lay between robbing and murdering him, or selling him into slavery. But aware that he had wealthy and influential friends across the frontier in Persia, the men hesitated to dispose of him there and then. Instead, in order to test reaction, they sent back word that he had been murdered. If no retribution followed, then they would know that they could safely proceed with their plan. Fortunately for Conolly, word of his capture had already reached his friends and a search party had been sent into the desert to look for him. In the end, minus many of his possessions and most of his money, and disappointed not to have reached Khiva, he got safely back to Astrabad, none the worse for his experience, but grateful to be alive.

Although Conolly had failed to get to Khiva, he nevertheless managed to acquire much valuable information about the Karakum–Caspian region, of which almost nothing was known in London or Calcutta, and across which ran one of the principal routes likely to be taken by an invader. He also learned, despite fears to the contrary, that the Russians were not yet in possession of the eastern shore of the Caspian, let alone Khiva. Fully recovered from his ordeal, Conolly now decided to press on towards Meshed, 300 miles to the east, and close to Persia's frontier with Afghanistan. From there he hoped to enter Afghanistan and reach the strategically important city of Herat, which no British officer had seen since Christie's clandestine visit twenty years earlier, and which many saw as the ideal staging point for an invading army because of its capacity to provide food and other essentials.

Conolly reached Herat in September 1830, and passed through the city gates with a mixture of apprehension and excitement. For Herat was then governed by the greatly feared Kamran Shah, one of the most ruthless and brutal rulers in Central Asia. The Englishman was to remain there for three weeks, this time posing as a *hakeem*, secretly observing and noting down everything of significance. He was especially interested in anything to do with the city's defences and its ability to provision an army from the produce of the great fertile valley in which it stood. How Conolly was able to do this without attracting the attention of Kamran's secret police, he does not disclose. The next stage of his reconnaissance, the hazardous, 300-mile journey to Kandahar, took him through bandit-infested country where, he was warned, the slave-raiders removed their captives' ears to make them ashamed to return home, and thus less likely to escape. Conolly was lucky, however, to be able to attach himself to a party of Muslim holy men. Such respected companions, from whom he learned much that was of interest to him, offered at least some protection from robbery, enslavement or murder.

Although he reached Kandahar safely, despite some anxious moments, Conolly had the misfortune to be struck down with illness shortly after his arrival. He became so weak that at one time he feared that he was going to die, but he was nursed back to health by one of the kindly holy men. Just as he was recovering, however, a dangerous rumour began to circulate that he was really an Englishman in disguise and spying for Kamran, who was then at war with Kandahar. This forced Conolly to drag himself from his sick-bed and leave town hurriedly after only nine days there. On November 22, this time in the company of some horse-dealers, he arrived at Quetta, at the head of the great Bolan Pass, the Khyber's southern twin, and an entry point to India for an invader. Two weeks later, after riding down the eighty-mile-long pass, Conolly reached the banks of the River Indus. The following morning he was rowed across by ferrymen. It took precisely eight minutes, he noted. His odyssey, which had brought him more than 4,000 miles from Moscow to India, was all but over.

Just to have come through alive was achievement enough. Others would be less fortunate. But Conolly had done a great deal more than that. By travelling the very routes along which a hostile Russian army was likely to advance, he was able to address many of the questions to which Lord Ellenborough and those responsible for India's defence needed answers. His more sensitive military and political observations were obviously kept for his superiors' eyes only. But he also wrote a book telling the full story of his adventures and misadventures. Entitled *Journey to the North of India, Overland from England,*

Through Russia, Persia and Affghaunistan, it was published three years later, in 1834. It included a lengthy appendix in which he examined in detail the possibilities open to a Russian general planning an invasion of India, and the likelihood of success.

Conolly argued that there were only two possible routes which a Russian army, large enough to stand any chance of success, could take. Put simply, the first involved seizing Khiva, followed by Balkh, and then crossing the Hindu Kush, as Alexander the Great had done, to Kabul. From there the army would march via Jalalabad and the Khyber Pass to Peshawar, and finally cross the Indus at Attock. The initial seizure of Khiva, he reasoned, might best be undertaken from Orenburg rather than from the eastern shore of the Caspian. This route, although longer, was better watered than the Karakum, and the tribes along its line of advance could be more easily subdued than the dangerous Turcomans. On reaching the northern shore of the Aral Sea, moreover, the Russian troops could be conveyed by boat or raft to the mouth of the Oxus, and continue up it to Khiva. The capture of Khiva, and subsequent advance on India, was a highly ambitious undertaking and might involve several successive campaigns, and take two or three years to carry out.

The second feasible route open to the Russian generals involved seizing Herat, and using it as a staging point where troops could be massed. From there they would march via Kandahar and Quetta to the Bolan Pass, the way he himself had entered India. Herat could be reached either overland through a compliant Persia, or by crossing the Caspian to Astrabad. Once Herat was in Russian hands, or had been annexed by a friendly Persia, then an army 'might be garrisoned there for years, with every necessity immediately within its reach'. Its very presence there might be sufficient to unsettle the native population of India, thus smoothing the way for an invasion when the British found themselves under attack from within.

A determined invader might even use both these routes simultaneously, Conolly pointed out. But whichever was chosen, one major obstacle remained which might rule out any hopes of success. By either route an invader would have to pass through Afghanistan. 'The Afghans', Conolly wrote, 'have little to gain, and much to fear, from letting the Russians enter their country.' Moreover they were fanatically hostile towards those on whom the Russians would most depend, the Persians. 'If the Afghans, as a nation, were determined to resist the invaders,' he declared, 'the difficulties of the march would be rendered well nigh insurmountable.' They would fight to the last drop of blood, harassing the Russian columns incessantly from their mountain strongholds, destroying food supplies and cutting off the invader's lines of communication and retreat.

If, however, the Afghans were to remain divided, as they then were, the Russians would be able to play one faction off against another with promises or other inducements. 'Singly,' Conolly wrote, 'the chief of a small state could not offer effectual opposition to a European invader, and it would be easy to gain him by encouraging his ambitions against his rivals at home, or doubly to profit by it, by directing it on India.' It was very much in Britain's interest therefore that Afghanistan be reunited under one strong and central ruler in Kabul. 'It would require great inducements to tempt a reigning prince from a sure and profitable alliance with us,' Conolly declared, 'and to engage him in an undertaking which, at best doubtful, would entail ruin upon him if he failed.' And if the Russians did succeed in holding out expectations 'sufficiently dazzling to seduce a prince', then either the stakes could be upped, or his overthrow could be arranged.

The Afghan chief whose claim to the throne should be supported, Conolly urged his superiors, was Kamran Shah of Herat. While his unsavoury character might be regretted, he and Britain shared one vital interest – that Herat, 'the Granary of Central Asia', should not fall into the hands of either the Persians, who had a long-standing claim to it, or the Russians. In Herat, moreover, it was no secret that Kamran was most anxious to ally himself to the British. If he were left to fend for himself against the Persians, Conolly warned, then it would only be a matter of time before Herat fell to their superior forces, 'and the road to India would be open to the Russians.'

*   *   *

During the year that Conolly was away, in London and Calcutta mistrust of Russian intentions continued to mount,
particularly among the hawks in Wellington's Cabinet, who
deplored the passive policies of the previous Tory administration. Particularly they feared the prospect of Turkey and
Persia, already crushed and shackled to St Petersburg by treaty,
becoming Russian protectorates. Lord Ellenborough, who had
been given a virtually free hand with regard to India by his
friend Wellington, was becoming increasingly convinced of
Russia's expansionist aims. It was his belief that the Tsar
would use stealth to get his armies within striking distance of
India. As Persia gradually became weaker, the Russians would
extend their influence and military presence throughout the
country, while elsewhere Russian troops would follow in their
merchants' footsteps, protection being the pretext. Thus,
merely by mapping the progress of their trading posts, the line
of advance towards India could be monitored. But two could
play at that game, Ellenborough believed, and the superiority
of British goods should be used to halt the advance of the
Russian merchants. This was the very strategy which Moorcroft had vainly urged on his superiors. Now, five years later,
it was official British policy.

It had been one of Moorcroft's dreams to see the River Indus
used to transport British goods northwards to the frontiers of
Central Asia, whence they could be carried across the mountains by caravan to the bazaars of the old Silk Road. His
impassioned arguments, however, had as usual fallen on deaf
ears. Now that Ellenborough himself had taken up the idea,
the Company's directors embraced it enthusiastically. Since
very little was known about this great waterway, it must first
be surveyed to ensure that it was navigable. This was much
easier said than done, for the Indus flowed through vast tracts
of territory which did not belong to the Company, notably
Sind in the south and the Punjab in the north, whose rulers
would almost certainly object. Then Lord Ellenborough hit
on a brilliant, if somewhat devious, solution.

Ranjit Singh, the ruler of the Punjab, had recently presented
to the King of England some magnificent Kashmiri shawls,
and the question now arose of what the British sovereign,

William IV, could send him in return. Women, who were known to be the ageing maharajah's favourite pastime, were clearly ruled out. Next on the list of his hobbies came horses, and this gave Ellenborough an idea. Ranjit Singh would be presented with five horses. But these would be no ordinary mounts. They would be the largest horses ever seen in Asia – massive English dray horses, four mares and a stallion. It was thought that they would make a suitably impressive and spectacular gift for this Asiatic potentate who had recently sent an envoy to St Petersburg. At the same time Sir John Malcolm, the Governor of Bombay, gave orders for the construction of a gilded state coach in which Ranjit Singh, drawn by his huge horses, could tour his kingdom in regal splendour and comfort.

However, there was more to it than just that. Because of their size, and the unsuitability of both the climate and the terrain, it was reasoned that the horses and the state coach could not possibly travel the 700 miles to Lahore, Ranjit's capital, overland if they were to survive. Instead, they would have to go by boat up the Indus. This would make it possible to conduct a discreet survey of the river, and ascertain whether it was navigable as far as Lahore. The officer chosen to lead this curious espionage mission was a young subaltern named Alexander Burnes, who, because of his unusual talents, had recently been transferred from his regiment, the 1st Bombay Light Infantry, to the élite Indian political service. At the age of 25, he had already shown himself to be one of the Company's most promising young officers. Intelligent, resourceful and fearless, he was also an excellent linguist, being fluent in Persian, Arabic and Hindustani, as well as in some of the lesser-known Indian tongues. Although of slight stature and mild appearance, he was a man of extraordinary determination and self-confidence. He also possessed remarkable charm, which he exercised to great effect on Asiatics and Europeans alike.

Ellenborough's scheme for the clandestine survey of the Indus did not, however, meet with universal approval in India. One of its severest critics was Sir Charles Metcalfe, a member of the all-powerful Supreme Council, and former Secretary of the Secret and Political Department. 'The scheme of surveying the Indus, under the pretence of sending a present to Rajah Runjeet Singh, is a trick . . . unworthy of our Government,' he complained. It was just the sort of deviousness, he added, which the British were often unjustly accused of, and would very likely be detected, thus confirming the suspicions of the native rulers. He and Sir John Malcolm, both powerful figures in India, represented the two extremes of strategic thinking then prevalent. Metcalfe, destined to become Governor-General of Canada, believed in the consolidation of the Company's existing territories and frontiers, while Malcolm, like Ellenborough in London, was convinced of the need for a forward policy.

It was at this moment that Wellington's government fell, taking Ellenborough with it, and the Whigs came to power. Fearing – needlessly, as it turned out – that the Indus project might now be cancelled, Malcolm urged Lieutenant Burnes to set out as soon as possible. The latter, eager for adventure, needed no second bidding. Wasting no time, he sailed from Kutch on January 21, 1831, accompanied by a surveyor, a small escort and the coach and five horses for Ranjit Singh.

·11·

Enter 'Bokhara' Burnes

'Alas, Sind is now gone,' a holy man was heard to say as he watched Lieutenant Alexander Burnes and his party sail past him up the Indus. 'The English have seen the river which is the road to our conquest.' This fear was echoed by a soldier who told Burnes: 'The evil is done. You have seen our country.' The real purpose of the expedition, as Sir Charles Metcalfe had warned, fooled no one, and at first the suspicious emirs had objected strongly to the passage across their dominions of the Company's vessel with its bizarre cargo. Finally, however, threatened with grave consequences if they held up Ranjit Singh's gifts, and sweetened with gifts themselves, they reluctantly agreed to allow Burnes and his companions to proceed. Apart from the occasional pot-shot taken at them from the river bank, they had no further trouble, although the emirs insisted that they could not be responsible for their safety as they made their way slowly northwards.

Working wherever possible at night to avoid arousing the hostility of the locals, they reached Lahore, Ranjit Singh's capital, five months after entering the mouth of the Indus system. In addition to charting the river, which involved taking discreet soundings of its muddy depths, they had proved by their arrival that the Indus was navigable up to that point, 700 miles from the coast, though only for flat-bottomed craft like their own. There, provided Ranjit Singh agreed, British goods could be unloaded and carried overland into Afghanistan and across the Oxus to the markets of Turkestan.

The five horses, which had miraculously survived the heat and other discomforts of the long voyage, caused a sensation among the court officials sent to the frontier to welcome them to the Punjab. 'For the first time,' Burnes noted, 'a dray horse was expected to gallop, canter and perform all the evolutions of the most agile animal.' Further astonishment was to follow when their massive feet were inspected. On it being discovered that just one of their shoes weighed four times that of a local horse, Burnes was asked whether one of these might be sent ahead to Lahore. 'The curiosity was forthwith dispatched,' he observed, 'accompanied by the most minute measure of each of the animals for Ranjit Singh's special information.' The coach too, with its lining of blue velvet, drew similar admiration from his officials, and hauled by the five huge horses ('little elephants', the locals christened them), this now set out overland for the capital.

A dazzling reception awaited Burnes in Lahore, Ranjit being as anxious to maintain cordial relations with the British as they were to keep on the right side of their powerful Sikh neighbour. For his highly trained and well-equipped army was thought in Calcutta to be almost a match for the Company's own forces, although neither side had any wish to put this to the test. The only cause for concern in London and Calcutta was Ranjit's health, and the inevitable struggle for power which would follow his death. One of Burnes's tasks was to report on the ruler's expectation of life, and on the political mood of the kingdom.

'We passed close under the walls of the city,' he wrote afterwards, 'and entered Lahore by the palace gate. The streets were lined with cavalry, artillery and infantry, all of which saluted as we passed. The concourse of people was immense; they had principally seated themselves on the balconies of houses, and preserved a most respectful silence.' Burnes and his companions were next led across the outer courtyard of the royal palace to the main entrance to the throne room. 'While stooping to remove my shoes,' he reported, 'I suddenly found myself in the arms and tight embrace of a diminutive, old-looking man.' He realised to his astonishment that it was the mighty Ranjit Singh himself who had come forward to greet

his guest, an unprecedented honour. The maharajah now led
Burnes by the hand to the interior of the court where he seated
him on a silver chair before the throne.

Burnes presented Ranjit Singh with a letter from Lord Ellenborough. Sealed in an envelope made from cloth of gold, and
bearing the British royal coat-of-arms, it conveyed a personal
message to the Sikh ruler from William IV. Ranjit ordered it
to be read aloud. 'The King', Lord Ellenborough had written,
'has given me his most special command to intimate to your
Highness the sincere satisfaction with which his Majesty has
witnessed the good understanding which has for so many years
subsisted, and which may God ever preserve, between the
British Government and your Highness.' Ranjit Singh was
clearly delighted, and even before it was finished gave orders
for a thunderous artillery salute – sixty guns, each firing
twenty-one times – to be discharged to make his pleasure
known to the people of Lahore.

Next, with Burnes at his side, Ranjit was taken to inspect
the five dray horses, which were waiting patiently in the heat
outside, together with the new state coach. Clearly pleased
with this spectacular gift from the English sovereign, he called
out excitedly to court officials as one by one the horses were
led past him. The following morning Burnes and his party
attended a military review, with five regiments of infantry
drawn up in line. Burnes was invited by Ranjit to inspect his
troops, who were dressed in white with black cross belts,
and armed with locally made muskets. The regiments now
manoeuvred for Ranjit's guests, 'with an exactness and precision', Burnes noted, 'fully equal to our Indian troops.' Ranjit
asked him many questions about military matters, and in particular whether British troops could advance against artillery.

In all, Burnes and his companions were to spend nearly two
months as Ranjit's guests. There were endless military parades,
banquets and other entertainments, including long sessions
spent imbibing with Ranjit a locally distilled 'hell-brew' of
which the latter was extremely fond. There was also a troupe
of Kashmiri dancing girls, forty in number and all dressed as
boys, to whom the one-eyed ruler (he had lost the other from
smallpox) appeared similarly addicted. 'This', he confided to

Burnes with a twinkle, 'is one of my regiments, but they tell me it is the only one I cannot discipline.' When the girls, all strikingly beautiful, had finished dancing, they were whisked away on elephants – much to the disappointment of the youthful Burnes, who also had a weakness for comely native girls.

There was plenty of time, too, for serious discussion on political and commercial matters, which was the real purpose of their coming. Burnes was profoundly impressed by the wizened old Sikh who, despite his diminutive size and unattractive appearance, had gained the respect and loyalty of this warrior people, every one of whom towered over him in stature, for so long. 'Nature', Burnes wrote, 'has indeed been sparing in her gifts to this personage. He has lost an eye, is pitted by the small-pox, and his stature does not exceed five feet three inches.' Yet he commanded the instant attention of all around him. 'Not an individual spoke without a sign,' Burnes noted, 'though the throng was more like a bazaar than the Court of the first native prince in these times.'

Like all native rulers, however, he could be ruthless, although he claimed that during his long reign he had never punished anyone by execution. 'Cunning and conciliation', Burnes wrote, 'have been the two great weapons of his diplomacy.' But how much longer would he remain in power? 'It is probable', reported Burnes, 'that the career of this chief is nearly at an end. His chest is contracted, his back is bent, his limbs withered.' His nightly drinking bouts, Burnes feared, were more than anyone could take. However, his favourite tipple – 'more ardent than the strongest brandy' – appeared to do him no harm. Ranjit Singh was to survive another eight years – greatly to the relief of the Company's generals, who saw him as a vital link in India's outer defences, and a formidable ally against a Russian invader.

Finally, in August 1831, laden with gifts and compliments, Burnes and his companions crossed back into British territory, making for Ludhiana, the Company's most forward garrison town in north-west India. There Burnes met briefly a man whose fate was to be closely bound to his own – Shah Shujah, the exiled Afghan ruler, who dreamed of regaining his lost throne by toppling its present occupant, the redoubtable Dost

Mohammed. Burnes was not impressed by this melancholy-looking man who was already turning to fat. 'From what I learn,' he noted, 'I do not believe that the Shah possesses sufficient energy to set himself on the throne of Cabool.' Nor, Burnes felt, did he appear to have the personal qualities or political acumen to reunite so turbulent a nation as the Afghans.

A week later Burnes reached Simla, the Indian government's summer capital, where he reported to Lord William Bentinck, the Governor-General, on the results of his mission. He had shown that the Indus was navigable for flat-bottomed craft, whether warships or cargo-boats, as far north as Lahore. As a result of this discovery it was decided to proceed with plans to open up the great waterway to shipping, so that British goods could eventually compete with Russian ones in Turkestan and elsewhere in Central Asia. Bentinck therefore dispatched Henry Pottinger, now a colonel in the political service, to begin negotiations with the emirs of Sind over the passage of goods through their territories. Ranjit Singh, Burnes reported, would present no problems. Apart from being friendly towards the British, he would also benefit from this passing trade. Burnes's superiors were delighted with the results of his first mission, and no one more so than the Governor-General who, on Sir John Malcolm's recommendation, had chosen him for it. He was commended by Bentinck for the 'zeal, diligence and intelligence' with which he had carried out his delicate task. At the age of 26, Burnes was already on his way to the top.

*   *   *

Having won the Governor-General's ear and confidence, Burnes now put forward an idea of his own for a second, more ambitious mission. This was to reconnoitre those hitherto unmapped routes to India lying to the north of the ones which Arthur Conolly had explored the previous year. He proposed travelling first to Kabul, where he would seek to establish friendly links with Ranjit Singh's great rival Dost Mohammed, and at the same time endeavour to gauge the strength and efficiency of his armed forces and the vulnerability of his capital. From Kabul he intended to proceed through the passes of the Hindu Kush and across the Oxus to Bokhara. There he hoped to do much the same as in Kabul, returning to India via the Caspian Sea and Persia with a mass of military and political intelligence for his chiefs. It was a highly ambitious scheme, for most people would have settled for either Kabul or Bokhara, not both.

Burnes expected strong opposition to his proposal, not least because of his junior rank and the extreme sensitivity of the region. It came as a pleasant surprise therefore when in December 1831 he was informed by the Governor-General that approval had been given for him to proceed. Burnes was soon to discover the reason for this. The timing of his suggestion could not have been better. In London the new Whig Cabinet under Grey was beginning to feel as uneasy as the Tories about the growing strength and influence of the Russians, both in Europe and in High Asia. 'The Home Government', Burnes wrote to his sister, 'have got frightened at the designs of Russia, and desired that some intelligent officer should be sent to acquire information in the countries bordering on the Oxus and the Caspian ... and I, knowing nothing of all this, come forward and volunteer precisely for what they want.'

He immediately set about making plans for the journey and choosing suitable companions – one Englishman and two Indians. The former was a Bengal Army doctor named James Gerard, an officer with a taste for adventure and with previous experience of travel in the Himalayas. One of the Indians was a bright, well-educated Kashmiri named Mohan Lal. He was fluent in several languages, which would come in useful when oriental niceties had to be observed. It would also be one of his tasks to record much of the intelligence gathered by the mission. The other Indian was an experienced Company surveyor named Mohammed Ali who had accompanied Burnes on the Indus survey and had already proved his worth. In addition to these three, Burnes brought his own personal servant who had been with him almost since his arrival in India eleven years earlier.

On March 17, 1832, the party crossed the Indus at Attock, turning their backs on the Punjab, where they had enjoyed

Ranjit Singh's hospitality and protection, and prepared to enter Afghanistan. 'It now became necessary to divest ourselves of almost everything which belonged to us,' Burnes was to write, 'and discontinue many habits and practices which had become a second nature.' They disposed of their European clothing and adopted Afghan dress, shaving their heads and covering them with turbans. Over their long, flowing robes they wore cummerbunds, from which they hung swords. But they made no attempt to conceal the fact that they were Europeans – returning home to England, they claimed, by the overland route. Their aim was to try to melt into the background, and thus avoid attracting unwelcome attention; 'I adopted this resolution', Burnes explained, 'in an utter hopelessness of supporting the disguise of a native, and from having observed that no European traveller has ever journeyed in such countries without suspicion and seldom without discovery.'

Robbery, he believed, was their greatest danger, and the expedition's small treasury was divided among its members for concealment on their persons. 'A letter of credit for five thousand rupees', Burnes wrote, 'was fastened to my left arm in the way Asiatics wear amulets.' His passport and letters of introduction were attached to his other arm, while a bag of gold coins hung from a belt beneath his robes. It was also agreed that Gerard should not dispense free medicines for fear that this might give the impression that they were wealthy. In Afghanistan, where every man carried a weapon and coveted the property of strangers, one could not afford to be off one's guard for a second.

They had been warned that if they attempted the Khyber Pass they would be unlikely to get through alive, so instead they crossed the mountains by a longer and more tortuous route. After passing safely through Jalalabad, they took the main caravan route westwards towards Kabul. All around them as they rode were snow-capped mountains, while in the far distance could be seen the mighty peaks of the Hindu Kush. Their problems proved fewer than they had feared, and one bitterly cold night they were allowed to sleep in a mosque, although the villagers knew they were infidels. 'They do not appear to have the smallest prejudice against a Christian,'

Burnes wrote, and nowhere did he or Dr Gerard attempt to conceal their religion. Nonetheless they were cautious, and most careful not to cause offence. 'When they ask me if I eat pork,' Burnes was to write, 'I of course shudder and say it is only outcasts who commit such outrages. God forgive me! For I am very fond of bacon and my mouth waters when I write the word.'

At midnight on April 30 they reached the pass leading down to Kabul, and the following afternoon entered the capital, proceeding first to the customs house. Here, to their alarm, their baggage was searched. This was something they had not anticipated, though fortunately it did not prove to be very thorough. 'My sextant and books, with the doctor's few bottles and paraphernalia, were laid out in state for the inspection of the citizens,' Burnes recounted. 'They did them no harm, but set us down without doubt as conjurors, after a display of such unintelligible apparatus.'

Six weeks after crossing the River Indus they had reached their first goal. It was here in Dost Mohammed's stronghold that their mission would really begin. By the time it was over, nine months later, it would have won for Burnes the kind of acclaim that Lawrence's exploits in Arabia were to attract seventy-five years later.

*   *   *

Although the name of Alexander Burnes will always be associated with Bokhara, it is to Kabul that it really belongs. For it was with the Afghan capital and its ruler that his destiny was to be fatally entwined. On this first visit to it, in the spring of 1832, he was to fall in love with the city, likening it to paradise. Its many gardens, so abundant in fruit-trees and song-birds, reminded him of England. 'There were peaches, plums, apricots, pears, apples, quinces, cherries, walnuts, mulberries, pomegranates and vines,' he wrote, 'all growing in one garden. There were also nightingales, blackbirds, thrushes and doves ... and chattering magpies on almost every tree.' So struck was Burnes by the song of the nightingales that an Afghan friend was later to have one delivered to him in India. Christened 'the nightingale of a thousand tales', it sang so loudly all night that it had to be removed from earshot so that he could sleep.

Burnes and Dost Mohammed hit it off from the start. The Englishman, who maintained his story that he was on his way home via Kabul and Bokhara, had brought with him valuable letters of introduction to the Afghan potentate, and very soon found himself invited to the royal palace within the Bala Hissar, the great walled citadel overlooking the capital. In contrast to his neighbour and foe Ranjit Singh, Dost Mohammed was a man of surprisingly modest tastes, and he and Burnes sat cross-legged together on a carpet in a room otherwise devoid of furniture.

Like all Afghan princes, Dost Mohammed had been schooled almost from birth in the arts of intrigue and treachery. In addition he had been born with other, more subtle qualities inherited from his Persian mother. All this had enabled him to outmanoeuvre his several older brothers in the struggle for the throne of Kabul which had followed the ousting of Shah Shujah, now in exile at Ludhiana, and by 1826 he had finally won it for himself. Unable to read or write, he had at once set about remedying this and at the same time restoring order and prosperity to his new domains. Burnes and his companions found themselves much impressed by what he had managed to achieve in this turbulent land in those six years.

'The reputation of Dost Mohammed', Burnes reported, 'is made known to the traveller long before he enters the country, and no one better merits the high character he has obtained. The justice of this chief affords a constant theme of praise to all classes. The peasant rejoices at the absence of tyranny, the citizen at the safety of his house and the strict municipal regulations, the merchant at the equity of his decisions and the protection of his property.' A potentate, Burnes concluded, could enjoy no higher praise than that. But Mohan Lal, the young Kashmiri in the party, was less convinced of the Afghan ruler's benevolence, observing later that while he was 'prudent and wise in cabinet, and an able commander in the field', he was no less able in the arts of 'treachery, cruelty, murder and falsehood'.

Welcoming Burnes at their first meeting, Dost Mohammed

declared that although he was unfamiliar with Englishmen, he had heard others speak well of both them and their nation. In his eagerness for knowledge of the outside world and how it managed its affairs, he showered Burnes with questions. He wanted to know all about Europe, how many kings it had, and how they prevented neighbouring ones from trying to overthrow them. The questions were so numerous and diverse that Burnes soon lost track of them, but they included law, revenue collection, the manner in which European nations raised their armies (he had heard that the Russians used conscription), and even foundling hospitals. He also wanted to know whether the British had any designs on Afghanistan, looking Burnes sharply in the eye as he asked. Aware that Ranjit Singh employed European officers to train and modernise his army, he even offered Burnes, whom he knew to be a Company officer, the command of his. 'Twelve thousand horse and twenty guns shall be at your disposal,' he promised, and when Burnes gracefully declined the honour he invited him to recommend a brother officer instead.

Dost Mohammed made no attempt to conceal his dislike of his powerful and arrogant Sikh neighbour, and asked Burnes whether the British would like his help in overthrowing him. It was an embarrassing offer, for the removal of the friendly Ranjit was the very last thing anyone in Calcutta or London wanted. To them it was not the Sikhs who were the worry, but the unruly Afghans. After all, only seventy-five years earlier they had poured down through the Khyber Pass and sacked Delhi, riding home triumphantly with all the treasures they could carry. Thanking Dost Mohammed for his offer, Burnes pointed out that his government had a long-standing treaty with Ranjit and could not afford to be on bad terms with so formidable a neighbour. As a political officer, Burnes knew that what Calcutta really needed on this, its most vulnerable frontier, was not two warring rivals, but two strong and stable allies, both friendly to Britain, to serve as a shield against invasion. However, he had been sent to report on these rulers' sympathies, not to try to reconcile them. That would come later, as would the crucial question of which of the several rivals for the throne of a united Afghanistan Britain should back. Conolly had argued for Kamran Shah, if only because it was vital to keep Herat out of Persian (and therefore eventually Russian) hands. Burnes had no doubts whatever about his candidate. Dost Mohammed, he believed, should be courted by Britain and kept firmly on his throne, as the only man capable of uniting this warlike nation.

Burnes and his party would happily have stayed much longer, sipping tea and gossiping with Afghan friends in this delightful town, but their journey to Bokhara still lay ahead of them. After one final meeting with Dost Mohammed which continued until long after midnight, they set off northwards towards the passes of the Hindu Kush, beyond which lay Balkh, the Oxus and, ultimately, Bokhara. Once they were clear of Dost Mohammed's territories they would be embarking on the most dangerous stretch of their journey, and the fate of Moorcroft and his two companions, only seven years earlier, was now never far from their thoughts. When they reached the once-great city of Balkh, by then reduced to ruins, they were determined to track down the men's lonely graves as an act of personal homage.

The first one they managed to locate, in a village several miles away, was that of George Trebeck, the last of Moorcroft's party to die. It lay, unmarked, beneath a mulberry tree. 'After burying his two European fellow-travellers,' Burnes wrote, 'he sank, at an early age, after four months' suffering, in a far distant country, without a friend, without assistance, and without consolation.' They finally came upon the graves of Moorcroft and Guthrie, buried side by side, beneath a mud wall outside Balkh. Because they were Christians, the locals had insisted that they be buried without a headstone of any kind. It was a clear, moonlit night, and Burnes was much affected, for Moorcroft was a man whom he, like all those who played the Great Game, much revered. 'It was impossible to view such a scene at dead of night without any melancholy reflections,' he wrote. 'A whole party, buried within twelve miles of each other, held out small encouragement to us who were pursuing the same track and were led on by nearly similar motives.'

But they had little time to spare for such morbid considerations. They had reached the Oxus safely, and there were important if discreet enquiries to be made about the great river, up which, it had long been feared, a Russian invasion force might one day sail from the Aral Sea to Balkh. In his published narrative Burnes gives little indication of how they set about this during their five days in the region, describing instead their search for coins and antiquities in the ruins of ancient Balkh. It is only when one reads Burnes's secret reports to his chiefs, whose faded transcripts are today in the archives of the India Office in London, that one realises how busy they must have been enquiring about the river's navigability, the availability of food and other supplies in the region, and further strategic considerations. This task completed, they now set out on the final stage of their journey, the gruelling, ten-day desert crossing to Bokhara. For this they attached themselves to a large, well-armed caravan. Although they were now nominally within the domains of the Emir of Bokhara, they knew there was a real risk of being seized by Turcoman slavers and ending up in shackles in the city's market square. But apart from a mysterious fever which afflicted Burnes and his companions, reminding them uncomfortably of the fate of their three predecessors, the journey passed off without mishap.

As they approached Bokhara, Burnes composed a letter, redolent with oriental flattery, which he sent ahead of them to the Koosh Begee, or Grand Vizier, expressing their wish to see the legendary glories of the holy city. His liberal use of phrases describing the vizier as 'the Tower of Islam', and 'the Gem of the Faith' clearly pleased the recipient, for a messenger soon returned to say that they would be welcome to visit Bokhara. Still weak from their illness, Burnes and Gerard, together with their native companions, finally rode through the city's main gateway on the morning of June 27, 1832, just six months after leaving Delhi. Later on that same day Burnes was summoned before the Grand Vizier at the Emir's palace in Bokhara's famous Ark, or citadel, some two miles from their lodgings. After changing into local garb, Burnes proceeded there on foot, for it was strictly forbidden for all but Muslims to ride within the holy city. He went alone, Gerard still being too ill to accompany him.

His interview with the Koosh Begee, a wizened old man with small, crafty eyes and a long grey beard, began with an interrogation lasting two hours. The vizier first wanted to know what had brought Burnes and his party to a kingdom so far from their own. Burnes explained as usual that they were returning overland to England, and that they wanted to take back with them word of Bokhara's splendours, already so renowned throughout the Orient. 'What', the vizier next asked him, 'is your profession?' Burnes hesitated for a moment before confessing to being an officer in the Indian Army. But he need not have worried, for this did not appear to perturb the Koosh Begee in the least. The Bokharan seemed to be more interested in Burnes's religious beliefs, asking him first whether he believed in God, and then whether he worshipped idols. Burnes denied the latter emphatically, upon which he was invited to bare his chest to show that he was not wearing a crucifix. When it transpired that Burnes was not, the vizier declared approvingly: 'You are people of the Book. You are better than the Russians.' He next asked whether Christians ate pork, a question which Burnes knew he had to answer with caution. Some did, he replied, though mainly the poor. 'What', his interrogator next asked, 'does it taste like?' But Burnes was ready for that one. 'I have *heard*', he replied, 'that it is like beef.'

Very soon, however, as he invariably did with Asiatics, Burnes was getting on famously with the vizier, to whom he was evidently a source of tantalising information from the sophisticated outside world. The friendship was to cost him one of his only two compasses, although this gift won for him and his companions the freedom to wander the city at will, and to observe its everyday life. They saw the grim minaret from which criminals were hurled to their deaths, and they visited the square before the Ark where beheadings were conducted with a huge knife. Burnes went to watch the slave-market in action, reporting afterwards: 'Here these poor wretches are exposed for sale, and occupy thirty or forty stalls where they are examined like cattle.' That morning there were only six being offered, none of them Russians. 'The feelings of a European', he added, 'revolt at this most odious traffic', which

Bokharans defended on the grounds that the slaves were kindly treated, and were often far better off than in their own land.

Burnes had discreetly let it be known that he wanted to meet one of the Russian slaves, of whom there were 130 or so in Bokhara. Not long afterwards a man of obvious European origin slipped into their house one night and flung himself emotionally at Burnes's feet. He told them that as a boy of 10 he had been captured by Turcoman slavers while asleep at a Russian outpost. He had been a slave for fifteen years now, and worked for his master as a carpenter. He was well treated, he said, and was allowed to go where he wished. But for reasons of prudence he pretended to have adopted Islam, although secretly ('and here', Burnes noted, 'the poor fellow crossed himself') he was still a Christian. 'For I live among a people', he explained, 'who detest, with the utmost cordiality, every individual of that creed.' After sharing the Englishmen's meal with them, he told them before departing: 'I may appear to be happy, but my heart aches for my native land. Could I but see it once again, I would willingly die.'

They had now been in Bokhara for a month, and their enquiries were complete. Burnes had hoped to press on to Khiva, and return home from there via Persia. However, the Koosh Begee warned him strongly against attempting the journey to Khiva, saying that the surrounding region was unsettled and extremely dangerous. In the end Burnes decided to head directly for Persia, via Merv and Astrabad, and forget Khiva. He managed to obtain from the vizier a firman bearing the Emir's personal seal and ordering all Bokharan officials to assist the party in every way possible. However, once they were outside the Emir's domains, he cautioned Burnes, they would be in treacherous country all the way to the Persian frontier, and should trust no one. For reasons he did not explain, the vizier had at no time allowed them to meet the Emir himself, although this may well have been done in their own interest. Newly installed on the Bokharan throne was the man who was to have the next two British officers to arrive there brutally put to death. Finally, as the Koosh Begee, who had been so kind to Burnes, bade them farewell, he asked them to pray for him when they reached home safely, 'as I am an old

man'. And Oh yes! One other thing. If Burnes ever returned
to Bokhara would he be kind enough to bring him a good pair
of English spectacles?

*   *   *

After a series of adventures and misadventures too numerous
to go into here, Burnes and his party reached Bombay by sea
from the Persian Gulf on January 18, 1833. There they were
to learn that a great deal had taken place elsewhere during their
thirteen months away, leading to a further sharp decline in
Anglo-Russian relations. On February 20, just as Burnes
arrived in Calcutta to report to the Governor-General on the
results of his reconnaissance into Central Asia, a large fleet of
Russian warships dropped anchor off Constantinople, causing
profound dismay in London and in India. This was the final
outcome of a chain of events which had begun in 1831, following a revolt in Egypt, then nominally part of the Ottoman
Empire, against the Sultan's rule. At first the revolt had seemed
purely a local affair, though very soon it began to represent a
serious threat. The man behind it was one of the Sultan's own
vassals, the Albanian-born Mohammed Ali, the ruler of Egypt.
Having first seized Damascus and Aleppo with his powerful army, he now advanced into Anatolia, and looked set on
marching on Constantinople and relieving the Sultan of his
throne. The latter appealed desperately to Britain for help,
but Lord Palmerston, the Foreign Secretary, hesitated to act
alone.

If Britain was slow to respond to the Sultan's pleas, however,
Tsar Nicholas was not, for he had no wish to see the present
compliant ruler in Constantinople replaced by an aggressive
new dynasty. He at once dispatched Nikolai Muraviev (of
Khiva fame, and now a general) to Constantinople to offer the
Sultan protection against Mohammed Ali's advancing army.
At first the Sultan hesitated, for he still clung to the hope
of receiving British assistance, which he would have much
preferred. London continued to do nothing, though, Palmerston being convinced that St Petersburg, officially an ally
of Britain's, would never act unilaterally. But finally, on the

urgings of his men on the spot, who viewed the crisis as a threat to Britain's Near Eastern interests, not to mention those of India, he allowed himself to be persuaded, though even now he preferred mediation to intervention. His decision, needless to say, proved too late. As Mohammed Ali's troops fought their way through Anatolia towards the capital, driving all before them, the Sultan had no choice but to accept gratefully Nicholas's offer of immediate help.

As it was, the Russian fleet arrived off Constantinople only just in time, for the invaders were now less than 200 miles away. The Sultan's throne, however, had been saved. Aware that they could not defeat both the Russians and the Turks, Mohammed Ali's commanders called a halt, and a settlement was duly arranged. British indecisiveness had enabled St Petersburg to realise at last its age-old dream of landing troops at Constantinople. When news of this latest Russian move reached Calcutta it was at once seen as part of a grand design, with India as its ultimate goal. The pieces seemed to be falling ominously into place. No longer were men like Wilson, Moorcroft, Kinneir and de Lacy Evans viewed as scaremongers. Such then was the mood when Burnes arrived in Calcutta. He could hardly have chosen a better moment to reappear. The Great Game was beginning to intensify.

After Burnes had reported to the Governor-General, Lord William Bentinck, he was ordered to sail at once for London where he was to brief the Cabinet, the Board of Control and other senior officials on the situation in Central Asia and the likelihood of a Russian threat to India. The reception he received was a heady one for a young subaltern, culminating in a private audience with the King, for he, like everyone else, wanted to hear Burnes's story at first hand. Overnight Burnes became a hero. Professionally, too, he was made. In addition to being promoted to captain, he was awarded the coveted gold medal of the Royal Geographical Society for his remarkable journey. He was also invited to join the Athenaeum, holy of holies of England's literary and scientific élite, without first having to stand for election, while society hostesses and would-be mothers-in-law joined in the pursuit of this dashing young officer.

John Murray, the leading publisher of the day, was quick to acquire Burnes's account of his journey. Entitled *Travels into Bokhara*, it was rushed through the press so as to steal a march on Arthur Conolly's book, which appeared a few months later, and Moorcroft's long-delayed posthumous work, which was not to be published for a further seven years. Burnes's epic, in three volumes, thus brought to the reader for the first time the romance, mystery and excitement of Central Asia. It was to prove an immediate bestseller, 900 copies being sold on the first day, a huge number for those times. Sadly, Dr Gerard was unable to enjoy any of this acclaim, being far away in India. Indeed, within two years he was dead, his health broken by the illness which had struck him and his companions on the final march to Bokhara.

But amidst all this adulation, Burnes had not lost sight of the real purpose of their journey. In addition to his book, which had mainly been written on the sea voyage home, he produced for his superiors two secret reports – one military and the other political – and two more, less sensitive, on the topography and commercial prospects of the region. In his military report he argued that it would be as dangerous for Kabul to fall into Russian hands as Herat. A hostile army, he reported, could get there from Balkh in a month. The passes of the Hindu Kush, where so many of Alexander's troops had frozen to death, would prove no obstacle to a well-equipped, modern army. Ferocious and courageous though they were in tribal warfare, the Afghans could not hope to defend Kabul for very long against a determined Russian army. Once in possession of Kabul, an invader would have little difficulty in advancing on India, there being several possible routes open to him.

As for reaching Balkh, this could be achieved by ferrying troops up the Oxus in barges towed by horses – 'as on a canal'. The river, he and his companions had ascertained, was fully navigable to that point. Its banks were low and firm, and horses plentiful in the region. Artillery could either be carried up the river by barge, or be dragged along the river bank. If the invasion force were to set out from Orenburg, rather than from the eastern shore of the Caspian, it would not even be necessary to occupy Khiva first. Bokhara too could be bypassed, although both oases might serve as valuable sources of food and other supplies if their rulers' co-operation could first be won. Because of the danger of Kabul thus falling into Russian hands, he argued, Britain should back Dost Mohammed rather than Kamran Shah for the throne of a united Afghanistan. Burnes made a Russian move against Kabul sound all too easy, and he, unlike Wilson, Kinneir or de Lacy Evans, had actually been there.

Eager to return to the region which had brought him such sudden fame, Burnes now lobbied vigorously to be allowed to establish a permanent mission in Kabul. Apart from maintaining close and friendly ties with Dost Mohammed, and keeping an eye on any Russian moves south of the Oxus, its purpose would be to ensure that British goods rather than Russian ones dominated the markets of Afghanistan and Turkestan. If the River Indus route, which he had shown to be navigable, was fully exploited by the Company, then British goods, being cheaper and better, would eventually drive out those of Russia. At first Burnes's proposal for a British trade mission (albeit with strong political undertones) at Kabul was turned down by his superiors, for they feared that it might, as one put it, 'degenerate into a political agency.' However, the newly appointed Governor-General, Lord Auckland, thought otherwise, and on November 26, 1836, Burnes was dispatched once more to Kabul.

Like his earlier visit to Dost Mohammed, and the month he had spent in Bokhara, this did not go unnoticed in St Petersburg. For some time now, and with growing concern, the Russians had been keeping a close watch on the movements of British travellers in Central Asia. Not only were their own goods beginning to suffer from increasing British competition, but political rivalry also appeared to be intensifying. No longer was the Great Game confined to the khanates of Central Asia. Play had spread to the Caucasus, which the Russians had hitherto regarded as theirs. Reports were beginning to reach St Petersburg from Circassia, on the north-eastern shore of the Black Sea, that British agents were operating among the tribes there, supplying them with arms and inciting them to resist the infidels who had come to seize their lands.

·12·

The Greatest Fortress
in the World

Although by now most of the Caucasian region, including Georgia and Armenia, was firmly in Tsar Nicholas's hands, and officially incorporated in the Russian Empire, in the mountains of the north fierce resistance continued among the Muslim tribes. The two principal areas still remaining to be conquered were Circassia in the west and Daghestan in the east. No longer at war with the Turks or Persians, the Russian generals now devoted all their energies to crushing the warlike inhabitants in these two strongholds. It was to take them a great deal longer than they had expected, for the local commanders showed a brilliant aptitude for mountain and forest warfare. In addition, they had discovered an unexpected ally.

David Urquhart, then aged 28, had acquired a passionate attachment to the Turks as a result of his experiences as a volunteer during the Greek War of Independence. In 1827, together with some eighty other Britons, he had gone to Greece to help drive out the Turks, but had soon found himself thoroughly disillusioned by the Greeks. His new devotion to the Turks, whose courage and other qualities he greatly admired, was to give rise in him to an equally intense dislike of their ancient foes the Russians. Educated at a French military academy and at Oxford, Urquhart also possessed remarkable skills as a propagandist, which he now directed against St Petersburg. Before long he was to become Britain's leading Russophobe. He enjoyed the added advantage of having friends in the highest realms of public life, including the King himself. As a result he was employed by the government on a number of secret diplomatic missions in the Near East, and it was during one of these, while in Constantinople, that he found himself caught up in the Circassian cause.

Not long before, with the ending of Mohammed Ali's threat to the Sultan's throne, the Russians had reluctantly agreed to withdraw their task-force from Constantinople, although not without first making the Turks pay heavily for their intervention. Under the terms of a treaty signed in the summer of 1833, Turkey had been reduced — at least in the eyes of Urquhart and his fellow Russophobes — to little more than a protectorate of the Tsar's. To London's alarm, it was soon discovered that under a secret clause the Turks were committed, if St Petersburg so demanded, to closing the Dardanelles to all foreign warships save those of Russia. Thus, in the event of war, the Russians would have exclusive rights of passage through the Turkish straits for their powerful Black Sea fleet.

Palmerston, the British Foreign Secretary, was incensed at this, and protested strongly to St Petersburg. He was beginning to wonder whether the redoubtable Mohammed Ali, who had made friendly overtures to Britain, would not have been better on the Turkish throne than the supine Sultan. His humour was not improved by the Russian reply to his protest, which argued that they had merely done what Britain would have liked to have done, but had beaten her to the draw. This Palmerston dismissed as 'flippant and impertinent', although he knew it to be uncomfortably near the truth. It did little, however, to improve the rapidly deteriorating climate between the two powers. Concern over Russia's long-term ambitions was intensified by the news that St Petersburg was greatly expanding its fleet, and the Royal Navy was accordingly enlarged to match this. Coming on top of Russia's victories over Persia and Turkey in 1828 and 1829, and the secret deal over the Dardanelles, this did indeed seem ominous. In such an atmosphere, almost anything, however trivial, served the cause of the Russophobes.

Such was the mood when David Urquhart took up the cudgels on behalf of the Circassians. He had first established contact with their leaders in 1834 while dwelling in Constantinople, and paid a secret visit to their mountain strongholds, the first of his countrymen ever to do so. The Circassian chiefs, fearless but unsophisticated, were much impressed by this visitor from the great world outside who represented and spoke for – or so they assumed – a nation as powerful as Great Britain. He offered them much encouragement and advice, and they begged him to stay on and lead them in their struggle against the Russians. Urquhart refused, however, insisting that he could be of far more use to them in London. He returned home convinced that it was Britain's moral duty to prevent the Russians from overrunning this small highland nation, which posed no threat to anyone and reminded him of his own native Scotland. It was strongly in her own interest, too, to help the Caucasian tribes to drive the Russians out of this vital bridgehead, from which Turkey, Persia and eventually India could be invaded. Not for nothing had one Russian general described the Caucasus as 'the greatest fortress in the world.'

Urquhart kept his word to his friends, and a torrent of articles, pamphlets and news items began to pour from his pen propagating their cause and execrating all things Russian. The following year he published a book entitled *England and Russia*, in which he warned of Russia's expansionist aims in the Near East and in Central Asia. Turkey, he forecast, would be the first to be swallowed up. 'The whole Ottoman empire passes at once from us to her, by then our open foe,' he wrote. 'The force, the arms, the frontiers, the fortresses, the treasures and the ships of Turkey, now placed against Russia, will be placed against us – disciplined, combined and directed by her.' Having absorbed Turkey, Russia would next subjugate Persia. The Persians were 'a numerous, patient and warlike people, to be disciplined and moved by Russia without inconvenience or expense'. Urquhart had little doubt against whom they would be moved. With their fondness for plunder, the Persians would require little urging if India's fabulous wealth were the prize held out to them.

Russia, he concluded, 'chooses her own time ... she cannot miscalculate on such a moment as this. Her whole mind, energies and resources are concentrated on it. She will be perfectly certain of success before she makes her move'. None of this was entirely original. Sir Robert Wilson had been the first to raise the spectre of the Ottoman Empire being overwhelmed by Russian armies, while the concept of St Petersburg using the Persians to invade India had been mooted by Kinneir seventeen years earlier. But much had changed since then. Urquhart's warning came at a time when the Russians appeared to be on the move again. In addition to enlarging their fleet, they had greatly strengthened their hand in the Caucasus, the bridgehead from which any further advances into Turkey or Persia would almost certainly be launched. With Russophobia now at an all-time high, Urquhart found no shortage of people who were willing to listen to him.

Possessing such powerful friends as William IV, the Turkish Sultan and Lord Ponsonby, then British ambassador to Constantinople, it was no surprise when early in 1836 Urquhart was posted to the Turkish capital as First Secretary at the British Embassy. But Urquhart was not a man to allow his new diplomatic status to curb either his Russophobe activities or his support for the Circassian cause, and it was while he was serving at Constantinople that the celebrated, if now long forgotten, affair of the *Vixen* took place. At that time, although Circassia was far from subdued, the Russians claimed it as their sovereign territory, acquired by treaty from the Turks. On the pretext of isolating the region because of an outbreak of plague, they had imposed a strict naval blockade of its Black Sea coastline.

Britain did not recognise this claim, but the government did not feel strongly enough about it to challenge Russia over the matter. Urquhart, however, was incensed by what he saw as Palmerston's acquiescence in St Petersburg's efforts to crush the gallant Circassians, as well as by his spinelessness in not challenging the blockade, which was aimed at keeping British goods, and possibly arms, out of the Caucasus. To force the issue, therefore, Urquhart persuaded a British shipping company to send one of its schooners, the *Vixen*, from Constantinople with a cargo of salt to the port of Sudjuk Kale, at the northern end of the Circassian coast. It was a deliberate act of provocation, intended to see how far the Russians were prepared to go to maintain their claim to Circassia. If the vessel was intercepted, Urquhart hoped that this would inflame public opinion at home and thus force the government to take direct action against the Russians to protect its merchant fleet. Such a move, necessitating the sending of British warships into the Black Sea, would also serve the purpose of challenging the new Russo-Turkish secret agreement over the Dardanelles. If, on the other hand, the Russians failed to seize the *Vixen*, then it showed that they could be forced to climb down if only one stood up to them. It would also show that supplies of arms for the beleaguered Circassians might be able to follow.

In November 1836, the *Vixen* left Constantinople and headed eastwards across the Black Sea. Her departure could hardly have escaped St Petersburg's notice, for Urquhart's newspaper contacts saw to it that this received widespread coverage. Urquhart and his co-conspirators, hawks to a man, clearly hoped that she would be intercepted. For they believed that only a showdown between London and St Petersburg could now halt Russian aggrandisement. Things got off to a promising start when the commander of a Russian brig arrested the vessel in the port of Sudjuk Kale, where she had been trading for two days. News of her seizure was promptly dispatched to London by British newspaper correspondents, mostly friends of Urquhart's, based in Constantinople. As had been expected, the tidings aroused the wrath of press and public, although few Britons had even the haziest idea where Circassia was. The Russophobe newspapers, temporarily out of ammunition, rose predictably to Urquhart's bait. While *The Times* chided the government for allowing the Russians to 'scoff at the pusillanimity of England', the *Edinburgh Review* examined the wider implications of the crisis. 'The Circassians once subdued,' it declared, 'the Caucasus is open and Persia lies at St Petersburg's mercy ... Thus we shall see the frontier of Russia advanced at one stride 1,200 miles nearer our Indian frontier.'

Palmerston himself was no less angered by the illegal seizure of the British vessel, and a heated correspondence commenced with St Petersburg. The Foreign Secretary was equally annoyed with Urquhart and his Russophobe friends, whom he knew to be behind it all. He had tried to block Urquhart's appointment to Constantinople, but it was no secret that this had had the King's personal backing, and he had been over-ruled by his Cabinet colleagues. Now feeling thoroughly vin-dicated, he at once set about getting the offender recalled to London before he could do any more damage to Anglo-Russian relations. Meanwhile, in the Turkish capital, Urquhart and his friends eagerly awaited the British government's response to the arrest and confiscation of the *Vixen*.

It was around this time that the Russians began to claim that there were British agents operating among the Circassians, supplying them with arms, advising them and encouraging them to resist. Indeed, in addition to its cargo of salt, they alleged that the *Vixen* had been found to be carrying weapons intended for the rebellious tribesmen. So concerned were they about the possible effects of this on the course of the war, that the Russian commander issued a warning to the Circassians suspected of harbouring the foreigners in their mountain lairs. 'The Englishmen in your midst', he declared, 'are merely unprincipled adventurers.' They had come, not to help the Circassian cause, but to try to acquire Circassia for Britain. They should be seized forthwith and killed. The Circassians themselves, he said, would be wise to lay down their arms, for no country had ever waged war against Russia and won. 'Are you not aware', he asked them, 'that were the heavens to fall, the Russians could prop them up with their bayonets?' It was far better for the Caucasian tribes to be ruled by the Tsar than by the King of England. However, if they listened to the British and chose to resist, then it would not be the Russians' fault if their valleys and homes were destroyed by fire and sword, and their mountains 'trampled into dust'.

As the Russians were to discover during the next quarter of a century or more, it would take more than bombast to intimi-date the Circassians, who continued to resist long after the other Caucasian peoples had submitted. But on one point the general was right. There were indeed Englishmen living with the Circassians at that moment. One, James Longworth, was a special correspondent of *The Times*, a newspaper sympathetic to the Circassian cause, who had come to see how they were faring in their David and Goliath struggle with the Russians. His companion, James Bell, was also a Circassian sympathiser. Indeed it was he, perhaps unwisely, who had lent the *Vixen* to further their cause. Encouraged by Urquhart, he had run the Russian gauntlet like Longworth in order to witness the war and to try to keep it in the headlines at home. He was also anxious to discover what had happened to his vessel and its cargo, and to endeavour to recover them.

During the months they were to spend with the *mujahedin*, living under the very noses of the Russians, the two men learned of the extraordinary veneration felt by the Circassians for 'Dauod Bey', as David Urquhart was known to them. When, more than two years earlier, he had landed on their shores he had found them divided and disorganised. He at once set about forming a central authority to organise and co-ordinate their resistance. He also wrote for them a formal declaration of independence, which he ensured was widely publicised in Europe. For their part, Longworth and Bell were able to offer the Circassians encouragement and advice while they and their hosts awaited news of the British government's response to the seizure of the *Vixen*, and St Petersburg's claim to Circassia. In the meantime they were able to observe some of the fighting, and Longworth to report on its progress to his newspaper, thus helping to keep the Circassian cause in the public eye.

At first, when the fighting had been confined to the frontier region, the Russians had used their Cossack cavalry to try to crush resistance. But with centuries of mountain and forest warfare behind them, and an intimate knowledge of the terrain, the Circassians had shown themselves to be more than a match for the Russians. They were also better mounted and armed than the Cossacks, and quite as skilled and ferocious in combat. The result was that the Russian commanders had to think again. Their next move was to use infantry supported by artillery, with Cossack cavalry to guard their flanks. In this way they were able to advance cautiously into hostile territory, destroying villages and crops as they went.

After disastrous attempts to break the Russian squares, during which, Longworth recounts, 'the best and the bravest of the warriors fell victim to their own rashness', the Circassians likewise changed their tactics. Instead of attempting to meet the Russians head on, they learned to steer them into skilfully laid ambushes and traps, striking from nowhere on their swift mounts and vanishing as quickly. The Russians next introduced grape-shot, an early form of shrapnel. 'Their guns,' one Circassian complained to Longworth, 'instead of sending a single ball which came whistling over our heads ... now vomit ten thousand of them at the very least which come tearing and smashing everything about us.' If only the British would provide them with such weapons, he pleaded, then the Russian troops 'would be no more able to keep their ranks than we are, and, being once dispersed, our cavalry would play the devil with them as before.'

Resistance in the Caucasus, the Englishmen learned, was not confined to Circassia. Across the mountains to the east, on the Caspian side of the Caucasus, a similar struggle was going on against the Russians in Daghestan. This was led by a Muslim divine of extraordinary charisma and genius at guerilla tactics called Shamyl. However, because of Daghestan's remoteness, and the fact that there was no Urquhart to publicise it, or Longworth to report it, this war went virtually unnoticed in Europe. But if the British had not yet heard of Shamyl, the Tsar's generals certainly had, for none of the usual tactics appeared to work against him. More than twenty years of incessant warfare lay ahead before Shamyl was defeated, and a further five before the Circassian tribes were finally overrun. The campaign was to prove extremely costly to the Russians, in both money and lives, but it was to inspire some of their greatest writers and poets, including Tolstoy, Pushkin and Lermontov. All that was still far off at the time of which we are writing, however, as Longworth and Bell awaited word from London on the outcome of the *Vixen* affair.

When news did finally reach them, in the shape of a cutting from *The Times*, it was profoundly disappointing. The British government, it was clear, was unwilling to make a major issue of the vessel's seizure, let alone risk going to war with Russia over it. To the fury of the Russophobes, Palmerston decided that while Circassia did not belong to the Russians, the port of

Sudjuk Kale, where the arrest had taken place, did. By this time Urquhart had been ordered back to London and sacked for his role in the confrontation between the two powers, officially allies. None of Urquhart's friends was powerful enough to intercede on his behalf, for a month before his return William IV had been taken ill and died. Instead, Urquhart launched a vituperative campaign against Palmerston, claiming that he had been bought with Russian gold. He even sought to have the Foreign Secretary impeached for treason, though nothing finally came of this.

The news that Britain had backed down came as a grave embarrassment to Longworth and Bell, for they had repeatedly assured their hosts that they would soon enjoy the support of the most powerful nation on earth, apparently firmly convinced of this themselves. Palmerston's decision was an even worse blow for Bell, who could now bid farewell to any hopes of recovering his vessel from the triumphant Russians. The two men decided that there was little further to be gained by staying on, although they promised their Circassian friends that they would continue the fight from England. Indeed, both were to publish detailed accounts of their adventures and experiences with the *mujahedin*. Meanwhile, though foiled by Palmerston in his attempt to bring Russia and Britain into collision, Urquhart had returned with fresh vigour to the Russophobe cause, and, among other things, was organising the smuggling of arms to the Circassians. John Baddeley, in his classic study *The Russian Conquest of the Caucasus*, published in 1908, attributes the successes of the Circassians in large part 'to these efforts'. However, he accuses Urquhart and his collaborators of thus prolonging a war which the Circassians could never win, and of feeding them with false hopes of receiving British support.

Urquhart eventually entered Parliament where he continued to pursue his campaign against Palmerston and his efforts to have him impeached for treason, as well as his Russian-baiting activities. But gradually he found himself caught up in other causes, and finally ill-health drove him to retire to the Swiss Alps. As the arch-Russophobe of the day, however, he had done much to turn British public opinion against St Petersburg, and to deepen the growing rift between the two powers. Indeed, modern Soviet historians lay some of the blame for today's problems in the Caucasus on British interference in the region, even claiming that Shamyl was a British agent. Certainly the resistance the Russians encountered there was to keep them stretched militarily, and to act for some years as a restraint on their ambitions elsewhere in Asia. The Caucasus, thanks to Urquhart and his friends, had thus become part of the Great Game battlefield.

*　　*　　*

Despite Urquhart's claims to the contrary, Palmerston was anything but in St Petersburg's pocket. He shared Urquhart's suspicion of Russia's intentions, but was far from persuaded that they yet posed a threat to Britain's interests. His main source of reassurance on this was Lord Durham, then British ambassador in St Petersburg. Durham was convinced that Russia's apparent military might was of defensive value only, and that Tsar Nicholas was not in a position to indulge in any expansionist dreams which he might harbour. Foreign adventures required huge resources that Durham knew, from his secret contacts in St Petersburg, Russia simply did not possess. 'The power of Russia has been greatly exaggerated,' wrote Durham in March 1836, in what Palmerston described as one of the most brilliant dispatches ever received at the Foreign Office. 'There is not one element of strength which is not directly counterbalanced by a corresponding ... weakness,' he went on. 'In fact her power is solely of the defensive kind. Leaning on and covered by the impregnable fortress with which nature has endowed her – her climate and her deserts – she is invincible, as Napoleon discovered to his cost.'

But not everyone at the Foreign Office was as confident as Durham about Russia's powerlessness to act aggressively. Among those who shared Urquhart's fears, even if they did not approve of his methods, were Lord Ponsonby, the British ambassador to Constantinople, and Sir John McNeill, the newly appointed Minister to Teheran, who had travelled as far as the Ottoman capital with Urquhart when they were taking up their respective posts. McNeill, an old Persia hand, had served for some years in Teheran under Sir John Kinneir, and had watched Russian influence grow there at the expense of Britain. He was strongly suspected by the Russians of having had a hand in the death of the unfortunate Griboyedov when their embassy had been attacked by a mob eight years earlier, although there was not a shred of evidence to support this. A man of considerable ability, not to say ambition, McNeill had originally come to Teheran as a doctor to the legation, but had quickly shown himself to possess great political acumen.

While waiting to take up his appointment as Minister, McNeill had written a book detailing Russia's territorial gains, in both Europe and Asia, from the time of Peter the Great. Published anonymously, at Palmerston's insistence, it appeared in 1836 under the title *The Progress and Present Position of Russia in the East*, and was the most carefully reasoned piece of Great Game literature so far. The book contained a large folding map which showed the alarming extent of Russia's expansion during the previous century and a half. Appended to the map was a table demonstrating Russia's population gains resulting from these annexations and other acquisitions. In all, since the time of Peter's accession, the number of the Tsar's subjects had increased nearly fourfold, from 15 million to 58 million. At the same time Russia's frontiers had advanced 500 miles towards Constantinople, and 1,000 miles towards Teheran. In Europe, Russia's acquisitions from Sweden were greater than what was now left of this once-powerful kingdom, while those from Poland were almost equal in area to the entire Austrian Empire. This was all in stark contrast to the picture of a purely defensive Russia painted by Lord Durham in St Petersburg.

'Every portion of these vast acquisitions', McNeill wrote, 'has been obtained in opposition to the views, the wishes and the interests of England. The dismemberment of Sweden, the partition of Poland, the conquest of the Turkish provinces and those severed from Persia, have all been injurious to British interests.' The Russians, he added, had achieved all this by stealth, gaining their objectives by means of 'successive encroachments, no one of which has been of sufficient importance to interrupt friendly relations with the great powers of Europe.' It was an apt description of a process which would be repeated again and again by St Petersburg in Central Asia during the coming years.

Russia's next two targets, McNeill forecast, would be those ailing twins the Ottoman and Persian empires, neither of which was in any position to withstand a determined attack by the Tsar's armies. If Turkey were to fall into St Petersburg's hands, it would gravely threaten Britain's interests in Europe and the Mediterranean, while Russia's occupation of Persia would very likely seal the fate of India. His prognosis was a gloomy one, but it was one with which many leading strategists, and all Russophobe commentators and newspapers, were in agreement. It was only a question of time, they were convinced, before the Russians made their next move, and a toss-up whether it would be against Turkey or Persia.

On arriving at his new post, McNeill discovered that Russia's influence at the Shah's court was even stronger than it had been before his departure for London. In Count Simonich, a general in the Russian army and now St Petersburg's man in Teheran, he found himself facing a formidable and none too scrupulous adversary. But McNeill, no novice himself when it came to political intrigue, was determined to do everything in his power to spoil Tsar Nicholas's game. Sure enough, within a very short time of his arrival in Persia, the Russians began to make shadowy moves towards Herat and Kabul, the two principal gateways leading to British India. The Great Game was about to enter a new and more dangerous phase.

·13·

The Mysterious
Vitkevich

In the autumn of 1837, while travelling through the remote borderlands of eastern Persia, a young British subaltern was startled to see, far ahead of him across the plain, a party of uniformed Cossacks riding towards the Afghan frontier. It was evident that they had hoped to enter the country unobserved, for when he approached them as they breakfasted beside a stream he found them evasive and reluctant to discuss the reason for their being in this wild spot. It was quite clear to Lieutenant Henry Rawlinson, a political officer on Sir John McNeill's staff in Teheran, that they were up to no good, though precisely what he could not be sure.

'Their officer', he reported, 'was a young man of light make, very fair complexion, with bright eyes and a look of great animation.' As the Englishman rode up, saluting politely, the Russian rose to his feet and bowed. He said nothing, however, obviously waiting for his visitor to speak. Rawlinson addressed him first in French – the language most commonly used between Europeans in the East – but the Russian merely shook his head. Speaking no Russian, Rawlinson next tried English, followed by Persian, but without success. Finally the Russian spoke, using Turcoman, of which Rawlinson had only a smattering. 'I knew just sufficient', he wrote later, 'to carry on a simple conversation, but not to be inquisitive. This was evidently what my friend wanted.'

The Russian told Rawlinson that he was carrying gifts from Tsar Nicholas to the newly enthroned Shah of Persia, who had just succeeded his deceased father following a family power struggle. This was reasonably plausible, for at that very moment the Shah was less than a day's march away, at the head of an army, on his way to lay siege to Herat. In fact Rawlinson himself was heading for the Shah's camp bearing messages from McNeill. However, he was far from convinced by the Russian officer's story, suspecting that he and his party were very likely making for Kabul. If this was so, Rawlinson knew, it would cause considerable alarm in London and Calcutta, where Afghanistan was seen as lying strictly within Britain's sphere of influence. As it was, Count Simonich had already begun to meddle in the country's affairs, using the Shah as his cat's-paw. For it was no secret in Teheran that it was he who had urged the Shah to march on Herat, which Persia had long claimed, and wrest it from Kamran, while assuring McNeill that he was doing everything in his power to restrain him.

After smoking a pipe or two with the Cossacks and their officer, Rawlinson bade them farewell and hastened on his way, determined to discover what their game really was. On reaching the Shah's camp that evening, Rawlinson at once sought an interview with him. Ushered into the royal tent, he reported his encounter with the Russians, who were supposedly bringing gifts from the Tsar. 'Bringing presents for me!' the Shah exclaimed with astonishment. Why, he assured Rawlinson, these had nothing to do with him, but were intended for Dost Mohammed at Kabul. Indeed, he had agreed with Count Simonich to allow the Cossacks safe passage through his domains. So much then for the Russian officer's tale. Rawlinson now knew that he possessed news of the utmost importance, and he prepared to hasten back to Teheran with it.

It was at that moment that the Russian party rode into the Persian camp, unaware that Rawlinson had discovered the truth about them. Addressing Rawlinson in perfect French, their officer introduced himself as Captain Yan Vitkevich from the Orenburg garrison. Apologising for his earlier coolness and evasiveness, he explained that he had thought it unwise to be too friendly or familiar with strangers in the desert. He now endeavoured to make up for this by being especially cordial towards the Englishman. This chance encounter, in the heart of Great Game country, was the first such meeting between players of either side. For the most part it was a shadowy conflict in which the contestants rarely if ever met. This particular meeting, however, was to have unforeseen and far-reaching consequences, for it would help to precipitate one of the worst catastrophes ever to befall a British army.

Lieutenant Rawlinson had already ridden a record 700 miles or more in 150 hours to reach the Shah's camp from Teheran. Travelling day and night, he now set about doing the same in reverse, reaching the British legation with his tidings on November 1. When McNeill's warning of what the Russians were up to was received in London and Calcutta it was to cause immense consternation. Not only were anti-Russian feelings already running high, but the news came close on the heels of the disclosure that Simonich was behind the Shah's advance on Herat. Were Herat to fall to the Persians, this would give the Russians a crucial and dangerous toe-hold in western Afghanistan. But Rawlinson's chance discovery showed that St Petersburg's interests in Afghanistan were not merely confined to Herat, threatening though that was in itself. All of a sudden Kabul too was at risk. If Vitkevich was successful in winning over Dost Mohammed, then the Russians would have succeeded, in one spectacular leap, in clearing the formidable barriers of desert, mountain and hostile tribes which lay between themselves and British India.

However, the authorities in London and Calcutta were at least able to comfort themselves with one thought, if not much else. At that very moment, by luck rather than by any foresight, they had an exceptionally able man on the spot. If anyone would prove a match for Captain Vitkevich, and could be relied upon to spoil his game (whatever that was precisely), then it was surely Captain Alexander Burnes, now safely at the court of Dost Mohammed in Kabul.

*   *   *

Ever since the collapse of the great Durrani empire, which had been founded by Ahmad Shah in the middle of the eighteenth century, Afghanistan had been at the centre of an intense and unceasing struggle for power. Currently Kamran was vowing to restore his own family's fortunes by overthrowing Dost Mohammed in Kabul, while the Persians, as we have seen, were on their way to try to recover their one-time eastern province. Indeed, in exchange for Herat, the Shah had even offered to help Kamran topple Dost Mohammed and seize the Afghan throne for himself, but had been turned down. For his part, Dost Mohammed had pledged himself not only to restore Afghanistan to its former glory, but also more immediately to wrest back from Ranjit Singh, who had occupied it while his back was turned, the rich and fertile province of Peshawar. He was still looking to the British for help over the latter, despite Burnes's earlier warning to him that they were committed to Ranjit Singh by treaty.

It was possibly with this in mind that in October 1835, unknown to the British, Dost Mohammed had made a discreet approach to the Russians. Tsar Nicholas, increasingly concerned about what the British were up to in Afghanistan, not to mention elsewhere in Central Asia, had promptly dispatched Vitkevich to Kabul to see what Dost Mohammed was offering, and to forge friendly links with him. Meanwhile, on discovering that a new Governor-General, Lord Auckland, had been appointed in India, Dost Mohammed had made a fresh appeal to him for assistance in recovering Peshawar. But Dost Mohammed and Kamran were not the only contenders for power in Afghanistan at that moment. There was also Shah Shujah, then in exile at Ludhiana in British India, from where he plotted endlessly against Dost Mohammed, who had seized the throne from him. His prospects of winning it back, however, seemed extremely remote. Not long before, he had suffered a humiliating defeat at the hands of Dost Mohammed when a 22,000-strong invasion force which he personally had led into Afghanistan was routed at Kandahar. Shah Shujah, it was said, had been in the forefront of the flight from the battlefield.

Such, in a nutshell, was the situation when, on September 20, 1837, Burnes returned in triumph to Kabul. Dost Mohammed was delighted to see his old friend back, and

Burnes was borne aloft on the back of an elephant to his quarters in the great Bala Hissar fortress, close to the royal palace. But the Afghan sovereign was also anxious to get down to serious business as soon as diplomatic decorum permitted. It proved to be politics rather than trade, moreover, which was uppermost in his mind, just as the East India Company directors had feared. For Dost Mohammed was aware, as Burnes was then still not, that Vitkevich and his Cossacks were on their way. He genuinely wanted an alliance with his near-neighbours the British, rather than with the Russians, who were too far away to be of much practical use. On the other hand, if the British hesitated to give him the help he needed, the arrival of the Russians might help to concentrate their minds. In the event his strategy, like everyone else's, was to backfire disastrously.

Meanwhile, with the return of Burnes to Kabul, another character had entered the narrative. This was a curious individual named Charles Masson, an itinerant antiquarian who had developed a passion for Central Asian history, and who for several years had been roaming Persia and Afghanistan in search of coins and other antiquities. Travelling usually on foot, and at times penniless and in rags, he had acquired a knowledge of the region unique among Europeans. He claimed to be an American from Kentucky, but it was discovered by Captain Claude Wade, the British political agent at Ludhiana, that he was not an American at all, but a deserter from the Company's army named James Lewis. In the summer of 1833 he had settled in the Afghan capital, living close to the Bala Hissar in the Armenian quarter.

At that time the East India Company employed a network of agents known as 'news-writers', who were often local Hindu traders, to supply intelligence on political and economic developments from some of the remoter areas where there was no European representative. This was rarely of much value, consisting for the most part of unreliable bazaar gossip. But when Wade discovered that Charles Masson had taken up residence in Kabul, he realised that he could be a valuable source of intelligence from this vital region. For Wade knew him to be a man of excellent judgement, capable of sifting truth from mere rumour. The only problem was that desertion from the Company's forces carried a death sentence. In the event it was agreed that Masson would be officially pardoned and paid a small salary if he supplied regular news from Kabul, while continuing to pursue his archaeological and historical researches.

Whether an element of jealousy arose between the two men or not will never be known, but Masson appears to have taken an intense dislike to Burnes. In a book he wrote after Burnes's death, Masson blamed him for everything which had gone wrong. Perhaps this antipathy was mutual, for Burnes must have known that Masson was a deserter from the Company's army. Masson, a highly sensitive man, may well have sensed his disapproval. In his own account of the mission, Burnes made only scant reference to Masson, although the two must have spent much time together during those crucial weeks. As it was, however, Masson was to have the last word.

Whatever the truth about Masson's criticism of Burnes, the mission was condemned to failure from the outset. Lord Auckland was totally opposed to any deal with Dost Mohammed which risked upsetting Ranjit Singh. If a choice had to be made between the two men, then it had to be the latter. Already Ranjit Singh had been restrained from seizing parts of Sind, and to try now to persuade him to hand Peshawar back to his arch-enemy Dost Mohammed would be both futile and dangerous. Burnes suggested a compromise – that Dost Mohammed be secretly promised Peshawar on Ranjit Singh's death, which could not be too far off. But this was turned down by the Governor-General, who disapproved of such a deal on principle. Dost Mohammed's offer to dispatch one of his own sons to the court of Ranjit Singh as a sort of diplomatic hostage, a not uncommon practice in the East, in exchange for the return of Peshawar, was also rejected.

On January 20, 1838, after prolonged negotiations, the Governor-General wrote personally to Dost Mohammed ruling out any remaining hopes he might have had of using the British to force Ranjit Singh's hand, and advising him to abandon any idea of recovering Peshawar. Instead, Auckland suggested, he should try to end his quarrel with the Sikh ruler.

'From the generosity of his nature,' the Governor-General wrote, 'and his regard for his old alliance with the British Government, Maharajah Runjeet Singh has acceded to my wish for the cessation of strife and the promotion of tranquility, if you should behave in a less mistaken manner towards him.' The letter could hardly have been more insulting, or more calculated to offend Dost Mohammed's pride. But worse was to follow.

By now Lord Auckland had learned that Captain Vitkevich was on his way to Kabul (he had in fact just arrived), and he went on to warn the Afghan ruler that were he to have any dealings with the Russian, without his own prior personal approval, then Britain would not feel under any obligation to restrain Ranjit Singh's armies. In case the message was still not clear, the unfortunate Burnes was instructed to spell it out to Dost Mohammed. Were he to enter into any alliance with the Russians, or any other power, which was considered detrimental to British interests, then he would be forcibly removed from his throne. When the letter's contents became known, they were to cause outrage in Kabul. Burnes himself was badly shaken by the letter's uncompromising terms which effectively cut the ground from under him. Addressing Dost Mohammed as though he was a naughty schoolboy, and instructing him on whom he might or might not have dealings with, Auckland offered him nothing in return besides Britain's vague goodwill. Despite his anger, however, Dost Mohammed managed to keep his composure, still evidently hopeful that the British could be won round. After all, he did have one last trick up his sleeve – the Russian card.

* * *

Although coming from a very different background, Captain Yan Vitkevich possessed many of the same personal qualities as men like Burnes, Rawlinson and Conolly. Born of an aristocratic Lithuanian family, he had become involved as a student in the anti-Russian resistance movement in Poland. Saved from execution by his youth, he had instead, at the age of 17, been exiled to Siberia as an ordinary conscript in the Russian army. To fill in the long months of tedium he began to study the languages of Central Asia, and very soon his linguistic and other gifts attracted the attention of senior officers at Orenburg. In due course he was promoted to lieutenant and widely used to gather intelligence among the Muslim tribes of the frontierlands. Finally General Perovsky, the Russian commander-in-chief at Orenburg, appointed him to his personal staff, proudly claiming that Vitkevich, the one-time dissident, knew more about the region than any other officer, past or present.

When it came to selecting an emissary for the delicate task of conveying to Kabul the Tsar's gifts, and his reply to Dost Mohammed's letter, there could be no other choice. After receiving his instructions personally from Count Nesselrode, the Foreign Minister, in St Petersburg, Vitkevich travelled to Teheran where he received a last-minute briefing from Simonich. So secret was his stay in the Persian capital that even Sir John McNeill, who maintained a close watch on all Russian activities there, failed to learn of it. It was only by sheer ill-chance that the Russian and his Cossack escort were spotted by Rawlinson, and the alarm raised. As a result, according to one Russian historian, the party had to fight off attacks by local tribesmen who, he claims, were put up to it by the British, although he produces no evidence to substantiate this. Whatever the truth, Vitkevich was received most courteously, and in true Great Game style, by his British rival Alexander Burnes when, on Christmas Eve 1837, he rode into Kabul. He was at once invited by Burnes, who must have been anxious to weigh him up, to join him for Christmas dinner.

Vitkevich made a good impression on Burnes, who found him 'gentlemanly and agreeable . . . intelligent and well-informed.' In addition to the languages of Central Asia, the Russian was fluent in Turkish, Persian and French. Burnes was somewhat surprised to learn that Vitkevich had made three visits to Bokhara, as against his one. However, this gave them much to talk about other than the delicate question of why they were both in Kabul. It was destined to be their only meeting, although in happier circumstances Burnes would have liked to have seen more of this unusual individual. But, as he explained, this was not possible 'lest the relative positions of our two

nations be misunderstood in this part of Asia.' Instead, therefore, the two rival contenders for Dost Mohammed's ear kept
a close watch on one another during the crucial weeks which
were to follow.

When Vitkevich first arrived in Kabul, Dost Mohammed
had not yet received Lord Auckland's ultimatum, and Burnes's
star was still very much in the ascendant at the Bala Hissar.
The Russian officer's reception had been cool and uncere-
monious, as Simonich had warned him it would be. Indeed,
at first he had been kept under virtual house arrest, Dost
Mohammed even consulting Burnes over the authenticity of
his credentials. Had Vitkevich really been sent by the Tsar, he
asked, and was the letter from the Russian Emperor genuine?
He had sent it round to Burnes's quarters for his inspection,
aware no doubt that a copy of it would, within the hour, be on
its way to Lord Auckland in Calcutta. It was at this point,
Masson was to claim afterwards, that Burnes made a cardinal
error, allowing integrity to overrule expediency.

Convinced that the letter, which turned out to be little more
than a message of goodwill, was indeed from Tsar Nicholas,
Burnes said as much to Dost Mohammed. Masson, on the
other hand, was convinced that it was a forgery, and that it had
been composed by Simonich, or perhaps even by Vitkevich
himself, to give the Russian mission more weight in its trial
of strength with the British. When Burnes pointed to the
impressive-looking imperial Russian seal it bore, Masson sent
a messenger to the bazaar to buy a packet of Russian sugar –
'at the bottom of which', he claimed 'we found precisely the
same kind of seal.' But by then, Masson added, it was too late.
Burnes had thrown away his one and only chance of spiking
his rival's guns by not allowing the Afghans – as Masson
sardonically put it – 'the benefit of their doubts'.

Following the arrival of Auckland's ultimatum, everything
began to change. Although Dost Mohammed officially continued to cold-shoulder the Russian mission, Burnes knew
that his own position was daily becoming weaker and that of
Vitkevich more promising. It was even whispered in Kabul
that Vitkevich had offered to approach Ranjit Singh on Dost
Mohammed's behalf, while Burnes faced the unenviable task

of demanding, at Lord Auckland's insistence, that his old friend write to the Sikh ruler formally renouncing his claim to Peshawar. If Masson is a reliable witness, Burnes was by this time in utter despair at what he saw as India's failure to realise the long-term value of Dost Mohammed's friendship. But what neither he nor Masson knew was that the Governor-General and his advisers already had other plans in mind for Afghanistan, and that in none of these did Dost Mohammed now feature.

By April 21, 1838, the die was cast. Instead of sending Vitkevich on his way as Auckland was insisting, Dost Mohammed received the Russian with every mark of respect and friendship at his palace within the walls of the Bala Hissar. Vitkevich, who was prepared to offer the Afghans the moon in order to displace the British in Kabul, had routed his rival simply by biding his time. Nothing remained now for Burnes but to leave Kabul and report to his chiefs in India on what he saw as the failure of his mission. On April 27, after a final audience with Dost Mohammed at which deep personal regrets were expressed by both sides, and with the Afghan insisting that his esteem for his British friend was unaffected by what had happened, Burnes and his companions departed for home. When he next returned to the Afghan capital it would be under very different circumstances.

But if Vitkevich appeared to have won the day in Kabul, elsewhere in Afghanistan Russian machinations were proving less successful. Despite the confident assurances of Simonich to the Shah, after weeks of bitter fighting the city of Herat was obstinately refusing to surrender. For there was one thing which the Count had not reckoned with. Shortly before the Persians had taken up position around it, a young British subaltern had slipped into the city in disguise and had quietly set about organising its defence.

·14·

Hero of Herat

His skin darkened with dye, and posing as a Muslim holy man, Lieutenant Eldred Pottinger of the Company's political service entered Herat on a routine Great Game reconnaissance on August 18, 1837, little suspecting that he would be there for more than a year. Aged 26, and the nephew of that veteran of the game Colonel Henry Pottinger, he had been sent into Afghanistan to gather intelligence. He had already visited Peshawar and, shortly before Burnes's arrival there, Kabul, without his disguise being penetrated. He had been in Kamran's capital for only three days when alarming rumours began to circulate in the bazaars that a powerful Persian force, led by the Shah in person, was marching from Teheran to attack the city. To an ambitious and adventurous young officer like Pottinger, the situation seemed to be full of possibilities. He decided to stay on and watch developments.

When word of the Persian advance reached Kamran he was campaigning in the south, and he hastened back to defend his capital. In his youth he had been a great warrior. With a single stroke of his sword, it was said, he could cut a sheep clean in half, while an arrow from his bow would go straight through a cow. But subsequently he had become dissolute, taking heavily to drink, and effective power now rested with his vizier, Yar Mohammed, whose reputation for cruelty exceeded even his. Orders were immediately issued for the seizure and incarceration of all those of doubtful loyalty, especially anyone with

Persian connections. Villagers were ordered to gather in their crops, and to transport all grain and other foodstuffs into the city. Anything else which might prove useful to the enemy, including fruit-trees, was to be destroyed, and troops were sent to ensure that this was done. Simultaneously intensive work began on Herat's massive ramparts, built mainly of earth, which had been allowed to fall into dangerous disrepair. Finally, all exits to the city were closed to prevent spies from leaving and conveying news of its defences to the enemy.

Until now Pottinger had not disclosed his presence to the authorities, happy to maintain his discreet role as an observer. But then one day in the bazaar he felt a gentle hand on his sleeve. 'You are an Englishman!' a voice whispered. By luck the man who had penetrated his disguise turned out to be an old friend of Arthur Conolly's, a Herati doctor who had travelled with him seven years earlier. He had been to Calcutta, moreover, and could spot European features, even when darkened with dye. The doctor strongly advised Pottinger to go to Yar Mohammed and put his services, including his knowledge of modern siegecraft, at his disposal. The vizier received the Englishman enthusiastically, for although the Heratis had successfully beaten off earlier Persian attacks, it was clear that this one was much more serious. Not only was the Shah believed to have a Russian general in his service, but also a unit composed of Russian deserters who had fled to Persia. Herati cavalry sent to harass the advancing enemy returned complaining that this time they were using unfair tactics. Instead of the usual straggling mass of troops who in the past had been so vulnerable to the Afghan horsemen, under Russian direction they were advancing in compact bodies protected by artillery.

Pottinger's determining role in the defence of Herat emerged only afterwards when other British officers entered the city and spoke to those who had lived through the ten-month siege. In his own official report to his superiors he played down his contribution, not to mention his own gallantry, although he wrote critically of the part played by others, especially Yar Mohammed. But he also kept a journal, and it was from this that the historian Sir John Kaye was later to piece together his graphic account of these stirring events in his celebrated

History of the War in Afghanistan. Subsequently this journal was lost in a fire which swept through Kaye's study.

Hostilities began on November 23 when the Shah's forces, supported by artillery, launched a vigorous attack on the city from the west. 'The garrison sallied out as they advanced,' recorded Kaye. 'The Afghan infantry disputed every inch of the ground, and the cavalry hung on the flanks of the Persian army. But they could not dislodge the enemy from the position they had taken up.' And so the siege commenced. It was to be conducted, wrote Kaye, 'in a spirit of unsparing hatred and savage inhumanity ... what was wanting on either side in science would be made up for in cruelty and vindictiveness.' One barbaric practice introduced by Yar Mohammed was to encourage his troops to cut off the heads of the Persian dead and bring these to him for inspection. His aim was to spread fear among the enemy, for the heads were displayed in rows along the ramparts for all to see. 'As rewards were always given for these bloody trophies,' Pottinger noted, 'the garrison were naturally very active in their endeavours to obtain them.' But as a soldier he considered this not only abhorrent but also counter-productive, for the Afghan sorties invariably petered out, the defenders being too busy severing heads to follow up their advantage.

It also led to temptation. On one occasion, after a sortie, an Afghan brought to Yar Mohammed a pair of ears. 'A cloak and some ducats', Pottinger recounted, 'were given him as a reward for his butchery.' However before he could be further questioned he vanished. Half an hour later another man appeared, this time carrying a mud-encrusted head. 'The Vizier, thinking it looked as though it had no ears, ordered one of his retainers to examine it,' Pottinger reported. 'On this, the bearer of the ghastly trophy threw it down and ran away with all the speed he could command.' When the head was more closely inspected it was discovered to belong to a defender who had died during the sortie. The man who had produced it was pursued, caught and brought back before Yar Mohammed, who ordered him to be severely beaten. But the man who had brought the ears and disappeared with his reward was never found, although Yar Mohammed promised the cloak and money to anyone who produced him. The Afghans were not alone in their barbarism, however. In the Shah's camp Afghans unfortunate enough to fall into Persian hands were subjected to similar atrocities, including disembowelling.

So the siege dragged on, week after week, month after month, with neither side making any progress. Although the Persians had managed to break through the city's outer defences, they never totally surrounded it. Even at the height of the fighting some fields close to the walls were still used for crops and grazing. Every night the beleaguered Afghans sallied out against the Persian positions, but were unable to dislodge them. Meanwhile the Persians kept up their bombardment of the ramparts, and the defenders continued to repair them. In addition to their cannons, the attackers had rockets, whose 'fiery flight as they passed over the city', Kaye recounts, 'struck terror into the hearts of the people, who clustered on the roofs of the houses, praying and crying by turns.' More accurate than either the cannons or the rockets were the mortars, which reduced many homes, shops and other buildings to rubble as the weeks passed. One mortar bomb, its fuse spluttering, plunged through the roof of the house next to Pottinger's, landing near a sleeping baby. The child's panic-stricken mother threw herself between it and her offspring, but seconds later it exploded, decapitating her and flinging her body on top of the baby, who was suffocated.

There were moments, too, of near farce. On one occasion the defenders were greatly disturbed by a mysterious drilling sound which appeared to come from the enemy lines where Russian soldiers could be seen digging a large hole. Immediately it was assumed that they were drilling a tunnel beneath the ramparts in order to plant mines under them. As the sound persisted, anxiety increased, and desperate attempts were made to find the tunnel and flood it. It was only later that the real source of the noise was discovered – 'a poor woman', Pottinger recounts, 'who was in the habit of using a hand-mill to grind her wheat.' Alarm again spread through the city's 70,000 inhabitants when, in the New Year, the besiegers brought up a massive cannon capable of hurling devastating eight-inch shells against the ramparts, and bigger than anything ever seen in Central Asia before. But after only half a dozen rounds had been fired from it the carriage collapsed beneath it and it was never used again. Yet in spite of their Russian advisers, even when the Persians did succeed in breaching the ramparts they failed to take advantage of it – discouraged perhaps by the sight of their late comrades grinning down at them from above.

All this time Pottinger had been working tirelessly, stiffening the defenders' resolve whenever it failed, which was often, and giving technical advice according to the latest European military precepts. 'His activity was unfailing,' wrote Kaye. 'He was always on the ramparts; always ready to assist with his counsel ... and to inspire with his animating presence new heart into the Afghan soldiery.' Pottinger himself, however, attributed the city's survival to the incompetence of the Persians and their Russian advisers. A single British regiment, he argued, could have taken Herat without much difficulty.

The Shah, who had been led by Count Simonich and his Russian advisers to expect a quick victory, was now becoming desperate over his failure to capture the city with his vastly superior force. He even sent Yar Mohammed's own brother, Shere Mohammed, who had earlier surrendered to him, to try to persuade the Heratis to submit. But the vizier refused to see him, denouncing him as a traitor and disowning him as a brother. Before returning to the Persian lines, however, Shere sent his brother a message warning him that when the Shah's troops stormed Herat he would be hanged like a dog and his women and children publicly dishonoured by the muleteers. Moreover, if the city continued to defy the Shah he himself would be put to death by the Persians. To this Yar Mohammed replied that he would be delighted if the Shah were to execute him as this would save him the trouble of having to do so himself.

Now and again, during lulls in the fighting, attempts were made by both sides to negotiate some kind of settlement. One of the Shah's proposals was that if Herat accepted nominal Persian suzerainty he would not interfere in the government of the province. All he would require of the Heratis was that they should supply him with troops. The present campaign, he insisted, was directed not so much against Herat as against

British India. If the Heratis would unite with him, then he himself would lead them against India, whose riches they would then share between them. It was a proposal which to Pottinger sounded suspiciously like the voice of Simonich. But Yar Mohammed was not that easily fooled, and he suggested that the best proof of Persian sincerity would be for them to lift their siege. A meeting was arranged between Yar Mohammed and the Shah's chief negotiator which took place on the edge of the ditch beneath the ramparts. It ended abruptly, however, when Yar Mohammed learned that the Shah expected both him and Kamran (who most of the time was too inebriated to take much interest in the proceedings) to make formal submission to him in front of the entire Persian army.

By now Sir John McNeill and Count Simonich, both of whom had expected Herat to fall quickly to the Persians, had arrived from Teheran and were staying in the royal camp. Officially they were there as neutral observers, but each was working overtime to spoil the other's game. McNeill was trying to persuade the Shah to abandon the siege, while Simonich was endeavouring to find a way of hastening the city's surrender. The Persian troops, McNeill reported to Palmerston on April 11, nearly five months after the siege began, were in desperate need of supplies, and were being forced to survive on what wild plants they could find. 'Without pay, without sufficient clothing, without any rations whatsoever,' he wrote, 'the same troops remain night and day in the trenches.' These, at times, were knee-deep in water or mud, and with the death toll running at between ten and twenty a day the men's morale and powers of endurance were beginning to fail. Unless the Shah was able to arrange regular supplies of food and clothing for his troops, McNeill believed, then the siege would eventually have to be abandoned.

Within Herat itself, however, the plight of the defenders was, if anything, worse. They faced grave food and fuel shortages, which increased as the siege dragged on, while sickness and starvation were beginning to claim as many lives as the Persian artillery. Houses were being torn down to provide fuel, and horses slaughtered for food. Everywhere there were huge mounds of refuse, while the unburied dead added to the stench and to the risk of pestilence. To try to ease the plight of the overcrowded city it was decided to let some of the population leave, the perils they faced outside the walls being considered no greater than those inside. Because they would have refused to agree to anything which would relieve the pressure on the garrison, the besiegers were not consulted. A batch of 600 elderly men, women and children were accordingly allowed out through the gates to chance their luck with the Persians. 'The enemy', Pottinger reported, 'opened a heavy fire on them until they found out who they were, when they tried to drive them back with sticks and stones.' To prevent this, however, the Herati official in charge of the operation fired on them from the ramparts, causing more casualties than the Persians, who finally let them pass.

Meanwhile, in the Persian camp, Count Simonich cast aside any remaining pretence of being there simply as a diplomatic observer and personally took over direction of the faltering siege. Word that Simonich, telescope in hand, had reconnoitred the beleaguered city soon reached the defenders, while a new vigour and an increased professionalism became apparent, causing Herati morale to plummet. To Pottinger's dismay they began to consider submitting, not to the Persians but to the Russians. To his relief a rumour reached the defenders the very next day which brought hopes of British intervention. McNeill, it was said, had warned the Shah that were Herat to fall the British would not only go to war with him but would also drive his troops out of the city, whatever the cost. Arrangements were already being made, moreover, to rush supplies of desperately needed food to Herat from British India. The rumour happened to be untrue, but it miraculously saved the city, so crucial to India's defence, from being handed over to the Tsar by its inhabitants.

By the time the Heratis discovered the truth it was too late for them to turn to the Russians, for on June 24, 1838, Count Simonich launched his great attack. It was destined to be Lieutenant Pottinger's hour of glory. The assault began with a heavy artillery barrage directed against the city from every side, and was followed by a massed infantry attack delivered at five different points simultaneously. At four of these the Afghans, fighting desperately for their lives, managed to drive the Persians back, but at the fifth the enemy succeeded in gaining the breach made in the ramparts by their artillery. 'The struggle was brief but bloody,' wrote Kaye, the defenders falling at their post to a man. 'A few of the most daring of the assailants, pushing on in advance of their comrades, gained the head of the breach,' he went on. But the Afghans rushed up reinforcements just in time to throw them back, although only temporarily. 'Again and again, with desperate courage,' wrote Kaye, the attackers tried to fight their way through the breach and into the city. One moment they were all but there, and the next they were forced back again. For a whole hour, as the fighting ebbed and flowed, the fate of Herat hung in the balance.

Immediately on hearing of the danger Pottinger and Yar Mohammed had rushed to the spot. But when the vizier, whom no one had ever before accused of cowardice, saw how close the Persians were to storming the city his resolution failed him. He began to walk more slowly towards the breach, finally halting. Then, to Pottinger's utter dismay, he sat down on the ground. The sight was not lost on the defenders who had seen him and Pottinger approaching. One by one those at the back began to sneak away on the pretence of carrying the wounded to safety. Pottinger knew that there was not a second to lose before the trickle became a flood and the defenders all took to their heels. By means of entreaties and taunts he managed to get Yar Mohammed to his feet again and impel him towards the parapet. For a moment disaster seemed to have been averted as the vizier roared at his men, in the name of Allah, to fight. This had always had magical results before, but this time they had seen his own hesitation. They wavered, and seeing this, his nerve again deserted him. He turned back, muttering that he was going to get help.

At this Pottinger lost his temper. Seizing Yar Mohammed by the arm, and loudly reviling him, he dragged him forward to the breach. The vizier called upon the defenders to fight to the death, but they continued to sneak away. What happened next was electrifying. 'Seizing a large staff,' Kaye tells us, 'Yar

Mohammed rushed like a madman upon the hindmost of the party, and drove them forward under a shower of heavy blows.' Finding themselves with no other way of escape, and even more frightened of the vizier than of the enemy, the defenders 'leapt wildly over the parapet, and rushed down the exterior slope upon the Persian stormers.' Panicked by this violent onslaught, the attackers abandoned their position and fled. The immediate danger was over. Herat was saved – thanks, in Kaye's words, 'to the indomitable courage of Eldred Pottinger'.

When news of the subaltern's role in Herat's defence, and in foiling Russian designs, reached London and Calcutta, he was to receive similar acclaim to that showered upon Alexander Burnes on his return from Kabul and Bokhara five years earlier. Unlike Burnes, however, he was not there to receive it in person. For although the moment of greatest danger had passed, Simonich had not given up, and the siege was to drag on for another three months. Long afterwards Pottinger's exploit was to be celebrated by Maud Diver, a romantic novelist, in *The Hero of Herat*, a bestseller in its day. But the ultimate compliment at the time came, ironically, from the Shah of Persia himself. Seeing Pottinger's presence in Herat as the principal reason for his failure to bring Herat to its knees, he demanded that McNeill order the young officer to leave the city, in return for which he would be guaranteed safe passage through the Persian lines. McNeill pointed out, however, that Pottinger was not under his command, and that he was therefore in no position to issue such an order. Only Calcutta could do that. The Shah next tried the Heratis, declaring that he would not discuss an ending to the siege while Pottinger remained with them. This too failed, Yar Mohammed fearing that he might lose the invaluable Pottinger only to find that, on some spurious excuse, the siege was resumed.

Nonetheless, unknown to either Pottinger or the Shah, an end to the seeming stalemate was in sight. Alarmed by Vitkevich's triumph in Kabul, and fearing a similar Russian gain at Herat, the British government had decided at last to act. The sending of a relief force across Afghanistan to the beleaguered city had been ruled out as too hazardous and too slow. Instead it was decided to dispatch a task-force to the

Persian Gulf. Threatening the other end of the Shah's domains while he was fully occupied in the East, might, it was thought, oblige him to release his grip on Herat. At the same time Palmerston stepped up the pressure on Nesselrode, the Russian Foreign Minister, to call a halt to Simonich's highly irregular activities. Both moves were to produce swift and satisfying results.

On June 19, British troops landed unopposed on Kharg Island, at the head of the Gulf, just off the Persian coast. Wild rumours quickly began to spread inland that a massive British invasion force had landed on the coast and had begun to advance on the capital, capturing town after town as it proceeded. At the same time McNeill, who had by now returned to Teheran, sent one of his staff, Lieutenant-Colonel Charles Stoddart, to the royal camp at Herat to warn the Shah of the grave consequences if he continued the siege. 'The British Government', McNeill's note declared, 'looks upon this enterprise in which your Majesty is engaged against the Afghans as being undertaken in a spirit of hostility towards British India.' Officially informing him of the seizure of Kharg Island, the note went on to caution the Shah that Britain's next move would be decided by what action he took over Herat. It advised him to have nothing more to do with 'the bad counsel of the ill-disposed persons' who had encouraged him to attack the city in the first place.

Somewhat to his surprise Stoddart was cordially received by the Shah, whom he had believed to be still firmly under Count Simonich's influence. He read aloud to the Shah the contents of McNeill's note, translating it into Persian as he went along. When he came to the mention of 'ill-disposed persons', the Shah interrupted, asking: 'The fact is that if I don't leave Herat there will be war — is that not it?' Stoddart replied that this was so. Dismissing Stoddart, the Shah told him that he would consider the British demands and give him an answer shortly. No one knows what transpired between the Shah and Count Simonich, although McNeill would dearly have liked to, but two days later Stoddart was summoned to the royal presence. 'We consent to the whole of the demands of the British Government,' the Shah told him. 'We will not go to war. Had we known that our coming here might risk the loss of their friendship, we certainly would not have come at all.'

The Persians had climbed down completely, and the Russians had suffered an ignominious defeat. Gunboat diplomacy had triumphed where conventional diplomacy had failed. Reporting the dramatic turn of events to McNeill, Stoddart wrote: 'I replied that I thanked God that his Majesty thus regarded the true interests of Persia.' The Shah now gave orders for the siege to be lifted, and for his troops to prepare to return to Teheran. At 8 o'clock on the morning of September 9, Stoddart sent the following dispatch by special messenger to Sir John McNeill: 'I have the honour to report that the Persian army has marched ... and that His Majesty the Shah is about to mount.' At 10.26 he added briefly: 'The Shah has mounted his horse ... and is gone.'

But there was more to come. All along Count Nesselrode had insisted that there was no Russian involvement in the siege, maintaining that Simonich had strict instructions to do all he could to dissuade the Shah from marching on Herat. He even offered to show the British ambassador, Lord Durham, the confidential book containing his instructions to Simonich. At first this had satisfied Palmerston, but by now it was embarrassingly obvious that he was being hoodwinked. Either Simonich had totally ignored his government's instructions, or he had been told unofficially to disregard these for as long as he could get away with it, by which time, with luck, Herat would be safely in Persia's compliant hands. The truth will probably never be known, and historians still ponder over it today. But whatever the truth, Palmerston was out for blood.

In London the Russian ambassador was summoned and informed that Count Simonich and Captain Vitkevich (who was still lurking in Afghanistan) were pursuing policies actively hostile to Britain which gravely threatened relations between the two governments. Palmerston demanded that the two men be recalled at once. Perhaps the Russians had gambled on the expectation that the British, as on earlier occasions, would do nothing. If so, this time they had badly miscalculated. Moreover, the evidence against Simonich was so damning that Tsar Nicholas had little choice but to accede to Britain's demands. 'We pushed Russia into a corner in the matter of Count Simonich,' Palmerston told McNeill in triumph. 'The Emperor has no other way out but to recall him and to acknowledge that Nesselrode made a whole string of untruthful declarations.'

Simonich, rather than Nesselrode, was made the scapegoat, however, being accused of exceeding his authority and ignoring his instructions. Even if this was unfair, and he was simply obeying covert orders, he had failed to deliver Herat, despite the many months he had had at his disposal while St Petersburg played for time. Few tears were shed on his behalf by his British adversaries, moreover, for he had made himself extremely unpopular with McNeill and others with whom he had had dealings. It was felt that he had got no more than he deserved. But the fate which was to befall Captain Vitkevich, a much respected rival, gave no one any satisfaction.

Recalled from Afghanistan, he was ordered to proceed to St Petersburg, which he reached in the spring of 1839. Precisely what happened there remains a mystery. According to one account, based on contemporary Russian sources, he was warmly received by Count Nesselrode who congratulated him on displacing the British at Kabul. He was promised that his status as a Lithuanian aristocrat, removed when he was sent into exile as a youth, would be restored to him, and that he would be promoted and found a place in an élite regiment. But according to Kaye, who had access to British government intelligence from the Russian capital, the young officer had returned full of hopes only to be cold-shouldered by Nesselrode. The latter, anxious to dissociate himself from the whole affair, refused even to see him, declaring that he knew of no such Captain Vitkevich – 'except for an adventurer of that name, who had been lately engaged in some unauthorised intrigues in Kabul and Kandahar.'

However, on one thing both versions do agree. Returning to his hotel shortly after visiting the Foreign Ministry, Vitkevich went up to his room and burned his papers, including all the intelligence he had brought back from Afghanistan. Then, after scribbling a brief letter of farewell to his friends, he blew out his brains with a pistol. The Great Game had claimed another victim. As had happened after Griboyedov's violent death in Teheran ten years earlier, there were suspicions in St Petersburg that the British somehow had a hand in this too. But any such thoughts were quickly forgotten in the wake of the momentous events which were soon to rock Central Asia.

·15·

The Kingmakers

The British could congratulate themselves that this time they had come out on top. Vitkevich was dead, Simonich disgraced, Nesselrode outmanoeuvred, and Herat, the outermost bastion of India's defences, saved from falling under Russia's influence. When put to the test, moreover, Tsar Nicholas had shown no great inclination to rush to the assistance of the Shah. Having thus forced the Russians and Persians to back off, the British might have been well advised to leave it at that. But from the moment that Dost Mohammed spurned Lord Auckland's ultimatum, and officially received Vitkevich, he was considered in London and Calcutta to have thrown in his lot with the Russians. With Herat then still under siege, and a British naval task-force on its way to the Gulf, Palmerston and Auckland were determined to settle the Afghan crisis once and for all. Despite the arguments of Burnes, now strongly supported by Sir John McNeill, that Dost Mohammed was still Britain's best bet, it was decided that he must be forcibly removed from his throne and replaced by someone more compliant. But by whom?

Arthur Conolly favoured Kamran, who had shown himself to be hostile to both Tsar and Shah, and anxious to ally himself with Britain against Dost Mohammed and other claimants to the Afghan throne. However, there were other advisers closer to the Viceroy than Conolly, Burnes or McNeill. Foremost among these was William Macnaghten, Secretary to the Secret and Political Department in Calcutta. A brilliant orientalist, he was said to be as fluent in Persian, Arabic and Hindustani as in English. His views, moreover, carried immense weight, especially with Lord Auckland, whose sister, Emily Eden, once described him effusively as 'our Lord Palmerston'. Macnaghten's candidate for the Afghan throne was the exiled Shah Shujah, to whom he claimed it legitimately belonged. He put forward a plan whereby Ranjit Singh, who loathed Dost Mohammed, might be prevailed upon to use his powerful army of Sikhs to help Shah Shujah overthrow their mutual foe. In return for the recovery of his throne, Shujah would abandon all claims to Peshawar. By using an invasion force of Ranjit Singh's troops and Shujah's irregulars, Dost Mohammed could be toppled without British troops becoming involved.

Both Palmerston and Auckland were strongly attracted to this plan which got others to do their dirty work, much as the Russians were doing with the Persians over Herat. To replace one ruler with another among a people who had transferred their allegiance no fewer than eight times in less than half a century did not seem to be unduly problematical or perilous. Among those who favoured Macnaghten's idea was Claude Wade, the Company's respected political agent at Ludhiana, where Shujah was living, who was an expert on the intricate politics of Afghanistan and the Punjab. He and Macnaghten were therefore sent by Lord Auckland to Lahore to sound out Ranjit Singh and see whether his co-operation could be counted upon. At first he appeared enthusiastic about the plan. However, the wily old Sikh was far more aware than the British were of the perils of taking on the Afghans in their own mountainous domains, and soon he began to prevaricate and bargain. Gradually it became obvious to Auckland that he could not be relied upon to fulfil his expected role in Macnaghten's grand design. The only sure way of removing Dost Mohammed, and putting Shujah on his throne, would be by using British troops.

Auckland, normally a cautious man, found himself under growing pressure from the hawks around him to do just that. One of their arguments was that if there was to be a war with the Persians over Herat – and the siege was still in progress at that time – then a British army in Afghanistan would be well placed to wrest it back if it fell, and to prevent any further advance towards India's frontiers by the Shah's troops. Auckland was finally persuaded. But even if Ranjit Singh would not send his own forces into Afghanistan, his blessing for the operation was vital if he and Shujah were to enjoy a stable relationship in future, and their two countries were to serve as a protecting shield for British India. The Sikh ruler, who knew that he lacked the strength to overthrow Dost Mohammed himself, was more than happy to go along with this. Not only would it cost him nothing (although Auckland still hoped that he would contribute troops to the expedition), but also Shujah would be signing away, once and for all, any Afghan claims to Peshawar. He had everything to gain and nothing to lose. Shujah, too, was delighted with the plan, for the British were at last doing what he had been begging them to do for years. In June 1838, a secret agreement was signed by Ranjit Singh, Shujah and Great Britain, swearing eternal friendship and giving approval to the plan. Auckland was now free to start preparing for the coming invasion.

Palmerston had in the meantime alerted the British ambassador in St Petersburg to the proposed operation. 'Auckland', he informed him, 'has been told to take Afghanistan in hand and make it a British dependency ... We have long declined to meddle with the Afghans, but if the Russians try to make them Russian we must take care that they become British.' On October 1, Auckland issued the so-called Simla Manifesto in which he made public Britain's intention of forcibly removing Dost Mohammed from the throne and replacing him with Shujah. In justification of this, Dost Mohammed was portrayed as an untrustworthy villain who had driven a patient British government to act thus, and Shujah as a loyal friend and rightful owner of the throne. 'After much time spent by Captain Burnes in fruitless negotiation at Cabool,' Auckland declared, 'it appeared that Dost Mohammed Khan ... avowed schemes of aggrandizement and ambition injurious to the security and peace of the frontiers of India; and that he openly threatened, in furtherance of those schemes, to call in every foreign aid which he could command.' So long as Dost Mohammed remained in power in Kabul, he went on, there was no hope 'that the tranquillity of our neighbourhood would be secured, or that the interests of our Indian empire would be preserved inviolate'.

Although it was obvious to whom he was referring, Auckland carefully avoided any mention of the Russians, for he was about to embark on the very kind of foreign adventure of which Britain was accusing Tsar Nicholas. At the same time the Viceroy announced the names of the political officers who would be accompanying the expedition. Macnaghten, who received a knighthood, was appointed as Britain's envoy to the proposed new royal court at Kabul, with Alexander Burnes as his deputy and adviser. Burnes, although privately dismayed by the plan to overthrow his old friend, was nonetheless ambitious enough to acquiesce rather than resign. Not only was he promoted to lieutenant-colonel, but he was also given something which he had never dreamed of. In a letter complimenting him on his valuable services, Auckland suggested that he take another look at the envelope. Rescuing it from the waste-paper basket, Burnes saw to his astonishment that it was addressed to Lieutenant-Colonel *Sir* Alexander Burnes, Kt. Another appointment was that of Lieutenant Eldred Pottinger, then still beleaguered in Herat, who was to become one of Macnaghten's four political assistants.

Colonel Charles Stoddart of McNeill's staff, who at that moment was at the Shah's camp at Herat, was to be dispatched to Bokhara to reassure the Emir that he had nothing to fear from the British attack on his southern neighbour, and to try to persuade him to release his Russian slaves so as to remove any excuse for an attack on him by St Petersburg. Stoddart was also authorised to hold out the prospect of a treaty of friendship between Britain and Bokhara. His mission, like so much else that was to follow, was destined to go tragically wrong. However, as we have already seen, in the autumn of 1838 things were suddenly looking very rosy for the British. The news had just come through from Herat that the Persians and their Russian advisers had abandoned the siege and departed.

The question immediately arose of whether the expedition should be called off, since the danger had greatly receded.

Much bitter wrangling ensued at home and in India, with many arguing that it was now no longer necessary to unseat Dost Mohammed. To occupy Afghanistan would not only be prohibitively expensive, and leave India's other frontiers ill-guarded, but it would also push the Persians even further into the welcoming arms of the Russians. The Duke of Wellington for one was strongly against it, warning that where the military successes ended the political difficulties would begin. But for Palmerston and Auckland, with the bit now firmly between their teeth and the army ready to march, there could be no turning back at this late stage. Moreover, with anti-Russian feeling running at near hysteria point in Britain and India, the coming adventure enjoyed immense popular support. It certainly had that of *The Times*, which thundered: 'From the frontiers of Hungary to the heart of Burmah and Nepaul ... the Russian fiend has been haunting and troubling the human race, and diligently perpetrating his malignant frauds ... to the vexation of this industrious and essentially pacific empire.'

Auckland's only concession, now the Persians would no longer have to be taught a lesson, was a slight reduction in the size of the invasion force. 'The Army of the Indus', as it was officially called, consisted of 15,000 British and Indian troops, including infantry, cavalry and artillery. It was followed by an even larger force, a raggle-taggle army of 30,000 camp-followers – bearers, grooms, dhobi-wallahs, cooks and farriers – together with as many camels carrying ammunition and supplies, not to mention officers' personal belongings. One brigadier was said to have had no fewer than sixty camels to transport his own camp gear, while the officers of one regiment had commandeered two camels just to carry their cigars. Finally there were several herds of cattle, which were to serve as a mobile larder for the task force. In addition to the British and Indian units there was Shujah's own small army. Burnes had pointed out to Auckland that he might be more acceptable to his fellow-countrymen were he to claim the throne at the head of his own troops rather than be placed on it by British bayonets alone. Few of Shujah's men, however, were Afghans, most of them being Indians, trained and led by British officers, and paid for out of British funds.

With Lieutenant-Colonel Sir Alexander Burnes riding ahead to try to smooth the way by means of threats, persuasion or bribes, the invasion force entered Afghanistan through the fifty-mile-long Bolan Pass in the spring of 1839. Its shortest route by far would have been across the Punjab and up the Khyber Pass, but at the last minute Ranjit Singh had objected. The approach therefore had to be made through Sind and the more southerly of the two great passes. The Sindi rulers had also objected, pointing out that their treaty with the British stated that no military supplies would be transported up the Indus. However, they were told that this was an emergency, and threatened with dire consequences if they attempted to resist the British force, which proceeded to tramp roughshod across their territory.

Although Burnes managed to buy a safe passage for the expedition through the Bolan Pass from the Baluchi chiefs across whose domains it ran, many stragglers, runners and cattle fell victim to the bands of brigands who lay in wait for them on its lonely stretches. For the main columns, too, the going soon proved much harder than had been anticipated. It had been assumed that the expedition would be able to live largely off the land, but blight had decimated the previous season's crops, forcing villagers to subsist on what wild plants they could find – something which careful reconnaissance could have revealed. The invasion force now found itself running dangerously short of food, causing the men's morale to plummet. 'These privations soon began to tell fearfully upon their health and their spirits,' wrote Sir John Kaye. 'The sufferings of the present were aggravated by the dread of the future, and as men looked at the shrunk frames and sunken cheeks of each other ... their hearts died within them.'

What seemed like inevitable disaster, so early on in the campaign, was retrieved just in time by Burnes. He managed to buy, at an exorbitant price, some 10,000 sheep from the Baluchis, and the expedition's strength and morale were restored. But the intelligence which he gathered from the khan from whom he purchased them, and which he passed to Macnaghten, was far from encouraging. The Baluchi warned him that while the British might succeed in placing Shujah on the

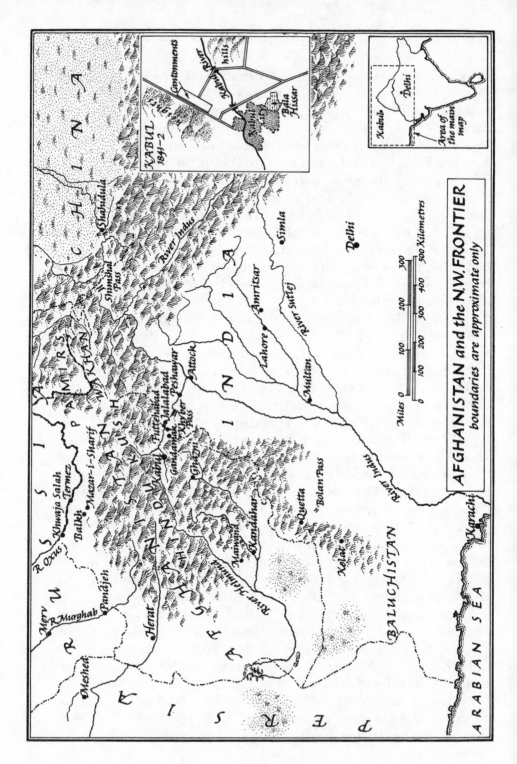

AFGHANISTAN and the N.W. FRONTIER
boundaries are approximate only

KABUL 1841-2

Area of the main map

throne, they would never carry the Afghan people with them, and would therefore fail in the end. The British, he declared, had embarked on an undertaking 'of vast magnitude and difficult accomplishment'. Instead of trusting the Afghan nation and Dost Mohammed, the British had 'cast them aside and inundated the country with foreign troops'. Shujah, he insisted, was unpopular among his fellow Afghans, and the British would be wise to point out to him his errors 'if the fault originated with him, and alter them if they sprang from ourselves'.

That was the last thing that Macnaghten wanted to hear, for he had repeatedly assured Lord Auckland that Shujah's return would be rapturously welcomed by the Afghans. Although there had been little sign of this so far, the first real test of the British puppet's popularity would come when they reached Kandahar, the country's southern capital, which was ruled by one of Dost Mohammed's brothers. As they approached the city, intelligence reached Macnaghten and Sir John Keane, the general commanding the expedition, that the ruler had fled north. Because there appeared to be no likelihood of any resistance, the British units were ordered to hold back to make it appear that Shujah's own troops had restored Kandahar to him. On April 25, with Macnaghten at his side, Shujah entered the city without a shot being fired. A large and curious crowd turned out to see him, with the men thronging the streets and their womenfolk lining the rooftops and balconies. Flowers were strewn in his path and he was greeted with shouts of 'Kandahar is freed' and 'We look to you for protection' as he rode in triumph through the city.

Macnaghten was delighted. He had been proved right, and Burnes wrong. 'The Shah made a grand entry,' he reported that night to Lord Auckland, 'and was received with feelings nearly amounting to adoration.' Dost Mohammed, he believed, would not defend Kabul but would flee when he learned of the wild scenes of welcome which had accompanied Shujah's bloodless victory. He decided to stage a durbar on the plains outside the city, at which the Afghans would be able to express their loyalty to their new ruler. A spectacular military parade was laid on at which General Keane's troops would pass in review order before Shujah, who would take the salute from a platform sheltered from the blazing heat by a brightly coloured canopy. On the chosen day Shujah rode out at sunrise to where the British and Indian units were lined up, and where Macnaghten, Keane and other political and military officers awaited him. As he ascended the saluting dais, the troops presented arms, a 101-gun salute thundered out, and the march-past commenced. Everything went perfectly – except for one thing. Barely a hundred Afghans turned up to witness the spectacle and to honour Shujah. 'The whole affair', wrote Kaye, 'was a painful failure … but the miserable paucity of Afghans who appeared to do homage to the King must have warned Shah Shujah, with ominous significance, of the feebleness of his tenure upon the affections of the people, as it bitterly disappointed his principal European supporters.'

Macnaghten may have been disappointed but was not going to admit to it. If all else failed, Afghan loyalty, or at least that of those who mattered, could always be bought with British gold. He was well provided with the latter, which he proceeded to distribute freely among the tribal chiefs through whose territories they advanced. 'He opened the treasure-chest,' wrote Kaye, and 'scattered abroad its contents with an ungrudging hand.' However, no amount of gold would buy the loyalty of the next town lying astride their line of advance. This was Ghazni, with its mighty fortress, perched on a mountainside and reputed throughout Central Asia to be impregnable. After inspecting its ramparts, sixty feet high and massively thick, General Keane and his engineers realised that they faced a serious problem. The Afghan fortress was infinitely more formidable than they had been led to believe. Assuming that he would not need them, Keane had left his siege guns behind at Kandahar. All he had with him were light field pieces which would make little or no impression on this great stronghold. They were once again running short of food, and it would take weeks for the enormously heavy siege guns, which would have to be dragged every inch of the way, to reach Ghazni.

There was, however, one other way of storming Ghazni without their use, and that was by blowing up one of its huge gates. This would be a near-suicidal mission for whoever placed the explosive charges and lit the fuse, calling for exceptional physical courage, as they would be working in full view of the defenders on the ramparts above. The young officer chosen to lead the small party of sappers detailed to carry out this task was Lieutenant Henry Durand of the Bengal Engineers, although he was still weakened by an attack of jaundice. The question now arose of which of the city's several gates should be attacked. Here the British were in luck. Accompanying the expedition as a native intelligence officer was Mohan Lal, Burnes's young friend and protégé, who managed to make contact with one of the defenders whom he had known previously. From this traitor he learned that all the gates save one – the great Kabul Gate – had been bricked up from the inside, making them virtually unassailable.

While General Keane and his staff were working out their plans for the attack, look-outs suddenly spotted a group of armed Afghans on the crest of a hill overlooking the British encampment. A bugler raised the alarm and cavalry and infantry were thrown against them, forcing them to flee, but not before a number of captives and a holy war banner had been seized. As the former were being paraded before Shujah, one of them, screaming that he was a traitor to the Faith, broke free and in the ensuing mêlée stabbed a royal attendant. Enraged at this, Shujah gave orders that all the prisoners were to be killed on the spot. Just as the bloodbath got under way a British officer passing the rear of the royal encampment heard a commotion and peered inside one of the tents. To his horror he came face to face with the executioners, laughing and joking as they set about their work, 'hacking and maiming the poor wretches indiscriminately with their long swords and knives'.

There were forty or fifty prisoners, he reported later, both young and old. 'Many were dead, others at their last gasp.' Some, sitting or standing with their hands tied behind their backs, were still awaiting their fate. Aghast at what he had seen, he ran to Macnaghten's tent to warn him. But the latter appears to have done little or nothing to stop the massacre, although it may already have been too late. Until then he had been fulsome in his praise for Shujah's humanity, Kaye notes.

It now became clear that this humanity 'was nowhere to be found except in Macnaghten's letters'. Even by Afghanistan's savage standards such barbarism was unacceptable, and news of this atrocity by the man who sought to be the country's ruler spread rapidly, swelling the ranks of his foes, and doing immeasurable harm to the reputation of his British sponsors.

*　　*　　*

By now Keane had finalised his plans and had issued his orders for the storming of Ghazni. The attack was to be made that night, under cover of darkness and the loud gusting of the wind. To draw the defenders away from the Kabul Gate, a diversionary attack was to be made on the far end of the fortress, while Keane's light artillery and sepoy infantry directed their fire from close range against those manning the ramparts. At all costs the defenders' attention had to be kept away from the Kabul Gate, against which Lieutenant Durand and his sappers would be placing their bags of gunpowder.

By three o'clock the next morning everything was ready, and everyone in his place. On Keane's signal the gunners and infantry opened up on the ramparts, a shell removing the head of an Afghan soldier in full view of the storming party which was waiting in the darkness for the gate to be blown up. Meanwhile the explosives party moved silently and swiftly towards its target. After placing their charges without detection, the men darted to safety, leaving Durand behind to light the fuse. As he crouched by the gate, through a crack in the woodwork he could see one of the defenders, long-barrelled *jezail* in hand. On the first attempt the fuse failed to light, and likewise on the second. For a grim moment, knowing that everything depended on him, Durand feared that he would have to sacrifice himself by igniting the actual explosives. But on the third attempt the fuse began to splutter. Durand dashed for cover, and seconds later the charges went off.

'The effect', recounts Kaye, 'was as mighty as it was sudden. A column of black smoke arose, and down with a crash came heavy masses of masonry and shivered beams in awful ruin and confusion.' As the roar of the explosion died away, the bugler sounded the advance. Led by Colonel William Dennie, a soldier of legendary bravery, the storming party poured through the smoking gateway and within seconds British bayonets and Afghan swords were locked in vicious combat. On hearing cheers from inside the walls, the main attacking force rose from their positions and raced for the gateway. But then, in the confusion and darkness, something happened which nearly cost the British the battle. Believing the gateway to be totally blocked by debris, and Dennie's men to be still outside, the bugler sounded the retreat, causing the attack momentarily to peter out, while inside the walls the storming party fought for their lives against overwhelming odds. The error was quickly realised, however, and the order again given to charge. Moments later, led by a brigadier wielding a sabre, the entire assault party was inside the fortress and had joined forces with Dennie's men.

The Afghans, who had never dreamed that their stronghold could be stormed, fought back with the utmost courage and ferocity. But it was the first time they had encountered highly trained European troops well versed in modern siege tactics, and soon the defence began to crumble. 'In the frenzy of despair,' Kaye wrote, 'the Afghans rushed out from their hiding places, sword in hand, upon our stormers, and plied their sabres with terrible effect, but only to meet with fearful retribution from the musket-fire of the British infantry ... Some, in their frantic efforts to escape by the gateway, stumbled over the burning timbers, wounded and exhausted, and were slowly burnt to death. Some were bayoneted on the ground. Others were pursued and hunted into corners like mad dogs, and shot down.' Those who managed to escape through the gateway or over the wall were cut down by the cavalry outside. Soon it was all over, and the Union Jack and regimental standards of the assault parties fluttered in triumph from the ramparts.

It was an overwhelming victory for the British, as the casualty figures showed. They had lost only 17 dead, with a further 165 wounded, 18 of them officers. At least 500 of the defenders had died during the fighting within the fortress, while many others had been cut down outside by Keane's cavalry. Hardly less important to the victors, however, were the large quantities of grain, flour and other foodstuffs found inside the city, for their own supplies were all but exhausted, gravely imperilling their hopes of reaching Kabul. Now, thanks largely to the enterprise of Mohan Lal, and the cool nerves of Lieutenant Durand (which would have won him a Victoria Cross had it then existed), the way was clear to the Afghan capital, less than a hundred miles away to the north.

*　　*　　*

The sudden and unexpected loss of Ghazni proved a devastating blow to Dost Mohammed. A 5,000-strong Afghan cavalry force commanded by his son, which he had sent to try to halt the advancing British, turned back rather than face annihilation. Everywhere Dost Mohammed's supporters began to melt away, preferring to watch developments from the sidelines. On June 30, 1839, Keane resumed his march, and a week later, opposed only by a line of abandoned cannon, the British appeared before the walls of Kabul. Dost Mohammed, they found, had fled, and the capital surrendered without a shot being fired.

The following day, with Macnaghten, Keane and Burnes riding at his side, Shah Shujah entered the city he had not seen for thirty years. His robes glinting with precious stones, he was borne through the streets on a magnificent white charger, its trappings embellished with gold. 'The jingling of money-bags, and the gleaming of the bayonets of the British,' observed Kaye, 'had restored him to the throne which, without these glittering aids, he had in vain striven to recover.' But nowhere was there any sign of the rapturous welcome which Macnaghten had so confidently forecast. 'It was more like a funeral procession,' added Kaye, 'than the entry of a King into the capital of his restored dominions.' Palmerston, however, was delighted with Auckland's neat exhibition of kingmaking. 'The glorious success of Auckland in Afghanistan', he wrote, 'will cow all Asia and make everything more easy for us.'

Lord Auckland's original plan had been for the British force to be withdrawn as soon as Shujah had been safely restored to his throne, and was cocooned by his own officials and protected by his own troops. However, it was now clear even to Macnaghten that he remained anything but secure while the able Dost Mohammed remained at large. A cavalry force led by one of Keane's best commanders was sent out to try to capture the deposed king, but returned to Kabul empty-handed after a month. A subsequent pursuit proved similarly fruitless. Only months later was Dost Mohammed to hand himself over to the British who – to the fury of Shujah, who wanted to 'hang him like a dog' – treated him with the utmost respect and sent him into honourable, albeit temporary, exile in India.

In the meantime, in Kabul, the British settled down to the daily routine of garrison life. Race-meetings were organised, business flourished in the bazaars as the British and Indian troops spent their earnings there, and the families of some of the officers began to travel up from India to join them in this exotic new hill-station. Among them was Lady Macnaghten, bringing with her crystal chandeliers, vintage wines, expensive gowns and scores of servants. General Keane, who had been given the title of Lord Keane of Ghazni by Queen Victoria, now returned to India with a major portion of the task-force. But a substantial part remained in Kabul, with smaller contingents at Ghazni, Kandahar, Jalalabad and Quetta, to protect British lines of communication with India. However, if Macnaghten was confident that Shujah could be maintained on his throne by force of British arms, Keane was certainly not. 'I cannot but congratulate you on quitting this country,' he remarked to Lieutenant Durand, who was due to return to India, 'for, mark my words, it will not be long before there is here some signal catastrophe . . .'

In late August 1839, two disturbing pieces of intelligence reached the British garrison in Kabul. The first was that Lieutenant-Colonel Charles Stoddart, who had been sent to Bokhara to reassure the Emir about British intentions in Afghanistan, had been arrested and thrown unceremoniously into a pit filled with vermin. The second, even more worrying item of news was that a large Russian expedition was on its way southwards from Orenburg to seize the khanate of Khiva.

·16·

The Race for Khiva

Ever since William Moorcroft's visit to Bokhara four-teen years earlier, concern had been growing in St Petersburg over British designs on Central Asia and its markets. By the autumn of 1838, this disquiet matched that of London and Calcutta over Russia's incursions into the regions surrounding India. In October of that year, shortly before learning of the British plan to replace Dost Mohammed with their own puppet, Count Nesselrode wrote to his ambassador in London to brief him on St Petersburg's fears. He warned him of 'the indefatigable activity displayed by English travellers to spread disquiet among the peoples of Central Asia, and to carry agitation even into the heart of the countries bordering our frontier'. Chief among these trouble-some travellers was Alexander Burnes, who was clearly intent on undermining Russian influence in Central Asia and replac-ing it with that of Britain, and also on driving out Russian goods in favour of British ones. 'For our part,' Nesselrode insisted, 'we ask nothing but to be allowed to partake in fair competition for the commerce of Asia.'

The ink was hardly dry on his letter when the news reached St Petersburg of Britain's proposed invasion of Afghanistan. And if that were not alarming enough, it was followed shortly by the ill-tidings that British action in the Gulf had forced the Shah to withdraw from Herat, thus removing any hopes that Russia might have had of gaining a surrogate foot-hold there. Realising that there was little or nothing they could do about either of these British moves, the Russians decided instead to embark on a bold initiative of their own. This was to seize Khiva, an old dream of theirs, before the British began to venture north of the Oxus, not merely with agents, but with armies and caravans of merchandise. With Britain behaving so aggressively in Afghanistan, the Russians could hardly have asked for a better moment to make their own first major thrust into Central Asia. Nor was their excuse for it easy to fault. Its officially proclaimed aims were to free the many Russian and other slaves known to be held by the Khivans, to punish the Turcoman raiders and slavers who regularly plundered the native caravans bearing Russian goods, and to replace the ruler – just as the British were doing in Afghanistan – with a compliant candidate of their own who would forswear the barbaric practices of his predecessor.

Even Burnes found it difficult to criticise these aims, although it was obvious to him and to his fellow hawks that the Russian advance southwards would not end there. Bokhara and Merv would probably be the next victims, with Herat after that. The only way to prevent this happening would be for British troops, using their newly won base at Kabul, to get there first. It was Macnaghten's view that Balkh, the crucial bridgehead on the Oxus, should be seized in the coming May, when the passes of the Hindu Kush would be free of snow. From there a swift and effective blow could be struck against Bokhara, where Britain's envoy, Lieutenant-Colonel Stoddart, was being held prisoner in appalling conditions by the cruel and tyrannical Emir. Next, before the Russians or the Persians could get their covetous hands on it, Herat should be taken into permanent British care. Having come so far, there seemed little point in not taking full advantage of it if the Russians were bent on seizing Khiva. It was classic forward school reasoning. Veterans of the Great Game began to feel that their hour of destiny had come at last.

What finally decided the Russians to press ahead with the seizure of Khiva was a wild (and totally false) report which reached them via Bokhara that a twenty-five-strong British mission had arrived in Khiva with offers of military assistance. On instructions from St Petersburg, General Perovsky, the commander-in-chief at Orenburg, immediately set about assembling a force consisting of 5,200 infantry, cavalry and artillery. He hoped to keep his intention secret until the very last moment. Apart from not wishing to alert the Khivans to his coming, he had not forgotten how one young British subaltern had foiled their plans at Herat, and had no wish for anything like that to happen again. Finally he wanted to see the British fully committed to their Afghan adventure, so that they would be in no position to protest about similar kingmaking activities by St Petersburg at Khiva. In case rumours began to leak out about the preparations, the expedition was to be officially described as a 'scientific' one to the Aral Sea, which lay on its route. Indeed, in the coming years 'scientific expeditions' were frequently to serve as covers for Russian Great Game activities, while the British preferred to send their officers, similarly engaged, on 'shooting leave', thus enabling them to be disowned if necessary.

In the event the Russians found it impossible to maintain secrecy for very long. As we have seen, the British first learned of Perovsky's preparations in the summer of 1839, three months before the expedition's departure. The warning had come from Khiva itself, after rumours reached the Khan's ears through his efficient network of spies. There are two versions of how it travelled from there to Herat, where there were still British officers stationed following the Shah's withdrawal. According to one, the Khan of Khiva, in a state of panic, sent an envoy post-haste to the Heratis to beg assistance, knowing that they had successfully held off the Persians and their Russian advisers. According to the British account, it was one of their own native agents who had returned from Khiva with the news that a Russian army – rumoured to be 100,000 strong – was about to set out from Orenburg. In any event, on hearing of it, Major d'Arcy Todd, the senior British officer at Herat, at once dispatched messengers to Teheran and Kabul to alert his superiors to the danger. In the meantime, he determined to do whatever he could from Herat to prevent Khiva from falling into the hands of the Russians.

It being impossible for him to desert his own post, he decided to dispatch Captain James Abbott, a resourceful officer on his staff, to Khiva to offer to negotiate with the advancing Russians on the Khan's behalf. If the Khan could be persuaded to release all his Russian slaves, then St Petersburg would no longer have any excuse for advancing into Khivan territory. The threat to the Khan's throne, not to mention that to British India, might thus be removed. It was Abbott's task to convince the Khan of the urgent need to jettison the slaves before Perovsky advanced too far to turn back. Wearing Afghan dress, and with the fate of Colonel Stoddart, the last British officer to be sent to one of the Central Asian khanates, very much in mind, Abbott set off alone for Khiva, 500 miles away to the north, on Christmas Eve 1839.

*   *   *

Meanwhile, 1,500 miles to the north, General Perovsky had also departed for Khiva. Accompanied by more than 5,000 troops, both Russian and Cossack, he was followed by a train of 10,000 camels bearing their ammunition and equipment. Before setting out on their long and gruelling march across steppe and desert, the general had assembled his men in Orenburg's main square and read out a special order of the day. 'By command of His Majesty the Emperor,' he declared, 'we are going to march against Khiva.' Although rumours of their destination had long been rife, this was the first that the troops had been told officially of the expedition's objective. Hitherto they had been informed that they were to serve as an escort to a scientific mission to the Aral Sea. 'Khiva', the general continued, 'has for many years tried the patience of a strong but magnanimous power, and has at last brought down upon itself the wrath which its hostile conduct has provoked.' Honour and glory would be their reward, he told them, for braving danger and hardship to rescue their brethren who were languishing in bondage. Thorough preparations, however, had been made for the journey, and these, together with their own determination to reach Khiva, would ensure them victory. 'In two months, with God's help,' he promised, 'we shall be in Khiva.'

At first everything went according to plan. The early winter months had been deliberately chosen because of the intense heat of the desert in summer and the difficulty of obtaining water for so large a force along the 1,000-mile route. It was the general's aim to reach Khiva before the worst of the Central Asian winter closed in on them in February. Nonetheless, the cold came as something of a shock to men who, in the words of the official report of the expedition, 'had always lived in warm houses, and rarely ventured out of doors except when hunting or performing short journeys'. At night in their felt tents the Russians covered themselves from head to foot with their sheepskin coats to protect their noses and other extremities from frostbite. Even so the men's breath and sweat caused their hair and moustaches to freeze to their sheepskins, and when they rose in the mornings 'it took them a considerable time to disentangle themselves'. Fortunately, however, the troops were extremely hardy and soon began to adjust to the sub-zero temperatures.

November now gave way to December, and the snow began to fall. It was far heavier and more frequent than Perovsky and his staff had expected. Even the local Kirghiz could not recall so much falling so early in winter. Soon it began to obliterate the tracks of the preceding columns, making navigation treacherous in the flat, featureless terrain. 'It was only now and again', the report declares, 'that the route pursued by the columns in front could be ascertained by the pillars of snow erected at some distance from each other by the Cossacks, by the snow heaps which marked the night camps, and by the camels, living and dead, some frozen and partly devoured by wild beasts, which lay along the line of march.' The deep snow and frozen earth made it increasingly difficult to find food for the camels, and soon they began to die at an alarming rate. 'Once a camel fell,' the report tells us, 'it rarely rose again.' Constantly having to transfer the loads from fallen camels to others greatly slowed the expedition's progress and exhausted the men. A subaltern was sent ahead to the Aral Sea region to try to buy fresh camels, but word came back that he had been captured by a Khivan patrol and carried off, bound hand and foot, to the capital.

By early January they had lost nearly half their camels, and the surviving beasts, crazed by hunger, began to gnaw through the wooden cases containing the men's rations. To prevent this, every night some 19,000 boxes and sacks had to be unloaded, and loaded again the following morning. Before fires could be lit for cooking and for warmth, fuel had somehow to be found beneath the snow. This consisted of the roots of small shrubs which had to be dug from the frozen earth. Large areas of snow also had to be cleared at every halt so that the felts could be laid down, tents erected and lines prepared for the camels and horses. 'Only towards 8 or 9 in the evening could the soldier or Cossack obtain a little repose,' the official record recounts, 'and by 2 or 3 the next morning he was obliged to rise and go through the same round of heavy duties.' Nonetheless they still pressed stoically on.

The snow-drifts were now so deep that the men had to work up to their waists in them to clear the way for the camels and artillery. As the snow continued to fall and temperatures to drop, their suffering increased, testing their strength and morale to the limit. 'In such cold,' the official report declares, 'it was impossible to wash clothes or observe personal cleanliness. Many of the men, during the whole march, not only did not change their soiled linen, but did not take off their clothes. They were covered with vermin and their bodies engrained with dirt.' Sickness now became a serious problem, with scurvy beginning to take an increasing toll. Yet they were still less than half-way to Khiva.

As January drew to a close, it became increasingly clear that the expedition was heading for disaster. More than 200 men had already died of sickness, while more than twice that number were too ill to fight. The camels, on which they were so dependent, were now dying at the rate of 100 a day. The weather was still deteriorating, and the Cossack scouts reported that ahead the snow lay even deeper, making it almost impossible to find fuel and forage of any kind, and reducing their likely progress to no more than a few miles a day, if that. On January 29, General Perovsky visited each of the columns to see for himself whether men and beasts were capable of continuing the march for another month – the minimum time it would take them to reach the nearest inhabited parts of the

Khivan khanate. It was the unanimous view of his column commanders that, if a catastrophe was to be averted, any further advance was now out of the question. From what he himself had seen of the men, Perovsky knew that they were right.

It must have been a moment of bitter disappointment, not to say humiliation, for them all, but especially for the general. By sheer ill-luck they had chosen to attack Khiva during the worst winter that anyone living on the steppe could remember. Had they only set out a little earlier they might have missed the worst of its fury and reached the rich and sheltered oasis of Khiva in safety. As it was, they had not so much as seen the enemy, let alone engaged him. On February 1, 1840, the general gave orders for the exhausted and depleted columns to turn about and head back to Orenburg. It had taken them the best part of three months to struggle this far, and the return march was unlikely to take them any less. Putting as brave a face on things as possible, Perovsky told his men: 'Comrades! Ever since we started out we have had to struggle against obstacles of the severest character, and a winter of unprecedented ferocity. These difficulties we have successfully overcome, but we have been denied the satisfaction of meeting the foe.' He assured them that their victory had merely been delayed, and that 'our next expedition will be more fortunate'.

But Perovsky's immediate problem was to extricate his force from its perilous situation with as little further loss of life as possible – not to mention loss of face. For this was the second time in little more than a century that a Russian expedition to Khiva had met with failure and humiliation. However, in the words of the official report: 'It was preferable to succumb to the insurmountable obstacles of nature, and to retreat at once, than to give the miserable opponents of Russia any pretext for exultation over an imaginary victory.' Nonetheless, those obstacles were to prove no less hazardous during the retreat than during the advance. In addition to the snow-drifts and blizzards, food shortages and sickness, there was the grisly trail of rotting camel carcasses, half eaten by wolves and foxes, to remind them of their plight. Having scented the carrion from far off, packs of wolves now plagued the columns when they halted at night.

In a misguided attempt to halt the ravages of scurvy, Perovsky managed with great difficulty to obtain supplies of fresh meat, believing that the deficiency of this, and not of fresh vegetables, was its cause. Sadly but not surprisingly, 'in spite of these preventive measures', the official report tells us, 'the scurvy, instead of diminishing, grew worse'. This was blamed on the men's general ill-health, and the filthy condition of their clothes and bodies. With the arrival of March, however, there was a slight but welcome improvement in the weather, though this gave rise to a new hazard – snow-blindness. Many of the men, their eyes weakened by months of vitamin deficiency, found themselves badly affected by the glare of the bright spring sunlight off the snow. Even improvised sun-glasses made from lattices of horsehair did little to ease the pain, which was aggravated by the acrid smoke from the green twigs used for fuel.

Throughout March and April, men and camels continued to drop, and by the time the last of the columns struggled into Orenburg in May, nearly seven months after their confident departure, the full magnitude of the catastrophe had become apparent. Of the 5,200 officers and men who had set out for Khiva, more than 1,000 had perished without a shot being fired, or the loss of one Khivan soldier. Fewer than 1,500 of the 10,000 camels which had accompanied the force were to return alive. Not one of the Russian slaves had been freed, the Turcoman caravan raiders remained unpunished, and the Khan who was to have been replaced was still firmly on his throne. Yet across the Oxus, for the whole world to see, the British had successfully carried out a not dissimilar operation with textbook professionalism. It could not have been more galling for the Russians, coming so soon after their setback at Herat, where again the British had outmanoeuvred them, in full view of everyone, on the Great Game battlefield. Furthermore, it was no secret that their campaign against the Circassians and Shamyl's Daghestanis in the Caucasus was going far from well.

One need hardly add that the Russophobe press in Britain

and on the Continent was rubbing its hands in satisfaction at this triple misfortune. For their part the St Petersburg newspapers sought to justify the Khivan adventure, rebuking the foreign press for denouncing it, and accusing the editors of hypocrisy. The Russians argued that the British, with considerably less justification, had occupied India, much of Burma, the Cape of Good Hope, Gibraltar, Malta, and now Afghanistan, while the French had summarily annexed the whole of Algeria on the dubious pretext that its Muslim ruler had insulted their consul. 'The guilt of the Algerian Bey', the official Russian report on the Khivan expedition was to argue, 'shrinks into insignificance when compared with that of the Khivan khans. For many years they have tempted the patience of Russia with their treachery, outrages, robberies and the detention of thousands of the Tsar's subjects as slaves and bondsmen.' Referring to the failure of the expedition, the report's anonymous authors declared that it was to be hoped that this would finally prove to the world 'the impracticability of all ideas of conquest in this region – even if they had existed', and would end, once and for all, such 'erroneous interpretations' of Russian policy in the East.

It was, of course, to do nothing of the sort, even if a further thirty years were to pass before the Russians dispatched another expedition to Khiva. By now suspicions and misunderstandings had progressed too far for that. Few in Britain or India were willing to see that it was largely panic over Britain's own forward move in Afghanistan which had driven St Petersburg into such precipitate action over Khiva. Russophobe propaganda was in full spate. British travellers returning from Russia insisted that Tsar Nicholas was aiming at nothing less than world domination. Robert Bremmer, in his *Excursions in the Interior of Russia*, published in 1839, warned that Nicholas was simply waiting for the most opportune moment to strike. 'That he will ultimately do so when Poland is more secure, Circassia conquered, and internal factions appeased, there can be little doubt,' he declared. Another British visitor, Thomas Raikes, writing in 1838, drew attention to the menace of Russia's rapidly growing military and naval power, and forecast that Britain and Russia would very soon be at war.

Nor were such views confined to the British. A celebrated French observer, the Marquis de Custine, who toured Russia in 1839, returned with similar forebodings about St Petersburg's ambitions. In his *La Russe en 1839*, a work still quoted by Kremlinologists today, he warned: 'They wish to rule the world by conquest. They mean to seize by armed force the countries accessible to them, and thence to oppress the rest of the world by terror. The extension of power they dream of ... if God grants it to them, will be for the woe of the world.'

The British press largely shared this sense of doom. In an editorial written shortly before the fate of the Khivan expedition was known, *The Times* declared: 'The Russians have well nigh mastered the whole of the northern kingdoms of Central Asia ... they are in possession of the great lines of inland traffic which once made Samarkand, and now make Bokhara, a position of first rate commercial importance; and ... having crossed a vast tract of horrid desert, they now stand preparing or prepared ... to launch their armed hordes towards the more fertile regions of Hindustan.' It blamed Palmerston for encouraging the Russians to indulge in such dreams by failing to deal firmly with them in the past. However, it had little doubt that when the inevitable collision came British arms would prevail. The news that the Russians had failed miserably to annex Khiva, and were back where they had begun, did little to moderate the newspaper's views. Despite the insistence of St Petersburg that the attempt would not be repeated, and that it had anyway intended to withdraw after its objectives had been achieved, it was generally assumed that it would only be a matter of time before a larger expedition set out for Khiva, at a more carefully chosen season of the year.

Another influential journal, the *Foreign Quarterly Review*, which hitherto had always preached restraint, now joined the ranks of the Russophobes, warning its readers of the 'extreme danger' posed by St Petersburg in both Asia and Europe. 'The silent and yet alarming progression of Russia in every direction', it declared, 'is quite evident now, and we do not know of one European or Asiatic power on which she does not meditate incursions. Poor Turkey is almost her own, and so is Greece. Circassia holds her at bay, but will share the fate of Poland if not assisted. Persia is already with her, India and China are obviously next in contemplation. Prussia and Austria must keep a sharp look-out, and even France is narrowly watched in the hope of some convulsion in the unpopular dynasty of Orleans to push forward a candidate for the throne, such as Prince Louis Napoleon.'

Such then was the low state of Anglo-Russian relations when, in late January 1840, Captain James Abbott approached Khiva, oblivious to any of this. He was unaware even that the Russian expedition had met with catastrophe, and that therefore he had won the race. However, as he was soon to discover, his own reception in this Muslim stronghold would be far from rapturous.

· 17 ·

The Freeing of the Slaves

When Captain Abbott rode through the gates of Khiva, having first changed from his Afghan disguise into British uniform, he found that alarming rumours about his real purpose in coming had already reached the capital. One of these maintained that he was a Russian spy, posing as an Englishman, who had been sent by General Perovsky to report on the city's defences. Not long before, he was disturbed to learn, two mysterious European travellers, claiming to be British but suspected by the Khan of being Russians, had been tortured with red-hot skewers in an effort to make them confess. This apparently having been achieved, their throats had been cut and their remains tossed into the desert as a dire warning to others. And here was he, also claiming to be British, turning up at a time when Khiva was gravely threatened. It was hardly surprising that Abbott found himself treated with the utmost suspicion.

To add to his predicament, there was considerable confusion, even in the Khan's mind, as to who precisely the British were. Until news of Eldred Pottinger's role in Herat's defence reached Khiva, few if any Khivans had ever heard of them. No Englishmen were held as slaves, and none, so far as anyone could recall, had ever visited Khiva. Many believed them merely to be a sub-tribe, or a vassal state, of the Russians. It was even rumoured that the British, having successfully seized Kabul, were proposing to join forces with the advancing Russians and divide Central Asia between them. In view of these wild tales, the prospect of Abbott persuading the Khivans to surrender their slaves in exchange for a Russian withdrawal seemed remote indeed. It appeared far more likely that he would end up with his throat cut like his unfortunate 'English' predecessors, or be thrown into a dungeon like Colonel Stoddart in neighbouring Bokhara.

But if Abbott was anxious about his safety, so too was the Khan about his. Believing the Russians to be advancing still towards his capital with an army said to be 100,000 strong, he was desperate for help from any quarter. He agreed to receive the British officer and consider what he had to offer, although, lest he be a spy, great pains were taken to ensure that he saw as little as possible of Khiva's defences. At the first of several audiences he was to have with the Khan, Abbott presented his credentials, together with the letter he bore from Major Todd, his superior at Herat. He was uncomfortably aware that these amounted to very little. 'I had been sent on the spur of the moment,' he wrote later, 'without even credentials from the head of the Indian Government.' The Khan was clearly disappointed by the contents of Todd's letter, evidently hoping that Abbott had been sent to offer him immediate military assistance, not merely expressions of goodwill. Abbott explained to him that so important a decision could not be made by Major Todd, but only by the British government in London. This would take time, and very soon the Russians would be at the gates. There was only one possible way of preventing this, and that was for the Khan to hand back all the Russian slaves he held, thereby removing the Tsar's widely proclaimed excuse for advancing on Khiva.

Abbott offered to travel northwards himself with the slaves, or a token party of them, to meet the Russians and try to negotiate a deal with them on the Khan's behalf. But the Khivan ruler, long versed in treachery, was suspicious of this. After all, although he did not quite say as much, the newcomer might well be in collusion with the Russians. He put it more delicately. What, he asked, was there to prevent the Russians from seizing both him and the slaves and continuing their advance? Abbott was forced to admit that he could not guarantee success. If London and St Petersburg were rivals in Asia, the Khan enquired, then was not Abbott concerned lest the Russians simply murder him? Abbott explained that the two countries were not at war, even if Britain had no wish to see Khiva occupied by Russia, and that each had an ambassador in the other's capital. The Russians, he added, had too much respect for British military and political power to risk molesting one of her subjects. The Khan pointed out that the Russians had shown no respect for his ambassadors, but had merely arrested them, his own brother among them. Such things, Abbott explained, might happen where retaliation was clearly impossible, but London and St Petersburg lay quite close to one another, and 'the naval and military force of England were too formidable to be trifled with'.

While the Khan mulled over Abbott's offer, they turned to other subjects. It soon became clear to Abbott that the Khan had little idea of the relative sizes of Britain, Russia and his own small kingdom. 'How many guns has Russia?' he asked Abbott. The Englishman replied that he did not know for sure, but that it would be a very large number indeed. 'I have twenty,' the Khan told him proudly. 'How many has the Queen of England?' Abbott explained that she had so many that no precise count was kept. 'The seas are covered with the ships of England, each bearing from twenty to one-hundred-and-twenty guns of the largest size,' he went on. 'Her forts are full of cannon, and thousands lie in every magazine. We have more guns than any nation in the world.'

'And how often can your artillerymen fire?' the Khan asked him.

'Our field artillery can fire about seven times in a minute.'

'The Russians fire their guns twelve times a minute.'

'Your Majesty has been misinformed,' Abbott replied. 'I myself belong to the artillery, and know such firing to be impossible.'

'The Persian ambassador asserts it,' the Khan insisted.

'Then he is misinformed. No artillerymen on earth are more expert than the British, yet we never by choice fire more than four rounds in a minute. We would not throw away our fire, as must happen when the gun is not freshly aimed each time.

We count not the number of shots fired, but the number which take effect.'

Never having seen modern artillery in action, however, the Khivans had no idea of its terrible destructive power against mud-built fortifications or cavalry charges. Some of the Khan's ministers even seemed confident that they could turn back Perovsky's force when it approached the capital. Abbott pointed out that if the Russians, who had almost unlimited resources, failed to free the slaves at their first attempt, they would simply return with an even more powerful force which the Khivans, however bravely they fought, would have no hope of defeating. In that case, the Khan's chief minister replied, 'if we die fighting the infidels, we will pass straight to paradise.' For a moment Abbott was lost for an answer. Then he asked them: 'And your women? What kind of paradise will your wives and daughters find in the arms of Russian soldiers?' The ministers fell silent at that uncomfortable prospect. Abbott began to feel that he was making some progress towards convincing them that their only salvation lay in freeing the slaves, and allowing him to act as intermediary with the Russians. However, he still had a long way to go yet, and in the meantime he found himself subjected to an endless catechism by the inquisitive Khan and other court officials – questions all too familiar to British officers visiting Muslim lands. The idea of a woman ruler, for instance, never failed to cause amazement and amusement.

'Is your king really a woman?' he was asked.

'She is.'

'Is your king married?'

'No, she is very young.'

'If she marries, does her husband become king?'

'By no means. He has no authority in the state.'

'How many cities has your king?'

'They are too numerous to count.'

And so it went on. Were the King's ministers all women? Did the English always choose women kings? Was it true that they had telescopes which could see through the walls of a fortress? Was England as cold in winter as Khiva? Did they eat pork? Was it true that they had taken Balkh? Was Russia much larger than England? On this last question, with so much at stake, Abbott felt it necessary to elaborate. 'This very issue', he told them, 'was the subject of a bet between the English and Russian missions at Teheran, which, after the most careful investigation, was decided in favour of the English.' Queen Victoria, he went on, 'has absolutely more territory, about five times the number of subjects, and several times more revenue than Russia.' But in addition to her land empire, there was also the sea. A glance at the map, he said, would show them that the seas occupied three times as much of the earth's surface as the land, adding that 'wherever the ocean rolls, there my Queen has no rival.'

By now the Khivans had learned that General Perovsky's invasion force had been halted by the terrible weather on the steppe, although they did not yet appear to know that the Russians were struggling back to Orenburg. It was assumed in Khiva that once the weather had begun to improve they would continue their advance. After days of prevarication and discussion, Abbott was summoned once again to the Khan's presence. It had been decided, he was informed, to make use of his services. Accompanied by a number of Russian slaves – as a token of Khivan goodwill – he was to proceed, not to Perovsky's headquarters, but to St Petersburg where he would negotiate on the Khan's behalf the return of the rest of the slaves. These would be freed if the Tsar agreed to abandon all military operations against Khiva and to return the Khivan hostages held at Orenburg. Abbott would be given a letter from the Khan stating these terms which he was to deliver in person to Tsar Nicholas.

To undertake such a mission was greatly in excess of Abbott's instructions from Major Todd, which had simply been to try to persuade the Khan to release his Russian slaves in the hope of preventing Khiva from falling into Russian hands. Abbott had, it later transpired, already exceeded his authority by discussing with the Khan the possibility of a treaty between Great Britain and himself. To be fair, however, there was no way in which he could obtain further instructions or advice from his superiors. Apart from the vast distances involved, he soon discovered that his dispatches to Todd were being intercepted by the suspicious Khan. Abbott therefore decided to risk official displeasure, calculating that were he to succeed in permanently lifting the threat towards Khiva, rather as Eldred Pottinger had done over Herat, nothing more would be said. Moreover, to travel from Khiva to St Petersburg, through the heart of Great Game country, offered the prospect of a rare adventure.

Although Abbott appeared to have allayed earlier Khivan suspicions that he was a Russian spy, even now the Khan was taking no chances. To protect himself from being double-crossed, he was anxious to obtain a hostage in place of the departing Abbott. Under the guise of altruism he proposed a plan for rescuing Colonel Stoddart from the clutches of his neighbour, the Emir of Bokhara, with whom he was currently at odds. He claimed to have information that Stoddart was allowed out of his prison cell each day to take exercise. His plan was to dispatch a small force of horsemen to try to snatch the Englishman from under the noses of his guards. But not only was Abbott suspicious of the Khan's motives for wishing to rescue Stoddart, he was also doubtful about the accuracy of his information. While it was his dearest wish to see his fellow countryman freed, he strongly opposed the rescue attempt on the grounds that if the Emir got wind of it he would immediately put Stoddart to death. The idea was dropped, but still fearful of being tricked, the Khan and his ministers decided at the last minute to go back on their offer to allow a number of Russian slaves to accompany Abbott. So it was that on March 7, 1840, with a small escort of Khivans, Abbott set out across the desert for Fort Alexandrovsk, the nearest Russian post, 500 miles away on the Caspian Sea, from where he hoped to make his way to the Tsar's court at St Petersburg.

*　　*　　*

Meanwhile, having heard nothing whatsoever from Abbott since his arrival in Khiva, and even fearing that he might be dead, Major Todd decided to dispatch a second officer to find out what was happening there, and to try, where Abbott had seemingly failed, to persuade the Khan to release his Russian slaves. The man he chose was Lieutenant Richmond Shakespear, aged 28, an able and ambitious career political, and a cousin of the novelist Thackeray. Unlike the evangelically minded Conolly and Abbott, he was less concerned with introducing the benefits of Christian civilisation to Central Asia than with keeping the Russians out – not to mention advancing his own career. 'The chances of distinction are so great and the hazards so slight,' he wrote to his sister, 'that the heart of a wren would be gladdened by the prospect.'

Wearing native dress and accompanied by eleven carefully chosen Heratis, including seven armed troopers, Shakespear left for Khiva on May 15. Four days out of Herat the party met a rider from the north who told them a wild tale. Abbott, he assured them, had reached St Petersburg where he had not only succeeded in negotiating a Russian withdrawal, but had also persuaded the Tsar to demolish all his forts on the eastern shore of the Caspian. If this was true, then there was clearly little point in Shakespear proceeding any further. But he was not convinced, and anyway had no intention of abandoning such an adventure. 'I don't believe this,' he noted in his diary. 'At any rate, I shall go on to Khiva.' Certainly there was no sign of any let-up in the activities of the slave-raiders, for that same day they came upon a Turcoman caravan bearing fresh victims northwards to the market in Khiva. There were ten of them in all, he observed, 'two females and the rest boys – mere children'. Although Shakespear's own well-armed party outnumbered the Turcomans, he felt unable to intervene. Such a move, he explained afterwards, would have destroyed all hope of his mission succeeding, and thereby ending 'this most detestable traffic'. Furthermore, he added, 'had I turned the poor children loose, they would soon have been retaken.' Instead he confined himself to lecturing the astonished slavers on the abomination of their ways, while his own men showered curses and abuse on them.

After passing safely through the ancient caravan town of Merv, they entered the most perilous stretch of the desert, on the far side of which lay the Oxus. Even by daylight the trail was hard enough to follow, for wind and sand quickly covered up the tracks of previous caravans. The only clues were the bones of animals, and the occasional skull of a camel which some public-spirited traveller had stuck on a thorn bush beside the way. Yet even at night, in total darkness, their young guide was able to find the trail. 'It was pointed out to me,' Shakespear noted, 'and though I dismounted and tried hard to distinguish it, I failed.' During the day the heat was extremely severe, and they were haunted by the fear of failing to find each successive well. 'Had anything happened to the guide,' Shakespear observed, 'or had he been less intelligent, the destruction of the party would have been inevitable.'

Three days later they were through the worst of it, and before long found themselves on the banks of the Oxus. From there it was only a hundred or so miles to Khiva, which they entered on June 12. They had covered some 700 miles in a little under a month, a day or two faster than Abbott. In Khiva Shakespear learned of the misadventure which had befallen his brother officer after setting out on his long journey to St Petersburg. Betrayed by his guide, Abbott had been attacked in the desert by raiders. He himself had been wounded, robbed of all his possessions and taken captive, while his men were carried off for sale. By a miracle, however, a messenger sent after him by Todd, carrying money and letters, caught up with him. Finding that he was being held by men who were nominally subjects of the Khan of Khiva, the messenger warned them of the terrible consequences when word of their treachery reached the capital. Abbott's captors had become even more alarmed when they learned that he was carrying a personal letter from the Khan to the Tsar of Russia, fearing retribution from the latter as well. The Englishman was hurriedly released, with profuse apologies and excuses. His men were freed, and his horse, uniform and other possessions were restored to him.

Abbott now continued his journey to Alexandrovsk, a tiny military fort on the Caspian, where he hoped to get his wounds treated before proceeding to St Petersburg. However, wild tales that he was leading a 10,000-strong force against the post had preceded him, and at first he was refused entry. Once it was realised who he was, and that he was injured, the gates were immediately opened, and he was welcomed by the Russian commandant and his strikingly beautiful wife, who saw to it that his wounds were carefully treated. When he was fit enough to travel again, Abbott set off for Orenburg and from there, bearing his letter to the Tsar, for St Petersburg. But in distant Khiva, Shakespear had no way of knowing any of this, or even whether Abbott was still alive. One thing was certain though. Abbott had clearly failed to persuade the Khan to surrender any of his Russian slaves. Here lay the ambitious Shakespear's chance.

*   *   *

On the evening of his arrival in Khiva, Shakespear was summoned to the Khan's presence. 'His Highness received me very graciously,' he reported, and the two men appear to have hit it off from the start. Shakespear was favourably impressed by the Khan's lack of ostentation. 'There is no pomp or show about his Court, no guards whatever, and I did not see a jewel of any sort,' he wrote. The tall, extrovert Shakespear – a handsome, commanding figure, according to contemporary accounts – appears to have cut more of a dash with the Khan than the rather shy and earnest Abbott. Certainly the outcome of his visit seems to suggest this. In fact, Shakespear had not chosen a particularly auspicious moment to arrive and seek to persuade the Khan to free his Russian slaves. For by now the full magnitude of the Russian disaster in the snowfields to the north had reached the capital, and the Khivans were cock-a-hoop over what they claimed as a monumental victory. Privately, however, the Khan himself was less sure, being anxious about what the Russians might do next. Abbott's warning that, even if they failed at their first attempt, the Russians would return in immensely greater strength, clearly worried him, thus making Shakespear's task of persuasion that much easier.

In his subsequent account of his mission, Shakespear gives us few details of his negotiations with the Khan, or of the arguments he employed to achieve his purpose. What does emerge, however, was that, like Abbott, he greatly exceeded his authority by holding out the bait of a treaty between Britain and Khiva. It was neither the first nor the last time that players on either side in the Great Game took the name of their government in vain to win advantage over their adversaries. But whatever the inducements used by Shakespear to persuade the Khan, he gradually found him more and more receptive to the argument that the best way to protect himself from Russian wrath would be by surrendering all his slaves. Finally, on August 3, Shakespear was able to record in triumph in his diary: 'The Khan ... has made over to me all the Russian prisoners, and I am to take them to a Russian fort on the eastern shore of the Caspian.'

He at once set up his headquarters in a garden outside the capital, lent him for the purpose by the Khan, where the slaves were brought to him for documentation as Khivan officials rounded them up. By the following day he had counted more than 300 males, 18 females and 11 children. On average, he discovered, the men had been in bondage for ten years, and the women for seventeen. 'With one exception,' he observed, 'they were all in fine health.' Most of the men had been seized while fishing in the Caspian, while the women had been taken from around Orenburg. 'They all seemed poor people, very grateful, and altogether it was one of the pleasantest duties I have ever executed,' Shakespear noted that evening. But his problems were far from over yet. Despite the Khan's edict that all Russian slaves were to be surrendered to him, there was a marked reluctance to comply with this among those who had paid a high price for their bondsmen. A sturdy male slave, after all, changed hands for £20 or more – the equivalent of four thoroughbred camels, Shakespear recounts. Word began to reach him via those who had been freed that a number of their countrymen were still being detained.

One such case, involving two young children, was brought to his attention by their desperate mother, who herself had just been liberated. It transpired that the two children, a 9-year-old girl and her younger brother, were in the service of a powerful lady at the Khan's court, who was determined to keep them. After much negotiation she was induced to free the boy, but insisted on keeping the girl. On hearing this the distraught mother told Shakespear that rather than leave without her child she would prefer to stay behind in bondage. 'She then taunted me', he wrote, 'with the promise I had made to obtain the child's release.' This was too much for him, and ordering his horse he rode to the Khan's palace. There the chief minister was anxious to know the reason for this sudden and unannounced visit, but Shakespear thought it wise 'to lead him astray on this point'. He was painfully aware that his request for this one child's release might put the entire operation at risk. It was imperative therefore that he spoke to the Khan in person, rather than through an intermediary, on so sensitive an issue.

On being ushered into the Khan's presence, Shakespear asked that the girl be allowed to go with her mother. The Khan assured him that she had no wish to leave her comfortable home in the palace, but Shakespear insisted that she was too young to know her own mind. The Khan remained undecided for a moment. Then he turned to the chief minister and ordered rather crossly: 'Give him the child.' Shortly afterwards she was produced and handed over to Shakespear. 'I have seldom seen a more beautiful child,' he wrote that night in his diary. It seemed clear that she was intended for the Khan's own harem. When she set eyes on Shakespear, who was in native dress, she at once mistook him for a slave-trader and began to scream. Nothing, she swore, would make her go with him. But fortunately Shakespear had with him a man she knew and trusted, and finally she was persuaded to accompany him, being lifted up behind him on his saddle. The following morning both children were brought to Shakespear by their grateful mother to thank him.

Even now, however, the party was not complete. Twenty or so Russians had still to be handed over, and once again Shakespear had to protest to the Khan that his edict was being defied. Showing him the list of those whom he knew to be detained, he argued that unless he could take all the Russians with him he would have to call the whole thing off. So long as any of the Tsar's subjects remained in Khivan hands, he pointed out, the Russians would have a pretext for invading their territory. 'His Majesty was astounded at my plain speaking,' Shakespear recounts, 'and gave his minister an order in a tone which made him shake.' Anyone found detaining a Russian slave, he declared, would be put to death. The next day seventeen more Russians were handed over, some still in chains. This now left only four unaccounted for, and finally just one. The headman of the village in which the latter dwelt came to Shakespear and swore on the Koran that the missing man was dead. But his father, also a slave, insisted that he was still alive and being held against his will. In the end, after a thorough search of the village, the Russian was found hidden in a vault beneath the granary.

On August 15, two months after Shakespear's arrival at Khiva, the party was ready to leave on its 500-mile march across the desert to Fort Alexandrovsk on the Caspian. In addition to the freed slaves – 416 of them in all – Shakespear was to be accompanied by an armed escort provided by the Khan. Although the latter had decreed that from now on the seizing of Russians would be punishable by death, Shakespear had no wish to see the slaves merely fall into the hands of the lawless Turcomans once again. The close shave of Abbott and his party a few months earlier on this very same route was a reminder of the need for both armed protection and extreme vigilance.

As it set out from Khiva the caravan must have presented an extraordinary spectacle. 'The plain was so open', wrote Shakespear, 'that the camels crowded together and marched *en masse*, the children and women riding on panniers, singing and laughing, and the men trudging along sturdily – all counting the few days which remained ere they should rejoin their countrymen.' Shakespear must have been feeling understandably pleased with himself, for he had achieved single-handed what a heavily armed Russian force had so abysmally and humiliatingly failed to do. His boldness and directness in dealing with the all-powerful Khan, risky though this was, had enabled him to succeed where Abbott too had failed. 'The release of these poor wretches has surprised the Turcomans amazingly,' he observed, 'and I humbly hope that it is the dawn of a new era in the history of this nation, and that ultimately the British name will be blessed with the proud distinction of having put an end to this inhuman traffic, and of having civilised the Turcoman race, which has for centuries been the scourge of Central Asia.' He appears to have forgotten, however, as the Khan clearly had not, that the Khivans still retained their far more numerous, if less valuable, Persian slaves.

As the caravan approached the Russian fortress at Alexandrovsk, Shakespear sent ahead one of the ex-slaves, bearing a letter in English from himself, to alert the commandant. At first the messenger was received with the gravest suspicion by his fellow-countrymen inside the fort, just as Abbott had been, for they clearly feared a trap. They had difficulty, too, in understanding Shakespear's letter, while news of the freeing by the Khan of all his Russian slaves was, the British officer noted, 'too astounding to be credited'. It took the Russian garrison a whole night to overcome their suspicions. This fear of treachery, however, was not confined to the Russians. When the party got to within six miles of the fortress, the Khivan escort and camelmen refused to advance any further lest they be taken captive by the Russian troops. They pointed out that in accompanying the caravan so far they had already exceeded the Khan's instructions. But it was still too far for some of the smaller children to walk, and many of the adults had possessions which they were unable to manage by themselves. Finally the nervous camelmen agreed to provide twenty animals for the final leg of the journey, while they waited at a safe distance for their return.

So it was that the slaves reached Alexandrovsk, and liberty at last. Their reception, Shakespear observed, would have made a most memorable painting. 'The worthy commandant', he wrote, 'was overpowered with gratitude.' He even gave Shakespear an official receipt for the rescued slaves, on which he scrawled: 'They expressed themselves unanimously grateful to you as their Father and Benefactor.' That night, writing to his sister to break the news to her, Shakespear declared triumphantly that 'not a horse nor even a camel has been lost'. The following evening the Russians laid on a banquet in his honour at which they drank to the health of Queen Victoria and Tsar Nicholas, as well as to that of their English guest.

Shakespear's own men were much alarmed at the ceremonial firing of guns and the cheering, not to mention the consumption of alcohol. Indeed, all devout Muslims, they were horrified by some of the infidel customs which they encountered for the first time at Alexandrovsk.

On the day after their arrival one of them came rushing to Shakespear in distress. He had just seen the Russian soldiers feeding their pet dogs – unclean creatures to Muslims – and thought that they were being fattened for eating. 'There was a woman there too,' he told Shakespear, 'whose face and neck was uncovered.' Worse still, he went on, her legs were bare, 'and I saw up to her knee!' He and his companions had also peered into the garrison chapel. 'They worship idols,' he exclaimed. 'I saw it. All of us saw it.' Muttering 'Repentance ... Repentance', he begged to be allowed to depart without further delay with the dispatches he was to carry back to Todd at Herat. The following day, amid vows of undying friendship, they set out on their long homeward journey. 'Never had a man better servants,' wrote Shakespear in his diary.

By now three vessels had been found to take Shakespear and his charges further up the coast, from where they continued overland to Orenburg. There, having shaved off his beard and exchanged native dress for European clothes, Shakespear was warmly received by General Perovsky, who thanked him profusely and immediately ordered the release of the 600 Khivans being held at Orenburg and Astrakhan. Not a man to overlook such an opportunity, Shakespear kept his eyes open for any signs of a second Russian expedition being mounted against Khiva. He was relieved to see none, although his hosts were careful to ensure that he observed as little of military value as possible while he was at Orenburg. On November 3, 1840, six months after setting out on his mission from Herat, Shakespear arrived in St Petersburg *en route* for London. There he was officially welcomed by Tsar Nicholas who formally thanked him for rescuing, at grave risk to his own life, so many Russian subjects from their heathen captors. It was no secret in court circles, however, that privately the Tsar was infuriated by the young British officer's unsolicited but now widely publicised act. For just as Shakespear's superiors had hoped, it effectively removed any excuse which St Petersburg might have had for advancing again on Khiva, seen by many strategists, both British and Russian, as one of the principal stepping-stones leading to India.

*   *   *

It is not surprising that Russian historians, whether Tsarist or Soviet, have ignored the role of Abbott and Shakespear in the freeing of the Khivan slaves. Their liberation by the Khan is attributed solely to his growing fear of Russian military strength, and the fright he received on learning of the first expedition launched against him. Russian historians, however, have had plenty to say about Abbott and Shakespear. Both, they claim, were British spies, sent into Central Asia as part of a grand design for paramountcy there at the expense of Russia, whose influence they aimed to destroy. The Afghan city of Herat, according to N. A. Khalfin, a leading Soviet authority on the Great Game era, was at that time 'a nest of British agents'. It served as the controlling point, he argues, for 'a wide network of British military-political sources of intelligence, and a system of communication for British agents.' There was, of course, an element of truth in this, although he credits the British with being far better organised in Central Asia than they really were. Indeed, Macnaghten, Burnes, Todd and other politicals would have been surprised, not to say flattered, by this Russian view of their omniscience.

Like Abbott before him, Khalfin claims, Shakespear was sent to Khiva to reconnoitre routes and fortresses along the Russian frontier between Alexandrovsk and Orenburg. 'As an excuse for entering Russia from Khiva,' he declares, 'Shakespear put forward the "necessity" of accompanying the Russian slaves. Taking advantage of the fact that the Khivan government was obliged by Russian pressure to free these prisoners, Shakespear travelled with them, passing himself off as their liberator.' In order to be allowed to proceed to Orenburg – 'the terminal point of his mission' – he represented himself, like Abbott before him, as a mediator between the Khivans and the Russians. Aware that both officers were really there as spies, General Perovsky had them placed under strict surveillance until they were safely out of the country.

Khalfin further alleges that the British even had a spy network in Orenburg itself. This was centred, he tells us, on the mission station there of the British and Foreign Bible Society, which had changed its name in 1814 to the Russian Bible Society. Its purpose, he quotes an earlier historian as having discovered, was to engage in espionage and to establish relations with Khiva and Bokhara, if possible turning them against Russia. Shakespear, Khalfin claims, had orders to make contact with the missionaries of this station. In fact, he adds, what neither Shakespear nor his superiors appeared to realise was that the mission had already been closed down by the authorities. He concludes, however, that possibly 'some remnants of the Society remained, and that it was these whom Shakespear was to enlist in subversive activities in Orenburg.' Needless to say, neither Shakespear nor Abbott make any mention of the mission in their own narratives.

Khalfin's claims are largely based on a cache of faded letters and other papers said to have been seized from the Turcomans in 1873, and to be found today in the Soviet Military Archives (file no. 6996). The letters, written between 1831 and 1838, together with the other papers, are believed by Khalfin to have belonged to Lieutenant Shakespear (although nowhere do they bear his name) which he somehow lost during his visit to Khiva. But as Colonel Geoffrey Wheeler, the British scholar who first reported Khalfin's allegations in the *Central Asian Review* in 1958, points out: 'It is difficult to believe that any responsible person would proceed on an allegedly secret mission to Central Asia carrying with him a collection of confidential letters, the latest of which had been written two years previously.'

The letters, which are unsigned and appear only to be copies, deal mainly with British policy – or naked ambition, as Khalfin sees it – in Central Asia. However, it is from the papers found with them, some of which bear the words 'secret and confidential', that the Russian scholar largely makes his deductions about the real purpose of Shakespear's and Abbott's missions. His article, which appeared in the Soviet journal *Istoriya*

SSSR, 1958, No. 2, includes no facsimiles of these documents, and therefore, as Wheeler points out, cannot be verified. Nor, without access to the originals in the Soviet Military Archives, can the accuracy of the quotations, or Khalfin's selection or use of them, be checked. If the papers and letters are what he claims, regardless of his interpretation of them, it is possible that they belonged to Abbott rather than Shakespear, and that they were taken from the former when he was attacked and robbed on his way to Alexandrovsk.

But whatever the Russians may have felt (and, apparently, still do feel) about Shakespear, his superiors were delighted by the way he had so skilfully spiked the Tsar's guns by liberating his subjects. On his return to London he was to receive a wild and enthusiastic welcome reminiscent of that accorded to Alexander Burnes eight years earlier. Although still in his twenties, he was knighted and promoted by a jubilant Queen Victoria, who, only 21 herself, was already showing signs of Russophobia. As for the modest Abbott, who had paved the way for Shakespear's feat, he was to receive scant recognition. His rewards were to come much later in his career, though. Not only was he knighted and made a general, but a garrison town – Abbottabad, today in northern Pakistan – was named after him.

All that lay far in the future, however. Both Shakespear and Abbott were now eager to get back to India, for during their long absence things had begun to go seriously wrong for the British in Central Asia.

·18·

Night of the
Long Knives

If the British had succeeded in liberating the Tsar's subjects from bondage in Khiva, they had failed miserably in their efforts to free their own man from the clutches of the Emir of Bokhara. All their attempts, not to mention those of the Russians, the Turks and the rulers of Khiva and Khokand, to persuade Emir Nasrullah to let Colonel Charles Stoddart go had so far proved futile. By now this unfortunate officer had been held captive for the best part of two years. His day-to-day fortunes were seemingly determined by Nasrullah's capricious moods, and by his current estimate of British power in Asia. Thus, when news of Kabul's capitulation to the British reached him, Colonel Stoddart's situation suddenly improved. Until then he had been kept at the bottom of a twenty-foot-deep pit, known locally as the 'Black Hole', which he shared with three common criminals and an assortment of vermin and other unpleasant creatures, and to which a rope was the sole means of access.

He was now hastily removed from here and instead placed under close house arrest in the home of the Emir's chief of police. But his misfortunes were far from over, for the Emir showed no signs of allowing him to leave Bokhara. Quite why he was held in the first place is not absolutely clear, although there are several possible explanations. Inevitably, in a region where treachery was the norm, a rumour had preceded him warning that he was not an emissary at all but a British spy sent to prepare the way for the seizure of the Emir's domains.

If so, he had already seen too much to be allowed to return home. But there was another reason for his having incurred Nasrullah's displeasure. On first arriving in Bokhara, on December 17, 1838, Stoddart had committed an extremely unfortunate gaffe. To the astonishment of the populace, he had ridden in full regimentals to the Emir's palace to present his credentials, instead of respectfully dismounting, as was customary in Bokhara.

By ill chance, Nasrullah happened to be returning at that moment to his palace, and saw the colonel and his servants from across the city's main square. Remaining in his saddle, in conformity with British military practice, Stoddart had saluted the Bokharan sovereign. Nasrullah, according to one source, 'looked at him fixedly for some time, and then passed on without saying a word'. At Stoddart's first audience with the Emir there had followed other misunderstandings, and in consequence he had found himself swiftly consigned to the rat-infested dungeon.

Some have blamed Stoddart himself for what happened, accusing him of arrogance and insensitivity, though this hardly justifies Nasrullah's treatment of him. Unlike Burnes, the Pottingers and Rawlinson, Stoddart was unschooled in the sycophantic ways of oriental diplomacy. As a brother officer put it: 'Stoddart was a mere soldier, a man of the greatest bravery and determination. To attack or defend a fortress, no better man could have been found. But for a diplomatic mission a man less adapted to the purpose could not readily have been met with.' Indeed, much of the responsibility for his fate rests with those who chose him for this most delicate mission, notably Sir John McNeill in Teheran, himself a veteran of the game, and well versed in the strict etiquette of the East.

Although no longer subjected to the horrors of the Emir's 'Black Hole', and enjoying the comparative comfort of house arrest, Stoddart had little reason to feel sanguine. His only hope, he realised, of being allowed to leave Bokhara lay in the advance of a British rescue expedition from Kabul. We know this from notes he managed to smuggle out to his family, which amazingly found their way to England. 'My release', he wrote in one of these, 'will probably not take place until our forces have approached very near to Bokhara.' But as the months passed, with no sign of a rescue operation, he must frequently have despaired. Only once, however, did his courage fail him. That was during his spell in the pit, when the official executioner had descended the rope with orders from the Emir to behead him there and then unless he embraced Islam. Stoddart had agreed, thereby saving his life, although when he was released from the pit into the custody of the chief of police he insisted that his conversion was invalid, having been made under extreme duress.

More than once the Emir had shown signs of wishing to come to an accommodation with the British against the Russians, and had even corresponded with Macnaghten in Kabul about it, thereby raising Stoddart's hopes. But on learning of the disaster which had befallen the Russians on their way to Khiva, he had lost interest. He complained that the British notes appeared to have no *mutlub* (meaning), and in the end nothing came of them. When it became clear, moreover, that the British were not proposing to dispatch an expedition to Bokhara to try to free Stoddart, the colonel's fortunes again took a turn for the worse. Twice he was thrown into prison, though not this time into the dreaded pit. Despite his deteriorating health, in his occasional letter home Stoddart continued to put a brave face on things. Eventually, he maintained, Nasrullah might come to realise that the British were his best protection against the Russians, who sooner or later would turn their attention to him. By being on the spot, Stoddart argued, he would be in a position to discuss terms, and perhaps even persuade the Emir to free his slaves, as he had heard that Shakespear had succeeded in doing in Khiva.

All this time the authorities in London and Calcutta had been wrestling with the problem of how to free their envoy from this monster's grip. Originally Macnaghten had been in favour of sending a punitive force to Bokhara from Kabul, but Lord Auckland, the Governor-General, was opposed to British troops venturing any further into Central Asia. Moreover, antagonism towards the British, and their puppet ruler Shah Shujah, was beginning to grow in Afghanistan, and Macnaghten needed all the troops he had to contain possible trouble there. Nor was the Cabinet in London anxious to embark on any fresh adventures in Asia, already having enough on its hands there and elsewhere. In addition to its heavy commitment in Afghanistan, in China the first of the Opium Wars was well into its second year, while nearer to home there were serious troubles brewing with both France and the United States. The plight of a comparatively junior British officer in a remote town in Central Asia did not figure high on Palmerston's list of priorities, although diplomatic efforts to secure his release continued through the good offices of the Turks and others, albeit unavailingly.

Stoddart's friends protested that he had been callously abandoned by the British government to the caprices of an evil tyrant. Reports that he had been forced to renounce Christianity and embrace Islam caused particular outrage. But their demands for action went unheeded, and as the winter of 1841 – Stoddart's third as Nasrullah's prisoner – approached, his prospects looked bleak indeed. Then, in November of that year, something happened which was to bring him fresh hope. For there rode into Bokhara, on a one-man rescue mission, a fellow British officer and veteran of the Great Game, Captain Arthur Conolly.

* * *

Conolly had been travelling in Central Asia on official government business. It had long been his dream to reconcile and unite, under British protection, the three quarrelling khanates of Turkestan – Khiva, Bokhara and Khokand. Such an arrangement, he was convinced, would not only bring Christian civilisation to this barbaric region, but would also serve, together with a friendly Afghanistan, as a protective shield for northern India against Russian encroachments. The total abolition of slavery throughout Turkestan would remove any remaining pretexts for interference by St Petersburg. It seemed, on the face of it, an attractive idea, and Conolly found no shortage of backers, especially in London where few people had any real grasp of Central Asian politics. Members of the Board of

Control were particularly attracted to his ideas for opening up the waters of the Oxus to steam navigation. Not only would the natives have the benefits of Christianity bestowed upon them, but they would also be able to buy British goods in their bazaars.

There were others, however, who strongly opposed Conolly's grandiose scheme. Among them was Sir Alexander Burnes. From his own experience of dealing with Asian potentates, he saw little prospect of Conolly bringing about any kind of alliance between these three disputatious neighbours. And even if he were to succeed, Burnes asked, 'is England to become security for barbarous hordes some thousands of miles from her frontier?' Ultimately, Burnes insisted, Russia could only be restrained in Central Asia through London putting strong pressure on St Petersburg, and not by means of vague alliances with capricious and treacherous khans. For although Burnes belonged to the forward school, he was less of a hawk than many imagined, and considered the British presence in Afghanistan quite forward enough.

Conolly, however, was a man not easily deterred. Using his considerable powers of persuasion, he gradually overcame all opposition. At first the Governor-General, Lord Auckland, had been hesitant about letting him go, believing that the Khivan disaster had removed any immediate Russian threat in the region. He therefore saw no point in getting unnecessarily involved there, or in needlessly provoking St Petersburg into retaliatory action. However, in the face of powerful pressure from London, and from Macnaghten in Kabul, he finally agreed to the venture, though with one important proviso. Conolly was to urge the three khans to resolve their ancient differences and to unite against the Russians. He was to try to persuade them of the urgent need to abolish slavery and introduce other humanitarian reforms in order to remove any pretext for a Russian attack on them. But under no circumstances was he to offer them British protection or assistance against the Russians.

He left Kabul for Khiva on September 3, 1840, with a considerably reduced brief, but intent nonetheless on changing the course of Central Asian history. He was to have been accompanied by Henry Rawlinson, but at the last moment the latter was required elsewhere in Afghanistan, which, as it turned out, proved fortunate for him. Conolly's journey to Khiva was uneventful, and he was well received by the Khan, who held the British in high regard following the visits of Abbott and Shakespear. But Conolly's visionary proposals for a voluntary Central Asian federation, and far-reaching social reforms, found no favour with him. The Khan clearly had no wish for any sort of an alliance with either Bokhara or Khokand. He seemed, moreover, to have lost his earlier fears of the Russians sending another invasion force against him now that he had freed their slaves. Disappointed, Conolly proceeded to Khokand, where he was also well received. But here too he failed to interest the Khan in an alliance with either of his neighbours. Indeed, at that very moment, the Khan was about to go to war with the Emir of Bokhara.

So far, as Burnes and others had warned, Conolly had achieved nothing beyond gathering useful intelligence on the latest political situation in Central Asia. Only one hope now remained of justifying his mission, and that was to secure the release of the unfortunate Stoddart. During his two-month stay in Khokand, Conolly had somehow managed to make contact with Stoddart, who was enjoying one of his spells of relative freedom. The latter sent him a message to say that the Emir would not be averse to his visiting Bokhara. 'The favour of the Ameer', he informed Conolly, 'is increased in these days towards me. I believe you will be well treated here.' They were fateful words. Little did Stoddart realise that he was being used by the wily Nasrullah to lure his fellow officer into a trap. For the Emir, whose spies had been following Conolly's movements, was convinced that the Englishman was conspiring with his enemies, the khans of Khiva and Khokand, to have him overthrown.

In October 1841, despite warnings from both khans to keep well clear of Bokhara, Conolly set out for the holy city, 400 miles away to the south-west, convinced that he could use his formidable powers of persuasion on the Emir to obtain Stoddart's freedom. It was a foolhardy venture, but Conolly, like most Great Game players, was not lacking in boldness or physical courage. There is another factor, impossible to ignore, which may have affected his judgement and led him to take an excessive risk. A few months before setting out on his journey, Conolly had been turned down for a rival by the woman he had dearly hoped to marry. He had been profoundly hurt by this, and it is possible that as a result he did not care too much whether he returned from his mission or not. Whatever the truth, he entered Bokhara on November 10, travelling via Tashkent so as to avoid being caught up in the war about to break out between the Emir and his neighbour.

Stoddart, pathetically thin after his months of privation, was overwhelmed at seeing Conolly. At first the Emir received the newcomer politely, but soon his mood began to change. This was apparently due to his failure to receive a reply to a friendly letter he had dispatched months earlier to Queen Victoria. This lapse he interpreted either as an intended slight, which caused him to lose face before his court officials, or as evidence that Stoddart and Conolly, who claimed to represent the Queen, were impostors and therefore, as he had suspected all along, spies. Neither was his mood improved when finally there arrived from Lord Palmerston (of whom he had naturally never heard) a note advising him that his letter had been passed to Calcutta for attention. To Nasrullah, who was under the firm belief that his kingdom was every bit as powerful as Great Britain, this appeared to be a deliberate snub. Had Stoddart and Conolly known that a second note, this time from the Governor-General, would soon be on its way, their sense of betrayal and abandonment by their superiors would have been complete. For this described them, inexplicably, not as British envoys but as 'private travellers', and demanded their immediate release. But when it eventually reached Nasrullah it was far too late to cause them any further harm. What finally sealed their fate was news reaching Bokhara from Kabul of a catastrophe which had befallen the British in Afghanistan.

*　　　*　　　*

Animosity towards the British in Shah Shujah's newly restored capital had been building up for months, although they themselves had been slow to recognise it. As experienced political officers, Sir William Macnaghten and Sir Alexander Burnes should have been aware of what was going on in Afghan hearts and minds, but relations between the two men had become badly strained. Burnes was to describe himself in a letter to a friend as 'a highly paid idler', whose advice was never listened to by his chief. Macnaghten, moreover, had largely lost interest in his present task, for he was shortly due to leave Afghanistan to take up the much-coveted Governorship of Bombay, his reward for successfully placing the British puppet on the throne. The last thing he wished to admit was that anything was amiss. Burnes, waiting to take over from him, and in the meantime having little to do, was too busy enjoying himself to notice the warning signs.

He was not alone in this. Ever since their arrival in Kabul two years earlier, the British had been making themselves thoroughly at home there. Kabul's exotic situation and invigorating climate had attracted the wives, and even the children, of British and Indian troops up from the hot and dusty plains of Hindustan. Every kind of entertainment was laid on, from cricket to concerts, steeplechasing to skating, with some of the Afghan upper classes joining in the fun. Much of what went on, particularly the womanising and drinking, was to cause great offence to the Muslim authorities and the devout majority. At the same time punitive action, often very severe, was taken against those tribes refusing to submit to Shujah's (but effectively Macnaghten's) rule, while others were bribed into submission with lavish helpings of gold, or 'subsidies' as they were officially termed. On November 3, 1840, realising that further resistance to the British was futile, Dost Mohammed had voluntarily surrendered to Macnaghten, and had been sent into exile in India. This had moved Macnaghten, impatient to begin his new job in Bombay, to report to Lord Auckland that Afghanistan – to use his own now celebrated phrase – was quiet 'from Dan to Beersheba'. All things considered, he remarked to one of his staff, 'the present tranquillity of this country is to my mind perfectly miraculous'.

Not everyone, however, was as easily persuaded as Macnaghten. Among the first to realise the mounting danger was Major Henry Rawlinson, who had very nearly accompanied Conolly to Bokhara, and who was now the political agent at Kandahar. 'The feeling against us', he warned in August 1841, 'is daily on the increase and I apprehend a succession of disturbances ... Their mullahs are preaching against us from one end of the country to the other.' Another of Macnaghten's politicals to sense this growing hostility was Eldred Pottinger, now a major and operating among the tribes to the north of Kabul. Their leaders, he reported, were preparing for a general uprising against Shah Shujah and the British. But Macnaghten, fearful lest Lord Auckland order him to stay on in Kabul, refused to listen to such forebodings. Both men, he persuaded himself, were merely being alarmist.

There were plenty of reasons for this antagonism towards the British and Shah Shujah. For one thing the presence of so many troops had hit the pockets of ordinary Afghans. Because of the increased demand for foodstuffs and other essentials, prices in the bazaar had soared, while taxes had risen sharply to pay for Shujah's new administration, not to mention his lavish personal lifestyle. Moreover, the British showed no signs of leaving, despite earlier assurances. It looked more and more as though the occupation would be permanent, as indeed some of the British were beginning to think it would have to be if Shujah was to survive. Then there was the growing anger, especially in Kabul, over the pursuit and seduction of local women by the troops, particularly the officers. Some Afghan women even left their husbands to move in with wealthier and more generous lovers, while there was a regular traffic in women to the cantonments. Strong protests were made, but these were ignored. Murderous feelings towards the British possessed those who had been cuckolded – some of them men of considerable influence. 'The Afghans', Sir John Kaye, the historian, was to write, 'are very jealous of the honour of their women, and there were things done in Caubul which covered them with shame and roused them to revenge ... It went on until it became intolerable, and the injured then began to see that the only remedy was in their own hands.' Nor did they have to wait for very long. All that was needed now was for someone to light the fuse.

*   *   *

The first signs of the coming explosion occurred on the evening of November 1, 1841, when Burnes was warned by his Kashmiri assistant and friend, the well-informed Mohan Lal, that an attempt was to be made on his life that night. It was Burnes whom many Afghans held responsible for bringing the British to Afghanistan, after first spying out the land under the pretence of friendship with Dost Mohammed. His blatant fraternisation with their womenfolk only served to deepen their hostility towards him. Burnes and several other officers were then living in a large and somewhat isolated house surrounded by a wall and courtyard in the heart of the old city. Because of its vulnerability to attack, he was urged by Mohan Lal to move to the safety of the cantonments, to the north of the city, where the British and Indian troops were quartered. Originally they had occupied the Bala Hissar fortress, but at the request of Shah Shujah, who wanted it to house his own troops and large household staff, Macnaghten had agreed to move the entire British force out of its walled security into hurriedly constructed cantonments. Confident that he could quell any trouble, Burnes eschewed his friend's advice. He knew, moreover, that the British and Indian troops were less than two miles away. Nonetheless, he did ask for the sepoy guard on the house to be reinforced that night.

Meanwhile, not far away in the darkness, a mob was gathering. It was led by men of whom Burnes had made personal enemies. At first it consisted of only a handful of demonstrators, but the conspirators let it be known that the house next door to Burnes's was the garrison treasury, in which was kept the soldiers' pay and the gold used by Macnaghten for buying allies. In no time the numbers had swelled, and the crowd needed little urging to march on the infidels' residence and surround it. At this point Burnes was still confident that he could talk the Afghans into dispersing, and he ordered his sepoy guards not to fire. As a precaution, however, he sent a runner to the cantonments to ask for immediate assistance. Then he went out on to the balcony and began trying to reason with the angry crowd in the street below.

When word of the danger facing Burnes and his companions reached Macnaghten, he immediately summoned his military advisers, and urgent discussions began as to how they should react. This soon developed into an argument between Macnaghten and the officer in command of his troops, General William Elphinstone. Macnaghten's secretary, Captain George Lawrence, suggested dispatching a regiment of troops at the double to the old city to rescue Burnes, disperse the mob and seize the ringleaders while there was still time. But this was rejected out of hand. 'My proposal was at once set down as one of pure insanity,' wrote Lawrence afterwards. Macnaghten and Elphinstone continued to argue, while reports started to come in that the situation at Burnes's house was rapidly deteriorating. The general, a sick and ageing man who should never have been in command of the troops, lacked the will or energy to take action, and could only come up with objections to the suggestions of others. Macnaghten was equally indecisive, being less concerned about rescuing Burnes than about the political consequences of using troops against the mob. Finally, however, it was agreed to send troops under a brigadier up to the Bala Hissar, and to decide there, in consultation with Shah Shujah, how best to deal with the demonstrators. There they learned that Shujah had already sent some of his own men into the city to try to disperse the rioters and rescue Burnes. Insisting that they were sufficient for the purpose, he refused to allow the British force to follow.

Meanwhile the plight of Burnes had become critical as he tried in vain to make himself heard by the screaming mob below. With him were two other officers – his young brother Charles, an Indian Army subaltern who had come up to stay with him in Kabul, and Major William Broadfoot, his political assistant. Sir John Kaye was to write afterwards: 'It was obvious now that nothing was to be done by expostulation – nothing by forbearance. The violence of the mob was increasing. That which at first had been an insignificant crowd had now become a great multitude. The treasury of the Shah's paymasters was before them, and hundreds who had no wrongs, and no political animosity to vent, rushed to the spot hungering after the spoil which lay so temptingly at hand.' Yet despite the increasing fury of the mob, Burnes continued to order his sepoys to hold their fire, in the belief that help must very soon arrive.

By now some of the bolder demonstrators had entered the compound and succeeded in setting fire to the stables. They next turned their attention to the house. Then came a single shot from the crowd. Major Broadfoot, standing beside Burnes and his brother on the balcony, clutched at his chest and fell. Hastily his two companions dragged him inside, only to find that he was dead. Burnes returned to the balcony in a last attempt to save the situation, shouting down to the mob that he would give them large sums of money if they would disperse. The demonstrators knew, however, that they had no need to bargain. The British gold would very soon be theirs anyway. Realising that no relief was coming, Burnes at last ordered the sepoys to fire on the mob. But, like everything else that had happened so far, it was too late. By now the house itself was ablaze, and the crowd was rampaging across the compound, ignoring the bullets and making for the entrance. It was clear to Burnes and his brother that their last moment had come. Charles decided to fight his way out through the mob.

Watching in horror from a nearby rooftop, but powerless to do anything, was Mohan Lal, whose warning Burnes had ignored. 'Lieutenant Charles Burnes', he wrote afterwards, 'then came out into the garden and killed about six persons before he was cut to pieces.' Sir Alexander Burnes's own death he did not witness, for some of the mob then turned towards the house on whose roof he was hiding, forcing him to flee. But he was told later by the servants that when Burnes finally emerged to face the mob he had tied a black cloth over his eyes so as not to see from where the blows came. Seconds later he was dead, wrote Burnes's friend, 'cut to pieces by the furious mob'. Inevitably, without reliable eye-witnesses, there are several versions of Burnes's death. According to one of these, a traitor managed to gain access to the house and, under Koranic oath, persuade Burnes that if he disguised himself in native dress he personally would lead him to safety through the crowd. Realising that he had nothing to lose, Burnes agreed. But the moment he stepped out of the house, the man denounced him to the mob. 'This', he screamed in triumph, 'is Alexander Burnes.' A frenzied mullah then struck the first blow, and moments later Burnes was on the ground, being hacked to death by the long murderous knives of the Afghans.

Another version maintains that Burnes's servants offered to carry him through the crowd wrapped up in a tent, as though they were bearing plunder, like so many others that night, but that he had refused. Whatever the truth about his last moments in this city he had once so loved, it appears that one of his old Afghan friends remained loyal to him to the last. According to Kaye, after the mob had moved on to plunder the treasury, a man named Naib Sheriff retrieved his badly mutilated body, together with that of his brother, and buried them both in the garden of the smoke-blackened residence. Major Broadfoot, Kaye records, was less fortunate, for 'the dogs of the city devoured his remains'.

All this had been allowed to happen just half an hour's march from where 4,500 British and Indian troops were quartered, and rather less from the Bala Hissar, where the British-led rescue party was standing by, awaiting orders. For reasons which are unclear, although the clamour and the firing could be heard quite distinctly from the cantonments, those orders were never given. Indeed, in the end the rescue party was employed, not to save Burnes and his companions, but to cover the inglorious retreat of Shujah's irregulars, of whom the angry mob had made short work. Yet seldom could a tragedy have been so easily averted. As one young officer noted in his journal: 'When 300 men would have been sufficient in the morning to have quelled the disturbance, 3,000 would not have been adequate in the afternoon.'

But it was far from over yet. Worse – much worse – was to follow.

·19·

Catastrophe

News of the appalling fate which had befallen Sir Alexander Burnes and his two companions, not to mention some thirty sepoy guards and servants, sent a wave of horror through the British garrison. At first it was rumoured that Burnes had managed to escape, and was lying low somewhere, but any such hopes were soon dashed. The mob, meanwhile, emboldened by the failure of the British to act, continued on its rampage, burning homes, looting shops and slaughtering anyone suspected of collaboration with the British. Now and again, above the tumult and the roaring flames, could be heard warning cries of 'They are coming ... they are coming', for the rioters were expecting swift and violent retribution. Indeed, so that they could make a quick get-away, the ringleaders, it was learned later, had their horses already saddled up. But in the cantonments Macnaghten and Elphinstone continued to vacillate and agonise, wasting even more precious time. And this despite reports that several other officers, as well as Mohan Lal, were still hiding out in the old city, hoping to escape the mob's vengeance.

By now it had become clear to everyone, even to Macnaghten, that this was something far more serious than a rabble out of control. Word was coming in that thousands of Afghans were joining the cause by the hour, and that similar disturbances were taking place in the surrounding countryside. Rumours also reached British ears claiming that Shah Shujah himself had called for a holy war against the British. Letters to this effect, bearing his personal seal, were discovered in circulation. For a while it was feared that these might be genuine, and that Shujah had been playing a double game with those who had restored him to his throne. But, on examination, the letters proved to be forgeries and the rumours to be false, deliberately spread by the conspirators. Indeed, it was clear that Shujah's own position was no less precarious than that of his sponsors. He, to be fair, was the only one who had tried to save Burnes and his companions on learning of their peril, but his troops had been ill-led. Instead of swiftly skirting the city to reach the quarter where Burnes's house stood, they had tried to advance through the crowded centre, with its narrow, winding streets, dragging their guns behind them. They soon found themselves trapped, and at the mercy of the rioters, many of whom were armed and who greatly outnumbered them. Two hundred of them were killed. The rest, having abandoned their guns, fled in disorder to the shelter of the Bala Hissar, their unseemly retreat covered by the British relief party.

The humiliating rout of Shujah's troops, supposedly there to protect him, reduced the Afghan ruler to 'a pitiable state of dejection and alarm', Kaye tells us, over his own personal safety. The British, too, were badly shaken by this violent and unexpected turn of events. 'The unwelcome truth was forced upon us', observed one officer in his diary, 'that in the whole Afghan nation we could not reckon on a single friend.' The champagne life, which the garrison had enjoyed for so long, was now clearly at an end. In a half-finished memorandum, which was found after his death, Macnaghten tried to justify his failure to anticipate the uprising. 'I may be considered culpable', he wrote, 'for not having foreseen the coming storm. To this I can only reply that others, who had much better opportunities of watching the feelings of the people, had no suspicion of what was coming.' He made no mention of Rawlinson or Pottinger, whose warnings he had ignored, and tried to blame Burnes, now conveniently dead, for failing to alert him to the danger. On the evening before his assassination, Macnaghten claimed, Burnes had congratulated him on leaving to take up his new post at a time of 'such profound tranquillity'.

It was no secret, however, that Burnes could hardly wait to see his chief go, and was unlikely to have said anything which might delay his departure, and therefore his own assumption of Macnaghten's mantle.

According to his friend Mohan Lal, Burnes had viewed the situation as anything but tranquil, even if he had gravely underestimated his own personal danger that night. On the previous evening he had declared that 'the time is not very far off when we must leave this country'. The Kashmiri took this to mean that Burnes was perfectly aware of the deepening hostility of the Afghans towards the British in their midst. However, he could equally well have been referring to the new policy towards Afghanistan which had just been announced in London. For in August of that year a Tory government led by Sir Robert Peel had replaced Melbourne's Whig administration and had immediately set about stringent economies. Maintaining troops in Afghanistan was costing a fortune, and it was felt that Shujah should now be made to stand on his own feet, especially as the Russian threat appeared to have receded. It was proposed, therefore, that while Shujah's own forces should be built up, the British military presence in Afghanistan, though not the political one, should be phased out. For a start, Macnaghten had been instructed to end the lavish payments he had been making to the tribes commanding the crucial passes between Kabul and British India. It was to prove a fatal move, for these previously quiescent tribes were among the first to join the insurrection.

Meanwhile, in the cantonments, instead of venturing out against the ill-armed and (as yet) ill-organised rebels, the British began preparing for a siege. It was only now that they realised their folly in agreeing to move out of the Bala Hissar. The cantonments, it transpired, were singularly ill-sited for defence, being built on low, marshy ground, overlooked by hills on all sides. They were surrounded, moreover, by orchards, which obstructed the defenders' lines of fire and observation, while the numerous irrigation channels which criss-crossed this dead ground offered an attacker excellent cover. A mud-built wall surrounded the British position, but this was no more than waist-high in some places, providing little protection from sniper or artillery fire. Macnaghten's engineers had warned him of this at the time of the move from the Bala Hissar, but unlike the majority of Great Game professionals he had little or no military experience, and anyway was confident that no such contingency would ever arise. He had thus ignored their advice, with the result that 4,500 British and Indian troops and 12,000 camp-followers, including some three dozen British wives, children and nannies, found themselves beleaguered in what Kaye described as little better than 'sheep-folds on the plain'.

Had Macnaghten and Elphinstone acted decisively and promptly at the first signs of trouble they would have been in time to move the entire garrison into the Bala Hissar, with its high, protective walls. But they continued to procrastinate until it was too late to embark on such a risky undertaking. Instead, Macnaghten sought another way out of the perilous situation into which his policies had plunged them all. Using the resourceful Mohan Lal as his go-between, he set about trying to buy the support of key Afghan leaders in the hope of turning the tables on the rebellious factions and tribes. Considerable quantities of largesse were dispensed, or promised (for much of Macnaghten's treasury was now in the hands of the mob), but it was to singularly little effect. 'There were too many hungry appetites to appease, too many conflicting interests to reconcile,' observed Kaye. 'It was altogether, by this time, too mighty a movement to be put down by a display of money-bags. The jingling of the coin could not drown the voice of an outraged and incensed people.'

With the situation deteriorating by the hour, something more drastic was obviously called for. It was not long before a solution was forthcoming, though whose idea it was is unclear. Mohan Lal was authorised to offer a reward of 10,000 rupees to anyone who succeeded in assassinating one of the principal rebel leaders. The instruction, together with a list of names, was issued to him by Lieutenant John Conolly, younger brother of Arthur and a junior political officer on Macnaghten's staff. Conolly was at that time inside the Bala Hissar, serving as liaison officer with the anxious Shujah. As elsewhere, contact was maintained by means of fleet-footed messengers, known as *cossids*, who took their lives in their hands running the gauntlet with secret dispatches concealed on them. On learning of the offer of blood-money, Macnaghten professed to be horrified by this thoroughly un-British stratagem. But he had certainly agreed to rewards being offered for the *capture* of hostile chieftains, and Kaye doubts whether Lieutenant Conolly would have acted on his own 'in a matter of such responsibility' without the prior approval of his chief. He concludes that Macnaghten almost certainly knew about the offer of blood-money and chose to turn a blind eye to it, even if he did not actually authorise it. As both Macnaghten and Conolly were shortly to perish, this is as near to the truth as we are likely to get.

Two rebel leaders, each high on Conolly's list, did in fact die not long afterwards in decidedly mysterious circumstances, and claims were immediately put in for the reward. One came from an individual who insisted that he had personally shot one of the men, while the other maintained that he had suffocated the second in his sleep. Mohan Lal was not convinced by their stories, however, and the money was never paid. The Kashmiri argued that he had offered it for the men's *heads*, and that the claimants had failed to produce these. As it turned out, their elimination did little to ease the plight of the garrison. This sudden gap in the ranks of the rebel leaders neither weakened their resolve nor divided them. For word had just reached them that Mohammed Akbar Khan, favourite son of the exiled Dost Mohammed, was on his way from Turkestan to take personal command of what had now become a full-scale insurrection against the British and their puppet ruler. This fiery warrior-prince had vowed to overthrow Shujah, expel the British and restore his father to the throne.

In the cantonments, meanwhile, things were going from bad to worse. News was coming in of the fall of outlying British posts to the rebels, with considerable loss of life, including the massacre of an entire Gurkha regiment. A number of officers had been killed and others wounded, among them Major Eldred Pottinger, the hero of Herat. The cruel Afghan winter had already begun, far earlier than usual, and food, water, medicines and morale were beginning to run low. So too, it appears, was courage, for the garrison's one and only major assault on the rebels had ended in a humiliating and costly defeat which saw the headlong flight of the British and Indian troops back to their own lines. Kaye was to call it 'disgraceful and calamitous'. It took place on November 23, when the Afghans suddenly moved two guns to the top of a hill over-looking the British position and began to bombard the crowded camp below.

Even General Elphinstone, who until now had expended more energy quarrelling with Macnaghten than in engaging the enemy, could not ignore this threat. He ordered a far from enthusiastic brigadier to venture forth with a force of infantry and cavalry. Having successfully seized the hill and silenced the guns, the brigadier turned his attention to the enemy-held village below. It was here that things began to go wrong. There had long been a standing order that guns must always move in pairs, but for some reason, perhaps to give himself greater mobility, the brigadier had only taken one 9-pounder with him. At first the grape-shot from this had had a devastating effect on the Afghans occupying the village, but soon it began to overheat, putting it out of action when it was most needed. As a result the attack on the village was driven back. Meanwhile the Afghan commanders had dispatched a large body of horse-men and foot-soldiers to the assistance of their hard-pressed comrades. Seeing the danger, the brigadier at once formed his infantry into two squares, massing his cavalry between them, and waited for the enemy onslaught, confident that the tactics which had won the Battle of Waterloo would prove as deadly here.

But the Afghans kept their distance, opening up a heavy fire on the tightly packed British squares with their long-barrelled matchlocks, or *jezails*. To the dismay of the brigadier's men, easy targets in their vivid scarlet tunics, their own shorter-barrelled muskets were unable to reach the enemy, the rounds falling harmlessly short of their targets. Normally the brigadier could have turned his artillery on the Afghans, causing whole-sale slaughter in their ranks, whereupon his cavalry would have done the rest. However, as Kaye observed, it seemed as though 'the curse of God was upon those unhappy people', for their single 9-pounder was still too hot for the gunners to use without the risk of it exploding, and in the meantime men were falling in scores to the Afghan marksmen. Then, to the horror of those watching the battle from the cantonments far below, a large party of the enemy began to crawl along a gully towards the unsuspecting British. Moments later they broke cover and flung themselves with wild cries upon their foes, who promptly turned and fled. Desperately the brigadier tried to rally his men, displaying remarkable courage in facing the enemy single-handed, while ordering his bugler to sound the *halt*. It worked, stopping the fleeing men in their tracks. The officers re-formed them, and a bayonet charge, supported by the cavalry, turned the tide, scattering the enemy. By now the 9-pounder was back in action, and the Afghans were finally driven off with heavy casualties.

The British triumph was short-lived, though, for the Afghans were quick to learn their lesson. They directed the fire of their *jezails* against the unfortunate gunners, making it all but impossible to use the 9-pounder. At the same time, from well out of range of the British muskets, they kept up a murderous hail against the exhausted troops, whose morale was once more beginning to crumble. It finally gave way when a party of Afghans, again crawling unseen up a gully, leaped unexpectedly upon them with blood-curdling screams and long, flashing knives, while their comrades kept up an incessant fire from near-invisible positions behind the rocks. This was too much for the British and Indian troops. They broke ranks and fled back down the hill all the way to the cantonments, leaving the wounded to their inevitable fate.

'The rout of the British force was complete,' wrote Kaye. 'In one confused mass of infantry and cavalry – of European and native soldiers – they fled to the cantonment walls.' In vain did General Elphinstone and his staff officers, who had watched the battle from the British lines, try to rally them and turn them back against the Afghans. They had lost all heart and discipline, not to mention 300 of their comrades. As Kaye coldly put it: 'They had forgotten they were British soldiers.' So intermixed were the advancing Afghans with the fleeing British that the cantonment guns could no longer be fired in safety. Had the triumphant enemy continued their pursuit, observes Kaye, the entire garrison would almost certainly have been slaughtered. But by some miracle they held back, apparently on the orders of their commander, and shortly afterwards melted away. 'They seemed astonished at their own success,' reported one young officer, 'and after mutilating in a dreadful manner the bodies left on the hill, they retired with exulting shouts to the city.'

*　　*　　*

The next day, to the surprise of the British, the Afghans offered them a truce. The rebels had now been joined, amid much jubilation, by Mohammed Akbar Khan, accompanied by 6,000 fighting men. This brought the Afghan strength to something like 30,000 foot-soldiers and cavalry, thereby outnumbering the British troops by about seven to one. No doubt Akbar, with such overwhelming force behind him, would have liked to put the whole British garrison to the sword in revenge for the overthrow of his father. However, if he was to restore him to the throne, he knew he must proceed with caution, for Dost Mohammed was still securely in British hands in India. Macnaghten, for his part, realised that he had little choice but to negotiate with the Afghans if the garrison was to be saved from annihilation or starvation. But before he agreed to do so he demanded from Elphinstone a written statement declaring their situation, militarily speaking, to be hopeless, unless reinforcements, reported to be on their way from Kandahar, arrived in a matter of days. For, still hopeful of salvaging his career, he was determined to pin the blame for their predicament on Elphinstone's ineptitude and the pusillanimity of his troops.

The general duly supplied him with what he wanted, together with a recommendation that they negotiate with the Afghans. The long catalogue of the garrison's woes (which Macnaghten already well knew) ended thus: 'Having held our position here for upwards of three weeks in a state of siege, from the want of provisions and forage, the reduced state of our troops, the large number of wounded and sick, the difficulty of defending the extensive and ill-situated cantonments we occupy, the near approach of winter, our communications cut off, and the whole country in arms against us, I am of the opinion that it is not feasible any longer to maintain our position in this country.' Elphinstone's gloom had been deepened by two further pieces of intelligence which had just reached him. The first was that Akbar had warned that any Afghan found selling or supplying food to the British would be killed instantly. The second was that the hoped-for relief expedition from the south had been forced back by heavy snowfalls in the passes, and would be unable to reach Kabul that winter.

Armed with the general's bleak prognosis, Macnaghten sat down to write an urgent dispatch to Lord Auckland describing their grave situation, and placing responsibility for it squarely on the shoulders of the military, whom he accused of being ill-led and cowardly. 'Our provisions will be out in two or three days, and the military authorities have strongly urged me to capitulate,' he wrote, adding smugly: 'This I will not do, till the last moment.' He was still convinced that he could outwit the Afghans by exploiting divisions which he knew to exist among their leaders. In response to their offer of a truce, therefore, he invited them to send a deputation to discuss terms. While the negotiations were proceeding, extraordinary scenes took place in the British lines, as crowds of Afghans, all armed to the teeth, swarmed across the low perimeter walls and began fraternising with the British and Indian troops. Many of them carried fresh vegetables which they pressed on those they had been trying to kill only hours before. At first it was feared that these might have been 'spiked' in some way, or even poisoned, but careful examination showed this suspicion to be groundless.

For a start the Afghan negotiators wanted Shah Shujah, still reasonably secure behind the massive walls and ramparts of the Bala Hissar, to be handed over to them. They would guarantee his life (although it was whispered that they intended to put out his eyes so that he could never again be a threat). Next they demanded that all British troops in Afghanistan, after first surrendering their arms, should leave at once for India, and that at the same time Dost Mohammed should be returned to them. And to make quite sure that they were not double-crossed, they intended to hold British officers and their families as hostages until all the troops had left the country, and Dost Mohammed was safely back in Kabul. Needless to say, these demands were totally unacceptable to Macnaghten. The euphoria and fraternising came to an abrupt end as the talks broke up with both sides vowing angrily to go to war again.

In the event this did not happen. Instead, a few days later, a second meeting was arranged, this time on the banks of the Kabul river, a mile from the cantonments. Akbar himself led the Afghan delegation, which consisted of most of the leading tribal chiefs. Macnaghten now put forward his own proposals. 'Whereas', he began, reading in Persian from a prepared statement, 'it has become apparent from recent events that the continuance of the British Army in Afghanistan for the support of Shah Shujah is displeasing to the great majority of the Afghan nation, and whereas the British Government had no other object in sending troops to this country than the integrity, happiness and welfare of the Afghans, it can have no wish to remain when that object is defeated by its presence.' The British, therefore, would withdraw all their troops, provided the Afghans would guarantee their safe passage to the frontier. Shah Shujah (who appears not to have been consulted) would give up his throne and return with the British to India. Akbar himself would accompany them to the frontier, and be personally responsible for their safety, while four British officers, but no families, would remain behind in Kabul as hostages. On the safe arrival of the British garrison in India, Dost Mohammed would be free to proceed to Kabul and the British officers to return home. Finally, despite recent events, it was to be hoped that the two nations would remain friends, and in return for British assistance if they ever needed it, the Afghans would agree not to enter into an alliance with any other foreign power.

This was not quite the capitulation that it appeared. Macnaghten, an intriguer to his very fingertips, was taking one last desperate gamble. He had learned from Mohan Lal that some of the more powerful chiefs privately feared the return of

Dost Mohammed, a tough and masterful ruler, and actually preferred the weaker, more compliant Shujah. Nor were they in such a hurry as Akbar to see the British, with their generous largesse, depart. After discussing Macnaghten's proposals among themselves, the Afghans, seemingly unanimous, agreed to them in principle. Preparations began at once for the evacuation of the garrison, and the implementation of the other parts of the agreement, before the winter made this impossible. But faced by the reality of Shujah's imminent departure, those who were apprehensive about Dost Mohammed's return began to have second thoughts, as Macnaghten had anticipated. Using Mohan Lal once again as his go-between, and with tempting promises of gold to come, Macnaghten set about trying to widen the divide in the Afghan ranks. 'If any portion of the Afghans wish our troops to remain in the country,' he told his Kashmiri agent, 'I shall think myself at liberty to break the engagement which I have made to go away, which was made believing it to be in accordance with the wishes of the Afghan nation.'

During the next few days the tireless Mohan Lal was kept feverishly busy endeavouring to spread strife among the Afghan leaders, and to turn as many as possible against Akbar. Macnaghten, wrote Kaye, was aware that there was no real unity between the Afghans, merely temporary alliances where it suited the respective parties. 'It is not easy', Kaye adds, 'to group into one lucid and intelligible whole all the many shifting schemes and devices which distracted the last days of the Envoy ... He appears to have turned first to one party, then to another, eagerly grasping at every new combination that seemed to promise more hope than the last.' Nor did he have to wait too long for signs that his strategy seemed to be working, and that Akbar and his supporters were finding themselves under powerful pressure from within.

On the evening of December 22, Akbar sent a secret emissary to the British lines to tell Macnaghten that he had an entirely new proposal to put to him. Its terms were startling, to say the least. Shah Shujah would be allowed to remain on the throne after all, but with Akbar as his Vizier. The British would stay in Afghanistan until the spring, whereupon they would leave, as though by their own choice, thereby saving face. At the same time, the individual known to be behind the assassination of Sir Alexander Burnes would be seized and handed over to the British for punishment. In return for all this, Akbar was to receive a lump sum of £300,000 and an annuity of £40,000, plus the help of the British against certain of his rivals.

Clearly, or so it seemed to Macnaghten, Akbar had been forced into this compromise by those parties whom he, with the aid of Mohan Lal and the promise of British gold, had won over to Shah Shujah's cause. Macnaghten was triumphant. He had saved the British from humiliation, the garrison from massacre, Shujah from abdication and his own career from ruination. A rendezvous was arranged for the following morning at which, amid great secrecy, the two would finalise the agreement. That night Macnaghten scribbled a note to Elphinstone saying that he had struck a deal with Akbar which would bring all their anxieties to an end.

*   *   *

The next day, accompanied by three of his political officers, Macnaghten set out for the spot where he and Akbar had agreed to meet. To Elphinstone, who had asked whether it might not be a trap, he answered sharply: 'Leave it all to me. I understand these things better than you.' Similar fears were expressed by one of the officers chosen to go with him, as well as by his own wife. Mohan Lal, too, had warned him that Akbar was not a man to be trusted. But Macnaghten, whom no one could accuse of lacking courage, refused to heed them. 'Treachery,' he declared, 'of course there is.' Success, however, would retrieve their honour, and more than make up for the danger. 'Rather than be disgraced,' he added, 'I would risk a thousand deaths.'

Akbar and his party were waiting for them on a snow-covered hillside overlooking the Kabul river, 600 yards from the south-eastern corner of the cantonments. 'Peace be with you!', the Afghans greeted the Englishmen as they rode up. Servants had spread horse-cloths on the ground, and after both sides had saluted from the saddle Akbar suggested that

Macnaghten and his companions dismount and seat themselves. Captain Kenneth Mackenzie, one of the officers, wrote afterwards: 'Men talk of presentiment. I suppose that something of the kind came over me, for I could scarcely prevail upon myself to quit my horse. I did so, however, and was invited to sit down among the *sirdars*.' When everyone was seated and quiet, Akbar turned to Macnaghten with a smile and asked him whether he accepted the proposal which had been put to him the previous evening. 'Why not?' replied Macnaghten. Those two short words were to seal not only his own fate but also that of the entire British garrison.

Unknown to Macnaghten, Akbar had learned of his duplicity and had decided to turn it to his own advantage. He warned the other chiefs of Macnaghten's willingness to cut them out and do a secret deal with him behind their backs. And now – for it appears that some of them were present – they had heard the Englishman's treachery with their own ears. Akbar had never intended to let either the British or Shujah stay on. His offer was designed solely to trap Macnaghten, and regain the allegiance of those whom Macnaghten had sought to turn against him. He had merely answered treachery with treachery, and had come off best.

Still suspecting nothing, Macnaghten enquired who the several strangers present were. Akbar told him not to be alarmed, then added: 'We are all in the secret.' No sooner had he uttered that, according to Captain Mackenzie, than he suddenly screamed to his men: '*Begeer! Begeer!*', meaning 'Seize! Seize!' At once Mackenzie and his two colleagues found themselves pinioned from behind, while Akbar himself, together with another chief, held Macnaghten. On Akbar's face, Mackenzie remembered, was an expression 'of the most diabolical ferocity'. As Macnaghten was dragged out of sight down the hill, Mackenzie got a brief glimpse of his face too. 'It was', he wrote afterwards, 'full of horror and astonishment.' He also heard him cry: '*Az barae Khooda*', which means 'For God's sake'. His immediate concern, however, was over his own fate, for some of the more fanatical of the Afghans were demanding his blood and that of his two fellow officers. But Akbar, it seems, had given orders that they were to be taken alive. Stripped of their weapons, they were ordered at gunpoint to mount the horses of three of his men, and ride behind them in the saddle. Then, hotly pursued by those who still wanted to kill them, they were swept away to the safety of a nearby fort where they were thrown into a dank cell. By ill luck, one of their number, Captain Trevor, either fell or was dragged from his mount during the chase, and was brutally hacked to death in the snow.

Precisely how Macnaghten died will never be known. His murderers apart, there were no witnesses to what happened to him after he was dragged, struggling, down the hill. Akbar himself swore later that he had intended to hold the Englishman hostage against his father's safe return, but that the captive had fought so fiercely that they had been forced to kill him lest he broke free and escaped to the British lines. Another version, however, maintains that Akbar, who blamed Macnaghten personally for his father's overthrow, shot him dead in a blind rage, using one of an ornate pair of pistols which Macnaghten had earlier presented to him, and even shown him how to load.

Meanwhile, realising that something was amiss, look-outs in the cantonments had reported this to General Elphinstone. But once again incompetence, irresolution and plain cowardice prevailed, for no move was made to try to save Macnaghten and his companions, although they were less than half a mile away from the cantonments. Macnaghten had asked Elphinstone to have troops standing by in case anything went wrong, but even this he had failed to do. The excuse given afterwards for this inaction was that Macnaghten and his three fellow officers were thought to have ridden off with Akbar to finalise the deal elsewhere. It was not until later, when they failed to return, that the appalling truth became known. That night reports reached the horrified garrison that Macnaghten's corpse, minus its head, arms and legs, could be seen suspended from a pole in the bazaar, while his bloodstained limbs were being passed round the town in triumph.

·20·

Massacre in the Passes

The Afghans now braced themselves for the vengeance they expected from the British, the destructive power of whose artillery they still greatly feared. Even Akbar wondered whether he had not gone too far, hastily denying responsibility for Macnaghten's death and expressing his regret over it. After all, only three years earlier, when they had easily routed his father's forces, he had seen the effectiveness of British troops properly led. And while he held British hostages, they had the ultimate hostage, his father.

But just as the murder of Sir Alexander Burnes had brought no retribution, so a similar paralysis seemed to grip the garrison now. Had the British, who were still a well-armed and potentially formidable force, been led with boldness and determination, they could even at this late stage have routed the Afghans and turned the tables on Akbar. However, the elderly Elphinstone, dragged down by gout and looking forward to a quiet retirement, had long before sunk into a torpor of indecision and despair, if not downright funk. This, in turn, had spread to his senior officers. 'That indecision, procrastination and want of method which paralysed all our efforts', wrote one subaltern, 'gradually demoralised the troops and, ultimately, not being redeemed by the qualities of his second in command, proved the ruin of us all.' Without the will to act decisively, and with just a few days' supplies left, the British could now hope to avert disaster only by renewed negotiation with the enemy.

On Christmas Eve Akbar, who had clearly recovered from his momentary fears over British vengeance, sent fresh emissaries to the cantonments. They again offered the garrison safe passage, but this time at a considerably higher price. With Macnaghten and Burnes dead, and most of the other politicals in Akbar's hands or otherwise out of action, Eldred Pottinger was given the thankless task of negotiating from a position of extreme weakness. Pottinger, who had so successfully organised the defence of Herat five years before, had all along urged Macnaghten and Elphinstone to move into the Bala Hissar while there was still time, fighting their way there if necessary, rather than attempting to defend the cantonments. But Elphinstone had always managed to find reasons for not doing this, and now they had missed their chance, for the Afghans, realising the danger, had destroyed the only bridge across the Kabul river.

Even now, although suffering from a severe wound himself, Pottinger tried to persuade his chiefs to launch an all-out onslaught against Akbar and his allies, who were still far from united. It was a strategy which enjoyed the support of all the younger officers, not to mention the troops, who were in a cold-blooded fury over the murder of Macnaghten. Pottinger argued strongly against having any dealings with Akbar, warning that he was totally untrustworthy, and that his treacherous murder of Macnaghten had invalidated any undertakings given to him by the British. Elphinstone overruled him, however, for he and the other senior officers wanted to get home as soon as possible, and with what they judged to be the least possible risk. With Macnaghten and Burnes gone, no one had the authority to challenge Elphinstone and his staff, least of all Pottinger, who was employed strictly as a political officer, and not in any military capacity. 'I was hauled out of my sick room', he wrote afterwards, 'and obliged to negotiate for the safety of a parcel of fools who were doing all they could to ensure their destruction.' With his superiors simply hoping for the best, and trusting that Akbar would prove merciful, it therefore became Pottinger's painful and distasteful task to appease him and to negotiate what was, in effect, the garrison's surrender.

In addition to demanding that the British stand by Macnaghten's original offer to leave Afghanistan forthwith, Akbar further insisted that they surrender the bulk of their artillery to him, as well as what was left of their gold, and that the hostages he already held be replaced by married officers, together with their wives and children. Elphinstone, ever ready to take the line of least resistance, at once asked for volunteers to serve as hostages, but not surprisingly got little response. One officer swore that he would rather shoot his wife than agree to surrender her to the mercies of the Afghans, while another declared that he would have to be taken at the point of a bayonet to the enemy. Only one officer volunteered, declaring that if it were for the common good he and his wife would remain behind.

The weather was now rapidly deteriorating, and they had little time to waste if they were to stand a chance of getting through the passes to Jalalabad before they were blocked for the winter. Pottinger was given no choice but to submit to most of Akbar's harsh demands. On January 1, 1842, as heavy snow fell on Kabul, an agreement was signed with Akbar under which he guaranteed the safety of the departing British, and promised to provide them with an armed escort to protect them from the hostile tribes through whose territories they must pass. In return, the British agreed to surrender all but six of their artillery pieces and three smaller mule-borne guns. For their part, the Afghans dropped their demand for married officers with families to stay behind, and Captain Mackenzie and his companion were freed. The first they had known of Macnaghten's fate was when his severed hand, attached to a stick, was thrust up in front of the window of their cell by a mob yelling for their blood outside. Instead of them, as a guarantee of good faith, Akbar insisted that three other young officers stay behind as their 'guests'. The British were in no position to argue.

As preparations for the garrison's exodus quickly got under way, an alarming rumour began to circulate in the cantonments. 'We are informed', noted one senior officer's wife in her journal, 'that the chiefs do not intend to keep faith.' After seizing the women, it was whispered, they proposed to slaughter all the men except one. He was to be taken to the entrance to the Khyber Pass, where he would be left, after his arms and legs had been hacked off, with a note pinned to him warning the British never again to try to enter Afghanistan. The British wives would then be used as hostages for the safe return of Dost Mohammed. Added to this were the warnings of Afghans who still had British friends that by agreeing to Akbar's terms they were signing their own death warrants. But in the desperate haste to get away, no one was prepared to listen to them. Also ignored was Mohan Lal's warning that they were all doomed unless the sons of the Afghan leaders accompanied them as hostages.

At first light on January 6, to the sound of bugles and drums, and leaving Shah Shujah and his followers to fend for themselves inside the Bala Hissar, the once proud Army of the Indus marched ingloriously out of the cantonments. Its destination was Jalalabad, the nearest British garrison, which lay more than eighty miles across the snow-covered mountains to the east. From there it would leave Afghanistan and enter India by the Khyber Pass. Leading the march was an advance guard of 600 red-coated troops of the 44th Regiment of Foot and 100 cavalry. Next came the British wives and children on ponies, and sick or pregnant women in palanquins borne by Indian servants. Then followed the main body of infantry, cavalry and artillery. Last of all came the rearguard, also consisting of infantry, cavalry and artillery. Between the main body and the rearguard wound a long column of camels and bullocks carrying ammunition and food. Left to struggle along as best they could, without any proper provision having been made for them, were several thousand camp-followers who attached themselves to the column wherever they could.

At the last moment a worrying discovery was made. Akbar's promised escort, which was supposed to be waiting for them ahead, was nowhere to be seen. Nor were the supplies of food and fuel which they were expecting. Pottinger at once suggested to Elphinstone that even at this late stage they could still change their plans and make straight for the protection of the Bala Hissar. But the general would not hear of it, ruling that there could be no turning back now. A messenger had been sent ahead to alert the British garrison at Jalalabad that they were on their way. So it was, on that icily cold winter's morning, that the long column of British and Indian troops, wives, children, nannies, grooms, cooks, servants and assorted hangers-on – 16,000 in all – set out through the snow towards the first of the passes.

*   *   *

A week later, shortly after noon, a look-out on the walls of the British fort at Jalalabad spotted a lone horseman in the far distance making his way slowly towards them across the plain. News of the capitulation of the Kabul garrison had already reached Jalalabad, causing intense dismay, and for two days, with increasing anxiety, they had been expecting the advance guard. For it was a march which normally took only five days. At once the look-out raised the alarm, and there was a rush for the ramparts. A dozen telescopes were trained on the approaching rider. A moment later someone cried out that he was a European. He appeared to be either ill or wounded, for he leaned weakly forward, clinging to his horse's neck. A chill ran through the watchers as it dawned on them that something was badly amiss. 'That solitary horseman', wrote Kaye, 'looked like the messenger of death.' Immediately an armed patrol was sent out to escort the stranger in, for numbers of hostile Afghans were known to be roaming the plain.

The horseman, whose head and hand were severely gashed, told them that he was Dr William Brydon, a physician who had been in Shah Shujah's service, but who had left Kabul with the British garrison. The tale he had to relate was indeed a dreadful one. As Mohan Lal and the few Afghans friendly to the British had warned, Akbar proved treacherous from the very outset. No sooner had the rearguard left the cantonments than the Afghans swarmed on to the walls and opened fire on the British with their deadly *jezails*, killing a subaltern and wounding a number of soldiers. From then onwards the harassment never ceased. The Afghan horsemen rode in among the troops, slaughtering and plundering, and driving off the baggage animals. Nor were the unarmed and helpless campfollowers spared. Soon the snow was crimson with blood, while the trail was lined with the dead and dying. Despite this the column pressed on, fighting off the Afghans as best they could. But weighed down by unnecessary baggage, and hindered by the presence of the terror-stricken camp-followers, the British only managed to cover five miles on the first day after leaving Kabul, with stragglers coming in until late at night.

The senior officers and some European wives and children slept in the one tent which had survived the pillage. The rest, Dr Brydon among them, spent the night out in the snow. Some built fires, though having no fuel they burned portions of their own clothing. Brydon wrapped himself in his sheepskin coat and managed to sleep, firmly clutching the bridle of his pony. In the morning it was discovered that many of the Indian troops and camp-followers, who came from the sultry plains and were without warm clothing, had frozen to death. Others, on waking, found to their horror that their feet were badly frost-bitten, looking, in Brydon's words, 'like charred logs of wood'. They had to be left behind in the snow to die. Yet Pottinger had urged Elphinstone to try to obtain horse-blankets for the troops to make into puttees, as the Afghans did at the first fall of snow each year. Like every other suggestion he had made, however, this too had been rejected – the tragic and costly result of the rivalry which existed between the military and the political officers.

And so the retreat continued, a struggling mass of soldiers and civilians, British and Indians, infantry and cavalry, baggage animals and guns. There was only one idea in everyone's minds – to escape the terrible cold and get down to the warmth and safety of the plains beyond the Khyber. Throughout the day sniping continued, taking a steady toll of lives. Small skirmishes also took place, and the Afghans managed to seize a pair of mule-guns and force the British to spike and abandon two other precious guns. All they had left now were one mule-gun and two heavier pieces. Yet the real fighting had scarcely begun.

Around midday on the second day, Akbar himself put in an unexpected appearance, claiming to have come to escort them safely through the passes to Jalalabad. He blamed the British for their heavy loss of life, claiming that they had left the cantonments before his escort was ready (although the time had, in fact, been agreed upon by both sides). In return for escorting them, however, he now demanded further hostages, including Pottinger and two other political officers. He also ordered Elphinstone to proceed no further that day, saying that he must first make arrangements with the chiefs of the tribe guarding the pass ahead, the Khoord-Cabool, to let them through. Once again, incredibly, Elphinstone believed him, and agreed to camp there after covering only ten miles in two extremely costly days. He also accepted Akbar's demand for the three hostages, and they duly left to join the Afghan camp. Although it can hardly have seemed so at the time, for them it was to prove a most providential move.

The next day, January 8, the straggling column entered the narrow, winding, four-mile-long pass. There was still no sign of Akbar's promised escort, but there could be no further delay, for frost-bite and hunger were beginning to take an alarming toll. Akbar had also promised them provisions, but there was no sign of these either. Nor was there any evidence of his having arranged a safe passage for them with those who guarded the pass. Indeed, it soon became evident to all but Elphinstone that he had persuaded them to halt so as to give the tribesmen time to position themselves with their *jezails* in the towering crags overlooking the pass.

'This morning we moved through the Khoord-Cabool Pass with great loss of life and property,' recorded Dr Brydon grimly in a diary reconstructed from memory on reaching Jalalabad. 'The heights were in possession of the enemy, who poured down an incessant fire on our column. Great numbers were killed . . . and many more were wounded.' As soon as the main body had reached the end of the pass, which involved crossing a partly frozen stream no fewer than thirteen times, the tribesmen descended from their positions and set about butchering the stragglers. Some 3,000 of the garrison, including many women and children, were left dead in the pass that day, their frozen corpses stripped of precious clothing by friend and foe alike. Although Brydon did not himself witness it, others claimed to have seen Akbar riding among the enemy urging them in Persian (a language known to many of the

British officers) to 'spare' the British, but in Pushto (the language of the tribesmen) to 'slay' them. Despite this and other evidence of his treachery, Elphinstone decided the very next day, January 9, to trust him once more. Akbar this time proposed taking under his protection the wives and children of the British officers, promising to escort them by a safer road to Jalalabad. Where the husbands had survived, he offered to take them too, as well as a number of wounded officers. To this Elphinstone agreed. Nineteen of them – two men, eight women and nine children – were escorted away by Akbar's men. It would be the last that would be seen of them, or of the political officers already being held, for many months.

Despite the surrender of the women and children, the attacks on the column soon resumed. Of the following day, Brydon wrote: 'This was a terrible march – the fire of the enemy incessant, and numbers of officers and men, not knowing where they were going from snow-blindness, were cut up.' Among those who perished were no fewer than three of Brydon's fellow doctors, and at least seven other officers. The cold and continual exposure, he recounts, had rendered the ill-clothed Indian troops almost powerless to defend themselves against the incessant Afghan onslaughts, which came from all sides. By the end of the day, as darkness fell, Brydon tells us, 'a mere handful' of the sepoys remained alive. According to one estimate, all but 750 of the troops, British and Indian, who had left Kabul only five days earlier, were now dead, while some two-thirds of the 12,000 civilians accompanying them had also perished.

While the massacre continued, Akbar himself hovered just out of sight, insisting that he was doing everything he could to restrain the local tribesmen. This was proving difficult, he protested, as even their own chiefs had little control over them. There may have been some truth in this latter claim, but there is no real evidence that he ever tried to get the chiefs to stop their men from attacking the retreating columns. Even so, astonishingly, Elphinstone continued to accept his solemn assurances that he was doing all in his power to try to save them. Two days later, on January 12, he once again offered them safe passage. By now Elphinstone's force was down to

The ill-fated Captain Conolly
(*left*) and Colonel Stoddart being
[le]n chains to the Emir of Bokhara's
[o]minous dungeon – a Victorian
[arti]st's impression.

(*right*) The notorious Emir
[Nasr]ullah of Bokhara who,
[emb]oldened by the British
[catas]trophe in Afghanistan, had
[Con]olly and Stoddart beheaded in
1842.

21. Turcoman slavers in action. Thousands of the Tsar's subjects were held in bondage in the Central Asian khanates – one of the pretexts for Russian expansionism.

22. General Konstantin Kaufman (1818–82), first Governor-General of Turkestan, and architect of Russia's conquests in Central Asia.

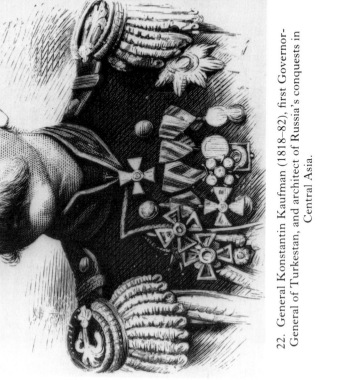

23. General Mikhail Skobelev (1843–82), whose brutal conquests in Transcaspia led to the building of a strategic railway threatening India.

24. Lieutenant Alikhanov (*seated left*), disguised as a merchant on his secret mission to Merv in 1882. His intrigues there paved the way for the surrender of this Turcoman stronghold.

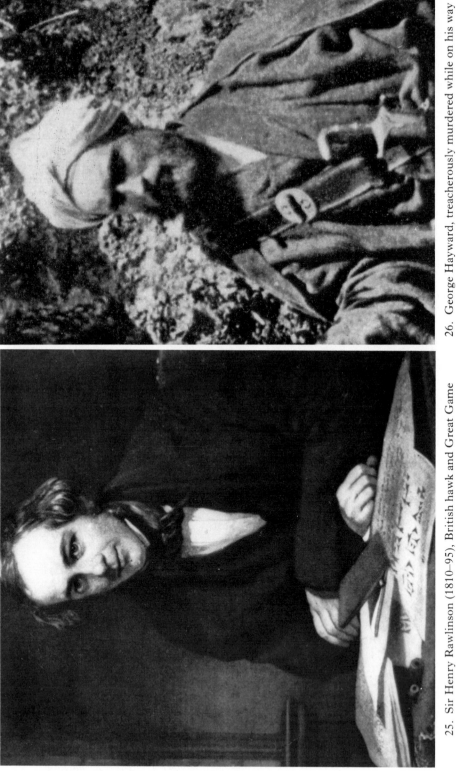

25. Sir Henry Rawlinson (1810–95), British hawk and Great Game strategist. His record-breaking ride, as a subaltern in 1837, brought news of a secret Russian mission entering Afghanistan.

26. George Hayward, treacherously murdered while on his way to map the Pamir passes in the no-man's-land between Russia and India.

27. A classic Great Game image – scanning the passes, with a rifle-case to steady the telescope.

28. Map-making in High Asia – one of the principal tasks of Great Game players on both sides.

fewer than 200 troops, plus some 2,000 camp-followers. The general felt that if any of them were to survive he had no choice but to come to terms with Akbar. Accordingly, with his second-in-command and another officer, he rode over to Akbar's camp. Once more, however, it proved to be a trick. For it soon became clear, even to Elphinstone, that Akbar was unable to protect them, even if he had wanted to. When the general asked to be allowed to return to his troops, Akbar refused, thus adding the British commander to his growing band of hostages. Nonetheless, Elphinstone managed to smuggle a secret message to the officer he had left in command of the surviving troops ordering him to press on immediately.

It was now dark and for once the British caught the Afghans off their guard, although not for long. The tribesmen had constructed a formidable barrier across the narrow gorge, intending to fire down on the redcoats as it forced them to a halt. But not expecting the British to move at night, they had left it unmanned. Yet even as the troops were trying to tear it down with their bare hands, the Afghans discovered what was happening and attacked them from the rear. 'The confusion was now terrible,' wrote Brydon, 'all discipline was at an end.' It was every man for himself. In the darkness he suddenly realised that he was surrounded. Before he could ride off he was dragged from his horse and felled by a savage cut from a long Afghan knife. Had he not by a miracle had a copy of *Blackwood's Magazine* stuffed in his cap, it would undoubtedly have killed him. As it was, the knife removed a large piece of his skull. 'I was nearly stunned,' he wrote, 'but I managed to get to my knees.' Seeing a second blow coming, he managed to parry it with the edge of his sword, slicing off some of his assailant's fingers. As the weapon fell to the ground, the man ran off into the darkness, leaving Brydon horseless and alone.

Despite his severe head wound, the doctor managed to clamber over the partly demolished barricade without attracting any further attention from the enemy, who seemed to have gone off in pursuit of the others. Stumbling weakly on over the piles of corpses, he came upon a mortally wounded cavalryman. The soldier, who had been shot through the chest and was bleeding profusely, begged him to take his pony before someone else did. Moments later he fell back dead. Profoundly grateful to his unknown benefactor, Brydon mounted the pony and rode hurriedly off into the darkness in search of his surviving comrades.

*   *   *

The handful of officers and men who had fought their way out of the gorge, leaving behind them many dead and dying, now found themselves divided into two groups, one mounted and the other on foot. The fifteen-strong former group, to which Brydon had attached himself, decided to ride on ahead in the hope of reaching Jalalabad before their pursuers could catch up with them. The second, far larger party, consisting of twenty officers and forty-five other ranks, fought their way to the village of Gandamak, less than thirty miles from Jalalabad. They knew that if they could survive one more day they would reach the safety of the British garrison. But they soon found their way blocked by the Afghans. Overwhelmingly outnumbered, they realised that they now stood little chance of reaching safety. Forming themselves into a square, and with only twenty muskets between them and two rounds of ammunition each, they prepared to sell their lives dearly in a last desperate stand.

The Afghans at first offered to negotiate, insisting that a ceasefire had been agreed at last, and that to be safe the British need only hand over their weapons. When they refused, suspecting another trap, the Afghans attempted to disarm them. Immediately hand-to-hand fighting broke out. With their ammunition all spent, the British fought on with bayonet and sword, one officer killing five Afghans before being cut down himself. Only four prisoners were taken by the Afghans, the rest of the group – most of them men of the 44th Regiment of Foot – being slaughtered to a man. In 1979, nearly a century and a half later, the British anthropologist Dr André Singer climbed to the top of the hill where they died. There, beneath the rocks of this grim and remote place, he found what were clearly the bones of those gallant men. Villagers told him that, long ago, visitors from British India occasionally made their way to the spot, where they stood in silent homage.

Meanwhile, twelve miles to the east, and unaware of the fate of their comrades, the mounted party pressed hastily on towards Jalalabad. The group consisted of Brydon, three captains, three subalterns, another doctor and half a dozen other ranks. At the village of Futtehabad, only fifteen miles from Jalalabad, they were offered food, and being desperately hungry they accepted, glad also of a rest while it was prepared. After all they had been through, the village seemed singularly peaceful and divorced from war. But it was an illusion, and while they rested a secret signal was given to those waiting in the hills nearby. The first the British knew of their danger was when suddenly they spotted scores of armed horsemen galloping towards the village from all sides. As they grabbed their weapons and dashed for their horses, villagers flung themselves on the small party, while others opened fire on those who managed to mount and ride off. Only five of them, including Brydon, got clear of the village. However, very soon the pursuing Afghans had disposed of all but Brydon, who by a miracle escaped. Even so, his trials were not yet over, for three more times during the fifteen-mile ride to Jalalabad he ran into hostile Afghans.

The first group, some twenty strong, threw stones at him and lunged at him with their knives. 'I with difficulty put my pony into a gallop,' he wrote, 'and taking my bridle in my teeth, cut right and left with my sword as I went through them. They could not reach me with their knives and I was only hit by one or two stones.' A mile or two further on he encountered a second group, one of whom was armed with a *jezail*. Jabbing his exhausted pony with the point of his sword, Brydon managed to force it again into a gallop. The Afghan with the *jezail* fired at him from close range, snapping short the blade of his sword and hitting his pony in the groin, but missing him. By the time the weapon could be reloaded he was out of range.

Finally, ahead of him on the plain, Brydon spotted a party of horsemen. Believing them to be a British cavalry patrol from Jalalabad, he rode eagerly towards them. Too late, he realised they were Afghans. As he quickly turned away they saw him and sent one of their number after him. Recognising him as an

Englishman, the man slashed at him with his sword. Brydon managed to block the blow with his own broken weapon. His enemy now turned and rode at him again. 'This time, just as he was striking, I threw the handle of my sword at his head,' wrote Brydon. Swerving to avoid it, the Afghan missed his aim, instead cutting the doctor's left hand, in which he held his bridle. Feeling it go numb, he reached for the bridle with his other hand. 'I suppose my foe thought it was for a pistol,' Brydon recounts, 'for he turned at once and made off as quick as he could.'

But his pistol, Brydon discovered to his dismay, had fallen from its holster, and he was now totally unarmed. His pony, bleeding badly from the wound in its groin, seemed unlikely to carry him much further. His own wounds, together with his hunger and exhaustion, had begun to take their toll. For the first time in those eight nightmarish days the doctor's strength began to fail him. 'All energy seemed to forsake me,' he wrote, and he feared that he would fall from the saddle from sheer exhaustion. Any moment he expected to be attacked by Afghans, and this time he knew he was unlikely to survive. 'I became nervous and frightened at shadows,' he recounts. But he was closer to Jalalabad than he realised. It was at that moment that the sharp-eyed look-out on the ramparts spotted him and his pony as they struggled painfully across the plain.

Dr Brydon was the only one of the 16,000 souls who had left Kabul to complete the terrible course and reach Jalalabad in safety – and the first, on that fateful thirteenth day of January, 1842, to break the news of the disaster which had overtaken Elphinstone's army to a horrified nation. But, as we shall see, he was not the sole survivor of the Kabul garrison. Besides the hostages held by Akbar, a number of sepoys and other Indians who had somehow escaped death by hiding in caves managed, during the ensuing months, to make their way home across the passes. Although Brydon himself recovered fully from his wounds to become the subject of one of the most celebrated paintings of Victorian times – Lady Butler's *Remnants of an Army* – sad to relate his gallant pony, also depicted in the work, died from its wounds. 'The poor pony, directly it was put in a stable, lay down and never rose again,' wrote the doctor.

Neither Brydon nor the garrison then knew of the fate which had befallen the men of the 44th Regiment of Foot at Ganda-mak. For many nights afterwards a large fire was kept blazing at Jalalabad's Kabul Gate, lights were placed on the ramparts and bugles were sounded regularly to guide in any stragglers trying to cross the exposed plain and reach the city under cover of darkness. But none ever came.

· 21 ·

The Last Hours of
Conolly and Stoddart

The dreadful tidings borne by Dr Brydon – the Messenger of Death, as he was to become known – reached
Lord Auckland, the retiring Governor-General, in
Calcutta, a fortnight later. The shock, his sister Emily noted,
was to age him by ten years. Things had gone wrong so terribly
fast. Only a few weeks earlier Sir William Macnaghten had
written from Kabul assuring him that everything was firmly
under control. And now his entire policy in Central Asia was
in ruins. Far from establishing a friendly rule in Afghanistan
to buttress India against Russian encroachments, it had led
instead to one of the worst disasters ever to overtake a British
army. A mob of mere heathen savages, armed with home-made
weapons, had succeeded in routing the greatest power on earth.
It was a devastating blow to British pride and prestige. The
ignominy suffered by St Petersburg following the Khivan
débâcle was nothing compared to this. To the bemused Auckland, who had been reluctant to use British troops to unseat
Dost Mohammed in the first place, it was 'as inexplicable as it
was appalling'. And now, with Akbar's forces beginning to
hammer at the gates of the two remaining British garrisons
in Afghanistan, Jalalabad and Kandahar, fears arose that the
warlike Afghans, flushed by victory, might pour down through
the passes into northern India, as they had done more than
once in the past.

London did not hear of the catastrophe for a further week.
First to break the news, using the largest headline type it

possessed, was *The Times*. 'We regret to announce', it declared, 'that the intelligence which this express has brought us is ... of the most disastrous and melancholy nature.' In a leading article a few days later it thrust an accusing finger at St Petersburg – 'whose growing influence amongst those tribes first called for our interference', and whose secret agents were 'examining with the greatest care' the passes leading towards British India. It insisted that the insurrection was far too well organised to have been spontaneous, and found it highly suspicious that the first to be murdered was Sir Alexander Burnes, 'the keenest antagonist of the Russian agents'. Others were less sure about Russia's implication. But everyone, including the Duke of Wellington, blamed General Elphinstone for failing to crush the insurrection at the outset, and Lord Auckland for embarking on such folly in the first place. 'Our worst fears regarding the Afghanistan expedition', declaimed *The Times* smugly, 'have been justified.'

The new Tory administration led by Sir Robert Peel could at least wash its hands of all responsibility for the disaster, placing this firmly on the shoulders of Melbourne's Whigs, who had approved the invasion plan. However, it was now faced with the task of clearing up the mess and deciding how the Afghans were to be punished for their treachery, for the nation was demanding vengeance. Fortunately, the Tories' own man – that old India hand Lord Ellenborough, thrice President of the Board of Control – was already on his way to replace Auckland as Governor-General, though he only learned of the catastrophe when he arrived off Madras on February 21. His brief from the government had been to withdraw the British garrisons from Afghanistan in line with its stringent new economic policies, but he now found himself facing a totally unexpected situation. That night, as his vessel bore him on to Calcutta, he wrote to Peel declaring that he proposed to restore Britain's honour and pride by teaching the Afghans a lesson they would not forget in a hurry.

On reaching the capital, Ellenborough learned that his predecessor had already dispatched a force to Peshawar to try to relieve the hard-pressed garrisons at Jalalabad and Kandahar, and to try to free the British hostages held by Akbar. The new Governor-General now took command. On March 31 the Khyber Pass was forced by Major-General George Pollock, using the tactics of the Afghans themselves, and at a cost of only fourteen British lives. As Pollock's flanking columns seized the heights, the astonished tribesmen for the first time found themselves shot down from above. Two weeks later the relief column was played into Jalalabad to the strains of the Scots air 'Oh, but ye've bin lang a'coming'. Meanwhile, in a series of actions around Kandahar, the able British commander, General Sir William Nott, had driven back the Afghans threatening the garrison. He, like Pollock, was now ready and eager to march on Kabul to avenge Elphinstone's humiliating defeat, not to mention the deaths of Burnes, Macnaghten and the countless soldiers and families who had perished on the death march.

It was at this point that Lord Ellenborough, so hawkish at first, began to get cold feet. Anxious about the continuing drain on India's already depleted treasury (for London was resolutely refusing to contribute to the expedition's costs), and perhaps fearing another catastrophe, the Governor-General argued that the Afghans had now received lesson enough at the hands of Pollock and Nott. 'At last we have got a victory,' he wrote to Peel, 'and our military character is re-established.' He ordered the two generals to return with their troops to India, leaving the hostages in Akbar's possession. After all, the British still held Dost Mohammed, while Shah Shujah (or so Ellenborough believed) continued to rule Afghanistan, nominally anyway, from the walled fastness of the Bala Hissar. Once the British troops had been withdrawn from Afghanistan, Ellenborough reasoned, negotiations for the freeing of the hostages could commence in a calmer atmosphere. But what he did not then know was that the unfortunate Shujah was no longer alive. As Pollock's men were fighting their way up the Khyber to Jalalabad, Shujah had been lured out of the Bala Hissar, ostensibly for talks, and instead had been riddled with bullets. Akbar's triumph, however, had proved short-lived, as fears spread among the other chiefs over the prospect of being ruled by him or his father. Just as Macnaghten had foreseen, a fierce power struggle now arose between Akbar's supporters and his foes.

Almost simultaneously, within the ranks of the British, a struggle of a different kind broke out. Ellenborough's order to Pollock and Nott to evacuate Afghanistan without further chastising the murderous tribes was received with dismay and disbelief by both officers and men, who wanted blood. A battle of wills now followed between the two generals and the new Governor-General, with other senior military officers in India and at home taking the side of the former. A succession of excuses – the weather, shortages of supplies, money, and so on – was found for delaying the departure of the two garrisons, while pressure grew on Ellenborough to change his mind. The hawks had a valuable ally at home in the Duke of Wellington, who still held a seat in the Cabinet. 'It is impossible to impress upon you too strongly', the India veteran warned Ellenborough, 'the notion of the importance of the restoration of reputation in the East.' Even Sir Robert Peel, the Prime Minister, who had from the start urged extreme caution on the Governor-General, began to waver under the pressure of public opinion, and wrote to him suggesting that sterner measures might be called for.

Feeling increasingly isolated, Ellenborough finally gave way. He realised that he would either have to admit that he had previously been wrong, or risk being accused of throwing away the opportunity of freeing the hostages and salvaging Britain's military reputation and pride. Without altering his order to evacuate Afghanistan, he told Pollock and Nott that they might, if they judged it militarily expedient, retire *by way of* Kabul. 'No change had come over the views of Lord Ellenborough', observed Kaye, 'but a change had come over the meaning of certain words of the English language.' Although Ellenborough was criticised for thus shifting the responsibility on to the shoulders of Pollock and Nott, neither complained. They had got their way, and a race began between the two to be the first into Kabul, although Nott's men in Kandahar had by far the furthest to march – some 300 miles against Pollock's 100.

As they fought their way back along the same route by which, only seven months earlier, Elphinstone's ill-fated columns had left Kabul, Pollock's troops soon came across harrowing evidence of the disaster. Everywhere there were skeletons. 'They lay in heaps of fifties and hundreds,' wrote one officer, 'our gun-wheels passing over and crushing the skulls of our late comrades at almost every yard.' Some even recognised the remains and possessions of former friends. Despite Ellenborough's orders to show restraint towards the populace, the growing fury of the troops led to numerous excesses being committed against those who resisted their advance. In one village, it is said, every male over the age of puberty was slaughtered, women were raped, and some even killed. 'Tears, supplications, were of no avail,' one young officer recalled. 'Fierce oaths were the only answer. The musket was deliberately raised, the trigger pulled, and happy was he who fell dead.' Shocked at what he saw, he described many of the troops as little better than 'hired assassins'. An army chaplain, who was present at the sacking of one village which fired on them after it had surrendered, declared that seldom had a clergyman been called upon to witness such a scene. But these painful things, he added, were almost impossible to prevent 'under such circumstances', and regrettably were common to all wars.

In the event, the race for the Afghan capital was won by Pollock's men, though only just. All the same it took them five times as long to fight their way there as it had taken Dr Brydon to travel the other way. They reached Kabul on September 15, to find that the enemy, including Akbar himself, had fled the city. That night they set up camp on the racecourse built by Elphinstone's men three years earlier, and next morning entered the Bala Hissar without having to fire a shot. A few minutes later the Union Jack was flying over Kabul once more. They found much to remind them of the events they had come to avenge, including the blackened ruins of Sir Alexander Burnes's house. 'It was a melancholy spectacle,' observed an officer with Nott's force, adding that 'the narrow street in which it stood, by the numerous scars of musket-balls, bore indubitable evidence of the fury of the conflict which had raged about it.' He and his companions returned to the camp 'little disposed for any conversation ... and fully occupied by the emotions of sorrow and mortification which such scenes were calculated to call forth.'

With Shah Shujah dead, Kabul was now kingless, and Pollock, the senior of the two commanders, who had been invested with political authority by Lord Ellenborough, immediately placed Shujah's son Futteh on the throne, thereby making him too a British puppet. Pollock's next priority was to try to free the British hostages held by Akbar. The officer he chose for this exacting and dangerous task was Captain (now Sir) Richmond Shakespear, whose aptitude for this sort of game had been amply demonstrated at Khiva two years earlier. Although he was provided this time with a powerful escort of Kizilbashi irregulars, sworn foes of Akbar's, there were many who feared that he would end up as one of the hostages. For roaming the Bamian area, where the latter were known to be held, were said to be 12,000 enemy troops. Undeterred by such warnings, and accompanied by his 600 armed Kizilbashis, Shakespear at once set out for Bamian, 150 miles to the north-west, having first sent messengers ahead to try to get word to the hostages that help was on the way.

By now the ranks of those held by Akbar had been swelled by the addition of a number of British captives taken by the Afghans, bringing the total to 22 officers, including Eldred Pottinger, 37 other ranks, 12 wives and 22 children. For some months they had been kept in the comparative comfort of Kabul, where they had been well treated, but with the advance of Pollock and Nott towards the capital they had been removed to a remote, mud-built fortress near Bamian. In August they heard from their servants that they were shortly to be moved northwards to Bokhara, well out of reach of any rescue attempt, where they would be presented as slaves to the tribes if the British occupied Kabul and Akbar was forced to flee. Aware that they had little time to spare, a number of the officers led by Pottinger, and aided by the wily Mohan Lal, set about trying to buy the party's freedom from the commander of their Afghan guards. At first he demurred, but news soon began to reach Bamian that the British were fast approaching Kabul and that Akbar was preparing to flee. Ignoring an order from the latter to march the hostages into Turkestan, he agreed to

free them for 20,000 rupees in cash and a monthly pension of
1,000 rupees.

Having thus obtained his co-operation, they next took over
the fortress in which they had been held, and prepared to
defend it until a relief expedition could get to them. They
deposed the Afghan governor, ran up the Union Jack, levied
taxes on passing merchants and established friendly contact
with local chiefs. At the same time they made plans for with-
standing a siege. As many of the British troops were too weak
because of illness to hold a musket, they promised their former
guards, more than 200 in number, four months' extra pay if
they remained with them until they were relieved. It was at
this moment that they heard that Kabul had fallen, Akbar had
fled, and that Shakespear was on his way to them with his
Kizilbashi escort. At once they abandoned the fort and
marched out to meet him.

After travelling for several hours, a scout spotted a large
body of horsemen winding its way down through the pass
towards them. For a moment it was feared that these might be
Akbar's men returning to seize them, but suddenly a horseman
in British officer's uniform was observed galloping ahead of
the others. It was Sir Richmond Shakespear. He had already
spotted them. The meeting was an extremely emotional one,
with many of the hostages in tears. They showered Shakespear
with questions, having been completely out of touch for eight
months. From them Shakespear learned that back in April
General Elphinstone, ailing and broken, had died, thus being
spared the ignominy of having to face a public enquiry, if not
a court martial, for his contribution to the catastrophe. He also
learned that four babies had been born to women in the party,
and that a sergeant's wife had run off with one of her captors.

With the hostages now freed, and on their way to Kabul,
there remained one last task for the British, and that was the
settling of accounts. Pollock had considered blowing up the
Bala Hissar, that symbol of Afghan might, but had been begged
by those who had remained loyal to the British not to do so,
as it would leave them defenceless. Instead therefore he decided
to raze Kabul's great covered bazaar, celebrated throughout
Central Asia, and where Macnaghten's dismembered corpse

had been hung nine months earlier. The task was carried out by Pollock's engineers using explosives. However, so massive was the structure that it was to take them two whole days. The general had issued strict orders that no one was to be harmed, and that property elsewhere in the old city was not to be touched. Guards were placed on the principal gates and in the area around the bazaar to ensure that no looting took place. But there followed a total breakdown of discipline. 'The cry went forth that Caubul was given up to plunder,' wrote Major Henry Rawlinson, a political officer with Nott's force. Troops and camp-followers streamed into the city, pillaging shops and applying torches to houses. Guilty and innocent alike, including the friendly Kizilbashis, saw their homes and businesses destroyed, and large areas of Kabul were laid low. Among those who lost everything they possessed were 500 Indian families who were now forced to beg their way home in the rear of the British troops. It was an inglorious episode with which to crown the victory of Pollock and Nott. Clearly it was time for the British to go.

On October 11 they hauled down the Union Jack over the Bala Hissar, and the next morning the first units marched away from Kabul. Once again they set out along the skeleton-strewn trail, the *via dolorosa* of the previous winter, leading towards the Khyber Pass, and home. Her honour nominally satisfied, Britain was content to leave Afghan politics to the Afghans – for the time being anyway. The First Afghan War, as historians now call it, was finally over. The British had received a terrible mauling, for all Lord Ellenborough's pretences, including a massive victory celebration, that it had ended in triumph. But no amount of medal-giving, triumphal arches, regimental balls and other extravaganzas could conceal the final irony. No sooner had the British left Afghanistan than the blood began to flow once more. Within three months Shah Shujah's son had been overthrown, and Dost Mohammed was allowed by the British to return unconditionally to the throne from which he had been removed at such terrible cost. No one now had any doubt that he was the only man capable of restoring order to Afghanistan. Events had come full circle.

*   *   *

But even now the Central Asian tragedy was not quite over for the British. Throughout that year the unfolding story had dominated the headlines both in India and at home. Deep anxiety had been felt over the fate of the hostages, particularly the women and children, and news of their release unharmed sent a wave of relief and rejoicing through the nation. Then, just as the celebrations ordered by Lord Ellenborough in India were getting under way, chilling news reached the British Mission in Teheran. It was brought by a young Persian, once employed by Arthur Conolly, who had just returned from Bokhara. Conolly and Stoddart, whose plight had been all but forgotten in the wake of the Kabul catastrophe, were, he reported, both dead. It had happened, he said, back in June, when Britain's reputation as a power to be feared in Central Asia was at rock bottom. Furious at receiving no reply to his personal letter to Queen Victoria, and no longer worried by any fear of retribution, the Emir of Bokhara had ordered the two Englishmen, then enjoying a brief spell of freedom, to be seized and thrown back into prison. A few days later they had been taken from there, with their hands bound, and led into the great square before the Ark, or citadel, where stood the Emir's palace. What followed next, the Persian swore, he had learned from the executioner's own lips.

First, while a silent crowd looked on, the two British officers were made to dig their own graves. Then they were ordered to kneel down and prepare for death. Colonel Stoddart, after loudly denouncing the tyranny of the Emir, was the first to be beheaded. Next the executioner turned to Conolly and informed him that the Emir had offered to spare his life if he would renounce Christianity and embrace Islam. Aware that Stoddart's forcible conversion had not saved him from imprisonment and death, Conolly, a devout Christian, replied: 'Colonel Stoddart has been a Mussulman for three years and you have killed him. I will not become one, and I am ready to die.' He then stretched out his neck for the executioner, and a moment later his head rolled in the dust beside that of his friend.

News of their brutal murder sent a wave of horror through the nation, but short of sending another expedition across

Afghanistan to deal with this petty tyrant, there was precious little that could be done about it. Even at the risk of losing further face in Central Asia, the Cabinet decided that it would be better if the whole unfortunate affair were quietly forgotten. However, angry friends of the dead men, who blamed their deaths on the government's abandonment of them, were determined not to let this happen. Some even believed that the Persian might have been lying, and that the two officers might, after all, still be alive. A subscription was raised, and a brave but highly eccentric clergyman, the Reverend Joseph Wolff from Richmond, Surrey, volunteered to travel to Bokhara to ascertain the truth. Unhappily, the Persian's story was to prove true in all but a few details, and the intrepid Wolff himself was lucky to escape with his own life, only doing so, it is said, because his bizarre appearance, in full canonicals, made the unpredictable Emir 'shake with uncontrollable laughter'. A detailed account of Wolff's courageous journey, not strictly part of the Great Game, is given in his own book, *Narrative of a Mission to Bokhara*, published in 1845, after his return to London.

Twenty years later a poignant footnote was added to the story of Conolly and Stoddart. Through the post one day a small parcel arrived at the home of Conolly's sister in London. It contained a battered prayer book which had been in her brother's possession throughout his captivity, and had evidently brought comfort to him and Stoddart during their long and painful ordeal. On the end-papers and in the margins were penned in a tiny hand details of their misfortunes. The last of these entries ended abruptly in mid-sentence. The prayer book had eventually found its way into the hands of a Russian living in St Petersburg who had managed to track down Conolly's sister. Sad to relate, this relic was subsequently lost.

For Conolly and Stoddart, like Burnes and Macnaghten, the Great Game was over. All had been victims of the forward policies which they themselves had so eagerly embraced and helped to shape. Within months, Eldred Pottinger, hero of Herat and Kabul, was also dead, struck down by fever at the age of 32. Another promising young player lost to the game was Lieutenant John Conolly, also of the political service. He had died of illness while Akbar's hostage in Kabul, without ever learning of the fate which had befallen his idolised brother Arthur. Thus, in swift succession, six prominent British players had gone to join William Moorcroft and their Russian adversaries, Griboyedov and Vitkevich, in the Valhalla reserved for Great Game heroes. Nor would they be the last.

For a while, however, it seemed that both Britain and Russia, chastened by their costly adventures in Central Asia, had learned their lesson, and that henceforward more cautious counsels would prevail. The period of *détente* which followed was to last for a decade, despite mutual fears and suspicions. The two powers were to use it to consolidate their frontiers, but in the end it proved merely to be half-time in the struggle for ascendancy in Central Asia.

· 22 ·

Half-time

Tsar Nicholas himself was the first to extend the olive branch. He did so when he came to Britain on a state visit in the summer of 1844. Queen Victoria, then aged 25, had expected her Russian guest to be little better than a savage, but found herself captivated by his striking good looks and graceful manners. 'His profile is beautiful,' she noted, 'but the expression of his eyes is formidable and unlike anything I ever saw before.' In his subsequent talks with Sir Robert Peel and the British Foreign Secretary, Lord Aberdeen, the Emperor assured them that he only wanted peace, and that he had no further territorial ambitions in Asia, and none whatsoever towards India. His principal concern was the future of the Ottoman Empire, or the 'Sick Man of Europe' as he called it. He professed to be deeply perturbed about what would happen when it broke up, something he judged to be imminent. But his real concern seemed to have more to do with ensuring that he got his share of the pieces when it did.

While Peel and Aberdeen were less convinced of the coming collapse of the Ottoman Empire, Nicholas found them sympathetic to his wish to avoid a free-for-all among the European powers, leading almost certainly to war, if it were to happen. Both sides also agreed on the desirability of maintaining the Sultan on his throne for as long as possible. Nicholas returned home under the impression that he had obtained an unequivocal commitment from Britain that, in the event of a crisis over Turkey, she would act in concert with him. To the British, however, the discussions, although most cordial, had produced little more than a vague statement of intent which could in no way be held to be binding on any future government. It was a misunderstanding which, in due course, would prove extremely costly to both sides.

In the meantime, while refraining from making any antagonistic or threatening moves towards one another's Asiatic domains, then still separated by vast stretches of desert and mountain, the two powers set about consolidating their existing frontiers by subduing troublesome neighbours. The Russians pushed forward their line of fortresses across the lawless Kazakh Steppe as far as the banks of the Syr-Darya, northern twin of the Oxus. By 1853, these stretched from the Aral Sea to Ak-Mechet, 250 miles up river and towards the Central Asian heartland. Two small steamers for supplying these outposts were brought overland in sections and reassembled on the Aral Sea. The British were even more active during this period of *détente*. In 1843, following their humiliation in Afghanistan, they had seized Sind – 'like a bully who has been kicked in the street and goes home to beat his wife in revenge,' observed one critic. They next fought two minor but bloody wars against the Sikhs of the Punjab, who had become increasingly unruly since the death of Ranjit Singh, adding this large and valuable territory to their domains in 1849. The northern state of Kashmir was detached from the Punjab and placed under the control of a ruler considered to be amenable to Britain. These rearrangements gave British India a new neighbour in Dost Mohammed, now firmly back on his throne and showing himself to be cautiously friendly towards his former captors, whom he had apparently come to like during his exile among them.

Such then was the position of the two powers in Central Asia in 1853 when the *détente* so keenly sought by Tsar Nicholas suddenly collapsed. It had been showing signs of strain for some time. In 1848 revolutions had broken out simultaneously in a number of European capitals, including Paris, Berlin, Vienna, Rome, Prague and Budapest. 'There is a general fight going on all over the Continent ... between governors and governed, between law and disorder, between those who have and those who want to have,' wrote Lord Palmerston, once more Foreign Secretary. Nicholas, who lived in perpetual fear of revolution at home, at once clamped down on the few freedoms which existed there. At the same time he dispatched an army under the able Paskievich to Hungary, which he believed to be the centre of the revolutionary movement and of a conspiracy against Russia. The uprising in Hungary was crushed, and its leaders executed. Nicholas had prevented the revolution from spreading to Russia, but had earned himself the enmity of liberals and others everywhere, as well as the title 'the Gendarme of Europe'. When he wrote to Queen Victoria pointing out that only Britain and Russia had been spared from anarchy, and proposing that they join forces to fight it, he got no reply.

However, it was a quarrel in which Britain was not involved, over the guardianship of the Christian sites of the Holy Land, then part of the Ottoman Empire, which finally led to the collapse of ten years of Anglo-Russian accord. The reasons for the squabble – between Russia, France and Turkey – are of no concern to us. But the ensuing crisis was to escalate to the point where Nicholas ordered his troops into the Sultan's northern Balkan provinces, purportedly to protect the Christians there. Nicholas ignored an ultimatum from the Turks to withdraw, and once again the two nations were at war. The British and the French, determined to keep the Russians out of the Near East, allied themselves to the Sultan. Tsar Nicholas, who believed he had forged a special relationship with the British over the question of Turkey, realised too late that he had badly misjudged matters. The Crimean War, which no one really wanted and which could easily have been avoided, had begun.

The story of that bloody conflict is too familiar to need retelling here. Nor was it a part of the Great Game, being fought by large armies on the open battlefield, far from the grim deserts of Central Asia and the lonely passes leading down into India. Yet the ripples were soon to be felt by those responsible for India's defence. For just as British hawks saw the war as an opportunity to prise the Russians from their Caucasian base, and thereby reduce the potential threat to India, there were Russian strategists who believed that a march on India would help speed their victory in the Crimea. Among the latter was Count Simonich's successor at the Persian court, General Duhamel, who put forward a detailed invasion plan aimed at forcing Britain to switch troops to India from the Near Eastern theatre. Such an attack, he argued, need not involve a very large Russian force if the Afghans, and perhaps the Sikhs, could be enticed to join in by the promise of plunder and territorial gains. While the British regiments were manning the frontier, the 'enemy within', India's vast native population, would require little encouragement to attack their masters in the rear.

There was nothing very new in Duhamel's plan. After considering the various alternative routes, all of which had been pointed out long before by Kinneir and others, he settled for a crossing of the Caspian to Astrabad, to be followed by an overland march to Herat. This, he believed, offered the shortest and least exhausting route for the invading troops, since it avoided deserts, mountains and major rivers, not to mention warlike tribes, some or all of which barred the other approaches. The final thrust, which would be made by Duhamel's hoped-for joint force of Russian, Persian and Afghan troops, would be launched from either Kabul or Kandahar. His own preference was for the former, since this led via the Khyber Pass to Lahore and Delhi, whose large native populations might be expected to throw in their lot with their 'liberators'. In the event, the general's plan was never put to the test. Already the war was beginning to go badly for the Russians, and no troops could be spared for such an adventure. Whether, in fact, it would ever have stood a chance of succeeding appears improbable. It seems highly unlikely that those two ancient adversaries, Persia and Afghanistan, would have agreed to forget their differences and join forces, let alone allow a Russian army to march across their domains. After all, they had no better reason to trust the Russians than they had the British. Even with such co-operation, moreover, the military authorities in Calcutta were confident that an invasion force could be destroyed. But Duhamel was right on one point. As the British were soon to discover, there was indeed an 'enemy within'.

If the general's plan achieved nothing for his own country, it was to provide British hawks with valuable political ammunition when word of it and another somewhat similar scheme leaked out. Here was damning evidence that St Petersburg, despite its frequent denials, still had designs on India. One cannot but be struck by the number of these invasion plans which somehow reached British ears over the years. It could well have occurred to the Russian military that there was profit to be gained from such leaks, since they obliged the British to garrison more troops in India than would otherwise have been necessary. After all, it was not only the British who were playing the *Bolshaya Igra*, the Great Game.

But if the British had their Achilles' heel in India, the Russians had theirs in the Caucasus where the local Muslim tribes were still holding out fiercely against the might of the Tsar. Because of the demands of the war in the Crimea, however, the Russian forces in the Caucasus had been drastically reduced. This was the moment, urged the hawks in London and Calcutta, to play Britain's trump card. Not only should arms be sent to the gallant Imam Shamyl and his followers, but also troops. For ever since the days of Urquhart, Longworth and Bell, who had given them such encouragement, not to mention false hopes, the tribesmen had been begging for British help, while Shamyl had even written to Queen Victoria, though in vain. 'An English corps operating in Georgia,' observed one British commentator, 'with the aid of Turkey and Persia, and backed by Shamyl and his hardy mountaineers, would certainly have driven the Russians back beyond the Caucasus.' Others saw the war with Russia as a chance to strike at the Russian fortresses being built along the Syr-Darya. This would not involve the use of British troops at all, it was argued. Arms and advice supplied to the local tribal leaders would enable them to turn the tables on the isolated and weakened Russian posts on the steppe, 'driving them back to the frontiers they occupied at the commencement of the century', as one advocate put it.

However, just as St Petersburg had shied away from Duhamel's plan, the British baulked at similar schemes directed against the Russians, although for different reasons.

With the horrors of the Afghan adventure still fresh in everyone's minds, there was an acute reluctance to meddle again in the affairs of the Muslim states of Asia, even by invitation. This cautious new approach was to become known as the doctrine of 'masterly inactivity', in sharp and obvious contrast to the aggressive 'forward' policy which, with such disastrous results in Afghanistan, had preceded it. Also the French were beginning to suspect that they had been dragged into the conflict in the Crimea in order to further British interests in the East, and London was most anxious to avoid doing anything which might appear to justify this suspicion. In fact, by now, the war was going very much in favour of the British and French. In September 1854 they had laid siege to Sebastopol, Russia's great naval stronghold on the Black Sea, since it was considered that its capture and destruction would secure Turkey's continued independence. The struggle was to last for 349 days and result in heavy casualties and much suffering on either side. But as the Russian surrender became inevitable, Tsar Nicholas, whose attack on Turkey had begun the war, sank deeper and deeper into despair. He finally died in the Winter Palace, from where he had personally commanded the Russian forces, on March 2, 1855. Officially the cause was said to be influenza, but many believed that he had taken poison rather than witness the defeat of his beloved army.

Following the surrender of Sebastopol, and a threat by Austria to join in against him, the new Tsar, Nicholas's son Alexander, agreed to a preliminary peace settlement on February 1, 1856. This was finalised a few weeks later at the Congress of Paris, called to settle the entire Eastern Question. The principal aim of the victors was to keep the Russians out of the Near East, and the harshest terms imposed on the losers concerned the Black Sea area. All warships, naval bases and other fortifications were banned from its waters and shores. While applying equally to all nations, this obviously hit the Russians hardest. At the same time the Black Sea ports were to be opened to the merchant ships of all countries, a somewhat belated victory for David Urquhart, James Bell and others involved in the celebrated *Vixen* affair of twenty years earlier. The Russians also surrendered the mouth of the Danube, the captured Turkish towns of Batum and Kars, and the northern Balkan territories they had occupied, as well as renouncing claims to a religious protectorate over Christians living in the Sultan's domains.

Inevitably, the hawks were dissatisfied, but Britain had achieved her main objectives. The Black Sea was now effectively neutralised, and Turkey's integrity guaranteed by the leading European powers. Russia's ambitions in Europe and the Near East had been blocked, and fifteen years were to pass before St Petersburg declared that it no longer considered itself bound by the Paris agreement, and began once again to build a powerful Black Sea fleet. Meanwhile, smouldering with resentment at their humiliation, the Russian generals once again turned their attention to the war against Shamyl and his followers in the Caucasus, determined this time to crush them once and for all. But if the British thought that their own immediate troubles were over, they were in for a disappointment. All of a sudden Afghanistan, the problem which would not go away, was back in the news.

*　　*　　*

On the outbreak of the Crimean War, the Shah of Persia, who had no great love for either the British or the Russians, found himself in a quandary over which side, if either, to ally himself to. He had hoped that, in exchange for his support, the British might help him to regain from the Russians his lost Caucasian territories. Instead they advised him to remain strictly neutral. Aware, however, that he was under strong pressure from the Russians, whom he greatly feared, to join in the war on their side by marching into eastern Turkey, the Indian government swiftly dispatched a warship to the Persian Gulf as a warning. It worked, and Persia remained neutral throughout the war. Russian machinations continued, however. In the hope of fomenting a war between Britain and Persia, St Petersburg worked on the Shah to lay claim once again to Herat, so crucial to India's defence, while the British were involved in the Crimea. Finally he was persuaded, believing that the British were less concerned now over Herat's ownership. By the time he set out, though, it was too late for the move to be of any benefit to the Russians, for the outcome of the war in the Crimea had already been decided.

Herat fell to the Persians on October 25, 1856, after only a brief siege. The news, which took a whole month to reach India, caught the British by surprise, despite the warnings of Dost Mohammed in Kabul that the Persians were planning such an adventure. He had asked for arms and other assistance from India so that he could repel any Persian incursions into Afghanistan, but in vain. For London, while instructing the Governor-General to maintain cordial relations with Kabul, ordered him to avoid at all costs interfering in the country's internal affairs. By the time it changed its mind it was too late. The Persians, nonetheless, had to be driven out, and quickly, lest Herat become an outpost for intrigue against India, or ultimately a base for invasion. For it had not been forgotten that the Russians had a long-standing agreement with Teheran under which they were entitled to establish consulates any- where in the Shah's domains that they wished. The British had two options. Either they could march an army, with Dost Mohammed's agreement, through Afghanistan, and drive the Persians back across the frontier, or they could dispatch a naval task force to the Gulf and bombard the Shah's ports until he saw sense and withdrew.

The current Governor-General, Lord Canning, was strongly opposed to forward policies – 'especially for India, which cannot raise the money to pay for them' – and par- ticularly averse to sending troops into Afghanistan, even as part of a joint force shared with Dost Mohammed. 'I believe it to be impossible', he wrote, 'for an English army to show itself in that country without at once alienating the common herd of the people, who do not care a straw for Herat but who have a lively recollection of 1838 and all that followed.' It was decided therefore to send a mixed naval and military force to the Gulf, as had been done to good effect when the Persians had laid siege to Herat seventeen years earlier. At the same time a state of war was proclaimed by the Government of India. A formal declaration of war by Britain would have meant the recall of Parliament, then in recess, and Palmerston, now

Prime Minister, knew that this recourse to gunboat diplomacy would prove unpopular, even among his Cabinet, so soon after the costly war with Russia. Indeed, when news of the expedition reached Britain there were anti-war demonstrations in a number of cities there.

After a brief but intensive bombardment, Bushire surrendered to the British on December 10, 1856. As the Union Jack was raised over the city the British troops gave a resounding cheer. Believing this to be the signal for a massacre, the defenders and other inhabitants fled into the desert. However, there was no ill-feeling among the attackers towards the Persians. The real culprits, most felt, were elsewhere. As one British gunner put it to his officer when the bombardment commenced: 'That's one in the eye for the Russians, sir!' But British belligerency did not have the immediate effect which Palmerston had hoped for. Two further engagements proved necessary before the Shah bowed to the inevitable, and agreed once again to withdraw from Herat, this time abandoning all claims to it. This was most fortunate for the British in India, who at that moment found themselves facing an internal upheaval which threatened their very survival.

*   *   *

The Indian Mutiny had been incubating for some time, though few had foreseen it. Among those who did was Eldred Pottinger. Not long before his death he wrote to a friend: 'If the Government does not take some decided steps to recover the affections of the Army, I really think a single spark will blow the sepoys into mutiny.' However, most of the British in India were convinced that the native soldier was, as one officer put it, 'perfectly happy with his lot, a cheerful, good-natured fellow, simple and trustworthy.' Details of the Mutiny, which broke out on May 10, 1857, at Meerut, are beyond the scope of this narrative. Like the Crimean War and the Persian Gulf expedition, it was not part of the Great Game, even if some hawks suspected Russian or Persian agents of having a hand in it. Indeed, the Persians were reported to be openly boasting of this. But even if the Russians were not involved, they did not hesitate to try to take advantage of it.

In the spring of 1858, Nikolai Khanikov, a Russian agent, crossed the Caspian and reached Herat, from where he intended to proceed secretly to Kabul and make overtures on behalf of his government to Dost Mohammed. As it happened, the Afghan ruler had just concluded an alliance with the British, towards whom he was feeling particularly well disposed since they had ejected the Persians from Afghanistan without so much as setting foot there themselves. He no doubt remembered too the painful consequences for himself, twenty years earlier, of his dallying with Captain Vitkevich, the last Tsarist agent to visit Kabul. And now he had witnessed the defeat of the Russians on the Crimean battlefield by the British and their allies, not to mention the failure of St Petersburg, for the second time in eighteen years, to come to the assistance of its Persian friends. There was little question in Dost Mohammed's mind as to which of the two rivals was the more powerful, and therefore worth remaining on good terms with. The one thing he most desired, moreover, was Herat, which the Russians were never likely to bestow upon him as this would finish them for ever with the Persians.

Khanikov was sent packing, without even seeing Kabul, despite the wild rumours then circulating in the capital that the British in India had all been slaughtered. Considering also the intense pressure that Dost Mohammed found himself under from the more fanatical of his followers to be allowed to join the uprising against the infidels, the British had good reason to feel profound gratitude towards the ruler they had once removed forcibly from his throne. For at a time when they were fighting for their very survival against the 'enemy within', the intervention of the Afghans would have been a stab in the back which would most likely have proved decisive. Dost Mohammed was to receive his reward some years later. In 1863, when he led his troops against Herat, the British raised no objection. They would have preferred the country to remain divided, lest under a less friendly successor to the ageing Dost Mohammed a united Afghanistan should prove a threat to India. As it was, just nine days after his victory, the old warrior died, happy in the knowledge that he had restored order to his kingdom, and regained control over this long-lost province. But what he did not know was that history would repeat itself with uncanny precision, and that within fifteen years Britain and Afghanistan would be at war again. A lot, however, was destined to happen before that.

*   *   *

The suppression of the Mutiny, which had been achieved by the spring of 1858, was to have the most far-reaching consequences for India. It was to lead to a massive shake-up in the way the country was ruled, and to mark the end of the East India Company's two and a half centuries of sway over 250 million people. At the time of the outbreak, India was still nominally run from the Company's headquarters in Leadenhall Street in the City of London, albeit with ever-increasing interference from Downing Street and Whitehall as improved communications made this easier. In August 1858, in an attempt to resolve the deep resentments and antagonisms which had led to the Mutiny, the British government passed the India Act, abolishing the powers of the Company and transferring all authority to the Crown. A new Cabinet post – that of Secretary of State for India – was created, and the old Board of Control, together with its powerful President, was abolished. In place of the Board an Advisory Council of fifteen members was appointed, eight of whom were chosen by the Crown and the others, initially, by the Company. At the same time the Governor-General was given the additional title of Viceroy of India, being the personal representative of the Queen.

There were radical changes too in the organisation of India's armed forces, then forming one of the largest armies in the world. A fresh start was obviously called for to restore the confidence of the sepoys in their officers and vice versa. The higher ranks of the Company's Army had long been filled with ageing, time-serving officers (of whom General Elphinstone had been merely one), in whose abilities and leadership the troops had little confidence. Worse, during the disastrous retreat from Kabul, many of the officers had deserted their men so as to make their own escape, leaving them to a chilling fate at the hands of the Afghan soldiery. Significantly, those native regiments which had fought in Afghanistan were among the first to join the Mutiny. Now, just as the East India Company ceased to exist, so too did its once formidable army. The regiments, both European and native, were transferred to the newly formed Indian Army, which was under the ultimate authority of the War Office in London. All artillery was henceforth placed under European control.

Altogether the Mutiny had been a close-run thing, and the nightmare experienced by the British during it served only to intensify their paranoia over Russian interference in India's affairs. Nonetheless, the enemy within had been crushed, and India was to remain relatively quiet for the rest of the century. But beyond the frontiers it was a very different matter. By defeating the Russians in the Crimea, the British had hoped not merely to keep them out of the Near East, but also to halt their expansion into Central Asia. As things turned out, it was to have quite the opposite effect.

THE CLIMACTIC YEARS

'Whatever be Russia's designs upon India, whether they be serious and inimical or imaginary and fantastic, I hold that the first duty of English statesmen is to render any hostile intentions futile, to see that our own position is secure, and our frontier impregnable, and so to guard what is without doubt the noblest trophy of British genius, and the most splendid appanage of the Imperial Crown.'

Hon. George Curzon, MP,
Russia in Central Asia, 1889.

· 23 ·

The Great Russian
Advance Begins

'Where the imperial flag has once flown,' Tsar Nicholas is said to have decreed, 'it must never be lowered.' Nor did his son Alexander have any reason to think differently. To those serving on Russia's Asiatic frontiers the inference soon became clear. Raise the two-headed eagle first, and ask permission afterwards. Those who did just that found that they were rarely, if ever, repudiated. This turning of a blind eye to such expropriations by St Petersburg was to coincide with the rise of a new and aggressive breed of frontier officer. Not surprisingly, in view of their country's defeat in the Crimean War, they were Anglophobes to a man. Between them, during the middle years of the nineteenth century, they were to add vast new tracts of Asia to Alexander's domains.

One such officer was Count Nikolai Ignatiev, a brilliant and ambitious young political, who enjoyed the ear of the Tsar, and burned to settle his country's scores with the British. As the latter would soon learn to their cost, he was to prove himself a consummate player in the Great Game. While serving as military attaché in London during the Indian Mutiny, he had repeatedly urged his chiefs in St Petersburg to take full advantage of Britain's weakness in order to steal a march on her in Asia and elsewhere. Although he attempted to conceal his anti-British feelings, and enjoyed considerable popularity in London society, he did not entirely fool the Foreign Office. Describing him in a confidential report as a 'clever, wily fellow', it had him closely watched after a London map dealer informed the authorities that he had been discreetly buying up all available maps of Britain's ports and railways.

In 1858, aged 26 and already earmarked for rapid promotion, he was chosen by Alexander to lead a secret mission to Central Asia. His task was to try to discover how far the British had penetrated the region, politically and commercially, and to undermine any influence which they might already have acquired in Khiva and Bokhara. For the Tsar was concerned about reports reaching Russian outposts on the Syr-Darya that British agents were becoming increasingly active in the region. If this were to turn into a race for the valuable markets of Central Asia, then St Petersburg was determined to win it. Ignatiev was instructed therefore to try to establish regular commercial links with both Khiva and Bokhara, if possible securing favourable terms and assured protection for Russian traders and goods. He also had orders to gather as much military, political and other intelligence as he could, including an evaluation of the khanates' capacity for war. Finally he was to discover all he could about the navigability of the Oxus, and about the routes leading into Afghanistan, Persia and northern India.

Ignatiev's mission, nearly a hundred strong, including a Cossack escort and porters, reached Khiva in the summer of 1858. The Khan had agreed to receive them, and they brought with them an impressive array of gifts, including an organ. These proved too bulky to be transported across the desert, having instead to be ferried across the Aral Sea and up the Oxus, thus providing the Russians with the opportunity to survey the latter's lower reaches. It was a Great Game subterfuge borrowed from the British, who had charted the River Indus in somewhat similar manner nearly thirty years previously. Nor was the gift of an organ to an Eastern potentate entirely original, the British Levant Company having presented the Turkish Sultan with one more than two centuries earlier. The Khan was not that easily fooled, however. He received Ignatiev politely, accepted the gifts, but adamantly refused to let the Russian vessels proceed any further up the Oxus towards Bokhara. Even so, Ignatiev persuaded the Khan to open his markets to Russian merchants, only to see this collapse at the last moment when a Persian slave sought asylum aboard a Russian vessel. Nonetheless he left Khiva for Bokhara with a good deal of valuable intelligence, not to mention hawkish views on the need to cut the Khan down to size by annexing his territories.

Ignatiev was to fare marginally better in Bokhara, where, sixteen years after the beheading of Conolly and Stoddart, the cruel and tyrannical Emir Nasrullah was still firmly on the throne. Nor had age mellowed him. When, not long before, his chief of artillery had displeased him, he had personally cut him in half with an axe. For Ignatiev, however, he was prepared to put himself out a little. Once again he was at war with his old adversary and neighbour, the Khan of Khokand, and was anxious to do nothing likely to provoke the Russians into supporting his foe. He promised to free all Russians then being held in Bokhara as slaves, and actively to encourage trade between their two countries. He even suggested that they should divide the Khan of Khiva's domains between them if the latter persisted in denying Russian vessels access to the Oxus from the Aral Sea. Finally he undertook not to receive any emissaries from the British, and to urge his Afghan neighbours not to allow any of them to cross the Oxus.

Ignatiev knew perfectly well that the Emir's promises were worthless, and that he had no intention of keeping any of them once the threat from Khokand was over. Nonetheless, as at Khiva, he and his men were able to gather valuable intelligence which was to come in useful later. Altogether it had been a bold journey, fraught with hardship and danger, and even if it had failed in its objectives it had helped to restore Russian self-esteem. Ignatiev returned to St Petersburg to find himself a celebrity and more highly regarded than ever by his superiors. In the detailed report which he produced on the mission he urged the immediate annexation of the Central Asian khanates, lest the British get there first. While this was being carefully considered by the Tsar and his advisers, he was assigned to an even more challenging task, this time 3,500 miles away to the east, in China. His new mission was to give Ignatiev considerable satisfaction, for not only was he raised to the temporary rank of general, so as to invest him with the authority he would require, but it also offered him the chance to pit his wits against the British.

A crisis had arisen over Alexander's fears for his new and ill-guarded possessions in the Far East, which his Siberian garrisons had acquired for him during the previous three or four years at the expense of the Chinese. Fearful lest the British gain possession of China, as they already had India, the Russian commanders had been driving remorselessly eastwards along the great Amur river, and southwards down the Pacific seaboard towards what is now Vladivostok. The Chinese Emperor, being fully engaged at this time with the Taiping rebellion, and with British and French demands for land concessions and other privileges, was in no position to stop them. Thus, at little cost to themselves, the Russians were able to relieve him of nearly 400,000 square miles of his empire. Now, however, they found their new possessions threatened by the British.

Just how this came about is too complex to go into in any detail here, but broadly it resulted from the Second Opium War, the so-called Arrow War, between Britain and China in 1856. Following their victory, the British had made various demands of the Emperor, to which he had reluctantly agreed. These included the right of European powers to have diplomats residing in Peking, the opening of more ports to foreign trade, and the payment of a huge indemnity to Britain. When the Emperor tried to go back on these, a powerful British and French force was dispatched to enforce them, with orders to march on Peking if necessary. The prospect of the British thus gaining a foothold in the Manchu capital struck fear into the Russians, lest it imperil their Far Eastern domains. Such was the situation when Ignatiev set out by sleigh and on horseback for distant Peking in the spring of 1859. His most urgent task was to secure the Tsar's new territories by coercing the Chinese Emperor into formally ceding them to Russia, thereby making them a permanent part of the Russian Empire. It was a classic Great Game mission, and St Petersburg could not have entrusted it to a more determined or resourceful player.

On reaching the Forbidden City, Ignatiev immediately

offered his services to the hard-pressed Emperor as an intermediary between himself and his European foes. At first these
were declined, for it was feared that despite his protests of
strict neutrality he might in fact be in league with the British
and French. Nor, as it would later transpire, were they that far
out, for Ignatiev was playing a double game. At first he assisted
the invaders, discreetly supplying them with maps of the
Chinese positions and with intelligence from inside the capital,
to which he had access. At the same time he did everything he
could to prevent them from coming to terms with the Chinese,
fanning the flames of discord, and encouraging them to press
on towards Peking. Finally, when the British and French
troops were at the very walls of the city, he again offered his
services to the Chinese as a mediator. By now the Emperor
had fled the capital, leaving his brother to cope with the enemy.
Already the latter had burned down the magnificent Summer
Palace, which lay five miles outside Peking, and fearing the
wholesale destruction of the city if foreign troops entered it,
the defenders gratefully accepted Ignatiev's offer.

Faced by the onset of the cruel winter of northern China,
the British and French were anxious to enforce the provisions
which the Emperor had originally agreed to, and then to depart.
Ignatiev, however, was careful to keep this from the Chinese.
Instead he played on their fears of the foreign troops staying
on, and indeed Lord Elgin, the British commander, did
momentarily toy with the idea, writing to Lord John Russell,
then Foreign Secretary: 'We might annex the Chinese Empire
if we were in the humour to take a second India in hand.'
Finally the British and French settled for their original
demands, both signing separate treaties with the Chinese, and
then made plans to leave at once. Ignatiev succeeded in convincing the Chinese that he had not only hastened the departure
of the foreign troops, but had also persuaded them to reduce
the indemnity they were demanding. He now set about negotiating a treaty with the defeated Chinese on behalf of his
own government, the formal ceding of Russia's new Pacific
territories being its main provision. When the Chinese hesitated over his demands, he used a brief, and purely administrative, delay in the troops' departure to frighten them into

agreement, claiming that he had ordered it. On November 6, 1860, the last of the foreign troops left. Eleven days later, without the British or the French suspecting what was afoot until it was too late to prevent it, the Russians, in the person of Ignatiev, and the Chinese signed the Treaty of Peking.

It had been a Machiavellian performance of the highest order by the young Ignatiev, then still in his late twenties, and a remarkable diplomatic triumph for the Russians. First, they had formally added a vast tract of territory, the size of France and Germany together, to their already huge northern Asiatic empire. Second, they had got the Chinese to agree to their opening consulates at Kashgar, in Eastern Turkestan, and at Urga, the capital of Mongolia, then both under Peking's rule. They had thereby stolen a march on their rivals, the British, who had obtained no such facility, for the establishment of consulates meant that Russian merchants and goods would have exclusive access to these important new markets. It was with considerable satisfaction, therefore, that Ignatiev left Peking on November 22 and rode hard for St Petersburg. 'Not since 1815', one British historian has written, 'had Russia concluded such an advantageous treaty, and probably never before had such a feat been carried off by so young a Russian diplomat. The successes of 1860 went far to obliterate the bitter memories of the Crimean defeat, the more especially as they had been achieved in good measure by hoodwinking the English.'

*   *   *

Six weeks after leaving Peking, Ignatiev arrived in St Petersburg. Once again he had ridden the whole way across Asia, this time in the middle of winter. After his filthy clothes, crawling with lice and fleas, had been removed and burned, he was summoned to report to the Tsar at the Winter Palace. There, in recognition of his remarkable services to his country, he was awarded the coveted Order of St Vladimir by the delighted Alexander. He was also allowed to retain his temporary rank of general. Finally, to make full use of his first-hand experience of the region and its peoples, he was made head of the recently formed Asiatic Department of the Foreign Ministry. Ignatiev thus joined the growing number of hawks and Anglophobes holding high positions in St Petersburg or on Russia's frontiers. Among these was the energetic War Minister, Count Dmitri Milyutin, who had been appointed at the age of only 34. Another was Count Nikolai Muraviev, the forceful Governor-General of Eastern Siberia. It was he who had originally seized the vast Pacific territories which Ignatiev had now secured permanently for the Tsar. A third was Prince Alexander Baryatinsky, Governor-General of the Caucasus, who viewed the halting of British political and commercial penetration in Asia as a matter of urgency. In 1859, using new strategies, he had finally forced the submission of Imam Shamyl, thereby bringing to an end, except in parts of Circassia, four decades of bloody resistance to Russian rule. He saw the Caucasus as a powerful base from which the Tsar's armies could 'descend like an avalanche on Turkey, Persia and the road to India.'

Nor was this new mood for empire-building confined to the highest echelons of government. Most of the younger army officers favoured forward policies in Asia, and were eager to spoil what they believed to be Britain's game there. Indeed the entire army, which Milyutin was drastically reorganising, was thirsting for fresh conquests following its successes in the Far East, not to mention the chance to expunge the memory of its Crimean defeat. As for the risks of a collision with Britain, most soldiers believed that sooner or later another war with Britain was inevitable anyway. In addition, Russian merchants and factory owners were pressing for the markets of Central Asia, as well as China, to be opened up to their goods, provided the caravans could be protected from plunder by Kazakh, Kirghiz and Turcoman raiders. Finally, the hawks at the top had an unexpected ally in Otto von Bismarck, then Prussian ambassador to St Petersburg, and soon to become his country's chief minister and the architect of the German Empire. Believing that the more the Russians became involved in Asia the less of a threat they would be in Europe, he strongly encouraged them to embark on what he called their 'great civilising mission'.

But those close to the Tsar who urged him to press southwards into Central Asia before the British got there had to bide
their time. For Alexander had more critical matters to attend
to at home. Largely as a result of the many shortcomings in
Russian society which the Crimean War had shown up, he
had embarked on a series of major liberal reforms aimed at
modernising the country. The most momentous of these was
the emancipation in 1861 of some forty million serfs, and the
distribution of land to them, which predictably was resisted
fiercely by many landowners. At the same time Alexander
faced yet another uprising in Poland, which took him eighteen
months to put down, and earned him much opprobrium in
Europe. There were senior officials around him, moreover,
who opposed forward policies in Central Asia. One was Count
Mikhail Reutern, the Minister of Finance, who strongly cautioned him against taking on any new financial burdens until
the country had recovered from the economic ruin resulting
from the Crimean War. Another was Prince Alexander Gorchakov, who in 1856 had succeeded Nesselrode as Foreign
Minister. It had been his uncomfortable task to try to justify
the crushing of the Polish uprising to the rest of Europe. He
now warned Alexander that the importance which the British
accorded to India would make any moves by Russian troops
towards its frontiers too perilous to contemplate.

Ignatiev and his allies were to win the day, however. Freed
finally from his other problems, Alexander allowed himself to
be persuaded by them of the need to steal a march in Central
Asia on the scheming British. Any fears of a strong British
reaction to moves there by Russia were brushed aside by Ignatiev. He pointed out that the British, after a succession of costly
wars – with Afghanistan, Russia, Persia and China – not to
mention a bloody insurrection in India, showed clear signs of
entering a passive phase, and of wishing to avoid becoming
embroiled in further conflicts. But what finally decided the
Tsar was something which had happened in America, whose
Southern States had long been Russia's principal source of raw
cotton. As a result of the civil war there, supplies of this vital
commodity had been cut off, badly affecting the whole of
Europe. The Russians, however, were more fortunate than

most. For some time they had known that the Khokand region of Central Asia, especially the fertile Ferghana valley, was particularly suitable for growing cotton, with the potential to produce it in very substantial quantities. Alexander was determined to get his hands on the cotton-fields of Central Asia, or at least on the crop itself, before anyone else did. And that meant the British.

Originally it had been hoped that cordial relations and commercial co-operation might be established with the individual khanates by means of alliances, thereby avoiding bloodshed, expense and any risk of provoking untoward British reaction. But Ignatiev insisted, from his own recent experience at Khiva and Bokhara, that this was merely naïve. The rulers of Central Asia, he said, were untrustworthy and totally incapable of keeping to any agreement. Conquest was the only way of being sure, and thus keeping the British out. His view, which enjoyed the support of Count Milyutin, was to prevail. By the end of 1863 any remaining hopes of imperialism by negotiation had been finally abandoned. The Russians were ready to move into Central Asia, albeit gradually at first.

Their initial move, in the summer of 1864, was to consolidate their existing southern frontier with Central Asia by closing a gap, 500 miles wide, in the middle. It involved seizing several small towns and forts situated in the northern domains of the Khan of Khokand, and was achieved without difficulty. Alarmed by these aggressive moves, which had robbed him of the oasis towns of Chimkent and Turkestan, the Khan immediately dispatched an emissary to India to beg for military assistance from the British. However, this was politely refused, for the doctrine of 'masterly inactivity' now guided British policy in Central Asia. What frontier activity there was, including mapping the hitherto unmapped and the construction of strategic roads, was confined to areas close to India's own frontiers, in the somewhat pious hope that the Russians might show similar restraint. It would take more than that, though, to convince St Petersburg that the British had lost interest in Central Asia.

The Russians now prepared for their next step, encouraged no doubt by Britain's failure to respond to the Khan of Khokand's plea for help. But anticipating the outcry, particularly from the British, which would follow any further advances into Central Asia, the Russian Foreign Minister, Prince Gorchakov, first sat down to prepare an official 'explanation' for such moves which, he hoped, would allay European fears and suspicions. It was skilfully designed, moreover, to make it difficult for powers like Britain, France, Holland, and even America, to object. For it compared Russia's position in Central Asia to theirs in their own extensive colonial territories. In December 1864 Gorchakov's memorandum was circulated, via the Tsar's ambassadors, to the major European powers.

'The position of Russia in Central Asia', declared this celebrated document, 'is that of all civilised states which are brought into contact with half-savage nomad populations possessing no fixed social organisation. In such cases it always happens that the more civilised state is forced, in the interests of the security of its frontiers and its commercial relations, to exercise a certain ascendancy over those whose turbulent and unsettled character make them undesirable neighbours.' In their turn these newly pacified regions had to be protected from the depredations of the lawless tribes beyond them, and so on. The Russian government therefore had to choose between bringing civilisation to those suffering under barbarian rule and abandoning its frontiers to anarchy and bloodshed. 'Such has been the fate', Gorchakov wrote, 'of every country which has found itself in a similar position.' Britain and the other colonial powers had been 'irresistibly forced, less by ambition than by imperious necessity, into this onward march'. The greatest difficulty, he concluded, lay in deciding where to stop. Nonetheless, having consolidated its frontier with Khokand, Russia was intending to advance no further.

'We find ourselves', he assured the other powers, 'in the presence of a more solid, less unsettled and better organised state, fixing for us with geographical precision that point at which we must halt.' Whether he himself really believed this, or whether he was merely playing for time on behalf of a government already bent on subjugating the khanates, is a question which still exercises scholars. Certainly N. A. Khalfin, the Soviet historian of this era, believes that it was a deliberate smokescreen aimed at deceiving the British. Needless to say, the Russian advance did not stop there as Gorchakov had promised. Within a few months they were driving south once more. The great Russian push into Central Asia was about to begin. It was not destined to halt until the khanates of Central Asia lay prostrate at the Tsar's feet.

· 24 ·

Lion of Tashkent

In the middle of the nineteenth century, the three warring khanates of Khiva, Bokhara and Khokand between them ruled the vast region of desert and mountain, half the size of America, which stretched from the Caspian in the west to the Pamirs in the east. But besides these three city-states, there were other towns of importance. One was ancient Samarkand, Tamerlane's one-time capital, now part of the Emir of Bokhara's domains. Another was Kashgar, cut off from the others by high mountains, which was then ruled by China. Finally there was the great walled city of Tashkent, once independent, but at that time belonging to the Khan of Khokand.

Tashkent, with its orchards, vineyards, pasturage and population of 100,000, was the richest city in Central Asia. It owed its prosperity not only to its abundance of natural resources, but also to the energy and enterprise of its merchants, and to its proximity to Russia, with which it had long traded. However, it was no secret that its powerful merchant families would only too happily have exchanged Khokand's rule, with its punitive taxation, for that of the Russians. It was no secret either that the clergy, who also wielded considerable influence, looked to the Emir of Bokhara, ruler of the holiest city in Central Asia, for their salvation. Given the opportunity, the Emir would have been more than willing to oblige them, thereby adding this rich prize to his possessions. In the spring of 1865, such an opportunity arose when he and his old adversary the Khan of Khokand found themselves once again at war.

But there was one other contender – the Russians. It was clear to the commander of the Khokand frontier region, Major-General Mikhail Cherniaev, that Tashkent and its valuable commerce were at risk. Cherniaev, who had had his eye on Tashkent for some time, decided to seize it before the Emir of Bokhara did, and while both rulers were fully occupied by their war. The Tsar and his advisers in St Petersburg were not yet ready to annex Tashkent, however. This was partly because they were unsure, despite Ignatiev's confident assurances, how the British would react, and partly because they were doubtful whether Cherniaev's forces, only 1,300 strong, were sufficient to take the city, with its estimated 30,000 defenders. They therefore telegraphed him ordering him not to attack. But suspecting what the envelope might contain, the general deliberately left it unopened, concealing it from his staff. He calculated that if he succeeded in adding this jewel to the Tsar's crown, at minimum loss of life and expense, his disobedience would be overlooked. Such an action by a British general would have brought the wrath of Parliament and press down upon his head, not to mention that of the Cabinet and his own superiors. In Russia, however, there was only one man ultimately to please or displease – the Tsar himself. The rewards for success could be considerable, moreover. Cherniaev decided that it was a gamble worth taking. There was another reason, too, why he acted as he did. His immediate chief, the Governor-General of Orenburg, was planning to visit the frontier region, and he feared that his chief would rob him of his chance by leading the attack himself.

Leaving word that the advance of Bokharan troops into the Khan of Khokand's domains posed a serious threat to Tashkent, giving him no alternative, he set out at the beginning of May 1865. On the way he seized the small fort of Niazbek, lying to the south of the city, thereby gaining control of the river which provided most of its water. His engineers now diverted the river so that none of its water reached Tashkent. Cherniaev was joined here by reinforcements which he had called up, bringing his numbers to 1,900, with 12 guns. Together they pressed on towards Tashkent, which they reached around May 8 after defeating a force sent by the Khan of Khokand to intercept them. Cherniaev immediately set about studying the city's defences, and making contact with those inside the walls who were friendly to the Russians. It was his hope that the latter would be able to persuade the rest of the population to surrender, opening the gates to their liberators, and handing the Khokand garrison over to his troops. But he quickly discovered that shortly before his arrival a small force of Bokharan officers and men had slipped into the city at the invitation of the Emir's supporters there and had taken over its defences. It also transpired that only a minority of the inhabitants relished the prospect of Russian rule.

There could be no turning back now, however. The humiliation of a Russian retreat would reverberate through Central Asia for years to come. Cherniaev was aware that he himself would face certain court-martial for disobeying orders and bringing disgrace upon the army. Yet his force was far too small for him to consider laying siege to a city surrounded by a high crenellated wall some sixteen miles long. There was nothing for it, Cherniaev knew, but to try to take it by storm. While extraordinarily daring, this was not quite so far-fetched or reckless as it appears. Although the defenders outnumbered his troops by something like fifteen to one, the Russian general knew that here lay their weakness. Provided he could keep the moment and exact point of his attack secret until the very last moment, the defenders were so thinly spread along the many miles of wall that they would be unable to concentrate there in time. Furthermore, not only were the Russians far better armed, trained and led, but they also knew that once they were inside the city they would find sympathisers and helpers among the population.

Cherniaev struck at first light on June 15. Late the night before, under cover of darkness, his men crept forward into position. The main assault party, carrying long scaling ladders, advanced towards one of the gates where reconnaissance had shown the wall to be at its lowest and the cover good. The wheels of the gun carriages were wrapped in felt to ensure silence as they were moved into position. At the same time a smaller force made its way to another of the city's gates, several miles to the east, ready to make a feint attack designed to draw off large numbers of the defenders until the storming party was inside. They would then endeavour to join their comrades in the struggle for the citadel.

At 2.30 a.m. volunteers unloaded the scaling ladders from the camels and bore them to the very foot of the walls beside the gate which was to be attacked. As they did so they stumbled over a sleeping sentry, whose presence outside the wall suggested the existence of a secret passage under the wall through which he had come. Rudely prodded by Russian bayonets, the prisoner was forced to reveal its whereabouts. Cleverly camouflaged with grey felt, which exactly matched the colour of the walls, it led upwards to a barbette, or platform, perched beside the gate. Its discovery was an extraordinary bit of luck for the Russians, for just then they heard the sound of heavy gunfire from the direction of the other gate. The diversionary force had begun its attack, immediately drawing large numbers of the defenders to the spot.

Here was the attackers' chance. Under cover of the noise of the bombardment, the Russians moved swiftly. Some crawling along the secret passage, and others swarming silently up their scaling ladders, they took the defenders totally by surprise. Within minutes, and without loss to themselves, they had seized the gates from inside and forced them open. Led by their chaplain, Father Malov, armed only with a cross, the main party now poured into the city, fanning out to attack the startled defenders manning barricades and the parapets above. At the same time a captain and 250 men fought their way along the wall to try to reach the diversionary force and let them into the city. Resistance at first was fierce, but very soon the superior fire-power and tactics of Cherniaev's seasoned troops began to tell. Even with their stiffening of Bokharan officers, the defenders lacked the fanatical spirit of resistance which the Russians were used to encountering in the Caucasus. Within an hour or so the diversionary force was also inside the city, and the citadel was firmly in Russian hands. By the middle of the afternoon the Russians were in possession of half the city. Meanwhile, outside the walls, 39 of Cherniaev's Cossacks had routed 5,000 enemy horsemen, many of whom had been drowned while fleeing across a river.

There was now a brief lull in the fighting as pro-Russian elements among the population tried to negotiate a ceasefire. But this failed to hold and fighting broke out again, continuing into the night. Until then Cherniaev had refrained from using his artillery for fear of destroying the city and threatening the lives and property of those friendly to Russia. By this time, however, after fighting all day, his men were utterly exhausted. He ordered his guns to be brought to bear on the enemy positions so as to keep them at bay. Very soon many of the buildings in the labyrinth of streets around the Russian positions were ablaze, creating a protective ring of fire around them and enabling the troops to snatch some desperately needed sleep and rest.

The next morning fierce fighting flared up again, but by evening the defenders, badly dispirited and now deserted by their Bokharan advisers, could see that further resistance was futile. The city elders realised, too, that unless they wanted to see Tashkent reduced to rubble they had no choice but to submit. A meeting was arranged with Cherniaev at which surrender terms were discussed. These were accepted by him on behalf of Tsar Alexander the following morning, although he had no authority to do so. At the same time, awed by the brilliant and daring generalship which had enabled the Russian to capture their city with so small a force, the elders gave him the honorific title of 'Lion of Tashkent'. It was indeed an astonishing victory. Russian losses were only twenty-five dead and eighty-nine wounded – a fraction of the casualties they had inflicted on the enemy.

Cherniaev now set about trying to win the goodwill of the people, particularly the religious authorities, by reconciliation and generosity in victory. He called on Tashkent's principal Muslim leader at his home, bowing respectfully as he entered, and pledged himself to allow the elders to run the city's affairs as before, and not to interfere in their religious life. Aware of the deep resentment felt over the crippling taxes which the Khan of Khokand had imposed, he absolved everyone from paying any taxes for a year – an immensely popular, if costly, move. He rode alone through the streets and bazaars, talking to ordinary people, and even accepting a bowl of tea from a total stranger. It was an early hearts-and-minds operation by Cherniaev and his troops, and their magnanimity was to win over many of those who had previously regarded the Russians as ogres. It was an admirable policy, but not one that subsequent Russian commanders in Central Asia always adopted.

Having appointed himself Military Governor of Tashkent, Cherniaev sat back to await word from St Petersburg of his own fate. There his report on the city's capture, and the pacification of its inhabitants, was being perused by his startled superiors, including Tsar Alexander. In it Cherniaev extolled the valour of his troops, singling out a number of officers and men for special praise. Among them was Father Malov, the crucifix-bearing chaplain, who had been in the thick of all the fighting, and who was to remain in Tashkent as a priest for the rest of his life. Cherniaev reasoned that once the imperial flag had been raised over Tashkent the Tsar would be loath to see it hauled down. He therefore recommended that the city should once again become an independent khanate, but from now on under Russian protection.

Cherniaev did not have to wait long to learn that his reckless gamble had paid off. 'A glorious affair,' the Tsar called it. Disobedience, it appeared, was acceptable – provided it was successful. For Cherniaev had achieved, with the minimum of fuss and casualties, what Alexander really wanted, but feared could not be achieved without the deployment of a far larger force. The Tsar immediately awarded Cherniaev the Cross of St Anne, while other officers who had distinguished themselves were fittingly rewarded. Other ranks received a bonus of two roubles each. Meanwhile, St Petersburg braced itself for the British protests which, in view of Prince Gorchakov's recent assurances, seemed inevitable. In a bid to pre-empt these, the official announcement of Cherniaev's victory published in the St Petersburg newspapers declared the occupation of Tashkent to be no more than temporary, insisting that it had been done strictly to protect Tashkent from Bokharan annexation. Once the danger was over, it would be restored to independence under a khan of its own.

The British government, as expected, duly protested. It pointed out that Tashkent lay far beyond the frontier which Prince Gorchakov had spelt out in his famous memorandum on Russia's southern limits. Moreover, the seizure of Tashkent, London added, was 'scarcely consistent with the professed intention of the Russian government to respect the independence of the states of Central Asia.' But by now no one seriously expected St Petersburg to keep its undertaking to withdraw from Tashkent, any more than it had kept its earlier promise. Nor did it. After waiting for things to calm down, it announced the permanent establishment of a new Governorate-General, that of Turkestan. Tashkent was to be its military and administrative headquarters, as well as the official place of residence of the Governor-General. Beyond declaring that this move had been forced upon it by 'military expediency', St Petersburg did not go out of its way to justify it. As Count Milyutin wrote: 'It is unnecessary for us to beg the forgiveness of ministers of the English Crown for each advance we make. They do not hasten to confer with us when they conquer whole kingdoms and occupy foreign cities and islands. Nor do we ask them to justify what they do.'

Having served his purpose, General Cherniaev, whose impulsiveness and ambition were viewed in St Petersburg as a liability, was recalled, and General Konstantin Kaufman, a veteran of the Caucasus war and a personal friend of Milyutin's, was appointed the first Governor-General of Turkestan. A soldier of exceptional ability and vision, he was given extraordinary powers by Tsar Alexander. Eventually he was destined to become the uncrowned king of Central Asia, and principal architect of Russia's empire there. To the dismay of the hawks in London and Calcutta, the British government's reaction to all this, beyond its initial protest, was surprisingly muted. So, too, was that of most of the press and public. 'To those who remember the Russophobia of 1838–39,' wrote Sir Henry Rawlinson, that veteran of the earlier phase of the Great Game, 'the indifference of the English public to the events now passing in Central Asia must appear one of the strangest instances in modern history.' The truth was that the Russophobes had cried wolf too often to expect much support this time. The spectre of the Cossacks pouring down through the passes into British India, raised on and off for nearly half a century, had so far not materialised. And yet, as Rawlinson pointed out in a long, anonymous article in the *Quarterly Review* of July 1865, the relative positions of Britain and Russia in Asia had changed considerably since the days of Wilson, Kinneir, de Lacy Evans and McNeill.

'We have, in the first place, greatly advanced our own frontier,' he wrote, referring to the annexation of Sind and the Punjab. British India had also extended its political influence northwards into Kashmir. At the same time the Russians had consolidated their position in the Caucasus, after crushing Imam Shamyl, thereby freeing large numbers of troops for deployment elsewhere, and had also begun to make forward moves in Turkestan. In addition to this, Rawlinson observed, the Russians had much improved their communications with Central Asia. A railway now ran all the way from St Petersburg to Nijni-Novogorod (formerly Gorky) on the Volga, while plying the latter, all the way down to the Caspian Sea, were 300 steamships. In time of war these, plus a further 50 vessels on the Caspian itself, could be used to transport men and supplies eastwards towards Afghanistan and India.

Rawlinson, who had retired from Indian government service to enter Parliament as a Conservative MP, next considered the reasons for the public's apathy. One, obviously, was the memory of the Afghan disaster, and a determination not to let such a thing happen again. Another was a widespread conviction that nothing could prevent the Russian advance and their eventual annexation of Khiva, Bokhara and Khokand. Any attempt by Britain to stop this would merely make them move faster, it was argued. Some doves reasoned that it would be better to have the Russians as neighbours than wild tribesmen, upon whom no reliance could be placed. A settled Central Asia ruled by St Petersburg would bring prosperity to the region, and open up new markets there for British goods. Rawlinson, needless to say, shared none of these views.

Ranged against him and his fellow hawks was the new Whig Cabinet, under Lord Russell, vigorously supported by the Viceroy, Sir John Lawrence, himself an old frontier hand of considerable distinction, and a former Governor of the Punjab. Lawrence was convinced that if the Russians tried to attack India through Afghanistan their troops would suffer the same fate at the hands of the fanatical tribes as the British had in the dreadful winter of 1842. He dismissed as highly improbable the fear that St Petersburg might persuade the Afghans to allow Russian troops to march across their country, or even to join forces with them, in order to attack India. The best way to restrain Russia, he argued, was by means of tough diplomacy from London. The Russian Achilles' heel, if it came to it, lay within easier reach of London than of Calcutta. Were Tsar Alexander ever to show signs of launching an attack on India through Central Asia or Persia then the immediate dispatch of a British battle fleet to the Baltic would force him to think again. Even so, it was not long before those responsible for India's defence, including Lawrence himself, began to feel distinctly uneasy.

*   *   *

Looking back now, it is obvious that from the moment General Kaufman took up his new post as Governor-General of Turkestan the days of the independent khanates of Central Asia were numbered. Despite all Gorchakov's assurances it is clear that their absorption, in one form or another, into the Russian Empire was his principal aim. As we have already seen, there were three main reasons for this. Foremost was the fear of the British getting there first and monopolising the region's trade. Russian merchants and manufacturers had long had their eyes on the untapped markets and resources of Central Asia, especially its raw cotton. Then there was the question of imperial pride. Blocked in Europe and the Near East, the Russians sought to work off their frustration by demonstrating their military prowess through colonial conquest in Asia. After all, it was no more than the other European powers were doing, or had already done, almost everywhere else in the world. Finally there was the strategic factor. Just as the Baltic was Russia's Achilles' heel in the event of trouble with Britain, it had long been obvious that the latter's most vulnerable point was India. Therefore to have bases in Central Asia from which its frontiers could be threatened greatly increased Russia's bargaining power.

This is not to say that from now on every Russian move in Central Asia was part of a grand design carefully thought out in St Petersburg, as Khalfin, the Soviet historian, rather suggests. Indeed, there had been considerable disagreement earlier among the Tsar's ministers and advisers over the wisdom of retaining Tashkent. Those on the spot, notably General Kaufman, had no such doubts, however. For they could see that possession of Tashkent was the key to the conquest of Central Asia. Its occupation by Russian troops effectively drove a wedge between the two territories of Bokhara and Khokand, enabling them to be dealt with in turn. Following his loss of Tashkent to Cherniaev, and the failure of the British to come to his assistance, the Khan of Khokand had concluded a treaty with the Russians which secured Kaufman's rear and enabled him to concentrate on Bokhara. Nor did he have to wait very long for an excuse to move against the Emir. For in April 1868 word reached Tashkent that Bokharan forces were massing at Samarkand, then lying within the Emir's domains, with the aim of driving the Russians out of Turkestan.

Kaufman immediately set out for Samarkand with a force of only 3,500 men, all that could be spared. He met with little resistance, however, for the Bokharan troops, whose commanders were divided among themselves, fell back at his approach. The following morning a deputation from the city came to Kaufman saying that the troops had all left and that they wished to surrender. Thus, on May 2, 1868, Samarkand was absorbed into the Russian Empire, at a cost of two lives and thirty-one wounded. To the Russians its fall had a special significance. For it was from here, nearly 500 years earlier, that the great Mongol commander Tamerlane had launched his fateful attack on Muscovy. The capture of this legendary city, with its dazzling architectural splendours, including the tomb of Tamerlane himself, was seen as the settling of an ancient score. Nor was the significance of its surrender lost on the people of Central Asia, on whom it was to have a crushing psychological effect, adding to the growing Russian reputation for invincibility.

Leaving behind him a small garrison to occupy Samarkand, Kaufman now set off in pursuit of the main Bokharan force, catching up with it at a spot 100 miles short of the Emir's capital. Despite the great disparity in numbers, Kaufman's superior tactics and seasoned troops won the day, putting the Bokharans to flight. But he was unable to pursue them further, for a second Bokharan force, which had managed to escape his notice, had attacked the Russian troops left to hold Samarkand. At the same time many of the townspeople joined the attackers, having surrendered merely to save their city from destruction. The plight of the Russians, who had withdrawn to the citadel, was becoming more desperate by the hour. Finally, rather than surrender, they decided to blow up the magazines – and themselves. But prompt action by Kaufman saved them. Racing back to Samarkand, he drove the attackers off, but not before 50 of the defenders had been killed and nearly 200 wounded.

Thrice defeated, and fearing for his capital, the Emir had little choice but to accept Kaufman's harsh surrender terms. These reduced him to a mere vassal of the Tsar's, and made his once-powerful kingdom a Russian protectorate. In addition Russian merchants were guaranteed free passage through his domains, and allowed to appoint local agents there. Russian goods, moreover, would be taxed at a favourable rate, thereby giving them an advantage over imports from India. Force had achieved what, ten years earlier, Ignatiev had tried and failed to obtain through negotiation – though the intelligence he returned with was now proving invaluable to Kaufman. Finally, in addition to paying a large indemnity, the Emir was obliged to surrender to the Russians the crucial Zarafshan valley, which controlled Bokhara's water supply, thereby giving them a permanent stranglehold on the capital. In return, so long as he abided by the terms of the treaty, the Emir was allowed to retain his throne. The Russians also gave vague assurances that once stability had been restored to the region they would return Samarkand to the Emir. But this, like their earlier undertaking over Tashkent, they never did, and the respective situations of the two cities were to remain unchanged until the Bolsheviks came to power, when Bokhara was 'liberated' and fully incorporated into the USSR.

*   *   *

Only the Khan of Khiva, in his remote desert fastness, continued to defy the might of the Tsar. Kaufman in Tashkent, and Ignatiev in St Petersburg, realised that if they were to absorb Khiva into Russia's new Central Asian empire they must greatly improve their lines of communication in the region. Troops could only reach Turkestan after a long and arduous march from Orenburg, while Khiva, as previous expeditions had shown, was even more difficult of access. What was needed was a direct route from European Russia, along which troops and supplies could be moved, as well as better communications within Turkestan to tighten Russia's grip on it. The most obvious way to link Central Asia to European Russia was by building a port on the eastern shore of the Caspian. Men and supplies could then be shipped down the Volga and across the Caspian to this point. They could also be ferried there from the Russian garrisons in the Caucasus. Eventually, when Khiva had been conquered and the troublesome Turcomans pacified, a railway could be constructed across the desert to Bokhara, Samarkand, Tashkent and Khokand.

So it was that, in the winter of 1869, just eighteen months after the submission of Bokhara, a small Russian force set sail from Petrovsk, on the Caucasian side of the Caspian, and a few days later landed in a desolate bay on its eastern shore. The spot was known as Krasnovodsk, and it was here that the Oxus was said to have once flowed into the Caspian. The whole operation was highly secret, for the Russians' task was to construct a permanent fortress there, and St Petersburg did not wish the British to learn of the move until it was complete. For this reason the officer in command had strict instructions to avoid clashing with the Turcomans, lest the British come to hear of this through the native spies they were known to have among the tribes of the region. Despite this, it was not long before news of what was going on at Krasnovodsk reached British ears. It was to cause considerable alarm in both London and Calcutta.

Until now, still pursuing its policy of masterly inactivity, the British government had done no more than protest to St Petersburg over its recent forward moves in Central Asia, pointing out that they ran contrary to its own official pronouncements. London was uneasily aware, moreover, that what the Russians had done in Central Asia differed little from what Britain had already done when adding Sind and the Punjab to its Indian possessions, and had tried but failed to do in Afghanistan when it placed Shah Shujah on the throne. To protest too vociferously would be to invite charges of hypocrisy. However, the construction of a Russian fortress on the eastern shore of the Caspian, and the garrisoning of troops there, was altogether more disturbing, for it was seen as posing a threat to Afghanistan. Not only would it enable the Russians to launch an expedition against Khiva, thereby adding it to their domains and dependencies in Central Asia, but it would also bring them within striking distance of Herat, strategic key to India.

For some time the forward school, with Sir Henry Rawlinson as its principal spokesman, had been urging the British government to abandon its policy of masterly inactivity. Rawlinson had even proposed that Afghanistan should be made a 'quasi-protectorate' of Britain's so as to keep it out of Russia's grasp. Some of those who had previously supported the government's passive policies now began to question their realism. Even the Viceroy, Sir John Lawrence, began to have second thoughts. The Russians, he advised, should be warned not to interfere in the affairs of Afghanistan or any other state sharing a frontier with India. It should be made clear to St Petersburg, moreover, that 'an advance towards India, beyond a certain point, would entail her in war, in all parts of the world, with England'. Lawrence proposed that Central Asia should be divided into British and Russian spheres of influence, the details of which should be worked out between the two governments.

The opportunity for some plain talking with the Russians arose shortly afterwards when Lord Clarendon, the British

Foreign Secretary, met his opposite number, Prince Gorchakov, at Heidelberg. Clarendon enquired bluntly of Gorchakov whether Russia's recent Asiatic conquests, which went so far beyond what he himself had spelt out in his celebrated memorandum, had been ordered by Tsar Alexander, or were the result of commanders on the spot exceeding their instructions. It was an embarrassing question, and it required an answer. Gorchakov chose to blame the soldiers, explaining that they thereby hoped to win distinction for themselves. Even now, though, the British were probably no nearer the truth than before, or than scholars are to this day. At the same time Gorchakov assured Clarendon that his government had no intention of advancing any further into Central Asia, and certainly harboured no designs on India.

The British had by now become used to such assurances and promises, and to seeing them broken. Pursuing Lawrence's expedient of trying to put a fixed limit on further Russian advances, Clarendon therefore proposed to Gorchakov that their two governments should establish, not so much spheres of influence in Asia, but a permanent neutral zone between their two expanding empires there. The Russian immediately suggested that Afghanistan would serve this purpose, his own government having no interest of any kind in it. The latter, if it could be believed, was welcome news to the British, and Clarendon assured Gorchakov that his government had no territorial ambitions there either. For a time the prospects for such an agreement looked quite promising, and discussions and correspondence continued between London and St Petersburg. In the end, however, they were to grind to a halt over the question of where precisely Afghanistan's remote and unmapped northern frontier ran, especially in the almost totally unexplored Pamir region. For it was here that the most advanced Russian military posts lay closest to British India.

Hitherto, British strategists had always worked on the assumption that the Khyber and Bolan passes were the most likely entry points for a Russian invasion of India. But now they were awakening to the uncomfortable realisation that further to the north, in a region that they knew virtually nothing about, there were other passes through which the Cossacks might one day pour down into India. For this unwelcome piece of intelligence they had to thank two British explorers who, lucky to be alive still, had just returned from Chinese Turkestan after a highly adventurous journey. And if that were not enough, they also brought back with them alarming tales of Russian intrigues there. The diplomatic process might have reached an impasse, but the Great Game certainly had not.

· 25 ·

Spies Along the
Silk Road

At the time that these events took place, Chinese Turkestan was shown on both British and Russian maps
as a vast white blank, with the locations of oasis towns
like Kashgar and Yarkand only approximately indicated. Cut
off from the rest of Central Asia by towering mountain ranges,
and from China by the huge expanse of the Taklamakan desert,
it was one of the least known areas on earth. Centuries earlier
the flourishing Silk Road, which linked imperial China to
distant Rome, had passed through it, bringing great prosperity
to its oases. But this traffic had long ago ceased, and most of
the oases had been swallowed up by the desert. The region had
then sunk back into virtual oblivion.

The Taklamakan desert, which dominates the region, had
always enjoyed an ill reputation among travellers, and over
the years a sad procession of men – merchants, soldiers and
Buddhist pilgrims – had left their bones there after losing their
way between the widely scattered oases. Sometimes entire
caravans had been known to vanish into it without trace. It is
no surprise to learn that Taklamakan, in the local Uighur
tongue, means 'Go in – and you won't come out'. As a result
very few Europeans had ever been to this remote region, for
there was little to attract them to it.

Chinese Turkestan, or Sinkiang as it is today called, had
long been part of the Chinese Empire. However, the central
authorities' hold over it had always been tenuous, for the
Muslim population had nothing in common with their Manchu

rulers and everything in common with their ethnic cousins in Bokhara, Khokand and Khiva, lying on the far side of the Pamirs. As a result, in the early 1860s, a violent revolt had broken out among the Muslims against their overlords. Chinese cities were burned to the ground and their inhabitants massacred. The insurrection, which had begun in the east, spread quickly westwards until the whole of Turkestan was up in arms. It was at that moment that a remarkable Muslim adventurer named Yakub Beg, claiming direct descent from Tamerlane, arrived on the scene. Veteran of a number of engagements against the Russians, in which he had acquitted himself with courage and distinction (having five bullet wounds to show for it), he was now in the service of Kashgar's former Muslim ruler, then living in exile in Khokand. It was the latter's hope to drive out the infidel Chinese and reclaim his throne.

In January 1865, accompanied by a small force of armed men, Yakub Beg and his patron crossed the mountains to Kashgar to find it in bloody turmoil, with rival factions fighting among themselves for possession of the throne, as well as against the Chinese. But within two years, by means of his own charismatic leadership and European tactics which he had picked up from the Russians, Yakub Beg had managed to wrest Kashgar and Yarkand from both the Chinese and his local rivals. The two Chinese governors, it is said, chose to blow themselves up rather than surrender to the Muslims. According to one colourful, but unsubstantiated, account, Kashgar's defenders had eaten their own wives and children before submitting, having first devoured every four-legged creature in the city, including cats and rats.

After ruthlessly pushing aside his patron, and making Kashgar his capital, Yakub Beg declared himself ruler of Kashgaria, as the liberated area now became called. From here he proceeded to fight his way eastwards, taking more and more of Chinese Turkestan under his wing. Before long his rule was to extend to Urumchi, Turfan and Hami, the latter lying nearly 1,000 miles from Kashgar. In addition to his own troops from Khokand, his authority was maintained by means of mercenaries recruited from the local ethnic groups and tribes, including Afghans and even a few Chinese, not to mention a handful of Indian Army deserters who had found their way across the mountains. So far as the Muslim population was concerned, Yakub Beg's expulsion of the Chinese from the region brought few, if any, benefits, as it merely replaced one unwelcome ruler with another. They found themselves, like the vanquished Chinese, the victims of plunder, massacre and rape at the hands of his rag-bag army. As each oasis town and village capitulated, moreover, Yakub Beg's secret police and tax-collectors moved in to terrorise and squeeze them.

Such was the situation in the former Chinese territory when, in the autumn of 1868, an adventurous British traveller named Robert Shaw crossed the mountains northwards, intent on being the first of his countrymen to reach the mysterious cities of Kashgar and Yarkand. It was no secret to him that one Russian officer, of Kazakh origin, had preceded him there in the guise of a trader, bringing back valuable military and commercial intelligence. But that was before Yakub Beg's seizure of power, and Shaw was convinced that Kashgaria now offered great commercial prospects to enterprising British merchants. Shaw had originally intended to be a regular soldier, and had passed first into Sandhurst from Marlborough. However, in his youth he had been struck down with rheumatic fever, and persistent ill-health finally forced him to abandon any hopes of a military career. What he lacked in bodily fitness, he more than made up for in determination. At the age of 20 he had moved to India, taking up residence in the Himalayan foothills as a tea-planter. It was as a result of talking to native traders who had visited Chinese Turkestan that he became persuaded that a great untapped market lay there, especially for Indian tea now that supplies from China had been halted by Yakub Beg's conquest of the region.

Journeys beyond India's frontiers were severely frowned upon by the authorities in Calcutta, and British officers and other officials were banned from attempting them. The lesson of Conolly and Stoddart had not been forgotten. As the Viceroy put it: 'If they lose their lives we cannot avenge them, and so lose credit.' He also felt that they tended to do more harm than good, though, as will be seen, he made an exception for Indian agents carrying out specific tasks for the government, since they could be more readily disowned. Robert Shaw, however, was not a government employee, and therefore felt bound by no such restrictions. On September 20, 1868, having sent a native messenger ahead to inform Yakub Beg's frontier officials of his coming, and of his friendly intentions, he set out from Leh with a caravan laden with tea and other merchandise.

What Shaw was unaware of was that following close behind him was a rival, also an Englishman. This was a young ex-army officer named George Hayward, who had a passion for exploration and whose one-man expedition had been financed by the Royal Geographical Society in London. He also enjoyed the vigorous support of Sir Henry Rawlinson, who was shortly to become the Society's President. Officially Hayward was there to explore the passes between Ladakh and Kashgaria, but the close personal interest taken in his journey by the Russophobe Rawlinson suggests that there may also have been a political motive behind it. Indeed, the dividing line at that time between exploration and intelligence-gathering was often extremely narrow. But whatever the truth about Hayward, both men were soon to find themselves inextricably caught up in the Great Game.

The first that Shaw knew of his rival's presence was when he received word that an Englishman, disguised as an Afghan and travelling light and fast, was following only a few days behind his own slow-moving caravan. Shaken by the news, he hastily penned a note to the stranger asking who he was and urging him to turn back lest he endanger the prospects of his own expedition, in which he had invested so much. Hayward, a man every bit as determined as Shaw, refused. However, the two rivals agreed to meet over Hayward's camp-fire to discuss the situation. In fact they were not really in competition, for whereas Shaw's objective was principally commercial, Hayward was there to explore and map the passes. Hayward had no particular wish to take part in a race for Kashgar or Yarkand, merely wishing to make them his base for map-making forays into the Pamirs, then still totally unknown.

He therefore agreed to give Shaw a two-week start while he explored some of the passes and river gorges of the Karakorams on the Indian side of the frontier.

Nonetheless, although they were often no more than a mile apart, their meeting on that bitterly cold night was to be their last for many months. For each strongly resented the other's presence, and from then on behaved as though he were not there. Indeed, Shaw comforted himself with the thought that very soon Hayward would not be there. For while he had been careful to send generous gifts ahead to Yakub Beg's frontier officials, with the hint of more to follow, he knew that Hayward had no such gifts to dispense, and had not even alerted them to his coming. Moreover, Hayward had no reason that would satisfy Yakub Beg for wishing to enter his domains. Almost certainly he would be turned back, if not arrested.

Shaw reached Yarkand, where he was cordially received, in the middle of December. But two weeks later, to his intense annoyance, he was joined there by Hayward. He had seriously underestimated his rival's resourcefulness and determination. After completing his explorations in the Karakorams, Hayward had talked his way past the border guards by assuring them that he was part of Shaw's caravan – or so the latter claimed afterwards – and was on his way to catch it up. In Yarkand the two men studiously ignored one another, occupying separate lodgings, while keeping a close watch on the other's movements. For their part, the authorities maintained a wary eye on both of them while awaiting further instructions from Kashgar, 100 miles further on. Shaw's careful preparations, not to mention his generous gifts, appear to have paid off, for on January 3, 1869, he was officially informed that Yakub Beg would receive him in his palace at Kashgar. Eight days later, after leaving his rival kicking his heels in frustration at Yarkand, Shaw saw in the distance across the treeless plain the great mud walls of the capital – the first Englishman ever to do so. Beyond it, on the horizon, rose the snow-capped Pamirs, while to the east stretched the endless sands of the Taklamakan. Soon afterwards he was met by an armed escort who led him and his caravan through the gates of the city to the quarters which had been prepared for him. Yakub Beg, he was told, was expecting to see him the next morning.

At the appointed hour, followed by thirty or forty servants bearing the gifts he had brought, including examples of the latest models of British firearms, he set off for the palace for his audience with the King – as Yakub Beg now styled himself. After passing through a large but silent crowd which lined the route, he entered the gateway. There followed a succession of large courtyards, each lined with rank upon rank of seated guards and attendants, all clad in brilliantly coloured silk robes. They sat so still, Shaw noted in his diary that night, 'that they seemed to form part of the architecture of the building'. Instead of firearms some of the guards carried bows and quivers full of arrows. 'The whole effect was curious and novel,' he wrote. 'The numbers, the solemn stillness, and the gorgeous colouring gave a sort of unreality to this assemblage of thousands.' Finally he and his escort reached the royal audience chamber in the heart of the palace. Here, seated on a rug, was a solitary figure. Shaw realised at once that this was the redoubtable Yakub Beg, descendant of Tamerlane, and conqueror of Chinese Turkestan.

'I advanced alone,' Shaw recalled, 'and when I drew near he half rose to his knees and held out both hands to me.' Mindful of the costly error in oriental etiquette committed by Colonel Stoddart at Bokhara, Shaw had briefed himself thoroughly on the courtesies of Yakub Beg's court. After grasping the latter's hands in the manner of Central Asia, he was invited by him to be seated. Yakub Beg, who Shaw was relieved to see was now smiling, began by asking him about his journey. In replying, Shaw first expressed regret for his poor Persian, but Yakub Beg assured him that he was able to understand it. Recalling that his own country had fought the Chinese three times, the Englishman congratulated Yakub Beg on his victory over them, and on re-establishing a Muslim kingdom in Turkestan. By now the ruler had signalled his visitor to sit closer, and the courtesies being over, Shaw explained the reason for his coming. He was there, he said, to try to open up trade between their two countries, especially the traffic in tea, which was his own particular business. He was not a representative of the

British government, however, and he apologised for the modesty of the gifts he had brought. In fact, these had been chosen with the utmost care. Laid out on large trays, they were a dazzling sight, and caused Yakub Beg's eyes to widen in satisfaction.

To allow his host ample time to inspect the gifts, which were intended to whet his appetite for a regular supply of British goods, Shaw suggested that more detailed discussions might be conducted at a subsequent meeting. It was a proposal that Yakub Beg happily fell in with. However, when the Englishman said he thought they might need an interpreter next time, because of the inadequacy of his Persian, his host replied: 'Between you and me no third person is requisite. Friendship requires no interpreter.' With that he stretched out his hand and gave Shaw's a powerful squeeze, declaring: 'Now enjoy yourself for a few days. Consider this place and all it contains as your own, and on the third day we will have another talk.' It would be a much longer one, he assured his visitor, and others would follow. Finally he summoned an attendant who arrived bearing a magnificent satin robe which Shaw was helped into.

That night Shaw noted in his diary with some satisfaction: 'The King dismissed me very graciously.' After so effusive a welcome, he might have been forgiven for believing that he had hit it off with the wily Yakub Beg, and that he had stolen a march on the Russians, who were known to have been actively pursuing the trade of Chinese Turkestan before its seizure by its present ruler. Already Shaw could see his dream of tea caravans streaming northwards across the passes coming true. After all, Kashgar's ancient trading links with China had been severed, and Yakub Beg badly needed new friends and commercial partners. It was no secret that his relations with St Petersburg were anything but cordial, for by driving out the Chinese he had brought to naught the special trading concessions obtained by Ignatiev for Russian merchants under the Treaty of Peking. It was strongly rumoured in Kashgar, moreover, that the Russians had moved their troops up to the frontier with a view to wresting the territory from its new ruler. What better ally could Yakub Beg want than Great Britain, which had been victorious in war against both Russia and China?

It was only as the days passed and there was no further word from Yakub Beg that Shaw began to feel less sure and to wonder what was going on. The days soon stretched to weeks, and Shaw found himself pondering gloomily on the fate of Conolly and Stoddart at Bokhara and asking himself whether he might not be being held as a hostage or privileged prisoner of some kind. Although most courteously treated, and provided with everything he asked for, he found that his movements were more and more restricted, until he was not even allowed to leave his quarters, let alone depart from Kashgar. Despite this, however, he did not waste his time. He had numerous visitors, and from them he endeavoured to glean as much political and other intelligence concerning Yakub Beg's rule as possible. He learned, for instance, that until his arrival virtually nothing had been known in Kashgar of the British in India, let alone of their power and influence in Asia. Hitherto it had been thought that they were merely vassals of the Maharajah of neighbouring Kashmir – very likely a piece of Russian disinformation.

He also learned at this time of the arrival in the town of two other travellers. One was his rival George Hayward, who had finally received permission to visit Kashgar, only to find that he had merely exchanged house arrest in Yarkand for house arrest there. Clearly Yakub Beg wanted to keep a closer eye on him. Like Shaw, he was being well treated, though he was guarded day and night, for in Yarkand he had made a brief but unauthorised foray from his quarters which had caused the authorities there considerable embarrassment. It was not long before he and Shaw, using trusted couriers, managed to make contact with one another and maintain an irregular but secret correspondence.

The other new arrival was something of a mystery. The first that Shaw knew of his presence was when he received a note from him, written in English, in which he made two rather curious requests. Signing himself simply Mirza, he claimed that he had been sent to Kashgar from India (by whom precisely he did not say) to conduct a clandestine survey of the region. He begged Shaw for the loan of a watch, explaining that his own was broken and that he desperately needed one in order to complete the astronomical observations essential to his task. For the same reason, he said, he needed to know the exact date by the European calendar. Mystified as to who he was, and fearing that he might be an *agent provocateur* sent by Yakub Beg to test him, Shaw decided to have nothing to do with him. 'I have grave doubts of his genuineness,' he noted in his diary, adding that were the man found to be in possession of a watch traceable to him this would cast dangerous suspicion upon himself. Shaw therefore sent the mysterious newcomer a verbal message explaining regretfully that he had no spare watch. In this way he avoided even having to reveal the date to the stranger.

Unbeknown to Shaw, the man was perfectly genuine. His full name was Mirza Shuja, and he was doing precisely what he claimed. An Indian Muslim in the service of the British Indian authorities, he had left Kabul the previous year and had made his way in mid-winter across the Pamirs. It had been a cruel journey, which he had been lucky to survive. Nonetheless he had managed to carry out his orders, which were to survey the route between Afghanistan and Kashgaria. His principal task in Kashgar, apart from generally keeping his eyes and ears open, was to try to fix its exact position on the map. It was something which could not be done without a watch, an instrument then unobtainable in Kashgar. He could not believe his luck therefore when he learned that an Englishman had arrived in Yakub Beg's capital shortly before him. Shaw's abrupt brush-off must thus have come as a cruel blow to one who risked so much for his British masters, and who would eventually give his life for them. But then Mirza Shuja was no ordinary man, for he belonged to an élite group of hand-picked and highly trained Indians known as the 'Pundits'.

*   *   *

The idea of using native explorers to carry out clandestine surveys of the lawless regions beyond India's frontiers had arisen as a result of the Viceroy's strict ban on British officers venturing there. Because of this the Survey of India, which had the task of providing the government with maps of the entire sub-continent and surrounding regions, found itself greatly hampered when it came to mapping northern Afghanistan, Turkestan and Tibet. Then a young officer working for the Survey, Captain Thomas Montgomerie of the Royal Engineers, hit upon a brilliant solution. Why not, he asked his superiors, send native explorers trained in secret surveying techniques into these forbidden regions? They were far less likely to be detected than a European, however good the latter's disguise. If they were unfortunate enough to be discovered, moreover, it would be less politically embarrassing to the authorities than if a British officer was caught red-handed making maps in these highly sensitive and dangerous parts.

Surprisingly perhaps, in view of the British and Indian governments' determination not to become entangled in Central Asia, Montgomerie's bold plan was approved, and over the next few years a number of Indian explorers, including Mirza Shuja, were dispatched in great secrecy across the frontier. All of them were hillmen, carefully chosen for their exceptional intelligence and resourcefulness. Because discovery, or even suspicion, would have spelt instant death, their existence and activities had to be kept as secret as possible. Even within the Survey of India they were known merely by a number or a cryptonym. They were trained personally by Montgomerie at Dehra Dun, the Survey's headquarters in the Himalayan foothills. Some of the techniques and equipment he devised were extremely ingenious.

Montgomerie first trained his men, through exhaustive practice, to take a pace of known length which would remain constant whether they walked uphill, downhill or on the level. Next he taught them ways of keeping a precise but discreet count of the number of such paces taken during a day's march. This enabled them to measure immense distances with remarkable accuracy and without arousing suspicion. Often they travelled as Buddhist pilgrims, many of whom regularly crossed the passes to visit the holy sites of the ancient Silk Road. Every Buddhist carried a rosary of 108 beads on which to count his prayers, and also a small wood and metal prayer-wheel which he spun as he walked. Both of these Montgomerie turned to his advantage. From the former he removed eight beads, not enough to be noticed, but leaving a mathematically convenient 100. At every hundredth pace the Pundit would automatically slip one bead. Each complete circuit of the rosary thus represented 10,000 paces.

The total for the day's march, together with any other discreet observations, had somehow to be logged somewhere safe from prying eyes. It was here that the prayer-wheel, with its copper cylinder, proved invaluable. For concealed in this, in place of the usual hand-written scroll of prayers, was a roll of blank paper. This served as a log-book, which could easily be got at by removing the top of the cylinder, and some of which are still preserved in the Indian State Archives. Then there was the problem of a compass, for the Pundit was required to take regular bearings as he journeyed. Montgomerie decided to conceal this in the lid of the prayer-wheel. Thermometers, which were needed for calculating altitudes, were hidden in the tops of pilgrims' staves. Mercury, essential for setting an artificial horizon when taking sextant readings, was hidden in cowrie shells and poured out into a pilgrim's begging bowl when required. Concealed pockets were added to the Pundits' clothing, and false bottoms, in which sextants could be hidden, were built into the chests which most native travellers carried. All this work was carried out in the Survey of India's workshops at Dehra Dun under Montgomerie's supervision.

The Pundits were also thoroughly trained in the art of disguise and in the use of cover stories. For in the lawless lands beyond the frontier their safety would depend on just how convincingly they could play the part of holy-man, pilgrim or Himalayan trader. Their disguise and cover had to stand the test of months of travelling, often in the closest intimacy with genuine pilgrims and traders. Some were away for years. One became the first Asiatic to be awarded the Royal Geographical Society's gold medal, having contributed 'a greater amount of positive knowledge to the map of Asia than any other individual of our time'. At least two never returned, while a third was sold into slavery, although he eventually escaped. In all, their clandestine journeys were to provide a wealth of geographical intelligence over some twenty years which Montgomerie and his fellow cartographers at Dehra Dun used to fill in many of the no-go areas on the British maps of Central Asia.

Just what drove men like Mirza Shuja to face such hardships and extreme dangers for their imperial masters has never been satisfactorily explained. Perhaps it was the inspirational leadership of Montgomerie, who took such a pride in their individual achievements, and who looked upon them as his sons. Or possibly it was the knowledge that they belonged to an élite, for each was aware that he had been hand-picked for this great task. Or maybe Montgomerie had managed to imbue them with his own patriotic determination to fill in the blanks on the Great Game map before the Russians did. In an earlier book, *Trespassers on the Roof of the World*, I have described some of the Pundits' more prodigious feats of exploration, which I shall not attempt to retell here. Sadly, very little is known of these men as individuals, for none of them left memoirs of any kind. However, it is in Kipling's masterpiece *Kim*, whose characters so clearly come from the shadowy world of Captain Montgomerie, that they have their just memorial.

*   *   *

In Kashgar, in the spring of 1869, neither Shaw nor Hayward had any idea of this. Mirza, the mysterious Indian, they learned, had been arrested and chained to a heavy log. More ominously for Shaw, Yakub Beg had been enquiring whether he and the Indian had been in communication, and whether he still had in his possession the two watches with which he was known to have arrived. Both he and Hayward were becoming increasingly perturbed as they received no further word from Yakub Beg, for it was now nearly three months since Shaw's audience with the ruler. Although both men were well treated, enquiries put to court officials produced no satisfactory explanation for this long silence. In fact, if they did but know it, there was a very good reason for Yakub Beg's procrastination – the Russians.

Having fought against them in the past, Yakub Beg was aware that his mighty northern neighbour represented an infinitely greater threat to his throne than the Chinese, whom he had defeated without much difficulty. He also knew that their troops were poised on the frontier, not many days' march from Kashgar. Altogether they represented a more immediate priority than his two British visitors, who could quite happily be kept on ice for the time being. For its part, St Petersburg was in something of a quandary over Yakub Beg. Not only was it worried by the prospect of Kashgar becoming a rallying-point for anti-Russian feeling in Central Asia, but with British help and encouragement the Muslim adventurer might even try to launch a crusade aimed at driving the Russians out of their newly acquired territories. The hawks were impatient to invade Kashgaria and place it under permanent Russian rule, while time was still on their side. Anxious not to allow this promising new market to slip from its grasp, St Petersburg was sorely tempted. But in the event, as always, the Tsar and his ministers were guided by what they felt they could get away with. For the Russians to march into Kashgaria would be bound to enrage and alarm both the British and the Chinese (the latter regarding it still as part of their empire, albeit momentarily lost). With the disaster of the Crimean War still fresh in Russian minds, Tsar Alexander did not yet feel confident enough to risk it. Instead of an army, therefore, an envoy had been sent to Kashgar to try to find another solution.

What St Petersburg most wanted from Yakub Beg was his recognition of the treaty rights, especially the trading concessions, which Ignatiev had obtained from the Chinese. It was particularly anxious to prevent these from going to the British. For his part, Yakub Beg was eager for Russian recognition of his rule, and a guarantee that his frontiers would be secure against invasion. However, St Petersburg was unwilling to grant his regime formal recognition, since this would permanently damage its relations with Peking. He, at least, was mortal. The Chinese would be around for a long time. Although Shaw did not realise it, these negotiations had still been in progress when he first arrived in Kashgar. Indeed, a Russian envoy had left for home shortly before, taking with him Yakub Beg's nephew as an emissary to St Petersburg. But Alexander had refused to receive him, fearing that this might be seen by both Peking and Yakub Beg himself as implying recognition. Yakub Beg was incensed. Realising that the Russians had no intention of recognising his authority, he decided to show his displeasure in a way calculated to cause them the maximum alarm and annoyance. He turned to those whom he knew by now to be their principal rivals in Central Asia – the British.

The first that Robert Shaw knew of this, although he had no idea what lay behind it, was when, to his great relief, he found himself summoned to an audience with Yakub Beg. 'Today,' he noted in his diary on April 5, 'I have some news to write. I have had my long expected second interview with the King.' Although he made no attempt to explain the long delay, Yakub Beg proved even more amiable than at their first meeting. Brushing aside Shaw's reminder that he did not represent the British government, but had travelled to Kashgar of his own accord, Yakub Beg told him: 'I consider you my brother. Whatever course you advise, I will take.' Other extravagant compliments followed. 'The Queen of England is like the sun, which warms everything it shines upon,' he declared. 'I am in the cold, and desire that some of its rays should fall upon me.' Shaw, he said, was the first Englishman he had ever met, although he had heard much of their power and truthfulness from others. 'It is a great honour for me that you have come. I count upon you to help me in your country.'

The compliments over, Yakub Beg now got down to business. 'I am thinking', he told Shaw, 'of sending an envoy to your country.' What did his visitor think? Shaw said he thought it was an excellent idea. In that case, Yakub Beg declared, he would dispatch a special emissary bearing a note to the 'Lord Sahib', as he called the Viceroy. Welcoming this, Shaw offered to brief the individual chosen, promising to smooth his path in every way possible. After a further exchange of compliments, Shaw withdrew, hardly daring to believe that he might soon be free to leave for home. Aware, though, of Yakub Beg's reputation for every kind of double-dealing, he knew that he would feel much happier once he was safely across the frontier.

But there remained one last problem – Hayward. Nothing

had been said about him during Shaw's audience with Yakub Beg. In view of the latter's evident eagerness to woo the British, Shaw had assumed that Hayward would be free to return home too, although perhaps not via the Pamirs, which was what his sponsors, the Royal Geographical Society, had hoped. Then one of Shaw's servants brought him 'an ugly rumour ... that I should be sent back to India with an envoy ... and that Hayward would be kept as a hostage for his safe return.' At the same time he received an anxious note from Hayward himself. In this he said that he had learned that Yakub Beg was proposing to hold on to him. Much as Shaw disliked Hayward – 'the thorn in my flesh', he calls him in his diary – he knew he could not simply abandon him to the whims of an oriental despot with an unsavoury reputation for cruelty and treachery. Still confined to his own quarters, he at once sent a note to one of Yakub Beg's senior officials, a man with whom he was on excellent terms. In this he warned that it would be a waste of time and effort for Yakub Beg to send an envoy to India seeking Britain's friendship, 'so long as an Englishman is kept here against his will'. It was a risky thing to do, he knew, but it worked. The following day he was informed that not only Hayward, but also the mysterious Mirza, whom Yakub Beg seemed to associate with them, would be free to return home. The envoy would follow later.

*　　*　　*

Shaw and Hayward got back to a hero's welcome, having been given up for dead by some. Despite their close confinement, they had managed, albeit quite independently, to bring back with them an immense amount of intelligence – political, commercial, military and geographical. The latter was to win for both men that ultimate prize among explorers, the gold medal of the Royal Geographical Society. For his part, however, Mirza Shuja was to receive no such reward or acclaim. Although it was due to his determined efforts that the Survey of India was able to produce its first, if somewhat rough, map of northern Afghanistan and the Pamirs, his activities had to be kept secret still. Only when a Pundit had made his final journey could his identity be disclosed. Sadly, Mirza would not live to enjoy this, for he was destined to be murdered in his sleep while on another mission to Central Asia, this time to Bokhara.

Both Shaw and Hayward, who saw eye to eye on very little else, returned to India convinced that the Russians were proposing to march into Kashgaria, overthrow Yakub Beg, and add his kingdom to their own Central Asian empire. After that it would only be a question of time before they continued southwards into northern India via the very passes by which the two British travellers had entered Kashgaria, and across which Shaw was hoping to send his tea caravans. Until then the great mountain systems to the north of India had been regarded by strategists in Calcutta and London as impenetrable to a modern army weighed down with artillery and other heavy equipment, and requiring regular supplies of food and ammunition. Shaw and Hayward, having crossed those mountains both ways, now questioned this, arguing that one pass in particular – the Chang Lung, lying north-east of Leh – offered an invader a back-door route into Ladakh, and thence into northern India. Although this rose to over 18,000 feet, both Shaw and Hayward (the latter a former army officer) believed that artillery could be dragged over it.

Had Sir John Lawrence still been Viceroy, no official notice would have been taken of their views. Indeed, they would almost certainly have been severely reprimanded for meddling in affairs of state, as Moorcroft had been half a century earlier. But during their absence he had retired and had been succeeded by a younger Viceroy with a more open mind. India's new chief was Lord Mayo, who had not only visited Russia but had also written a two-volume work about the country. It was not surprising, therefore, that he was eager to hear what these two enterprising young travellers had to say about Yakub Beg and Russian machinations beyond the Pamir and Karakoram passes.

Their warnings, however, would not go unchallenged by the military establishment, even if none of the latter had ever set foot themselves in the passes they discussed with such intimacy. 'It is conceivable', one War Office colonel wrote, 'that 10,000 Kirghiz horsemen might be able to traverse a difficult road ... with nothing but what can be carried at the saddle bow. But turn these into European soldiers with their trains of artillery, ammunition, hospital supplies, and the innumerable requirements of a modern army, and the case is totally different. The resources of the country that might suffice for the one would be utterly insufficient for the other.' However, if Shaw and Hayward had failed to convince the defence chiefs that the Cossacks were about to swarm down through the northern passes into India, they did succeed in opening up a great debate on the general vulnerability of the region to Russian incursion. And they did more than that, for they also managed to interest the new Viceroy in Yakub Beg's diplomatic overture. Their hand was strengthened here by the timely arrival in India of the latter's special envoy.

Lord Mayo was convinced that India's best defence lay, not in forward policies or military adventures, but in the establishment of a chain of buffer states friendly to Britain around its vast and thinly guarded frontiers. The most important of these was obviously Afghanistan, now ruled by Dost Mohammed's son Sher Ali, with whom Calcutta enjoyed cordial relations. Here was Mayo's chance to add another link to the chain by making a friend of Yakub Beg. With these two powerful rulers as Britain's allies, India had little to fear from the Russians. In a crisis Mayo was willing to assist them with arms and money, and perhaps even military advisers. With a handful of British officers and generous helpings of gold, he declared, 'I could make of Central Asia a hotplate for our friend the Russian bear to dance on'. It was much what Moorcroft had proposed many years before when he outlined to his superiors a strategy whereby British officers commanding local irregulars would halt an invading Russian force in the high passes by rolling huge boulders down on it from above.

Lord Mayo gave orders for a small British diplomatic mission, thinly disguised as a purely commercial one, to return with Yakub Beg's special envoy to Kashgar. It was led by Sir Douglas Forsyth, a senior political officer. Its purpose was to make exploratory contacts with this powerful Muslim ruler who, it appeared, preferred the friendship of the British to that of the Russians, and also to investigate the possibility of establishing regular caravan traffic across the Karakorams. Sir John Lawrence, fearing the political consequences of the latter, had always opposed any such initiatives. But Mayo took the opposite view, seeing commerce as a means of extending British influence into Central Asia with the minimum of risk. He also saw it as a way of combating the growing influence of the Russians, with their manifestly inferior goods, in the states beyond India's northern frontiers. Nor was he blind to the commercial advantage to be gained from opening up Kashgaria where, according to Robert Shaw, there were anything up to sixty million potential customers, each one a tea-drinker and a cotton-wearer, eagerly awaiting the British caravans. Shaw was invited by Mayo to join the Forsyth mission, and immediately accepted. George Hayward, the loner, had other plans. He too was preparing to venture into the unknown once again. His objective was the Pamirs, beyond whose towering peaks and unmapped passes lay the nearest Russian outposts. And this time no one was going to stop him.

· 26 ·

The Feel of Cold Steel Across His Throat

When word of George Hayward's plans reached the ears of the authorities, considerable pressure was brought to bear on him to call off his expedition. Not only were the dangers to a lone European traveller in this wild and lawless region immense, but it was also a highly sensitive area politically. Indeed, it was for just such hazardous operations as this that the Pundits had been conceived and trained. To a man like Hayward, however, the risks merely made it more attractive. In a revealing moment he had once written to Robert Shaw: 'I shall wander about the wilds of Central Asia possessed of an insane desire to try the effects of cold steel across my throat.' From anyone else this would simply have sounded like bravado. But Hayward, as his few friends would confirm, genuinely relished danger, though in retrospect it appears more like a death wish. Having no close ties or family, moreover, he had little to lose, and a great deal to gain if he succeeded. For on one thing everyone was agreed. Hayward was a first-rate explorer and a surveyor of great skill. If he did get back alive, his discoveries were likely to be of immense value.

Originally, like his Kashgar journey, the Pamir expedition was to have been sponsored by the Royal Geographical Society, which now had Sir Henry Rawlinson as its President, and some of whose operations in Central Asia smacked as much of the Great Game as of geography. But in the meantime something had happened which had caused Hayward reluctantly to distance himself from the Society for fear of embarrassing it. It had also greatly increased the dangers of the expedition, for it had made an enemy of the Maharajah of Kashmir, through whose territory the explorer would have to pass on his journey northwards. The affair had sprung from an earlier visit which Hayward had made to a remote region beyond the Maharajah's domains known as Dardistan. Here lived the Dards, a fiercely independent people with whom the Maharajah was constantly at war. It was from them that Hayward had learned of an appalling series of atrocities which Kashmiri troops had carried out in the Yasin area of Dardistan some years earlier. Details of these, which had included tossing babies into the air and cutting them in half as they fell, had been sent by Hayward to the editor of *The Pioneer*, the Calcutta newspaper. They had been published in full, under Hayward's name, although he insisted that this had been done expressly against his instructions. Inevitably, a copy of the paper had found its way into the hands of the Maharajah, a ruler whose goodwill and co-operation the British authorities were most anxious to preserve, and who was now reported to be extremely displeased.

Even Hayward could hardly fail to see that this affair, and his own involvement in it, was highly embarrassing to both the British government and the Royal Geographical Society. He therefore wrote to the latter formally severing all connections with it for the duration of the expedition. The anger at the Maharajah's court, he declared, 'is very great, and it cannot be doubted that they will in every way secretly strive to do me harm'. Although he had been strongly advised to postpone or abandon his venture, he was nonetheless determined to proceed, despite the greatly increased risk. The fact that the matter was now public knowledge, he argued, would make it difficult for the Kashmiri ruler to harm him. Indeed, it might even oblige him to protect the party during its passage through his domains, lest he be blamed for any harm which befell it. Hayward made it clear, however, that the expedition was being undertaken entirely at his own risk and on his own decision. He hoped to reach Yasin, he said, in twenty-two days, and from there to enter the Pamir region by the Darkot Pass.

At the very last minute the Viceroy, Lord Mayo, had tried

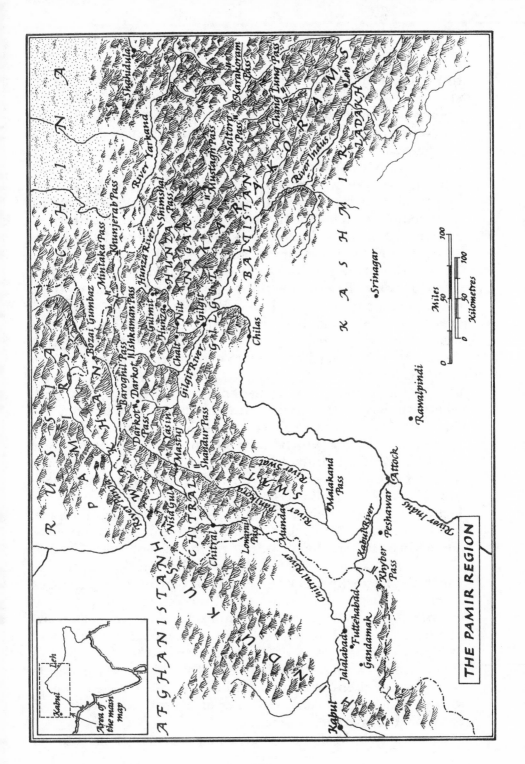

THE PAMIR REGION

to persuade him to change his mind, warning him: 'If you still resolve on prosecuting your journey it must be clearly understood that you do so on your own responsibility.' But Hayward had already defied officialdom once by visiting Kashgar, and ultimately there was little that anyone could do to stop him this time. After all, he was not a government official, and was now no longer answerable to the Royal Geographical Society. He was a free agent. Undeterred therefore, and accompanied by five native servants, he set out northwards across the Maharajah's territories in the summer of 1870. Travelling via Srinagar, his capital, and the small town of Gilgit, on Kashmir's northern frontier, the party passed without incident into Dardistan. By crossing the no-man's-land separating these two warring peoples, they had risked incurring the suspicions of both. Nonetheless, on July 13, they rode safely into Yasin, where they were warmly greeted by the local Dard chief, Mir Wali, whom Hayward knew from his earlier visit and believed to be his friend.

The true story of what ensued in this wild and desolate spot, where human life counted for little, will never be known. But during his brief halt in Yasin it seems that Hayward quarrelled with his host over which route he should take out of Dard territory into the Pamirs. Mir Wali, it is said, had been ordered by his own chief, the ruler of Chitral, to send Hayward to see him before being allowed to continue on his journey. But Hayward, already delayed, was anxious to press on. To travel to Chitral would have meant a considerable detour westwards, and anyway he was suspicious of the ruler's motives. He thus refused, and an angry scene is said to have followed, during which the Englishman called Mir Wali by what was described as 'a hard name' in public. Other accounts challenge this, claiming that it was invented as an excuse for what was being planned. What is certain is that Hayward was bearing a number of highly desirable gifts which were intended for the chiefs of areas through which he had still to pass. These, according to several subsequent witnesses, had attracted the covetous gaze of Mir Wali, and possibly the ruler of Chitral, who were loath to see them leave their domains.

By now Mir Wali had abandoned his efforts to re-route

Hayward via Chitral, even lending him coolies to see his party as far as the village of Darkot, twenty miles to the north, which marked the limits of his own territory. After an outwardly friendly parting from Mir Wali, Hayward left Yasin for Darkot, arriving there on the afternoon of July 17, and setting up his camp on a nearby hillside, 9,000 feet above sea level. Hayward, who had performed a great service for the Dards by exposing the Kashmiri atrocities, had no reason at that point to suspect treachery. However, that evening he was surprised to learn that a party of Mir Wali's men had arrived unexpectedly in Darkot. They told the villagers that they had been sent to see the Englishman safely over the Darkot Pass on the following day. It seems, though, that they made no attempt to contact him. Hayward was puzzled by this, for he was not expecting the men, and Mir Wali had not mentioned them at their parting.

Something else worried him too. One of his servants now confided to him that shortly before they left Yasin an attempt had been made by Mir Wali to persuade him to desert. Hayward decided to take no chances. He would sit up all night, in case treachery was afoot. 'That night,' the village headman reported later, 'the Sahib did not eat any dinner, but only drank tea.' He sat alone in his tent, writing by the light of a candle. On the table before him were his firearms, loaded and ready. In his left hand he held a pistol, while he wrote with the other. But the night passed quietly. At first light everything appeared normal. Nothing stirred in the camp. Perhaps he had been worrying needlessly. Hayward rose and made himself some tea. Then, exhausted by the long night's vigil, he fell asleep.

This was the moment Mir Wali's men had been waiting for. One of them crept silently into the camp from the nearby undergrowth, where he and his accomplices had been hiding. He asked Hayward's unsuspecting cook whether his master was asleep. On discovering that he was, he made for his tent. One of Hayward's servants, a Pathan, spotted him and tried to stop him, but the rest of Mir Wali's men now rushed in. The struggle was over in seconds. Hayward's servants were all seized, and he himself pinioned while a noose was slipped around his neck. He had no time to reach for his firearms.

Their arms tightly bound, the captives were next led into the forest. According to the headman's account, which he obtained from the men themselves, Hayward tried to bargain with them for his own and his servants' lives. First he offered them the contents of his baggage, including the gifts he was carrying, but they pointed out that these were already theirs for the taking. He next offered them substantial rewards of money which his friends would provide in exchange for the party's release. However, the men clearly had their orders and showed no interest.

There are two different accounts of what followed. According to one – that of the village headman – Hayward's ring was next torn from his finger. Then the leader of Mir Wali's men drew his sword. Realising that he was going to die, Hayward uttered what those present took to be a prayer. Seconds later he was dead, slain by a single stroke of the sword. So that there might be no witnesses to the crime, his five servants were killed. The murderers then hastened to Hayward's camp, which they proceeded to ransack in search of his own personal possessions and the gifts he was carrying. Their task now complete, they rode back to Yasin to report to their master, and to hand over to him the Englishman's valuables. The other account of Hayward's death, said to have come from one of his murderers, and which was to gain wide currency at the time, maintains that he asked his captors for one last favour before they killed him – to be allowed to watch the sun rise over the mountains. If the story is true, then the Mir's men let him walk forward to a piece of rising ground. There, with his arms still tightly bound, Hayward stood in silence while the sun rose. Then he strode back to his captors, declaring: 'I am ready'.

It was just how the Victorians liked their heroes to die. Hayward's treacherous murder, in one of the world's most desolate spots, stirred the nation profoundly when word of it reached London by telegraph from India nearly three months later. Surprisingly, no painter tried to immortalise the scene, although the popular poet Sir Henry Newbolt would later do so in verse. His poem – 'He Fell Among Thieves' – ends thus:

And now it was dawn. He rose strong to his feet,
　　And strode to his ruined camp below the wood;
He drank the breath of the morning cool and sweet,
　　His murderers round him stood.

Light on the Laspur hills was broadening fast,
　　The blood-red snow-peaks chilled to a dazzling white;
He turned, and saw the golden circle at last,
　　Cut by the Eastern height.

'O glorious Life, Who dwellest in earth and sun,
　　I have lived, I praise and adore Thee.'
　　　　　　　　　　　　　　　　A sword swept.
Over the pass the voices one by one
　　Faded, and the hill slept.

Whatever the outrage felt by Victorian England towards Hayward's murderers, there was very little that could be done about it short of dispatching a punitive expedition into these dangerous wilds, and that was something that the Viceroy had no intention of doing. The tragedy proved all too clearly the point which Sir John Lawrence and others had made – that one should not allow Europeans, however willing or brave, to venture into regions where their deaths could not be avenged. Immediate efforts were nonetheless made to try to discover the precise circumstances of the murder, as well as to retrieve Hayward's body so that he could be given a proper burial. It was obviously too dangerous to send investigators to the spot, and nothing very useful was to emerge as to whether Mir Wali was solely responsible for the murder, or whether others were behind him, as some suspected. Both the Maharajah of Kashmir and the ruler of Chitral were rumoured to have been involved, although there is no evidence against either of them.

Hayward's body was recovered on the initiative of one of his friends, a British geologist named Frederick Drew, who was in the employ of the Maharajah of Kashmir. Unable, for reasons of personal safety, to visit Yasin or Darkot himself, he sent instead a highly trusted British Indian sepoy to discover all he could about Hayward's death, and to try to find and bring back his remains. The resourceful soldier, at considerable risk to his own life, succeeded in recovering Hayward's corpse from beneath a pile of rocks which had been heaped on it, and in conveying it back to Drew at Gilgit. He also rescued some of the explorer's possessions, including books, maps and papers, which his murderers had judged valueless.

On December 21, Drew was able to report to the Royal Geographical Society that he had buried its gold medallist in a garden beside the fort in Gilgit, a detachment of troops firing three volleys over the grave. Later a headstone was erected bearing these words: 'To the memory of G. W. Hayward, Gold Medallist of the Royal Geographical Society of London, who was cruelly murdered at Darkot, July 18, 1870, on his journey to explore the Pamir steppe. This monument is erected to a gallant officer and accomplished traveller at the instance of the Royal Geographical Society.' It remains there to this day in what was to become Gilgit's Christian cemetery, though now one has to obtain the key from the cobbler's shop opposite if one wishes to see it. At the time of Hayward's burial there grew beside it an apricot tree which, it is said, never bore fruit again. Today only a weeping willow stands there.

As for the treacherous Mir Wali, he was never brought to justice. However, shortly afterwards he was forced to flee from Yasin, for the ruler of Chitral, using British wrath over Hayward's murder as a pretext, forcibly relieved him of his authority. This was supposedly by way of punishment, but it soon became obvious that the real motive was to enable him to reward one of his relatives with Yasin's rule. Mir Wali's sins finally caught up with him, though. After evading pursuit for several years, he met with a violent and dramatic end at the hands of his enemies – according to one account plunging over a precipice locked in a deadly embrace with an assailant. More than a century later Hayward's name is widely remembered throughout the region. At Darkot, hardly less remote today than in his time, villagers took me to the bleak spot beside a small stream where, they say, Hayward was killed. My guide, as it happened, was a direct descendant of Mir Wali. According to a British traveller, Colonel Reginald Schomberg, who passed through Darkot in the 1930s, Hayward's pistol, telescope and saddle were said still to be in the possession of local families. More recently, in the 1950s, six topographical watercolours by the murdered explorer turned up in the Bombay bazaar, and were subsequently sold at auction in London. Just how they found their way on to the market will forever remain a mystery – like so much else about George Hayward.

*　　*　　*

The Russians had long been concerned about the activities of British officers, explorers and other travellers in a region which they had come to look upon as lying within their sphere of influence. Thus the journeys of Shaw and Hayward (and perhaps even the Pundits, of whose existence they were by now very likely aware) had not gone unobserved by General Kaufman in Tashkent. Even more disturbing to him, however, was the British mission, ostensibly commercial, which Lord Mayo had dispatched under Sir Douglas Forsyth to the court of Yakub Beg. For the Muslim leader was currently showing himself to be extremely hostile to St Petersburg, strengthening his military posts along their common frontier, and prohibiting the entry of all Russian goods and merchants. To Kaufman it must have looked as though the British had at last abandoned their policy of masterly inactivity, and were preparing to bring Kashgaria under their protection and to monopolise its trade. In fact, though the Russians did not yet know it, the British had met with a reverse. On reaching Yarkand, the mission had discovered that Yakub Beg was at the eastern end of his kingdom, nearly a thousand miles away, and was not expected back for quite some time. There were those who suspected that he had done this deliberately, fearing on careful reflection that he might needlessly risk St Petersburg's wrath by receiving the British. Whatever the reason, the mission had no choice but to return empty-handed to India. Coupled with the unavenged murder of Hayward and his servants, this rebuff, intended or otherwise, represented a serious blow to British esteem in Central Asia.

It was at this moment that St Petersburg launched the first of a series of major moves which were to strengthen greatly its political and strategic position in the region. Spurred on by Count Ignatiev, who had shortly before been appointed as his country's ambassador to Constantinople, it unilaterally renounced the humiliating Black Sea clauses forced on it under the Treaty of Paris after the Crimean War. These, it may be recalled, banned Russian warships and naval installations from the Black Sea. The news caused consternation in London, for the ban's purpose had been to keep the Russian fleet as far away as possible from the Turkish straits and the Mediterranean, and so safeguard Britain's imperial lifeline with India. However, not having the full backing of the other major European powers, the British were unable to do much about it short of going to war with St Petersburg, and that the government was unwilling to do.

Russia's next forward move followed soon afterwards, in the summer of 1871, though because of the remoteness of the region where this occurred it took the British three months to hear about it. The Muslim territory of Ili, which commanded important strategic passes into southern Siberia, had shaken off Chinese rule during the recent insurrection and won temporary independence. Lying adjacent to Yakub Beg's domains, to the north-east of Kashgar, it had not yet been annexed by him. But believing, or at least claiming, that Yakub Beg was about to seize it, General Kaufman ordered his troops to pre-empt any such move, lest the Muslim ruler's occupation of the territory threaten Russia's southern borders. For it was across these passes, it should in fairness be said, that in Mongol times the destructive hordes had poured into Russia, causing them to be likened by Russian strategists to the Khyber Pass. However, that was not the Ili valley's only significance. It was also rich in minerals, as Kaufman's geologists were well aware, while for good measure it served as the principal granary of this desolate region, a fact which can hardly have escaped his generals. On June 24, the Russians marched through the passes into Ili, where they defeated a force more than twice their strength which attempted to stop them. The following day they entered Kuldja, the capital, the Russian commander proclaiming it to have been annexed 'in perpetuity' although he had no authority to do so. Later St Petersburg corrected this, declaring that the occupation was merely temporary.

So distant was Ili from the nearest Chinese outposts, since their expulsion from Turkestan, that Peking was totally unaware of the Russian incursion until officially informed of it by St Petersburg. It was explained to the Chinese that the Tsar's forces had recovered Ili from the rebels for the Emperor, and would hold on to it until he was once again able to defend it against Yakub Beg or anyone else. This did not deceive the Chinese, who immediately demanded that it be restored to them. St Petersburg refused, and relations between the two powers became extremely chilly. No longer worried by the prospect of upsetting Peking, the Russians decided to reopen discussions with Yakub Beg over the old questions of recognition and trade. In the spring of 1872, they dispatched a senior political officer to his court at Kashgar with instructions to offer him full recognition in exchange for opening his markets to Russian goods on specially favourable terms which would effectively keep out the British. This time the talks were successful, or so the Russians thought.

It was Yakub Beg's aim, however, to keep foreign influence to a minimum in Kashgaria. The best way to achieve this, he reasoned, was by playing one side off against the other. No sooner had the Russian envoy departed than he sent a special emissary to the British in India expressing his profound regrets at his unavoidable absence the previous year, and inviting them to dispatch a second mission to Kashgar for talks with him. Alarmed by news of the Russian visit, Lord Northbrook, the new Viceroy (Lord Mayo had been assassinated the previous year), accepted gratefully, and in the summer of 1873 a second British mission set out across the Karakorams. Far larger than the earlier one, it consisted of political and military officers, trade experts, surveyors and other specialists, and was headed once again by Sir Douglas Forsyth. His instructions were to obtain from Yakub Beg a trade deal similar to that which he had granted to the Russians, and to gather as much intelligence as possible from this little-known region, whether political, strategic, economic or scientific. With its escort of infantry and cavalry from the Corps of Guides, and its numerous interpreters, secretaries, clerks and servants, the mission totalled 350 men and 550 baggage animals. After thirty years,

Britain's policy of masterly inactivity in Central Asia, condemned by its hawkish critics as craven surrender to Russia's designs, was at last coming to an end.

* * *

At first the tougher line which London was beginning to take appeared to yield gratifying results, momentarily allaying fears of further Russian moves towards India. For an unprecedented climb-down by St Petersburg brought to a conclusion the long-standing disagreement with London over the location of Afghanistan's northern frontier. This had arisen over the sovereignty of the remote and mountainous regions of Badakhshan and Wakhan, on the upper Oxus, where the Russian outposts lay closest to British India. London had all along insisted that they formed an integral part of eastern Afghanistan, while St Petersburg argued that they did not, maintaining instead that the Emir of Bokhara had a better claim to them. Then, in January 1873, the Russians suddenly and unexpectedly gave way, acknowledging that they lay within the domains of the Emir of Afghanistan. Furthermore, they reaffirmed that Afghanistan itself lay within Britain's sphere of influence, and outside their own. In return they expected Britain to restrain the Emir from embarking on military adventures beyond his northern frontier or inciting his co-religionists there to make war on them. The British were delighted, believing themselves to have won an important diplomatic victory, although the agreement was not incorporated into a formal treaty, the Russians merely accepting it in principle. Indeed, even now, the frontier was little more than a vague line on an even vaguer map, for almost nothing was known about the wild Pamir region of eastern Afghanistan – a deficiency which George Hayward had intended to put right. But what the British did not then realise was that Russia's capitulation over Badakhshan and Wakhan was merely a smoke-screen for a further advance, the boldest yet by far, which was being planned at the highest level in St Petersburg.

Only a month before the Afghan frontier agreement, at an extraordinary session of the Council of State, presided over by

Tsar Alexander in person, it had finally been decided to launch an all-out expedition against Khiva. Secret preparations had been in hand for this for many months, but the agreement over the Afghan frontier appeared to provide the ideal moment for such a move. By conceding to the British what they wanted, the Tsar and his advisers reasoned, they had made it more difficult for London to object to the seizure of Khiva. The British, however, had already got wind of the fact that something was afoot. Assurances were demanded from St Petersburg that no further conquests were being planned in Central Asia. These were given without so much as a blush, although a 13,000-strong force commanded by Kaufman was by now ready to march towards Khiva. Finally it had to be admitted that an expedition was about to be launched. But even then St Petersburg insisted that it had no intention of occupying the city permanently. Indeed, the British Foreign Secretary was assured, the Tsar had given 'positive orders' to this effect.

Following their two earlier disasters, in 1717 and 1839, the Russians were taking no risks this time, advancing across the desert from three directions simultaneously – from Tashkent, Orenburg and Krasnovodsk. Aware of the enormous distances which an attacker had to cover, the Khan had at first felt secure. But as Kaufman's troops advanced ever further into his domains, he became increasingly alarmed. In an attempt to buy off the invaders he released twenty-one Russian slaves and captives held in Khiva, though to no avail. Finally, when the nearest Russian troops were only thirteen miles from his capital, the Khan sent his cousin to Kaufman offering to surrender unconditionally and submit permanently to the Tsar if the Russian commander agreed to halt the attack. Kaufman replied that he would only negotiate from inside the city. To help the Khan make up his mind, the Russians turned their new, German-made artillery on the mud-built walls. On May 28, 1873, the Khan fled, and the following day Kaufman entered Khiva in triumph.

Although, as at Tashkent, Samarkand and Bokhara, the Russians had done no more than defeat ill-armed and undisciplined tribesmen, the fall of Khiva represented to St Petersburg a resounding psychological victory. Not only did it help to alleviate the humiliation of the earlier Khivan disasters, as well as that of the Crimean defeat, but it also greatly enhanced the Tsar's military prestige and growing reputation for invincibility throughout Central Asia. In addition, it won the Russians control over navigation on the lower Oxus, with its attendant commercial and strategic benefits, as well as total domination of the eastern shore of the Caspian. It also closed a large gap in Russia's southern Asiatic flank, and brought Kaufman's jubilant troops to within 500 miles of Herat, India's ancient strategic gateway. After half a century, the forebodings of men like Wilson, Moorcroft, de Lacy Evans and Kinneir were beginning to look ominously justified. By seizing Khiva, the British ambassador in St Petersburg warned the Foreign Office, the Russians had secured a base from which they could 'menace the independence of Persia and Afghanistan, and thereby become a standing danger to our Indian Empire.'

A terse exchange of notes now followed between London and St Petersburg, with the latter once again assuring the British government that the occupation was only temporary. In November, however, *The Times* published details of a secret treaty, signed by the Russians and Khivans, under which the Khan became a vassal of the Tsar's and his country a Russian protectorate. The British realised that they had been duped once again, while the Russians insisted that military imperatives and changed circumstances had overridden all earlier undertakings – an excuse the British had heard before. To this Prince Gorchakov, the Russian Foreign Minister, added the following reproof. 'The Cabinet of London', he reminded the British, 'appears to derive, from the fact of our having on several occasions spontaneously and amicably communicated to them our views with respect to Central Asia, and particularly our firm resolve not to pursue a policy of conquest or annexation, a conviction that we have contracted definite engagements toward them in regard to this.' It fooled nobody, of course, but once again, short of war, there was little or nothing that could be done about it – or about the Russians' next move.

Worried perhaps lest this time he might have overtaxed British forbearance, Gorchakov volunteered yet another assurance. 'His Imperial Majesty', he declared, 'has no intention of extending the frontiers of Russia such as they exist at present in Central Asia, either on the side of Bokhara, or on the side of Krasnovodsk.' He omitted to mention Khokand, however, whose ruler had been closely tied to Russia by treaty since the fall of Tashkent. In the summer of 1875, an uprising there directed against both the Russians and their puppet khan gave Kaufman the opportunity he needed to impose a tighter grip on this unstable territory, then still nominally independent. On August 22 his troops routed the main rebel army, and four days later he entered Khokand, over which he raised the imperial Russian flag. After further fighting, in which the rebels suffered heavy losses, the towns of Andijan and Osh also fell to him. Not long afterwards the khanate was formally proclaimed to be part of the Tsar's Central Asian empire, and renamed the province of Ferghana. Alexander, the official announcement declared, had 'yielded to the wishes of the Khokandi people to become Russian subjects'. So it was that the Russians, in a period of just ten years, had annexed a territory half the size of the United States, and erected a defensive barrier across Central Asia stretching from the Caucasus in the west to Khokand and Kuldja in the east.

For India's defence chiefs this was highly disturbing. The incorporation of the Khanate of Khokand into the Russian Empire had brought Kaufman's battle-hardened troops to within 200 miles of Kashgar. It could only be a matter of time before the Russians seized that too, together with Yarkand, which would give them control of the passes leading into Ladakh and Kashmir. Then the ring around India's northern frontiers would be complete, allowing the Russians to strike southwards from almost any point or points of their choosing. Only the great mountain ranges of the north – the High Pamirs and the Karakorams – stood in their way. Until recently these had been regarded as impenetrable to a modern army with its artillery and other heavy equipment. Shaw and Hayward had been the first to challenge this, only to have their warnings rebutted by the experts. Now others, whose opinions could not be so lightly dismissed, were expressing similar fears about the vulnerability of the northern passes.

*　　　*　　　*

By now the mission headed by Sir Douglas Forsyth which the Viceroy had dispatched to the court of Yakub Beg at Kashgar had returned to India. Their reception this time had been splendid, and the many promises which the Muslim ruler had made to them greatly exceeded anything he had offered his earlier Russian visitors. However, despite the vows of undying friendship between Kashgaria and Britain, and visions of a great new trading partnership, in the end nothing was to come of it. The vast markets for European goods which both the British and the Russians had believed to exist in the region were to prove illusory. It soon became clear, moreover, that Yakub Beg was merely stringing his two powerful neighbours along, exploiting their mutual jealousies to safeguard his own position. After all, an oriental could play the Great Game too. But if Forsyth's mission failed to extract from the wily ruler anything other than what would prove to be worthless promises, it did succeed in one thing. Lieutenant-Colonel Thomas Gordon and two other officers had been allowed by Yakub Beg to return home across the Pamirs with a small escort of the Indian Corps of Guides. The route they took was much the same, though in reverse, as that which Hayward had hoped to follow. Their aim, like Hayward's, was to explore and map the passes leading from the Russian frontier southwards into Kashmir, and gauge whether a modern army could enter India by them.

· 27 ·

'A Physician from the North'

Struggling at times through snow which came up to the bellies of their ponies, and frequently forced to halt by violent storms, Lieutenant-Colonel Gordon and his party nonetheless rode 400 miles across the Pamirs in three weeks. Unlike the other great mountain systems which converge there – the Hindu Kush, the Karakorams and the Tien Shan – the Pamirs consist of a vast plateau broken by mountains and broad valleys. Known to the tribes living in the surrounding regions as the Bam-i-Dunya, or Roof of the World, they are almost destitute of human habitations, trees and other vegetation. It was the objective of Gordon's party to fill in as many of the blanks on the British staff maps of this little-known region as possible, and to answer certain other crucial strategic questions. The intelligence they returned with in the spring of 1874 was profoundly disturbing.

Provided the right season was chosen, the Pamirs were far from impenetrable to a modern army, even one encumbered with artillery. Indeed, there was little to prevent a Russian force from the Tsar's new garrisons in the Khokand region, just across the Oxus, from crossing the river and swarming down through the passes into Dardistan and Kashmir, and from there into northern India. The most vulnerable of the passes, they learned, were the Baroghil and the Ishkaman, a hundred miles or so north-west of Gilgit. Although they lay roughly equidistant from the nearest British and Russian outposts, the approaches to them from the north were far easier than from the south. In the event of a race between the two powers for their possession, Gordon reported, the Russians would almost certainly win. For much of the year, both these passes could be crossed without any great difficulty. Not many years earlier, one of the native rulers to the north had even managed to get cannons over them, or so it was said.

In his report to his chiefs, Gordon concluded that by means of the Baroghil Pass the Russians could reach the Indian frontier in thirteen marches via Chitral, while the Ishkaman would bring them there in much the same time via Gilgit. These two passes, he and his fellow officers agreed, were far more vulnerable than the Chang Lung, which Hayward and Shaw had envisaged as a back-door route into India for a Russian force occupying Kashgaria, not to mention the formidable Karakoram Pass, whose difficulties the mission had experienced. Possession of Kashgar by the Russians, Gordon believed, was less worrying than their present occupation of Khokand, although in the event of a war the former might serve either as a supply centre for an invasion force crossing the Pamir passes, or as a base from which the British could attack its lines of communication. To preserve the friendship of Yakub Beg was therefore vital for India's interests.

In addition to all this, Gordon and his companions made another disturbing discovery. They found that Afghanistan and Kashgaria did not, in fact, meet in this great mountain fastness. A crucial gap fifty miles wide remained between them. Were the Russians to discover this too, then they would be able to claim, through their possession of Khokand, that it belonged to them. They would thus, in Sir Douglas Forsyth's words, be able to interpose 'a narrow wedge of actual Russian territory' between eastern Afghanistan and Kashgaria, thereby bringing them even closer to northern India. Gordon's party also heard worrying tales of Russian agents and caravans regularly visiting Afghanistan, access to which was still barred to British merchants and others. They further learned that Mir Wali, Hayward's murderer, had fled the region on their approach, fearing that the British had come to seize him.

In his military report Gordon urged that immediate action be taken to strengthen Britain's position in the southern approaches to the Baroghil and Ishkaman passes. This could be achieved by building a road northwards from Kashmir to the latter, which would also ensure control of the Baroghil. Officially its purpose would be to serve as a trade route between India and the extreme north. 'It would attract not only the Eastern Turkistan traders who at present toil over the Karakoram,' Gordon declared, 'but also the Badakhshan merchants who trade with Peshawar through Kabul.' However, its real purpose would be to enable the British to move troops northwards 'at the shortest notice' in the event of a Russian incursion across the Oxus towards the Baroghil and Ishkaman passes.

But in so desolate a region, much of which lay at 20,000 feet or more, how would it be known in time if a Russian invasion force had set out? Apart from native traders or travellers from the Khokand region bringing back word of obvious military preparations there, the British would be unlikely to get any warning until the invader was well on his way. One solution proposed by Forsyth was to appoint a British Agent at Gilgit. From there, where an Englishman would be reasonably safe, he would be able to gather intelligence on regions 'which at present are a sealed book to us'. This could be done by establishing a regular network of paid native spies, as had already been done in areas where it was too dangerous, or politically unwise, for Europeans to venture. His recommendation was adopted, though not before a further reconnaissance of the Baroghil and Ishkaman passes had been carried out by one of Gordon's party, who not only confirmed their original view but also reported that in the summer months there was ample pasturage for an invading army along the entire route.

As a result of these unwelcome discoveries, it was decided in Calcutta to encourage the Maharajah of Kashmir, who was allied to Britain by a treaty, to extend his political influence, if not his actual territories, northwards to include Chitral and Yasin, thereby enabling him to exercise some sort of control over the Baroghil and Ishkaman passes. If actual conquest proved necessary, then Britain would be prepared to give him material support. There were those in Calcutta and elsewhere who questioned the wisdom of this, however, for there were unsubstantiated rumours circulating that the Kashmiri ruler had secretly received Russian agents. If this were true, then his expansion northwards might merely result in bringing the Russians closer to India's frontiers. While not himself questioning the Maharajah's loyalty, Sir Douglas Forsyth warned the Viceroy that Britain was in grave danger of losing the confidence of those very states which she saw as her allies against an expanding Russia. In parts of Central Asia, he declared, it was widely held that 'Russia is the rising power, that she is destined to rise still further, that England is afraid of her, and will do nothing to oppose her progress or help those who would preserve themselves from being swallowed up.' As a result, he claimed, some rulers were beginning to wonder whether it would not be wiser to transfer their loyalty to what they judged to be 'the coming power' in Asia.

Just as Calcutta was alarmed at the presence of Russian garrisons across the Pamir passes, so too was St Petersburg at the escalation in British military and political activity in regions which the Russians now regarded as lying within their own sphere of influence. This had begun innocently enough with Shaw and Hayward, ostensibly independent travellers, but already British diplomatic missions were coming and going between India and Kashgaria, undermining Russia's gains at Yakub Beg's court, while British military surveyors were energetically mapping the Pamir passes. What were London and Calcutta brewing up between them? As the cycle of mistrust intensified, and relations between Britain and Russia continued to deteriorate, one thing was becoming clear. While Afghanistan remained the focal point of the Great Game, with the Khyber and Bolan passes as the most likely routes for an invading army to take, the options facing the Russian generals, if that was indeed their intention, were far greater than had hitherto been thought. The imperial chessboard had been considerably extended, and play on it was about to be stepped up.

*　　*　　*

In the spring of 1874, following the fall of Gladstone's Liberal administration, the Tories were returned to power with a massive majority. At their head was Benjamin Disraeli, who believed passionately in Britain's imperial destiny and in maintaining a vigorous foreign policy, views which he shared with Queen Victoria. He had long been critical, moreover, of what he considered to be his predecessor's display of weakness towards the Russians. This he was determined to put right. From now on forward policies were to return with a vengeance, and Anglo-Russian relations to cool at an ever-increasing rate. Following St Petersburg's dramatic gains in Central Asia, India naturally commanded much Cabinet attention. Disraeli and Lord Salisbury, his new secretary of state for India, feared not so much an imminent Russian attack as attempts by St Petersburg, despite Gorchakov's 1873 undertaking, to gain some kind of a toe-hold in Afghanistan. If this was successful it might be used as a base from which trouble could be stirred up against the British in India, or even as a springboard for a combined invasion. Disraeli was anxious, therefore, to establish a permanent British mission in Kabul, while the hawks around him urged similar representation at Herat and Kandahar.

To institute his new policies, the Prime Minister decided to appoint Lord Lytton as Viceroy in place of the Liberals' man, Lord Northbrook, who had resigned over the government's decision to meddle thus with Afghanistan's highly combustible domestic affairs. On the eve of his departure for home, Northbrook had warned London that to abandon its policy of masterly inactivity would expose Britain to the risk 'of another unnecessary and costly war' with her unpredictable neighbour. His warning, however, was to go unheeded, and Lord Lytton, armed with detailed instructions regarding the new forward policies he was to enact, set about his task with vigour. One of his first duties was to proclaim Queen Victoria Empress of India, Disraeli's way of pleasing the sovereign while at the same time signalling to the Russians, 'in language that cannot be mistaken', that Britain's commitment to India was permanent and absolute. In other words 'hands off'.

Two other moves made by Britain around this time greatly strengthened her hand in India. One was the purchase from the Khedive of Egypt, amid intense secrecy, of 40 per cent of the shares in the newly opened Suez Canal. This waterway reduced the distance by sea between Britain and India by some 4,500 miles, and Disraeli wished to make absolutely sure that this crucial lifeline, for both troops and goods, could never be threatened or even severed by a hostile power – notably by the Russians in the event of their acquiring Constantinople and the Turkish straits. The purchase of the Egyptian ruler's entire holding, which effectively rescued him from bankruptcy, made Britain the largest shareholder in the Suez Canal Company. A second major improvement in communications with India was the opening, in 1870, of a direct submarine cable link with London. Five years earlier an overland telegraph line had been completed, but traffic went via Teheran and was thus vulnerable to interference or severance in time of war. The new submarine cable was far less vulnerable. 'As long as England holds the empire of the sea the cables will be safe from enemies,' declared *The Times*. 'To grapple and raise them would require not only a knowledge of their exact position, and a ship specially fitted with proper apparatus and trained hands, but also more time than could be given to the task. The electric lines will lie beneath the great highways of traffic, and no grappling ship in search of them could escape notice.' The inauguration of the new link, moreover, enabled Whitehall to maintain a tighter control over the affairs of India than ever before, it now taking hours to elicit a reply from either end where once it had taken weeks or even months.

Disraeli's instructions to the new Viceroy, Lord Lytton, included bringing not only Afghanistan but also the neighbouring state of Baluchistan into a defensive alliance with Britain. For there lay the Bolan Pass, leading out of Afghanistan into India. Baluchistan was then torn by internal strife which threatened the throne of its ruler, the Khan of Kelat. Worried by the region's instability, and the Khan's inability to control the turbulent tribes, Calcutta considered deposing him and replacing him with someone more able. This was strongly opposed, however, by British political officers on the spot, who argued that it was likely to do far more harm than good. Instead, it was decided to allow Captain Robert Sandeman, an officer possessing a remarkable influence over the Baluchi chiefs, to try to bring them to heel by persuasion. In the winter of 1875, alone and armed only with a revolver, Sandeman visited the insurgent tribesmen in the mountains where he succeeded in resolving their conflict with the Khan. The following autumn, in gratitude to Calcutta for thus securing his throne, not to mention a generous annual subsidy, the Khan agreed to lease both the Bolan Pass region and the nearby garrison town of Quetta permanently to Britain.

Afghanistan, as might be expected, was to prove a far tougher proposition. Part of the problem arose from the previous policy of non-interference in Afghanistan's affairs. In 1873, fearing the Russians more than the British, the Emir, Dost Mohammed's son Sher Ali, had approached Lord Northbrook with the offer of a defensive treaty against a threat from the north. The Viceroy had been instructed by Gladstone's government to turn this down, as well as to reprimand Sher Ali over certain other matters. Understandably the Emir had been angered by this rebuff from those he had considered to be his friends. It was not long after this that reports began to reach India that he was in communication with General Kaufman at Tashkent. Lytton's orders from Disraeli were to try to undo the damage done by Northbrook's snub by offering the Emir the treaty he had previously sought, but with the added proviso that he accept a permanent British representative at Kabul or Herat. This was so that a close eye could be kept on Kaufman's activities at the royal court, for the Emir was now strongly suspected of being partial to the Russians and therefore not to be fully trusted. But as the less hawkish among Lytton's advisers had warned, the presence of British officers anywhere in Afghanistan was to prove totally unacceptable to the Emir. Indeed, he would not even agree to a temporary British mission visiting Kabul to discuss such matters, arguing that he would then have no grounds for refusing a Russian one. Talks must take place, he insisted, either on the frontier or in Calcutta. Needless to say, this did little to relieve Lytton's growing distrust of Sher Ali – not to mention St Petersburg, whose malign influence he believed to be behind it all.

'The prospect of war with Russia immensely excites,' he wrote to Lord Salisbury in September 1876, 'but so far as

India is concerned does not at all alarm me. If it is to be –
better now than later. We are twice as strong as Russia in this
part of the world, and have much better bases for attack and
defence.' In the event of war, he added with gusto, 'a sea of
fire' could be spread around India's northern frontiers by
inciting the khanates to turn against their Russian masters.
Coming from a man like Lytton – a liberal-minded and somewhat Bohemian ex-diplomat, more interested in poetry than
in politics – such bellicose talk may seem out of character.
However, like most men of letters and intellectuals of his day,
he had an inborn dislike of Russia's autocratic system of rule.
To this were now added not only grave misgivings about
St Petersburg's intentions towards Afghanistan, but also the
universally held conviction that another showdown with Russia
was inevitable, either in Central Asia over Afghanistan or in
the Near East over Constantinople.

Concern over Russian ambitions had been heightened by
the recent publication of a book, *England and Russia in the
East*, by the leading British authority on the subject, Sir Henry
Rawlinson, now a member of the government's advisory body,
the Council for India. Although it added little to what he and
other forward school writers had been saying since the days of
Wilson, McNeill and de Lacy Evans, the book was to have
a considerable influence on Cabinet thinking and on those,
including the new Viceroy, responsible for the defence of India.
As always with the literature of the Great Game, timing was
everything. There were other books and articles which questioned the opinions of Rawlinson and his school, but they
received scant attention in the largely Russophobe press.
Although Rawlinson denounced those who scorned his warnings as 'dangerous enemies', it would be unfair to regard him
and his allies as wild men spoiling for a fight. Indeed, Lord
Salisbury, while a believer in forward policies, was anything
but a warmonger or scaremonger. 'A great deal of mis-
apprehension arises from a popular use of maps on a small
scale,' he once told a worried fellow peer. 'If the noble lord
would use a larger map, he would find that the distance between
Russia and British India was not to be measured by the finger
and thumb, but by a rule.' However, while he did not for a

moment believe that a Russian invasion of India could succeed, he was concerned lest they incite the Afghans to attempt it at a time when British troops were desperately needed elsewhere. As he was to put it later: 'Russia can offer the Afghans the loot of India. We can offer them nothing, because there is nothing in Turkestan to loot.'

The airing of hawkish views in print was not this time confined to the British forward school. Warning of Britain's ambitions in the East, one St Petersburg newspaper declared: 'They will attempt to extend their influence to Kashgar, Persia and all the Central Asian states bordering on us, and then will pose a direct threat to our interests in Asia ... We must watch them vigilantly and take swift measures to parry the blow being prepared for us by them.' The words might easily have come from a London newspaper issuing a similar warning about Russian designs. Indeed, it was from the St Petersburg press that the British embassy there obtained much, if not all, of its intelligence about what was going on in Central Asia, albeit usually long after it had happened.

In 1876, the year after Rawlinson's book appeared, an English translation of a Russian Great Game classic – Colonel M. A. Terentiev's *Russia and England in the Struggle for the Markets of Central Asia* – was published in Calcutta in two volumes. Intensely Anglophobic, among many other things it accused the British of secretly distributing rifles among the Turcoman tribes for use against Russia. It also alleged that Sir John Lawrence, that staunch believer in masterly inactivity, had been sacked as Viceroy of India for not being sufficiently Russophobic. The Indian Mutiny, Terentiev maintained, had only failed because the Indians lacked a proper plan and outside support. They continued to suffer from British misrule and exploitation. 'Sick to death,' Terentiev went on, 'the natives are now waiting for a physician from the north.' Given such assistance, they had every chance of starting a conflagration which would spread throughout India, and thus enable them to throw off the British yoke. In the event of such an uprising, the Russian claimed, the British would find themselves unable to rely on the support of their native troops, who formed the major part of their army in India.

Turning to the question of a Russian invasion of India, Terentiev declared that if the two powers were to go to war 'then we shall clearly be obliged to take advantage of the proximity of India to our present position in Central Asia'. He rated highly the chances of such an expedition succeeding in ending British rule in India, particularly in view of what he claimed to be the seething discontent of the native population. As for the many natural obstacles in the path of an invading army, he saw no insurmountable problems. If such an expedition had been judged feasible during the reign of Tsar Paul, more than seventy years earlier, then it should pose considerably fewer difficulties now that the intervening distance had been dramatically reduced. This latter argument said little for the colonel's powers of reasoning, for it will be recalled that the invasion force sent against India by the half-mad Paul in 1801 was saved from almost certain annihilation only by its hasty recall on his assassination.

It need hardly be said that Terentiev's views on the Great Game were precisely the reverse of those which Prince Gorchakov was trying to convey to the British government. Yet in Russia, where the printed word was so rigidly controlled by the censor, the colonel's exposition must have enjoyed high-level approval for it to have been published. Very likely it was intended for internal consumption only, and not for British eyes. It serves nonetheless as yet another example of Russia's twin-policy strategy. One, emanating from St Petersburg, was official and conciliatory. The other, unofficial and aggressive, was left to those on the spot, and could always be repudiated if necessary. Terentiev's book clearly reflected the thinking of the Russian forward school. As such it was extremely valuable, for very little was known about what lay in the minds of the Russian military in Central Asia, let alone about what was going on in the Tsar's new domains north of the Oxus. One British officer, who had read Terentiev's work in the original Russian, was determined to discover more. And that could only be done by going there.

· 28 ·

Captain Burnaby's Ride to Khiva

Captain Frederick Gustavus Burnaby of the Royal Horse Guards was no ordinary officer. For a start he was a man of prodigious strength and stature. Standing six-foot-four in his stockinged feet, weighing fifteen stone, and possessing a forty-seven-inch chest, he was reputed to be the strongest man in the British Army. Indeed, it was even said that he could carry a small pony under his arm. Another Herculean feat of Burnaby's was to grasp the tip of a billiard cue between his middle and index fingers, and hold it out horizontally, his arm fully extended and the butt end steady. Nor was this son of a country parson entirely brawn. He also displayed a remarkable gift for languages, being fluent in at least seven, including Russian, Turkish and Arabic. Finally he was born with an insatiable appetite for adventure which he combined with a vigorous and colourful prose style. Inevitably these two latter qualities brought him into contact with Fleet Street, with the result that during his generous annual leaves he served abroad on several occasions as a special correspondent of *The Times* and other journals, on one occasion travelling up the Nile to interview General Gordon at Khartoum.

It was during one of these periods of leave that Burnaby made up his mind to visit Russian Central Asia, which was then said to be closed to British officers and other travellers. His plan was to journey to St Petersburg and apply direct to Count Milyutin, the Minister of War, for permission to travel to India via Khiva, Merv and Kabul. It was a bold approach, though it appeared to offer little prospect of success, especially at a time when Anglo-Russian relations were anything but cordial. But where the slightest chance of adventure was concerned, Burnaby was willing to try anything. He had carefully avoided doing one thing, however, and that was seeking permission for his journey from the British Foreign Office or from his own superiors. The answer, he knew very well, would be no.

Burnaby, carrying only 85 lbs of baggage, left Victoria by the night mail train for St Petersburg on November 30, 1875. In the Russian capital he was advised by friends that the authorities would never agree to his journey. 'They will imagine that you are being sent by your government to stir up the Khivans,' he was told. 'They will never believe that an officer, at his own expense, would go to Khiva.' Surprisingly, his friends proved wrong, for the following day he received a reply to his request to Milyutin which gave partial approval for his journey. The Minister informed him that the authorities along his route had been instructed to help him on his way, but that 'the Imperial Government could not give its acquiescence to the extension of the journey beyond Russian territory', as it was unable to accept responsibility for his life in regions outside its control. This, Burnaby decided, was ambiguous. Either Milyutin meant that he could not go as far as Khiva, then nominally still self-governing – and certainly not to Merv, which lay outside Russian control – or that he could go there, though strictly at his own risk. Given the circumstances, most people would have taken it that Milyutin meant the former. Burnaby decided to assume he meant the latter. Quite why the Minister agreed to Burnaby travelling in the Tsar's Central Asian territories at all is puzzling, unless he feared that the British authorities might apply similar restrictions on Russians travelling in India or elsewhere in the Empire, which at present they were free to do.

Burnaby was not the first British officer to have attempted recently to reach Merv, which many felt might very shortly become the flashpoint of an Anglo-Russian conflagration if Kaufman attempted to seize it. The previous year, while travelling in north-eastern Persia, Captain George Napier, an

Indian Army intelligence officer, had gathered an impressive amount of strategical and political information on the line of advance likely to be taken by a Russian force marching on Merv from Krasnovodsk, their new base on the eastern shore of the Caspian. Although invited to visit Merv by the Turcomans, who were anxious for British protection from Kaufman's troops, Napier had reluctantly declined lest this raise the tribesmen's 'undue expectations'. Only five months before Burnaby's arrival in St Petersburg, a second British officer, Colonel Charles MacGregor, who was later to become chief of military intelligence in India, had reached Herat, intending to visit Merv. But at the last moment he had received an urgent message from his superiors in Calcutta ordering him not to proceed. It was feared that a visit to this strategically sensitive oasis by a British officer known to be involved in intelligence work might expedite its seizure by Kaufman. Indeed, on his return MacGregor had been reprimanded for having gone as far as he had, although he, like Napier, had managed to collect much valuable information on this little-known region.

Burnaby, answerable only to himself, was not a man to allow such considerations to deter him. Travelling part of the way by rail, and the remainder by troika, he reached Orenburg shortly before Christmas. On the way there he had met the Governor and his wife returning to St Petersburg. 'You must remember', the Russian had told him, 'that on no account are you to go to India or Persia. You must retrace your steps to European Russia along the same road by which you go.' It was all too evident to Burnaby that the Governor had received instructions about him from Milyutin. He made little attempt to conceal his own disapproval of the visit, or to assist Burnaby with advice. It was also clear that he had been warned by St Petersburg that this British officer spoke Russian, something highly unusual in those days, although at their roadside meeting Burnaby had addressed him in English. Nonetheless he made no attempt to prevent Burnaby from continuing to Orenburg, although it was still left somewhat in the air just how far he could proceed from there. He was well aware, however, that wherever he went the Russians would keep a close watch on him, and ensure that he saw nothing he was not supposed to see. At Orenburg he met the former Khan of Khokand, exiled there by the Russians but evidently enjoying his new lifestyle, having recently thrown a ball for the garrison officers and their wives. He also learned that Kaufman had asked for two more regiments to be sent to Central Asia for his unspecified use.

After hiring a Muslim servant, and horses to carry their baggage, Burnaby next set out through the snow by sleigh for the Russian fortress town of Kazala, 600 miles away on the northern shore of the Aral Sea, from where he hoped to reach Khiva, and finally Merv, before crossing into Afghanistan. The winter of 1876 was one of the worst in memory, and the journey southwards proved to be an extremely harsh one as the two men fought their way through blizzards and snow-drifts. Although Burnaby was to make light of it later, he was lucky not to lose both his hands from frostbite, being unwise enough to fall asleep with them exposed. Fortunately some friendly Cossacks he encountered managed to restore the circulation by vigorously massaging his arms with naphtha. 'If it had not been for the spirit,' one of the soldiers assured him, 'your hands would have dropped off, and you might very well have lost both arms.' As it was, he did not regain full use of his hands for several weeks.

In Kazala Burnaby was cordially received by his Russian fellow officers. However, they informed him with relish that they were greatly looking forward to the coming struggle with the British for possession of India. 'We will shoot at each other in the morning,' one Russian told Burnaby, handing him a glass of vodka, 'and drink together when there is a truce.' The next morning Burnaby boldly asked the Governor, with whom he was staying, how best he could reach Khiva, 400 miles further south. He was told firmly that he must not proceed there direct, but must go first to the nearest Russian garrison town, Petro-Alexandrovsk, where he could seek permission to visit the khanate. When Burnaby asked him what would happen if he made straight for Khiva, the Governor warned him that the Turcomans who roamed the desert around it were extremely dangerous, as were the Khivans themselves. 'Why,' he told Burnaby, clearly hoping to frighten him, 'the Khan would very likely order his executioner to gouge out your eyes.'

To protect the Englishman from the marauding Turcomans, he offered him a small Cossack escort. But Burnaby knew that the tribesmen had been largely pacified by Kaufman's troops, and that anyway they were well disposed towards the British, as Captain Napier had discovered, hoping for assistance from them if the Russians advanced on Merv. Having learned what he needed to know, Burnaby was determined to head straight for Khiva, and thence try to make his way, via Bokhara if possible, to Merv. He therefore politely declined the offer of an escort, but found himself instead provided with a guide, whose task it obviously was to ensure that he did not stray from the sleigh-route to Petro-Alexandrovsk. This man, it transpired, had served as guide to the Russian force which had conquered Khiva three years earlier. To someone as single-minded and resourceful as Burnaby, however, his presence was not to represent an insurmountable problem.

Khiva, Burnaby discovered, could best be reached by turning off the trail to Petro-Alexandrovsk at a point just two days short of the latter. On January 12, having hired horses for himself, his servant and the guide, and three camels to carry their baggage, including a *kibitka*, or Turcoman tent, he left Kazala, ostensibly bound for the Russian garrison town. 'Although I had hired the camels as far as Petro-Alexandrovsk,' he wrote afterwards, 'I had not the slightest intention of going there if it could be avoided.' He knew that the Russian garrison commander would find a dozen reasons why it was impossible for him to proceed to Khiva, let alone to Bokhara or Merv, and even if he did agree it would be under the strictest supervision. For a start, in order to get his servant on his side, he promised him a 100-rouble note the day they reached Bokhara or Merv, via Khiva. 'The little Tartar', wrote Burnaby, 'was well aware that if we once entered Petro-Alexandrovsk he had but little chance of earning his promised reward.' Nothing, however, was said to the guide.

Khiva lay two weeks' march away across the frozen desert. The savage wind and cold were so severe at times that Burnaby was forced to abandon his dark glasses, whose metal arms froze to his face, and try instead to peer through the fur of his hat in order to avoid snow-blindness. As they struggled on he recalled the terrible suffering experienced by the Russian troops who had tried to reach Khiva from Orenburg in 1839, only to be driven back by the cold. Later he learned that two unfortunate Cossacks had frozen to death while travelling, at the same time as his own party, between Petro-Alexandrovsk and Kazala, their uniforms offering far less protection against the sub-zero temperatures than the furs and sheepskins worn by himself and his men.

Eventually Burnaby reached the remote spot where the trails to Petro-Alexandrovsk and Khiva divided. Here he set about trying to deflect the guide from the path of duty by exploiting a cupidity which he had detected in him. The man's brother-in-law, Burnaby was aware, was a horse-dealer dwelling in a village near Khiva. He therefore let it be known that, when they arrived at Petro-Alexandrovsk, he intended to purchase fresh horses, their own now being thoroughly exhausted. The guide was quick to swallow the bait, swearing that far better horses could be obtained from a dealer known personally to him who lived on the way to Khiva. Knowing that the guide would receive a substantial cut from any purchases he made, Burnaby also indicated that he might require fresh camels for his onward journey. At first the man had insisted that the horses and camels be brought from the village for Burnaby's inspection, but finally, when the Englishman suggested that they press on to Petro-Alexandrovsk, he weakened. Eventually it was agreed that they would bypass the Russian garrison altogether and proceed direct to Khiva. There was one proviso, however. The guide insisted that Burnaby must first obtain the Khan's permission to enter the capital. The mullah of a nearby village helped to compose a suitable letter, which was sent off by messenger to the Khan. In it Burnaby explained that he was a British officer travelling in the region who wished to visit the renowned city and pay his respects to its celebrated ruler.

A day later, as Burnaby and his companions arrived on the far bank of the frozen Oxus, sixty miles from the capital, they were met by two Khivan nobles who had been sent by the Khan to welcome him. As they entered the city, Burnaby noticed the unmistakable silhouette of a gallows. On this, his companions informed him, convicted thieves were hanged. Murderers were executed by having their throats cut with a huge knife, like sheep. Of the Khan's executioner, whom the Governor of Kazala had warned might be on hand to prise out Burnaby's eyes, there was no sign. Any remaining fears the Englishman might have had were quickly dispelled when he found himself installed in the Khan's state guest-house, a building of great splendour, whose dazzling tiles and ornate style reminded him of the Arab architecture of Seville, and whose living-room was lavishly furnished with fine rugs. Despite it being mid-winter, melons, grapes and other lush fruits were brought to him on trays by servants, and he was told that the Khan had ordered that he was to be given anything that he chose to ask for.

The next morning Burnaby was informed that the Khan would receive him that afternoon, and at the appointed time his horse was brought so that he could ride to the palace. Guards armed with scimitars and wearing long, brightly coloured *khalats*, or silk coats, stood at its gates, while an excited crowd of Khivans lined the way to see the giant figure of the Englishman pass. For word had spread that he was an emissary from British India, tales of whose stupendous wealth had long ago reached the khanates of Central Asia. Burnaby had been careful to impress upon officials of the Khan that he did not come as a representative of his government or sovereign. They, in their turn, had expressed astonishment that he had managed to evade the Russians, one telling him: 'They do not much love you English people.'

The Khan, who was seated on a Persian rug, reclined against some cushions, warming his feet before a hearth filled with glowing charcoal. He looked about 28, and was powerfully built, with a coal-black beard and moustache surrounding an enormous mouth filled with irregular but white teeth. To Burnaby's relief he was smiling, with a distinct twinkle in his eye. 'I was greatly surprised,' Burnaby wrote later, 'after all that had been written in Russian newspapers about the cruelties and other iniquities perpetrated by this Khivan potentate, to find him such a cheery sort of fellow.' The Khan motioned to

Burnaby to be seated beside him, after which tea was brought. When the courtesies were over he began to question his visitor about the relationship between Britain and Russia, and how large and far apart their territories were.

With the Khan's permission, Burnaby produced a map and pointed out the respective positions of India, Russia and the British Isles. The Khan was greatly struck by the disparity in size between Britain and India, between conqueror and conquered, and also by how much larger the Tsar's domains were than the two of them put together. To demonstrate his point to Burnaby he showed how it took both his hands to cover up Russia on the map, and only one to cover India. To this Burnaby replied that the British Empire was so vast that the sun never set on it, and that only part of it could be included on his map. Furthermore, a nation's strength did not depend only on the size of its territories. India's population, for instance, was three times that of the whole of Russia. Moreover, for all its apparent size and might, Russia had been defeated by Britain in one war, and would assuredly be beaten in any subsequent ones. Nonetheless, despite Britain's great strength, she was a peaceable nation who preferred to be on cordial terms with her neighbours.

After remaining silent for a while, the Khan turned to the question of Russia's ambitions in Central Asia. 'We Mohammedans used to think that England was our friend because she helped the Sultan,' he told Burnaby, 'but you have let the Russians take Tashkent, conquer me, and make their way into Khokand.' Their next move, he forecast, would be to seize Kashgar, Merv and Herat. They had many soldiers, but little to pay them with. India, he understood, was very rich. 'You will have to fight some day, whether your government likes it or not.' He wanted to know whether the British would come to the assistance of Kashgar if the Russians attacked it. However, Burnaby explained that he was not privy to the secrets of his government on such matters, although he deeply regretted that the Russians had been allowed to seize the Khan's domains, since this could easily have been prevented.

Despite St Petersburg's protestations that it had withdrawn all its troops from Khiva, and restored power to the Khan, it was obvious to Burnaby that this was mere sham. The Khan was firmly under the Russian thumb. He was allowed no army of his own, and despite his request that their own troops be withdrawn, the Russians maintained a 4,000-strong garrison at Petro-Alexandrovsk, within easy striking distance of the capital, and commanded by one of their ablest frontier soldiers, Colonel Nikolai Ivanov. In addition, the Khivans had to pay a considerable annual tribute to the Tsar. This Burnaby had seen being counted out in silver coins and rouble notes by the Khan's treasurer as he passed through the palace on the way to his audience.

The Khan now gave a low bow, a signal that Burnaby's meeting with him was over. Thanking him for his gracious welcome, and for allowing him to visit Khiva, the Englishman withdrew and rode back to his quarters. By this time word had spread that he had been favourably received by the Khan, and those lining the streets and rooftops bowed respectfully as he and his official escort passed by. The Khan had ordered that Burnaby was to be shown anything in the capital that he wished to see, and the following morning he set out on a grand tour of inspection. Among many other things he was shown were the royal gardens where he saw apple, pear and cherry trees, melon beds and vines, and the summer palace, from where the Khan dispensed justice during June and July, Khiva's two hottest months. He next visited the prison. 'Here', he wrote, 'I found two prisoners, their feet fastened in wooden stocks, whilst heavy iron chains encircled their necks and bodies.' They were accused of assaulting a woman, but denied the charge. Burnaby enquired what happened when a man pleaded not guilty to a charge he was known to have committed. 'Why,' he was told, 'we beat him with rods, put salt in his mouth, and expose him to the burning rays of the sun, until at last he confesses.' This admission said little for St Petersburg's claims that it had freed its subject peoples from the barbaric practices of the past, its principal justification for their conquest.

The following morning, on returning from a visit to the camel market, Burnaby found two solemn-faced strangers waiting for him in his quarters. One of them handed him a letter which he said was from Colonel Ivanov at Petro-

Alexandrovsk. The Russians, it appeared, had discovered that the Englishman had given them the slip. The letter informed Burnaby that an urgent telegram awaited him at Petro-Alexandrovsk. But instead of giving it to the courier to deliver to him, the colonel instructed him to come to Petro-Alexandrovsk to collect it. Thus Burnaby had no way of ascertaining who the mysterious telegram was from, or how important it was. All he could discover was that it had been telegraphed as far as Tashkent, where the overland line to Central Asia at present ended, and then borne 900 miles across the steppe and desert by a succession of horsemen. Clearly the Russians judged its contents important. He could, of course, ignore it, and head quickly for Bokhara or Merv. However, he was informed that Colonel Ivanov had given strict orders to the Khan that if he had already left Khiva he was to be rounded up and brought straight to Petro-Alexandrovsk. Bitterly disappointed, Burnaby could see that he had no choice but to return with the two couriers, his prospects of reaching Bokhara and Merv at an end. For the Russians were unlikely to let him slip through their fingers so easily again.

Before Burnaby left Khiva, the Khan asked to see him once more. Expressing regret that his visit had been thus cut short, he assured Burnaby that he or any of his countrymen would always be welcome in his capital. 'He was very kind in his manner,' noted Burnaby, 'and shook hands warmly when I took my leave.' That night they halted at the home of a senior Khivan official who had been sent, in vain, to India to seek help from the British at the time of the Russian attack on Khiva. Despite the failure of his mission, he had been much impressed by what he saw, and by the way he had been received. He, like the Khan, warned Burnaby that India was the Tsar's ultimate objective. In his view British troops were far better than their Russian counterparts. However, the latter were numerically superior. Were they to invade India, he declared, the Russians could afford to lose as many men as the British had to defend it, 'and begin again with double the original force'. When Burnaby tried to suggest that the Russians bore the British no ill-will, the official asked him: 'If they like you so much, why do they prevent your goods coming here?' Indian teas, for example, were either totally banned, or bore such heavy duty that no one could possibly afford them.

Considering that he had obviously caused the Russian military authorities in Turkestan much inconvenience, not to say embarrassment, Burnaby's reception at Petro-Alexandrovsk was surprisingly cordial, perhaps because they knew what his telegram contained. Indeed, its contents must have shaken even the intrepid Burnaby. For it was from the Commander-in-Chief of the British Army, Field Marshal the Duke of Cambridge, ordering him to return immediately to European Russia. 'Too bad, letting you get so far, and not allowing you to carry out your undertaking,' observed Colonel Ivanov with ill-concealed satisfaction to his British guest. 'It is the fortune of war,' replied Burnaby. 'Anyway, I have seen Khiva.' The Russian was determined to belittle even that. 'Khiva, that is nothing,' he said. It was Burnaby's suspicion that St Petersburg, never dreaming that he would succeed in reaching Khiva in one of the worst winters on record, had leaned on the British Foreign Office to get him removed from Central Asia. This was strongly denied in the House of Commons, however, the government insisting that it was its own decision to order him out, lest the Russians be led to believe that he was there in an official capacity.

During his brief stay at Petro-Alexandrovsk, Burnaby found Ivanov and his fellow officers full of war-talk, and convinced that hostilities with Britain were inevitable. Merv, they told him, they could take any time they wanted, it only needing St Petersburg's go-ahead. The mood of these officers, Burnaby noted, was the same as all those he had spoken to in Central Asia. 'It is a great pity,' seemed to be the view, 'but our interests clash, and though capital friends as individuals, the question of who is to be master in the East must soon be decided by the sword.' It was while Burnaby was at Petro-Alexandrovsk that the Khan of Khiva's treasurer arrived with the money due to the Russians, and breakfasted with Ivanov, struggling gallantly with a knife and fork, and showing himself not at all averse to French champagne.

With any hope of further travels in Central Asia now dashed, Burnaby was anxious to get home as soon as possible to begin work on a book he was planning about his journey and his views on the Russian threat to India. Ivanov had received strict instructions from Kaufman that this troublesome British officer, who had already been allowed by St Petersburg to see far more than he should, must return by the way he had come. As it happened, two Russian officers and a party of Cossacks were about to leave Petro-Alexandrovsk for Kazala, and it was agreed that Burnaby would accompany them. This arrangement suited him well, for it gave him a unique opportunity to observe, at close quarters and under severe conditions, Cossack troops on the march, thus providing further material for his book. The going was extremely hard, with even the Cossacks complaining, its rigours made a little less unbearable by recourse to the four-gallon cask of vodka they carried. The discipline too was harsh, with punishments meted out for the slightest misdemeanour. One camel driver was flogged for being slow in saddling up, the captain snatching the whip from the Cossack administering it, declaring that it was not hard enough, and completing the task himself. Nonetheless Burnaby formed a high opinion of his companions during the nine days they spent together crossing the great snowy plain. 'The Cossacks were fine, well-built fellows, averaging about eleven stone in weight,' he wrote. In the saddle they carried a further seven stone or more, including twenty pounds of grain for their horses, and six pounds of biscuits for themselves, sufficient to feed them for four days. The horses too were impressively sturdy. His own stalwart mount had borne him the best part of 900 miles in appalling conditions, without once going lame or falling sick, despite the twenty stone it had carried all that way. And yet in England, Burnaby noted, due to its modest stature it would have been looked upon as a polo pony.

During Burnaby's brief halt in Kazala, he heard that 10,000 more Russian troops were being moved from Siberia to Tashkent in preparation, it was rumoured, for a campaign against Yakub Beg in Kashgaria. On his way northwards to Orenburg he encountered the commander of one of these units travelling in a large sleigh with his family many miles ahead of his troops. He also heard that there had been serious trouble recently in some of the Cossack regiments, and that a number of the ringleaders were to be shot. On reaching London at the end of March 1876, he immediately set about the task of writing his book. He also found himself lionised, for everyone, including Queen Victoria herself, wished to hear of his adventures and listen to his views on the Russian menace. He was received by the Commander-in Chief, the Duke of Cambridge, who had been leaned on by the Cabinet to order him out of Central Asia. Afterwards, writing to the secretary of state for war, the Duke declared: 'I saw Captain Burnaby yesterday, and a more interesting conversation I never remember holding with anybody. He is a remarkable fellow, singular-looking, but of great perseverance and determination. He has gone through a great deal, and the only surprise is how he got through it.' He strongly recommended that the secretary of state should listen to what Burnaby had to say, and that the Foreign Office and India Office should do likewise.

Burnaby's graphic, 487-page narrative of his adventures, which included lengthy appendices on Russian military capabilities and likely moves in Central Asia, appeared later that year under the title *A Ride to Khiva*. Its strongly anti-Russian flavour caught the mood of the moment, and it was to prove a bestseller, being reprinted eleven times in its first twelve months. While the Foreign Office deplored it, for it did little for Anglo-Russian relations, the hawks and the largely Russophobe press were delighted by its jingoistic tone. Flushed by the book's success, and by a £2,500 advance on his next, Burnaby set his sights on Eastern Turkey, a wild and mountainous region where Tsar and Sultan shared an uneasy frontier. His aim was to try to discover what the Russians were up to in this little-known corner of the Great Game battlefield, and how capable the Turks were of holding out against a Russian thrust towards Constantinople from their Caucasian stronghold. For relations between the two powers were deteriorating rapidly in the wake of a serious quarrel over Turkey's Balkan possessions. War appeared imminent, and likely to involve Britain.

The trouble began in the summer of 1875, with an uprising against Turkish rule in a remote village in Herzegovina, one of the Sultan's Balkan provinces. From there it quickly spread to Bosnia, Serbia, Montenegro, and Bulgaria. Whether it was a genuinely spontaneous movement, or the result of Russian intrigue, is uncertain. In May 1876 the crisis deepened when Turkish irregular troops, known as *bashi-bazouks*, put 12,000 Bulgarian Christians to the sword in a frenzy of blood-letting. This massacre was to result in almost universal condemnation of the Turks, and to bring the likelihood of war between the Tsar, who claimed to be the protector of all Christians living under Ottoman rule, and the Sultan even closer. In Britain the Russophobes, Turcophiles almost to a man, tried hard to pin the blame on the Tsar, whom they accused of fomenting the trouble in the first place. Disraeli, the Prime Minister, dismissed first reports of the Bulgarian massacres as 'coffee-house babble'. Gladstone, on the other hand, demanded that the Turks be cleared 'bag and baggage' out of the Balkans.

With the storm clouds gathering once more over the East, Burnaby set out from Constantinople in December 1876 to ride the length of Turkey. His arrival in the capital was not to go unnoticed by the astute Count Ignatiev, the Russian ambassador, and when he reached the important garrison town of Erzerum, in Eastern Turkey, a friendly official confided to him that the Russian consul there had received a telegram ordering him to keep a close watch on the British officer. 'Two months ago,' it declared, 'a certain Captain Burnaby left Constantinople with the object of travelling in Asia Minor. He is a desperate enemy of Russia. We have lost all traces of him since his departure from Stamboul. We believe that the real object of his journey is to cross the frontier into Russia.' The consul was ordered to discover the whereabouts of Burnaby, and at all costs prevent him from entering Russian territory. A portrait of Burnaby, he was also to discover, had been posted prominently at all Russian frontier posts. Having seen all he needed to of Turkey's ill-preparedness against a sudden attack, Burnaby cut short his 1,000-mile ride and caught a steamer back along the Black Sea coast to Constantinople, from where he returned hurriedly by train to London to start work on his book before events overtook it. Entitled *On Horseback Through Asia Minor*, it was even more anti-Russian than his previous book. In April 1877, while he was still writing it, news reached

London that the Russians had declared war on Turkey, and had begun their advance on Constantinople through the Balkans, while simultaneously marching into eastern Anatolia.

With the British bracing themselves once again for war over Constantinople, and anti-Russian feeling running at an all-time high, Burnaby's new book was assured an eager readership, being reprinted in all seven times. Its author now set off for the Balkan front where, although ostensibly a neutral observer, he managed to obtain unofficial command of a Turkish brigade fighting against those recent travelling companions of his, the Cossacks. At this point, however, having achieved his self-appointed task of drumming up public opinion at home against the Russians and in favour of the Turks, Burnaby makes his exit from this narrative.

*   *   *

'If the Russians reach Constantinople, the Queen would be so humiliated that she thinks she would abdicate at once.' So wrote Queen Victoria herself to Disraeli, urging him to 'be bold'. To the Prince of Wales she declared: 'I don't believe that without fighting ... those detestable Russians ... any arrangements will be lasting, or that we shall ever be friends! They will always hate us and we can never trust them.' Her sympathies were shared by the masses, even if few of them had a very clear idea of where either Bulgaria or Herzegovina were, let alone any grasp of the issues involved. But their mood was well summed up in the words of a jingoistic song which was then doing the rounds of the music halls. It went like this:

> 'We don't want to fight,
> But, by jingo, if we do,
> We've got the men, we've got the ships,
> We've got the money too.
> We've fought the Bear before,
> And while we're Britons true,
> The Russians shall not have Constantinople.'

Against all expectations, the Russian advance towards the Ottoman capital was slow. For five months it was held up by the gallant and resolute defence by the Turks of their stronghold at Plevna in Bulgaria, which cost the invaders 35,000 lives and the Romanians, who had been persuaded to join them, a further 5,000. In the east, too, despite initial successes, the Russian Caucasian forces found themselves facing tougher opposition than St Petersburg had anticipated, as well as nationalist uprisings among the Muslim tribes behind their own lines. Finally, however, Turkish resistance crumbled, and in February 1878 the Russian armies stood at the gates of Constantinople, their age-old dream seemingly about to be realised, only to find the British Mediterranean fleet anchored in the Dardanelles. It was a blunt warning to the Russians to proceed no further. War now seemed certain.

Meanwhile, having foreseen such a possibility, in Turkestan General Kaufman had been assembling a 30,000-strong force, the largest ever to be deployed in Central Asia. The moment war broke out it was his intention to strike against India through Afghanistan. At the same time he sent a powerful military mission, led by Major-General Nikolai Stolietov, to Kabul to try to obtain Afghan co-operation against the British. Ideally Kabul would be the springboard for the attack, with the Khyber Pass as the principal point of entry. Ahead of the invasion force, which it was hoped would consist of both Russian and Afghan troops, would go secret agents to prepare the way. They would be well supplied with gold and other inducements. For Kaufman was convinced that the Indian masses were ripe for revolt, and that once it was known that a large Russo-Afghan force was on its way to liberate them, the powder-keg would ignite. Although not yet aware of what Kaufman was planning, to the British a joint Russian-Afghan thrust at India represented the ultimate nightmare.

In the event, confronted by the prospect of another war with Britain, and to the immense disappointment of the hawks on either side, Tsar Alexander backed down. With the Russian armies only two days' march from Constantinople, a hasty truce was agreed between the Russians and the Turks. This gave Bulgaria independence from Ottoman rule and the Russians large tracts of eastern Anatolia. Immediately the British objected. They feared Bulgaria would merely become a satellite state of St Petersburg, giving the Russians a direct overland route to the Mediterranean. This, like their threatened occupation of Constantinople, would enable them to menace India's lines of communication at will in time of war. Thus, despite the ending of hostilities between Russia and Turkey, the threat of war between Russia and Britain had not lessened. Not only had Austria-Hungary now allied itself with Britain over the issue of Bulgaria, but 7,000 British troops had been moved to Malta from India in an effort to induce the Tsar to withdraw his own forces from before Constantinople. In the end, however, the crisis was settled without recourse to war. In July 1878, at the Congress of Berlin, the contentious treaty was revised to the satisfaction of all the major powers except for Russia. The Tsar, under strong pressure, agreed to withdraw his troops in exchange for some limited gains from the Turks. The Sultan, on the other hand, had two-thirds of the lands he had lost in the war restored to him. For their parts, the British occupied Cyprus while the Austrians acquired Bosnia and Herzegovina. So it was that St Petersburg saw its costly victory wrenched from its grasp by the other major European powers, with the British playing a key role.

This setback was not to go wholly unavenged, however. Although Kaufman's planned invasion of India was called off when the risk of war with Britain receded, he nonetheless allowed the mission to Kabul to proceed. This was partly due to pique, for Kaufman was aware of the anguish it would cause the British, and partly to explore the possibilities of a joint invasion in case it ever became necessary to revive the plan. Intelligence that the Russian mission was on its way to the Afghan capital reached India through native spies while the Congress of Berlin was still deliberating. The Emir, Sher Ali, was said to have tried to persuade the Russians to turn back, only to be told by Kaufman that it was too late to recall his men, and that he would be held personally responsible for their safety and for ensuring them a cordial reception. When challenged about the mission by the British, the Russian Foreign Ministry denied all knowledge of it, insisting that no such visit was being contemplated. Once again St Petersburg was vowing one thing while Tashkent was doing precisely the reverse.

Lord Lytton, the Viceroy, was by now well aware of the truth, and was incensed by Sher Ali's apparent duplicity. Having repeatedly refused to receive a British mission to discuss relations between the two countries, the Emir was now secretly welcoming a Russian one. What the Viceroy did not fully appreciate was the degree of pressure being applied by the Russians on the Afghan ruler, who was already in a state of profound distress over the death of his favourite son. Kaufman had warned him that unless he agreed to a treaty of friendship with the Russians, they would actively support his nephew and rival for the throne, Abdur Rahman, then living under their protection in Samarkand. Fearing the might of Russia more than that of Britain, Sher Ali reluctantly yielded. Having accomplished his task, and leaving some of his subordinates to work out the details, General Stolietov left Kabul for Tashkent on August 24. Before departing he cautioned the Emir against receiving any British missions, at the same time promising him the support of 30,000 Russian troops if the need arose.

By now Lord Lytton, with London's telegraphed approval, had decided to dispatch a mission to Kabul, using force if necessary. The officer chosen to lead it was General Sir Neville Chamberlain, an old frontier hand who was known to be on excellent personal terms with the Emir. He was to be accompanied by a senior political officer, Major Louis Cavagnari, and an escort of 250 troopers of the Corps of Guides – precisely the same number of men as had gone with General Stolietov. On August 14, the Viceroy wrote to the Emir announcing his intention of sending a mission to Kabul and asking for a safe conduct for it from the frontier. The letter remained unanswered. Chamberlain was now ordered to proceed to the entrance to the Khyber Pass. From there Major Cavagnari rode forward with a small escort to the nearest Afghan post and demanded leave to enter the country. However, he was informed by the officer commanding it that he had received orders to oppose the mission's advance, by force of arms if necessary, and were Cavagnari not an old friend he would already have opened fire on him and his party for illegally crossing the frontier.

Angered by the Emir's rebuff, Lord Lytton now urged the Cabinet to waste no further time and to authorise an immediate declaration of war. But London decided that a final ultimatum should first be presented to the Emir. This warned him that unless, by sundown on November 20, he had apologised in full for his discourtesy in refusing a British mission while welcoming a Russian one, military operations would begin against him forthwith. In the meantime, to exacerbate matters, the Russian Foreign Ministry, which had earlier denied all knowledge of Stolietov's mission, had come up with a highly unsatisfactory explanation, insisting that it was purely a matter of courtesy and in no way conflicted with their former assurances that Afghanistan lay outside their sphere of influence. It did little to subdue Lytton's fear of what they were really up to in Afghanistan, or his suspicion that Britain was being made a fool of.

By the time the ultimatum to Sher Ali expired on November 20, no answer had been received from him. The following day three columns of British troops began their advance on Kabul. Ten days later a letter arrived from the Emir agreeing to the dispatch of a British mission. But it failed to offer the apology also demanded by the Viceroy. Anyway it was far too late now, for the Second Afghan War had already begun. Lytton was determined to teach the Emir a lesson he would not easily forget, and at the same time make it perfectly clear to St Petersburg that Britain would tolerate no rivals in Afghanistan.

· 29 ·

Bloodbath at the Bala Hissar

Events now moved swiftly, as the hastily assembled, 35,000-strong British force crossed the frontier into Afghanistan at three points. Its first objectives were to seize the Khyber Pass, Jalalabad and Kandahar, and after some brief but fierce engagements these were achieved. On learning of the British incursion, the Emir had hastily turned to General Kaufman, asking for the urgent dispatch of the 30,000 troops he believed he had been promised. But to his dismay he was told that this was out of the question in mid-winter, and was advised instead to make his peace with the invaders. As the British consolidated their positions, while awaiting further orders from Calcutta, the desperate Emir decided to go in person to St Petersburg to plead with the Tsar for help, as well as to the other European powers. But first he released his eldest son, Yakub Khan, whom he had been holding under house-arrest, and appointed him Regent, leaving him to contend with the British. He then set off northwards, accompanied by the last of the Russian officers from General Stolietov's mission.

On reaching the Russian frontier, however, he was refused entry on Kaufman's orders. So much for the treaty of friend-ship which the latter had persuaded him to sign. Abandoned by the Russians, at war with the British, the unfortunate Sher Ali had no one left to turn to. His spirit and health broken, and refusing all food and medicine, he died at Balkh in February 1879. A few days later the British received word from Yakub Khan that his father had 'cast off the raiment of existence, obeyed the voice of the Great Summoner, and hastened to the land of Divine Mercy'. The accession of Yakub Khan, who had long opposed his father, to the throne offered both sides the chance to reconsider the situation. It soon became apparent to the British that the new Emir lacked the whole-hearted support of many of the chiefs and therefore was anxious to hold the discussions which his father had so adamantly refused.

Having written to Yakub Khan to express the condolences of the British government over the death of his father, Cavagnari followed this with a letter proposing terms for ending the war and for the withdrawal of British troops from his kingdom. The terms were fairly harsh, and included the Emir surrendering control of Afghanistan's foreign policy to London, his agreeing to the stationing of British missions at Kabul and elsewhere, and the ceding to Britain of certain territories lying close to the Indian frontier, including the Khyber Pass. In fact, the invasion had more or less come to a halt, for the British com-manders were finding the going difficult, what with fierce resistance from the local tribes, the harsh winter, widespread sickness, and inadequate transport. But the Emir was aware that with the arrival of spring it would be merely a question of time before the invaders, reinforced from India, reached Kabul. After much hard bargaining, therefore, he agreed to most of the British demands. In return he received a guarantee of protection against the Russians, or for that matter his covetous neighbours the Persians, and an annual subsidy of £60,000.

The treaty was signed by the Emir in person at the village of Gandamak, where forty years earlier the remnants of the ill-fated Kabul garrison had made a gallant last stand against the Afghans. Somewhat tactlessly, Yakub Khan and his com-mander-in-chief arrived dressed in Russian uniforms. On May 26, to the anger of the majority of Afghans, the agreement was signed. Under the Treaty of Gandamak, as it is known, Cavagnari was to proceed to Kabul as the first British Resident there since the murders of Sir Alexander Burnes and Sir William Macnaghten in the disastrous winter of 1841. Lord Lytton was delighted with the outcome. Firm action had produced the intended results, including the departure of the last of the Russians from Kabul, and a demonstration to the Afghans of just how much Kaufman's promises were worth. There was much self-congratulation in London and Calcutta. Queen Victoria, who followed Central Asian and Indian affairs very closely, was especially pleased at seeing Tsar Alexander outmanoeuvred thus. Cavagnari, whose father had been one of Napoleon's generals and who himself was perhaps the outstanding frontier officer of the day, was given a knighthood as a reward for his highly successful handling of the negotiations, and to give him the necessary status for his new and delicate role at Yakub Khan's court. But not everyone was so sanguine about the deal he had struck with the notoriously slippery Afghans. Some felt that the Emir had given in to British demands rather too easily. They remembered the treachery, not to mention the consequent disaster, which had followed India's last interference in Afghanistan's affairs after similar Russian intrigues at Kabul. 'They will all be killed,' Sir John Lawrence, the former Viceroy, declared on hearing of Cavagnari's appointment. However, in the general euphoria, such warnings went unheeded.

The night before Sir Louis Cavagnari's departure for Kabul he was entertained to dinner by General Sir Frederick Roberts, VC, who had also been knighted for his part in the successful campaign, but who harboured grave doubts about the mission's dispatch. Roberts had intended to propose a toast to Cavagnari and his small party, but had found himself utterly unable to do so because of his fears for their safety. The following day he saw them depart. 'My heart sank', he wrote afterwards, 'as I wished Cavagnari goodbye. When we had proceeded a few yards in our different directions we both turned back, retraced our steps, shook hands once more, and parted for ever.' Despite the anxieties of his friends and colleagues, Cavagnari was confident that he could handle any difficulties that might arise. Indeed, at his own suggestion, he took only a modest escort with him, fifty infantrymen and twenty-five cavalrymen, all from the Corps of Guides. Commanding them was Lieutenant Walter Hamilton, who had won a Victoria Cross during the recent battle for the Khyber Pass, while Cavagnari's own staff consisted of two other Europeans, a secretary and an Indian Army medical officer.

After an uneventful journey the mission reached the Afghan capital on July 24, 1879. Although there was an uneasy atmosphere, they were well received. There were artillery salutes and an attempted rendering by an Afghan military band of 'God Save the Queen', while Cavagnari himself was borne into the capital on the back of an elephant. He and his party were then conducted to the Residency which had been prepared for them inside the walls of the Bala Hissar and not far from the Emir's own palace. For a few weeks all went well, but then Cavagnari reported that a large body of Afghan troops had arrived in Kabul at the end of a tour of duty at Herat. They were said to be extremely disgruntled because they were owed three months' pay, and also angry at discovering the British mission's presence in the capital. Cavagnari and his companions were strongly advised by Afghan officials not to venture outside the Bala Hissar as trouble was expected. Nonetheless, on September 2, he sent a message which concluded with the words 'All well'. They were the last that were ever to be heard from the mission.

*　　*　　*

As Calcutta anxiously awaited further news from Kabul, St Petersburg was endeavouring to restore its *amour propre* in Central Asia following the hurried departure of its mission from Afghanistan and the disappointing outcome of its recent war with Turkey. Nor had these been its only disappointments. Kashgar, on which it had long had its eye, had suddenly reverted to Chinese rule, together with the rest of Sinkiang. After years of procrastination, the Emperor had finally moved against Yakub Beg, dispatching a large army westwards with orders to recover the lost territories. The force, whose leisurely progress included the planting and harvesting of its own crops, took three years to reach its destination. On hearing of its approach, Yakub Beg hastily assembled a 17,000-strong army and set out eastwards to meet the Chinese. But this time they were more than a match for him. Following the rout of his army, he was forced to flee to Kashgar. There, in May 1877, to the relief of his subjects, he died. Some said it was from a stroke, others from poison. Whatever the truth, by December of that year Kashgar was safely back in the Emperor's hands, and three powerful empires – those of Britain, Russia and China – now faced one another across the Pamirs. Only Ili and its principal town Kuldja remained in Russian hands.

This snatching of Kashgar from their grasp must have been a blow to the Russians, and particularly to Kaufman, the architect of the Tsar's Central Asian empire. However, worse was to follow. During the recent war with Turkey, Kaufman's plans for further expansion had been momentarily checked while his energies were directed towards getting ready the invasion force for its march on India. And yet it was quite evident, at least to the hawks in London and Calcutta, that Russian ambitions in Central Asia were still far from satisfied. Significantly, as Burnaby had noticed, their latest staff maps showed no southern frontier to the Tsar's territories there. Sure enough, when the immediate threat of war with Britain faded, it became apparent that fresh moves were being planned. In the autumn of 1878, a Russian staff officer, Colonel N. L. Grodekov, rode from Tashkent via Samarkand and northern Afghanistan to Herat, carefully surveying the route. In Herat he carried out a thorough examination of the city's defences, and claimed on his return that its inhabitants were eager for Russian rule. At the same time other Russian military explorers were busy surveying the Karakum desert and the Pamirs, while further east Colonel Nikolai Prejevalsky, accompanied by a Cossack escort, was endeavouring to reach Lhasa, the Tibetan capital, from the north.

These renewed Russian activities were hardly calculated to add to the peace of mind of those responsible for the defence of India. Then, on September 9, 1879, St Petersburg made its first forward move in Central Asia since the annexation of Khokand four years earlier. This time the Russians struck against the great Turcoman stronghold of Geok-Tepe, on the southern edge of the Karakum desert, roughly half-way between the Caspian Sea and Merv. Their aim was to conquer this wild and lawless region, thereby stabilising their southern flank from Krasnovodsk to Merv, and eventually to construct a railway through it linking up with Bokhara, Samarkand and Tashkent. Used to fighting rabble armies of ill-led and untrained tribesmen, the Russians had not reckoned on the warlike qualities of the Turcomans. At first the Russians looked set to bombard the huge, mud-built fortress into submission with their artillery. But then, impatient for victory, they called off the guns and attempted to storm it with their infantry. The Turcomans, fighting for their lives, flung themselves on the Russians, whom they greatly outnumbered, forcing them to flee. Only with difficulty were the pursuing Turcomans beaten off, and the Russians able to retreat back across the desert towards Krasnovodsk. It was the worst defeat they had suffered in Central Asia since the ill-fated Khivan expedition of 1717. It also represented a shattering blow to Russian military prestige, and the general who had commanded the force was brought back to St Petersburg in disgrace. However, the bad news that month was not confined to the Russians, for four days earlier the British had received tidings every bit as alarming.

*　　*　　*

The first to learn of them was General Sir Frederick Roberts at Simla. He was awoken in the early hours of September 5 by his wife who told him that a man bearing an urgent telegram was wandering around the house looking for someone to sign for it. Roberts tore open the envelope. The news it contained was horrifying. A native agent sent by Cavagnari at Kabul had arrived exhausted at the frontier to say that the Residency was being attacked by three regiments of mutinous Afghans. The British were still holding out when the runner left Kabul. Nothing further was known. It was just as Roberts had feared, and Lawrence had warned. After informing the badly shaken Viceroy, who had so keenly backed the dispatch of Cavagnari, Roberts telegraphed the frontier posts nearest to Kabul ordering them to spare no efforts or money to discover what was happening in the Afghan capital. He did not have to wait long. That same evening it was learned that the Residency had been stormed by the mutineers and that all those inside had been killed after a desperate but hopeless resistance.

In fact, several members of the escort survived, being else-where in the city at the time of the attack, and from them and from others a detailed account of the mission's last hours was later pieced together. Spurred on by their mullahs, the disaffected troops had marched on the Bala Hissar to demand their pay from the Emir. There they had jeered at their com-rades of the Kabul garrison for their defeat by the infidel British during the recent campaign. In an attempt to appease them, the Emir ordered them to be given one month's back pay, but this was not enough to satisfy them. Someone then suggested that they should obtain the rest from Cavagnari, who was known to have money at the Residency, which was only 250 yards away. When he refused to give them anything, they began stoning the building. Others attempted to force their way in, and shots were fired at them by the escort. Swearing vengeance, the angry Afghans ran back to their bar-racks to collect their rifles, before returning in force to the Residency. An all-out attack was now launched on the building, which was neither chosen nor designed to resist a siege. Little had been learned, it appears, from the massacre, in almost identical circumstances, of Sir Alexander Burnes, some forty years earlier. Surrounded by other buildings from which fire could be directed from close range against the defenders, the Residency consisted merely of a cluster of bungalows inside a compound.

Directed by Lieutenant Hamilton, the escort managed to hold off the attackers for most of the day. Considering that the Emir's palace was so close, he could hardly have failed to hear the shooting or the uproar. In addition, three messengers were sent to him asking for immediate assistance. The first two were killed, but the third got through. Yet Yakub Khan made no attempt to interfere, or to pay off the troops. To this day his role in the affair remains uncertain, though there is no real evidence to suggest that he was anything other than powerless to control his rampaging troops, and feared that if he tried to they might turn their fury against him too. Meanwhile, the fighting around the Residency had been getting fiercer. Already Sir Louis Cavagnari had been killed, gallantly leading a sortie aimed at driving the attackers back and clearing a space around the main building. The Afghans next brought up two small field guns and opened up with these at point-blank range. Immediately Hamilton led a charge against them, seizing both guns before they could do further damage. The mission surgeon was mortally wounded while taking part in this sortie. Despite several attempts, under heavy fire, the defenders were unable to drag the guns into a position from where they could be turned against the attackers.

For several hours Lieutenant Hamilton and those of the seventy-strong escort who remained alive continued to defy the Afghans, although by now several of the outbuildings were ablaze. But finally, using ladders, some of the attackers managed to clamber on to the roof of the main Residency building, in which the defenders were preparing to make their last stand. Savage hand-to-hand fighting followed, and soon Hamilton and his surviving European companion, the mission secretary, were both dead, leaving only a dozen Guides still fighting. The Afghans called on the Indians to drop their rifles and surrender, declaring that they intended them no harm, all their hostility being directed against the British. Ignoring this, and led by one of their officers, the Guides made one last desperate charge, dying to a man. No fewer than 600 of the attackers, it was later ascertained, had perished during the twelve-hour battle. 'The annals of no army and no regiment can show a brighter record of bravery than this small band of Guides,' declared the official report of the enquiry. 'By their deeds they have conferred undying honour, not only on the regiment, but on the whole British Army.' Had Indian troops then been eligible for the Victoria Cross, almost certainly at least one would have been awarded. As it was, the two words 'Residency, Kabul' were added to the long list of battle-honours on the Guides' regimental colours.

Within hours of news of the massacre being confirmed, General Roberts was on his way up to the frontier to take command of a hurriedly assembled punitive force, with orders to march as soon as possible on the Afghan capital. At the same time other units were ordered to reoccupy Jalalabad and Kandahar, which had only just been returned to the Afghans under the Treaty of Gandamak. The Emir, meanwhile, had hastily sent a message to the Viceroy expressing his deepest regrets for what had happened. Having learned of the British advance towards his capital, however, he dispatched his chief minister to intercept Roberts and beg him to advance no further, declaring that he personally would punish those responsible for the attack on the mission and the deaths of Cavagnari and the others. But Roberts was convinced that he was merely trying to delay the advance until the onset of winter, and to give his subjects time to organise resistance. Thanking the Emir for his offer, he replied: 'After what has recently occurred, I feel that the great British nation would not rest satisfied unless a British army marched to Kabul and there assisted Your Highness to inflict such punishments as so terrible and dastardly an act deserves.' The advance would therefore proceed, as ordered by the Viceroy, 'to ensure Your Highness's personal safety and aid Your Highness in restoring peace and order at your capital.'

Early in October, having encountered little opposition, Roberts reached Kabul. Almost the first thing he did was to visit the spot where Cavagnari and his men had died. 'The walls of the Residency, closely pitted with bullet holes, gave proof of the determined nature of the attack and the length of the resistance,' he wrote. 'The floors were covered with bloodstains, and amidst the embers of a fire we found a heap of human bones.' He ordered an immediate search to be made for any other remains of the victims, but no further traces were found. His next move was to set up two commissions of enquiry. One was to determine whether the Emir had, in fact, played any part in the massacre, while the other was to establish who the ringleaders and principal participants were. The enquiry into Yakub Khan's role was to prove inconclusive, although he was indicted of having been 'culpably indifferent' to the mission's fate. In the meantime, however, he had announced his abdication as Emir, declaring that he would rather be a humble grass-cutter in the British camp than try to rule Afghanistan. In the end he was given the benefit of the doubt, and sent into exile in India with his family.

In his efforts to bring the murderers to justice, Roberts

offered rewards for information leading to convictions. This inevitably served as an invitation to some to settle old scores. As a result, a number of those accused were convicted on very dubious evidence. Others, however, were undoubtedly guilty, like the Mayor of Kabul, who had carried Cavagnari's head in triumph through the city. In all, nearly a hundred Afghans were hanged on gallows erected by Roberts's engineers inside the Bala Hissar, overlooking the spot where Cavagnari and his companions had fought vainly for their lives. On the morning of their execution, a large crowd looked down in angry silence from the surrounding walls and rooftops, while British troops with fixed bayonets stood guard over the condemned men. 'Facing the ruined Residency', wrote an officer of the Guides, 'is a long grim row of gallows. Below these, bound hand and foot and closely guarded, is a line of prisoners. A signal is given, and from every gibbet swings what was lately a man. These are the ringleaders . . . who hang facing the scene of their infamy.'

At home a fierce controversy broke out over the harshness of Roberts's methods, and he himself was widely criticised. In fact, he had been told to act mercilessly by Lord Lytton, who had advised him before his departure: 'There are some things which a Viceroy can approve and defend when they have been done, but which a Governor-General in Council cannot order to be done.' Lytton had even considered burning Kabul to the ground, though he had later abandoned the idea. Among the first to criticise Roberts was *The Times of India*, which declared: 'It is to be regretted that a good many innocent persons should have been hanged while he was making up his mind as to their degree of guilt.' Four days later, the equally respected *Friend of India* observed: 'We fear that General Roberts has done us a serious national injury by lowering our reputation for justice in the eyes of Europe.' Other newspapers warned that Roberts was – in the words of one – 'sowing a harvest of hate'. Certainly trouble was not slow in coming. What followed that Christmas not only gravely threatened the British garrison in Kabul, but was also ominously reminiscent of what had followed Sir Alexander Burnes's murder in 1841.

Inflamed by their hatred of the British, and possibly encouraged by rumours that a 20,000-strong Russian force was on its way to support them, a number of tribes had begun to advance towards Kabul from the north, south and west. They were led by a 90-year-old Muslim divine who called for a holy war against the infidel invaders. Learning of this threat, Roberts decided to forestall the Afghans by dispersing them before they could join forces for a combined attack on Kabul. For unlike the ageing General Elphinstone, whose professional incompetence and procrastination had led to the 1842 disaster, Roberts was a fighting soldier of outstanding ability (some said the best since Wellington), who had won a Victoria Cross in the Indian Mutiny. Nevertheless, he at first gravely underestimated the numerical strength of the advancing enemy, and as a result failed to defeat or disperse them. By this time, following a series of unexplained explosions in the Bala Hissar which had partially demolished it, the 6,500-strong British garrison was quartered in cantonments which Sher Ali had built for his own troops just outside the capital. Here, in December 1879, the British braced themselves for an onslaught by the combined Afghan force, which was said to number anything up to 100,000 armed tribesmen.

But this time, despite the Afghans' overwhelming superiority in sheer numbers, Roberts held most of the trump cards. Not only were his troops highly trained and experienced, but they were also equipped with the latest breech-loading rifles and two Gatling machine-guns, enabling them to direct a murderous fire against anyone approaching the British position. In addition he had a dozen 9-pounder field guns and eight 7-pounder mountain guns, whereas the Afghans had no artillery. Furthermore, he had enough ammunition to last for four months, and had gathered enough food and fuel to see them through the long Afghan winter. To deprive the enemy of any advantage they might gain at night, he had star shells which could light up the entire countryside. Finally, thanks to one of his spies, he knew precisely when and how the Afghans intended to attack. So it was that in the early hours of December 23 the entire British garrison was standing to, fingers on triggers, peering into the darkness of the surrounding plain.

Then suddenly, an hour before first light, wave after wave

of screaming tribesmen, led by suicide-bent Muslim fanatics known as *ghazis*, began to hurl themselves against the British positions. In all, Roberts estimated, they numbered some 60,000. Star shells from his artillery now lit up the battlefield, bewildering the Afghans and making their white-robed and turbaned figures easy targets for the British infantry and gunners. At one time, through sheer weight of numbers, the charging Afghans managed to get perilously close to the perimeter wall, but they were driven back before they could swarm across it. After four hours of fierce and bitter fighting, as the Afghan dead piled up around the British positions, the attack began to lose its momentum. Realising that all hopes of victory were now lost, some of the tribesmen started to slip away. Finally, hotly pursued by Roberts's cavalry, the rest turned and fled towards the hills. By noon the battle was over. The Afghans had lost at least 3,000 men, the British only 5.

However, although the struggle for the capital had been decisively won, the war was still far from over. So long as the British remained in Afghanistan, and the country was without a ruler, any hopes of peace being restored were remote. Equally remote were the prospects of Britain being able to look to Afghanistan as a bastion against a Russian invasion of India. All that Lytton had succeeded in doing was to turn the hand of every Afghan against the British. It was at this moment, when the Viceroy was despairing of what to do next, that a possible solution arose, albeit from an entirely unexpected quarter.

*   *   *

For twelve years, Abdur Rahman, grandson of the great Dost Mohammed, and nephew of the late Sher Ali, had been living in exile in Samarkand under the protection of General Kaufman and in receipt of a pension from the Tsar. He had been forced to leave Afghanistan after losing the throne, to which he was the legitimate heir, to Sher Ali following his grandfather's death. Confident that he more or less had Sher Ali in his pocket (and papers found by Roberts in Kabul showed this to be so), Kaufman had been perfectly content to let things remain as they were. But Sher Ali's death, and Britain's aggressive new policy towards Afghanistan, had changed all that. With the clear intention of putting his own candidate on the vacant throne before the British installed theirs, Kaufman now urged Abdur Rahman to return home at once and claim his birthright. Accordingly, in February 1880, accompanied by a small force of supporters armed with the latest Russian rifles (not to mention promises of further assistance if required), Abdur Rahman crossed the Oxus into northern Afghanistan.

News of his advance soon reached Roberts in Kabul, to be followed by reports that the tribes of the north were rapidly flocking to his banner as he rode southwards. The sudden appearance on the scene of this contender for the throne was to lead to some rapid thinking in London and Calcutta. For there, at that very moment, British plans for the future of Afghanistan were under urgent discussion. All question of a permanent occupation, with its enormous cost in lives and money, had been ruled out. The consensus was that the country should be broken up, thereby making it more difficult for the Russians, or any other potential enemy, to gain control of it. But, more immediately, it had to be decided who was to rule in Kabul when the British garrison there was withdrawn. Until this was settled, General Roberts and his troops would obviously have to remain, with the former to all intents and purposes occupying the throne. Obviously Kaufman was gambling on Abdur Rahman, whom he knew to be extremely able and to enjoy considerable popularity, eventually gaining sufficient support to drive the British out. This would effectively turn Afghanistan, or a large part of it anyway, into a Russian dependency. Or so Kaufman must have reasoned.

For once, however, the British displayed a rare stroke of imagination towards Afghanistan. On the face of it, Abdur Rahman was a protégé of Russia's, whose claim to the throne represented a serious threat to India's security. But more likely, it was reasoned, at heart he was neither pro-Russian nor anti-British, but pro-Afghan. In which case it might be better if, instead of opposing his claim to the Emirship, the British welcomed it, thereby pre-empting Kaufman. From everything that was known about Abdur Rahman, moreover, it appeared that he was the only Afghan leader with the necessary qualities of character and personality to rule and unite this turbulent people. Moreover, having seen his predecessors let down by the Russians on more than one occasion, despite extravagant promises, he might even prefer to look to the British in future for protection or other assistance. It was therefore decided to offer Abdur Rahman the throne. Talks followed, and an agreement was reached. Under the terms of this, the British would withdraw from Kabul, leaving a Muslim agent as their sole representative. In return Abdur Rahman agreed to have no relations with any foreign power other than Britain, which for its part undertook not to interfere in any territories ruled by him. On July 22, 1880, at a special durbar to the north of Kabul, the 40-year-old Abdur Rahman was publicly proclaimed Emir, making a ceremonial entry into his capital a little later. He was to prove a tough and capable ruler, and a reliable neighbour to the British, though certainly no lackey.

His own position, however, was still far from secure. He only controlled the Kabul region and parts of the north. Much of the rest of Afghanistan was still in turmoil, for his accession to the throne had not gone unchallenged. Moreover, he dared not show himself to be friendly with the British, who had put him on the throne, lest, like Shah Shujah, he be accused of being their puppet and of being kept in power by the force of their bayonets. 'I was unable to show my friendship publicly,' he wrote years later, 'because my people were ignorant and fanatical. If I showed any inclination towards the English, my people would call me an infidel for joining hands with infidels.' His trump card, however, was the fact that the British were going, and he did not hesitate to make it appear to his people as though this was all his doing. In fact, it was with considerable relief that the British handed over control of Kabul to Abdur Rahman. For two things had happened which precipitated the need for a speedy departure.

One was a change of government at home. The Tories had been heavily defeated, largely because of their handling of the Afghan crisis, and Gladstone's Liberals were once again in power after six years in opposition. Lord Lytton, who had been appointed Viceroy by Disraeli, had gone, following vicious criticism by Gladstone, and been replaced by Lord Ripon, a former Lord President of the India Council. Even before the defeat of the Tory administration, it had been decided to evacuate Kabul, but the Liberals now pledged themselves to abandon totally Disraeli's forward policies. Gladstone believed the Russian threat to India to be greatly exaggerated, despite the seemingly incriminating evidence of Kaufman's machinations which Roberts had uncovered in Kabul. Forward policies, Gladstone was convinced, merely provoked or panicked the Russians into acting similarly. He likewise refused to publish details of Kaufman's secret correspondence with Sher Ali, or of the treaty they had signed, lest this rock the boat needlessly at a time when Anglo-Russian relations were momentarily tranquil. By the time these were finally published, in the Tory newspaper *The Standard* a year later, they had lost most of their impact.

The other, far more pressing reason for the departure of Roberts and his troops from Kabul was a dreadful piece of news which reached them from Kandahar just six days after Abdur Rahman had been proclaimed Emir. The trouble had originated in Herat, then ruled by Ayub Khan, Abdur Rahman's cousin, and a rival for his throne. It was Ayub Khan's declared aim to drive the infidel British from Afghanistan and then wrest the throne from his cousin. Towards the end of June 1880, accompanied by an 8,000-strong force of infantry and artillery, and gathering support as he advanced, Ayub Khan set out for Kandahar, then occupied by a small British garrison. When word of his unexpected advance reached Kandahar, 2,500 British and Indian troops were hastily dispatched westwards to intercept him. However, intelligence was scanty, and it was not realised quite how formidable Ayub Khan's force was, nor that he possessed modern artillery. Worse, local Afghan troops, supposedly loyal to Abdur Rahman, who had been sent to reinforce the British units, began to desert to the advancing enemy, whose ranks had by now swelled to at least 20,000.

The engagement took place at the tiny mud village of Maiwand, on the open plain forty miles west of Kandahar.

The officer commanding the British force, Brigadier-General George Burrows, had orders to do battle with Ayub Khan's troops only 'if you consider yourself strong enough to do so'. But not realising the strength of the enemy, and anyway confident that British troops could always defeat a far larger Afghan army by means of superior tactics and weapons, he decided to attack. By the time he realised his error it was too late. The result was one of the worst defeats ever suffered by the British in Asia. Ayub Khan was an able commander, well versed in modern warfare. Unlike Burrows he was a veteran of numerous engagements, and he used this experience to advantage by quickly seizing what high ground there was before hostilities began. So well trained were his artillerymen, moreover, that the British afterwards insisted that there were Russians among them.

Outnumbered, outmanoeuvred and outgunned, and tormented by heat and thirst, the British and Indian troops nonetheless fought magnificently. Much of the fighting was hand-to-hand. Afghans were pulled on to British bayonets by their beards, while other attacks were beaten off with rocks as ammunition ran low. Finally the order was given for a fighting withdrawal to Kandahar under cover of darkness. By the time the shattered remnants of the force reached Kandahar to break the appalling news to the garrison there, Burrows had lost nearly a thousand of his men, even if they had left nearly five times that number of the enemy dead or dying on the plain around Maiwand. Having buried his own dead (leaving the British corpses to the vultures), Ayub Khan now turned his attention to the capture of Kandahar. Immediately, the garrison prepared to face a siege. For a start, because of the risk of treachery from within, it was decided to take the drastic step of expelling from the city all male Afghans of fighting age. More than 12,000 were ordered out, many at gunpoint, by the 3,000 defenders.

The first that anyone in India knew of the disaster was when the telegraph operator at Simla received an urgent, clear-the-line signal. Moments later came the grim tidings from Kandahar. 'Total defeat and dispersion of General Burrows's force. Heavy loss in both officers and men.' The final death toll was not yet known, the message added, as small groups of survivors were still coming in. The troops of the garrison had been moved into the citadel and were preparing to face a siege by a victorious and vastly superior enemy. When word of the calamity reached Kabul, the first British troops had already begun to leave for India. Immediately, the evacuation was halted. The garrison had been considerably reinforced since General Roberts's victory there, and it was decided to dispatch him at once at the head of a 10,000-strong force to destroy Ayub Khan's army and relieve Kandahar. The 300-mile forced march was expected to take him a month, for all supplies had to be carried, and the route lay across harsh and hostile territory. In fact, it was one of the most rapid marches in military history. The entire force, including infantry, cavalry, light artillery, field hospitals, ammunition and even mutton on the hoof, reached the beleaguered city in twenty days.

On hearing that the greatly feared Roberts was on his way to avenge the British defeat, Ayub Khan took fright and withdrew from his positions around Kandahar. He even sent a message to Roberts insisting that the British had forced him to do battle with them at Maiwand, and asking the general how matters could best be resolved between himself and the British, with whom he insisted he wished to be friends. But Roberts was in no mood for such dalliance. Within hours of reaching Kandahar he had reconnoitred the new Afghan positions in the hills to the west of the city. The following morning he struck. This time, numerically speaking, the two sides were evenly matched, although the Afghans enjoyed considerable superiority in artillery. At first Ayub Khan's troops resisted ferociously, pouring down a heavy fire on the advancing British. Soon, however, the bayonets of the 72nd Highlanders and the *kukris* of the 2nd Gurkhas began to tell. By lunchtime all the Afghan artillery was in Roberts's hands, and as darkness fell the battle was over. British losses totalled only 35 dead, while the Afghans left more than 600 corpses on the battlefield, taking as many others with them as they fled. Although weakened by illness, Roberts had commanded the entire operation from the saddle, taking occasional sips of champagne to keep up his strength.

With Britain's military prestige in Central Asia now restored, thanks to Roberts's two brilliant victories, and with a strong and friendly ruler on the throne in Kabul, only one obstacle remained in the way of the government's decision to evacuate Afghanistan. This was the contentious question of Kandahar. In view of the fact that it lay astride the approach route from Herat to the Bolan Pass, many argued that it should not be evacuated, warning that Russian agents would move in the moment the British garrison left. Even the military were split down the middle, though all were agreed that it should be immediately reoccupied if the Russians seized Herat. In the end the Cabinet decided to offer Kandahar to Abdur Rahman on the grounds that the less the British interfered in the affairs of Afghanistan, the less hostility there would be towards them, and the more inclined the Afghans would be to resist the Russians as they previously had the British. Abdur Rahman was slow in taking up the British offer, and as a result his cousin Ayub Khan seized Kandahar shortly after the British had evacuated it. He did not hold it for long, however. Following Roberts's route southwards, Abdur Rahman led his own troops against Kandahar, wresting first it and then Herat from his rival, who escaped into Persia. These two victories now left Abdur Rahman master of virtually the whole of Afghanistan.

The British had successfully if painfully eradicated all Russian influence at Kabul, and had at last established a reasonably stable and united buffer state, under a friendly ruler, in Afghanistan. But they would not be allowed to rest on their laurels for long. While London might have decided to abandon forward policies in Central Asia, St Petersburg certainly had not. Within weeks of the last British troops leaving Afghanistan, the Russians were once more on the move.

· 30 ·

The Last Stand of the Turcomans

Had one been crossing the desert to the east of Isfahan, in central Persia, on the morning of October 1, 1880, one might have chanced upon a curious sight. At a lonely spot beside a disused well, a European of obvious military appearance and bearing was divesting himself of his clothes and struggling into those of an Armenian horse-trader. As he donned a long quilted coat and black lambskin hat, the two men with him watched in silence. They were similarly dressed, the only difference being that they were genuine Armenians while he was a British officer. Lieutenant-Colonel Charles Stewart of the 5th Punjab Infantry was preparing to set out, thus disguised, for a remote part of Persia's north-eastern frontier. From there he hoped to monitor Russian troop movements in the empty Turcoman lands to the north, where lay the great oasis of Merv, known since ancient times as 'the Queen of the World'.

For some months, intelligence had been reaching India that pointed to the likelihood of a major military initiative by the Russians in the region to the east of the Caspian – Transcaspia, as the geographers called it. For it was no secret that a powerful force was being prepared at Krasnovodsk under the formidable command of General Mikhail Skobelev, one of the Tsar's most outstanding and colourful soldiers, who had risen to prominence during the recent war with Turkey. Nicknamed 'the White General' by his troops because he invariably rode into battle in a dazzling white uniform and on a white charger, he also had a reputation for ruthlessness and cruelty which had earned him the name of 'old Bloody Eyes' among the Turcomans. A leader of great daring, he had made a number of clandestine reconnaissances behind Turkish lines during the war, even secretly visiting Constantinople.

Skobelev's presence in this strategically sensitive region was a matter of considerable concern to those responsible for India's defence, for it was he who had prepared the master plan for its invasion during the Anglo-Russian crisis of 1878. Like every other soldier in the Russian army, he had been bitterly disappointed when it was called off, and still dreamed of driving the British out of India. Now, with the full blessing of the Tsar, he was proposing to march eastwards. Where, the British defence chiefs asked themselves, would he halt? To make things more difficult for them, Skobelev's likely line of advance lay across some of the most inaccessible and least populated regions on earth. It might take days, if not weeks, for news of a Russian advance to reach the nearest British outpost. Indeed, as had happened before, very likely the first that would be known of it would be from the St Petersburg newspapers. The obvious solution would be to send British officers to sit it out on the spot, for Captain Napier had found the Turcomans to be friendly towards their hoped-for ally against the Russians. However, London had decreed otherwise following the abandonment of forward policies, fearing that any British activity in the region might provide the Russians with the pretext they needed to seize Merv. Provocation was to be avoided at all costs.

Such prohibitions on travel in sensitive regions by British officers and politicals were nothing new in the Great Game, and were rarely allowed to inhibit individual enterprise, as Moorcroft, Hayward, Shaw, Burnaby and others had demonstrated. Apart from knowing that they might incur official displeasure, or even be ordered out like Burnaby, there was nothing really to stop those on leave from going where they liked. Indeed, so long as they could be officially disowned if need be, the intelligence they brought back from 'shooting leave' or other such thinly disguised ventures was often extremely welcome to the military. Whether a nod and a wink had been given to Colonel Stewart's enterprise, or perhaps even more, is uncertain, for there is no evidence either way in the archives of the time in the India Office Library. But what Stewart himself does admit is that part of the purpose of his disguise was to protect him from discovery by British diplomats in Teheran, who would have done everything in their power to stop him from proceeding. For there was a perpetual war between the Foreign Office, which was traditionally opposed to forward policies, and the military over anything which might conceivably upset St Petersburg. A somewhat similar conflict existed between the Russian Foreign Ministry and the Tsar's generals, particularly the hawks in Tashkent and Tiflis.

Stewart reached the remote frontier town of Mahomadabad, which was to be his listening-post, on November 25. He told the Persian governor that he was an Armenian from Calcutta who had come to purchase the famed Turcoman horses of the region. In keeping with this pretence he began to inspect and acquire a number of horses from the governor's own stud. At the same time he was making friends and contacts in the bazaar, for there, without arousing anyone's suspicions, he was able to learn what was going on across the frontier from traders and other native travellers who came and went almost daily. But Colonel Stewart was not the only person intent on watching General Skobelev's movements in southern Transcaspia. When he had been in Mahomadabad for several weeks, he learned to his astonishment that another Englishman had arrived in town. This turned out to be Edmund O'Donovan, special correspondent of the *Daily News*, hell-bent on witnessing the coming campaign against the Turcomans. His original intention had been to accompany Skobelev's troops, but this had been blocked personally by the general. His aim now was to reach the Turcoman stronghold of Geok-Tepe before the Russians launched their attack on it, a move which appeared imminent. For after months of preparation, Skobelev's great advance had begun. O'Donovan, delayed by Persian obstructiveness and by illness, was engaged in negotiations with Turcoman contacts at Mahomadabad for a safe passage to Geok-Tepe.

Although Stewart saw O'Donovan almost daily for the next three weeks, he decided not to reveal his true identity. His disguise must have been extremely convincing, for he was even congratulated by O'Donovan, a man more astute than most, on his mastery of English. To this Stewart replied quite truthfully: 'Calcutta Armenians receive a very fair education'. In the end, before they parted, he confessed the truth to his friend, who refused to believe him until shown his passport. In O'Donovan's subsequent account of his adventures, *The Merv Oasis: Travels and Adventures East of the Caspian*, he admits to being totally taken in by Stewart's disguise. Finally, in January 1881, O'Donovan received word that he was welcome to visit Geok-Tepe. The Turcoman chiefs, who had little idea of what a newspaper correspondent's functions really were, had got the idea that he had been sent by the British government to help them. O'Donovan at once set out across the frontier, hoping to reach Geok-Tepe before Skobelev. But the invitation had come too late, for he soon learned that the Russians had surrounded the fortress and begun to bombard it. He arrived just in time, however, to witness through binoculars from a nearby hilltop the flight of the defeated and panic-stricken Turcomans, and to hear survivors' accounts of the pitiless and vengeful massacre which Skobelev had ordered. For the Russian troops had not forgotten the humiliation of their earlier defeat by Geok-Tepe's defenders.

All this gave O'Donovan a wealth of material for a long and graphic dispatch on the fall of the desert fortress, which was to cause uproar in Europe. There had been 10,000 Turcoman troops inside its massive walls, most of them cavalry, as well as nearly 40,000 civilians. Skobelev himself had 7,000 infantry and cavalry, and 60 guns and rocket batteries. Resistance at first had been fierce and determined, and the Russians found themselves under heavy fire from the ramparts. The defences had been greatly strengthened, moreover, since the Russians' earlier attempt to storm them, the work having been directed by a Turcoman who had studied Russian fortifications in the Caspian region. Although Skobelev's artillery and rockets were wreaking devastation inside the fortress, they failed to make much impression on the walls. Fearing the arrival of Turcoman reinforcements if the siege was allowed to drag on, Skobelev realised that something drastic was called for. He ordered his engineers to tunnel to a point beneath the wall where a mine could be exploded, thereby breaching the defences. To hasten their progress, the general seated himself each day at the entrance to the tunnel and timed the teams as they worked. If they dug quickly, the officer in charge would be rewarded with vodka and champagne, and warmly embraced. If they dug too slowly, he would be violently abused in front of his men.

By January 17, as fierce fighting continued overhead, the sappers had got to within twenty-five yards of the wall without detection. Progress now began to slow, due to the difficulty of getting air to the diggers, but finally the tunnel was ready. Two tons of explosives were carried along it by volunteers to a position directly beneath the wall. Shortly before noon on January 24, as the storming parties waited in readiness, the mine was ignited. Simultaneously the full fury of Skobelev's artillery and rocket batteries was turned against the same part of the wall. The result was an enormous explosion, which sent a huge column of earth and rubble skywards. Together with the artillery fire it blew a gap nearly fifty yards wide in the wall, instantly killing several hundred of the defenders. The Russian storming party now poured into the fortress, while at other points, using scaling ladders brought up under cover of darkness the previous night, Skobelev's troops swarmed over the walls. Ferocious hand-to-hand fighting followed for possession of the fortress. Unprepared for the sudden appearance of the Russians in their midst, and still stunned by the violence of the explosion, the Turcomans soon began to give ground. Before long this had turned into a headlong flight as the defenders took to their horses and made off across the desert followed by thousands of terrified civilians and hotly pursued by Skobelev's cavalry.

It was then that the real slaughter began, as the victors avenged their earlier defeat at the hands of the Turcomans. No one was spared, not even young children or the elderly. All were mercilessly cut down by Russian sabres. In all, 8,000 of the fugitives are said to have perished, while a further 6,500 bodies were counted inside the fortress itself. 'The whole country was covered with corpses,' an Armenian interpreter with the force later confided to a British friend. 'I myself saw babies bayoneted or slashed to pieces. Many women were ravished before being killed.' For three days, he said, Skobelev had allowed his troops, many of whom were drunk, to rape, plunder and slaughter. In justification for this afterwards, the general declared: 'I hold it as a principle that the duration of peace is in direct proportion to the slaughter you inflict upon the enemy. The harder you hit them, the longer they remain quiet.' It was, he claimed, a far more effective way of pacifying troublesome neighbours than the British method, employed by Roberts at Kabul, of publicly hanging the ringleaders, since that merely engendered hatred and not fear. Certainly the Turcomans, who for nearly two centuries had plundered Russian caravans, attacked their frontier posts and carried off the Tsar's subjects into slavery, were never to give trouble again. Skobelev's own losses he put at 268 killed and 669 wounded. The dead included a general, two colonels, a major and ten junior officers, while the wounded numbered forty other officers. Unofficial sources put Skobelev's casualty figures higher, claiming that the Russians always understated their own losses and exaggerated the enemy's.

As for the mysterious Colonel Stewart, he had hastily departed from Mahomadabad, his listening-post on the frontier, the moment word reached him of the fall of Geok-Tepe. Having gone to such lengths to be the first to hear the news, it seems almost certain that he passed it immediately to the British Mission in Teheran. If his visit to the frontier was unauthorised, he would now feel free to admit to it, since it was too late for the Foreign Office to do much about it, as he was already making his way home. Indeed, in Teheran, he visited the British Mission, reporting to the Minister, whom he had previously taken such pains to avoid. In his own account of the exploit, entitled *Through Persia in Disguise* and published many years later, Stewart is extremely circumspect about what he was really up to in this sensitive area disguised as an Armenian horse-trader. The Mission archives, today in the India Office Library in London, throw no further light on this. Certainly his clandestine and unauthorised (if indeed they were that) activities were to do his career no harm. For within a few months he was back on the Persian frontier, this time as a member of the Mission staff, on what was euphemistically termed 'special duty'.

General Skobelev, the flamboyant victor of Geok-Tepe, was less fortunate. Following the outcry in Europe over the massacre of the Turcoman innocents, the Tsar was to relieve him of his command, moving him to Minsk, a backwater so far as any fighting soldier was concerned. Officially this was to appease European public opinion. However, according to some, the real reason was quite different. Skobelev, it was feared in St Petersburg, was suffering from delusions of grandeur and showing signs of political ambition. He even offered to meet Bismarck, the German Chancellor, whom he denounced as Russia's greatest foe, in mortal combat before their two armies. Skobelev, who had outlived his usefulness, clearly had to be cut down to size. Not yet 40, and deprived of the chance of further glory, which was all that he lived for, Skobelev began to have nightmares about dying in his bed, and not on the battlefield. Within a year of his victory at Geok-Tepe those fears were to be realised, for he was found dead from a heart attack, sustained, it was whispered, during a visit to a Moscow brothel.

The seizure of Geok-Tepe did not, in itself, cause undue alarm in London or Calcutta (except among the Russophobes), for this mud-walled stronghold in the middle of nowhere was of little strategic significance. Its annexation, moreover, had not been entirely unexpected. There was even a feeling that the 'man-stealing Turcomans', who had been responsible for so much human misery themselves, had got no more than they deserved, although the subsequent massacre of their women and children was universally condemned as abhorrent and unnecessary. What really disturbed the British, though, was whether the Russians would now press on eastwards towards Merv, from where they would quite easily be able to march into Afghanistan and occupy Herat. St Petersburg, which was not yet ready to move again, was aware of these British fears, and was concerned lest London decide on a pre-emptive strike, seizing Herat and – as some hawks were urging – perhaps even

Merv. To calm such British fears, St Petersburg issued a succession of assurances that it had no further ambitions in Transcaspia, and certainly no intention of occupying Merv. 'Not only do we not want to go there,' Nikolai Giers, the Tsar's Deputy Foreign Minister, declared, 'but happily there is nothing which can require us to go there.' To this, in a personal message to Lord Dufferin, the British ambassador, Tsar Alexander himself had added his own solemn assurance that he had ordered a permanent halt. What the British could not have known was that very shortly Alexander would be dead – killed by an assassin's bomb as he rode back to the Winter Palace after reviewing his troops.

*   *   *

Hopes that the Russians might at last have abandoned their forward policies in Central Asia, as the British had done, were encouraged by two apparently conciliatory moves which they made at this time. One was their peaceful settlement of a large part of their previously undemarcated frontier with Persia, extending from the Caspian Sea to a point well to the east of Geok-Tepe, although further east still the frontier remained wide open. Here lay Merv, nominally belonging to Persia, but now in Turcoman hands. The other Russian move, admittedly carried out with great reluctance, was their withdrawal from Kuldja, to the north-east of Kashgar, and its return to Chinese rule. Apart from their sale of Alaska to the United States in 1867 for $7 million (after St Petersburg had decided it was neither easily defended nor economic), the Russians had never been known to haul down their flag anywhere. The town and neighbourhood of Kuldja, it may be recalled, had been annexed by Russia ten years earlier to prevent it (or so St Petersburg claimed at the time) from falling into the hands of Yakub Beg. There had been some justification for this, for Kuldja, or Ili as the Chinese called it, commanded important strategic routes leading northwards into Russia. But despite earlier assurances that it would be returned to China once Peking had regained control of Sinkiang from Yakub Beg, St Petersburg had failed to honour this pledge, and a long and bitter diplomatic quarrel had followed.

Finally, in the spring of 1880, the Chinese had threatened to take Kuldja back by force, and began assembling an army for that purpose. The Russians were neither willing nor able to go to war with China at that moment, so in line with their age-old policy of maximum acquisition at minimum risk they gave way, accusing the British of being behind Peking's unexpected bellicosity. Under the Treaty of St Petersburg, signed the following year, the Russians agreed to return Kuldja, while retaining control of a small parcel of territory to the west, and receiving heavy 'occupation costs' from the Chinese for safeguarding it for them. For the Russians to back down in face of threats by an Asiatic power was unprecedented. 'China', declared Lord Dufferin, 'has compelled Russia to do what she has never done before – disgorge territory that she has once absorbed.'

But if all this was viewed by Gladstone and the Cabinet as an earnest of St Petersburg's future good intentions in Central Asia, then disillusionment was soon to follow. For despite the solemn pledges made with regard to Merv, plans were soon being laid, amid the greatest secrecy, for its annexation. Among those invited to the coronation of Alexander III, following his father's assassination, were a number of Turcoman chiefs from Merv. The purpose of this was to remind them of Russia's military might, and convince them that any further resistance would be futile. It worked. Awed by the pageantry and splendour of the occasion, and by the sight of vast bodies of armed troops and artillery everywhere, the chiefs returned home to Merv, the last of their strongholds, convinced that it would be insane to oppose the Tsar's armies. At the same time native agents were busy spreading the story in the surrounding towns and villages that the British had left Afghanistan because the Tsar had ordered them out. No one on earth, they declared, not even Queen Victoria, dared to defy the will of the Tsar. Any hopes that the Turcomans might entertain of the British marching to their assistance were in vain.

Having thus sown the seeds of doubt among the Turcomans, the Russians next decided to send a spy to Merv to try to gauge the mood there. It was hoped that, with the memory of Geok-Tepe still fresh in their minds, the Turcomans would no longer have the heart to fight, and that they would submit without further resistance when faced by Russian military might. But in case they did decide to make a stand, a thorough study of Merv's defences would also have to be made. It would be a hazardous enterprise, in classic Great Game mould, and one calling for exceptional courage and resource. However, the ideal man was at hand in the person of Lieutenant Alikhanov.

*　　*　　*

In February 1882, a Turcoman caravan laden with goods could be seen approaching Merv from the west. Its leader was a prominent native trader, secretly friendly with the Russians. Half a dozen armed horsemen, all Turcomans, accompanied him. There were two other men in the party, both apparently native merchants. In fact, they were Russian officers. The senior of the two was Alikhanov, while his companion was a young Cossack ensign who had volunteered to accompany him. Alikhanov was a Muslim from an aristocratic Caucasian family. After distinguishing himself on numerous battlefields, he had been promoted to the rank of major and made aide-de-camp to Grand Duke Mikhail, Viceroy of the Caucasus. Like many Caucasians, however, he was quick-tempered, and following a duel with a senior officer he had been court-martialled and reduced to the ranks. Gradually he had redeemed himself by his gallantry and ability, and was once more a lieutenant. If he succeeded in this mission, he knew that almost certainly he would be given back his original rank.

The caravan entered Merv at night so that he and his companion would not be too closely scrutinised. There were in the city a number of Turcoman elders who had already been won over to the Russian cause, and who favoured submission to the Tsar. They had been secretly alerted to Alikhanov's coming. After welcoming him and his Cossack companion, they decided to announce the following morning that two Russian merchants had arrived in Merv hoping to establish regular caravan traffic between Ashkhabad, the nearest Russian settlement, and the

Turcoman traders in the bazaars. It was obviously a risky move, but one, Alikhanov agreed, which had to be taken. When word of their presence in the town got round, it caused a sensation, and an urgent meeting of all Turcoman elders and notables was immediately summoned. Alikhanov and his companion were ordered to appear before them in the great council tent. It was here that Alikhanov's affinity with his fellow Muslims was to prove invaluable. Already he had paved the way by seeing to it that the most senior among the Turcoman chiefs had received lavish Russian-made gifts which had been brought especially for that purpose. And now he addressed the tense assembly, explaining why they had come, and asking leave to unpack their goods and offer them for sale to the city's merchants.

When one of the elders proposed that first talks should be conducted between the two governments, Alikhanov dismissed the idea. 'Do you want us to return home?' he asked scornfully. 'We don't need your business that badly, and are not prepared to waste time travelling backwards and forwards. If we go back this time, you won't ever see our faces again.' It was a bold, if perilous, strategy, but Alikhanov could see from the elders' expressions that it was beginning to work. He had forced them on to the defensive. Maintaining the pressure, he asked: 'Do you call a meeting every time a caravan arrives, or do you do this only to the Russians?' There was a long silence. Then one of the chiefs spoke. The desert between Merv and the nearest Russian settlements was in the grip of lawless brigands whom they could not control, he said. 'We don't want anything to happen to you, the merchants of the great Russian Tsar.' Alikhanov replied that the armed escorts accompanying the caravans would be able to deal with any raiders unwise enough to attack them. All that St Petersburg would ask was for their safety to be guaranteed once they reached Merv.

The Turcomans had now run out of arguments. Seeing that they were sharply divided among themselves, Alikhanov decided to press home his advantage. If they still wished to prevent him and his companions from trading, he declared, then they would immediately pack their bags and depart. He could not say for sure how the new Tsar, who was currently well disposed towards the Turcomans, would react to news of this rebuff, but he imagined that he would be greatly angered. This was all too much for the elders, who remembered painfully their defeat at Geok-Tepe. A heated discussion followed, at the end of which Alikhanov was told that he was welcome to sell his goods, and that if he so wished he could remain in Merv permanently. 'God forbid,' laughed Alikhanov, anxious not to appear grateful. 'Two or three days will be long enough for us to judge what business is like.' In fact, he and his party were to remain in Merv for a fortnight – long enough for Alikhanov and his Cossack companion to conduct a discreet survey of the city's defences by taking a stroll early each morning while most of the Turcomans were still asleep. Finally, when the caravan left for home, it took a different route to that by which it had come so that this too could be mapped.

Alikhanov was now entrusted with making preparations for the annexation, preferably peacefully, of Merv. He was aware that many of the Turcoman chiefs were still extremely hostile towards Russia, and were totally opposed to submitting to Tsarist rule. To agree to let him sell Russian goods was one thing; surrender was quite another. Making skilful use of agents and contacts he had set up while in Merv, Alikhanov continued to intrigue against the anti-Russian faction among the Turcoman elders. Gradually this undermined their influence. At last, in February 1884, he reported that everything was ready. As luck would have it, the British government was then facing grave difficulties in the Sudan where it had a holy war on its hands. The last thing that Gladstone wanted, as St Petersburg was quick to realise, was a fight with Russia in Central Asia.

The Russians' first move was to occupy the oasis of Tejend, eighty miles west of Merv. This they had done once before, withdrawing soon afterwards, so the Turcomans were not too worried when they learned of it. After all, there was no reason why they should fear trouble from the Russians, having been careful, ever since the fall of Geok-Tepe, not to attack their caravans or give them any other excuse for making war. The first they knew that anything was amiss was when Alikhanov, whom they had believed to be a Russian merchant, arrived at the city gates with a detachment of Cossacks, and wearing the uniform of the Imperial Russian Army. He was accompanied by a number of Turcoman chiefs and notables who had already submitted and taken an oath of allegiance to the Tsar. Summoning the city's elders together, he advised them to surrender at once, explaining that the force currently occupying Tejend, from where he had just come, was merely the advance guard of a large Russian army, equipped with heavy artillery, which was already on its way. If they agreed to accept the sovereignty of the Tsar, he assured them, there would be no question of a Russian garrison being stationed in Merv. At most there would be a governor, a few assistants and an escort. Otherwise things could carry on much as before. Although some of the Turcomans wanted to resist, the majority had by now lost their stomach for the fight. Elsewhere the tribes had already submitted, so they could expect no help from them, while the British had shown no interest in their plight, and anyway were said to go in fear of the Russians themselves. After an agonised debate, the once-proud Turcomans, for so long the lords of Transcaspia, agreed to surrender their capital and submit to the rule of St Petersburg.

Telegraphing the news to Tsar Alexander III, the Governor of Transcaspia declared: 'I have the honour to inform Your Majesty that the khans of the four tribes of the Merv Turcomans, each representing 2,000 tents, have this day formally taken the oath of allegiance to Your Majesty.' They had done so, he added, 'being conscious of their inability to govern themselves, and convinced that Your Majesty's powerful authority alone can establish order and prosperity in Merv.' Shortly afterwards, a column of troops from Tejend entered Merv and took possession of the great fortress. Thanks to the audacious, if none too scrupulous diplomacy of Alikhanov, the Russian victory had been entirely bloodless, and had cost almost nothing. On the personal orders of the Tsar, Alikhanov was immediately restored to the rank of major, and his medals, stripped from him at his court martial, were pinned back on his tunic. Not long afterwards he was promoted to colonel, and fittingly made governor of the city which, virtually single-handed, he had annexed for his Tsar and country.

News of Merv's fall was broken, almost casually, to the British ambassador by Nikolai Giers, now Foreign Minister, on February 15, the day after Alexander had been told. It was painfully clear to the British that St Petersburg, with its repeated reassurances, had been hoodwinking them all along. Once again the Russians were gambling on Gladstone's Liberals not going beyond their customary remonstrances on finding themselves confronted by a *fait accompli*. The announcement, however, did not take the British government entirely by surprise, even if it was in no position, with a major crisis on its hands in the Sudan, to do much about it. Early the previous year, Lord Granville, the Foreign Secretary, had advised Queen Victoria that the Russians were 'moving and feeling their way towards the border of Afghanistan', while only a month before Merv's surrender a senior Foreign Office official had warned that the uprising in the Sudan served as 'an encouragement to the Russians, as it is to every enemy of this country'.

The capitulation of Merv was almost as much a triumph for the Russophobes as it was for the Russians, for it was precisely as they had forecast. General Roberts, shortly to become Commander-in-Chief, India, described the move as 'by far the most important step ever made by Russia on her march towards India'. It would not be long now, warned the hawks, before the Cossacks were watering their horses on the banks of the Indus. Even the government had to recognise that Russia's seizure of Merv posed a greater menace to India than its earlier annexation of Bokhara, Khiva and Khokand. For whereas vast mountain ranges and deserts lay between the conquered khanates and India's frontiers, no such obstacles blocked the line of march from Merv, via Herat and Kandahar, to the Indus. Moreover, now that the tribes of Transcaspia had been crushed, there was nothing to stop the Tsar's armies in the Caucasus and in Turkestan from acting together, under a joint command, against India. To add to British worries, the Russians had begun to build a railway eastwards across Transcaspia towards Merv, which clearly, when completed, could be used to bring troops up to the Afghan frontier region, and eventually to link the garrison towns and oases of Central Asia.

Its patience and credulity finally at an end, the British government once again protested to St Petersburg about the broken promises and false assurances which had led to the seizure of Merv. In a long memorandum, the Foreign Office accused the Russians of acting with cynical disregard for the solemn and frequently repeated pledges of both the Tsar and his ministers. Ignoring the question of the broken promises, the Russians replied that their annexation of Merv had not been premeditated, insisting that it had been at the request of the Turcomans themselves, who wished to end their state of anarchy and enjoy the benefits of civilisation. Having got what it wanted, however, St Petersburg now showed itself anxious to let the matter cool. It therefore proposed that to prevent any such problem from happening in the future, the two governments should get together amicably and work out a permanent frontier between northern Afghanistan and Russia's Central Asian territories. Disregarding warnings that the Russians were not to be trusted, the Cabinet decided that any settlement with St Petersburg was better than none at all and welcomed the proposal. Once a line had been formally agreed, then any Russian move across it would amount to a hostile act against Afghanistan. Because, under her treaty with Abdur Rahman, Britain was responsible for Afghanistan's foreign policy, such a step would be tantamount to a hostile act against her too. The Russians, or so the Cabinet was convinced, would consequently think twice before making any further move towards Herat.

After lengthy official correspondence, and much quibbling, it was finally agreed that representatives of both powers – together known as the Joint Afghan Boundary Commission – would rendezvous on October 13, 1884, at the oasis of Sarakhs. This lay in the remote and desolate region, to the south-west of Merv, where Afghanistan, Persia and Transcaspia met. Their task was to delineate the frontier scientifically and permanently, thereby replacing the old 1873 line which had merely been drawn from maps, and extremely vague ones at that. The Russians appeared to be in no hurry to begin work, however, and a series of delays occurred, including the illness, almost certainly tactical, of their chief commissioner, General

Zelenoy. Finally the grim Central Asian winter began to close in, making it impossible – or so the Russians insisted – for the general and his staff to reach the spot before the spring. Nonetheless, the chief British commissioner, General Sir Peter Lumsden, managed to get to the rendezvous on time, only to find considerable Russian military activity going on. It immediately became clear what they were up to. Whatever St Petersburg might have decided, the Russian military were determined to extend their southern frontier with Afghanistan as close as possible to Herat before the Commission began its work. They were gambling on the belief that with the Liberals in power, and with the British already heavily committed in the Sudan, London would be unwilling to go to war over a worthless stretch of desert in Asia's back-of-beyond. But for once, the Russians soon discovered, they had misjudged their adversary.

· 31 ·

To the Brink of War

Russia's annexation of Merv, and the deceitful manner in which this had been carried out, had already set the presses rolling in Britain, as a new generation of Wilsons, Urquharts and Rawlinsons took up their pens. General Lumsden's warning that the Russians were on the move once more was followed shortly by a report from the British military attaché at St Petersburg that the Tsar's generals planned to seize Herat on some pretext in the spring – 'or as soon as a large portion of our forces are locked up in Egypt and the Sudan'. Then came the news that General Gordon had been butchered on the steps of the Residency at Khartoum by a fanatical mob. It put the nation in a belligerent mood. With the hawks convinced that their moment had come, the year 1885 was destined to be a vintage one for Great Game literature.

Of the new breed of forward school commentators, the most prolific was probably Charles Marvin, already the author of several works on the Russian menace, including *The Russian Advance Towards India*, and *The Russians at Merv and Herat and Their Power of Invading India*. Another, *Reconnoitring Central Asia*, detailed secret missions and journeys made by Russian officers in the regions surrounding British India. A former correspondent in St Petersburg for the London *Globe*, he had the advantage over his rivals of being fluent in Russian, and knowing a number of the Tsar's leading generals personally. A facile and persuasive writer, he also turned out countless newspaper articles on Russian aims in Central Asia, and how best these could be thwarted.

Marvin had first come to the attention of the public, not to mention the authorities, in May 1878, when he was involved in a *cause célèbre* concerning a Whitehall leak. It occurred at the time of the Congress of Berlin, following the Russo-Turkish War of 1877, when Marvin was working as a part-time official at the Foreign Office, as well as contributing to the *Globe*. Discovering that the government intended to leak details of agreements reached between Britain and Russia to *The Times*, he decided instead to pass them to his own news-paper. The result was a world scoop, although the story was hastily denied by the government. However, the following day the *Globe* published the text of the agreements. Soon afterwards Marvin, the most obvious suspect, was arrested and charged with stealing a top-secret document. When a search of his home failed to find any trace of this, he was acquitted, the court ruling that he had broken no law – there being no Official Secrets Act at that time. In fact, Marvin had committed the entire text to memory as he copied it. The affair was to do Marvin no harm, for within five years, while still only in his late twenties, he was to become the most widely read writer on Anglo-Russian matters of his day.

In 1885, that *annus mirabilis* for all who addressed themselves to the Russian menace, Marvin published no fewer than three books on various aspects of the subject, including one on the threat posed to India by the new Transcaspian Railway. Another, *The Russians at the Gates of Herat*, was written and published in the space of one week (demonstrating that there is nothing new in the 'instant' book). Like other works by Marvin, it was to become a bestseller, 65,000 copies being sold in all. In general, Marvin's line was that successive British governments, especially Liberal ones, had brought the problem upon themselves by their spineless and vacillating policies towards St Petersburg. Of the present administration he declared: 'Mr Gladstone's Cabinet is notoriously given to making concessions, and Russia, well aware of this, is resorting to every artifice to squeeze it.' Other Great Game works appearing that year included Demetrius Boulger's *Central*

Asian Questions, Colonel G. B. Malleson's *The Russo-Afghan Question and the Invasion of India*, and H. Sutherland Edwards's *Russian Projects against India* – to name just three. In addition there were innumerable pamphlets, articles, reviews and letters to the editor by these and other commentators, mostly backing the Russophobe cause.

But perhaps the best known of the writers on the Russian peril, after Charles Marvin, was not an Englishman at all. He was an Anglophile Hungarian orientalist named Arminius Vambery, who had taken up the cudgels on behalf of Britain. Twenty years earlier, disguised as a ragged dervish, or Muslim holy man, he had made a long and daring journey through Central Asia, drawn by the belief that the Hungarians originally came from there. A brilliant linguist, who already spoke Arabic and Turkish, he quickly mastered the languages of the region, which enabled him to visit Khiva, Samarkand and Bokhara without detection. At that time all three still enjoyed independence, but Vambery returned to Budapest convinced that they would very soon be seized by Russia. Finding little interest in Central Asia among his own countrymen, Vambery turned his attention to Britain, hoping that people there would heed his warnings, particularly over India. When he arrived in London in 1864, he discovered that word of his remarkable exploits in Central Asia had preceded him, and he was immediately lionised. The son of a poor Jewish family, he was overwhelmed by the warmth of his reception, which had included meetings with the Prince of Wales, Palmerston and Disraeli. Although everyone wanted to hear at first hand of his adventures as a dervish, in one thing he failed. It will be recalled that forward policies were out of favour at this time, as Sir Henry Rawlinson was finding, and Vambery likewise was unable to persuade anyone other than the hawks to take his warnings seriously.

On returning to Budapest, where he became Professor of Turkish, Arabic and Persian at the university, Vambery proceeded to bombard *The Times* and other British newspapers with letters urging the government to take a far tougher line with the Russians, as one by one the Central Asian khanates fell to them, bringing them ever closer to what he considered to be their ultimate goal, India. But now, with the fall of Merv, and with the Russians showing no real signs of halting, Vambery sensed that his moment had come, and in the spring of 1885 he set out for London intent on expounding his views on St Petersburg's ambitions towards India. Once again he was lionised, but this time people listened to his warnings at a series of packed meetings which he addressed up and down the country. He received so many invitations that he was forced to turn most of them down. One admirer placed at his disposal, during his stay in London, a luxurious apartment, complete with cook, servants and wine cellar. More than once during his travels in the provinces luncheon baskets filled with expensive delicacies were thrust into his railway carriage, their donors signing themselves simply 'an admirer' or 'a grateful Englishman'. After three exhausting but triumphant weeks, during which he met many leading figures of the day, Vambery returned to Budapest to work on a book entitled *The Coming Struggle for India*. Completed in twenty days, it contained very little that he had not said before. But this time both mood and moment were right. With its eye-catching, vivid yellow cover, it was quickly to join Charles Marvin's latest work among the year's bestsellers.

Yet most of these books, hastily written following the fall of Merv, were little more than polemics. Aimed at alerting the public to what the authors believed to be the rapidly growing Russian menace, they relied heavily on the arguments and strategic reasoning originally put forward by Kinneir, de Lacy Evans, McNeill and others. Admittedly, since their time the Russians had moved that much closer to India's frontiers. However, none of the new generation of analysts had any first-hand experience or knowledge of the military realities involved. Only Vambery had ever set foot in these regions, and that many years earlier, and he knew nothing at all of modern strategy or tactics. Colonel Malleson, it was true, had served in the Indian Army, but he had long been retired after years in non-combative employment (including sanitation and finance), ending his career as guardian to the young Maharajah of Mysore.

There was one analyst who really did know what he was

talking about, but copies of his book – a veritable encyclopedia of the Great Game – could not be obtained for love or money. Its author, Major-General Sir Charles MacGregor, was uniquely qualified to examine the Russian threat to India in all its aspects. As Quartermaster-General of the Indian Army, he was also head of its newly formed Intelligence Department. Not only was he a veteran of numerous frontier campaigns, but he had also travelled extensively in Afghanistan and north-eastern Persia, even visiting Sarakhs. Needless to say, since this was his job, he had access to the latest intelligence, both military and political, to reach India. If there was a definitive work to be written on the Russian peril, then MacGregor, not Marvin or Vambery, was the man to undertake it.

Until MacGregor's appointment, the collecting of military intelligence had been extremely haphazard, and compared badly with the well-organised and efficient Russian system. The new Intelligence Department – based at Simla, since this was a good deal closer to the areas of Russian activity than Calcutta – consisted at first simply of five officers, two of whom were only part-time, and a number of trusted native clerks and cartographers. It was principally concerned with gathering and evaluating information about Russian troop dispositions and strengths in Central Asia, and their potential threat to India in the event of war. It also arranged the translation into English of relevant Russian books, articles and other matter. Political intelligence continued to be collected by frontier officers, who passed it back to the Political Department, by whom they were employed, and which was, in effect, the Indian government's Foreign Office. Topographical intelligence, much of which was of military value, was largely the responsibility of the Survey of India, based at Dehra Dun. This organisation, which until very recently had employed native agents or 'pundits' for gathering geographical information in sensitive areas, had the task of mapping the entire sub-continent, both within and beyond India's frontiers, and of keeping these maps up to date. Military, political and topographical intelligence were additionally contributed by enterprising young officers and other travellers, as we have seen, although unofficially. But contrary to the impression given by Rudyard Kipling in *Kim*, there was no overall intelligence-gathering or co-ordinating body in India at that time. Indeed, there was a good deal of rivalry and jealousy between the three existing departments.

MacGregor's role as head of military intelligence was one of his responsibilities as Quartermaster-General, but being an ardent forward school man, like most of his fellow generals, he embraced it with particular enthusiasm. While on leave in London in the summer of 1882, he had devoted considerable time to examining the workings of the Intelligence Branch of the War Office, and to combing its files for data useful to his own department. However, back in India he had soon encountered obstruction and resentment from the Political Department, most of whose members at that time favoured a policy of masterly inactivity, as well as from some members of the India Council. MacGregor, who was convinced that the Russians meant trouble, was determined to shake his political and civilian colleagues out of their complacency by demonstrating how easily, as things stood, an attack could be launched against India. It was largely with this in mind that in the summer of 1883 he had set about gathering material for a confidential handbook which was to be called *The Defence of India*.

It took him the best part of a year to assemble his material. In addition to his own intelligence files on Russian capabilities and dispositions, he was able to draw on the thinking of the most senior officers and best strategic brains in the Indian Army. Many of those whom he consulted were personal friends, including General Roberts, under whom he had served as a column commander during the Second Afghan War. From them he sought an answer to the crucial question of how long it would take a 20,000-strong Russian force to reach Herat, in the event of a race, as against a similar sized British force. Other key points around India's frontiers from which an invasion could be launched were likewise evaluated. Finally, in June 1884, his report and recommendations – running to more than 100,000 words, with extensive appendices, tables and a large map of Central Asia – were ready for the printer.

MacGregor warned that if the Russians decided to attack India they would probably do so at five different points simultaneously. It was a spectre that no one had raised before. One column would go for Herat, another for Bamian, a third for Kabul, a fourth for Chitral and a fifth for Gilgit. Careful calculations showed that in this way the Russians could position 95,000 regular troops around India's northern frontiers, and from there, when they were ready, pour into India. As things stood, MacGregor argued, the Indian Army had neither the numbers nor the capacity to resist such an attack. Only determined action now by the British and Indian governments would 'make Russia see the hopelessness of attacking us', he declared. He urged that the Indian Army be greatly expanded so that it might be in a position to meet such a threat. He also proposed the immediate occupation of Herat by Britain, so as to pre-empt any Russian move in that direction, together with the reoccupation of Kandahar. Delay, he warned, might be very costly. Were Herat to fall in the meantime to the Russians, then the expansion of India's armed forces would need to be even greater, while if Kandahar fell too, it would have to be greater still. He also called for increased urgency to be given to the construction of strategic roads and railways to and within the frontier regions, pointing out that the Russians were working flat out to advance their own railway system towards Afghanistan.

Recalling St Petersburg's record of broken pledges, Mac-Gregor dismissed any hopes of ever coming to terms with the Russians. The only way to restrain them, he argued, was by squaring up to them, preferably in alliance with Germany, Austria and Turkey. In giving this piece of gratuitous advice, in what was supposedly a military assessment, the general was clearly going far beyond his brief and trespassing in domains regarded by statesmen and diplomatists as theirs and strictly out of bounds to soldiers. But MacGregor was not content to leave it there, for he ended his report with words so provocative that even his fellow hawks must have reread them to make sure they had understood him correctly. 'I solemnly assert my belief', he wrote, 'that there can never be a real settlement of the Anglo-Russian question *till Russia is driven out of the Caucasus and Turkistan.*' (The italics are MacGregor's.)

The report, which bore the word CONFIDENTIAL in red type

29. Sir Louis Cavagnari (1841–79), seated on the ground among Afghan leaders not long before his murder at Kabul, where he was British Resident.

30. Gateway to the Bala Hissar fortress, Kabul. Inside its walls stood the British Residency where Cavagnari and his escort were slaughtered by mutinous Afghan troops in 1879.

31. General Sir Frederick Roberts, VC (1832–1914), who led the punitive expedition to Kabul to avenge Cavagnari's murder.

Echo

Thursday December 5th

BRILLIANT VICTORY

by General Roberts

ROUT of the AFGHANS

DESPERATE FIGHTING

Opening of Parliament

QUEEN'S SPEECH

32. Newsbill announcing Roberts's triumph. Ringleaders and rebels were summarily hanged outside the Bala Hissar.

"SAVE ME FROM MY FRIENDS!"

"IF AT THIS MOMENT IT HAS BEEN DECIDED TO INVADE THE AMEER'S TERRITORY, WE ARE ACTING IN PURSUANCE OF A POLICY WHICH IN ITS
INTENTION HAS BEEN UNIFORMLY *FRIENDLY* TO AFGHANISTAN."—*Times*, Nov. 21.

35. In addition to household names like Pottinger and Burnes, many minor players were involved in the Great Game. An anonymous political officer (rifleless), hardly distinguishable from his companions, is seen here with friendly Afghan tribesmen.

Opposite:
33. (*above*) Abdur Rahman (1844–1901), whom the Russians hoped would be a compliant Emir when they encouraged him to claim the Afghan throne in 1880, but who proved a trustworthy neighbour to the British.

34. (*below*) A contemporary cartoon from *Punch* depicting the pressures applied to Abdur Rahman by his two superpower neighbours.

36. Cossacks manning a machine-gun post in the Pamirs – scene of Russia's last thrust towards India.

37. The celebrated meeting of Captains Younghusband and Gromchevsky north of Hunza in 1889, at which they discussed over a bottle of brandy their countries' rivalry in Central Asia.

38. Francis Younghusband (1863–1942), at the time of the Lhasa
Expedition of 1904, the last major move by either side in the
Great Game.

39. An imperial gesture – Gurkha troops showing the flag in Tibet. Contrary to expectations, they found no Russians there.

on its title page, was officially intended for the eyes of India
Council members and senior government and military men
only. However, on the author's instructions some copies were
sent to carefully selected politicians and editors in London.
For he was convinced that the Great Game had first to be won
at Westminster if there was to be any hope of winning it in
Asia, and he was determined to jolt the home government into
vigorous if belated action. Aware, though, that much of the
material in the report would be of considerable value to Russian
planners, he impressed upon the recipients the need for
secrecy. At the same time he urged them to use their influence
to get the government to act while there was still time. Then
he sat back to await the results. They were not long in coming.

Gladstone's Cabinet, already hard-pressed in the Sudan,
and genuinely worried about Herat, saw MacGregor's move
as a flagrant attempt to undermine their authority. Frantic
telegrams began to pass between Whitehall and Calcutta
demanding an explanation. The Government of India presses
at Simla, which were still running off copies of the report, were
hurriedly stopped on the orders of the Viceroy. Where possible,
copies were called in. MacGregor was officially reprimanded,
although most senior officers in India agreed with his conclusions, if not necessarily with his methods. For it was widely
known that their opposite numbers in the Imperial Russian
Army were now openly boasting of their coming conquest of
India, despite what St Petersburg might be saying. Indeed,
hardly had the presses been stopped than the Russians made
their next move. It was to bring Britain and Russia to the
brink of war – and a glow of grim satisfaction, no doubt, to
MacGregor, Marvin, Vambery and others who had long been
forecasting it.

The flashpoint was the remote and little-known oasis of
Pandjeh, lying half-way between Merv and Herat, and destined
shortly to become a household word. The British had always
regarded it as belonging to Afghanistan, as did the Afghans.
But for some time, following their annexation of Merv, the
Russians had had their eye on it. During the correspondence
leading to the appointment of the Anglo-Russian boundary
commission, St Petersburg had challenged Afghanistan's claim

to it, insisting that the oasis belonged to Russia by virtue of its possession of Merv. London had strongly resisted this, since Pandjeh lay astride the strategic approach to Herat, which clearly explained St Petersburg's keen interest in it, not to mention the furtive Russian troop movements which General Lumsden, the chief British commissioner, had detected in the vicinity on his arrival there. It soon became obvious to him, as he sat out the winter of 1884–5 at nearby Sarakhs, that the Russians had no intention of sending a representative to join him until they had wrested Pandjeh from the Afghans. This they were unlikely to attempt until the spring, when the snows melted, and more troops could be brought up to ensure success. All this Lumsden reported to his chiefs in London, where Gladstone and his Cabinet colleagues were becoming increasingly disturbed.

The Russians, aware that there were considerable risks in what they were doing, were obliged to proceed cautiously. For it was known in St Petersburg that Britain had pledged herself – albeit in somewhat vague terms – to help Abdur Rahman if ever he were attacked by his northern neighbour. What the Russians could not be sure of was just how far the British would be prepared to go to honour their pledge. Would they risk a full-scale conflict over a distant oasis which they did not even own, and which few people in Britain had ever heard of? With Gladstone in power, and the Sudan in flames, it seemed unlikely. And even if they did decide to intervene it would take their troops weeks, if not months, to reach the spot. Nonetheless, the Russians advanced stealthily, playing their old game of Grandmother's Footsteps – carefully observing British reactions to each move forward, while maintaining their long-running correspondence with London over the Afghan Boundary Commission as though nothing untoward was going on.

By now, however, the British knew exactly what was going on. In India two army corps, one under the command of General Roberts, were being mobilised in readiness to march across Afghanistan to defend Herat if it became necessary. At the same time three engineer officers attached to General Lumsden's party were sent to Herat to examine its fortifications and decide how best the city could be defended, while others of his staff set to work to map the route a Russian army would take to reach it. General MacGregor wrote to Roberts observing that at last there were hopeful signs that 'our miserable government' was beginning to heed their repeated warnings. Meanwhile the Afghans, partly as a result of British prompting, had dispatched troops to Pandjeh and strengthened its defences. When the Russian commander, General Komarov, learned of this he was furious. Declaring that the oasis was Russian, he ordered them to leave at once. The Afghan commander refused. Komarov now turned to Lumsden, demanding that he instruct the Afghan troops to leave. This Lumsden declined to do.

Determined not to let Pandjeh slip from his grasp, Komarov now switched tactics. On March 13, pressed by Britain, St Petersburg had given a solemn assurance that their forces would not attack Pandjeh, provided the Afghans refrained from hostilities. Three days later Nikolai Giers, the Foreign Minister, repeated this, adding that the undertaking was given with the Tsar's full approval. Earlier, Queen Victoria herself had telegraphed to Alexander, appealing to him to prevent the 'calamity' of a war. There was only one way now in which Komarov could justify the seizure of Pandjeh. The Afghans had to be seen as the aggressors. It was here that the wily Alikhanov, now governor of Merv, came in. Already, according to rumours reaching Lumsden's camp, he had secretly visited Pandjeh, disguised as a Turcoman, and studied its defences. He was now entrusted by Komarov with the task of goading the defenders into firing the first shot. Aware that the Afghans were both proud and quick-tempered, Alikhanov wrote a personal letter to their commander couched in highly offensive and insulting terms. It accused him, among many other things, of cowardice, a charge guaranteed to enrage an Afghan, to whom fighting was almost a way of life. But Lumsden, warning him of the Russian's game, urged him not to react, explaining that the British were in no position to help him if he did. The Afghans, despite intense provocation, managed to control their tempers – and trigger fingers.

All this time, despite St Petersburg's repeated pledges,

Komarov's troops had been gradually closing in on Pandjeh. By March 25 they were in positions less than a mile from those of the defenders. Having failed to provoke the Afghans into firing at them, Komarov now presented their commander with an ultimatum. If, in five days, he had not withdrawn every one of his men, then the Russians would drive them from what, the general claimed, rightfully belonged to the Tsar. Until then Lumsden had been closely monitoring developments and reporting these back to London. But having done everything he could to prevent a clash, he now decided to withdraw his camp to a position some distance away to avoid being caught up in the fighting. As a result we have only the Russian account of what followed.

On March 31, when General Komarov's ultimatum expired, and the Afghans showed no sign of giving way, he ordered his troops to advance, but not to fire unless first fired upon. In the event, if Alikhanov is to be believed, the Afghans opened fire first, wounding the horse of one of his Cossacks. It was just what he was waiting for. 'Blood has been shed,' he declared, and gave orders for his troops to open fire on the Afghan cavalry, who were massed within easy range. Thrown into confusion by the murderous hail, they broke and fled. But the Afghan infantry fought with great bravery, Alikhanov recounted later, two entire companies dying to a man as the Russians gradually overran their positions. Finally they too fled, leaving behind them more than 800 dead, many of them drowned while trying to escape across a flooded river. Komarov's casualties amounted to only 40 dead and wounded.

The news that the Russians had seized Pandjeh reached London a week later. It was received with a mixture of fury and dismay, and even the government admitted that a situation of 'the utmost gravity' had arisen. Most people, including foreign diplomats in London, assumed that war between the two great powers was now inevitable. Gladstone, who had been made a fool of by Giers, not to mention by the Tsar himself, denounced the slaughter of the Afghans as an act of unprovoked aggression, and accused the Russians of occupying territory which unquestionably belonged to Afghanistan. He told the House of Commons that the situation was grave, though not hopeless. As something approaching panic swept the Stock Exchange, he obtained an £11 million vote of credit from excited MPs of both parties, the largest such sum since the Crimean War. Official announcements of the outbreak of hostilities were prepared in readiness by the Foreign Office. The Royal Navy was placed on full alert, with instructions to monitor the movements of all Russian warships. In the Far East the fleet was ordered to occupy Port Hamilton in Korea, so that it might be used as a base for operations against the great Russian naval stronghold at Vladivostok and other targets in the North Pacific. At the same time, the possibility of striking at the Russians in the Caucasus, preferably with Turkish help, was being considered.

So that the Tsar and his ministers could have no doubt whatever about the government's firmness of intent, the British ambassador in St Petersburg was instructed to warn Giers that any further advances towards Herat would definitely mean war. In case this failed to stop the Russians, the Viceroy prepared to move 25,000 troops to Quetta, where they would be held poised, awaiting Emir Abdur Rahman's approval, ready to race to Herat. In Teheran meanwhile, the Shah of Persia, profoundly alarmed himself by these aggressive Russian moves so close to his own frontier with Afghanistan, was urging Britain to seize Herat before St Petersburg did, while declaring that he intended to remain strictly neutral in the event of a war between his two powerful neighbours.

By now the tremors from the crisis were being felt throughout the rest of the world. In America, where the news had rocked Wall Street, all talk was of the coming struggle between the two imperial giants. Beneath the banner headline ENGLAND AND RUSSIA TO FIGHT, the normally sober *New York Times* began its story with the words: 'It is war.' And so it might well have been, had not one man kept his head when all about him were beginning to lose theirs.

·32·

The Railway Race to
the East

While the world's newspapers and statesmen were predicting that the two greatest powers on earth were about to go to war over a remote Central Asian village, the ruler in whose domains it lay was temporarily absent from his throne on a state visit to India. Indeed, it may well have been Russian fears that Abdur Rahman and his British hosts were scheming against them, plus the fact that he was away from his kingdom, that had precipitated their seizure of Pandjeh. The prospect of the British, with the Emir's blessing, occupying Herat was a worrying one to St Petersburg. For just as their own annexation of Merv, and now Pandjeh, menaced India, a strong British military presence at Herat would similarly threaten Russia's new Central Asian possessions. The spectre might then arise of the British and Afghans joining forces to liberate the Muslim khanates from Russian rule. By occupying Pandjeh, however, the Tsar's generals knew that if it came to a race for Herat they could be certain of getting there first.

The news of Pandjeh's fall, and the massacre of the Afghan garrison, was broken to Abdur Rahman by Sir Mortimer Durand, Foreign Secretary to the Indian government and, as it happened, the son of Henry Durand, the subaltern who had blown up the gates of Ghazni during the First Afghan War. No one was sure how the Emir, who was both hot-tempered and ruthless, would take the ill tidings. It was thought very likely that he would demand that the affront be expunged by the spilling of Russian blood and, under the terms of the Anglo-Afghan agreement, with British help. If so, it was hard to see how war was to be avoided, unless Britain was prepared to abandon its buffer state, so painfully and expensively acquired, to the tender mercies of the Russians.

'We received the news about dinner time,' Durand reported, 'and I drove at once to tell him of the slaughter of his people.' To Durand's relief and astonishment, the Emir took it quite calmly, considering the alarm it was generating in Britain, India and elsewhere. 'He begged me not to be troubled,' Durand wrote. 'He said that the loss of two hundred or two thousand men was a mere nothing.' As for the death of their commander, 'that was less than nothing.' Lord Dufferin, the former British ambassador to Russia, who had recently become Viceroy of India, was to observe later: 'But for the accidental circumstances of the Amir being in my camp at Rawalpindi, and the fortunate fact of his being a prince of great capacity, experience and calm judgement, the incident at Pandjeh alone, in the strained condition of the relations which then existed between Russia and ourselves, might in itself have proved the occasion of a long and miserable war.'

The plain truth was that the Emir had no wish to see his country turned once more into a battlefield, this time by his two quarrelling neighbours. Some authorities have even doubted whether, until then, he had ever heard of the village of Pandjeh. Nonetheless, his restraint did much to defuse a highly incendiary situation. Even so, for the next few weeks, the outbreak of war was expected daily, with the British newspapers demanding that the Russians be taught a lesson, and those of St Petersburg and Moscow insisting that their government annex Herat, and warning Britain to keep away. But there were other restraining influences, besides Abdur Rahman, at work behind the scenes. The fact was that it was in neither side's interest to go to war over Pandjeh, although Herat was another matter. This time, moreover, the Russians could see that if they advanced any further the British were prepared to fight, even with the Liberals in power. Throughout the crisis, a line was kept open between Lord Granville, the British Foreign Secretary, and Giers. Gradually calm was restored. Pandjeh, it was agreed, should be neutralised until its future could be decided by all three powers. Until then Russian troops would withdraw a short distance from the village. It was further agreed that negotiations over the frontier should commence as soon as possible. In the meantime, the immediate threat of war having faded, both the Royal Navy and British troops in India were stood down.

The Joint Afghan Boundary Commission now commenced its work, which was to drag on, with numerous disagreements, until the summer of 1887, when the protocols for the settlement of all except the eastern part of the frontier were finally signed. Under these the Russians retained Pandjeh, which they exchanged with Abdur Rahman for a strategic pass lying further west which he and his British advisers were anxious to control. But once again the Russians had got more or less what they wanted (even if their generals were opposed to the restraints imposed on them by a frontier), showing themselves to be the masters of the *fait accompli*. Very roughly the new frontier followed the line originally agreed in 1873, except for the southward bulge in the Pandjeh region which brought it much closer to Herat. War, nevertheless, had been averted. Moreover, the Russians had been shown, by the vigour of Britain's response, that any further move towards Herat would be taken as a declaration of war. Even so, many commentators were far from convinced that any of this would halt the Russian advance for long. Yet history was to prove them wrong. Almost a century would pass before Russian troops and tanks crossed the Oxus into Afghanistan in the winter of 1979.

But further to the east, in the Pamir region, the frontier had still to be fixed. It was to this desolate region, where today Afghanistan and Pakistan share a border, that the focus of the Great Game was now to switch, as for the next ten years Britain and Russia manoeuvred against one another for military and political ascendancy. There was another development, though, which was to make for a further change in the rules of the game. During the Pandjeh crisis, depending upon one's point of view, Gladstone's government had displayed 'consummate statecraft, lamentable vacillation, or abject surrender' – as one commentator put it. Many of the British electorate evidently judged it to be the latter, especially as it came so soon after Gordon's death at Khartoum, which was widely blamed on the government. As a result, in August 1886, the Tories swept back into office under Lord Salisbury, a man intensely interested in India's defence.

*   *   *

Thanks largely to courageous travellers like George Hayward and Robert Shaw, the British had been aware for some time of the vulnerability of the passes leading across the Pamirs, the Hindu Kush and the Karakorams into northern India. Even so, despite the pioneering journeys of a few such individuals, and the brief reconnaissance of Sir Douglas Forsyth's party in 1874, very little was known militarily about India's far north, where it merged with Afghanistan and China. Yet already Russian explorers, invariably soldiers, were busy mapping and probing well south of the Oxus in this vast no-man's-land, while at least one of their generals was reported to have drawn up plans for invading Kashmir via the Pamirs. To remedy this deficiency, in the summer of 1885 a British military survey party was dispatched to the region to explore and map a large swathe of terrain stretching from Chitral in the west to Hunza and beyond in the east. One of its most urgent tasks was to explore the passes leading northwards towards the upper Oxus, and settle once and for all the worrying question of whether or not they represented a threat to India's defence.

Leading the party was Colonel William Lockhart, a highly regarded officer from MacGregor's Intelligence Department, who was eventually destined to become Commander-in-Chief of India's armed forces. Accompanying him were three other officers, five native surveyors and a military escort. During the remainder of that year and in the first few months of the next, they were to map 12,000 square miles of previously unsurveyed territory beyond India's northern frontiers. In a lengthy report written on his return, Lockhart argued that earlier fears attached to the region, especially to the Baroghil Pass, were exaggerated, although a secondary Russian thrust might be directed across the Pamirs in support of a full-scale invasion via the Khyber and Bolan. But because the Pamir passes were closed every winter by snow, while in summer the numerous rivers became raging torrents, only during the short spring and autumn would the region be vulnerable. Even then a military road would first have to be built if a sizeable force, including artillery and other heavy equipment and supplies, was employed. A more likely strategy, Lockhart thought, would be for four small, highly mobile units to be used.

Lockhart's initial study of the passes leading northwards suggested that such a force would very likely come via Chitral. In a region entirely without roads or railways, it would take some time to get British troops to the spot, and then they might well find themselves fighting the Chitralis as well as the Russians. With the Viceroy's full approval, therefore, Lockhart had signed a defensive agreement with Chitral's ageing ruler, Aman-al-Mulk, a man once suspected of complicity in Hayward's murder. In return for a generous subsidy, plus a guarantee that the throne would always remain in his family's possession, the ruler undertook to unleash his fierce tribesmen against an advancing Russian force until British troops could come to their assistance.

This reconnaissance by Lockhart was not the only forward move ordered at this time by Lord Dufferin. For the fall of the Liberal government at home had lifted the taboo on dispatching officers and politicals on missions beyond India's frontiers. One area the Viceroy was particularly anxious about was Sinkiang, where the Russians appeared to have stolen a considerable march on the British. Under the Treaty of St Petersburg, which had restored Kuldja, or Ili, to China, the latter had agreed to the Russians having a consul in Kashgar. The man chosen by St Petersburg to fill this post was a formidable individual named Nikolai Petrovsky. A militant Anglophobe, he had vowed at all costs to keep the British out of Sinkiang, both politically and commercially. During the three years he had been there, by sheer force of character he had already made himself virtual ruler of Kashgar, intimidating Chinese officials and terrorising the Muslim population. The Chinese, only too aware that the nearest Russian garrisons lay just across the frontier, went in perpetual fear of annexation by St Petersburg – something which the Russian consul was not averse to threatening them with. They were most careful in their dealings with him never to cause him offence, or to give the Russians any other excuse for wresting Kashgar from them. Petrovsky's hand was considerably strengthened by the fact that there was no British representative there. He had the field to himself, and fully intended to keep it that way.

Lord Dufferin was determined to end Petrovsky's monopoly in Kashgar before it spread throughout the whole of Sinkiang. For a start the Viceroy wished to obtain for Indian merchants the right to trade with Sinkiang on equal terms with their Russian rivals. Although the market was a far smaller one than had once been believed, it was dominated by cheap but shoddy Russian goods, there being no alternative. Dufferin also wanted to see a permanent Indian government official stationed there. Ostensibly his function would be to safeguard the interests of British-Indian subjects living in Sinkiang, many of them Hindu money-lenders and their families. His real role, though, would be to keep a close eye on Petrovsky, and to report back on his and other Russian activities in the region. At present this was done unofficially by an enterprising young Scottish trader named Andrew Dalgleish, who travelled regularly between Leh and Kashgar. However, the Viceroy wanted to see this put on a firmer footing.

The man chosen by Dufferin for the task of trying to secure for Britain equal rights with Russia in Kashgar was an experienced political officer and Central Asian traveller with the somewhat curious name of Ney Elias. Currently he was serving as the Indian government's representative at Leh, where for six years he had been engaged in gathering political and other intelligence from travellers arriving from all parts of Central Asia, especially from Kashgar and Yarkand. Dalgleish was one of his principal and most reliable sources. The British Legation in Peking was asked by the Viceroy to obtain diplomatic accreditation for Elias, and to arrange for him to be received in Kashgar by a senior Chinese official with whom he could conduct discussions on both British representation and trading rights there. To Dufferin's intense annoyance, however, the Chinese refused his request, arguing that the volume of trade between India and Sinkiang was too small to justify a special treaty or arrangement of any kind. Nonetheless, they agreed to grant Elias a passport, although this gave him no diplomatic status. There were two possible explanations for this rebuff. One was that Peking was still smarting from Britain's attempts, during Yakub Beg's years as Sinkiang's ruler, to ally herself with him. The other was that the scheming Petrovsky, with his usual mixture of threats and bribes, was leaning hard on the Chinese to keep Elias out.

Despite this setback to his plans, the Viceroy ordered Elias to proceed, even without diplomatic accreditation, for he might at least be able to discover at first hand something of what was going on across the Karakorams, and what threat this might represent to British India. But even before he left Leh, a second piece of bad news reached Elias from Kashgar. The Chinese authorities had ordered Dalgleish to leave, pointing out that he had no passport. Previously they had turned a blind eye to this, and had always welcomed him. He told Elias that he was pretty certain that the Russian consul was behind his expulsion. If so, it certainly did not bode well for Elias's own prospects. And so it turned out, for he was to get no further than Yarkand. Although he was received there by a guard of honour of sorts, Elias found the Amban, or senior Chinese official, openly hostile. Barred, despite his passport, from proceeding to Kashgar, Elias quickly saw that any hopes of his negotiating what the Viceroy wanted were in vain. He also learned of a third possible reason for the obstructiveness of the Chinese. At one time they would have welcomed a British presence in Kashgar to counter the powerful influence of Petrovsky. But now, unnerved by the painful experience of having one bullying Westerner in their midst, they had no wish to saddle themselves with another.

Although his mission had proved abortive, Elias was not a man to return empty-handed from Yarkand, using the opportunity to check at first hand on various political and military matters, news of which normally reached him via often dubious sources in the bazaars of Ladakh. The Viceroy had been hoping, for example, that in the event of a Russian advance into Sinkiang, or even the eastern Pamirs, there might be some kind of military co-operation between Britain and China to halt this. Indian Army officers, it was thought, might be used as advisers, or perhaps even to command Chinese units. One glance, though, at the guard of honour which had lined the way as he rode into Yarkand, together with subsequent observations, showed Elias the hopelessness of this. Ill-armed, poorly trained and undisciplined, the troops slouched, chatted, joked, ate fruit and commentated loudly on the 'foreign devil' as he passed by. 'These are the people', Elias noted with exasperation in his diary, 'we are asked to ally ourselves with against the Russians. Ye Gods!'

But the tasks which Elias had been set were not yet over. It was the Viceroy's hope that he would be able, on his return to India, to travel via the eastern Pamirs and upper Oxus, including regions lying beyond those explored and mapped by Lockhart's party. Having little interest themselves in this godforsaken area, where Russia, Afghanistan and Kashmir merged with their own territories, the Chinese raised no objection. In addition to surveying this previously unexplored (except by the Russians) terrain, Elias had been asked to discover all he could about the locally recognised frontiers there, whether Russian, Chinese, Afghan or merely tribal. Finally, he was to examine the worrying gap, formed of undemarcated and as yet unclaimed lands, known to lie between the easternmost part of Afghanistan and the westernmost part of Sinkiang. Its existence had first been reported by Sir Douglas Forsyth following his mission to the court of Yakub Beg, and subsequent reconnaissance, twelve years earlier. India's defence chiefs had hoped that the Russians would not spot it until a way could be found of sealing it against an invader.

Elias's task, much of it undertaken in the middle of winter, took him seventeen months. During this time, although dogged by illness, he covered 3,000 miles and explored no fewer than forty passes. His conclusion, like that of Lockhart, was that the Russians were unlikely to launch a full-scale invasion across a region incapable of supporting a large body of men. Political penetration, however, was another matter, and this he saw as the principal threat posed by the Russians in this far northern region. As for the vulnerable gap between the Afghan and

Chinese frontiers, he recommended that the two powers should be persuaded to join their frontiers up, thereby making any Russian incursions an act of violation. Thus far, Elias and Lockhart were broadly in agreement. However, on the question of how best to keep the Russians out of Chitral, the soldier and the political differed strongly. Elias considered the Chitrali ruler, with whom Lockhart had just signed a treaty, to be totally untrustworthy, and certainly not to be relied upon if faced by Russian blandishments. 'No guarantee given by an irresponsible barbarian of this kind could ever be effective,' Elias warned. The only way to prevent Britain's new ally from selling out to the Russians, he suggested, would be to garrison troops on his southern border, so that the threat from behind would be greater than that from in front. Such differences of opinion between the Viceroy's military and political staffs were a familiar theme of the Great Game, there being little love lost between the two. But of more immediate concern than Chitral to India's defence chiefs at that moment was the Transcaspian Railway. With its obvious capacity for transporting troops and artillery, this was being extended eastwards by Russian engineers at an alarming rate.

*   *   *

Work on this line had begun in 1880 on the orders of General Skobelev when he was preparing for his advance on Geok-Tepe. He had originally envisaged it merely as a means of moving ammunition and other supplies across the desert from the Caspian port of Krasnovodsk. It was intended to be no more than a light, narrow-gauge track, along which heavy equipment could be hauled by traction engine, or even by camels, and which could be dragged forward as the force advanced. This had very soon been dropped, however, for a more ambitious and permanent rail link. One hundred miles of standard track from European Russia was shipped across the Caspian, and a special railway battalion, commanded by a general, was formed to lay it. In the event, Skobelev moved faster than the railway builders, and he stormed Geok-Tepe without waiting for them. But the railway had continued to creep forward as the neighbouring tribes were pacified, reaching Merv only a year after its capitulation to Lieutenant Alikhanov. The ensuing threat of war with Britain over Pandjeh led to the formation of a second railway battalion, and a rapid increase in the line's rate of advance. By the middle of 1888, it had reached Bokhara and Samarkand, and work on the final leg of its journey to Tashkent had begun.

Among the first to sound the alarm over the new Russian railway, and the strategic threat it posed to India, was Charles Marvin. In 1882, when the line had still not progressed very far eastwards, and long before the Pandjeh crisis, he had warned of the railway's threat, and particularly of the Russians seizing Herat and then consolidating their position there by extending the line to it. This, he argued, could be completed by Russian military engineers in a few short months. Since then the threat to Herat had been lifted following the Afghan boundary settlement. Even so, in the event of hostilities at some future date, the nearest Russian railhead was considerably closer to Herat than the nearest British one. Indeed, a few years later, not long after Marvin's death, the Russians were to close the gap even further, by advancing their rail network southwards to well below Pandjeh.

The glaring inadequacy of India's frontier communications, particularly its roads and railways, was now beginning to dawn on Calcutta and London. Foremost of those calling for Russia's railway encirclement of northern India and Afghanistan to be matched by a similar construction programme within India's frontiers was General Roberts, Commander-in-Chief of its armed forces. Following a thorough study made by him on the spot, he argued that India's defence budget, which was always tight, would be better spent on enabling commanders to rush troops to a threatened sector of the frontier, than on building forts and entrenchments which might never have to be defended. 'We must have roads, and we must have railways,' he wrote in a secret report to the Viceroy. 'They cannot be made at short notice, and every rupee spent upon them now will repay us tenfold hereafter . . . There are no better civilisers than roads and railways, and although some of those recommended to be made may never be required for military purposes, they will be of the greatest assistance to the civil power in the administration of the country.' In the longer term, if Abdur Rahman could be persuaded to agree, Roberts favoured the extension of the railway into Afghanistan, with lines to Jalalabad and Kandahar, and the stationing of British troops there. Without this, Roberts believed, the Russians would gradually occupy the whole of Afghanistan, absorbing it bit by bit as they already had Pandjeh. And when Abdur Rahman died, St Petersburg was likely to take every advantage of the ensuing power struggle.

But even extending the railway up to the Afghan frontier was to prove difficult, for not every member of the India Council was persuaded of the need for such heavy expenditure. Several years later, despite continuous pressure from the military, there were still fewer than fifty miles of track in the frontier region, although the road network was improved. To force through the expansion in railways, roads and telegraphs which Roberts deemed vital for India's defence called for someone at the very top who was not only convinced of the long-term Russian threat but who also possessed the power and determination to sweep aside all obstacles and objections. And such an individual had yet to occupy Government House. However, at around this time, the man who was destined to achieve precisely that was travelling eastwards across Russian Central Asia at a steady fifteen miles an hour on the very railway which was causing so much concern to Roberts and his fellow generals.

*　　*　　*

The Honourable George Nathaniel Curzon, then a young and ambitious Tory backbencher, had set out for Central Asia in the summer of 1888 determined to see for himself what the Russians were really up to there, and to try to fathom their intentions towards British India. Already, at the age of 29, he had set his sights on one day becoming Viceroy. Turning his back on the London social scene, this aristocratic and eligible bachelor took a train across Europe to St Petersburg and Moscow, whose political mood he first wished to gauge, before heading south into the Caucasus. From Baku he caught the ageing paddle-steamer and sometime troopship, the *Prince Bariatinski*, across the Caspian to Krasnovodsk. It was here that Curzon's personal reconnaissance of Central Asia, not to mention his lifelong passion for it, really began. For he now set off eastwards across the desert by the new Russian railway whose operations he was so keen to examine. His eventual destination was Tashkent, the nerve-centre of all Russian military operations in Central Asia, but the route took him via Geok-Tepe, Ashkhabad, Merv, Bokhara and Samarkand. At first, for nearly 300 miles, the line ran parallel, and close, to the Persian frontier. Because of its capacity for carrying troops and artillery, Curzon later observed, the railway represented to the Shah 'a sword of Damocles perpetually suspended above his head'. Further east, where it curved northwards from Merv in the direction of Bokhara, it served as a similar reminder of the Russian military presence to Afghanistan and British India.

The journey to Samarkand, where the line currently ended, normally took three days and three nights. But Curzon broke the 900-mile run more than once, catching the next train onwards when he had seen all he wanted to. As he travelled, he filled his notebooks with everything he could gather about the railway itself and the oasis-towns along the route. When it came to discussing rolling-stock – in other words the railway's capacity for transporting troops and equipment – he found the Russians particularly tight-lipped. Indeed, apart from what he could observe with his own eyes, information was difficult to come by. 'It is as hard to extract accurate statistics ... from a Russian', he complained, 'as to squeeze juice from a peach-stone.' The authorities were perfectly aware of who he was, however, and it would have been surprising if they had not warned railway officials and others not to discuss certain matters with him. Nonetheless, Curzon was able to gather sufficient material on the workings of the Transcaspian Railway, and its strategic significance to British India, to fill a 478-page narrative entitled *Russia in Central Asia and the Anglo-Russian Question*.

The first halt of note was at Geok-Tepe, where eight years earlier Skobelev's men had blasted their way into the massive

Turcoman stronghold and slaughtered so many of the fleeing inhabitants. As the train approached the barren spot from across the desert, Curzon could see the ruined fortress, its mud walls nearly three miles in circumference and pitted with shell holes. He also saw the huge breach which Skobelev's engineers had blown in it, and through which his infantry had stormed. The train halted at Geok-Tepe station, built only sixty yards from the ghostly fortress, just long enough for Curzon to explore parts of it. 'The bones of camels, and sometimes of men,' he wrote, 'may still be seen lying within the desolate enclosure, and for long after the assault it was impossible to ride over the plain without one's horse-hooves crushing into human skulls.' In the distance he could see the hills from whose vantage-point Edmund O'Donovan of the *Daily News* had witnessed the flight of the defeated Turcomans across the plain.

Ancient Merv, once known throughout Central Asia as the 'Queen of the World', proved disappointing, having lost all traces of its former glory. Four years of Russian occupation had stripped it of any romance, and reduced it to just another small garrison town, with shops selling cheap Russian goods and a club where a dance was held once a week. The once greatly feared Turcomans had been thoroughly tamed, and Curzon saw a number of Russia's erstwhile enemies sporting the Tsar's uniform as officers in his service. 'I do not think that any sight could have impressed me more profoundly with the completeness of Russia's conquest', he wrote, 'than the spectacle of these men, only eight years ago the bitter and determined enemies of Russia on the battlefield, but now wearing her uniform, standing high in her service, and crossing to Europe to salute as their sovereign the Great White Czar.'

From Merv the train toiled all day across the bleak solitude of the Karakum desert – 'the sorriest waste that ever met the human eye', Curzon called it – before coming to the great wooden bridge which carried it across the Oxus. Even today few foreigners have ever set eyes on this river, so remote is its course. Certainly the experience was not lost on Curzon, who wrote: 'There in the moonlight gleamed before us the broad bosom of the mighty river that from the glaciers of the Pamir rolls its 1,500 miles of current down to the Aral Sea.' He found himself haunted, moreover, by Matthew Arnold's poem *Sohrab and Rustum*, which tells the story of the legendary Persian warrior who, by a dreadful mistake, slays his own son on the banks of the Oxus. As the train inched its way across the creaking structure, taking a full fifteen minutes to reach the far side, Curzon broke off from such musings to record in his notebook that it rested on more than 3,000 wooden piles, was over 2,000 yards long, and had taken 103 days to construct. He also learned that a permanent iron bridge, costing £2 million, was expected to replace it before long.

Both Bokhara and Samarkand came fully up to Curzon's expectations. Few non-Russians had ever seen these fabled Silk Road cities, still redolent with romance and mystery, and Curzon was to devote many pages in his book to describing their dazzling mosques, tombs and other celebrated monuments. In Bokhara, where he remained for some days, he was accommodated, as a British VIP, at what the Russians officially called their embassy. For St Petersburg still maintained the fiction that the Emir was an independent ruler and not a vassal of the Tsar's. In the city itself the only Russian presence, therefore, was the ambassador, together with a small escort and staff. However, only ten miles away, as if to remind the Emir of his position, a Russian garrison was stationed, ostensibly to protect the railway.

It was in Bokhara that nearly half a century earlier Conolly and Stoddart had been brutally put to death in the great square before the Ark, as the citadel was called. 'Somewhere in this pile of buildings', Curzon wrote, 'was the horrible hole, or bug-pit, into which Stoddart and Conolly were thrown.' He was assured that this had long ago been sealed up, but when he tried to enter the Ark to see for himself he was turned back by a crowd of natives who gesticulated him away. In view of the tales he heard of prisoners being held in the innermost parts of the Ark, 'chained to each other by iron collars ... so that they could neither stand, nor turn, nor scarcely move', Curzon strongly suspected that the verminous pit was still in use. Certainly other barbaric methods of punishment were practised in the holy city. There was, for example, the notorious Minaret of Death. From the top of this, malefactors –

including murderers, thieves and forgers – were regularly pushed to their deaths. 'The execution', Curzon reported, 'is fixed for a bazaar day, when the adjoining streets and the square at the base of the tower are crowded with people. The public crier proclaims aloud the guilt of the condemned man and the avenging justice of the sovereign. The culprit is then hurled from the summit and, spinning through the air, is dashed to pieces on the hard ground at the base.' To humour the Emir and the religious authorities, the Russians had interfered as little as possible with the people's customs and traditions, although slavery had been stamped out. To annex the Emirate formally, however, would have meant needless expense and trouble. As it was, Curzon observed, 'Russia can do in Bokhara what she pleases'.

In Samarkand, where the railway then ended, he found no such pretence of independence, although the Russians had repeatedly declared their intention of returning the city and its fertile lands to the Emir of Bokhara, from whom they had seized it. 'It is unnecessary to say', Curzon wrote, 'that there was never the slightest intention of carrying out such an engagement.' Only a Russian diplomat, he added sardonically, could have given such an undertaking, while only a British one would have believed him. Among the signs suggesting permanent Russian occupation were the large and pretentious governor's residence, standing in its own park, the new Orthodox church, and the carefully planned European quarter lying at a comfortable distance from the noise and squalor of the old city.

When not pursuing his other enquiries, Curzon spent much time wandering among Samarkand's many architectural treasures, their dazzling blue tiles now rapidly crumbling away. Like today's tourists, more than a century later, he stood in awe in the mighty Registan, gazing up at the surrounding buildings, which include some of the finest architecture in Central Asia, if not anywhere. Even in its then derelict state, Curzon judged it to be 'the noblest public square in the world', while Samarkand itself he described as 'the wonder of the Asiatic continent'. He chided the Russians for doing nothing to preserve its great monuments for future generations, something which happily has since been put right. From Samarkand, using that peculiarly Russian means of transport, the springless, horse-drawn *tarantass*, Curzon reached Tashkent by the post road in thirty uncomfortable hours. But the discomforts were soon forgotten amid the civilised amenities of Government House, where he stayed with the Governor-General, a successor to the formidable Kaufman, who had died six years earlier and is buried in Tashkent.

Curzon was now at the very heart of the Tsar's vast Central Asian empire – a unique position from which to try to fathom Russian intentions towards India. During his stay in Tashkent, which he found to be one huge armed camp ruled entirely by the military, he took every opportunity to try to ascertain the views of senior officers, including his host, on Russia's long-term ambitions in Asia. He was not surprised to discover their mood to be distinctly bellicose, especially towards Britain. He was aware, however, that not too much significance should be attached to this. 'Where the ruling class is entirely military,' he observed, 'and where promotion is slow, it would be strange if war, the sole available avenue to distinction, were not popular.' Tashkent, he reminded his readers, had long served as a refuge for those 'of damaged reputations and shattered fortunes, whose only hope of recovery lay in the chances afforded on the battlefield'. Indeed, shortly before his arrival, promising rumours had been circulating the garrison of an impending invasion of Afghanistan. On the frontier such dreams helped to keep men sane.

Curzon returned to London by the route along which he had come, and at once sat down to write his book. He was forced to concede that Russian rule had brought considerable benefits to the Muslim peoples of Central Asia, while the new railway would serve to hasten the region's economic development. But the existence of the Transcaspian line had dramatically altered the strategic balance in the region. Previously, Russian armies advancing towards India had faced the almost insuperable task of moving large bodies of troops, artillery and other heavy equipment across vast distances and nightmarish terrain. When the final 200-mile stretch of the railway, linking Samarkand and Tashkent, was completed, it would enable St Petersburg to concentrate as many as 100,000 troops on the Persian or Afghan frontiers. These could be drawn from as far away as the Caucasus and Siberia. Curzon was convinced that the full significance of the railway had been gravely underestimated in Britain. 'This railway', he wrote to a friend, 'makes them prodigiously strong. And they mean business.'

He was not of the belief that their remorseless advance across Central Asia was part of some grand design, or in fulfilment (as some still thought) of Peter the Great's supposed deathbed command. 'In the absence of any physical obstacle,' he wrote, 'and in the presence of any enemy ... who understood no diplomatic logic but defeat, Russia was as much compelled to go forward as the earth is to go round the sun.' But while the prospect of invading India may not have been the original motive for their advance towards it, Curzon believed that the numerous plans worked out by their generals showed that 'for an entire century the possibility of striking at India through Central Asia has been present in the minds of Russian statesmen.' He concluded that although neither Russian statesmen nor generals dreamed of the *conquest* of India, 'they do most seriously contemplate the invasion of India, and that with a very definite purpose which many of them are candid enough to avow'. Their real objective was not Calcutta but Constantinople. 'To keep England quiet in Europe by keeping her employed in Asia,' he declared, 'That, briefly put, is the sum and substance of Russian policy.'

Others had said it before. However, what made it significant this time was that within ten years the man who uttered it was to realise his ambition by becoming, at the age of 39, the Viceroy of India. Even so, that was still a long way off. But his was not the only promising career taking shape at that time in what Curzon called 'the Central Asian game'. For just back from a secret reconnaissance of Sinkiang was a young Indian Army officer whose exploits were before long to thrill a whole generation of Englishmen.

· 33 ·

Where Three Empires
Meet

Moulded in what Curzon later termed 'the frontier school of character', Lieutenant Francis Younghusband of the 1st King's Dragoon Guards seemed to possess all the virtues required by a romantic hero of those times. Indeed he might almost have been a model for such John Buchan heroes as Richard Hannay and Sandy Arbuthnot – men who pitted themselves single-handed and in lonely places against those threatening the British Empire. Born into a military family at Murree, a hill-station on the North-West Frontier, he was commissioned in 1882, aged 19, and sent to join his regiment, then serving in India. Early in his career he was spotted by his superiors as a natural for intelligence work, and while still in his twenties he carried out a number of successful reconnaissances on and beyond the frontier. Such activities, however, were in his blood, for he was the nephew of that earlier player in the Great Game, Robert Shaw, whose career he had dreamed since boyhood of emulating. In the event, he was destined to eclipse it. By the age of 28 he would be a veteran of the game, sharing the confidences of men in high places with whom few subalterns ever came into contact. His secret work made him privy to the latest intelligence reaching India on Russian moves to the far north, while it was his boast that he knew General MacGregor's *Defence of India*, then the bible of the forward school, by heart.

The great Asian journey from which Lieutenant Younghusband had just returned when Curzon was making his more leisurely one by railway, was a 1,200-mile crossing of China from east to west by a route never before attempted by a European. It had happened almost by chance. In the spring of 1877, after travelling through Manchuria on leave (in reality in pursuit of intelligence), he found himself in Peking at the same moment as Colonel Mark Bell, VC, his immediate chief. Bell was about to set out on an immense journey of his own across China. His object was to try to ascertain whether its Manchu rulers would be able to withstand a Russian invasion. Younghusband at once asked the colonel if he might accompany him on his mission. Bell refused, arguing that this was a waste of valuable manpower. It would be far better, he suggested, if Younghusband returned to India across China, but by a different route. This would avoid duplication of effort, and enable them to gain between them a more complete picture of the country's military capabilities. On his return, Younghusband could then present a separate report on his own findings and conclusions.

It was a generous offer, and Younghusband needed no second bidding. With that, Bell set out, leaving Younghusband to seek the necessary extension to his leave by telegraphing to India. Approval was granted by the Viceroy himself, and on April 4, 1887, the young officer rode out of Peking on the first leg of his long march westwards across China's deserts and mountains. It was to take him seven months and to end with a dramatic winter crossing of the then unexplored Mustagh Pass, leading over the Karakorams – a formidable achievement for someone ill-equipped for climbing, and with no previous mountaineering experience. The valuable information he brought back delighted his chiefs. Ostensibly the purpose of his journey was purely geographical, and on his return to India he was granted a further three months' leave by General Roberts, the Commander-in-Chief, so that he could travel to London and lecture on the scientific results of his journey to the august Royal Geographical Society. Elected its youngest ever member, at 24, he was not long afterwards awarded its highly coveted gold medal. At an age when most young officers were regarded by senior officers with ill-disguised disdain, Francis Younghusband was already accepted by those who mattered as a member of the Great Game élite.

During the next few years he was to be kept extremely busy. The Tsar's generals had begun to show an alarming interest in that lofty no-man's-land where the Hindu Kush, Pamirs, Karakorams and Himalayas converged, and where three great empires – those of Britain, Russia and China – met. Russian military surveyors and explorers like Colonel Nikolai Prejevalsky were probing further and further into the still largely unmapped regions around the upper Oxus, and even into northern Tibet. In 1888, one Russian explorer had got as far south as the remote, mountain-girt kingdom of Hunza, which the British regarded as lying within their sphere of influence, and well outside that of Russia. The next year another Russian explorer, the formidable Captain Gromchevsky, had the temerity to enter Hunza accompanied by a six-man Cossack escort. He was reported to have been cordially received by the ruler, and to have promised to return the following year with some interesting proposals from St Petersburg. To British officers stationed on the frontier, and their masters in Calcutta, it looked as though the long feared Russian penetration of the passes had now begun.

Not long afterwards it was learned that three travellers, all believed to be Russians, had crossed the highly sensitive Baroghil Pass and entered Chitral after a gruelling journey. The ruler, now on the British payroll, had the men seized and sent under escort to Simla, where they were interviewed in person by Lord Dufferin, the Viceroy. To everyone's relief it turned out that they were not Russians but French, led by the well-known explorer Gabriel Bonvalot. Indeed, their account of their misadventures, including the loss of their horses and baggage, was listened to with some satisfaction by the British. The Frenchmen had made their crossing in the spring, when the passes were supposedly at their most vulnerable, yet they had very nearly come to grief. The severe hardships they had encountered were a welcome foretaste of what Russian troops might expect. Nonetheless, the British were beginning to feel increasingly uneasy at the prospect of Russian political penetration of the region – especially of officers like Gromchevsky seeking to establish friendly relations with the rulers of the small northern states lying in the path of their advancing armies. Kipling made use of this theme in his classic spy story *Kim*, in which Tsarist agents posing as hunters are sent to infiltrate and suborn the 'five kingdoms of the north'. John Buchan used it, too, in his now little-known Great Game novel, *The Half-Hearted*, written a year earlier, in 1901. In this the hero dies a lonely death in the Hunza region, defending with his rifle and a large boulder a secret pass which the Russians have discovered and are swarming through.

In response to the (real-life) Russian moves in the ill-guarded far north, the Viceroy took a number of urgent steps to counter any threat of infiltration or other interference – at least until the Pamir region boundaries had been agreed with Russia, Afghanistan and China. He dispatched to Gilgit, at the northern extremity of the Maharajah of Kashmir's domains, an experienced political officer. This was Colonel Algernon Durand, whose brother, Sir Mortimer Durand, was Foreign Secretary to the Government of India. From this safe and friendly vantage-point he was to monitor any Russian movements to the north, and at the same time to try to establish good relations with local rulers there. Simultaneously the Viceroy announced the establishment of a new, 20,000-strong force, which was to be contributed by the Indian princes and others possessing private armies. Known as Imperial Service troops, these were intended primarily for the defence of India's frontiers. Finally General Roberts, the Commander-in-Chief, visited Kashmir in person to advise the Maharajah on how best to strengthen and modernise his armed forces. It was thus hoped that the latter would be able to hold the passes against the Russians until help could arrive in the form of Imperial Service troops or Indian Army units.

More immediately, though, there was the problem of Captain Gromchevsky, known to be skulking somewhere in the Pamirs, and said to be planning to return to Hunza shortly to renew his acquaintance, made the previous year, with its ruler. And that was not the only worry involving Hunza. For years, using a secret pass known only to themselves, raiders from Hunza had been plundering the caravans which plied the lonely trail across the mountains between Leh and Yarkand.

Not only was this strangling what little traffic there was in British goods, but, much more disturbing to India's defence chiefs, if armed raiders could slip in and out of Hunza that way, so too could the Russians. The secret pass, it was decided in Calcutta, had to be located. And who better to attempt this than Lieutenant – recently promoted to Captain – Francis Younghusband? 'The game', Colonel Durand noted at Gilgit with satisfaction, 'has begun'.

*　　*　　*

In the summer of 1889, Younghusband received a telegram ordering him to Simla, the headquarters of the Intelligence Department, to be briefed in person by the Foreign Secretary, Sir Mortimer Durand. It could hardly have come at a better moment, for he had just had turned down a request to be allowed to visit Lhasa – on which Russian military explorers were known to have set their sights – disguised as a Yarkandi trader. One reason for this refusal was the news that another lone traveller, the enterprising Scottish trader Andrew Dalgleish, had been brutally hacked to death while on his way to Yarkand. For his new mission, which would take him past the spot where Dalgleish had been murdered, Younghusband was to be accompanied by an escort of six Gurkhas and a party of Kashmiri soldiers from Leh. In addition to locating the secret pass used by the Hunza raiders, he was to visit the capital and warn their ruler that the British government was no longer prepared to tolerate such activities against innocent traders, many of whom were the Empress of India's subjects, carrying British goods. He was also to warn him off having anything to do with the Russians.

Younghusband and his party left Leh on August 8, 1889, heading northwards across the Karakoram Pass towards the remote village of Shahidula. Here, at 12,000 feet, lived many of the traders who plied the Leh–Yarkand caravan route and suffered at the hands of the raiders. From them Younghusband hoped to learn the whereabouts of the secret pass – the mysterious Shimshal – leading westwards into Hunza. It was his plan to block it by posting his Kashmiri troops there, before entering Hunza himself for his audience with its ruler. Fifteen days after leaving Leh, Younghusband and his party reached the village, a bleak spot consisting of a dilapidated fort and some nomadic tents in which the traders lived. From their chief, Younghusband learned that appeals to the Chinese authorities for protection against the Hunzas had fallen on deaf ears. Peking, it was clear, had no wish to encourage trade between India and Sinkiang, especially in tea, since it threatened their own trade. Although the village, nominally anyway, lay in Chinese territory, its chief offered to transfer his allegiance to the British government if it would protect them. Explaining that he was not empowered to accept this offer, Younghusband nonetheless promised to refer it to the Viceroy. However, there was one thing which he could do for them he told the chief, and that was to station a detachment of well-armed Kashmiri troops in the pass, which would help to curb the activities of the raiders. Furthermore, he had instructions from his government to enter Hunza and convey a warning to its ruler of the serious consequences for himself if the raids continued.

The Shimshal Pass, Younghusband learned from the villagers, was dominated by a fort currently occupied by the raiders. Colonel Durand, based at Gilgit, had been instructed by Calcutta to advise the ruler of Hunza — officially allied to Britain's friend the Maharajah of Kashmir by treaty – that Younghusband was on his way. But the latter had no way of being sure that the raiders, in their stronghold, had been warned of this. Nonetheless, as there was no other way of entering Hunza from where he was, Younghusband decided to proceed directly to the fortress and see what sort of a reception he and his Gurkhas got. Led by the village chief in person, they set off up the narrow, precipitous pass towards the fortress. It was a desolate landscape. 'A fitter place for a robbers' den could not be imagined,' Younghusband wrote, observing that, apart from the villagers, they had not seen another soul for forty-one days. Suddenly, high above them, they spotted the raiders' lair. It was perched dramatically at the top of a near-vertical cliff, and was known locally as 'the Gateway to Hunza'. Leaving the rest of his Gurkhas to give covering fire in case they had to withdraw rapidly, he and two others, together with an interpreter, crossed the still frozen river at the bottom of the gorge and began to ascend the zig-zag pathway winding up the precipitous rock face. It was a bold move, but Younghusband knew that audacity usually paid off in Central Asia.

On nearing the top they were surprised to find the gates of the fortress wide open. For a moment it seemed as though it was unoccupied. But this was merely an old Hunza trick. As Younghusband and his two Gurkhas cautiously approached the gates, these were suddenly slammed shut from within. In a split-second, Younghusband wrote, 'the whole wall was lined with the wildest-looking men, shouting loudly and pointing their matchlocks at us from only fifty feet above.' For a moment he feared that they were about to be mown down. However, although the clamour continued, the men on the wall held their fire. Trying to make himself heard above the uproar, Younghusband shouted back: '*Bi Adam!*' *Bi Adam!*' – 'One man! One man!' He held aloft one finger, indicating to those inside that they should send out a man to parley with him.

After an interval the gates opened and two men emerged and made their way over to where Younghusband and his men were waiting. He explained to them that he was on his way to Hunza to see their ruler. The two men returned to the fort to report to their chiefs, and shortly afterwards Younghusband and his companions were invited inside. It was almost the last thing the British officer ever did, for as he rode through the gateway a man suddenly stepped forward and seized his bridle. It looked like treachery, and the Gurkhas, although greatly outnumbered, raised their rifles, ready to sell their lives dearly. Their commanding officer, Younghusband learned later, had told them that if they allowed any harm to befall him they need not bother to return, as the honour of the regiment was at stake. Fortunately, however, it turned out to be a somewhat bizarre joke, albeit an extremely perilous one. The man who had grabbed his bridle began to shake with laughter, and soon everyone, including Younghusband, was joining in. They had merely wanted to test the Englishman's courage, and see how he would react. It transpired, moreover, that they had been expecting him all along, but had no very precise orders as to how to receive him. The ice had now been broken, though, and after this the two sides got on famously, sitting round a huge fire which the raiders had built inside the fort. 'And when the little Gurkhas produced some tobacco,' Younghusband recalled afterwards, 'and with their customary grins offered it to their hosts, they were completely won.'

Younghusband had begun to suspect that the raiders were in fact not there entirely of their own choice, but were acting on the orders of the ruler. 'They had all the risks and danger,' he wrote, 'while their chief kept all the profits to himself. They raided because they were ordered to raid, and would have been killed if they refused.' He explained to them therefore that his government was angry that the traders, who included some of its own subjects carrying goods from India, were being robbed, murdered or sold into slavery. He had been sent to discuss with their ruler how the raiding could be brought to an end. The men listened intently to all he had to say, but told him nervously that the question of raiding was not one they could discuss, which appeared to confirm Younghusband's suspicions.

The next day, escorted by seven of their new Hunza friends, Younghusband and his Gurkhas set off up the pass, whose secrets Calcutta was so anxious to have explored and mapped. They had proceeded only about eight miles when they were met by an emissary sent by the ruler, Safdar Ali. He bore a letter welcoming Younghusband to Hunza, and informing him that he was free to travel anywhere he wished in the kingdom. When he had seen everything he wanted, the ruler hoped that Younghusband would visit the capital as his official guest. Younghusband gave the emissary gifts, including a fine Kashmir shawl, to take back to his master, together with a note thanking him for his generous offer of hospitality. The latter, Younghusband added, he would be delighted to accept shortly, when he had seen a little more of his renowned kingdom. For not only did Younghusband wish to explore the Shimshal Pass, but he also needed to discover whether there were any other passes in the region through which Russian troops or agents might enter Hunza.

Not long afterwards a second messenger arrived, this time bearing mail which had been carried by a runner all the way from India. It included an urgent note from Younghusband's chiefs in Simla warning him that the Russian agent Gromchevsky was back in the area, making his way southwards towards Ladakh. Younghusband was instructed to keep a close eye on the Russian's movements. This was followed a few days later by a third messenger, this time bearing a letter from Captain Gromchevsky himself. The Russian, who had somehow learned of his presence in the region, cordially invited his English rival to dine with him in his camp. Younghusband needed no urging, and the next morning set out for where the Russian had pitched his tents.

'As I rode up,' he wrote later, 'a tall, fine-looking bearded man in Russian uniform came out to meet me.' Gromchevsky, who had an escort of seven Cossacks, greeted his guest warmly, and that night, after the British officer had pitched his own camp nearby, the two men dined together. 'The dinner was a very substantial meal,' Younghusband reported, 'and the Russian plied me generously with vodka.' As the latter flowed freely, and the meal progressed, Gromchevsky talked more and more frankly about the rivalry between their two nations in Asia. He told Younghusband that the Russian army, both officers and men, thought of little else but the coming invasion of India. To make his point, he called his Cossacks over to the tent and asked them whether they would like to march against India. They answered him with a rousing cheer, swearing that there was nothing they would like more. It was much what Burnaby, Curzon and others had reported after returning from the Tsar's Central Asian domains.

Younghusband could not help noticing that on Gromchevsky's map the worrying Pamir 'gap' was picked out in red. There could be no hiding the fact that the Russians were aware of the existence of this stretch of no-man's-land where Russia, China, Afghanistan and British India met. The British, Gromchevsky insisted, had invited Russian hostility towards themselves in Asia because they persisted in meddling in the Black Sea and Balkan region, and in trying to thwart what St Petersburg believed to be its legitimate interests there. When Russia did attack India – and Gromchevsky thought it only a question of time – then it would not involve a small force, as British strategists seemed to think, but one anything up to 400,000 strong. Younghusband was aware that British experts, including MacGregor, judged 100,000 to be the maximum number of men who could be deployed in this type of terrain. How, he asked Gromchevsky, were they proposing to transport and supply so vast an army once they had left the railway behind and found themselves crossing the great mountain barriers which protected northern India? His host replied that the Russian soldier was a stoical individual who went where he was told, and did not trouble his head too much about transport and supplies. He looked upon his commander as a child did its father, and if at the end of a gruelling day's march or fighting he found neither water nor food he simply did without, carrying on cheerfully until he dropped.

The debate next turned to the question of Afghanistan, the linchpin of India's defence, and whose side it would take if there was a war over India. The British, Gromchevsky declared, should long ago have annexed it for their own protection, together with the other, lesser kingdoms of the region. Their preferred use of subsidies and treaties, he argued, offered no safeguard against treachery. The Emir Abdur Rahman, he claimed, was no real friend of Britain's. In the event of war the promise of a share of India's riches would prove too much for him, and he would throw in his lot with the Russians, among whom he had lived for so long before coming to the throne. Furthermore, India's native population would rise against its British oppressors if help seemed at hand. But that argument, Younghusband pointed out, was double-edged, for what was there to prevent the British from unleashing the Afghans and others against Russia's Central Asian territories, with the legendary treasures of Bokhara and Samarkand as the prizes? The Tsar's vast possessions to the east of the Caspian were highly vulnerable. While India's weakest points were strongly fortified, Russia's were not. And so the argument continued over the vodka and blinis until far into the night. It was conducted with more bombast perhaps than science, but nonetheless with much good humour. What made it memorable, however, was the fact that this was the first time that rival players had met face to face on the frontier while actively engaged in the Great Game. It would not be the last time.

Two days later, after sharing Younghusband's remaining bottle of brandy, the two men prepared to go their own ways. Before parting, the Gurkhas saluted the Russian officer by presenting arms. The latter, Younghusband reported 'was quite taken aback' by the precision of their drill, for his own Cossacks, sturdy as they were, were irregulars. On being congratulated by the Russian, the Gurkha havildar, or sergeant, whispered anxiously to Younghusband that he should inform the towering Gromchevsky that they were unusually small and that most Gurkhas were even taller than he was. The Russian was immensely amused when Younghusband told him of this ingenuous attempt to deceive him. After ordering his Cossacks to 'carry swords', their equivalent of presenting arms, Gromchevsky bade Younghusband a cordial farewell, saying he hoped that one day they would meet again – in peace at St Petersburg, or in war on the frontier. He added, Younghusband recalled, 'that in either case I might be sure of a warm welcome'.

While his British rival continued his exploration of the region prior to his meeting with the ruler of Hunza, Gromchevsky and his Cossacks set off southwards towards Ladakh and Kashmir. He hoped to obtain permission to spend the coming winter there from the British Resident, who had effective control over such matters. Younghusband had already warned him that the British would never allow a uniformed Russian officer and a party of seven armed Cossacks to enter Ladakh. Although he did not say as much, this was even more unlikely in the case of an officer known to be heavily engaged in the political game. However, this did not discourage Gromchevsky, a man used to getting his own way. While waiting at Shahidula for an answer from the British, the Russian decided to make good use of the time by heading eastwards and exploring the remote Ladakh-Tibetan border region. He failed, though, to foresee the severity of the winter at this altitude, and the reconnaissance was to prove catastrophic. His party lost all its ponies and baggage, while the Cossacks, stricken by frostbite and hunger, were finally too weak even to carry their own rifles. They were lucky to get back to Shahidula alive, and months later Gromchevsky was said still to be on crutches.

Although Gromchevsky himself blamed the British for his misfortunes by denying him permission to enter Ladakh, a certain amount of mystery surrounds the incident. Indeed, it appears that Younghusband may well have been partially responsible for the near-tragedy. In a confidential note written at the time he reported that he had conspired with his newly acquired friends at Shahidula to steer the Russians out of harm's way by encouraging them to embark on this perilous journey. Perhaps he had not fully realised its dangers, although he frankly admitted that he aimed to 'cause extreme hardship and loss to the party'. In his several subsequent accounts of his meeting with Gromchevsky, he significantly makes no mention of this. It goes to show, however, that the Great Game was not always the gentlemanly affair it is sometimes portrayed as being.

Many years later, after the Russian Revolution, Younghusband was surprised to receive from out of the blue a letter from his old rival. Accompanying it was a book he had written about his Central Asian adventures. Under the old regime, he told Younghusband, he had risen to the rank of Lieutenant-General and received numerous honours and high appointments. But in 1917 the Bolsheviks had seized all his property and thrown him into prison in Siberia. Thanks to the Japanese he had managed to escape and flee to Poland, from where his family had originally come. The contrast between the two men's situations could hardly have been more stark. Younghusband, then at the height of his renown, had been knighted by his sovereign, was President of the Royal Geographical Society, and was laden with awards and honours. The unfortunate Gromchevsky was now destitute, alone in the world, and so ill that he could not leave his bed. Not long afterwards Younghusband learned that the man who had once struck fear into the hearts of India's defence chiefs was dead. However, at the time which concerns us here, Gromchevsky still loomed large on the frontier.

*   *   *

After leaving his Russian rival, and completing his own exploration of the region, Younghusband crossed the mountains into Hunza for his meeting with Safdar Ali, the ruler. It was an unusually tricky and responsible task for a junior officer to be entrusted with, but he was held in exceptional esteem by his superiors in Calcutta and Simla. On his approach to the village of Gulmit, where the ruler awaited him, a thirteen-gun salute was fired (a court official having first been sent ahead to warn him not to be frightened), followed by the deafening beating of ceremonial drums. In the middle of the village, through which the tourist buses now race on their way up the Karakoram Highway to Kashgar, a large marquee had been erected. It was, in fact, an earlier gift from the British government. As Younghusband, who had changed into his scarlet, full-dress Dragoon Guards uniform, approached it, Safdar Ali emerged to meet him. This was the man, Younghusband knew, who in order to secure the throne had murdered both his father and mother, and tossed two of his brothers over a precipice. It was he who was responsible for the murderous attacks on the caravans. And now – the ultimate sin in Calcutta's eyes – he had begun to intrigue with the Russians on India's very doorstep.

Inside the marquee, in silent rows beside the throne, squatted the leading men of Hunza, all eyeing the newcomer with the keenest interest. Younghusband was quick to see that, apart from the throne, there was no other chair. Clearly he too was expected to kneel respectfully at Safdar Ali's feet. Keeping the courtesies going while both parties were still standing, Younghusband hastily dispatched one of his Gurkhas, now all dressed in smart green regimentals, to fetch his own camp chair. When this arrived, he had it placed alongside the ruler's throne. He wanted it made plain from the start that he was there as the representative of the greatest sovereign on earth, and that he expected to be treated as such. Indeed, as Younghusband soon discovered, the principal difficulty in dealing with Safdar Ali arose from his misconception of his own importance. 'He was under the impression', Younghusband reported, 'that the Empress of India, the Czar of Russia and the Emperor of China were chiefs of neighbouring tribes.'

When envoys such as himself and Gromchevsky arrived at his court, he took it that they were competing for his friendship. In fact, by and large, this was what they were doing. Younghusband, however, was determined to cut him down to size, although aware of the danger of pushing him further into the arms of the Russians.

For a start, Younghusband let it be known to Safdar Ali that the British government was aware of his secret dealings with Gromchevsky. No doubt this point would have been made even more forcefully had it been realised just how far these had gone. For not long afterwards it reached the ears of Colonel Durand in Gilgit that Safdar Ali had agreed with Gromchevsky to allow the Russians to establish a military outpost in Hunza and to train his troops, although this never appears to have been confirmed. However, it was the permanent task of Durand, rather than that of Younghusband, to foil such intrigues. Younghusband's primary concern was to stop the caravan raiding, so that trade with Sinkiang could be expanded. Safdar Ali admitted freely that the raids were carried out on his instructions. His kingdom, he said, as his visitor must have seen for himself, 'was nothing but stones and ice', possessing little pasturage or cultivable land. Raiding was its only source of revenue. If the British wanted this stopped, then they must compensate him with a subsidy, or his people would have nothing to eat. The only flaw in this argument, Younghusband observed, was that Safdar Ali took most of the proceeds of the raids for himself – just as he would do with any subsidy.

Younghusband told the ruler that the British government would never agree to subsidise him for ceasing to rob its caravans. 'I said that the Queen was not in the habit of paying blackmail,' Younghusband wrote, 'that I had left soldiers for the protection of the trade route, and that he might see for himself how much revenue he would get now from a raid.' To Younghusband's surprise, Safdar Ali shook with laughter at this, congratulating his visitor on his candour. With the aim of impressing on his Hunza host just how useless his own matchlock-wielding soldiers would be against modern, European-trained infantry, Younghusband decided to lay on a demonstration of his Gurkhas' fire-power. He ordered them to discharge a volley at a rock 700 yards away across the valley (though not before Safdar Ali had first demanded that a cordon of his own men should surround him). When everyone was ready, Younghusband gave the order to fire. The Gurkhas' six bullets struck the rock simultaneously, and impressively close together. 'This', noted Younghusband, 'caused quite a sensation.'

But it did not have the effect on Safdar Ali that he had hoped. Entering into this new game with gusto, the ruler decided that shooting at rocks was tame. Spotting a man descending the cliff path opposite, he asked Younghusband to order his Gurkhas to fire at him. Younghusband laughed, but explained that he could not do this as they would almost certainly hit the man. 'But what does it matter if they do?' the ruler declared. 'After all, he belongs to me.' This merely confirmed the highly unfavourable opinion of Safdar Ali that Younghusband had acquired during their discussions. 'I knew that he was a cur at heart,' he wrote afterwards, 'and unworthy of ruling so fine a race as the people of Hunza.' By now Younghusband had had more than enough of him, as he became increasingly arrogant and demanding. He had delivered his warnings, and was anxious to head south before the snow closed the passes, trapping him and his men in Hunza for the winter. The British party left for Gilgit on November 23, with Younghusband hardly on speaking terms with Safdar Ali. It is conceivable that the latter, persuaded by Gromchevsky that he enjoyed Russian protection, felt safe in pursuing his demands to the limit. If so, he would not be the first Asiatic ruler to put such misplaced trust in an emissary of the Tsar.

Younghusband and his men reached India shortly before Christmas 1889. During nearly five months away they had crossed seventeen passes, including two previously unknown ones, and found several, including the Shimshal, to be easily accessible to determined parties and to individuals like Gromchevsky. Younghusband now had to part from his six Gurkhas, whom he had come so much to admire. The sergeant and corporal were on his strong recommendation promoted, while the others were financially rewarded. 'Tears were in their eyes', he wrote, 'as we said goodbye.' He next settled down to prepare a detailed confidential report on the results of his journey. In this he said he saw no alternative to military action against the wayward Safdar Ali, lest he invite the Russians into Hunza. His other concern was over how to close the fifty-mile-wide Pamir gap, through which Gromchevsky had entered Hunza from the north the previous year. At present there was little to prevent the Russians from planting their flag there and claiming it as theirs. But if the frontiers of Afghanistan and Chinese Central Asia could be made to meet, thus eliminating this stretch of no-man's-land altogether, then any such danger would be forestalled. Younghusband suggested that he should be sent to investigate the gap, and then try to resolve the problem with senior Chinese officials in Kashgar. To his delight the proposal met with Calcutta's approval, for the authorities there were becoming increasingly nervous about the security of the northern states. In the summer of 1890 he once again left for the frontier. He was to be away for more than a year, and before it was over he was to be caught up in a confrontation with the Russians which was very nearly to lead to a war in Central Asia.

Younghusband was accompanied this time by a young Chinese-speaking colleague from the Political Department named George Macartney. Aged 24, he was two years Younghusband's junior. Like him, he was destined to become a legend in the Great Game. For the next two months they were to travel together through the whole of the Pamir region, filling in the blanks on the British maps, and trying to discover to whom the few small tribes living there owed their allegiance, whether to Afghanistan or to China. More often than not, in this inhospitable realm where neither Afghan nor Chinese trod, they owed allegiance to no one. At times, even in autumn, it was so cold that the water froze in the basins in the two men's tents, while dwelling at a high altitude for long periods caused them to suffer badly from physical weakness and lassitude, or what today would be called mountain sickness. Younghusband remarked that he did not envy Russian troops sent to occupy this region for any length of time. The temptation, he added, would be for them to continue southwards in search of an easier climate.

In November, as further work in the Pamirs became impossible, he and Macartney rode down into Kashgar. Relations
between London and Peking had improved considerably since
Ney Elias's ill-fated mission five years earlier, and the Chinese
had agreed to allow the two men to winter in Kashgar, even
providing them with a residence. Known as Chini-Bagh, or
Chinese Garden, this was eventually to become the British
consulate, and an important listening-post during the closing
years of the Anglo-Russian struggle. It was also to be George
Macartney's home for the next twenty-six years. But if the
Chinese were willing to forget Britain's flirtation with Yakub
Beg and welcome the two Englishmen, there was one man
in Kashgar who looked upon their arrival with the utmost
suspicion. This was Nikolai Petrovsky, the Russian consul,
who for eight years had successfully kept the British out of
Sinkiang.

If Petrovsky felt hostility towards the two newcomers, he
was careful to conceal it. His sole concern was to discover what
they were up to, and what they were discussing with Chinese
officials. He entertained them generously, and discoursed
expansively on the roles of their respective governments in
Asia, in the evident if vain hope of drawing them out. 'He was
agreeable enough company in a place where there was no
other,' wrote Younghusband of him. 'But he was the type of
Russian diplomatic agent that we had to fight hard against.'
He shocked Younghusband with his complete lack of scruples,
admitting frankly that he lied whenever it suited him, and
declaring that he thought the British naïve for not doing likewise. However, Younghusband and Macartney found him
singularly well-informed, not only about Sinkiang but also
about British India. He had a network of spies, moreover,
whose tentacles reached everywhere.

Younghusband had instructions to try to persuade the
Chinese to send troops into the Pamirs to claim and occupy
the undemarcated lands lying immediately to the west of their
present outposts, thereby filling part, at least, of the gap. So
well did the talks appear to be going that he felt able to report
to his superiors that the gap would very soon be closed, and
that the Russians would then be unable to advance through the

Pamirs 'without committing an act of very open aggression'. He had naturally hoped to keep his discussions with the Chinese secret. But he had not reckoned with Petrovsky. Just as Younghusband could have outmanoeuvred his Russian adversary in the Pamir passes, here, on his own home ground, Petrovsky was master. Later he was to boast that everything that passed between Younghusband and the Taotai, the Chinese governor, was immediately communicated to him. This was supported many years later by N. A. Khalfin, the Soviet historian of this period, who claimed that Petrovsky had discovered what the British were up to, and had alerted St Petersburg accordingly. What followed next certainly appears to bear this out.

In July 1891, while Younghusband and Macartney were still in Kashgar, reports began to reach London that the Russians were planning to send a force to the Pamirs to annex them. These were strongly denied by the Russian Foreign Minister, who declared them to be totally false. However, only a week later he admitted that a detachment of troops was on its way to the Pamirs 'to note and report what the Chinese and Afghans are doing in these regions'. Very soon rumours of the Russian move reached the ears of Younghusband and Macartney. Although they thoroughly distrusted Petrovsky, they had no suspicion of what he had been up to behind their backs. Nonetheless Younghusband at once set out for the Pamirs to try to discover the truth, leaving Macartney behind in Kashgar to keep an eye on things there, not least on Petrovsky. But as we know, they were too late. Younghusband quickly found out that the rumours were true. The Russians had got there before the troops the Chinese had promised to send. A force of 400 Cossacks had entered the Pamir gap from the north with orders to seize it in the name of the Tsar. On August 13, at a lonely spot high up in the Pamirs, Younghusband came face to face with the invaders.

· 34 ·

Flashpoint in the High Pamirs

'As I looked out of the doors of my tent,' Francis Younghusband wrote afterwards, 'I saw some twenty Cossacks with six officers riding by, and the Russian flag carried in front.' Apart from the new arrivals, and his own small party, the place was uninhabited. Situated 150 miles south of the Russian frontier, and known to the wandering tribes of the region as Bozai Gumbaz, it belonged, so far as the British were concerned, to Afghanistan. Younghusband at once sent one of his men, bearing his card, to where the Russians had pitched their camp, half a mile away, and invited their officers over for refreshments. They were not long in taking up the invitation, for they were clearly keen to know what he was up to. Shortly afterwards, led by a colonel wearing the coveted Order of St George, the nearest Tsarist equivalent to the Victoria Cross, several of their officers rode across to Younghusband's modest camp.

The meeting was friendly, even convivial. The Englishman had no vodka to offer his guests, only Russian wine which he had brought from Kashgar. He told the colonel, who was called Yanov, that he had heard that the Russians were annexing the whole of the Pamir region. Explaining that he was anxious not to cause unnecessary alarm in Calcutta and London by reporting mere native rumours on so serious a matter, he asked Yanov whether in fact this was true. The Russian's answer was unequivocal. 'He took out a map,' Younghusband recounted, 'and showed me, marked in green, a large area extending right

down to our Indian watershed.' It included much which was
unquestionably Afghan or Chinese territory. Yet all of it was
now being claimed as belonging to the Tsar. Carefully avoiding
discussion of the implications of the move, Younghusband
merely remarked to Yanov that the Russians were 'opening
their mouths pretty wide'. At this the colonel laughed, but
added that it was 'just a beginning'. The Russians remained
in Younghusband's camp for about an hour before excusing
themselves, saying that they had their own camp to prepare.
On leaving, however, Colonel Yanov invited Younghusband
to join them for dinner that evening.

Once more it was a cordial affair, with the seven officers
squatting round a tablecloth spread in the centre of one of the
low-slung Russian tents, which at night three of them shared.
Although Younghusband noted with satisfaction that his own
tent, with its bed, table and chair, was considerably larger and
more comfortable than those of his rivals, the Russians did not
stint themselves when it came to eating. 'There followed a
dinner,' he wrote, 'which for its excellence astonished me
quite as much as my camp arrangements had astonished the
Russians.' There were soups and stews 'such as native servants
from India never seem able to imitate', together with relishes,
sauces and fresh vegetables. The latter were an unbelievable
luxury to Younghusband, just as they are today to travellers in
Pakistan's far north. Besides the inevitable vodka, there was a
choice of wines, followed by brandy.

Younghusband soon discovered why his hosts were so elated.
In addition to claiming the whole of the Pamir region for the
Tsar, they had that very moment 'returned from a raid across
the Indian watershed into Chitral territory', entering it by one
pass and leaving by another, mapping as they proceeded. This
was an area which India's defence chiefs regarded as lying
strictly within their sphere of influence. Yanov even expressed
surprise to Younghusband that the British had no representative of any kind in Chitral, in view of its strategic
importance to India, and seemed content to rely on a treaty
with its ruler. The Russian pointed out to his guest on the map
how they had ridden to the summit of the highly sensitive
Darkot Pass, and peered down into the Yasin valley, which led

by an easy route towards Gilgit. It was, Younghusband knew, enough to make the blood of British generals run cold. But that was not all, as Younghusband was soon to discover.

At midnight, after toasts had been drunk to Queen Victoria and Tsar Alexander, the party broke up. The Russian officers, including Colonel Yanov, insisted on escorting the young British captain back to his camp. There, after exchanging compliments and amid protestations of friendship, they parted. Early next morning the Russians struck camp, before heading northwards to join their main force and report on their encounter in this desolate spot with a British intelligence officer. Younghusband himself stayed on, for unknown to the Russians he was expecting to be joined shortly at Bozai Gumbaz by a colleague. This was Lieutenant Davison, an adventurous subaltern in the Leinsters, whom he had met in Kashgar and co-opted to investigate Russian moves further to the west. He needed to know what Davison had discovered before racing for Gilgit, the nearest British outpost, to report to his chiefs in India on the Russian incursion.

Three nights later, just as he was turning in, Younghusband was surprised to hear the clatter of hoofs in the distance. Peering out of his tent, he saw in the bright moonlight some thirty Cossacks drawn up in line. While he slipped into his clothes, he sent one of his men to ask what had brought them. The man returned to say that Colonel Yanov wished to speak to him urgently. Invited into Younghusband's tent, together with his adjutant, the Russian said that he had something disagreeable to tell his guest of a few days earlier. He had been given orders, he explained, to escort the British officer from what was now Russian territory. 'But I am not in Russian territory,' Younghusband protested, adding that Bozai Gumbaz belonged to Afghanistan. 'You may think this Afghan territory,' Yanov replied grimly, 'but we consider it Russian.' What if he refused to move, Younghusband asked. Then they would have to remove him by force, Yanov replied, looking extremely uncomfortable. 'Well, you have thirty Cossacks, and I am alone,' the Englishman told him, 'so I must do as you wish.' However, he would agree to leave only under the strongest protest, and would report the outrage to his government so that it could decide precisely what action to take.

The colonel thanked Younghusband for making his unpleasant task easier, and expressed his deep personal regret at having to carry out the order, particularly in view of the cordial relationship which they had established such a short time before. Younghusband assured the Russian that he would not hold it against him, but against those who had given this unlawful order. Meanwhile, having ridden so far, might not Yanov and his adjutant like something to eat? He would happily instruct his cook to produce some supper. Much moved by this gesture, the Russian colonel seized Younghusband in a bear hug, thanking him emotionally for the gracious way he had taken it all. It was, he declared, a most unpleasant task for one officer to have to act like this towards another in what was more properly a policeman's job. He had hoped, he added, to find the Englishman gone, which would have saved them both considerable embarrassment.

To show his appreciation to Younghusband, Yanov suggested that he might like to proceed to the frontier by himself, instead of being escorted there. There was one proviso, however. He had been given strict instructions by his superiors that Younghusband, whom they regarded as a trespasser, must leave via the Chinese frontier and not the Indian one. Furthermore, he must not use certain passes. The reason for these requirements was not entirely clear, though it was presumably to delay for as long as possible news of the Russian moves, not to mention his own expulsion. There may also have been an element of revenge in it for the earlier British refusal to allow Captain Gromchevsky to winter in Ladakh, and perhaps Younghusband's suspected role in the near disaster which had ensued. The British officer, who was quite confident that he would be able to discover passes unknown to the Russians, and therefore not on their list, undertook to abide by this, and signed a solemn statement to that effect.

It was now long past midnight, and the two Russians gratefully accepted Younghusband's offer of a meal, although they did not linger long over what must have been a somewhat awkward occasion. The next morning, as Younghusband prepared to leave for the Chinese frontier, Yanov came over to his camp to thank him again for accepting the situation with such grace, and bearing with him a haunch of venison as a parting present. But if the colonel's superiors had hoped to delay the news of Younghusband's expulsion by making him return by a roundabout route, they were to be disappointed. For within an hour of parting from the Russians, the British officer had dispatched one of his men post-haste to Gilgit with a detailed report of what had happened, as well as of the latest moves by St Petersburg on the Roof of the World. He now rode eastwards towards the Chinese frontier, intending to find his way home from there across one of the passes not on Colonel Yanov's proscribed list. He was in no hurry, though, and lingered on the Chinese frontier just north of Hunza, hoping to meet up with Lieutenant Davison, and meanwhile to monitor any further Russian moves. This was Great Game playing at its most enthralling, and the 28-year-old Younghusband was in his element.

Some days were to pass before Davison appeared. 'Away in the distance,' Younghusband wrote, 'I saw a horseman approaching dressed in the peaked cap and high boots of the Russians, and at first I thought that another Russian was going to honour me with a visit. This, however, proved to be Davison. He had been treated in an even more cavalier manner than I had, and had been marched back to Turkestan.' There he had been interrogated by the Russian governor in person, before being escorted to the Chinese frontier and released. His arrest and detention had, however, served one useful purpose. His captors, Younghusband noted, had taken him northwards by a route which no British officer or explorer had previously traversed. The two officers now made their way back to Gilgit across a pass whose existence was revealed to them by friendly shepherds. It was the last that Younghusband was to see of his friend, for Davison was to die of enteric fever during a subsequent reconnaissance. He was, Younghusband wrote afterwards, an officer of remarkable courage and determination, with 'all the makings of a great explorer'.

By now news of the incident had reached London, and in Whitehall frantic efforts were being made to hush it up while the government decided how best to deal with this latest

Russian forward move. Rumours soon began to reach Fleet Street via India, however, it even being reported in *The Times* that Younghusband had been killed in a clash with the intruders. This was hastily denied, but details of the Russians' high-handed behaviour towards two British officers on Afghan territory could no longer be kept quiet. Press, Parliament and public were incensed, and once again anti-Russian feelings hit fever pitch. Lord Rosebery, the Liberal peer, who was shortly to become Foreign Secretary, went so far as to describe Bozai Gumbaz, the barren spot where Younghusband had been intercepted by the Russians, as 'the Gibraltar of the Hindu Kush'. In India the Commander-in-Chief, General Roberts, told Younghusband he believed that the moment had come to strike the Russians. 'We are ready', he said, 'and they are not.' At the same time he ordered the mobilisation of a division of troops in case the Russian seizure of the Pamirs led to war.

Other hawks were quick to join the fray. 'The Russians have broken all treaty regulations with impunity so far,' wrote E. F. Knight, special correspondent of *The Times*, then travelling in Kashmir and Ladakh. 'By marching their troops into the territory of Chitral, a state under our protection and subsidised by the Indian Government, they have deliberately taken steps which are generally looked upon as equivalent to a declaration of war.' Were Britain to ignore such incursions into states which she guaranteed against foreign invasion, he warned, then 'the natives cannot but lose faith in us'. They would conclude that Russia was the stronger power, 'to which we are afraid to offer resistance'. Inevitably, therefore, they would turn towards the Russians. 'We must', he concluded, 'expect intrigue against us, if not more open hostility, as the result of our apathy.' His forebodings were seemingly confirmed by secret intelligence from Chitral. This suggested that the expulsion from Afghanistan of Younghusband had seriously undermined British prestige among the Chitralis, and that they were no longer to be trusted where the Russians were concerned. Similar doubts, as we have already seen, existed with regard to Safdar Ali, the ruler of Hunza, whose personal sympathies were known to lie with St Petersburg.

A strong protest over Russia's aggressive moves in the

Pamirs was delivered on Lord Salisbury's orders by the British ambassador at St Petersburg, the forthright Sir Robert Morier. In addition to challenging Russia's claims to the Pamirs, he demanded an outright apology for the illegal expulsion of Younghusband and Davison from the region, adding a warning that unless this was immediately forthcoming, 'the question would assume very grave international proportions'. The unexpected vehemence of the British response, coupled with the knowledge that a division of the Indian Army had been placed on a war footing at Quetta, had the Tsar and his ministers rattled. At home things were in poor shape. Much of Russia was in the grip of famine and serious political unrest, and consequently the economy was in no position to sustain a fullscale conflict with Britain. St Petersburg therefore decided with reluctance to back down. To the indignation of the military, it withdrew its troops and its claim to the Pamirs pending a permanent settlement of the frontier. Blame for the entire incident was pinned on the unfortunate Colonel Yanov, who was accused of greatly exceeding his orders by proclaiming the annexation of the Pamirs, and in expelling Younghusband. Only later did it become known that by way of compensation for acting as a scapegoat he had been presented with a gold ring by Tsar Alexander in person, and quietly promoted to general. Nonetheless, Britain had got her apology, and for the time being at least the Pamirs were clear of Russian troops.

The Russian military held to the view that the British had brought the crisis upon themselves. Their decision to annex the Pamirs, they insisted, had been forced upon them by a British government determined to break up their Central Asian empire. As evidence of this they cited General MacGregor's hawkish tome *The Defence of India*, supposedly secret, but a copy of which had somehow found its way into their hands and been translated into Russian. Indeed, as recently as 1987, a Russian scholar seized upon MacGregor's long-forgotten work to prove what he calls 'the age-old dreams of British strategists'. Leonid Mitrokhin, in his *Failure of Three Missions*, quotes MacGregor's view that Britain should 'dismember the Russian state into parts which would be unable to represent a danger to us for a long time'. In fact, if one turns to Mac-

Gregor's original text, it is quite evident that he advocated such a move *only* if the Russians attacked India – something that Mitrokhin and his Tsarist predecessors found it convenient to ignore, or which may even have been omitted from the St Petersburg translation.

But even if determined British action, and St Petersburg's fear of war, had this time forced the Russians to step back, the incursion by Yanov and his Cossacks to within a few hours' march of Chitral and Gilgit had given India's defence chiefs a nasty fright. If the past was anything to go by, the Russian military would perceive this as no more than a temporary reverse, and before long would once again begin to creep southwards into the Pamirs and eastern Hindu Kush in this unending game of Grandmother's Footsteps. While no one in Calcutta saw the Pamirs any longer as a suitable route for an all-out invasion of India, the presence there of hostile agents or small bodies of troops could, as one commentator put it, cause 'far-spreading mischief' in the event of war between the two powers. The answer, wrote Knight of *The Times*, was 'to lock the door on our side', which was precisely what the British now set out to do, beginning with Hunza, which was regarded as the most vulnerable of the small northern states. From that moment, as Britain went over to the offensive, Safdar Ali's fate was sealed.

The Viceroy did not have to look far for an excuse to remove him from his throne. For many months he had been giving trouble, in the evident belief that the Russians would come to his assistance if needed. Following the withdrawal of Younghusband's Kashmiri detachment from the head of the Shimshal Pass, which became uninhabitable in winter, he had resumed his raids on the Leh–Yarkand caravan route, not to mention on other neighbouring communities. He had even been unwise enough to seize and sell into slavery a Kashmiri subject from a village lying well within Kashmir. Furthermore, he had let it be widely known that he regarded the British, who tried to curb his excesses, as foes, and the Russians and Chinese as his friends. Then, in the spring of 1891, shortly before Yanov's appearance in the Pamirs to the north of Hunza, Colonel Durand at Gilgit learned that Safdar Ali was planning to seize the Kashmiri fort at Chalt, which he had long coveted. By sending men to cut the rope bridges on the Hunza side, and reinforcing the Kashmiri garrison there, Durand was able to foil this, though it was clear that sooner or later Safdar Ali would try again, perhaps even with Russian help. As it was, he had managed to persuade the ruler of the small neighbouring state of Nagar to join forces with him against the meddlesome British and their Kashmiri clients.

In November 1891, amid great secrecy, a small force of Gurkhas and Kashmiri Imperial Service troops was assembled at Gilgit, under Colonel Durand's command, preparatory to marching northwards against Hunza and Nagar. While this was going on, the Kashmiris succeeded in capturing a Hunza spy sent by Safdar Ali to report on the strength of the British forces in Kashmir. Among other things, he revealed to his interrogators his master's ingenious new plan for surprising the garrison at Chalt. A number of men from Hunza, carrying loads on their backs to make them appear like coolies from Gilgit (whom they closely resembled), but with weapons hidden about them, were to seek shelter in the fort for the night. Once inside, they would fall upon the unsuspecting defenders, engaging them for long enough to allow Safdar Ali's troops, concealed nearby, to pour in after them.

Clearly it was time for Durand's force to get moving. It consisted of nearly 1,000 Gurkhas and Kashmiris, all regulars, and several hundred Pathan road-building troops. They were accompanied by a battery of mountain artillery, seven engineers and sixteen British officers. The going was so difficult in places that it took them more than a week to reach Chalt, only twenty miles north of Gilgit, and their forward base for operations in Hunza and Nagar. Here Durand received a bizarre missive from Safdar Ali, who by now had learned of the British advance towards his frontier. Declaring that Chalt was 'even more precious to us than the strings of our wives' pyjamas', he demanded that it be handed over to him. He warned Durand, moreover, that if the British entered Hunza they should be prepared to take on three nations – 'Hunza, Russia and China'. Already, he claimed, 'the manly Russians' had promised to come to his assistance against 'the womanly

British'. He added that he had given orders for Durand's head to be brought to him on a platter if he and his troops dared to enter Hunza. At the same time, George Macartney learned in Kashgar, Safdar Ali dispatched envoys to Petrovsky, the Russian consul, reminding him of Gromchevsky's promises of help. Similar pleas for arms and money were made to the Chinese governor.

On December 1, the British force crossed the Hunza river by an improvised bridge built by Durand's engineers, and headed eastwards towards Safdar Ali's mountain capital, today called Baltit, but then known simply as Hunza. Progress was slow, the columns having to ascend and descend the almost vertical sides of a succession of deep gorges. At the summits of these the enemy sharpshooters waited for them in *sangars*, or rock-built entrenchments, each of which had to be taken before the advance could safely continue. The first major obstacle to bar their way, however, was the formidable stone fortress at Nilt, belonging to the ruler of Nagar. With its massive walls and tiny loopholes, it was said, like so many Asiatic strongholds, to be impregnable. Certainly Durand's seven-pounder mountain guns made little impression on it, while his Gurkha marksmen found themselves unable to pick off the defenders behind their narrow slits. To add to Durand's difficulties, his only machine-gun kept jamming, while he himself was wounded, forcing him to hand over his command. But before doing so he gave orders for the main gate to be blown open by the sappers, led by Captain Fenton Aylmer. It was an extremely hazardous enterprise, singularly like the blasting of Ghazni's gates by Durand's father sixty years before. What followed, wrote E. F. Knight, who accompanied the expedition, 'will long be remembered as one of the most gallant things recorded in Indian warfare'.

Covered by heavy fire from the rest of the force, intended to keep the defenders back from their loopholes, Captain Aylmer, his Pathan orderly and two subalterns succeeded in reaching the fortress wall safely. Close behind them were 100 Gurkhas, ready to pour inside the moment the gate was destroyed. Then, as the subalterns with Aylmer emptied their revolvers into the loopholes at point-blank range, he and his orderly, both carrying explosive charges, dashed through a hail of fire to the foot of the main gate. There they placed their gun-cotton slabs, carefully covering them with stones to concentrate the effect. Finally, after igniting the fuse, both men withdrew hurriedly along the wall to a safe distance to await the explosion. None came. The fuse had gone out.

At that moment Aylmer was hit – shot in the leg at such close range that both his trousers and his leg were burnt by the powder. Nonetheless, he crawled back to the gate to try once more to light the fuse. Trimming it with his knife, he struck a match and after several attempts managed to re-ignite it. The defenders, fully aware of what he was up to, began to shower heavy stones down on him from above, one of which crushed his hand severely. Again Aylmer crept back along the wall to await the explosion. This time the fuse did not let him down. 'We heard a tremendous explosion above the din of guns and musketry, and perceived volumes of smoke rising high into the air,' wrote Knight. As the entire gateway disintegrated in a huge cloud of dust and rubble, the Gurkhas, led by the wounded Aylmer and the two subalterns, charged into the fort, where fierce hand-to-hand fighting began for its possession. At first the storming party found itself greatly outnumbered and hard-pressed, for amid the smoke and confusion of the explosion the main force failed to realise that the Gurkhas were inside, and kept up a heavy fire against the walls and loopholes. Realising that they would be slaughtered if the others delayed much longer, Lieutenant Boisragon, one of the subalterns, ran back to the ruined gateway to call for help, exposing himself to the fire of both friend and foe. His action was to save the day, for moments later the rest of the force charged into the fortress.

Knight had a grandstand view of what followed. On hearing the explosion, he had clambered to the top of a high ridge, from where he peered down into the smoke-filled interior of the fortress, 'spread out beneath us like a map'. He recounts in his book *Where Three Empires Meet*: 'In the narrow lanes there was a confusion of men, scarcely distinguishable from the dust and smoke, but in a moment we realised that fighting was going on within the fort.' It was clear, however, that those outside did not yet realise this. But then suddenly he and his companions heard cheer after cheer from below, in which they enthusiastically joined 'with what breath we had left in us after our long climb'. From their vantage-point they now saw the main body of troops pour through the gateway, putting the defenders to flight over the walls and through small, secret exits known only to them.

For the loss of just six British lives, against eighty or more enemy dead, Nilt the impregnable had fallen. Not long afterwards, Knight ran into Aylmer. Covered with blood, and supported by one of his men, *The Times* reporter found him 'as jolly as ever', despite the further wound he had received inside the fortress. 'When he set out for that gateway,' wrote Knight, 'he must have known that he was going to meet an almost certain death', adding that his gallantry had made a deep impression on both sides. One local chief, friendly to the British, who had witnessed the assault on the gate, declared to Knight afterwards: 'This is the fighting of giants, not of men.' It was a view evidently shared by the authorities at home, for both Captain Aylmer and Lieutenant Boisragon were later awarded the Victoria Cross. But despite their unexpected loss of Nilt, the enemy continued to harass and defy the British as they fought their way towards the Hunza capital. Finally, in the middle of December, the invaders found their way blocked by an obstacle even more formidable than the fortress at Nilt.

This time an entire mountainside had been turned by the enemy into a stronghold. Covered with *sangars*, manned by an estimated 4,000 men, it totally dominated the valley, 1,200 feet below, along which the British had to pass. To attempt to proceed up the valley without first driving the enemy from the heights would clearly be little short of suicide. Yet repeated reconnaissances failed to discover a route by which these positions could be approached. As at Nilt, something drastic was called for if the British were not to be forced to abandon the campaign and withdraw, which was utterly unthinkable. The solution came from an unexpected quarter. One night, at grave risk to his life, a Kashmiri sepoy succeeded in scaling the precipitous rock face leading up to the enemy positions without being detected by them. A skilled cragsman himself, he told his officers that he believed that a determined party of Gurkhas and other experienced climbers could reach the enemy by this route. It was so sheer in places, he reported, that the defenders would have difficulty in seeing, or firing down on, the ascending troops. A very careful examination was made of his suggested route through binoculars, after which it was decided to go ahead with this daring plan – if only because there appeared to be no alternative.

Arrangements for the assault went ahead amid the greatest possible secrecy, for inside the British camp, which included large numbers of locally hired bearers, were thought to be enemy spies. To make it appear that the expedition was pre-paring to withdraw, 200 Pathans, used principally for road-building and not essential to the operation, were ordered to start packing up. Meanwhile the attack was scheduled for the night of December 19. Chosen to lead the scaling party was Lieutenant John Manners Smith, a skilled mountaineer of 27, who had been seconded to the force from the Political Department. Only the fifty Gurkhas and fifty Kashmiris, each hand-picked, who were to accompany him were briefed on the perilous mission they were shortly to undertake. On the night of the attack, before the moon was up, the best marksmen among the remaining troops were moved as silently as possible to a vantage-point 500 yards away from, and overlooking, the enemy positions. The two seven-pounder mountain guns were also placed there under cover of darkness. At the same time the scaling party made its way noiselessly across the valley to some dead ground at the base of the cliff they were to ascend. As it was, by a happy coincidence the enemy had chosen that night for one of their periodic celebrations, the sounds of which effectively drowned any noise resulting from these various troop movements.

As dawn broke, the marksmen and gunners began to direct a steady fire on to the enemy *sangars* across the valley. This was concentrated on those positions from which the climbers below were most likely to be spotted. The moment they were detected, however, as they clung perilously to the rock face, this was to be greatly intensified. Otherwise Manners Smith and his 100-strong force would have little hope of survival, let alone of reaching their objectives. Half an hour after the firing commenced, the scaling party began its long and hazardous climb. 'From our ridge', wrote Knight, 'we could see the little stream of men gradually winding up, now turning to the right, now to the left, now going down for a little way when some insurmountable obstacle presented itself, to try again at some other point.' They looked, he added, very much like 'a scattered line of ants picking their way up a rugged wall'. At the front he could just make out Manners Smith, 'as active as a cat', scrambling ahead of his men. But then, 800 feet above the valley bottom, came a serious setback. Manners Smith halted. 'It was obvious to him,' wrote Knight, 'and still more so to us who could see the whole situation, that the precipice above him was absolutely inaccessible.' Somehow they had taken the wrong route. There was nothing else to do but to return to the starting point. Two hours had been wasted. Miraculously, however, the enemy had not yet spotted them.

Wasting no more time, Manners Smith scanned the rock face to see where they had gone wrong. Minutes later, unseen by the defenders, he semaphored back across the valley that he was going to make a fresh attempt. Hardly able to breathe, Knight and the rest of the force watched as once more the party began to work its way slowly upwards. This time the route proved right, and the climbers progressed uninterrupted. After what seemed like an eternity to their comrades across the valley, Manners Smith and a handful of the best climbers had got to within sixty yards of the nearest *sangars*. It was at this moment that the alarm was raised, and all hell was let loose. Someone, it appeared, who was friendly to the defenders, had seen what was going on from across the valley and had shouted a warning. Realising their danger, and disregarding the heavy fire which was concentrated against them, those in the *sangars* nearest to the cliff edge ran forward and began to rain heavy rocks down on the scaling party.

Several of the men were hit and seriously injured, though miraculously no one was swept into the abyss below. Fortunately the majority of the climbers had passed the points where they would have been most exposed to danger, and the boulders bounced harmlessly over their heads. By now

Manners Smith had been joined by the other subaltern in the scaling party. 'The two officers', wrote Knight, 'manoeuvred their men admirably, watching their opportunities, working their way from point to point with cool judgment between the avalanches, and slowly gaining the heights foot by foot.' Then, *The Times* man recounts, 'we saw Lieutenant Manners Smith make a sudden dash forward, reach the foot of the first *sangar*, clamber round to the right of it, and step on to the flat ground beside it.' Seconds later he was joined by the first of the Gurkhas and Kashmiris, their *kukris* and bayonets glinting in the winter sunlight. Forming into small parties, they began to move from *sangar* to *sangar*, entering them from behind and slaughtering their occupants. At first the defenders fought bravely, but then, realising that they stood no chance against these highly trained troops, they began to slip away, in ones and twos, from their positions. Soon this turned to wholesale panic, and the entire enemy force took to its heels. Many of the fugitives were picked off as they ran by the scaling party, or by the marksmen and gunners across the valley, leaving the mountainside strewn with dead and wounded.

The fall of their second stronghold, and the realisation that neither the Russians nor the Chinese were coming to their assistance, proved too much for the enemy. All along the route to the capital, which lay less than twenty miles ahead, they threw down their arms and surrendered, or made for their homes. For his conspicuous role in the victory, Manners Smith was later awarded the Victoria Cross, the third of the three-week campaign, while a number of sepoys received the Indian Order of Merit, the highest award for bravery then open to native troops. Meanwhile, in his great palace overlooking the capital, Safdar Ali was frantically packing up his treasures preparatory to flight. It was clear to him, too, that Grom-chevsky's promises had been empty ones. As the British advance guard, its progress slowed by the mountainous terrain, got closer to the capital, the ruler slipped away northwards, setting fire to village after village as he fled. The victors had expected to find his palace, in Knight's words, 'full of the spoil of a hundred plundered caravans'. But they were to be disappointed. Accompanied by his wives and children, and those of his entourage remaining loyal to him, he had taken almost everything of value with him, carried on the backs of 400 coolies, it was said. A thorough search of the palace did reveal, however, a secret arsenal hidden behind a false wall, containing Russian-made rifles. Also in the palace were Russian household goods, including samovars and prints, and a portrait of Tsar Alexander III. Among a massive correspondence, much of it unopened, with the Russian and Chinese authorities, were letters between Younghusband and Gilgit which his agents had intercepted during the 1891 Pamir crisis.

Most anxious to capture Safdar Ali, lest he try to rally support or attempt other mischief, the British hurriedly dispatched a party of horsemen after him, hoping to cut him off before he crossed the frontier into China, or even Russia. But somewhere in the snow-filled passes, whose secrets he knew better than his pursuers, he managed to give them the slip and escape into Sinkiang, where the Chinese governor of Kashgar reported his arrival to Macartney. Having placed Safdar Ali's more amenable half-brother on the throne, the British now had to decide what to do next. Should they stay on or withdraw? Fearing that to leave would be seen as weakness rather than magnanimity, they decided to stay. In addition to stationing a small garrison of Imperial Service troops there to keep out unwelcome intruders like Gromchevsky and Yanov, they appointed a permanent political officer to assist the new ruler with his decisions. To all intents and purposes Hunza and Nagar (whose elderly ruler had been allowed to remain on the throne) were part of British India. 'They have slammed the door in our face,' Giers, the Russian Foreign Minister, is reported to have complained indignantly on hearing the news.

For once the British had got there first. But any satisfaction, or peace of mind, which they might have gained over Hunza was to prove short-lived. Elsewhere in the extreme north the Russians were once more on the move. The military, it was becoming clear, had regained their ascendancy over the Foreign Ministry. Even Colonel Yanov, so recently carpeted by St Petersburg, was reported to be back in the Pamirs. By the summer of 1893 Russian troops had twice clashed with the

Afghans, and torn down a Chinese fort on territory they claimed as theirs. Although this time the Russians avoided a confrontation with the British, to both Durand in Gilgit and Macartney in Kashgar one thing appeared certain. Regardless of the consequences, and before the British could prepare any counter-moves, the Russians were planning to occupy the Pamirs. Little comfort could be expected from the Afghans or the Chinese, moreover, whose will to resist these Russian incursions was rapidly crumbling.

Even Gladstone, who had been returned to power at home following the Tory defeat in the 1892 general election, began to get anxious. 'Matters have now come to such a pass', warned Lord Rosebery, his Foreign Secretary and subsequent successor, 'that Her Majesty's Government cannot remain purely passive.' Gladstone's solution was to press St Petersburg to agree to a joint boundary commission, an idea which the Russians professed to welcome. However, as Rosebery warned, the military were clearly trying to delay any settlement of the frontier until they had got all they wanted. In other words, it was Pandjeh all over again. His warning was underlined by the news that the Russians had occupied Bozai Gumbaz, flashpoint of the previous Pamir crisis. But that was not all. A serious crisis had arisen in Chitral, which many strategists had long regarded as more vulnerable to Russian penetration than Hunza. Following the death of its ageing ruler, it had been plunged into turmoil as family rivals fought for the throne. As a result, Chitral was to have five successive rulers in three years.

Hitherto, the British had been content to rely on their treaty with Chitral to keep out any Cossacks or other undesirables. With Aman-ul-Mulk's death, however, the British were by no means confident that this arrangement would survive. That would depend upon which of his sixteen sons came out on top. In the meantime, or so some thought, there was a grave risk of the Cossacks filling the vacuum. 'With Russian posts on the Pamirs,' warned Durand from Gilgit, 'a Chitral in anarchy is too dangerous a neighbour for us, and too tempting a field for Russian intrigues and interferences to be tolerated.' Indeed, if the St Petersburg press was anything to go by, then the British had every reason for concern. Calling for a military highway to be built southwards across the Pamirs, and for the imperial Russian flag to be raised over the Pamir and Hindu Kush passes, the newspaper *Svet* demanded that Chitral be taken under the Tsar's 'protection'. Although conflicting sharply with what the Foreign Ministry was saying, it undoubtedly voiced the sympathies of every officer and man in the Russian army, and very likely those of the War Minister himself.

According to N. A. Khalfin, the Soviet historian of this period, the Tsar's ministers and advisers were at loggerheads over what action they should take in the Pamir region. They had become genuinely alarmed, he insists, over the activities of British politicals like Durand and Younghusband, and the annexation of Hunza and Nagar, although the return of a Liberal government offered, as always, some comfort. While the hawks, headed by the War Minister, urged the Tsar to take an aggressive stance, the doves, led by Giers, favoured a diplomatic solution, arguing that Russia's grave internal problems (the famine alone had cost half a million lives) ruled out any question of confrontation. And why quarrel with Britain now over territories which could always be seized in time of war? The British knew nothing of this, of course, and considering the bellicose tone of the Russian editorials, and St Petersburg's record of saying one thing and doing another, they could hardly be blamed for their disquiet.

Meanwhile, in Chitral itself, the struggle for the throne continued, getting bloodier at every turn. At first the British remained neutral, hoping to patronise the eventual winner. But very soon they found themselves in the thick of it. Getting out again was to prove a good deal more difficult.

· 35 ·

The Race for Chitral

Even today Chitral has lost little of its remoteness. In the great empty valleys surrounding it, the only sounds to be heard are the melancholy cry of the eagle, the occasional whine of a jeep, and the perpetual thunder of the glacier-fed torrents as they race through the precipitous gorges. But in the days of the Great Game, a more ominous sound sometimes met the traveller's ear – the crack of a matchlock. For this was a land where strangers were unwelcome, and into which Europeans did not venture except at the ruler's invitation, and then only with an armed escort.

Just getting there is still something of an adventure. From Gilgit, to the east, it can only be reached after a hair-raising, 200-mile drive by jeep, most of it in bottom gear, along a narrow track just one vehicle wide, and with sickening views of the valley floor hundreds of feet below. Even this route is often severed for days on end when sections of it break away and plunge into the abyss. The rewards are great, however, for the journey takes one through some of the most stupendous mountain scenery anywhere. In winter the road – if it can be so described – is closed, unless one is prepared to struggle waist deep through the snow which blocks the 12,000-foot Shandur Pass, the highest point on the route. The only other way, except by air, to reach Chitral is from the south, via Swat, along a road which cost 500 lives to construct. Even so, in winter, the telegraph poles are sometimes buried in snow to within a foot of the wires. But whichever way he comes, the traveller is in no doubt when he has reached his destination. For there, set dramatically on the bend of the river, is the great fortress of Chitral, once the palace of its rulers, and in which much of the action in this chapter occurred.

On the death of Aman-ul-Mulk in August 1892, the first of his heirs to seize the throne was his son Afzul, who happened to be in Chitral at the time, and who immediately set about murdering his numerous half-brothers lest they try to unseat him. But his principal rival was the real heir to the throne, his elder brother Nizam, who was away hunting in Yasin. He now set out with a large armed following in search of Nizam, intending to dispose of him also. Nizam was too quick for him, though, and fled to Gilgit where he sought British protection. This was granted, while the British authorities awaited the outcome of the struggle. At that moment a third contender entered the fray. He was the late ruler's brother Sher, who had long been living in exile in Kabul, as the guest of Abdur Rahman, who had a close interest in neighbouring Chitral. Encouraged by Abdur Rahman, who was anxious to see his own candidate on the throne, Sher now made his way secretly to the capital with a small band of supporters. There, by means of a trick, he lured Afzul to the gates of the fortress-palace, where he shot him dead. Thereupon, the Chitralis switched their loyalty to the new claimant to the throne, though not for very long.

On hearing in Gilgit of the death of his younger brother, Nizam immediately set out for Chitral to try to wrest his birthright from his uncle. In this he now enjoyed the support of the British who had by this time decided that they preferred him to Sher, or to anyone else. As he advanced westwards he was joined by large numbers of followers, including 1,200 Chitrali troops sent against him by Sher. Already, during the latter's brief reign, they had begun to see through his extravagant promises of houses, land, riches and beautiful wives for all. Seeing that his prospects of retaining the throne were hopeless, Sher fled hastily back into Afghanistan. On reaching the capital, the triumphant Nizam immediately proclaimed himself his father's rightful successor. His rule was officially recognised by the British, relieved to see their own man on the throne and stability once more restored to Chitral. Another door leading to India had been slammed in Russia's face.

Calcutta's relief was destined to be short-lived, however. Within a year Chitral had been plunged yet again into turmoil. This time the victim was Nizam himself, assassinated by his teenaged half-brother Amir while they were on a hunting trip together. Nizam had, in fact, wanted to dispose of Amir in time-honoured fashion, but had been dissuaded from doing so by the British. The reckless Amir now proclaimed himself Chitral's fourth new sovereign in little more than two years, a role for which he was hopelessly ill-equipped. At the same time he demanded immediate recognition by Calcutta via the political officer, Lieutenant Gurdon, who had been based in Chitral at Nizam's request. Aware that this would never be granted to Nizam's assassin, Gurdon played for time, declaring that only the Viceroy could make so important an announcement, and that he was awaiting his reply. Simultaneously he warned Gilgit that serious trouble could be expected when it dawned on Amir that retribution and not recognition would be forthcoming. Indeed, it was rumoured that he was already seeking allies against the British.

Fortunately, it was not to the Russians that he turned, but to his southern neighbour, Umra Khan, ruler of what today is called Swat. Word soon reached Gilgit that Amir's supposed new ally was preparing to advance into Chitral with an army of 3,000 Pathans. Ostensibly coming to Amir's assistance, he was, it was whispered, in fact intending to annex Chitral to his own kingdom. Whatever his motive, however, one thing was clear to the British. The door to northern India was once more dangerously ajar, if the Russians chose to take advantage of it. In Gilgit, the nearest British outpost, the senior British officer was now Major George Robertson, an army doctor turned political, who had succeeded Durand. Realising that Lieutenant Gurdon was in grave danger, as was the stability of this strategically crucial state, Robertson at once set out for Chitral with 400 troops, all he could muster. On reaching the capital he removed the feckless Amir from the throne, replacing him temporarily with his youngest brother, an intelligent boy of 12. At the same time he sent a stern warning to Umra Khan, ordering him and his troops to turn back. If he had not done so by April 1, 1895 – four weeks hence – a powerful British punitive force would advance northwards through his own domains from Peshawar and evict him from Chitrali territory. This force, he was advised, was already being mobilised in case it proved necessary.

It was at this moment that events took a turn for the worse for Robertson and his men. Quite unexpectedly, Sher returned to the fray from Afghanistan, this time as the unlikely ally of Umra Khan. The two men had agreed that if they succeeded in driving the British out of Chitral, they would divide the kingdom between them. Sher would occupy the throne, while Umra Khan would receive territories in the south which he had long coveted. Whether either of them intended to keep his word to the other is another question, but their combined armies represented a serious threat to Robertson's small force at Chitral. Seeing the danger, Robertson moved his troops into the fortress as the best place in which to withstand a siege. In so doing, he was to cause profound offence to the Chitralis, for the stronghold also served as the royal palace, harem and treasury. To see it overrun by European officers and their Kashmiri and Sikh troops was extremely humiliating. At first Robertson had enjoyed the support and sympathy of most Chitralis, who had no love for Umra Khan and his warlike Pathans, and certainly had no wish to be occupied by them. However, by commandeering the royal palace, he had forfeited their goodwill.

Hostilities began on March 3, when word reached the fortress that Sher was approaching Chitral with a large party of his supporters. As Robertson had little idea of the strength or capacity of the forces ranged against him, or of Sher's precise intentions, he decided to send out a reconnaissance party. Being a political officer himself, and not a professional soldier, he had placed Captain Colin Campbell in charge of the garrison's defences. Campbell, who led the party, gravely underestimated the strength of the advancing foe. After a fierce engagement, he and his Kashmiris were driven back into the fortress with heavy casualties. Campbell himself was badly wounded, while another officer subsequently died from his injuries, a Victoria Cross being awarded to the young army doctor who, under fierce fire, carried the mortally wounded man back to the fortress. In all, it had cost the British twenty-three lives and thirty-three wounded, an expensive way of gauging the enemy's strength, and a severe blow to the garrison's morale.

Nor was that all. Unknown to Robertson, a small party of Kashmiri troops led by two British subalterns was on its way from Gilgit bringing him badly needed ammunition when it was ambushed by Chitralis. After losing a number of men, the party managed to reach the temporary safety of a cluster of stone houses. For several days they remained there under siege. Then, under a white flag, a messenger arrived claiming that he had been sent by Sher with orders to stop the fighting. He told the two British officers that, following a clash with Robertson's troops at Chitral, amicable relations had now been restored, and that Sher guaranteed them a safe onward passage. A cease-fire was agreed, and a meeting took place between the senior of the two subalterns and the enemy commander at which the latter and other leading Chitralis solemnly assured him of the genuineness of the offer. As a gesture of apparent sincerity, they even supplied the defenders with much-needed food and water. Aware that they could not hold out indefinitely, and that help was unlikely to be forthcoming, the two British officers knew that they had little choice but to trust the Chitralis.

A bizarre piece of Central Asian treachery now ensued. The Chitrali commander announced that in order to celebrate the new-found accord his men would give a display of polo, their national game, on a piece of open ground before the British positions. The two officers were invited to watch this as guests of honour. Not wishing to risk offence, they agreed, but carefully placed themselves where their troops could cover them in the event of duplicity. The game took place without anything untoward happening. But the moment it was over, the Chitralis began to dance, as was their custom. For a few brief seconds some of them came between the two subalterns and the marksmen covering them, temporarily blocking the line of fire. It had been carefully planned. The two officers were seized and quickly bound hand and foot. Seeing what was happening, the Kashmiri troops opened fire, though too late. Dragging their two captives with them, the Chitralis dashed for cover behind a stone wall. Deprived of their officers, the Kashmiris were soon overrun and most of them slaughtered. There being no time to destroy the ammunition intended for Robertson, this now fell into the hands of the enemy. Before very long they would be putting it to alarming use.

Meanwhile in Chitral the situation was worsening. Robertson and his men now found themselves under heavy siege from a greatly superior force armed with modern rifles, though not, fortunately, with artillery. In addition to 5 British officers and nearly 400 native troops, Robertson had with him in the fortress more than 100 non-combatants, including servants, clerks and some Chitralis who had thrown in their lot with him. All had to be fed, and as there was only enough food to last a little more than a month, everyone was put on half rations. Furthermore, ammunition was short, there being barely 300 rounds per man. The fortress itself, eighty yards square, stood on the Chitral river, which ensured them a ready supply of water. Constructed from heavy blocks of stone, its walls were twenty-five feet high and eight feet thick. At each of its four corners rose a square tower, twenty feet higher than the walls. A fifth tower, built to protect those carrying water, jutted out towards the river, and a covered way was now built from this to the water's edge, a distance of twenty paces.

Such were the fortress's strengths. However, it also had a number of serious weaknesses. Surrounding it were clusters of tall trees from which snipers could easily fire down into its interior. Those manning the far walls were thus vulnerable to being shot in the back, and to protect them bullet-proof shelters had to be constructed from earth-filled boxes and thick wooden doors. There were also a number of mud-built outbuildings standing close to the fortress walls which both obstructed the defenders' lines of fire and provided the attackers with cover. Nor had the fortress been planned with modern rifles in mind, for it was within easy range of the towering crags which overlooked it from across the river. Another weak point was the amount of timber used in its construction, making it extremely vulnerable to incendiary attacks. Fire pickets and patrols were organised among the non-combatants, and the men always slept with their filled water-skins beside them. To boost morale, and to signal the garrison's defiance to the enemy, a makeshift Union Jack was stitched together and run up on one of the towers. In the meantime, amid great secrecy and at dead of night, trusted messengers were dispatched to alert the nearest British posts to the garrison's plight.

Apart from continuous sniping, which took a number of lives, the enemy made no major assault on the fortress during the first month. At one stage, peace talks even took place, but with Sher demanding that the British evacuate Chitral under a guarantee of safe passage. Aware of the great numerical superiority of those surrounding them, and the weakness of their own position, Robertson played along with this, hoping thereby to give a relief force as long as possible to reach them. Furthermore he deliberately leaked it to the enemy that, although well supplied with ammunition, the defenders were growing seriously short of food. He hoped thus to persuade Sher and Umra Khan, who had by now joined forces at Chitral, that the fortress could fairly quickly be starved into surrender. But soon his purpose became apparent to the enemy, and contacts ceased abruptly. A number of determined attacks were now launched against the fortress, including several attempts to set it on fire. However, these were successfully beaten off by the defenders. Even so, all the time the Chitralis were gradually pushing forward their *sangars*, and getting closer and closer to the walls. By April 5 they were in possession of an old summer-house only fifty yards away, and on the following day constructed a *sangar* from heavy timber only forty yards from the main gate.

Then came the most serious threat so far to the fortress. On April 7, under cover of a diversionary attack on the covered way down to the river, and heavy fire from marksmen hidden in the trees, a small party of the enemy managed to creep up to the far wall unobserved. With them they bore incendiary materials. They chose their moment well, for there was a strong wind blowing. Within minutes the south-east tower was blazing fiercely, largely due to its timber joists. Robertson could see that if it were not extinguished quickly it would collapse, leaving a large gap in the wall which would be almost impossible to defend against such superior numbers. Directed personally by Robertson, every man who could be spared was brought in to fight the flames. A heavy concentration of fire was directed against them as they worked, killing two and wounding nine others, including Robertson himself, who was hit by a bullet in the shoulder. But after five hours the flames were out.

It had been a close shave, though an even closer one was to follow. Four nights later the defenders heard the sounds of revelry coming from the summer-house, now occupied by the enemy. The loud beating of drums and the cacophony of pipes was at intervals interrupted by screams of derision directed at those in the fortress. The clamour was repeated on each successive night, but it was some time before the defenders realised what the enemy's game was. It was almost certainly intended to drown the tell-tale sounds of a tunnel being dug towards the nearest point of the wall. The besiegers had found a good use for the explosives captured from the British ammunition party. That night one of the sentries reported hearing the faint sounds of a pick being used underground. The officers were unable to hear anything, but by the following morning there was no mistaking it. The Chitrali miners were within twelve feet of the wall. Normally the threat would have been dealt with by means of a counter-mine, but the tunnel was now far too close for that. There was not a moment to lose lest the enemy realise that they had been detected and ignite the mine. There was only one thing to do. The summer-house would have to be stormed immediately, and the tunnel destroyed.

Forty Sikhs and sixty Kashmiris, led by a British subaltern, were chosen for the task. At four o'clock that afternoon the eastern gate of the fortress was opened swiftly and silently, and the assault party raced out, making straight for the summer-house. The enemy were caught by surprise, only managing to kill two of the attackers. Within seconds the assault party was inside the house, whose thirty or so occupants fled out of the back at the sight of the British bayonets. While some of the party positioned themselves to fight off any counter-attack, the officer and the others began frantically to search for the entrance to the tunnel. They soon found it, behind the garden wall, and from it no fewer than twenty-two Chitralis were dragged blinking into the daylight. There, one by one, they were bayoneted to death by the Sikhs. Two, however, were saved by the subaltern, for he had orders to bring back prisoners for interrogation. The explosive charges left by the enemy were then detonated, destroying the tunnel, the violence of the blast knocking over the officer and singeing the beards and turbans of several of the Sikhs.

Now came the most hazardous part of the operation – getting the party safely back to the fortress through murderous enemy fire. Miraculously, thanks to the covering fire maintained from the walls, this was achieved without further loss of life. In all the raid had cost the British eight lives, though undoubtedly it had saved many more, perhaps those of the entire garrison. As the men poured back through the gate, Robertson, who had observed the operation from one of the towers, hastened down to congratulate them. 'The Sikhs,' he wrote afterwards, 'still raging with excitement, crowded forward to recite the numbers they had killed, and to exhibit their stained bayonets and splashed faces.' They had, he noted, 'the ecstatic look of religious fanatics'. By now the garrison had been under siege for forty-seven days. Not a word of what was going on outside had reached them, or even of whether any of their messengers had got through. Food, ammunition and morale were running dangerously low, and many of their rifles, far from new at the start, had ceased to function. Robertson and his officers knew that if help did not arrive soon they would be forced to surrender, or be overrun. However, with the destruction of the tunnel had come a slender ray of hope. Interrogation of the two prisoners revealed that there had been fighting of some kind on the road from Gilgit. Could this mean, everyone wondered, that a relief party was on its way at last? The answer was to come very shortly.

*   *   *

Although the defenders had no way of knowing it, two British forces were at that moment racing to get to Chitral, one from the south and the other from the east. When word of the garrison's plight first reached India, preparations for an expedition to Swat and Chitral had been proceeding at a somewhat leisurely pace, for Robertson was not thought to be in any immediate danger. The enemy, moreover, had been given until April 1 to withdraw, which it was rather assumed they would. But as intelligence began to come in that Robertson and his small party were now under siege, and that the ammunition convoy from Gilgit had been ambushed, leaving two officers in Sher's hands, this complacency turned to something little short of panic. The vision of a handful of British officers, with their loyal native troops, holding out against overwhelming odds in a remote and picturesque fortress, brought to mind the recent tragedy in the Sudan. 'It is Khartoum all over again,' declared *The Graphic*. Those with slightly longer memories remembered Burnes, Macnaghten, Cavagnari, Conolly, Stoddart and other victims of oriental treachery beyond India's frontiers. With dread visions of the main relief party arriving too late, as had happened at Khartoum, the defence chiefs decided to send ahead a second, smaller column from Gilgit.

There were by now growing fears in Gilgit that the troubles might spread eastwards from Chitral. The only troops therefore who could be spared from garrison duties were 400 Sikh Pioneers. Although mainly used for road-building, these sturdy men were also trained soldiers who had shown themselves to be formidable fighters. Furthermore, they were commanded by an extremely able and experienced frontier soldier, Colonel James Kelly. Even so, despite the addition of forty Kashmiri sappers and two mountain guns, it was a pitifully small force for so crucial a mission. However, the day was saved by the unexpected offer of 900 irregulars by those erstwhile adversaries of Britain, Hunza and Nagar. 'Splendid men,' one of Kelly's officers called them. 'Hardy, thickset mountaineers, incapable of fatigue.' The offer was gratefully accepted, and in Gilgit they were issued with modern rifles. So that they would not be mistaken for the enemy, each man was given a strip of red cloth to wrap around his cap. One hundred of them were attached to Kelly's force, while the rest were deployed to guard the passes while British backs were turned.

Kelly had little or no time in which to prepare his force or make any plans. His orders were to leave at once, for if Robertson and his men were to avoid the fate of General Gordon, every day, perhaps every hour, was crucial. Ahead lay a forced march, often through deep snow and across some of the harshest terrain in the world, of more than 200 miles. Every man's hand would be against them, and every pony-track and gorge commanded by sharpshooters from the heights above. Kelly's force, which took no tents to enable it to travel at maximum possible speed, left Gilgit on March 23. One week later, the main relief column, 15,000 strong and commanded by Major-General Sir Robert Low, marched northwards from Peshawar. The race for Chitral was on.

Accompanying Low's force was Captain Francis Younghusband, who had served for a while in Chitral as a political officer, and who had been invited by *The Times* to act as its special correspondent with the expedition. After some hesitation the authorities had agreed to this, as he was officially on leave at the time. Unlike some, Younghusband did not suspect the Russians of being behind the crisis, but he regarded the expedition's mobilisation as a rehearsal for crushing any future Russian moves against India's northern frontiers. The force, consisting of three infantry brigades, two cavalry units, four batteries of mountain guns and numerous smaller units, was regarded by many as unnecessarily large and unwieldy for a task in which speed was more crucial than fire-power. Nonetheless it made rapid progress once it had started, overwhelming several strongly defended enemy positions in a succession of swift engagements. On April 3, Low's men stormed the 3,500-foot Malakand Pass, leading into Swat, and held by 12,000 of Umra Khan's Pathan warriors. The latter were taken partly by surprise following a feint attack made against a parallel pass further to the west. They fought with great ferocity and bravery, but they faced some of Britain's finest infantry regiments, including the King's Royal Rifles and the Gordon Highlanders, and were finally forced to flee, leaving behind many dead and wounded. British casualties in this key engagement amounted to only seventy killed and wounded.

Two days later a squadron of Guides Cavalry caught a party of 2,000 of the enemy out in the open, cutting down many of them and putting the rest to flight at little cost to themselves. On April 13, a battalion of Guides Infantry engaged a far stronger enemy force, killing 600 of them for the loss of only a dozen of their own ranks, although these included their own colonel, shot through the stomach while standing in full view of the enemy issuing orders. Four days after that, their morale rapidly crumbling, Umra Khan's followers prepared to make a stand at his palace-stronghold at Munda. However, finding themselves facing overwhelming odds, they soon melted away into the hills. Inside the fortress, Low's officers came upon a letter from a Scottish firm based in Bombay offering Umra Khan, in Younghusband's words, 'every luxury in the way of arms and ammunition, from Maxim guns at 3,700 rupees, down to revolvers at 34'. None, in fact, had been delivered, for British political officers had got wind of it, and the firm had been ordered to leave India.

Worryingly, there was still no news of the beleaguered garrison at Chitral. For all anyone knew, Robertson and his men might already have been slaughtered. Nor was there any word of the progress of Colonel Kelly. However, with Munda now in their hands, the only remaining obstacle between Low's triumphant troops and their objective was the 10,000-foot, snow-filled Lowarai Pass, the southern gateway to Chitral. Once they were across that, then it would merely be a race against time, not to mention against Kelly's little force advancing from the east. For, with the entire nation looking anxiously on, Low and his officers were determined to be the first to reach Chitral.

*　　　*　　　*

All this time, Kelly and his men had been painfully making their way across the mountains. At first they had not encountered any opposition, the Chitralis never suspecting that anyone would attempt this formidable route at that time of year. On March 30 the column crossed the snowline, 10,000 feet up, and the going began to get progressively worse. As they trudged on upwards, amid heavy snowfalls, the men were issued with tinted glasses to prevent blindness. At night, having no tents, the troops slept in the open. This was too much for the coolies who had been hired to carry the expedition's rations, and during the first night in the snow they deserted, together with their laden ponies. However, they were forcibly rounded up and from then on kept under close guard. Still there was no sign of the enemy.

Two marches ahead lay the first real test – the 12,000-foot Shandur Pass. To cross this, with their two mountain guns, everyone knew would prove an awesome, perhaps even impossible, undertaking. At their first attempt they were driven back, for the exhausted mules carrying the guns and ammunition soon found themselves in difficulties. Already two of them had nearly been lost, together with their vital loads, after rolling down a 100-foot decline into deep snow. For the men things were little easier. Already soaked to the skin, and some of them beginning to suffer from frostbite, they found themselves sinking into the snow, in places up to their armpits. Had the Chitralis been guarding the pass, the entire force might well have been massacred. Two days later, on April 3, they tried again. This time Kelly divided the column into several parties. First to head for the snow-blocked pass were 200 hardy Sikh Pioneers. Their job was to cut a way through for the guns. These were to follow next day, borne on makeshift sledges fashioned by Kelly's engineers. Late that night, after an anxious twelve-hour wait, word came back that the Sikhs had got through. It had been an appalling journey, and it left the force temporarily divided on either side of the pass, and therefore extremely vulnerable. Early next morning began the slow and hazardous task of dragging the guns over. At times they had to be lifted from the sledges and borne physically through the waist-deep snow. But by nightfall it was done.

It was a remarkable feat, accomplished by sheer grit and fine leadership, though not without cost, for the following day Kelly's doctors treated no fewer than fifty-five cases of snow-blindness and frostbite. Miraculously, however, there was still no sign of the enemy, and two days later the rest of the force was safely across the Shandur Pass. They were now only sixty miles from Chitral, but from here they would have to fight every inch of the way, for the following day the enemy suddenly became aware of their presence. Hitherto the Chitralis had devoted all their efforts to the siege, and latterly to the threat posed by Low's advancing force. Kelly's mountain guns were to more than prove their worth in the struggle which followed, and by April 13 he had driven the enemy from their two main positions on the approach route to Chitral. Five days later, although there was still no word from the beleaguered garrison, his men found themselves within two marches of it, and with every sign that the enemy had fled.

*　　　*　　　*

Meanwhile, inside the fortress, things had reached a very low ebb, with no news of a relief expedition being on the way. Many of the troops were ill or wounded, and the officers were reduced to eating their horses to keep up their strength. No one could escape the appalling stench of putrefying animal carcases and the faeces and urine of the several hundred inmates. Then, quite suddenly, it was over. The first that Robertson knew of the enemy's collapse was on the night of April 18, when it was reported that a man had crept up to the wall outside and had called out, though no one caught his words. The man then retreated into the darkness, evidently fearing that he would be fired at. A little later, though, he returned, and this time the troops manning the wall did hear what he said. 'Word flashed through the fort that all our besiegers had fled,' wrote Robertson in his account of their ordeal. But he was taking no chances that night, suspecting it almost certainly to be a trick.

At first light the next morning he sent out a heavily armed party to ascertain the truth. It did not take them long to confirm that the enemy had indeed vanished – nor to discover why. A message was hurriedly sent off to Kelly, and that night a reply was received from him saying that he hoped to reach Chitral the following day. Even after his column had crossed the Shandur Pass, the Chitralis had remained convinced that so small a force would never be able to drive them from their strongholds, which they considered to be unassailable. Umra Khan, moreover, had promised to send Sher 2,000 more of his Pathans so that they could together launch a final assault on the fortress, but these had not materialised, being desperately needed in the south. With that Sher and his remaining followers had fled. The siege, which had lasted a month and a half and cost the lives of forty-one of the defenders, was over.

Kelly's force marched into Chitral on April 20 to find Robertson and his men resembling 'walking skeletons'. The Gilgit column had won the race, for the vanguard of General Low's force was still struggling over the Lowarai Pass. Although the enemy had fled, no one doubted that it was Kelly's bold dash across the mountains, and his brilliantly fought engagements, which had forced the Chitralis to abandon the contest. When word of the garrison's relief reached London, Kelly's feat was lauded by the newspapers as 'one of the most remarkable marches in history', a judgement with which few would disagree. The first to reach Chitral from the south, just one week later and riding far ahead of Low's troops, were Captain Younghusband, temporarily of *The Times*, and his friend Major Roderick Owen, representing the Lucknow *Pioneer*. They had carefully avoided seeking Low's permission to ride thus through hostile territory, knowing full well that this would have been refused. That night they dined with Robertson and Kelly over a precious last bottle of brandy in the house which had been Younghusband's own residence back in Aman-ul-Mulk's day, and more recently had served as Sher's headquarters. The fanatical bravery of the enemy, especially of the Pathans, was highly praised by the British officers. But the real heroes, all agreed, were the sturdy Sikh Pioneers, men of the lowliest caste, who, serving under both Robertson and Kelly, had fought with extraordinary fortitude and professionalism. The worse conditions had become inside the fortress, and the heavier the enemy's fire, the keener the Sikhs had been to get to grips with them. It was they, Younghusband wrote later, who had really saved the garrison.

Not long afterwards word reached Chitral that Umra Khan, too, had fled the field. Accompanied by eleven mule-loads of treasures from his palace, he had crossed safely into Afghanistan, out of reach of his pursuers. Before doing so, though, he had freed the two British subalterns who had been seized at the polo match and entrusted to him by Sher. They had been well treated, and he had even apologised to them for the devious way in which they had been captured. 'Umra Khan', observed Robertson, 'had behaved like a gentleman.' He was, moreover, to prove luckier than his Chitrali ally Sher. Ten days after fleeing his capital, Sher had the misfortune to run into one of his foes, who starved him into surrender before handing him over to the British, together with 1,500 of his followers. He was marched off to exile in India, where he was to declare bitterly of Umra Khan: 'I don't ever want to set eyes on him again. He destroyed us with promises – and fled like a fox.' Needless to say, from his bolt-hole in Afghanistan, Umra Khan had much the same to say about him.

At home the nation was euphoric over the news from Chitral, for everyone had been fearing the worst. Surgeon-Major Robertson, the doctor turned political, was at once rewarded with a knighthood by an overjoyed Queen Victoria. Kelly was recommended for one, but instead was made ADC to the Queen and given a CB. Even if he failed to get the knighthood which many believed he deserved, Kelly will always be remembered among soldiers for his celebrated forced march across the mountains with his ragtag army. In addition, eleven DSOs were awarded, not to mention the VC won by Surgeon-Captain Henry Whitchurch for carrying back a dying fellow officer after the disastrous reconnaissance at the outset of the siege. Finally, there were decorations and awards for a number of native officers and men who had distinguished themselves, while all ranks who had taken part in the affair were given an extra six months' pay and three months' leave. It may only have been 'a minor siege', as Robertson modestly subtitled his own account of it, but those who took part in it included one future field-marshal, at least nine future generals and a number of knights. From a career point of view, Chitral was clearly a good place to have on one's CV.

The crucial question now arose of what to do with Chitral. Should it be annexed like Hunza, or be restored to independence under a ruler friendly to Britain? The issue was to become the subject of heated debate in military and political circles, with the forward school inevitably at loggerheads with those who favoured masterly inactivity. Hunza had been occupied to keep it out of Russian hands, and so had Chitral. But even during the previous month or so circumstances had changed dramatically in the Pamir region. Going almost unnoticed amid the drama surrounding the siege, London had concluded a deal with St Petersburg which finally settled the frontier between Russian Central Asia and eastern Afghanistan. The Pamir gap, moreover, which had for so long worried British strategists, had at last been closed. With Abdur Rahman's approval, a narrow corridor of land, previously belonging to no one and stretching eastwards as far as the Chinese frontier, now became Afghan sovereign territory. Although no more than ten miles wide in places – the closest that Britain and Russia had yet come to meeting in Central Asia – this corridor ensured that nowhere did their frontiers touch. Admittedly it left the Russians in permanent possession of most of the Pamir region. But the British were aware that if St Petersburg decided to seize this area, they were virtually powerless to prevent it. At least, from Britain's point of view, there was now an officially agreed frontier beyond which St Petersburg could not advance – except, of course, in time of war.

This settlement naturally had a close bearing on the question of Chitral. The forward school argued that because the new frontiers brought the Russians even closer to the passes leading to Chitral and northern India, the need to hold on to the territory was greater than ever. The Indian government also subscribed to this view, informing London that it proposed to establish a permanent garrison in Chitral, and build a strategic road to it across the Malakand Pass from Peshawar. For the only other way of getting troops from India to Chitral in the event of a crisis was via Gilgit, and even in late spring, as Kelly had found, this route was still blocked by snow (as indeed was the road leading up to Gilgit from India). However, despite these arguments in support of retention, the Liberal Cabinet of Lord Rosebery had made up its mind not to become entangled again with Chitral. It therefore overruled Calcutta's decision, decreeing that neither troops nor political officers were to be stationed there. Among the reasons given for this was the enormous expense of maintaining such a garrison, and also of building and protecting a road which would run for nearly 200 miles through hostile, Pathan-controlled territory. Furthermore, London argued, such a road might prove to be a two-edged weapon, serving invader as well as defender.

Then, less than two months later, the ruling was abruptly reversed as the Liberals fell from power and Lord Salisbury was back once more in Downing Street. More important perhaps for India, Curzon was appointed Under Secretary of State for Foreign Affairs. Strongly urging the Prime Minister to retain Chitral, he warned of the likelihood of the Russians seizing it if Britain withdrew. Even if they did not, a British withdrawal would be viewed by the frontier tribes as a sign of weakness, especially following Russia's gains in the Pamirs. Already serious trouble was brewing among the tribes in parts of the north, and such a move would only encourage them into believing that the British could be driven out. Curzon's arguments prevailed, and it was decided to retain Chitral. A permanent garrison was to be maintained there, consisting of two battalions of Indian infantry, mountain batteries and sappers, while two further battalions would guard the Malakand Pass and other points on the route northwards.

The hawks had won the day, and subsequently it emerged that very likely they were right in urging the retention of Chitral. In the spring of 1898, while on a 'shooting expedition' in the Pamirs, an officer of the 60th Rifles – Captain Ralph Cobbold – learned from a Russian frontier officer he met there that they had orders to take immediate possession of Chitral if the British evacuated it. 'Very complete plans' had been drawn up for this eventuality, and a Russian officer had visited Chitral in disguise in order to examine its defences and approach routes. Cobbold's informant added that plans for the invasion of Chitral 'are a matter of common discussion at the dinner table of the Governor of Ferghana', while other Russian officers told him that they looked upon the present frontier with Afghanistan as a 'purely temporary arrangement' and 'by no means

permanent'. Cobbold was much impressed by how well informed they were about the British and Afghan side of the frontier.
This he put down to 'the extensive system of espionage which
is encouraged by the Russian Government along the Indian
frontier'. He added: 'Trusty men in disguise are constantly
coming and going between the Russian frontier, Kabul and
Chitral, and these are encouraged to gain all the information
possible compatible with their own safety.' The Russian officers he met 'all look forward to war with the greatest eagerness',
he reported.

Russian officers serving on the frontier had long been given
to such bellicose talk, as we have noted before. Its encouragement was one way of keeping up morale, while the preparation of invasion plans, and the gathering of intelligence, was
merely part of a staff officer's routine in most armies. Allowing
word of it to reach British ears, moreover, was an effective way
of encouraging them to keep more troops in India than they
would otherwise have needed. That was all part of the Great
Game. Whatever the truth of this Pamir gossip, in the event
St Petersburg was to stick firmly to the agreement, making no
further moves towards Afghanistan or India. The Russians
had got pretty well what they wanted. Not only had they
secured their long southern frontier, but they had also placed
themselves advantageously if ever it came to a war with Britain.
After the best part of a century, the Tsar's empire in Central
Asia had finally reached its limits. But the British, so often
hoodwinked in the past, were still far from convinced. The last
round of the Great Game was about to begin. Once again the
play moved eastwards – this time to Tibet, a secretive land
long closed to foreigners, and protected from the inquisitive
by some of the highest mountains on earth.

· 36 ·

The Beginning of the End

Although the British had not yet grasped the fact, far grander visions now occupied the mind of the new Tsar Nicholas than the annexation of Chitral, or even the conquest of India. Under the persuasive influence of his Finance Minister, Count Witte, he dreamed of opening up to Russia the whole of the Far East, with its vast resources and markets, before these fell to other predators. It would thus become his India. Russia would be a great economic power, as well as a great military one. Witte knew just how to feed his sovereign's dreams with visions of a golden future for Russia. 'From the shores of the Pacific, and the heights of the Himalayas,' he declared, 'Russia will not only dominate the affairs of Asia, but those of Europe also.' And while his grand design would extend Russia's resources to the full, it involved no risk of war – or so he believed. To wrest India from the British was one thing, but to capture its trade was another.

Witte's plan involved the construction of the greatest railway the world had ever seen. It would run for 4,500 miles across Russia, from Moscow in the west to Vladivostok and Port Arthur in the east. Indeed, work had already begun on it, starting simultaneously at either end, although it was not expected to be completed for at least twelve years. When finished, Witte calculated, it would be capable of carrying merchandise and raw materials from Europe to the Pacific and vice versa in less than half the time it took by sea. It would thus attract not merely Russian commercial traffic, he reasoned, but also that of other nations, thereby seriously threatening the sea routes which served as Britain's economic arteries. But there was much more to it than that. The railway would enable Russia to exploit its own enormous but still untapped resources in the inhospitable Siberian wastes through which it would run. Entire communities from overcrowded parts of European Russia could be moved eastwards by railway, to work both on its construction and also in the new towns along its length. And in time of war its role could be crucial, for it could be used to rush – at 15 miles an hour – troops and munitions eastwards to a Far Eastern war zone, without risk of interference by the navies of Britain or any other power.

Even that, however, was not all that Witte dangled before the impressionable Nicholas in his vision of the future. In 1893, the year before Nicholas's accession, an astute Buryat Mongol named Peter Badmayev, a lecturer in Mongolian at St Petersburg, had submitted to Alexander III an ambitious plan for bringing parts of the Chinese Empire, including Tibet and Mongolia, under Russian sway. This could be done, he assured Alexander, without any risk of war and at comparatively little cost by fomenting large-scale insurrections against the already enfeebled and universally disliked Manchus. To accomplish it he proposed the setting up of a trading company, to be run by himself, whose real purpose would be to incite the population against their alien rulers. Alexander, however, turned the scheme down, calling it: 'so fantastic ... that it is hard to believe in the possibility of success'. But that did not deter Count Witte from reviving it after Alexander's death, and using it to excite Nicholas's expansionist dreams. And in this he appears to have had some success. Badmayev's company, with an initial capital of two million roubles, was set up, and Nicholas expressed to his Minister of War, General Kuropatkin, a wish to add Tibet to his domains. It is perhaps more than a coincidence, therefore, that around this time a growing number of reports began to reach Calcutta of shadowy Russian agents, usually Buryat Mongol subjects of Tsar Nicholas's, travelling between St Petersburg and Lhasa. All appeared to be somehow connected with the mysterious Badmayev.

Whatever the truth about Badmayev's machinations in Tibet

and Mongolia, elsewhere in the Far East the major European powers were at that moment engaged in a frantic scramble for their share of the dying Manchu empire, and anything else that was going. The Germans, late starters in the colonial game, began the immediate rush, fearing lest the other powers gain a monopoly of the world's markets and resources. Their first requirement was a naval base and coaling station for their new Far Eastern fleet somewhere on China's northern coastline. The murder of two German missionaries by Chinese bandits in November 1897 gave them their chance. By way of reprisal, Kaiser Wilhelm's troops seized nearby Kiaochow, known subsequently as Tsingtao, on which the Russians already had their eye. Peking was given little choice but to grant Germany a ninety-nine-year lease on it, together with mining and railway concessions. In the ensuing scrimmage, Britain and France gained further concessions, while Russia, ever posing as China's protector, obtained the warm-water naval base of Port Arthur and its immediate hinterland. The Russians further gained a crucial strategic concession – agreement to link the base by rail to the now half-completed Trans-Siberian line. The United States, too, joined the Far Eastern scramble, acquiring in 1898 Hawaii, Wake, Guam and the Philippines, which Russia, Germany and Japan were known to covet.

While this was taking place on the periphery of Great Game territory, something occurred in India which was to have a profound effect on the game itself. George Curzon, that arch-Russophobe, had been appointed Viceroy of India. At the age of only 39, and newly raised to the peerage, he had thus achieved his boyhood dream. Needless to say, the hawks were delighted, for Curzon's views on the Russian threat to India were well known. St Petersburg's ultimate ambition, he was convinced, was the domination of the whole of Asia, a goal it sought to achieve step by step. It was a remorseless process which must be resisted at every stage. 'If Russia is entitled to these ambitions,' Curzon wrote, still more is Britain entitled, nay compelled, to defend that which she has won, and to resist the minor encroachments which are only part of a larger plan.' He was confident, moreover, that with firm action the Russian steamroller could be halted. 'I will no more admit', he declared,

'that an irresistible destiny is going to plant Russia in the
Persian Gulf than at Kabul or Constantinople. South of a
certain line in Asia her future is much more what we choose
to make it than what she can make it herself.' It need hardly
be said that his appointment as Viceroy was to cause alarm in
St Petersburg.

Persia, particularly the Gulf, was seen by Curzon as an area
especially vulnerable to further Russian penetration. Already
St Petersburg was beginning to show an interest in acquiring
a port there, and even in building a railway for the Shah from
Isfahan to the coast. It was worrying enough, he wrote to Lord
George Hamilton, the Secretary of State for India, in April
1899, having to defend India from a Russian overland attack,
without the added menace of a seaborne one. He urged the
Cabinet to make it quite clear to both St Petersburg and
Teheran that Britain would never allow southern Persia to fall
under any foreign influence other than her own. Nor were the
Russians alone in showing an interest in the Gulf, for both
Germany and France were beginning to challenge British
supremacy there. The Cabinet, however, did not appear
unduly perturbed, causing Curzon to write to Hamilton: 'I do
not suppose that Lord Salisbury will be persuaded to lift a
little finger to save Persia ... We are slowly – no, I think I may
say swiftly – paving the way for the total extinction of our
influence in that country.' Afghanistan, too, was a worry to
Curzon, despite Britain's long-standing treaty with Abdur
Rahman and the settlement of the northern frontier with
Russia. For intelligence began to reach Calcutta that Russian
officials in Transcaspia, including the governors of Ashkhabad
and Merv, were endeavouring to communicate with the Emir
directly, and not, as St Petersburg had agreed, through the
Foreign Office in London. In the event, the Russians were
rebuffed by Abdur Rahman, and a crisis was averted. It was
to Tibet, however, that the focus of the Great Game now
shifted, as word was received in India that twice within twelve
months an emissary from the Dalai Lama had visited St Petersburg, where he had been warmly welcomed by the Tsar.

The Russians have always insisted that the comings and
goings of this emissary – a Buryat Mongol named Aguan

Dorjief – were purely religious, and without any political significance. Indeed, it could not be denied that the Tsar had many
Buddhists of the Tibetan school among his Buryat subjects in
southern Siberia. What was more natural, therefore, than for
spiritual contacts to be made between a Christian head of state
and a Buddhist one? But Curzon, for one, was unconvinced.
He felt fairly certain that Dorjief, far from being a simple
Buddhist monk, was working on behalf of Tsar Nicholas
against Britain's interests in Asia. The discovery that Dorjief
was a close friend of Peter Badmayev's, who was now the Tsar's
adviser on Tibetan affairs, served only to confirm Curzon's
suspicions. The final truth will almost certainly never be
known, although most scholars today believe that British fears
were largely groundless, Nicholas being beset by too many
problems of his own to be thinking about Tibet. However,
writing in 1924, a respected German traveller and Central
Asian scholar, Wilhelm Filchner, claimed that between 1900
and 1902 there was an all-out drive by St Petersburg to secure
Tibet for Russia. In *Storm Over Asia: Experiences of a Secret
Diplomatic Agent*, Filchner described in detail the activities of
a Buryat Mongol named Zerempil, a man even more shadowy
than Badmayev or Dorjief, with whom he was closely associated. Among other things, Filchner claims, Zerempil was used
by the 'Indian Section' of the Russian General Staff to smuggle
arms into Tibet. If Zerempil, who was said to go under a
variety of names and guises, did in fact exist, then he managed
to go undetected by the British intelligence services, for there
are no references to him in the archives at that time.

But it was the behaviour of the Tibetans themselves rather
than of the Russians that finally convinced the new Viceroy
that something underhand was going on between Lhasa and
St Petersburg. Twice he had written to the Dalai Lama raising
the question of trade and other matters, but each time the letter
had been returned unopened. And yet the Tibetan God-king
appeared to be on excellent terms with the Russians, as even
the St Petersburg newspapers were beginning to claim. Curzon
was both genuinely alarmed, lest some secret treaty was being
forged behind his back, and also personally affronted by this
rebuff to his authority by a political nonentity like the Dalai

Lama. By the beginning of 1903 he was convinced that the only effective course of action was for the Indian government to dispatch a mission to Lhasa – using force if necessary – to discover the truth about Russian activities there, and to put Britain's relations with Tibet on a firm and proper basis.

Curzon found the home government – which had only just extricated itself from a humiliating and unpopular war with the Boers – reluctant to embark on any further adventures, especially in Central Asia where there was the added danger of a Russian countermove. Nonetheless, that April he managed to get the Cabinet's approval for a small escorted mission to visit Khamba Jong, just inside Tibet, where it would endeavour to hold talks with the Tibetans. The political officer chosen by Curzon to lead the mission was one whose earlier Great Game exploits he much admired – Major Francis Younghusband, now aged 40, and promoted to colonel for the occasion. However, the Tibetans refused to negotiate – except on the British side of the frontier – and withdrew into their fortress, or *jong*. After a stalemate lasting several months, the mission was recalled to India, having achieved nothing and lost considerable face.

Stung by this second rebuff by his puny neighbours, the Viceroy persuaded London to agree to a second mission. This time it would be accompanied by a 1,000-strong military escort, and would venture considerably further into Tibet. Such a show of force, Curzon believed, would surely bring the Tibetans to heel. Strict orders were given, however, that the mission was to proceed no further than the great fortress at Gyantse, half-way to Lhasa. At the same time St Petersburg and Peking – the latter being the nominal ruler of Tibet – were officially notified of Britain's intended move. The Russians immediately lodged a strong protest. But this was brushed aside by London, it being pointed out firmly that this move was purely temporary, and in no way comparable with their own permanent annexation of vast areas of Central Asia. Again Colonel Younghusband was chosen to head the mission, with a brigadier-general in command of the Gurkha and Sikh escort. Led by a sepoy bearing a Union Jack, the party crossed the passes into Tibet on December 12, 1903. Behind, in the snow, trailed a straggling column of 10,000 coolies, 7,000 mules and 4,000 yaks, together carrying the expedition's baggage, including champagne for the officers. So began the last forward move in the Great Game, and what would prove to be one of the most contentious episodes in British history. At the same time the Russians, seemingly at the height of their power in Asia, were about to suffer a succession of spectacular disasters there. Between them, these two events were to mark the beginning of the end of Anglo-Russian rivalry in Asia.

*   *   *

As the Younghusband mission made its way northwards towards Gyantse, much was happening elsewhere in Asia, particularly in China. In the summer of 1900, taking the European powers by surprise, had come the Boxer Uprising. It sprang from a bitter resentment among the Chinese towards the 'foreign devils' who, taking advantage of their weakness, were acquiring treaty ports and other commercial and diplomatic privileges. The rebellion began in Tientsin with the massacre of Christian missionaries and the lynching of the French consul, and was finally put down by a six-nation relief force which occupied (and looted) Peking. But although the uprising was over, it was to have far-reaching consequences in Manchuria, where the Russians had feared for the safety of their newly-built railway at the hands of the Boxers. For, among many other grievances, the rebels were convinced that the construction of railways had upset the natural harmony of man, and had thus been responsible for recent droughts and flooding. In order to protect their expensive investment there – or so St Petersburg insisted – the Russians had at once moved 170,000 troops into Manchuria. It was one of the largest such concentrations of military might ever seen in Asia, and it caused considerable alarm among other powers with interests there, especially Japan.

During the protracted negotiations which followed the crushing of the Boxers, considerable pressure was put on St Petersburg to withdraw its troops now that the danger was over. The Russians were clearly extremely reluctant, though finally they agreed to do so, but in three stages. As it turned out, they only honoured the first of these promised withdrawals, for in the meantime Count Witte and the more moderate of his ministerial colleagues had been eased out of power by those close to Tsar Nicholas who favoured a more aggressive foreign policy. 'Russia has been made, not by diplomacy, but by bayonets,' declared the new Minister of the Interior, 'and we must decide the questions at issue with China and Japan with bayonets and not with pens.' It now became increasingly obvious that the Russians, as so often before in Asia, intended to stay put. To the British it was merely another broken promise by St Petersburg, but to the Japanese it was the last straw.

For many months the Japanese had watched with growing apprehension the Russian military and naval build-up in the Far East, which directly threatened their own interests there. They had noted with particular alarm the Russians' relentless infiltration of Korea, for this brought them dangerously close to Japan's own shores. The Japanese knew, moreover, that time was against them. Once the Trans-Siberian Railway was finished, the Russians would be able to bring up vast numbers of troops, heavy artillery and other war materials from Europe in the event of war. For these reasons, and after much agonis-ing, the Japanese High Command decided to do what the British , wisely or otherwise, had never risked doing in Central Asia. This was to meet the Russian threat head on. On Feb-ruary 8, 1904, the Japanese struck without warning. Their target was the great Russian naval base at Port Arthur. The Russo-Japanese War had begun.

News of its outbreak reached the Younghusband mission as it approached the small village of Guru, half-way to Gyantse, now only fifty miles off. Without spilling a drop of Tibetan blood, Younghusband and his escort had successfully over-come three major obstacles – the 14,000-foot Jelap Pass, a defensive wall which the Tibetans had built across their path, and the fortress at Phari, which at 15,000 feet was said to be the highest in the world. Each had fallen without a fight. It was at this moment that the Tibetan mood began to change, with the arrival at Guru of a group of warrior monks from

Lhasa, the capital, who had orders to halt the British advance. They were accompanied by 1,500 Tibetan troops armed with matchlocks and sacred charms – each one bearing the Dalai Lama's personal seal. These, their priests promised them, would make them bullet-proof.

Younghusband's escort commander, Brigadier-General James Macdonald, quickly moved his Gurkhas and Sikhs into position around the Tibetans, wholly surrounding them. Then the mission's Tibetan-speaking intelligence officer, Captain Frederick O'Connor, was sent to call for them to lay down their arms. But the Tibetan commander ignored him, muttering incomprehensibly to himself. Orders were now given by Macdonald for the Tibetans to be disarmed, forcibly if necessary, and sepoys detailed for this task began to wrestle the matchlocks from their reluctant hands. This was too much for the Tibetan commander. Drawing a revolver from beneath his robes, he blew the jaw off a nearby sepoy, at the same time calling on his troops to fight. The Tibetans immediately hurled themselves on the escort, only to be shot down by the highly trained Gurkhas and Sikhs. In less than four minutes, as their medieval army disintegrated before the murderous fire of modern weaponry, nearly 700 ill-armed and ragged Tibetans lay dead or dying on the plain.

'It was a terrible and ghastly business,' wrote Younghusband, echoing the feelings of all the officers and men. As head of the mission, however, he had taken no part in the killing, and had hoped for another bloodless victory. Why Macdonald did not order an immediate ceasefire the instant he saw what was happening is not clear. As it was, the firing continued while the Tibetans, not realising perhaps what was happening, streamed slowly away across the plain. Possibly Macdonald did try to halt the killing, but was not heard above the sound of the machine-guns and other clamour. As the subaltern commanding the machine-guns wrote in a letter to his parents: 'I hope I shall never have to shoot down men *walking* away again.' When word of the massacre reached London, it was to outrage liberal opinion, even though the mission doctors worked around the clock trying to save the lives of as many of the Tibetan wounded as possible. Remarkable stoicism was shown by the latter, some of whom were badly mutilated. One man, who had lost both his legs, joked pitifully with the surgeons: 'Next time I shall have to be a hero, as I can no longer run away.' The wounded found it hard to understand, Younghusband noted, 'why we should try to take their lives one day and try to save them the next.' They had expected to be shot out of hand.

Far from slackening, Tibetan resistance grew stiffer as the British advance on Gyantse was resumed. Tibetan casualties, too, continued to mount. At the spectacular Red Idol Gorge, twenty miles from Gyantse, 200 more perished before the mission could safely pass through the defile. In what was possibly the highest engagement ever fought, a further 400 Tibetans died in the fierce struggle for the 16,000-foot Karo Pass. British casualties amounted to only 5 killed and 13 wounded. In view of their unexpected resistance (organised by the mysterious Zerempil, according to the German traveller Filchner), London foresaw that the Tibetans were unlikely to agree to talks with Younghusband at Gyantse. Younghusband was instructed therefore to warn the Tibetans that unless they did so within a given period, the British would march on Lhasa itself. In view of the sanctity with which they regarded their capital, it was reasoned that this would bring the Tibetans to the negotiating table. But the expiry date passed without any sign of them. Ten days later, on July 5, 1904, the order was given to advance on Lhasa. Considerable excitement was felt by all ranks at the prospect of entering the most secretive city on earth, while the outbreak of the war between Russia and Japan had dispelled any fears of countermoves by St Petersburg.

Before the British could advance, though, the great fortress of Gyantse, perched on a precipitous outcrop of rock high above the town, had to be taken. Macdonald's attack was launched at four in the morning, after the wall had been breached by concentrated artillery fire. A storming party, led by Lieutenant John Grant, crept forward in the darkness and began the hazardous climb towards the breach. Soon, however, the Tibetans spotted them and began showering large boulders down on them. Grant, revolver in hand, had almost reached the breach when he was knocked violently backwards by a rock. Despite his injuries, the young Gurkha subaltern tried again. This time, watched from below by the entire British force, he made it through the hail of missiles. With several Gurkhas at his heels, he entered the fortress, shooting down a number of the defenders. Moments later the rest of the storming party were through the breach. A fierce struggle for the Tibetan stronghold, which was said to be invincible, ensued. This continued until late afternoon, when Tibetan resistance finally broke. The defenders, who had fought with great courage, now fled, slipping away through secret underground tunnels known only to themselves, or over the walls using ropes. They left behind more than 300 dead and wounded, while British casualties totalled just 4 killed and 30 wounded. Grant was later awarded the Victoria Cross, the only one ever to be won on Tibetan soil.

When news of Gyantse's fall reached Lhasa, it caused utter dismay. For there was an ancient belief that were the fortress to fall into an invader's hands the country was doomed. At last this had happened. After overcoming one last stand by the Tibetans, the British reached the banks of the wide and swift-flowing Tsangpo river, the only remaining obstacle between them and Lhasa. The crossing, using canvas boats, took five full days to complete, an officer and two Gurkhas being swept to their deaths in the course of it. The road to the Tibetan capital, barred for so long to the outside world, was now open. Two days later, on August 2, 1904, the British got their first glimpse of the holy city from a nearby hill. Turning in his saddle to his intelligence officer, Younghusband said simply: 'Well, O'Connor, there it is at last.' Fifteen years earlier, as a young subaltern, he had dreamed of entering Lhasa disguised as a Yarkandi trader, but his superiors had turned down the idea as too perilous. Since then, a succession of European travellers had tried to get there, though all had been turned back. The next day, with only a small escort, and in full diplomatic regalia, Younghusband rode into the holy city.

· 37 ·

End-game

The war in the East, meanwhile, had been going badly for the Russians. When, seven months earlier, the Japanese launched their surprise attack on Port Arthur, few people believed that they stood a chance against the awesome might of Tsar Nicholas. In addition to his powerful Pacific fleet, he had a million-strong regular army, supported by twice that number of reservists, to call on, while Japan had only 270,000 regulars and 530,000 reservists. The Russians were quite confident, therefore, that they could swiftly crush this upstart Asiatic nation of 'yellow apes', as they called the Japanese, which had dared to challenge them. After all, they had immense experience of warfare in Asia, and no one there had managed to withstand their onslaught.

In their initial attack on the great Russian naval base of Port Arthur, the Japanese had clearly hoped to destroy their fleet, as they were to do with the American Pacific fleet thirty-seven years later at Pearl Harbor. In the event, their ten destroyers only managed to damage three battleships, albeit one seriously, as they lay at anchor in the roads. In a second attack a few hours later another battleship and three cruisers were damaged, while off the Korean coast a fourth cruiser and a gunboat were sunk. Despite heavy fire from the Russian shore batteries, the Japanese warships, led by the brilliant Admiral Togo, got off singularly lightly. But even if they had failed to sink the Russian Pacific fleet, they had gravely undermined its morale. The following day both governments declared war on one another. The conflict was to last eighteen months, and lead indirectly to the fall, thirteen years later, of the Russian monarchy.

From then on, little seemed to go right for the Russians. Very early on they lost both their commander-in-chief and their flagship when the latter struck a mine which the Japanese had laid in the approaches to Port Arthur. Soon the Russians found themselves virtually imprisoned in the heavily defended naval base, as the Japanese, through superior tactics and leadership, made themselves masters of the sea. On land, too, the Japanese rapidly began to gain the upper hand, inflicting a series of defeats on the Russians, albeit often at great cost to themselves in lives. In May Russian troops were defeated on the Yalu river, and the following month the Japanese occupied the commercial port of Dalny, only twenty miles from Port Arthur. At St Petersburg, meanwhile, it had been decided to send the Russian Baltic fleet half-way round the world to the Far East in a desperate attempt to relieve beleaguered Port Arthur.

It was during this epic voyage that the Russian warships became involved in a bizarre international incident which raised Russophobia in Britain to fever pitch and very nearly led to war between the two powers. As a result of faulty intelligence, nervousness and inexperience, Russian sailors opened fire in fog in the North Sea on a fleet of Hull trawlers, believing them, incredibly, to be Japanese torpedo boats. One was sunk, five others were hit, and there were a number of casualties. In the panic of the moment, the Russian warships even fired on one another. Then, convinced that they had successfully fought off a Japanese attack, they continued on their way. While London remonstrated angrily with St Petersburg over what became known as the Dogger Bank incident, four British cruisers shadowed the Russian fleet across the Bay of Biscay. Meanwhile a large British naval force was hastily got ready for action. There were anti-Russian demonstrations in Trafalgar Square and outside Downing Street, while Count Benckendorff was booed as he left his embassy. In the end an abject apology by Tsar Nicholas, and promises of generous compensation, cooled British tempers, and war was averted. It was an inauspicious start, however, to this great Russian relief expedition designed to save Port Arthur.

By now the savage land battle for the naval base had begun. The first Japanese attack was driven back with heavy loss. Two more followed, which were also repulsed. But gradually the Japanese troops closed in on the Russian positions, using sappers to tunnel beneath the defences, and observers in balloons to spot the garrison's weaknesses. Moreover, the capture of a hill overlooking Port Arthur enabled the Japanese to direct a murderous artillery barrage against the defenders below. With nearly half the garrison either dead or wounded, and with little or no hope of relief reaching them in time, morale among the Russian rank and file had reached rock bottom. Although many of the officers still wanted to fight to the bitter end, the Governor, fearing a mutiny among the troops, decided to discuss surrender terms with the Japanese commander. On January 2, 1905, after a siege lasting 154 days, Port Arthur capitulated. Before doing so, the Governor sent a last message to Tsar Nicholas. 'Great Sovereign, Forgive!' it declared. 'We have done all that was humanly possible. Judge us, but be merciful.'

The loss of the great eastern stronghold to the 'yellow apes' was an appalling blow to Russian prestige throughout the world, but particularly in Asia. However, it was merely the start of St Petersburg's humiliation at the hands of the Japanese. On February 18 the biggest and bloodiest battle of the war began. The prize was the heavily defended railway centre of Mukden, today call Shenyang, which lay 250 miles north of Port Arthur. Russian military experts considered its defences virtually impenetrable. However, while the number of troops engaged on either side was roughly equal, around 300,000, the Japanese enjoyed a number of advantages. For a start, their troops had just won a resounding victory. Despite very heavy casualties, they were utterly determined to defeat the Russians, against whom they displayed a fanatical courage in close quarters combat with bayonet and grenade. No one questioned the bravery of the Russian troops, despite their recent defeat, but what counted in the end was the superiority of the Japanese commanders. In less than a month, after one of the longest and most savage battles of modern times, Mukden fell to the Japanese, although most of the Russian garrison managed to escape northwards. However, they left behind them 27,000 dead in what has been described as the most disastrous battle in Russian history. Yet their humiliation was still not over, though this time it was to be the turn of the navy.

News of the fall of Port Arthur and of Mukden reached the Russian Baltic fleet as it halted at Madagascar on its long voyage eastwards. The surrender of the former removed the main purpose of the expedition. Nonetheless it was decided to allow it to proceed, with the aim of winning back mastery of the seas from the Japanese, thereby preventing them from reinforcing or supplying their forces on the mainland. Shadowed from now on by Japanese agents, the armada finally entered the war zone in the middle of May. There Admiral Togo lay in wait for the weary Russians. On the morning of May 26, the two fleets met in the Tsushima Straits, which divide Japan from Korea. The outcome was catastrophic for the Russians. In the space of a few hours they suffered one of the worst defeats in naval history, losing eight battleships, four cruisers, five minelayers and three transports. Four more battleships were forced to surrender, while three cruisers which sought sanctuary in neutral ports were interned together with their crews. Nearly 5,000 Russian sailors perished. The Japanese lost just 3 torpedo boats and 110 lives. It was an astounding victory. St Petersburg's humiliation was complete, and Tsar Nicholas's dreams of building a great new empire in the East had been destroyed for ever.

To all intents and purposes, the war was over, although Russia, with its vast reserves of troops, was far from defeated. But the will to continue with this highly unpopular war was no longer there. Economic hardship, the succession of disasters on the battlefield and at sea, and general disillusionment with Tsar Nicholas's autocratic rule had given birth to widespread political and social unrest at home. The government therefore needed all the troops it possessed to put down the rising tide of revolution which threatened the very throne. St Petersburg was not alone in wishing to end hostilities in the Far East. Despite their spectacular victories, the Japanese knew that they could not win a long drawn-out war against the Russian colossus, with its inexhaustible manpower. Already the war was imposing a critical strain on their resources which could not be sustained indefinitely.

Both governments were therefore grateful when the United States offered to act as mediator between them. As a result, on September 5, 1905, a peace treaty was signed at Portsmouth, New Hampshire, between the warring powers. This effectively brought to an end Tsarist Russia's forward policy in Asia. Under its terms both countries agreed to evacuate Manchuria, which was restored to Chinese rule. Port Arthur and its immediate hinterland, including control of the Russian-built railway, was transferred to Japan. Korea was declared to be independent, albeit within Japan's sphere of influence. For their part, the Japanese were persuaded to drop their earlier demands for huge indemnities, while, apart from the southern half of Sakhalin Island which went to Japan, the Russians were not required to surrender any of their sovereign territory. Nevertheless St Petersburg had lost virtually everything it had gained in the region during ten years of vigorous military and diplomatic endeavour. The war, moreover, had exploded forever the myth of the white man's superiority over Asiatic peoples.

But if the Japanese had blocked Russia's last forward move in Asia, the Tibetans had signally failed to halt Britain in hers. In the summer of 1904, it will be recalled, Colonel Francis Younghusband had ridden unopposed into Lhasa at the head of a small army. However, if he and Lord Curzon, the Viceroy, had expected to find damning evidence of Russian intrigue there they were to be disappointed. Not only were there no arsenals of Russian weapons, no political advisers, no drill sergeants, but there was also no sign of any treaty of friendship between Tsar Nicholas and the Dalai Lama. Nonetheless, it does appear from other evidence that some sort of a promise may have been made by Nicholas, possibly through Dorjief, to the Dalai Lama whereby he would come to his assistance if the British ever invaded Tibet. This was claimed at the time by a senior Chinese Foreign Ministry official in conversation with the British ambassador to Peking, and later repeated in the memoirs, published after the Revolution, of a former Tsarist diplomat. If Nicholas did, in fact, give such an undertaking, it was very likely in the belief that Britain would never invade Tibet, and that therefore he would not be called upon to honour it.

Of more immediate concern to Younghusband was the question of what to do next. He had been sent all this way not merely to look for evidence of Russian skulduggery, but also to extract political and commercial concessions from the Tibetans. And here arose an unexpected problem. As everyone knew, only the Dalai Lama could negotiate on behalf of his country, and he was nowhere to be found. He had fled the Potala Palace, from where he ruled Tibet, at the approach of the British, and was rumoured at that moment to be on his way to Mongolia. Younghusband considered giving chase, but no Tibetan could be found who was willing to disclose the God-king's escape route. The situation was eventually saved, somewhat unexpectedly, by the Chinese, who were still recognised by Britain as the sovereign power in Tibet (albeit in little more than name). Peking, like St Petersburg, had protested strongly when the British announced their intention of entering Tibet. However, having no means of driving the British out themselves, they were anxious to give them no excuse for staying on. They therefore formally deposed the Dalai Lama for deserting his post during his people's hour of need, and appointed the benign and elderly Regent as the country's ruler. The negotiations for Britain's withdrawal from Tibet were thus able to proceed.

I have already described what followed in *Trespassers on the Roof of the World*, an account of the forcible opening up of Tibet, and will not therefore dwell on it here. Sufficient to say, the British mission left for home on September 23, having gained its objectives, or at least as these were perceived by Younghusband. However, partly due to Russia's defeat in the Far East, which had revealed it to have feet of clay, the mood at home had begun to change during Younghusband's absence. The old fear of Russia was at last waning in the face of a new spectre – that of an aggressively expansionist Germany. Indeed, as Germany's ambitions in Asia began to assume threatening aspects, Russia was already being seen by some as a potential ally against this new power. What had to be avoided at all costs was anything which might drive St Petersburg into the arms of the Germans. Consequently, for fear of alarming Russia, most of the gains which Younghusband had painfully wrung from the Tibetans – including the exclusive right of access to Lhasa by a British official – were considerably watered down. Younghusband, furthermore, was publicly censured for exceeding his instructions. Quite what the Tibetans made of this remarkable climb-down is not recorded.

Then, in December 1905, the Liberals drove the Tories from power. The new Cabinet, headed by Sir Henry Campbell-Bannerman, was genuinely determined to reach a permanent accommodation with the Russians. Shortly after coming to office, the new Foreign Secretary, Sir Edward Grey, began to put out feelers towards St Petersburg on the question of the two powers' long-standing differences in Asia. Decades of mutual suspicion had to be overcome. The British government was under powerful pressure from the hawks, and from the authorities in India, to treat any Russian proposals with the utmost suspicion, while St Petersburg was under similar pressure from its Anglophobes, especially the military. Indeed, following the débâcle in the Far East, there had been wild talk in some Russian circles of invading India to try to expunge the shame of defeat, for many were convinced that the British had incited the Japanese to attack them. One major obstacle so far as British public opinion was concerned was the autocratic nature of Nicholas's rule. Attitudes softened somewhat when, following the short-lived 1905 Revolution, he introduced Russia's first parliament, the Duma, but hardened again when he dissolved it shortly afterwards. Despite this, though, both governments were eager to settle once and for all the Asian question, which over the years had absorbed so much of their energy and resources.

The negotiations, spread over many wearisome months, confined themselves to just three countries – Tibet, Afghanistan and Persia – all of which were crucial to India's defence. In August 1907, after repeated disagreements and setbacks, accord was finally reached between Sir Edward Grey and the

Russian Foreign Minister, Count Alexander Izvolsky. The Great Game was now rapidly drawing to a close. The agreement was designed not only to resolve permanently the regional differences between the two powers, but also to curb Germany's eastward march (although it carefully made no mention of this). At the same time St Petersburg was advised that in future Britain would no longer oppose its wish to control the Turkish straits. It was a German presence there which Britain now feared most.

On August 31, amid great secrecy, the historic Anglo-Russian Convention was signed in St Petersburg by Count Izvolsky and Sir Arthur Nicolson, the British ambassador. With regard to Tibet, the two powers agreed to abstain from all interference in its internal affairs, to seek no concessions for railways, roads, mines or telegraphs, to send no representatives there, but to deal with Lhasa only through China, the suzerain power. Afghanistan the Russians formally recognised as lying within Britain's sphere of influence and outside their own. They pledged themselves to send no agents there, and to conduct all political relations with Kabul through London, though they would be free to trade there. For their part, the British guaranteed not to change the political status of Afghanistan. Acknowledging, moreover, St Petersburg's fear of Britain and Afghanistan combining against Tsarist rule in Central Asia, the British solemnly undertook never to do so and also to discourage Kabul from ever behaving in a hostile manner.

The agreement over Persia was more complicated. While both powers pledged themselves to respect its independence and allow other countries to trade freely there, they agreed to divide it into two spheres of influence, with a neutral zone between. Russia was assigned the north and centre, including Teheran, Tabriz and Isfahan, while Britain was granted the south, which included the vital entrance to the Gulf. As Sir Edward Grey put it: 'On paper it was an equal bargain. The part of Persia by which India could be approached was made secure from Russian penetration. The part of Persia by which Russia could be approached was secured from British penetration.' Nonetheless, he argued, Britain got the better deal.

'In practice,' he wrote, 'we gave up nothing. We did not wish to pursue a forward policy in Persia. Nor could a British advance in Persia have been the same menace to Russia that a Russian advance in Persia might have been to India.' It was hardly surprising, he added, that Count Izvolsky had difficulty in persuading the Russian generals to surrender so much, 'while we gave up what was of little or no practical value to us'.

But not everyone in Britain saw the new convention that way. The hawks, like their Russian opposite numbers, denounced it as a sell-out. Foremost among them was the congenital Russophobe Lord Curzon, now back in London after resigning as Viceroy following a row with the Cabinet. Already fuming at the way the government had emasculated Younghusband's hard-won treaty with the Tibetans, he declared of the convention: 'It gives up all we have been fighting for for years, and gives it up with a wholesale abandon that is truly cynical in its recklessness ... the efforts of a century sacrificed, and nothing or next to nothing in return.' The Russian sphere of Persia, he protested, was unduly large, and contained all the major cities, while that apportioned to Britain was small and economically valueless. As for the agreement over Afghanistan, Britain had gained nothing, while the Tibetan clauses of the convention amounted to 'absolute surrender'. He was joined in his condemnation of it by another veteran Russophobe, Arminius Vambery, now aged 76. From Budapest he wrote to the British Foreign Office, which paid him a small pension for his services to the Crown: 'I do not like it at all. You have paid too high a price for temporary peace, for such it is, and the humiliation will not enhance British prestige in Asia. You have shown excessive caution in the face of a sick adversary, although England was not in need of doing so.'

No less angered by the deal were the Persians and Afghans themselves when they learned that they had been shared out between London and St Petersburg in this ignominious fashion without even being consulted. Quite what the Tibetans felt is not known, for, with Younghusband gone, there was no one in Lhasa to take note. But whatever its critics thought of it, the Anglo-Russian Convention of 1907 finally brought the Great

Game to an end. The two rival empires had at last reached the limits of their expansion. There nonetheless remained, in India and at home, lingering suspicions over Russian intentions, especially in Persia, on which St Petersburg continued to tighten its grip. These were not enough, however, to cause the authorities in India to feel seriously threatened. At last the Russian bogy had been laid to rest. It had taken the best part of a century, and cost the lives of many brave men on either side, but in the end it had been resolved by diplomacy.

Or had it? Certainly it seemed so in August 1914, when the British and Russians found themselves fighting as allies in both Asia and Europe. Any remaining suspicions were hastily forgotten as the two ancient rivals joined forces to keep the Germans and Turks out of their Asian territories and spheres of influence. For the first time, instead of glowering at one another across the mountains and deserts of innermost Asia, Sepoy and Cossack fought together. Their common aim was to exclude these new rivals from the Caucasus, Persia and Afghanistan – the fuse which led to both British India and the Tsar's Central Asian domains.

But time was running out for Nicholas. The intolerable strain which the war effort placed on his people and on the Russian economy gave his own 'enemy within' the chance they had long been waiting for. In October 1917, the Russian Revolution led to the collapse of the entire eastern front, from the Baltic to the Caucasus. At once the Bolsheviks tore up all the treaties made by their predecessors. Overnight the Anglo-Russian Convention, on which such hopes had been staked by Britain, became a worthless piece of paper. Far from being over, the Great Game was destined to begin again in a new guise and with renewed vigour, as Lenin vowed to set the East ablaze with the heady gospel of Marxism. However, that is another story which I have already told elsewhere.

*　　*　　*

It is now more than eighty years since the imperial struggle between St Petersburg and London ended. Momentous changes have taken place in the vast arena in which it was contested. The political ones continue, as today's headlines show, but they are too complex and fluid to dwell on here. A change which would have astonished the Great Game players, however, is the opening up of this once forbidden region to foreigners. It is comparatively easy now to reach Chitral, where the grey stone fortress still dominates the river bend, and Hunza, where Manners Smith won his Victoria Cross storming the vertical rockface. Bokhara, where Conolly and Stoddart are buried under the square before the citadel, can be visited thanks to Intourist, as too can Khiva, Samarkand and Tashkent – although the latter has been largely rebuilt following an earthquake. Also at the time of writing, the Chinese allow tourists to visit Kashgar, Yarkand and Lhasa, though for how long is anyone's guess.

Some regions, once accessible, are now closed, like the skeleton-strewn Karakoram Pass, then the principal route through the mountains from northern India into China, but today superseded by the Karakoram Highway. Somewhere on the ancient pass stands a lonely monument to Andrew Dalgleish, brutally hacked to death there in 1888, although no one has seen it for many years, the last caravan having passed that way in 1949. The young Scotsman's remains were retrieved at the time of his murder, however, and buried behind the British commissioner's bungalow at Leh. Although some of the most celebrated players in the Great Game – notably Moorcroft, Burnes, Macnaghten and Cavagnari – have no known resting place, the graves of others can still be visited. General Kaufman, architect of the Russian conquest of Central Asia, is buried near the old Orthodox cathedral in Tashkent, George Hayward in the little-frequented European cemetery at Gilgit, while Francis Younghusband lies in the small Dorset churchyard of Lytchett Minster.

Men such as these, of either side, had few doubts about what they were doing. For those were the days of supreme imperial confidence, unashamed patriotism and an unswerving belief in the superiority of Christian civilisation over all others. With the benefit of hindsight, modern historians may question whether there was ever any real Russian threat to India, so immense were the obstacles that an invasion force would first have had to overcome. But to Burnes and the Pottingers, Burnaby and Rawlinson, it seemed real enough and ever present. Indeed, India's history appeared to bear out their fears. As one Russian general pointed out with ill-concealed relish, of twenty-one attempted invasions of India over the centuries from the north and west, eighteen had been successful. Was there any reason to think that a powerful Russian force might be any less so? Equally, men like Kaufman and Skobelev, Alikhanov and Gromchevsky, feared that unless they staked Russia's claim to the Central Asian khanates, the British would eventually absorb these into their Indian empire.

As for the Indians themselves, they were neither consulted nor considered in any of this. Yet, like their Muslim neighbours across the frontier, it was largely their blood which was spilt during the imperial struggle. All they ever wanted was to be left alone, something they achieved in 1947, when the British packed their bags and departed. But the peoples of Central Asia were less fortunate at their conqueror's hands. For more than a century the vast Russian empire there served as a monument to the Tsarist heroes of the Great Game. Only in 1991 did it finally come crashing down following the worldwide collapse of Communism.

The British heroes of the Great Game had no such memorial, and there is little or nothing to show on the map for all their efforts and sacrifices. Today they live on only in unread memoirs, the occasional place name, and in the yellowing intelligence reports of that long-forgotten adventure.

Bibliography &
Index

Bibliography

The literature of the Great Game, in all its many aspects, is vast. The following list of titles, although far from exhaustive, includes those works which I found most valuable while researching and writing this book. Many of the books are long out of print, and can only be obtained from specialist libraries – or at great expense. The Afghan wars, the Crimean War, the Eastern Question, Anglo-Russian relations and the Russo-Japanese War, although inseparable from the Great Game, are major subjects on their own, with substantial literatures devoted to them. I have therefore listed only those works which I found most useful. Also, for the sake of brevity, I have omitted reports and articles from contemporary newspapers from which I have quoted, although these are usually identified in the text. For the same reason, and because they are unlikely to interest the general reader, I have not listed the file numbers where I have drawn on the Political and Secret files of the day, now in the India Office Library and Records. Except where otherwise indicated, all the works below were published in London.

Abbott, Capt. James, *Narrative of a Journey from Heraut to Khiva, Moscow and St Petersburg, during the late Russian invasion of Khiva*. 1843.

Adam, Mme, *Le Général Skobeleff*. Paris, 1886.

Addy, Premen, *Tibet on the Imperial Chessboard*. Calcutta, 1984.

Adye, Gen. Sir John, *Indian Frontier Policy*. 1897.

Alder, Dr Garry, *British India's Northern Frontier, 1865–1895*. 1963.

—— *Beyond Bokhara. The Life of William Moorcroft*. 1985.

Alder, L., and Dalby, R., *The Dervish of Windsor Castle. The Life of Arminius Vambery*. 1979.

Alexander, Michael, *The True Blue. The Life and Adventures of Colonel Fred Burnaby, 1842–85*. 1957.

Ali, Mahfuz, *The Truth about Russia and England. From a Native's Point of View*. Lucknow, 1886.

Allen, W. E. D., and Muratoff, P., *Caucasian Battlefields. A History of the Wars on the Turco-Caucasian Border, 1828–1921*. Cambridge, 1953.

Anderson, M. S., *Britain's Discovery of Russia, 1553–1815*. 1958.

—— *The Eastern Question, 1774–1923*. 1966.

Andrew, C., and Noakes, J., *Intelligence and International Relations, 1900–1945*. Exeter, 1987.

Andrew, Sir William, *Euphrates Valley Route to India, in connection with the Central Asian and Egyptian Questions*. 1882.

'An Indian Army Officer', *Russia's March towards India*. 2 vols. 1894.

'An Old Indian', *Russia Versus India. Or observations on the present political relations of England with the East*. 1838.

Anon., *Invasions of India from Central Asia*. 1879.

Anon., *Notes on the Relations of British India with Some of the Countries West of the Indus*. 1839.

Anon., *Russia's Next Move Towards India*. 1885.

Anon., *The Dardanelles for England. The True Solution of the Eastern Question*. 1876.

Argyle, Duke of, *The Eastern Question*. 2 vols. 1879.

Armstrong, T. (ed.), *Yermak's Campaign in Siberia*. 1975.

'Arthur Vincent', *The Defence of India*. 1922.

Baddeley, John F., *The Russian Conquest of the Caucasus*. 1908.

Baker, J. N. L., *A History of Geographical Discovery and Exploration*. 1931.

Baker, Col. Valentine, *Clouds in the East. Travels and Adventures on the Perso-Turkoman Frontier*. 1876.

Barr, Lt. W., *Journal of a March from Delhi to Peshawur and from thence to Cabul with the Mission of Lieut.-Colonel Sir C. M. Wade.* 1844.

Bartlett, E. A., *Shall England Keep India?* 1886.

Barton, Sir W., *India's North-West Frontier.* 1939.

Baskakov, V. (trans.), *A History of Afghanistan.* Moscow, 1985.

Baxter, W. E., *England and Russia in Asia.* 1885.

Becker, S., *Russia's Protectorates in Central Asia. Bokhara and Khiva, 1865–1924.* Cambridge, Mass., 1968.

Bell, Maj. Evans, *The Oxus and the Indus.* 1869.

Bell, James S., *Journal of a Residence in Circassia during the Years 1837, 1838 and 1839.* 2 vols. 1840.

Bell, Col. M. S., *Afghanistan as a Theatre of Operations and as a Defence to India.* Calcutta, 1885.

Bellew, Surg.-Maj. H. W., *Journal of a Political Mission to Afghanistan in 1857.* 1862.

—— *From the Indus to the Tigris, a Journey through the Countries of Balochistan, Afghanistan, Khorassan and Iran in 1872.* 1873.

—— *Kashmir and Kashgar. A Narrative of the Journey of the Embassy to Kashgar in 1873–74.* 1875.

Benyon, Lt. W. G. L., *With Kelly to Chitral.* 1896.

Beresford, Col. C. E., 'Russian Railways towards India', *Proceedings of the Central Asian Society.* 1906.

Blanch, Lesley, *The Sabres of Paradise.* 1960.

Blood, Gen. Sir Bindon, *Four Score Years and Ten.* 1933.

Bonvalot, Gabriel, *Through the Heart of Asia. Over the Pamirs to India.* 2 vols. 1889.

Boulger, Demetrius, *England and Russia in Central Asia.* 2 vols. 1879.

—— *Central Asian Portraits.* 1880.

—— *Central Asian Questions. Essays on Afghanistan, China and Central Asia.* 1885.

Bower, Capt. Hamilton, *Diary of a Journey Across Tibet.* Calcutta, 1893.

Bremner, Robert, *Excursions in the Interior of Russia, including Sketches of the Character and Policy of the Emperor Nicholas.* 2 vols. 1839.

Bruce, R. I., *The Forward Policy and its Results.* 1900.

Buchan, John, *The Half-Hearted*. 1900.

Buckland, C. E., *Dictionary of Indian Biography*. 1906.

Burnaby, Capt. Frederick, *A Ride to Khiva. Travels and Adventures in Central Asia*. 1876.

—— *On Horseback through Asia Minor*. 2 vols. 1877.

Burnes, Sir Alexander, *Travels into Bokhara*. 3 vols. 1834.

—— *Cabool. Being a Personal Narrative of a Journey to, and Residence in, that City in the Years 1836, 7 and 8*. 1842.

Burslem, Capt. R., *A Peep into Toorkistan*. 1846.

Cameron, Lt.-Col. G. P., *Personal Adventures and Excursions in Georgia, Circassia and Russia*. 2 vols. 1845.

Campbell, Sir George, *The Afghan Frontier*. 1879.

Caroe, Sir Olaf, *The Pathans, 550 BC–AD 1957*. 1958.

Cazelet, E., *England's Policy in the East. Our Relations with Russia*. 1876.

Chakravarty, S., *From Khyber to Oxus. A Study of Imperial Expansion*. Delhi, 1976.

Chavda, V. K., *India, Britain, Russia. A Study in British Opinion, 1838–1878*. Delhi, 1967.

Chirol, Sir Valentine, *The Middle Eastern Question, or Some Problems of Indian Defence*. 1903.

Chohan, A. S., *The Gilgit Agency, 1877–1935*. Delhi, n.d. (1980s).

Churchill, R. P., *The Anglo-Russian Convention of 1907*. Cedar Rapids, USA, 1939.

Clayton, G. D., *Britain and the Eastern Question. Missolonghi to Gallipoli*. 1971.

Cobbold, Ralph, *Innermost Asia. Travel and Sport in the Pamirs*. 1900.

Coen, T. C., *The Indian Political Service*. 1971.

Collen, Lt.-Gen. Sir E., *The Defence of India*. 1906.

Colquhoun, A. R., *Russia Against India*. 1906.

Colquhoun, Capt. J., *Essay on the Formation of an Intelligence Department for India*. 1874.

Conolly, Lt. Arthur, *Journey to the North of India, Overland from England, Through Russia, Persia and Affghaunistaun*. 2 vols. 1834.

Cory, Col. A., *Shadows of Coming Events*. 1876.

Costin, W. C., *Great Britain and China, 1833–1860*. Oxford, 1937.

Cotton, Sir S., *The Central Asian Question*. Dublin, 1878.

Curzon, Hon. George N., *Russia in Central Asia*. 1889.

—— *Persia and the Persian Question*. 2 vols. 1892.

—— *The Pamirs and the Source of the Oxus*. 1896.

—— *Frontiers*. Oxford, 1907.

Custine, Marquis de, *Journey For Our Time. Russia in 1839*. 1953.

Dabbs, Jack, *History of the Discovery and Exploration of Chinese Turkestan*. The Hague, 1963.

Dacosta, J., *A Scientific Frontier*. 1891.

Dallin, D., *The Rise of Russia in Asia*. New Haven, USA, 1949.

David, Maj. C., *Is A Russian Invasion of India Feasible?* 1877.

Davies, C. C., *The Problem of the North-West Frontier, 1890–1908. With a Survey of Policy since 1849*. Cambridge, 1932.

Davis, H. W. C., *The Great Game in Asia, 1800–1844*. Raleigh Lecture, 1926.

Dekhnewala, A., *The Great Russian Invasion of India*. 1879.

Dictionary of National Biography. Oxford, 1921.

Dilke, Sir C., and Wilkinson, W., *Imperial Defence*. 1892.

Dobson, G., *Russia's Railway Advance into Central Asia*. 1890.

Durand, Col. Algernon, *The Making of a Frontier. Five Years' Experience and Adventures in Gilgit, Hunza, Nagar, Chitral and the Eastern Hindu Kush*. 1899.

Durand, Sir Henry, *The First Afghan War*. 1879.

Edwardes, Maj. Herbert, *A Year on the Punjab Frontier, in 1848–9*. 2 vols. 1851.

Edwardes, Michael, *Playing the Great Game. A Victorian Cold War*. 1975.

Edwards, H. S., *Russian Projects against India, from Czar Peter to General Skobeleff*. 1885.

Ellenborough, Lord, *Political Diary, 1828–30*. 2 vols. 1881.

Elliott, Maj.-Gen. J. G., *The Frontier, 1839–47*. 1968.

English, Barbara, *John Company's Last War*. 1971.

Entner, M. L., *Russo-Persian Commercial Relations, 1828–1914*. Gainsville, USA, 1965.

Evans, Col. George de Lacy, *On the Designs of Russia*. 1828.

—— *On the Practicability of an Invasion of British India*. 1829.

Eyre, Lt. Vincent, *The Military Operations at Cabul, which* ended in the Retreat and Destruction of the British Army, January 1842. 1843.

Fairley, Jean, The Lion River: The Indus. 1975.

Faris, Selim, The Decline of British Prestige in the East. 1887.

Fisher, A. W., The Russian Annexation of the Crimea, 1772–1728. Cambridge, 1970.

Fleming, Peter, Bayonets to Lhasa. The British Invasion of Tibet in 1904. 1961.

Forsyth, Sir Douglas, Report of a Mission to Yarkand in 1873. Calcutta, 1875.

Forsyth, E. (ed.), Autobiography and Reminiscences of Sir Douglas Forsyth. 1887.

Fraser-Tytler, Sir W. K., Afghanistan. A Study of Political Developments in Central Asia. 1950.

Frechtling, L. E., 'Anglo-Russian Rivalry in Eastern Turkistan, 1863–1881', Journal of the Royal Central Asian Society. Vol. XXVI. 1939.

Fredericks, P. G., The Sepoy and the Cossack. 1972.

Geyer, Dietrich, Russian Imperialism. The Interaction of Domestic and Foreign Policy, 1860–1914. Leamington Spa, 1987.

Gillard, David, The Struggle for Asia, 1828–1914. 1977.

Gleason, J. H., The Genesis of Russophobia in Great Britain. Cambridge, USA, 1950.

Glover, M., A Very Slippery Fellow. The Life of Sir Robert Wilson, 1777–1849. Oxford, 1977.

Golder, F. A., Russian Expansion on the Pacific, 1641–1850. Cleveland, USA, 1914.

Goldsmid, Col. Sir F., Central Asia and its Question. 1873.

—— Eastern Persia. 2 vols. 1876.

Gopal, S., British Policy in India, 1858–1905. Cambridge, 1965.

Gordon, T. E., The Roof of the World. Edinburgh, 1876.

—— A Varied Life. 1906.

Grant Duff, M. E., The Eastern Question. Edinburgh, 1876.

Greaves, R. L., Persia and the Defence of India, 1884–1892. 1959.

Green, Col. Sir H., The Defence of the North-West Frontier of India, with Reference to the Advance of Russia in Central Asia. 1873.

Grover, Capt. John, *An Appeal to the British Nation on Behalf of Colonel Stoddart and Captain Conolly, Now in Captivity in Bokhara*. 1843.
—— *The Bokhara Victims*. 1845.
—— *The Ameer of Bokhara and Lord Aberdeen*. 1845.
Habberton, W., 'Anglo-Russian Relations concerning Afghanistan, 1837–1907', *Illinois Studies in the Social Sciences*. Vol. 21. 1937.
Hall, L., *A Brief Guide to Sources for the Study of Afghanistan in the India Office Records*. 1981.
Hanna, Col. H. B., *Can Russia Invade India?* 1895.
—— *India's Scientific Frontier. Where is it? What is it?* 1895.
—— *Backwards or Forwards?* n.d. (1895).
—— *The Second Afghan War, 1878–79–80*. 3 vols. 1899–1910.
Harris, J., *Much Sounding of Bugles. The Siege of Chitral, 1895*. 1975.
Harrison, J. A., *The Founding of the Russian Empire in Asia and America*. Miami, USA, 1971.
Havelock, Capt. H., *Narrative of the War in Afghanistan*. 1840.
Haxthausen, Baron A. von, *The Tribes of the Caucasus. With an Account of Schamyl and the Murids*. 1855.
Hayward, George, 'Journey from Leh to Yarkand and Kashgar'. Read Dec. 13, 1869. *Journal of the RGS*. 1871.
—— 'Letters from Mr G. W. Hayward on his Explorations in Gilgit and Yassin'. Read Nov. 15, 1870. *Journal of the RGS*. 1872.
Heathcote, T. A., *The Afghan Wars, 1839–1919*. 1980.
Hellwald, F. von, *The Russians in Central Asia*. 1874.
Henze, P. B., 'Fire and Sword in the Caucasus. The 19th century resistance of the North Caucasian Mountaineers', *Central Asian Survey*. Oxford, 1983.
Heumann, Capt., *Les Russes et les Anglais dans L'Asie Centrale*. Paris, 1885.
Holdich, Sir Thomas, *The Indian Borderland, 1880–1900*. 1901.
—— *The Gates of India*. 1910.
Holdsworth, M., *Turkestan in the 19th Century. A Brief History of the Khanates of Bukhara, Kokand and Khiva*. Oxford, 1959.

Hopkirk, Peter, *Trespassers on the Roof of the World. The Race for Lhasa*. 1982.

—— *Setting the East Ablaze. Lenin's Dream of an Empire in Asia*. 1984.

Hoskins, H. L., *British Routes to India*. New York, 1928.

Hsu, I. C. Y., *The Ili Crisis*. Oxford, 1965.

Hue, F., *Les Russes et les Anglais dans L'Afghanistan*. Paris, 1885.

Hunt, Capt. G. H., *Outram and Havelock's Persian Campaign*. 1858.

Hutchinson, A. H., *The Next Battlefield*. 1871.

Hutton, J., *Central Asia: From the Aryan to the Cossack*. 1875.

Ingle, H. N., *Nesselrode and the Russian Rapprochement with Britain, 1836–1844*. Berkeley, USA, 1976.

Ingram, Edward, *The Beginning of the Great Game in Asia, 1828–1834*. Oxford, 1979.

—— *Commitment to Empire. Prophesies of the Great Game in Asia, 1797–1800*. Oxford, 1981.

—— *In Defence of British India. Great Britain in the Middle East, 1775–1842*. 1984.

James, Lionel, *With the Chitral Relief Force*. Calcutta, 1895.

Jelavich, B., *A Century of Russian Foreign Policy, 1814–1914*. Philadelphia, USA, 1964.

Jerningham, H. E., *Russia's Warnings. Collected from Official Papers*. 1885.

Kalmykow, A. D., *Memoirs of a Russian Diplomat. Outposts of the Empire, 1893–1917*. New Haven, USA, 1971.

Kaye, Sir John, *History of the War in Afghanistan*. 2 vols. 1851. (Revised in 3 vols., 1874.)

—— *Life and Correspondence of Major-General Sir John Malcolm*. 2 vols. 1856.

—— *Lives of Indian Officers*. 2 vols. 1867.

Kazemzadeh, F., *Russia and Britain in Persia, 1864–1914*. New Haven, USA, 1968.

Keay, John, *When Men and Mountains Meet*. 1977.

—— *The Gilgit Game*. 1979.

Kelly, J. B., *Britain and the Persian Gulf, 1795–1880*. Oxford, 1968.

Kessler, M. M., *Ivan Viktorovich Vitkevich, 1806–39. A*

Tsarist Agent in Central Asia. Washington, USA, 1960.

Khalfin, N. A., *Russia's Policy in Central Asia, 1857–63.* (Condensed and translated from the 1960 Moscow edn.) 1964.

Khanikoff, M., *Bokhara, its Amir and its People.* (From the Russian.) 1845.

Khiva. A Narrative of the Russian Military Expedition to Khiva under General Perofski in 1839. (From the Russian.) Calcutta, 1867.

Kinneir, J. M., *Geographical Memoir of the Persian Empire.* 1813.

—— *Journey through Asia Minor, Armenia and Koordistan in 1813–14.* 1818.

Kipling, Rudyard, *Kim.* 1901.

Knight, E. F., *Where Three Empires Meet.* 1894.

Kostenko, Capt. L. F., *Description of the Journey of a Russian Mission to Bokhara in 1870.* (From the Russian.) Secret and Political Department, India Office. n.d.

Krausse, A., *Russia in Asia.* 1899.

Kuropatkin, Col. A. N., *Kashgaria. Historical and Geographical Sketch of the Country, its Military Strength, Industries and Trade.* (From the Russian.) Calcutta, 1882.

—— *Les Confins Anglo-Russes dans L'Asie Centrale.* (From the Russian.) Paris, 1885.

Lal, Mohan, *Journal of a Tour through the Panjab, Afghanistan, Turkestan, Khorasan and Part of Persia.* Calcutta, 1834.

—— *Life of the Amir Dost Muhammed Khan of Kabul.* 2 vols. 1846.

Lamb, A., *Britain and Chinese Central Asia. The Road to Lhasa, 1767–1905.* 1960.

'Late Resident at Bhagulpore', *The Dangers of British India from French Invasion.* 1808.

Lawrence, Sir George, *Forty-three Years in India.* 1874.

Lobonov-Rostovsky, Prince A., *Russia and Asia.* New York, 1933.

Lockhart, Col. William, *Confidential Report of the Gilgit Mission, 1885–6.* 1889.

Longworth, J. A., *A Year Among the Circassians.* 2 vols. 1840.

Lunt, James, *Bokhara Burnes.* 1969.

MacGregor, Col. C. M., *Narrative of a Journey through the*

Provinces of Khorassan and on the N.W. Frontier of Afghanistan in 1875. 2 vols. 1879.

—— *Wanderings in Baluchistan*. 1882.

—— (Gen. Sir Charles), *The Defence of India*. Simla, 1884.

MacGregor, Lady (ed.), *The Life and Opinions of Major-General Sir Charles MacGregor*. 2 vols. Edinburgh, 1888.

MacKenzie, D., *The Lion of Tashkent. The Career of General M. G. Cherniaev*. Athens, USA, 1974.

Maclean, Sir Fitzroy, *Eastern Approaches*. 1949.

—— *A Person from England*. 1958.

—— *To Caucasus. The End of All the Earth*. 1976.

McNeal, R. H., *Tsar and Cossack, 1855–1914*. Oxford, 1987.

McNeill, Sir John (anon.), *Progress and Present Position of Russia in the East*. 1836.

Macrory, Sir Patrick, *Signal Catastrophe. The Retreat from Kabul, 1842*. 1956.

Malcolm, Sir John, *History of Persia from the Most Early Period to the Present Day*. 2 vols. 1815.

—— (anon.), *Sketches of Persia from the Journals of a Traveller in the East*. 2 vols. 1827.

Malleson, Col. G. B., *History of Afghanistan*. 1878.

—— *Herat: The Granary and Garden of Central Asia*. 1880.

—— *The Russo-Afghan Question and the Invasion of India*. 1885.

Malozemoff, A., *Russian Far Eastern Policy, 1881–1904*. Berkeley, USA, 1958.

Marriott, J. A. R., *The Eastern Question*. 1917.

—— *Anglo-Russian Relations, 1689–1943*. 1944.

Marvin, Charles, *The Eye-Witnesses' Account of the Disastrous Russian Campaign against the Akhal Tekke Turkomans*. 1880.

—— *Merv, the Queen of the World, and the Scourge of the Man-Stealing Turkomans*. 1881.

—— *The Russian Advance towards India*. 1882.

—— *The Russians at Merv and Herat, and their Power of Invading India*. 1883.

—— *The Russian Railway to Herat and India*. 1883.

—— *The Russian Annexation of Merv*. 1884.

—— *Reconnoitring Central Asia*. 1884.

—— *The Region of Eternal Fire. An Account of a Journey to the Petroleum Region of the Caspian in 1883.* 1884.

—— *The Railway Race to Herat.* 1885.

—— *The Russians at the Gates of Herat.* 1885.

—— (trans. and ed.), *Colonel Grodekoff's Ride from Samarkand to Herat.* 1880.

Mason, Philip, *A Matter of Honour. An Account of the Indian Army.* 1974.

Masson, Charles, *Narrative of Various Journeys in Balochistan, Afghanistan and the Panjab, including a Residence in those Countries.* 3 vols. 1842.

—— *Narrative of a Journey to Kalat.* 1843.

Masters, John, *The Lotus and the Wind.* 1953.

Maxwell, Col. Leigh, *My God – Maiwand! Operations of the South Afghanistan Field Force, 1878–80.* 1979.

Mayer, S. R., *Afghanistan. Its Political and Military History . . . and an Appendix on the Prospects of a Russian Invasion of India.* 1879.

Mehra, P., *The Younghusband Expedition. An Interpretation.* 1968.

Menon, K. S., *The 'Russian Bogey' and British Aggression in India and Beyond.* Calcutta, 1957.

Meyendorff, Baron, *Voyage d'Orenbourg à Boukhara fait en 1820.* Paris, 1826.

Michell, Robert (trans.), *A Narrative of the Russian Military Expedition to Khiva, conducted by Prince Alexander Bekovitch Cherkasski in 1717.* 1873.

Miller, C., *Khyber. British India's North-West Frontier.* 1977.

Monteith, Lt.-Gen. W., *Kars and Erzeroum, with the Campaigns of Prince Paskiewitch in 1823 and 1829, and an Account of the Conquests of Russia Beyond the Caucasus.* 1856.

Moorcroft, William, and Trebeck, G., *Travels in the Himalayan Provinces of Hindoostan and the Punjab.* 2 vols. 1841.

Morgan, Gerald, *Ney Elias. Explorer and Envoy Extraordinary.* 1971.

—— *Anglo-Russian Rivalry in Central Asia: 1810–1895.* 1981.

Morrell, J. R., *Russia and England. Their Strength and Weakness.* New York, 1854.

Morris, James, *Pax Britannica*. (Trilogy.) 1968, 1973, 1978.

Morrison, J. L., *From Alexander Burnes to Frederick Roberts. A Survey of Imperial Frontier History*. Raleigh Lecture, 1936.

Moser, L., *The Caucasus and its People, with a Brief History of their Wars, and a Sketch of the Achievements of the Renowned Chief Schamyl*. 1856.

Muraviev, Nikolai, *Journey to Khiva through the Turkoman Country, 1819–20*. Calcutta, 1871.

Napier, Capt. G. C., *Collection of Journals and Reports received from Captain the Hon. G. C. Napier, Bengal Staff Corps, on Special Duty in Persia*. 1876.

Nazem, Hossein, *Russia and Great Britain in Iran, 1900–1914*. Teheran, 1975.

Nemirovitch-Dantchenko, V. I., *Personal Reminiscences of General Skobelleff*. (From the Russian.) 1884.

Nevill, Capt. H. L., *Campaigns on the North-West Frontier*. 1912.

North, Lt.-Col. R., *The Literature of the North-West Frontier. A Select Bibliography*. Peshawar, 1945.

O'Connor, Sir Frederick, *On the Frontier and Beyond*. 1931.

O'Donovan, Edmond, *The Merv Oasis. Travels and Adventures East of the Caspian, 1879–80–81*. 2 vols. 1882.

'O.K.' (Mme Olga Novikoff), *Russia and England, from 1876–1880*. 1880.

Pahlen, Count K. K., *Mission to Turkestan, 1908–09*. 1964.

Parliamentary Papers, 'Russian Agents in Persia and Afghanistan'. Vol. 40. 1839.

Pasley, R., *'Send Malcolm!' The Life of Major-General Sir John Malcolm, 1769–1833*. 1982.

Piassetsky, P., *Russian Travellers in Mongolia and China*. 2 vols. (From the Russian.) 1884.

Pierce, R. A., *Russian Central Asia, 1867–1917*. Berkeley, USA, 1960.

Popowski, J., *The Rival Powers in Central Asia*. 1893.

Pottinger, G., *The Afghan Connection. The Extraordinary Adventures of Major Eldred Pottinger*. Edinburgh, 1983.

Pottinger, Lt. Henry, *Travels in Beloochistan and Sinde*. 1816.

Prejevalsky, Lt.-Col. Nikolai, *Mongolia, the Tangut Country and the Solitudes of Northern Tibet.* 2 vols. (From the Russian.) 1876.

—— *From Kulja across the Tian Shan to Lob Nor.* (From the Russian.) 1879.

Prioux, A., *Les Russes dans L'Asie Centrale.* Paris, 1886.

Quested, R. K. I., *The Expansion of Russia in East Asia, 1857–1860.* Kuala Lumpur, 1968.

Rahman, Abdur, *The Life of Abdur Rahman, Amir of Afghanistan.* 2 vols. 1900.

Ramazani, R. K., *The Foreign Policy of Iran, 1500–1941.* Charlottesville, USA, 1966.

Ravenstein, E. G., *The Russians on the Amur.* 1861.

Rawlinson, Sir Henry, *England and Russia in the East.* 1875.

Rawlinson, Canon G., *A Memoir of Sir Henry Rawlinson.* 1898.

Rayfield, Donald, *The Dream of Lhasa. The Life of Nikolay Przhevalsky, 1839–88, Explorer of Central Asia.* 1976.

Roberts, Field Marshal Lord, *Is An Invasion of India Possible? Confidential Report.* Madras, 1883.

—— *Forty-One Years in India.* 2 vols. 1897.

Roberts, P. E., *History of British India. Under the Company and the Crown.* 1921.

Robertson, Sir George, *Confidential Report on a Journey to Kafirstan.* 1894.

—— *Chitral. The Story of a Minor Siege.* 1898.

Robinson, G., *David Urquhart. Some Chapters in the Life of a Victorian Knight-Errant of Justice and Liberty.* Oxford, 1920.

Robson, B., *The Road to Kabul. The Second Afghan War, 1878–1881.* 1986.

Rodenbough, Brig. T. F. (US Army), *Afghanistan and the Anglo-Russian Dispute.* New York, 1885.

Romanovski, M., *Notes on the Central Asiatic Question.* (From the Russian.) Calcutta, 1870.

Russell, R., *India's Danger and England's Duty.* 1885.

Russian Missions into the Interior of Asia. 1. Nazaroff's Expedition to Kokand. 2. Eversmann and Jakovlew's Account of Buchara. 3. Captain Muraviev's Embassy to Turkomania and Chiva. 1823.

Sale, Lady, *Journal of the Disasters in Afghanistan.* 1843.

Schofield, Victoria, *Every Rock, Every Hill. The Plain Tale of the North-West Frontier and Afghanistan.* 1984.

Schuyler, Eugene, *Turkistan. Notes of a Journey in Russian Turkistan, Khokand, Bokhara and Kuldja.* 2 vols. 1876.

Seaver, George, *Francis Younghusband. Explorer and Mystic.* 1952.

Seton-Watson, Hugh, *The Decline of Imperial Russia, 1855–1914.* 1952.

—— *The Russian Empire, 1801–1917.* Oxford, 1967.

Seton-Watson, R. W., *Disraeli, Gladstone and the Eastern Question.* 1935.

Shakespear, Sir Richmond, 'A Personal Narrative of a Journey from Herat to Orenburg, on the Caspian, in 1840', *Blackwood's Magazine.* June 1842.

Shaw, Robert, *Visits to High Tartary, Yarkand and Kashgar.* 1871.

Showers, Maj.-Gen. C. L., *The Central Asian Question, and the Massacre of the Cabul Embassy.* 1879.

—— *The Cossack at the Gate of India.* 1885.

Shukla, R. L., *Britain, India and the Turkish Empire, 1853–82.* Delhi, 1973.

Sidebottom, J. K., *The Overland Mail. A Postal Historical Study of the Mail Route to India.* 1948.

Simond, C., *L'Afghanistan. Les Russes aux portes de L'Inde.* Paris, 1855.

Singer, André, *Lords of the Khyber.* 1984.

Skobeleff, Gen. M. D., *The Siege and Assault of Denghil Tepe.* (From the Russian.) 1881.

Skrine, C. P., and Nightingale, P., *Macartney at Kashgar. New Light on British, Chinese and Russian Activities in Sinkiang, 1890–1918.* 1973.

Skrine, F. H., and Ross, E. D., *The Heart of Asia. A History of Russian Turkestan and the Central Asian Khanates.* 1899.

Spiers, E. M., *Radical General. Sir George de Lacy Evans, 1787–1870.* Manchester, 1983.

'Stepniak', *The Russian Storm-Cloud. Russia in Her Relations to Neighbouring Countries.* 1886.

Stewart, Col. Charles, *Through Persia in Disguise.* 1911.

Stuart, Lt.-Col., *Journal of a Residence in Northern Persia and the Adjacent Provinces of Turkey*. 1854.

Stumm, H., *Russia's Advance Eastward*. (From the German.) 1874.

—— *Russia in Central Asia*. (From the German.) 1885.

Swinson, A., *The North-West Frontier, 1939–1947*. 1967.

Sykes, Sir P. M., *A History of Afghanistan*. 2 vols. 1940.

Terentiev, M. A., *Russia and England in Central Asia*. (From the Russian.) Calcutta, 1876.

Thomson, H. C., *The Chitral Campaign*. 1895.

Thorburn, S. S., *Asiatic Neighbours*. Edinburgh, 1894.

Tikhvinsky, S. L. (ed.), *Chapters from the History of Russo-Chinese Relations, 17th to 19th centuries*. (From the Russian.) Moscow, 1985.

Trench, Capt. F., *The Russo-Indian Question, Historically, Strategically and Politically Considered*. 1869.

Tynianov, Y., *Death and Diplomacy in Persia*. (From the Russian.) 1938.

Urquhart, David, *Turkey and its Resources*. 1833.

—— *England, France, Russia and Turkey*. 1834.

—— *England and Russia*. 1835.

—— *The Spirit of the East*. 2 vols. 1839.

—— *Diplomatic Transactions in Central Asia*. 1839.

—— *The Progress of Russia in the West, North and South*. 1853.

Valikhanov, Capt. C. (*et al.*), *The Russians in Central Asia*. (From the Russian.) 1865.

Vambery, Arminius, *Travels in Central Asia*. 2 vols. 1864.

—— *Sketches of Central Asia*. 1868.

—— *Central Asia and the Anglo-Russian Frontier Question*. 1874.

—— *Arminius Vambery, His Life and Struggles*. 2 vols. 1883.

—— *The Coming Struggle for India*. 1885.

'Vladimir', *Russia on the Pacific, and the Siberian Railway*. 1899.

Warburton, Sir Robert (anon.), *The Russian Warning*. Privately printed. Peshawar, 1892.

Waters, Brig.-Gen. W., *'Secret and Confidential'. The Experiences of a Military Attaché*. 1926.

Weil, M., *L'Expédition de Khiva*. Paris, 1874.

Westmacott, Capt. G. E., *Indian Commerce and Russian Intrigue*. 1838.

Wheeler, Col. Geoffrey (trans.), 'British Policy in Central Asia in the Early Nineteenth Century. The Mission of Richmond Shakespear'. Translation and review by G. Wheeler of article by N. I. Khalfin on 'British Expansion in Central Asia' in *Istoriya SSSR*. *Central Asian Review*. Vol. VI, No. 4. 1958.

Whitteridge, Sir Gordon, *Charles Masson of Afghanistan*. Warminster, 1986.

Wilson, Sir Robert, *A Sketch of the Military and Political Power of Russia in the Year 1817*. 1817.

Wisely, G. A., *Table of Distances in Russia, Central Asia and India*. 1885.

Wood, Maj. H., *The Shores of Lake Aral*. 1876.

Wood, Lt. J., *A Journey to the Source of the River Oxus*. 1841.

Worms, Baron H. de., *England's Policy in the East*. 1877.

Wright, Sir Denis, *The English Amongst the Persians. During the Qajar Period, 1787–1921*. 1977.

Yapp, Malcolm, *Strategies of British India. Britain, Iran and Afghanistan*. Oxford, 1980.

Yate, Lt. A. C., *England and Russia Face to Face in Asia. Travels with the Afghan Boundary Commission*. Edinburgh, 1887.

Yate, Maj. C. E., *Northern Afghanistan*. Edinburgh, 1888.

Younghusband, Col. Sir Francis, *Confidential Report of a Mission to the Northern Frontier of Kashmir in 1889*. Calcutta, 1890.

—— *The Heart of a Continent*. 1896.

—— *India and Tibet*. 1910.

—— *Wonders of the Himalaya*. 1924.

—— *The Light of Experience*. 1927.

Younghusband, G. J. and F. E., *The Relief of Chitral*. 1895.

Zimmerman, Lt. C., *Khiva. Memoir on the Countries about the Caspian and Aral Seas*. (From the German.) 1840.

Index

Abbas Mirza, 63–5, 66, 75, 109–10

Abbott, Capt. James, 204–5, 212, 219, 220–1, 224, 225; criticism of by Soviet historians, 227–9; town named after him, 229

Abdur Rahman, Emir of Afghanistan: protégé of Russians, 382, 395–6; recognised as Emir by British, 396–7, 398; good neighbour to Britain, 397; takes over Herat and Kandahar, 401; Britain's treaty obligations towards, 397, 416, 426, 429; his statesmanlike qualities, 397, 430–1; cedes Pandjeh to Russians, 432; Britain's ally against Russia, 440, 456, 499, 505; supports Sher in Chitral crisis, 484

Aberdeen, Lord, 281

Aboukir Bay, 26

Adrianople, see Edirne

Afghan Wars

First (1839–42), 188–91, 202, 203, 204, 232–3, 236, 237–42; disaster at Kabul, 239–60; retreat from Kabul, 260–9; Brydon (q.v.) only survivor, 268; news of catastrophe reaches Calcutta & London, 270–1; relief of Jalalabad, 271–2; retaliation against Kabul, 273–4, 276–7; 282, 286, 302, 430

incompetence of British leaders, 240, 242, 248–50, 251, 257, 260, 262, 263, 264, 394

Second (1878–81), 291; the Cavagnari Mission, 382–3, 384–7, slaughter of Mission, 389–91; Roberts marches on Kabul, 391–2, hangs ringleaders, 393, fights off Afghan attack, 394–5, installs Abdur Rahman as Emir, 396–7; decision to evacuate Kabul, 398, battle of Maiwand, 398–9, relief of Kandahar, 400; 423

see also Kabul

Afghanistan, 12, 30, 31, 32, 38, 41, 42, 88, 92, 135, 186, 235, 279, 329, 330, 335, 356, 368, 410, 422, 440, 484, 498, 521, 522

as invasion route to India, 3, 24, 27, 36, 42, 69, 72, 73, 74, 75, 117, 118, 128, 131, 139, 151, 189–91, 284, 287–8, 296, 313, 314, 352, 358, 360, 380, 388, 408, 415, 424, 437, 446, 455–6

British relations with, 7, 30, 31, 139, 168, 170–1, 173–4, 181, 183, 202, 210, 233, 234, 288, 318, 359, 361, 382–3, 505

as British sphere of influence, 166, 188–9, 319, 337, 350–1, 456, 520

Russian relations with, 7, 20, 117, 165–6, 167, 168, 172–4, 183, 185, 188, 356, 359, 361, 362, 380, 381–2, 383, 440, 524

delineation of northern border, 350, 416–17, 425–8, 430, 431, 432, 433, 437, 440, 450, 455, 462, 465–70, 471, 480–1, 500, 505

Afghanistan (*cont.*)
struggles over leadership, 167–8, 188–9, 273, 275
see also Afghan Wars; Kabul, Herat etc.; visitors and Emirs by name
Akbar Khan, Mohammed, 247, 250–6, 258, 259, 260, 270, 272; flees Kabul, 274; 275, 276
treachery of, 255–6, 257, 261, 262, 263–4
Ak-Mechet, 282
Alaska, 409
Alder, Dr Garry, 95, 106–7
Alexander I, Tsar, ruled 1801–25: 3, 29–30, 32, 34, 43, 56, 58–63, 65, 74, 87, 93–4, 102, 109, 110
Alexander II, Tsar, ruled 1855–81: territorial ambitions, 295, 296, 297, 298; decorates Ignatiev, 300; emancipates serfs, 302; expansion into Turkestan, 302–3, 305, 307; Tashkent annexed in his name, 310–11; appoints Kaufman, 312; British fears for India, 314; Emir of Bokhara becomes his vassal, 316; Gorchakov blames military for expansionism, 319; Tsar sends envoy to Yakub Beg, 333; 349; Khiva attacked, 351; 352, 353, 373, 378; Treaty of Berlin, 380–1; 384, 386, 403, 408; death, 409
Alexander III, Tsar, ruled 1881–94: 410, 412–13; continues Russian advances in Turkestan, 414–15; Pandjeh incident, 427–8; brink of war with Britain, 429; 442, 459, 464, 467, 471, 480, 482, 503
Alexandria, 26
Alexandrovsk, *see* Fort Alexandrovsk
Alikhanov, Lt., 411–14, 427–8, 439, 524

Aman-al-Mulk (ruler of Chitral), 434, 481, 484, 497
American Civil War, 302
Amu-Darya river, *see* Oxus
Amur river, 298
Andijan, 353
Anglo-Afghan agreement, 397, 416, 431
Anglophobia, 295, 363, 431, 434, 445, 519
Anglo-Russian Convention of 1907, 8, 519–22
Anne, Tsarina, ruled 1730–40: 20
Aral Sea, 17, 29, 117, 130, 146, 204, 205, 206, 282, 296, 297, 368, 442
Aras river (Araxes), 63, 66
Ark (or Citadel, at Bokhara), 146, 147, 278, 443
Armenia, 32, 110, 153
Armenians, 112–13
Arnold, Matthew, 443
Ashkhabad, 411, 441, 505
Astrabad, 27, 126, 128, 130, 148, 284
Astrakhan, 14, 15, 17, 83, 226
Athenaeum (London club), 150
Attock, 72, 130, 140
Auckland, Lord, Governor-General of India, 152, 168; offends Dost Mohammed, 170–1, 173, 174, 188; role in starting 1st Afghan War, 189–92, 195, 200; 232, 234, 237, 238, 251, 270, 271
Austria, 33, 59, 115, 163, 212, 286, 371, 424
Aylmer, Capt. Fenton, 474–6
Ayub Khan, ruler of Herat, 398–401

Badakhshan, 350, 357
Badmayev, Peter, 7, 503, 506
Baghdad, 13
Baku, 66, 79, 83, 86, 441
Bala Hissar, 143, 169, 173, 174; failure of British to make use of in 1st Afghan War, 239, 240, 242, 244, 245–6, 258, 260; 246,

251, 260, 272, 274; British consider blowing up, 276; 277; Cavagnari takes up residence, 387; mutinous troops arrive, 390, attack British, 390–1; Roberts sets up gallows, 393; explosions in, 394

Balkans, the, 283, 287, 377–9, 455

Balkh, 73, 74, 105, 106, 107, 117, 130, 145, 146, 151, 203, 216, 384

Baltic, the, 314, 522

Baltic fleet (Russian), 514, 516

Baltit, 474

Baluchistan, 24, 36; Christie and Pottinger in, 38–41, 43, 44, 45, 51, 52, 54, 55; 73, 193, 360

Bamian, 100, 275, 424

Bampur, 50

Baroghil Pass, 355–8, 433, 449

Baryatinsky, Prince Alexander, 301

Bashi-Bazouks, 378

Basman, 51

Batum, 287

Bekovich, Prince Alexander, 17–20

Bell, James, 159–62, 285, 286

Bell, VC, Colonel Mark, 448

Benckendorff, Count, 514

Bentinck, Lord William, 139, 150

Berlin, Congress of, 381, 419

Birmingham, 91

Bismarck, Otto von, 301, 408

'Black Hole', verminous pit at Bokhara (q.v.), 1, 230, 231, 232, 443

Black Sea, 21, 22, 27, 61, 71, 83, 115, 152, 154; Russian naval blockade, 156, 157; harsh terms after Crimean War, 286, 287, 348; 378, 455

Boer War, 507

Boisragon, Lt., 475, 476

Bokhara, 4, 13, 21, 28, 30, 42, 74, 78, 117, 119, 151, 172, 203, 211, 228, 235, 275, 306, 309, 310, 311, 313, 315, 316–17, 322, 328,
336, 353, 369, 374, 420, 456, 523

visited by Russians (1820), 102–4, 119

visited by Moorcroft (1825), 91, 92, 97, 98, 101–2, 105, 107, 202

visited by Burnes (1832), 140, 143, 145, 146–9, 151, 183

slavery in, 78, 104–5, 146, 147–8, 275, 297

perversions in, 103–4

Stoddart sent there, 191, & held prisoner, 201, 203, 214, 218, 230–3, 235; death, 1, 2, 278–9

Conolly arrives, 233, 236; death, 1, 2, 278–9

visited by Ignatiev (1858), 296–7, 303

annexed by Russia, 316, 351, 415

Transcaspian Railway link, 389, 439, 441

seen by Curzon, 443–4

Bokhara, Emir of, 19, 102–5, 306, 307, 308, 350, 443–4

as executioner of Stoddart & Conolly, 1, 2, 101, 148, 201, 203, 218, 230, 233, 236, 278–9, 297

depravity of, 104

abortive attempt to oust Russians, 315–17

becomes vassal of Tsar, 316

Bolan Pass, 42, 72, 129, 130, 193, 319, 358, 360, 361, 401, 434

Bolsheviks, 317, 458, 522

Bombay, 24, 25, 26, 39, 42, 118, 133, 149, 237, 347, 494

Bonvalot, Gabriel, 449

Bosnia, 378, 381

Bosporus, the, 22

Boulger, Demetrius, 419

Boxer Uprising, 508

Bozai Gumbaz, 465, 467, 470, 481

Bremmer, Robert, 210

British & Foreign Bible Society, 228

Broadfoot, Major William, 240–2

Brydon, Dr William, 261, 262, 263, 264; seriously wounded in head, 265, acquires pony from dying soldier, 266, only survivor of massacre at Futtehabad, 267, pony wounded, 267, & dies, 268, he reaches safety, 268–9; shock caused by his news, 270; 274

Buchan, John, 447, 450

Budapest, 282, 420, 521

Bulgaria, 114, 378, 379, 380–1; massacre of Christians by Turks, 378

Burnaby, Capt. Frederick, 364, 365–79; his strength & size, 365; fluent linguist, 365; almost loses hands from frostbite, 368; Russians warn him off Khiva, 368–9, his ruse to outwit them, 369–70, arrives in Khiva, 370–1, relations with Khan, 371–3, 374; summoned to Petro-Alexandrovsk, 373–4; ordered back to England, 375; arrives in London, 377; journey to Turkey, 378–9; 388, 403, 455, 524

Burnes, Alexander, Lt. (later Sir), 107, 133, 134; visits Ranjit Singh, 135–8; meets Shah Shujah, 138–9; visits Dost Mohammed, 139–45; locates Moorcroft's grave, 145; visits Bokhara, 146–9; 150, 151–2, 167; second visit to Kabul, 168–71, 172–4, 175, 190; 183, 188; receives knighthood, 191; appointed Macnaghten's deputy, 191; 1st Afghan War, 191–5, 197, 200, 237–42; 202, 203, 227, 229, 231, 234, 235; his death, 241–2, 243, 254, 257, 271, 272, 274, 385, 390, 393; Macnaghten tries to blame him, 244–5; 258, 279–80, 492, 523, 524

Burnes, Lt. Charles, 240–2

Burrows, Brig.-Gen. George, 399–400

Burton, Sir Richard, 56

Buryat Mongols, 5, 503, 505–6

Bushire, 34, 36, 289

Butler, Lady, 268

Calcutta, 24, 26, 95, 96, 97, 99, 101, 124, 176, 188, 340, 422, 446, 459

Cambridge, Field Marshal the Duke of, 375, 377

Campbell, Capt. Colin, 486

Campbell-Bannerman, Sir Henry, 519

Canning, Lord, 288

cantonments, Kabul: unsuitable position of, 239, 245–6, 251; British leave & begin retreat to Jalalabad (1842), 260, 261, 263; British garrison under Roberts forced to move there (Dec. 1879), 394, successfully defend, 394–5

Caspian Sea, 15, 17, 27, 65; comes under Russian control, 66, 73; 75, 78, 79, 83; Russians build port, 84, 317, 367, 438, 441; 86, 87, 110, 117, 119, 126, 128, 130, 140, 151, 160; Russian forts on, 218, 219, 220, 222, 318, 367; domination of, 352; forts extended east of, 282; 284, 290, 306, 313, 388

Castlereagh, Lord, 58

Catherine the Great, ruled 1762–96: 2, 20, 21, 22, 26, 27

Caucasus, 2, 12, 17, 123, 309, 312, 353, 411, 429, 441, 522

Russian expansion into, 19, 20, 22, 32, 67, 75, 114, 115–16, 124–5, 152, 153, 155–62, 209, 283, 285, 287, 313, 317

struggles with Persia over, 20, 21, 32, 35, 56, 63, 109–11

as threat to India, 4, 61, 67, 73, 301, 415, 424, 446

as threat to Constantinople, 61, 62, 377

see also Shamyl, Urquhart, Long-worth, Bell

Cavagnari, Maj. Louis, 382–3, 384–7; takes leave of Gen. Roberts, 386; arrives Kabul, 387; last message, 387; last hours, 389–90; 392, 492, 523

Central Asian Review, 228

Chalt, 473

Chamberlain, Gen. Sir Neville, 382

Chang Lung Pass, 336, 356

Cherniaev, Maj.-Gen. Mikhail: annexes Tashkent, 307–12, 315

Chimkent, 303

China, 12, 13, 89, 301, 328, 333, 410, 437, 448, 450, 473, 479, 504, 509, 517, 518, 520, 523

Ignatiev Mission, 297–300

Chinese Empire, 306, 321, 333, 349, 388, 409–10, 433, 434, 449, 455, 503, 504

Chinese Emperor, 298, 299, 388, 459

Boxer Uprising, 508

Chinese Turkestan, 2, 92, 93, 94, 98, 104, 212, 300, 301, 320, 321–9, 330, 363, 409, 462, 468, 480, 481, 499

and Yakub Beg (q.v.), 322–3, 325–6, 387

Russian designs on, 327, 332–4, 336, 347, 349, 376, 387, 466

see also Kashgaria and Sinkiang

Chini-Bagh, Kashgar, 463

Chitral, 342, 343, 345, 346, 356, 357, 424, 433, 434, 438, 449, 483, 497, 499, 500, 501, 502, 523

Russian incursions into, 466–7, 470, 472

death of Aman-al-Mulk, 481

struggle for succession, 481–2, 484–5

siege of, 486–96

Chitral river, 488

Christie, Capt. Charles, 7; Mission to Herat, 39–43, 48, 52, 54, 55, 128; trains Shah's troops, 56, 64–5, 67; death in action, 65; 68, 73, 118

Circassia, 152, 153, 154–61, 210, 212, 301

Circassians, 125, 209

Clarendon, Lord, 318–19

Cobbold, Capt. Ralph, 500–1

Conolly, Capt. Arthur, 1–2, 5, 8, 101; background, 124; religious faith, 124; 1st Great Game mission, 123, passes through Caucasus, 124–5, fails to reach Khiva, 125–8; visits Herat, 128, Kandahar, 129, reaches India, 129; reports on possible invasion routes, 130–1; supports Kamran Shah, 131, 145, 188; 139, 151, 171, 176, 219; travels in Turkestan, 233–5; goes to Bokhara, 233, 235–6; his disappointment in love, 236; death, 278–9; his prayer book recovered, 279–80; 297, 323, 328, 443, 492, 523

Conolly, Lt. John, 246–7, 279–80

Constantinople, 71, 103, 155, 156, 158, 162, 348, 378, 403

Russian designs on, 20, 21, 22, 34, 60, 61, 62, 74, 114–16, 149–50, 154, 163, 360, 362, 377, 379–81, 446, 505

Crimea, the, 14, 15, 21, 22, 61

Crimean War, 283–4, 285, 286, 287, 288, 289, 429; effects of Russian defeat, 290, 292, 295, 300, 301, 302, 333, 348, 352

Curzon, Hon. George (later Lord), 293, 440–6, 447, 455, 500, 504–7, 517, 521; his book on Central Asia, 441; appointed Viceroy of India, 504

Custine, Marquis de, 211

Daghestan, 83, 153, 160, 209
Daily News, 404, 442
Dalai Lama, 505, 506, 510, 517, 518
Dalgleish, Andrew, 435, 436, 451, 523
Dalny, 514
Danube river, 27, 287
d'Arcy Todd, Maj., 204, 214, 217, 218–19, 220, 226, 227
Dardanelles, 114, 115, 154, 157, 348, 360, 380, 520
Dardistan, 340, 342, 343, 344, 355
Darkot Pass, 340, 343, 466
Darkot village, 343, 344, 345, 346; visited by author, 346
Davison, Lt., 467, 469, 471
Dehra Dun, 330, 331, 332, 422
de Lacy Evans, Col. George, 116–18, 150, 152, 313, 352, 362, 421
Delhi, 69, 70, 144, 146, 284
Dennie, Col. William, 199
Derbent, 86
Disraeli, Benjamin (Tory PM), 359, 360, 361, 378, 379, 398, 420
Diver, Maud, 183
Dnieper river, 58
Dogger Bank incident, 514
Don river, 27
Dorjief, Aguan, 506, 517
Dost Mohammed, 138–9, 142, 152, 189, 190, 192, 195, 202, 247, 250, 251–2, 253, 260, 270, 288, 361, 395
    visited by Burnes, 143–5, 152, 168–71, 239
    wooed by Nicholas I, 166, 167, 168, 172–4, 188; & Alexander II, 290
    flees Kabul, 200–1
    exiled to India, 201, 237, 250, 272
    restored to throne, 277, 282
    his good relations with Britain, 282, 290
    death of, 290–1

Drew, Frederick, 345–6
Dufferin, Lord, 409, 410, 431, 434–6, 449–50
Duhamel, Gen., 284, 285
Dundas, Henry, 22, 24, 25
Durand, Col. Algernon (Political Officer, Gilgit), 450–1, 452, 460, 472–4, 481, 482
Durand, Lt. Henry (hero of Ghazni), 197–200, 201, 430, 474
Durand, Sir Mortimer, 430–1, 450, 451
Durham, Lord, 162, 163, 185

East India Company (principal refs.), 2, 3, 20, 22, 24, 25, 26, 27, 30, 43, 69, 88, 91, 93, 97, 116, 124, 133, 169–70, 189, 233–4; end of, 291
Eden, Emily, 189, 270
Edinburgh Review, 157
Edirne, 114, 115
Edwards, H. Sutherland, 420
Egypt, 22, 24, 25, 26, 30, 117, 149, 418; Khedive of, 359
Elgin, Lord, 299
Elias, Ney, 435–8, 463
Ellenborough, Lord, 118–19, 123, 129, 132, 133, 134, 137, 271; organises retaliatory expedition to Kabul, 271–3; but has cold feet, 272; public & private pressure forces him to act, 273; 274, 275, 277, 278
Elphinstone, Gen. William, 240, 243, 246, 248, 249, 250, 251, 254, 256; his indecisiveness demoralises his troops, 257; ignores Pottinger's advice, 258; tries to appease Akbar, 259; overrules Pottinger, 260, 262; agrees to Akbar's new demand for hostages, 263, 264; taken hostage himself, 265; blamed by Wellington, 271; expedition to avenge his defeat, 272–7; his

death in captivity, 276; 291, 394
Erivan, 32, 109, 110, 111
Erzerum, 114, 115, 378
Eversmann, Dr, 102–4

Ferghana, 303, 353, 500
Filchner, Wilhelm, 506, 511
First World War, 522
Foreign Quarterly Review, 211
Forsyth, Sir Douglas: 1st Mission
    to Yakub Beg, 337–8, 347; 2nd
    Mission, 349, 354; 356, 357,
    358, 433, 437
Fort Alexandrovsk, 218, 220, 224,
    225–6, 227, 229
44th Regiment of Foot, 260; last
    stand of, 266, 269
'Forward School', or forward poli-
    cies, 6, 286; end of, 521
  by Britain, 6, 25, 88, 134, 189–90,
    210, 234, 288, 318, 337, 359,
    362–3; Liberals renounce, 398,
    401; Foreign Office opposed to,
    404; 418, 420, 423, 425, 434,
    499, 500, 504–5, 508, 517
  by Russia, 203, 210, 283–4, 301,
    302, 318, 348, 363–4, 375, 388,
    401, 403, 409, 418, 425, 434,
    446, 455–6, 482, 500–1, 504–5,
    509, 517
  victims of, 279
France (and the French), 70, 115,
    117, 210, 212, 304, 504, 505,
    508
  as allies of Russia, 3, 27, 34, 36,
    56
  as enemies of Russia, 32, 33, 57–
    8, 60
  as allies of Britain, 283, 286, 298,
    299–300
  as enemies of Britain, 22, 25, 26,
    31, 32, 33, 36, 233
  see also Napoleon
Frankenburg, Maj., 18–19
Friedland, battle of, 33
Friend of India, 393

Futteh, son of Shah Shujah, 275,
    277
Futtehabad, 267

Gandamak: last stand of 44th, 266,
    269; treaty of, 385, 392
Geok-Tepe, 388, 404–6; slaughter
    of inhabitants, 406–7, 408; 409,
    411, 413, 438; seen by Curzon,
    441–2
George III, King, 35
Georgia, 32, 66, 77, 115, 153, 285
Gerard, Dr James, 140–2, 146, 151
Germany, 13, 301, 424, 505; Far
    Eastern acquisitions, 504;
    expansionist policies, 518–19,
    520, 522
Ghazni, 69, 196–200, 201, 430
Giers, Count Nikolai, 409, 415, 427,
    428, 429, 431, 480, 482
Gilgit, 342, 355, 452, 460, 461, 469,
    472, 473, 481, 483, 484, 485,
    487, 491, 493, 497, 499, 523;
    as invasion route to India, 356,
    357, 424, 450, 451, 467
Gladstone, Mr (Liberal PM), 358,
    361, 378, 397–8, 410, 413, 415;
    accused of appeasement, 419;
    425, 426; brought to brink of
    war over Pandjeh, 428; loses
    election as a result, 432–3; 481
Globe, The, 418, 419
Gorchakov, Prince Alexander, 302,
    304, 319, 352–3, 364; the Gor-
    chakov memorandum, 304–5,
    311, 312, 314, 319, 359
Gordon, Gen. Charles, 365, 418,
    433, 493
Gordon, Lt.-Col Thomas, 354, 355–
    7
Gordon Highlanders, 493
Grant, Lt. John, 511–12
Grant, Capt. W. P., 50
Granville, Lord, 415, 431
Graphic, The, 492
Great Game, origin of phrase, 123

Greek War of Independence, 110, 153

Grey, Earl (Whig PM, 1830–4), 140

Grey, Sir Edward (Liberal Foreign Secretary, 1905–16), 519, 520

Griboyedov, Alexander, 112–14, 163, 187, 280

Grodekov, Col N. L., 388

Gromchevsky, Capt., 7; enters Hunza, 449, 450; meets Younghusband, 455–7; almost dies in the Pamirs, 457–8; 460, 461, 462, 468, 474, 479, 480, 524; death in poverty after Revolution, 458

Guides, Corps of, 349, 354; escort for Cavagnari Mission, 386; gallant defence of residency, 391; 393, 494

Gulistan, Treaty of, 66, 109, 111

Gull, 48

Gulmit, 459

Gurdon, Lt., 485

Gurkhas, 92, 247, 400, 451, 452–3, 454, 457, 459, 460–1; their affection for Younghusband, 461; at the storming of Nilt, 473, 474, 475, 479; on Younghusband Expedition, 507, 510, 512

Guru, 509; massacre, 510–11

Guthrie, George, 92, 105, 106, 145

Gyantse, 507, 508, 509, 511; storming of fortress, 511–12

Hami, 322

Hamilton, Lord George, 505

Hamilton, Lt. Walter, 386, 390–1

Hayward, George: surveying trip to Ladakh & Kashgaria, 324; meets Shaw, 324–5, reaches Yarkand, 325, allowed to proceed to Kashgar, 328, but kept under guard, Shaw arranges his release, 334–5, goes home, 335; 336, 337, 338;

his Pamir expedition, 339–47, his article in *The Pioneer*, 340, quarrel with Mir Wali, 342, taken by treachery, 343, death, 344–5; Newbolt's poem, 344–5; his body recovered by Drew, 345–6, and buried at Gilgit, 346; 347, 350, 353, 354, 356, 358, 403, 433, 434, 523

Heber, Bishop Reginald, 124

Helmund Desert, 44

Herat, 13, 38, 39, 42–3, 128–9, 166, 167, 168, 189, 219, 226, 227, 290, 359, 361, 367, 372, 387, 398, 401, 430, 432

siege of (1837), 174, 175–83, 184, 185, 186, 191, 202, 204, 209, 213, 218

Persians attack (1856), 287–8, & withdraw, 289

as gateway to India, 42–3, 128, 130, 131, 151, 164, 167, 183, 185, 188, 203, 284, 287–8, 318, 352, 388, 408, 415, 416, 417, 418; MacGregor's assessment, 423–5; Roberts prepares to defend, 426–7; Britain warns Russia over, 429; fear of Russia extending railway to, 439

Herzegovina, 377, 379, 381

Heytesbury, Lord, 119

Himalayas, 91, 107, 449

Hindu Kush mountains, 140, 141, 145, 203, 355

as bulwark against invasion of India, 72, 74, 117, 130, 151, 433, 449, 472, 482

Hungarian uprising of 1848, 282–3

Hunza, 433; considered British sphere of influence, 449; entered by Gromchevsky, 449, 450; raiders plunder caravans, 450–4, 472; Younghusband visits & locates secret pass (Shimshal), 451–4; meeting between Gromchevsky &

Younghusband, 455–7; meeting between Younghusband & Safdar Ali, 459–61; 482, 492, 498, 523
as invasion route to India, 451, 462, 469, 470, 472, 481
Hunza Expedition, 473–80
Hyderabad, 40–1

Ignatiev, Count Nikolai, 295; mission to Turkestan, 296–7, returns to acclaim in St Petersburg, 297; mission to China, 297–300, his celebrated ride from Peking to St Petersburg, 300; joins other Anglophobes in Foreign Ministry, 301; 302, 303, 307, 316, 317, 327, 333; appointed ambassador to Constantinople, 347–8, 378
Ili (Kuldja), 348–9, 353, 388, 409–10, 434
Ili valley, 348
Imperial Service Troops, 450, 473, 480
India, communications with, 360; Duhamel's proposed invasion of, 284; Kaufman's proposed invasion of, 380–1
India Act, the, 291
Indian Army, institution of, 291–2
Indian Mutiny, 289–91, 292, 295, 302, 363, 394
Indus river, 3, 27, 28, 30, 72, 73, 88, 98, 118, 129, 130, 132, 142, 152, 193, 415
Army of the Indus, 192, 260
Burnes's survey of, 133, 134, 135, 139, 140, 296
Intelligence Department (of the Indian Army), 422–3, 433, 451
Isfahan, 42, 43, 55, 402, 505, 520
Ishkaman Pass, 355–8
Istoriya SSSR, 228–9
Ivan III (the Great), ruled 1462–1505: 14, 15

Ivan IV (the Terrible), ruled 1547–84: 15
Ivanov, Col. Nikolai, 373–5
Izvolsky, Count Alexander Petrovich, 520, 521

Jalalabad, 130, 141, 201, 259, 260, 261, 262, 263, 266. 267; reached by Brydon, 268; beacon lit for any more survivors, 269; at risk from Akbar, 270, 271; relief of, 272; 384, 391, 440
Japan, 89, 458, 504, 508, 509, 516, 517
see also Russo-Japanese War
Jeddah, 24
Jelap Pass, 509
Jingoism, origins, 379
Jones, Sir Harford, 35–6

Kabul, 21, 69, 72, 100, 117, 118, 130, 131, 164, 166, 167, 168, 190, 195, 200, 204, 213, 231, 232, 234, 236, 270, 284, 290, 329, 357, 359, 361, 365, 424, 484, 501, 505
visited by Burnes (q.v.), 139, 140, 141, 142, 168–71, 175, 183; his military report on, 151–2
visited by Vitkevich (q.v.), 172–4, 183, 186
taken over by British (1st Afghan War), 200–1, 203, 236–60
British insensitivity to local feelings, 237, 238
riots lead to death of Burnes, 239–42
Pottinger negotiates British evacuation, 258–9
British retreat from (1842), 260–9, 274, 278, 291–2; hostages, 259, 263, 264, 265, 268, 272, 273, 275–6, 278, 280; sufferings of Indian troops & camp-followers, 262, 263, 264, 268, 292; Afghans' treachery, 261, 262–4,

Kabul (*cont.*)

British retreat from (1842) (*cont.*)
266, 267; news of catastrophe
reaches London, 270–1; evidence of massacres, 266, 274,
277; retaliatory expedition by
British, 271–7; revenge by
British troops, 274; razing of
bazaar, 276–7

visited by Stolietov, 380–2

the Cavagnari Mission arrives,
387 (2nd Afghan War); slaughtered, 389–91; Roberts arrives,
392; punitive actions, 393;
battle, 394–5; Abdur Rahman
proclaimed Emir, 397; decision
to evacuate, 398, halted to allow
relief of Kandahar, 400

Kabul river, 252, 254, 258

Kailas, Mount, 89–90

Kamran Shah, ruler of Herat, 128–
9, 131, 145, 152, 166, 168, 175,
180, 188

Kandahar, 129, 168, 186, 195, 196,
201, 238, 250, 271, 272, 273,
384, 391; Abdur Rahman takes
it over, 401; 415, 424, 440

as invasion route to India, 72, 130,
270, 284, 359

siege of, 398–400

Karakoram mountains, 92, 95, 325,
338, 349, 355–7, 436, 448

as invasion route to India, 336,
353, 356, 433, 449

Karakoram Pass, 356, 451, 523

Karakoram Highway, 459, 523

Karakum Desert, 77, 79–80, 117,
125, 126, 128, 130, 388, 442

Karo Pass, 511

Kars, 115, 287

Kashgar, 42, 92, 94, 104, 300, 306,
321; conquered by Yakub Beg,
322; 323, 324; 1st Englishman
to see (Shaw), 325, Shaw's visit,
325–9, 335; Hayward's visit,
328–9, 335; Pundit Mirza tries

to fix position, 329; 332; British
send envoy to, 337, 349, 354;
Russians send mission to, 349;
Russian designs on, 353, 356,
363, 372, 387, 435; Russia
appoints consul, 434; reverts to
Chinese rule, 387–8; Yakub
Beg dies there, 388; 435, 436,
459, 462; Younghusband &
Macartney arrive, 463–4; 465,
467, 474, 480, 481, 523

Kashgaria, 322, 323, 324, 329, 333,
336, 338, 347, 348, 349, 354,
356, 358, 376

see also Chinese Turkestan

Kashi, 101

Kashmir, 26, 93, 96, 98, 107, 119,
282, 313, 328, 342, 353, 355,
357, 433, 437, 457, 470

Maharajah of, 340, 342, 345, 357–
8, 450, 452

Kashmiri atrocities in Dardistan,
340, 343

Kaufman, Gen. Konstantin: appointed Gov.-Gen. of Turkestan, 312; beginning of the
end of the Khanates, 314, 315;
annexes Bokhara, 316–17; consolidates Russian position in
Turkestan, 317; 347; annexes
Ili, 348–9, and Khiva, 351–2,
and Khokand, 353; approached
by Sher Ali, 361; 395; British
fear he will seize Merv, 366,
367–8; 376; assembles force for
possible invasion of India, 380–
1; protector of Abdur Rahman,
382, 395, 396; appealed to in
vain by Sher Ali, 384, 386;
expansionist aims in Central
Asia continue, 388; death in
Tashkent, 445, 523; 524

Kaye, Sir John: comments on Pottinger & siege of Herat, 176–7,
178, 179, 182–3, 186; comments
on 1st Afghan War, 193, 196,

197, 198, 199, 200, 238, 240, 242, 244, 246, 247, 248, 249, 250, 253, 261, 273

Kazakh Steppe, 73, 95, 282

Kazakh tribes, 74, 103, 301

Kazala, 368, 369, 370, 376

Kazan, 14, 15

Keane, Gen. Sir John, 195–201

Kelat, 38, 40, 41, 46, 54, 360–1

Kelly, Col James, 492–3, 494–6, 496–8, 499

Kerman, 39, 42, 47, 52, 55; Prince of, 53–5

Khalfin, N.A., 227–9, 304, 315, 464, 482

Khamba Jong, 507

Khanikov, Nikolai, 290

Kharg Island, 184

Khartoum, 365, 418, 433, 492

Khiva, 4, 16, 28, 29, 30, 42, 104, 117, 118, 119, 130, 148, 151, 201, 203, 228, 230, 233, 234, 235, 296, 306, 313, 317, 318, 322, 420, 523

British journeys to: Conolly's attempt to get there, 125–8; Abbott's visit, 212, 213–18, 235, relations with Khan, 214–16, 221; Shakespear's visit, 219–29, 235, secures release of slaves, 222–4, relations with Khan, 221, 223; Burnaby's ride to, 365–74

gardens of, 373

Russian expeditions to: expedition of 1717 (Bekovich), 16–20, 73, 75, 77, 103, 351, 389; expedition of 1819 (Muraviev), 77–87, 91; expedition of 1839 (Perovsky), 203–9, 210, 211, 217, 221, 232, 234, 270, 351, 370; expedition of 1858 (Ignatiev), 296–7, 303; expedition of 1873 (Kaufman), 210, 351–2

annexation by Russia, 351, 415

Khokand, 42, 230, 233, 235, 297,

310, 322, 357, 368

Russian designs on, 4, 119, 303–4, 306–8, 313, 315, 317

khanate annexed by Russia, 353, 355, 356, 372, 388, 415

Khwaja Salah, 100, 101

Khyber Pass, 98, 100, 129, 141, 193, 260, 262, 272, 277, 382, 384, 385, 386

as invasion route to India, 42, 72, 73, 117, 123, 130, 144, 284, 319, 348, 358, 380, 434

Kiaochow, 504

Kim, 1, 332, 422, 450

King's Royal Rifles, 493

Kinneir, John Macdonald (later Sir), 67–8; his detailed study of invasion routes, 70–5; 116, 117, 118, 150, 152, 156, 163, 284, 313, 352, 421

Kipling, Rudyard, 1, 332, 422, 450

Kirghiz Steppe, 29, 85

Kirghiz tribes, 78, 85, 206, 301, 337

Knight, E. F., 470, 472, 474–6

Komarov, Gen., 427–8

Koosh Begee (Grand Vizier of Bokhara), 146–9

Korea, 429, 509, 513, 516, 517

Kotliarevsky, Gen., 63–6

Krasnovodsk: Russians plan to build port, 84, 317–18; 351, 353, 367, 389; starting point for Transcaspian Railway, 438, 441

Kullugan, 46, 47

Kuropatkin, Gen., 503

Kutch, 134

Kutuzov, Marshal, 60

Ladakh, 324, 336, 353, 436, 455, 470

Moorcroft travels there, 92–3, 96–8, 106

Gromchevsky refused entry, 457–8, 468

see also Leh

Lahore, 94, 98, 133; Burnes's visit to, 135–8; 139, 189, 284

Lawrence, Capt. George, 240

Lawrence, Sir John, 313–14, 318–19, 336, 338, 345, 363; foresees Cavagnari's murder, 386, proved right, 389

Leh, 92, 93, 94, 98, 324, 336, 435, 436, 451, 523
  Moorcroft first Englishman to see, 92
  plundering of Leh-Yarkand caravans, 450, 451, 472

Lenin, V. I., 522

Lenkoran, 65, 79, 83, 110

Lermontov, Mikhail, 160

Lewis, James, see Masson

Lhasa, 90, 106, 107, 388, 451, 503, 507, 510, 511; entered by Younghusband, 512, 517–19, 521; 523

Lindsay, Lt. Henry, 64–5

Lithuania, 13

Lockhart, Col. William, 433–4, 437, 438

London, 202, 295, 347, 421, 423, 425

Longworth, James, 158–62, 285

Low, Maj.-Gen. Sir Robert, 493–4, 496, 497

Lowarai Pass, 494, 497

Ludhiana, 138, 143, 168, 169, 189

Lumsden, Gen. Sir Peter, 417, 418, 426, 427, 428

Lytton, Lord (Viceroy), 359, 360, 361–2, 382–3, 385, 393, 395, 397–8

Macartney, George, 462–4, 474, 480, 481

Macdonald, Brig.-Gen. James, 510–11

MacGregor, Col. (later Sir) Charles, 367, 422–5, 427, 433, 456
  his Defence of India, 423–5, 447, 471

Mackenzie, Capt. Kenneth, 255, 259

Macnaghten, Lady, 201, 254

Macnaghten, Sir William, 188–9; supports Shujah, 189, appointed political head of mission to Kabul, 191, sets off on invasion of Afghanistan (1st Afghan War), 193–8, enters Kabul, 200–1; 203, 227, 232, 234; political misjudgement, 237–8, 239, 270; vacillation leads to death of Burnes, 240–2; fails to stem ensuing riots, 243–5; fails to move to safety of Bala Hissar, 245–6; 247, 248; negotiates with Akbar, 250–4; Akbar's treachery, 254–6; death of Macnaghten, 256, 257–9; 272, 276, 279, 385, 492, 523

McNeill, Sir John, 162; his book on Russian expansion, 163–4; 165, 166, 167, 172; his role over siege of Herat, 180, 181, 183, 184, 185, 186; 188, 191, 231, 313, 362, 421

Madras, 26

Mahomadabad, 404, 407

Maiwand, battle of, 398–9, 400

Makran, the, 46, 50

Malakand Pass, 493, 499, 500

Malcolm, Capt. (later Gen. Sir), John: successful mission to Teheran (1800), 31–2, tries to return in 1808 but blocked by French pressure, 34–5, new agreement reached, 35–6; sends spies to reconnoitre Baluchistan & Afghanistan, 36–7, 39, 40, 53, 54, 55; invites Christie to stay on in Persia, 56; his officers train Shah's troops, 36, 56, 63, 64, 67–8; Governor of Bombay, 118; orders state coach for Ranjit Singh, 133; believer in forward policies, 134; 139

Malleson, Col. G. B., 420, 421

Malov, Father, 309, 311

Manchu Dynasty, 94, 321, 448, 503–4

Manchuria, 448, 508, 517

Manners Smith, Lt. John, 477–9, 523

Maragheh, 55

Marvin, Charles, 418–20, 421, 422, 425, 439

Masson, Charles (James Lewis), 169–70, 173, 174

'masterly inactivity', school of, 6, 286, 303, 318, 347, 350, 359, 363, 423, 499

Mayo, Lord, 336, 337–8, 340–1, 347, 349

Meerut, 289

Melbourne, Lord (Whig PM), 245, 271

Merv, 42, 148, 219, 365, 366, 368, 369, 372, 374, 439, 505
  fears of Russian seizure, 203, 366, 367, 369, 372, 375, 388–9, 402, 403, 408–9, 410, 416
  annexation, 411–15, seen as threat to India, 415, 418, 421, 425–6; Alikhanov governor of, 427; 430
  visited by Curzon, 441, 442

Meshed, 42, 43, 128

Metcalfe, Sir Charles, 133–4, 135

Mikhail, Grand Duke, 411

Milyutin, Count Dmitri, 301, 303, 312, 365, 366, 367

Minto, Lord, 34, 35, 36

Mir Wali, 342, 343, 344, 345, 356; death, 346

Mirza Shuja, Pundit, 328–9, 330, 332, 335–6

Mitrokhin, Leonid, 471–2

Mohammed Ali, ruler of Egypt, 149–50, 154

Mohammed Ali, surveyor & colleague of Alexander Burnes, 140

Mohan Lal: joins Burnes on mission to Kabul & Bokhara, 140, 143; helps at Ghazni, 197, 200; tries to protect Burnes at Kabul, 239; sees mob attack Burnes's house, 241; 243, 245; used by Macnaghten as go-between with Afghan leaders, 246, 247, 252, 253, 254; his warnings ignored over retreat from Kabul, 260, 261; helps with release of hostages, 275

Mongol invasion of Russia & effects of, 11–15, 16, 21, 315, 348

Mongolia, 89, 300, 503–4, 518

Mongols, 73

Monteith, Lt. William, 64–5

Montenegro, 378

Montgomerie, Capt. Thomas, 330–2

Moorcroft, William, 88, 90–2; first Englishman to visit Leh, 92; his Russian rival, 93–6; negotiates commercial treaty with ruler of Ladakh, 96, but disowned by Calcutta, 96; attempts on his life, 97; suspended by East India Company, 97; sets off for Bokhara, 98; suggests annexation of Afghanistan, 99, first Englishman to see Oxus, 100, reaches Bokhara, 101, beaten to it by Russians, 102; mystery surrounding his death, 105–7; his posthumous repute, 107; Burnes finds his grave, 107, 145; 109, 116, 117, 119, 132, 150, 151, 202, 280, 336, 337, 352, 403, 523

Morier, Sir Robert, 471

Moscow, 14, 124, 129, 408, 440, 502
  and Napoleon, 3, 57, 59

Mughsee, 49

Mukden (Shenyang), 515, 516

Multan, 72

Munda, 494

Muraviev, Capt (later Gen.)

Muraviev, Capt. (*cont.*)
Nikolai, 7; chosen for mission to Khiva, 77–9; his caravan sets out across Karakum, 79–80; detained outside Khiva for 7 weeks, 81, finally enters Khiva, 82; received by Khan, 83–4; meets Russian slaves, 84–5, leaves Khiva, 85; arrives Baku, 86, argues for conquest of Khiva, 86–7, summoned by Tsar, 87–8; 91, 104, 105, 116, 149, 301
Murray, John, publisher, 151
Muscovy, 14, 15, 315
Mustagh Pass (Karakorams), 448

Nagar, 473, 474, 480, 482, 492
Naib Sheriff, 242
Nakitchevan, 111
Napier, Capt. George, 366–7, 369, 403
Napoleon: his plans to invade India, 2–3, 22–3, 24–8, 29, 30; 32, 33–4, 36, 43; his disaster in Russia, 3, 56, 57–8; 59, 60, 63, 64, 67, 68, 75, 78, 96, 118, 162, 386
Nelson, Admiral Horatio, 26
Nesselrode, Count, Foreign Minister to Nicholas I, 94, 112, 172, 184, 185, 186, 188, 202, 302
New York Times, 429
Newbolt, Sir Henry, 344
Ney, Marshal, 58
Niazbek, 307
Nicholas I, Tsar, ruled 1825–55: his ruthlessness in the Caucasus, 110, 111; 114, 115, 116, 117, 132; offers to help Sultan, 149, 150; 153, 154, 158, 162, 164, 165, 166; sends Vitkevich to Kabul, 168, 172, 173; 181, 185–6, 188, 191; sends Perovsky expedition to Khiva, 205; 210, 217, 220, 225; thanks Shakespear for rescuing slaves, 226;

229; state visit to Britain, 281–2; fear of revolution, 283; death, 286; 295
Nicholas II, Tsar, ruled 1894–1917: 502, 503, 505–6, 509, 513–19, *passim*, 522
Nicolson, Sir Arthur, 520
Niemen river, 33
Nijni-Novogorod (Gorky), 313
Nilt: storming of fortress, 474–6; taking of the mountain stronghold, 476–9
Nizam, ruler of Chitral, 484, 485
Northbrook, Lord (Liberal Viceroy), 349, 359, 361
Nott, Gen. Sir William: retaliatory action against Afghans at Kandahar, 272, and Kabul, 273–4, 275, 277
Nushki, 38–41 *passim*, 43, 46, 47, 55

O'Connor, Capt. Frederick, 510, 512
O'Donovan, Edmund, 404–5, 442
Opium Wars, 233, 298, 302
Orenburg, 28, 29, 78, 102, 104, 166, 172, 201, 204, 221, 222, 307, 317, 351, 367–8, 376
departure of Perovsky's disastrous expedition, 205, 370
return of Perovsky's expedition, 208–9, 217
as staging point for invasion of India, 73, 74, 130, 151
Shakespear's activities in, 226, 227–8
Osh, 353
Ottoman Empire
threats from Russia, 61, 114, 115, 155, 156, 164
support from Russia, 149
Russia suggests joint action with Britain, 281, 283
Crimean War starts, 283
another war with Russia narrowly averted, 378, 380

see also Turkey

Owen, Maj. Roderick, 497

Oxus river (principal refs.): Peter the Great believes it a source of gold, 16, 17; once flowed into Caspian?, 17, 317; 29, 88, 99; Moorcroft is first Englishman to see, 100; 140, 203, 219, 220, 297, 350, 357, 370, 396, 433, 442

as means of ferrying Russian troops towards India, 73, 74, 117, 130, 146, 151, 296, 352

Pacific seaboard, 12, 15, 298, 299, 301, 502, 504

Pakistan, 432

Palmerston, Lord (Whig Foreign Secretary & later PM), 149; and the *Vixen* affair, 154, 156, 157–8, 160–1, 162; 163; and the siege of Herat, 180, 184, 185–6, 188; and the 1st Afghan War, 188–90, 192, 200; 211, 233, 236, 283, 288–9, 420

Pamirs, 5, 100, 306, 322, 325, 432

known as Roof of the World, 355

as invasion route to India, 319–20, 336, 353, 354, 355–6, 358, 433–4, 436, 481–2, 500

British exploration of, 324, 329, 335, 338, 340, 342, 346, 350, 354, 355–6, 433, 437, 500

Russian exploration of, 388, 433, 449, 480

Pamir gap, 356, 437–8, 449, 450, 455, 462, 463–4, 465–6; British protest, 471; 472, 499

Pandjeh, 425–8, 430, 431, 432, 439, 440, 481

Paris, 58, 282

Congress of (1856), 286, 287, 348

Paskievich, Count, 110, 114–16, 283

Paul I, Tsar, ruled 1796–1801: 2, 26, 27, 28–9, 58, 364

Pearl Harbor, 513

Peel, Sir Robert (Tory PM), 245, 271, 272, 273, 281

Peking, 298–300, 435, 448, 517

Treaty of, 300, 327

looting of, 508

Perovsky, Gen., 172, 203–9, 213, 216, 217, 226, 228

Persia (principal refs.), 2, 3, 12, 20–1, 30, 39, 40, 43, 50, 84, 140, 145, 148, 192, 212, 302, 366, 367, 385, 416

as Russian invasion route to India, 27, 34, 36, 61, 70–1, 73, 75, 111, 116, 118, 130–1, 132, 155, 157, 164, 284, 296, 301, 314, 352, 446

British relations with, 3, 31–3, 34–6, 66–8, 110–11, 163–4, 165–7, 184–5

Russian aggression against, 32, 62, 63–6, 109–11, 115

Pottinger's visit, 52–6

Christie remains in Persia & dies in action, 56, 64, 65

Griboyedov's death, 112–14

attack on Herat (1837), 175–85, 188, 189

attack on Herat (1856), 287–9

in Anglo-Russian Convention, 519, 520–1, 522

Persia, Shah of: wooed by Britain, 3; Tsarina Anne hands back Russia's Caucasian gains, 20; receives Captain Malcolm, 31, signs treaty with Britain, 32; threatened by Russia's annexation of Georgia, 32, appeals in vain for British help, 32–3; wooed by Napoleon, 33–4; refuses to receive Malcolm, 34–5, but receives Sir Harford Jones, 35–6, concludes new agreement with Britain, 36; allies himself with Sultan against Russia, 63, his troops cause Russian regiment to sur-

Persia, Shah of (*cont.*)
render, 63, Kotliarevsky's revenge, 65, he accepts British mediation, 66; Russia accepts his son Abbas Mirza as heir apparent, 66; disappointed by reduced British military aid, 67; Kinneir fears Russia will seize throne when he dies & his 40 sons struggle over succession, 74–5; new dispute with Russia over Caucasus, 109; Vitkevich visits new Shah & meets Rawlinson, 165–6; sets out to besiege Herat, 167, 168, 174, 176–85, 188, 191, 202; remains neutral in Crimean War, 287; alarmed by Russian aggression at Pandjeh, 429; threatened by Transcaspian Railway, 441

Persian Gulf, 7, 31, 34, 117, 149, 184, 188, 202, 287, 288–9, 520

as possible invasion route to India, 61, 70, 71, 505

Peshawar, 117, 130, 168, 170, 175, 189, 190, 271, 357, 486, 499

Peter the Great, ruled 1682–1725: 15–20, 21, 60, 62, 73, 116, 163, 446

Petro-Alexandrovsk, 368, 369, 370, 373, 374, 375, 376

Petrovsk, 317

Petrovsky, Nikolai, 434–5, 463–4, 474

Phari, 509

Pioneer, The, 340, 497

Plevna, 380

Poland, 12, 13, 58, 59, 163, 171, 210, 212, 302, 458

Pollock, Maj.-Gen. George, 272–7

Ponsonby, Lord, 156, 162

Port Arthur, 502, 504, 509, 513, 514, 515, 516, 517

Port Hamilton (Korea), 429

Portsmouth, New Hampshire, Treaty of, 517

Portuguese navigators, 70

Potemkin, Count, 21

Pottinger, Eldred, 174, 175, 176, 177, 178; his crucial role in defence of Herat, 179–83, 204, 213, 218; 231; warns Macnaghten of hostility among Afghans, 238, 244; is wounded, 247; is forced to handle negotiations for British withdrawal from Kabul, 258–9, warns Elphinstone against Akbar, 260, tries to protect Indian troops from frostbite, 262, taken as hostage by Akbar, 263, 275; death, 279–80; 289, 524

Pottinger, Lt. (later Sir) Henry, 7, 8, 39–41, 43–56, 64, 68, 73, 116, 118, 139, 175, 231, 524

Prejevalsky, Col. Nikolai, 388, 449

Prussia, 33, 59, 212, 301

see also Germany

Puhra, 49

Pundits (native explorers), 5, 328–32, 335, 339, 347, 422

punishments
Bokharan, 104, 443–4
Cossack, 59–60, 376
Khivan, 85, 86, 371, 373
Persian, 54

Punjab, 26, 92; Russians try to send envoy there, 94; 96; Moorcroft travels through *en route* for Afghanistan, 98; 117; Ellenborough decides to send horses to Ranjit Singh, 132–3, Burnes arrives with them, 136; 140, 189, 193; Britain annexes, 282, 313, 318

see also Ranjit Singh

Pushkin, Alexander, 113, 160

Quarterly Review, 313

Quetta, 129, 130, 201, 361, 429, 471

Rafailov, Mehkti (Aga Mehdi), 93–6, 98

Raikes, Thomas, 210–11
Ranjit Singh, 94; regarded as valuable friend by East India Company, 96; 97, 98, 117; British gift of horses to, 132, 133, 134, 135–8; 139, 141, 143; disliked by Dost Mohammed, 144; seizes Peshawar, 168, 170–1, 173–4; 189, 190, 193, death, 282
Rawalpindi, 431
Rawlinson. Lt. (later Maj., Gen. & Sir) Henry: meets Vitkevich in Persia, 165–7; 171, 172, 231; almost accompanies Conolly to Bokhara, 235, 238; warns of Afghan hostility in 1841, 238, warning ignored by Macnaghten, 244; accompanies Nott to Kabul on retaliatory expedition, 277; warns of Russian threat to India, 312–13, 318; encourages Hayward, 324; president of RGS, 339; more hawkish views, 362–3, 420, 524
Red Idol Gorge, 511
Red Sea, 24, 25, 70, 71
Regan, 52
Reutern, Count Mikhail, 302
revolutions of 1848, 282
Ripon, Lord, 398
Roberts, Gen. Sir Frederick VC (later Lord): fears for Cavagnari's safety, 386; hears news of disaster at Kabul, 389–90; takes charge of punitive force, 391, arrives Kabul, 392, & hangs ringleaders, 393; fights off Afghan attack, 394–5; obliged to stay in Kabul, 396, installs Abdur Rahman as Emir, 397; called to rescue Kandahar garrison, 398, 400, 401; warns of Russian advance towards India, 415; advises head of Indian Intelligence, 423; prepares to defend Herat, 426–7; urges railway & road construction in North India, 439–40; helps Younghusband, 448; visits Kashmir, 450; mobilises division after Russians seize Pamirs, 470
Robertson, Maj. George, 485–94, 496–8
Romania, 61, 380
Rosebery, Lord, 470, 481, 499
Royal Geographical Society, 55, 150, 324, 331, 335, 339, 340, 342, 346, 448, 458
Russell, Lord John, 299, 313
Russian Bible Society, 228
Russian Far East, 298, 299–300, 301, 502–4, 508, 513–16, 518
Russian Revolution (1905), 519
Russian Revolution (1917), 458, 518, 522
  contributory factors, 514, 516
Russo-Japanese War, 509, 511, 513–17, 519
Russophobia
  in the early 19th century, 5–6, 62, 67, 91, 97, 116–19
  at the time of the *Vixen* affair, 153–64 *passim*
  over Russian annexations in Turkestan, 192, 209–12, 229, 312, 408, 415, 420
  over Afghanistan, 361–2, 363, 424, 431, 470
  over Turkey, 377–9
  at the time of the Dogger Bank incident, 514
  over the Anglo-Russian Convention, 521
Russo-Turkish Pact, *see* under Turkey
Russo-Turkish War, *see* under Turkey

Safdar Ali, ruler of Hunza, 454,

Safdar Ali, ruler of Hunza (*cont.*)
459–61, 462, 470, 472, 474
Younghusband's unfavourable
opinion of, 461
bizarre ultimatum to British, 473
flees after fall of Nilt, 479–80
St Genie, Monsieur de, 21
St Petersburg, 19, 87, 91, 93, 94,
114, 119, 133, 162, 163, 186,
190, 217, 218, 219, 221, 279,
300–1, 384, 418, 429, 471, 503,
520
Treaty of, 1881: 410, 434
visited by Shakespear, 226
improved communications with
Central Asia, 313
visited by Burnaby, 366–7
visited by Curzon, 440
visited by Dorjief, 505–6
Sakhalin Island, 517
Salisbury, Lord, 359, 361, 362, 433,
471, 500, 505
Samarkand, 4, 13, 42, 211, 306, 382,
388, 395, 420, 456, 523
annexed by Russia, 315–17, 351
Russian rail link, 317, 389, 439,
441, 445
visited by Curzon, 441, 443, 444
Sandeman, Capt. Robert, 360–1
Sarakhs, 416–17, 422, 426
Saxony, 59
Schomberg, Col. Reginald, 346
scurvy, 86, 209
Sebastopol, 22, 286
Serbia, 378
serfs, emancipation of, 302
Sevan, Lake, 109
72nd Highlanders (at Kandahar),
400
Shahidula, 451, 457–8
Shakespear, Lt. (later Capt. & Sir)
Richmond, 219–29; sets out for
Khiva, 219, meets Khan, 221,
negotiates release of slaves,
222–4; arrives Fort Alexan-
drovsk, 225; arrives St Peters-

burg, 226; sent to free British
hostages in Afghanistan, 275–
6; 232
criticised by Soviet historians,
227–9
Shamyl, Imam, 160, 162, 209, 285,
287, 301, 313
Shandur Pass, 483, 495–6
Shaw, Robert, 323; his visit to
Yakub Beg, 324–9, meets
Hayward, 324–5, under house
arrest, 328, but leaves on good
terms, 334–5; his assessment of
threat from Russia, 335–7;
commercial opportunities in
Turkestan, 338; 339, 347, 353,
356, 358, 403, 433, 447
Shenyang, 515
Sher, contender for throne of
Chitral, 484, 486, 487, 489, 492,
497, 498
Sher Ali, 337, 361, 381–3; appoints
Yakub Khan regent, 384, dies,
384–5; 394, 395, 396, 398
Shimshal Pass, 450, 451, 452, 454,
461, 472
Shiraz, 55
Shujah, Shah: Burnes's opinion of,
138–9; 143, 168; backed by
Macnaghten, 189, and Ranjit
Singh, 190, Britain considers
him rightful ruler of Afghanistan, 190; Auckland raises
invasion force, 192, & 1st
Afghan War begins, 193, 194–
201 *passim*; atrocities by, 197;
232–55 *passim*, 260, killed, 272;
275, 318, 397
Siberia, 2, 12, 15, 29, 171, 301, 348,
376, 446, 458; building of
railway, 502–3; 506
Sikhs, 94, 96
Sikh troops, 486, 490–1
Sikh Pioneers, 492, 495, 497
on Younghusband expedition,
507, 510

see also Ranjit Singh & Punjab

Silk Road, 4, 102, 132, 321, 330, 443

Simla, 139, 389, 399, 422, 425, 449, 451, 455, 459

Simla Manifesto, 190

Simonich, Count, 164, 166, 167, 172, 173, 174; at siege of Herat, 179–84, British protest at his conduct, 185–6, downfall, 186, 188; 284

Sind, 26, 40, 70, 123, 132, 135, 139, 193; annexed by Britain, 282, 313, 318

Singer, Dr André, 266

Sinkiang, 93, 321, 387, 409, 434–7, 446, 452, 460, 463, 480

see also Chinese Turkestan & Kashgaria

Skobelev, Gen. Mikhail, 4, 402–8, 438, 441–2, 524

his methods contrasted with those of Gen. Roberts at Kabul, 407

slaves

Kurdish, 85, 87

Persian, 85, 87, 225, 297

Russian, 78, 79, 80, 82, 84–6, 87, 105, 124, 148, 191, 203, 205, 209, 214, 217, 218, 219; rescued by Shakespear, 222–4, 227, arrival back in Russia, 225, 235; 297, 351

slavery (in general), 126–7, 128, 129, 146, 147, 232, 233, 234, 275, 444, 454, 472

see also Turcomans

Smolensk, 57

snow-blindness, 209, 264, 370, 495

Soviet Military Archives, 228, 229

Srinagar, 342

Standard, The, 398

Stewart, Lt.-Col. Charles, 402, 404–5, 407

Stoddart, Col. Charles, 1–2, 5, 8, 101, 184, 185, 191, 205, 323, 328, 492, 523

taken prisoner in Bokhara, 201, 203, 214, 218, 230–3, 235, 236

death of, 278–80, 297, 443

Stolietov, Maj.-Gen. Nikolai, 380, 381–2, 384

Sudan, 413, 415, 417, 418, 425, 426, 492

Sudjuk Kale, 156, 157, 161

Suez Canal, 360

Sultan of Turkey, 63, 114, 115; threatened by Mohammed Ali, 149–50, 154; 156, 281; in Crimean War, 283; 296, 372; Bulgarian massacres and Congress of Berlin, 377, 378, 381

Survey of India, 330–1, 335, 422

see also Montgomerie & Dehra Dun

Svet, 482

Swat, 483, 485, 492, 493

Sweden, 13, 16, 163

Syr-Darya river, 282, 285, 296

Syria, 24, 71, 117

Tabriz, 520

Taiping rebellion, 298

Taklamakan Desert, 321, 325

Tartars, *see* Mongols

Tashkent, 4, 100, 306–12, 317, 347, 351, 376, 382, 388, 404, 523

annexed by Russia, 308–12, 315, 353, 372

as centre of Russian military activities in region, 441, 445

end of telegraph line to Central Asia, 374

Transcaspian Railway link, 389, 439, 445

visited by Curzon, 445

Teheran, 42, 62, 65, 117, 118, 185, 204, 360, 429

Malcolm's missions, 31, 32, 34–5, 36, 40, 67

French mission, 34

Harford Jones's mission, 35–6

Griboyedov posted there, 112, killed by mob, 113, 187

Teheran (*cont.*)
  Count Simonich as ambassador, 164, 166, 172
  Sir John McNeill as ambassador, 162–3, 165, 167, 184, 231, 278
  Col. Stewart's secret mission, 404, 407
  Russia's sphere of influence in 1907 Convention, 520
Tejend, 413, 414
Terentiev, Col. M.A., 363–4
Tibbee, 123
Tibet, 2, 89, 90, 330, 388, 449, 457, 502, 503, 505–6, 520, 521
  Younghusband expedition, 507–8, 509–12, 517–19
Tien Shan mountains, 355
Tientsin, 508
Tiflis, 77, 79, 83, 84, 86, 110, 113, 124, 404
Tilsit, 33, 59
The Times: and the *Vixen* affair, 157, 158, 160; 1st Afghan War, 192, 271; Russian annexations in Turkestan, 211, 352, and threat to India, 211; 360, 365, 419, 420, 470; erroneous report of Younghusband's death, 470; 472, 493, 497
Times of India, 393
Todd, Major d'Arcy, *see* d'Arcy
Togo, Admiral, 513, 516
Tolstoy, Count Lev, 160
Tora Bahadar, Prince, 101
Transcaspia, 402–15, 416, 456, 505
Transcaspian Railway, 317, 389, 415, 419, 438–40; Curzon travels along, 441–5, 448; military potential of, 445–6
Trans-Siberian Railway, 502–3, 504, 508, 509, 517
Trebeck, George, 92, 97, 105, 106, 145
Trespassers on the Roof of the World, 332, 518
Trevor, Capt., 256

Tsangpo river, 512
Tsingtao, 504
Tsushima Straits, 516
Turfan, 322
Turcoman horses, 90, 91, 105, 107, 404
Turcoman tribes, 79, 81, 84, 127, 228, 363, 367, 388, 403, 410–11, 411–14, 416
  warlike qualities, 17, 27, 30, 87, 130, 317, 368–9, 389
  fall of Geok-Tepe, 404–6, 441–2
  slaughter of inhabitants, 406–7, 408, 442
  evil reputation as slavers, 77, 78, 126–7, 146, 148, 203, 209, 219, 224–5, 301, 407, 408
Turkestan (region), 4, 16, 27, 75; Muraviev prepares way for Russian expansion, 87–8; Moorcroft foresees this, 88, 90, 92, 98; 127, 233, 247, 275; Ignatiev presses for conquest of region, 303, policy begins 305, 307 *et seq.*; Kaufman appointed Gov.-Gen., 312, British anxiety, 313, 314; Bokhara fails to oust Russians, 315–17; Russians construct fortresses, 219, 317, 318, 367, 368; 375; Kaufman raises force to invade India, 380–1; Skobelev's activities there, 402–8; threat to India from, 415, 421, 424
  as market for British & Russian goods, 88, 90, 92, 98, 135, 139, 152, 301, 313
Turkestan (town), 303
Turkey, 16, 21, 22, 59, 73, 285, 424, 429, 522
  as invasion route to India, 24, 34, 71, 116, 155, 301
  relations with Russia, 62, 63, 110, 111, 114, 115–16, 125, 132, 149–50, 153; Russo-Turkish Pact, 154, 157; 163–4, 212, 281;

Crimean War, 283, 286, 287; Russo-Turkish War, 379–81, 387, 388, 402, 419
attempt to mediate with Emir of Bokhara over Stoddart, 230, 233
Burnaby's journey, 377–9
Turkmanchi, Treaty of, 111

Ugra river, 14
Umra Khan, ruler of Swat, 485–6, 489, 493, 494, 497–8
United States of America, 233, 304, 409, 429, 513
Civil War, 302
Far Eastern acquisitions, 504
mediator in Russo-Japanese War, 517
Urga, 300
Urquhart, David, 153–8, 285, 286
Urumchi, 322

Vambery, Arminius, 420–1, triumphal visit to England, 421; 422, 425, 521
Viceroy of India, institution of title, 291
Victoria, Queen, 201; Abbott's replies to Khan of Khiva, 215–17; her health drunk by Shakespear & Russians at Fort Alexandrovsk, 225; her incipient Russophobia, 229; 236, 278; meeting with Nicolas I, 281, disapproves of his autocratic behaviour, 283; 285, 291; Yakub Beg's extravagant compliments, 334; accord with Disraeli, 359, proclaimed Empress of India, 359; receives Burnaby, 377; urges forward policies over Balkan crisis, 379; approves of Treaty of Gandamak, 386; 410, 415; telegraphs Tsar over Pandjeh, 427; 451, 459, 460; her health drunk by Younghus-

band & Yanov at Bozai Gumbaz, 467; knights Robertson after siege of Chitral, 498
Vienna, Congress of, 58, 59
1848 revolution in, 282
Vilnius (Vilna), 57
Vitkevich, Capt. Yan, 7; meeting with Rawlinson, 165–7; visit to Dost Mohammed, 169, 171–4, 183, 185; disgrace & death, 186, 188; 280, 290
Vixen (vessel), 156–61, 286
Vladivostok, 298, 429, 502
Volga river, 15, 27, 29, 87; as link with Turkestan, 313, 317

Wade, Capt. Claude, 169–70, 189
Wakhan, 350, 499
Wellesley, Lord, 24, 25, 26, 31, 34
Wellington, Duke of, 115, 118, 132, 134; opposes British policy in Afghanistan, 192, 271, 273; 394
Wheeler, Col. Geoffrey, 228–9
Whitchurch, Surg.-Capt. Henry, 487, 498
Wilhelm II, Kaiser, 504
William IV, King, 133, 137, 150, 154, 156, 158, 161
Wilson, Gen. Sir Robert: father of Russophobia, 59, 91; experiences in Russia during war with Napoleon, 59–60; his anti-Russia polemic, 60–2; 67, 68, 70, 74, 75, 111, 114, 116, 117, 150, 152, 156, 313, 352, 362
Witte, Count Sergei, 502–3, 509
Wolff, Rev. Joseph, 279

Yakub Beg: becomes ruler of Kashgaria, 322–3; his reign of terror, 323; contacted by Shaw, 324–5, receives Shaw, 326–7; keeps Shaw and Hayward under house arrest, 328; has Pundit Mirza chained up, 332; receives Shaw again, 334, and allows

Yakub Beg (*cont.*)
    him, Hayward & Mirza to go,
    335; 336, 356; routed by
    Chinese, 387–8; dies, 388; 409,
    436, 437, 463
    diplomatic overtures to Britain,
    334, 335, 337; avoids Forsyth
    Mission, 347, but relents, 349,
    354
    relations with Russia, 332–4, 348–
    9, 358, 376
Yakub Khan, 384–7, 390, 392
Yalu river, 514
Yanov, Col.: claims Pamirs for the
    Tsar, 465–6; regretfully ejects
    Younghusband, 467–9; made
    scapegoat after international
    incident, 471; 472, 480
Yar Mohammed, 175–80; cruelty of,
    175, 177; 182–3
Yarkand, 92, 93, 321, 323, 324, 353,
    435, 436, 450, 451, 472, 523
    conquered by Yakub Beg, 322
    visited by Shaw, 325, & Hayward,
    325, 328
    visited by Forsyth (1871), 347
Yasin: Kashmiri atrocities in, 340;
    Hayward arrives in, 342, leaves,
    343, dies, 344, Drew sends
    sepoy to investigate, 345; 346,
    357, 466, 484
Yermolov, Gen. Alexis: desire to
    annex Turkestan, 75, 77; sends
    Muraviev to Khiva, 78, 82, 84,
    86; his fall from grace, 87; starts
    war with Persia, 109, suffers
    unexpected defeat, 110, sacked,
    110; 112
Younghusband, Lt. (later Col Sir)
    Francis, 8; character, 447;
journey across China, 448;
youngest member of RGS, 448;
chosen for Hunza mission, 451,
locates Shimshal Pass, 452,
parleys with raiders, 453, maps
pass, 454, meets Gromchevsky,
455–7, sends him the wrong
way, 457–8, hears from him
after the Revolution, 458; meets
Safdar Ali, 459–61, returns to
India, 461; sets out on new
expedition to Pamirs, 462,
arrives Kashgar, 463, outwitted
by Petrovsky, 464; returns to
Pamirs & meets Yanov at Bozai
Gumbaz, 465–7, rendezvous
with Davison, 467, 469, Yanov
is instructed to eject him from
Pamirs, 467–9, outcry in
London, 469–70, reported dead
by *The Times*, 470, formal com-
plaint by Britain, 471; his
letters found in Safdar Ali's
palace, 480; cause for Russian
alarm, 482; accompanies Low
on relief expedition to Chitral,
493–4, arrives at Chitral, 497;
chosen to lead mission to
Khamba Jong, 507, then Lhasa,
507–8, 509–12, enters Lhasa,
512, 517, finds Dalai Lama
gone, 518, his treaty emasculated, 519, 521; his grave, 523
Younghusband Expedition (to
    Lhasa), 507–8, 509–12, 517–19

Zarafshan valley, 316
Zelenoy, Gen., 416–17
Zerempil (Russian Buryat agent),
    506, 511

About the Author

Before becoming a full-time author, Peter Hopkirk was a staff writer for *The Times* of London for nineteen years, five as its chief reporter and also as a Middle and Far East specialist. He has travelled extensively in Russian and Chinese Central Asia, the Caucasus, Mongolia, eastern Turkey, Persia, Afghanistan, Pakistan and northern India. Peter Hopkirk's three previous books are also set in this region and have been translated into seven languages.